PHILIPS'
SMALL WORLD
ATLAS

D1555681

George Philip

World

Europe

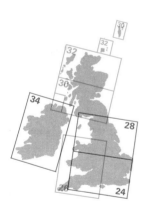

Edited by
B. M. Willett, Cartographic Editor
David Gaylard
Lilla Prince-Smith
  George Philip and Son Ltd., London

Maps prepared by
Cox Cartographic Ltd., and
George Philip Cartographic Services Ltd.,
London under the direction of Alan Poynter.

© **1985 George Philip & Son, Ltd., London**

British Library Cataloguing in Publication Data
Philips' small world atlas.
  1. Atlases, British
  912   G1021

ISBN 0-540-05496-8

Printed in Italy.

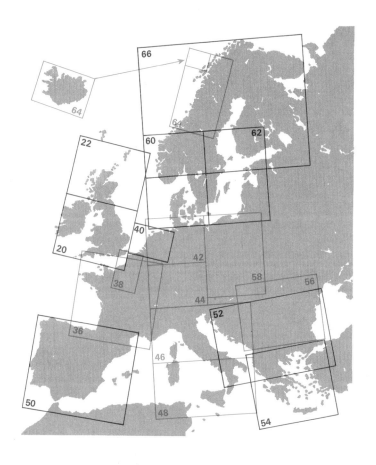

Asia

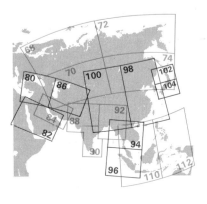

68-75 **U.S.S.R.**
  68-69 West
  70-71 South West
  72-73 North East
  74-75 South East and Mongolia

76-77 **Asia: Physical**
78-79 **Asia: Political**
80-81 **Turkey and the Middle East**
82-83 **Arabian Peninsula**
84-85 **The Gulf**
86-87 **Central Asia and Afghanistan**
88-89 **Pakistan and North West India**

90-91 **Central and Southern India, Sri Lanka**
92-93 **Eastern India, Bangladesh and Burma**
94-95 **Mainland South East Asia**
96-97 **The Malay Peninsula**
98-99 **China: East**
100-101 **China: West**

102-109 **Japan**
  102-103 North
  104-105 South
  106-107 Tokyo, Kyoto, Osaka
      108 Kyushu
      109 West Honshu and Shikoku

110-111 **Indonesia: West**
112-113 **Indonesia: East**

Australasia

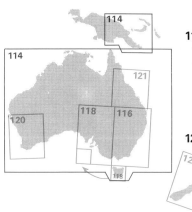

114-115   **Australia, New Zealand and Papua New Guinea**

116-121   **Australia**
116-117 Brisbane, Sydney, Melbourne
118-119 Adelaide, Melbourne, Tasmania
   120 Perth
   121 North East Queensland

122-123   **New Zealand, Central and South West Pacific**

Africa

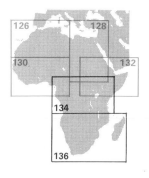

124-137   **Africa**
   124 Physical
   125 Political
126-127 North West
128-129 North East
130-131 West
132-133 East
134-135 Central
136-137 South

North America

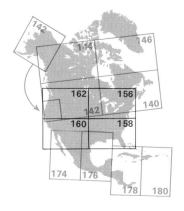

138   North America: Physical
139   North America: Political

140-155 Canada
  140-141 South East
  142-143 South West and Alaska
  144-145 North West
  146-147 North East
  148-149 Saint Lawrence Estuary
  150-151 The Great Lakes
  152-153 Southern Saskatchewan and
           Manitoba
  154-155 Southern British Columbia and
           Alberta

156-173 U.S.A.
  156-157 North East
  158-159 South East
  160-161 South West
  162-163 North West
      164 Boston, New York,
           Washington
      165 Washington, Atlanta
  166-167 Upper Mississippi
  168-169 Lower Mississippi and Gulf
           Coast
      170 Florida
      171 Columbia Basin
  172-173 California

174-175 Mexico: West
176-177 Mexico: East
178-179 Caribbean: West
180-181 Caribbean: East

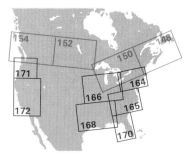

South America

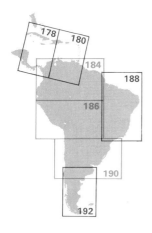

182-192	**South America**
182	Physical
183	Political
184-185	North West
186-187	West
188-189	East
190-191	Central
192	South

Index

Map Symbols

Settlement symbols in order of size

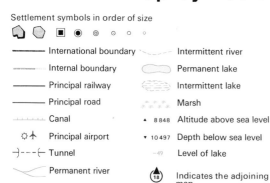

International boundary

Internal boundary

Principal railway

Principal road

Canal

☼✈ Principal airport

⊣---⊢ Tunnel

Permanent river

Intermittent river

Permanent lake

Intermittent lake

Marsh

▲ 8 848 Altitude above sea level

▼ 10 497 Depth below sea level

−49 Level of lake

(18) Indicates the adjoining map

As far as possible the de facto situation of international boundaries is shown

Scale note
To the right of each map title there is a number representing the scale of the map for example, 1 : 2 000 000. This means that one centimetre on the map represents 2 million centimetres or 20 kilometres on the ground. Or, if the number is 1 : 40 000 000, one centimetre represents 40 million centimetres or 400 kilometres.

Height and depth colours
Height of land above sea level

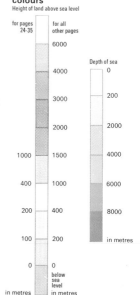

World: Northern Part

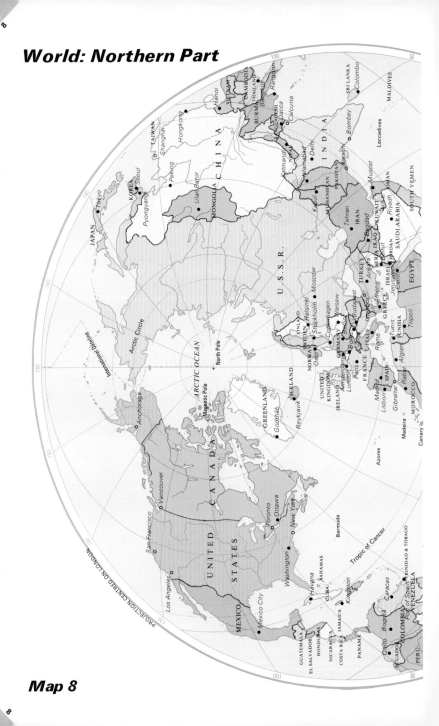

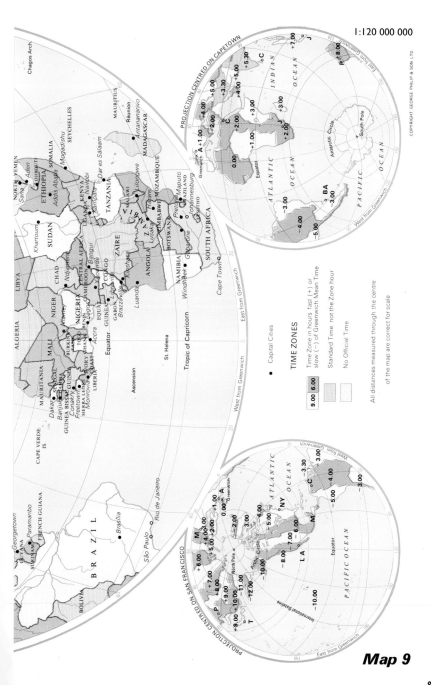

1:120 000 000

PROJECTION CENTRED ON CAPETOWN

INDIAN OCEAN

ATLANTIC OCEAN

PACIFIC OCEAN

South Pole

Antarctic Circle

Equator

East from Greenwich

COPYRIGHT GEORGE PHILIP & SON LTD

Chagos Arch.

MAURITIUS
Réunion
Antananarivo
MADAGASCAR
SEYCHELLES

NORTH YEMEN
Sana
Aden
DJIBOUTI
ETHIOPIA
Addis Ababa
SOMALIA
Mogadishu
KENYA
Nairobi
UGANDA
Kampala
TANZANIA
Dar es Salaam
MALAWI
Lilongwe
ZAMBIA
Lusaka
ZIMBABWE
Harare
MOZAMBIQUE
Maputo
SWAZILAND
Pretoria
Johannesburg
LESOTHO
Maseru
SOUTH AFRICA
Cape Town
NAMIBIA
Windhoek
BOTSWANA
Gaborone

Khartoum
SUDAN
ZAIRE
Kinshasa
ANGOLA
Luanda
CONGO
Brazzaville
GABON
Libreville
EQUAT. GUINEA
CAMEROON
Yaoundé
CENTRAL AFRICAN
Bangui
CHAD
Ndjaména
NIGER
LIBYA
ALGERIA
MALI
NIGERIA
Lagos
BENIN
TOGO
GHANA
Accra
IVORY COAST
BURKINA
MAURITANIA
SENEGAL
Dakar
GAMBIA
Banjul
GUINEA BISSAU
GUINEA
Conakry
SIERRA LEONE
Freetown
LIBERIA
Monrovia

CAPE VERDE IS.

St. Helena

Ascension

Tropic of Capricorn

Equator

West from Greenwich   East from Greenwich

Georgetown
GUYANA
Paramaribo
SURINAM
FRENCH GUIANA

B R A Z I L

Rio de Janeiro
São Paulo
Brasília

BOLIVIA

• Capital Cities

TIME ZONES

| 9.00 | 6.00 |

Time Zone in hours fast (+) or slow (−) of Greenwich Mean Time

Standard Time not the Zone hour

No Official Time

All distances measured through the centre

of the map are correct for scale

PROJECTION CENTRED ON SAN FRANCISCO

ATLANTIC OCEAN

PACIFIC OCEAN

North Pole
Arctic Circle
Equator
International Dateline

Greenwich
West from Greenwich   East from Greenwich

+1.00 0.00 −3.00 −4.00
+2.00 −2.00 −5.00
+3.00 +4.00 −6.00 −7.00
+5.00 +6.00 −8.00 −10.00
+7.00 +8.00 +9.00 −11.00 −12.00
+10.00

Map 9

World: Southern Part

PROJECTION CENTRED ON THE ANTIPODES OF LONDON

PACIFIC OCEAN

PACIFIC OCEAN

INDIAN OCEAN

Galapagos Is.

Easter I.

Marquesas Is.

Tuamotu Arch.

Pitcairn I.

Tropic of Capricorn

FRENCH POLYNESIA

Tahiti

Hawaiian Is.

Kiritimati

Tropic of Cancer

Equator

Cook Is.

SAMOA

TONGA

FIJI

Midway I.

Wake I.

Marshall Is.

KIRIBATI

TUVALU

Auckland

Wellington

NEW ZEALAND

Antipodes I.

Auckland Is.

Macquarie I.

Antarctic Circle

Victoria Land

Adélie Land

VANUATU

New Caledonia

SOLOMON IS.

Bonin I.

Northern Marianas

Guam

Caroline Is.

PAPUA NEW GUINEA

Port Moresby

AUSTRALIA

Sydney

Canberra

Perth

PHILIPPINES

Manila

VIETNAM

BRUNEI

Ho Chi Minh City

MALAYSIA

Singapore

Kuala Lumpur

INDONESIA

Jakarta

West from Greenwich

East from Greenwich

International Dateline

Map 10

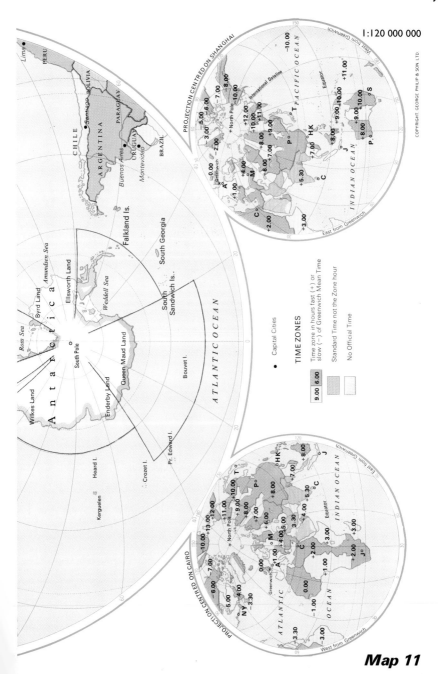

1:120 000 000

PROJECTION CENTRED ON SHANGHAI

West from Greenwich

−10.00

P A C I F I C   O C E A N

+8.00
−7.00
−6.00
−5.00
−3.00
−2.00
International Dateline
+North Pole +10.00
+12.00
+11.00
+10.00
+9.00
+8.00
+7.00
Equator
+11.00
T°
+9.00 +10.00
+10.00
P°
S°
−2.00
0.00 Greenwich
−4.00
+1.00
+4.00
+6.00
+8.00
+9.00
HK°
+8.00
+9.00
+8.00
+10.00
P°
A°
M°
+7.00
+5.30
C°
J°
+7.00
C°
+2.00
I N D I A N   O C E A N
+3.00

East from Greenwich

COPYRIGHT GEORGE PHILIP & SON LTD

Lima
PERU
BOLIVIA
Santiago
CHILE
ARGENTINA
PARAGUAY
Buenos Aires
URUGUAY
Montevideo
BRAZIL
Falkland Is.
South Georgia
South
Sandwich Is.

Amundsen Sea
Ross Sea
Byrd Land
Ellsworth Land
Weddell Sea
A n t a r c t i c a
Wilkes Land
South Pole
Queen Maud Land
Enderby Land
Bouvet I.
Pr. Edward I.
Crozet I.
Heard I.
Kerguelen

A T L A N T I C   O C E A N

• Capital Cities

TIME ZONES

| 9.00 | 6.00 |

Time zone in hours fast (+) or
slow (−) of Greenwich Mean Time

Standard Time not the Zone hour

No Official Time

PROJECTION CENTRED ON CAIRO

East from Greenwich

HK°
T°
+7.00
J°
+8.00
+10.00 +11.00 +12.00 +13.00
+10.00
+9.00
P°
+8.00
+8.00
C°
+5.30
+6.00
+4.00
+7.00
+North Pole
+11.00
+6.00
M°
A°
+4.00 +5.00
+3.00
Equator
+1.00
0.00 Greenwich
+2.00
+3.00
C°
+2.00
+1.00
J°
0.00
I N D I A N   O C E A N
−1.00
−3.30
−6.00
−5.00
−7.00
−10.00
NY°
−4.00
−3.30
−3.00
A T L A N T I C   O C E A N

West from Greenwich

Map 11

Arctic

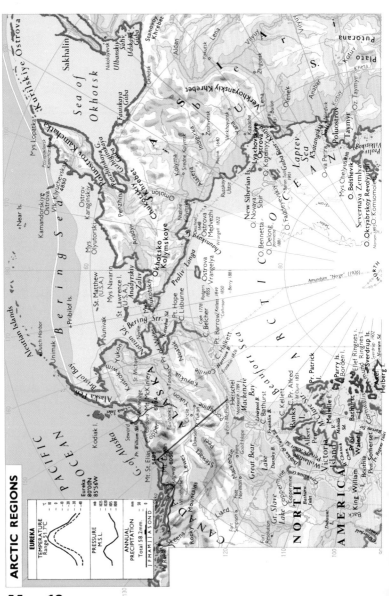

ARCTIC REGIONS

EUREKA
80°00N
85°56W

TEMPERATURE
Range 51.7°C

PRESSURE
M.S.L.

ANNUAL
PRECIPITATION
Total 58.2mm.

J F M A M J J A S O N D

Map 12

1:42 000 000

Progress of Exploration

Coasts explored before 1800
        ,,   ,,   between 1800 & 1850
        ,,   ,,   between 1850 & 1900
        ,,   ,,   since   1900

+ Byrd Highest latitudes reached by explorers
   1926   with date

Seas open all year

Extreme limits of
drift-ice

Seas covered by
pack-ice in Spring

Seas permanently
covered by pack-ice
ice caps and
permanent ice shelf

COPYRIGHT GEORGE PHILIP & SON LTD

Arctic Explorers

Cook 1778	
Franklin 1826–47	
McClure 1850–53	
Nansen (Fram) 1893–96	
Sverdrup 1902	
Peary 1892–1906	
Amundsen 1903–6 & 1926	
Bernier 1906–1913	
Peary 1908–9	
Knud Rasmussen 1912	
Stefánsson 1914–15	
Byrd 1926 (by air)	
Wilkins 1928 (by air)	
Lindsay 1934	
Papanin (Drift of Soviet	
Expedition) 1937–8	
Sedov 1937–40	
Knuth (Danish Pearyland	
Expedition) 1948–49	
Skate (Nuclear submarine) 1959	
Manhattan (Tanker) 1969	

Map 13

13

Antarctic

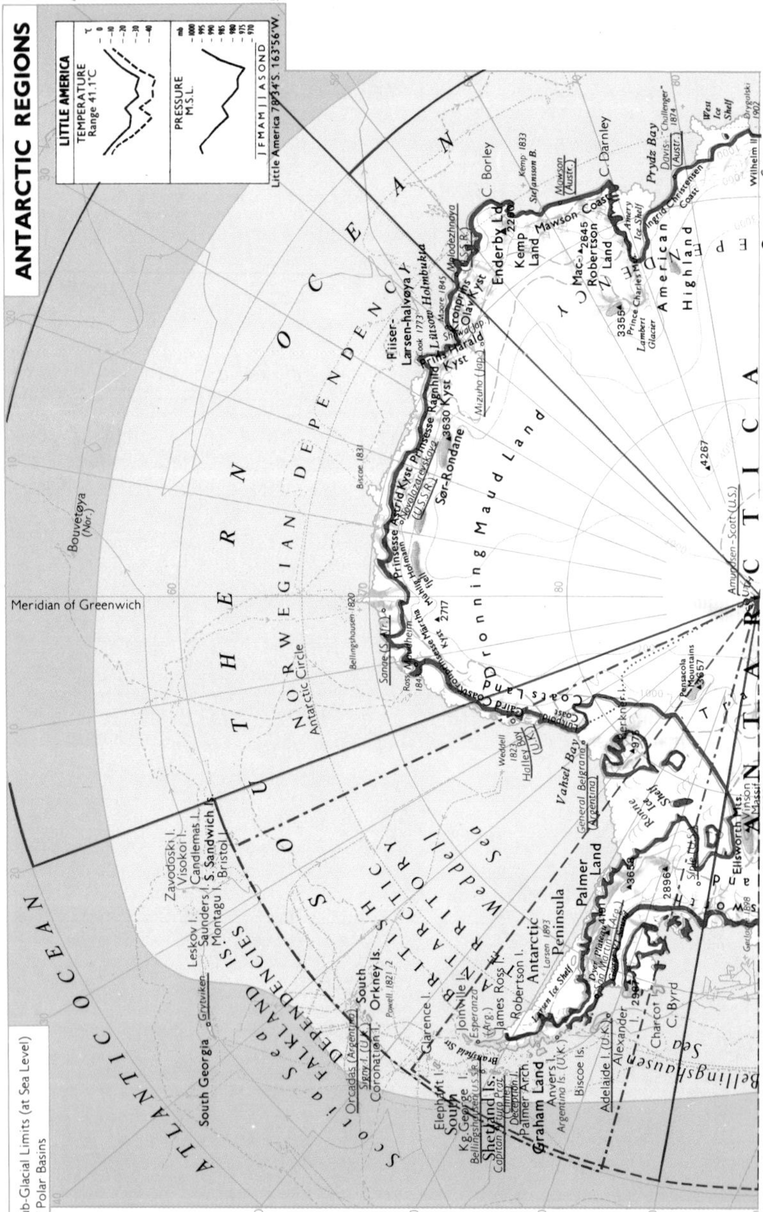

ANTARCTIC REGIONS

LITTLE AMERICA
TEMPERATURE Range 41.1°C
PRESSURE M.S.L.
J F M A M J J A S O N D
Little America 79°14'S. 163°56'W.

Sub-Glacial Limits (at Sea Level) of Polar Basins

Map 14

ATLANTIC OCEAN

Bouvetøya (Nor.)

SOUTHERN OCEAN

NORWEGIAN DEPENDENCY

Meridian of Greenwich

Antarctic Circle

Zavodoski I.
Visokoi I.
Leskov I.
Candlemas I.
Saunders I.
Montagu I.
Bristol I.
Grytviken
South Sandwich Is.

South Georgia

Scotia Sea

FALKLAND ISLAND DEPENDENCIES

South Orkney Is.
Orcadas (Argentina)
Coronation I.
Powell I. 1821
Signy I. (U.K.)

BRITISH ANTARCTIC TERRITORY

Elephant I.
Clarence I.
Kg. George I.
Joinville I.
Esperanza (Arg.)
James Ross I.
Robertson I.

South Shetland Is.

Palmer Arch.
Anvers I.
Biscoe Is.

Graham Land
Antarctic Peninsula
Palmer Land

Adelaide I.
Charcot I.
Alexander I.
C. Byrd

Bellingshausen Sea

Weddell Sea

Ronne Ice Shelf
Filchner Ice Shelf

Coats Land

Vahsel Bay
General Belgrano (Argentina)

Amundsen–Scott (U.S.)

A N T A R C T I C A

Dronning Maud Land

Fimbulheimen
Sør-Rondane

Prinsesse Astrid Kyst
Prinsesse Ragnhild Kyst
Princess Martha Coast

Larsen-halvøya

Enderby Ld.
Kemp Land
Mac·Robertson Land
American Highland

C. Borley
C. Darnley
Prydz Bay
Mawson (Aust.)
Wilhelm II Coast

Prince Charles Mountains
Lambert Glacier

Ellsworth Land
Ellsworth Mountains
Vinson Massif

1:42 000 000

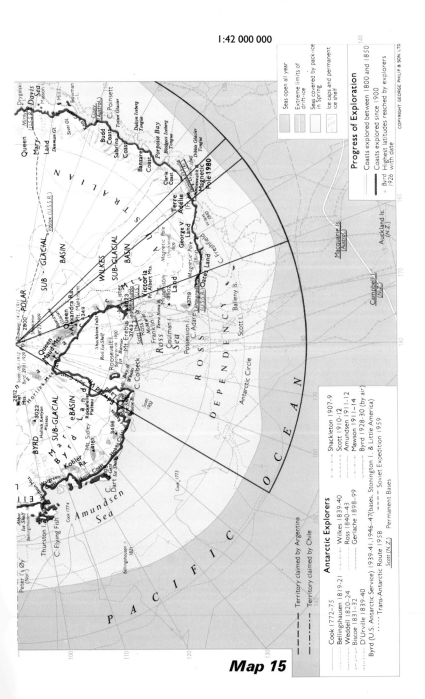

Seas open all year

Extreme limits of drift-ice

Seas covered by pack-ice in Spring

Ice caps and permanent ice shelf

Progress of Exploration

— — — Coasts explored between 1800 and 1850

——— Coasts explored since 1900

＋ Byrd Highest latitudes reached by explorers
1926   with date

COPYRIGHT GEORGE PHILIP & SON LTD

Antarctic Explorers

—— Cook 1772–75	—·—·— Wilkes 1839–40	·····•···· Shackleton 1907–9
—— Bellingshausen 1819–21	—··—··— Ross 1840–43	— — — Scott 1910–12
—— Weddell 1820–24	—···—···— Gerlache 1898–99	— — — Amundsen 1911–12
—— Biscoe 1831–32		—·—·— Mawson 1911–14
—— D'Urville 1839–40		—— Byrd 1928–30 (by air)

Byrd (U.S. Antarctic Service) 1939–41, 1946–47 (bases, Stonington I. & Little America)
····· Trans-Antarctic Route 1958   — — — Soviet Expedition 1959

Scott (N.Z)   Permanent Bases

— — — Territory claimed by Argentina
—·—·— Territory claimed by Chile

Map 15

Europe: *Physical*

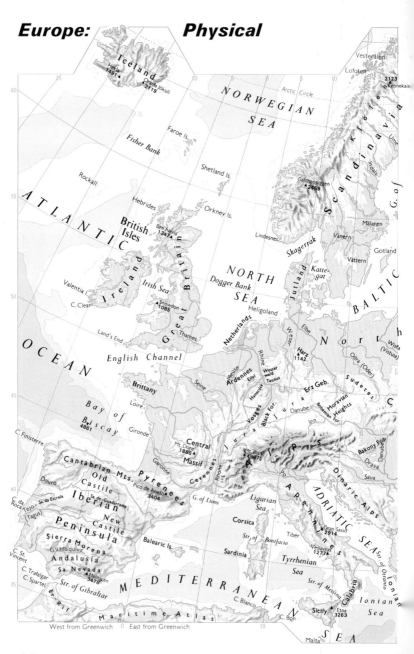

Iceland
Hekla 1491
Oraefa Jökull 2119

NORWEGIAN SEA

Vesterålen
Lofoten
2123 Kebnekais

Arctic Circle

Fisher Bank
Faroe Is.
Shetland Is.

Scandinavia
Galdhøpiggen 2469
Ume
Indals

ATLANTIC

Rockall
Hebrides
Orkney Is.
British Isles
Ben Nevis 1347

Lindesnes
Skagerrak
Kattegat
Jutland
Mälaren
Vänern
Gotland
Vättern

G. of

BALTIC

North

Valentia I.
C. Clear
Ireland
Irish Sea
Great Britain
Snowdon 1085

NORTH SEA
Dogger Bank
Heligoland
Netherlands

Weser
Elbe
Harz 1142
Odra (Oder)
Wista (Vistula)

Land's End
Thames

OCEAN
English Channel

Brittany
Seine
Meuse
Ardennes
Eifel
Rhine
Wester wald
Taunus
Hunsruck
Erz Geb.
Sudetes
C

Bay of Biscay 4861

Loire
Gironde

Vosges
Black For.
Jura
Danube
Bohemian For.
Moravian Heights
Bakony For.
Drava

C. Finisterre

Cantabrian Mts.
Old Castile
Douro
Sa. de Guadarrama
Pyrenees
Pico de Aneto 3404

Mt. Dore 1886
Central Massif
Cévennes
Rhône
Mt. Blanc 4807
ALPS
Po
Inn
Sava
Dinaric Alps

da Roca
Tejo (Tagus)
Sa. da Estrela
Iberian Peninsula
New Castile
Sierra Morena
Guadalquivir
Andalusia
Sa. Nevada
Mulhacén 3478

Balearic Is.

G. of Lions
Corsica
Str. of Bonifacio
Sardinia

Ligurian Sea
Tiber
Apennines
Gran Sasso 2914
Vesuvius 1277

ADRIATIC SEA
Str. of Otranto
Ionian

C. St. Vincent
C. Trafalgar
C. Spartel
Str. of Gibraltar

MEDITERRANEAN
C. Blanco
C. Bon

Tyrrhenian Sea
Str. of Messina
Sicily
Etna 3263
Calabria
Ionian Sea

Maritime Atlas

West from Greenwich   0   East from Greenwich   10

Malta

SEA

Map 16

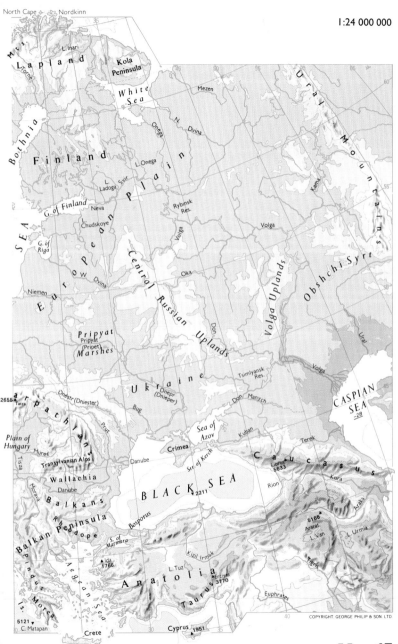

1:24 000 000

North Cape   Nordkinn

Mts. Lapland
L. Inari
L. Torne
Kola Peninsula
White Sea
Mezen
Ural Mountains
60
Bothnia
Finland
Onega
N. Dvina
L. Onega
L. Ladoga Svir
Kama
55
G. of Finland Neva
European Plain
Rybinsk Res.
Volga
Chudskoye
Volga
SEA
G. of Riga
Oka
Volga Uplands
Obschi Syrt
Niemen
W. Dvina
Central Russian Uplands
Don
Ural
Pripyat
Pripyat (Pripet) Marshes
Don
Tsimlyansk Res.
Volga
CASPIAN SEA
-28
45
2655 ▲ Tatra
Carpathians
Dnestr (Dniester)
Ukraine
Dnepr (Dnieper)
Bug
Prut
Don Manych
Plain of Hungary
Mures
Sea of Azov
Kuban
Terek
Elbrus 5633
Caucasus
Transylvanian Alps
Crimea
Str. of Kerch
Rion
Kura
Araks
Tisza
Wallachia
Danube
Danube
▲2211
BLACK SEA
Morava
Balkans
Bosporus
5166 ▲ Ararat
L. Van
L. Urmia
R.
Balkan Peninsula
Rhodope
S. of Marmara
Tigris
Aegean Sea
Pindus
▲ Ida 1766
Kizil Irmak
Anatolia
Erciyas 3770
Euphrates
40
Is.
Morea
5121 ▲ C. Matapan
Crete
Taurus
Cyprus ▲1951
35

Map 17

Europe: *Political*

Map 18

18

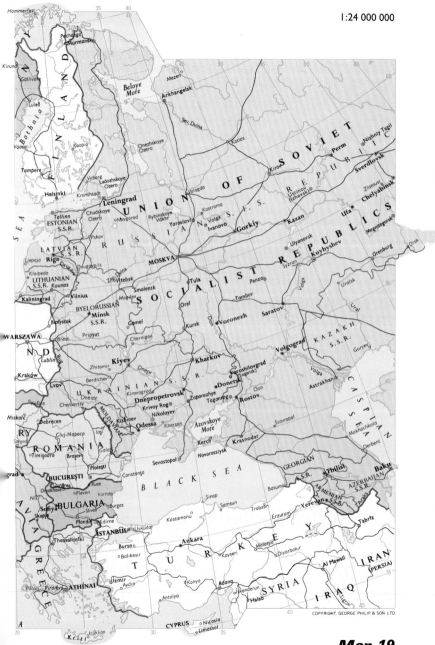

1:24 000 000

COPYRIGHT GEORGE PHILIP & SON. LTD.

Map 19

Map 20

British Isles: South

1:4 000 000

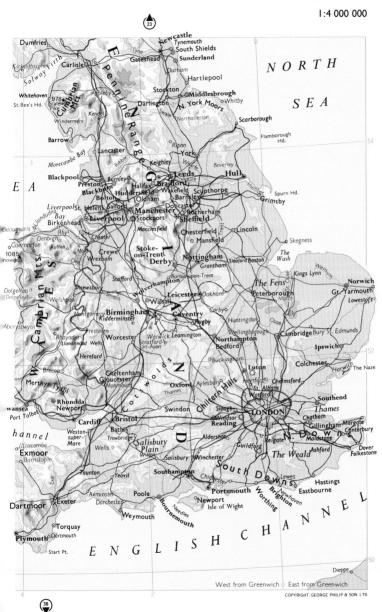

Dumfries
Kirkcudbright
Solway Firth
Whitehaven
St. Bee's Hd.
978
Scafell Pike
Windermere
Kendal
Appleby
Carlisle
Newcastle
Tynemouth
South Shields
Gateshead
Sunderland
Durham
Hartlepool
Stockton
Darlington
Middlesbrough
Whitby
N. York Moors
Northallerton
Swale
Scarborough

NORTH
SEA

Barrow
Lancaster
Morecambe Bay
Ribble
Ripon
Flamborough Hd.
York
Beverley
Wharfe
54

Blackpool
Preston
Burnley
Keighley
Leeds
Hull
Blackburn
Bolton
Halifax
Bradford
Wakefield
Liverpool
Bay
Birkenhead
St. Helens
Salford
Manchester
Stockport
Macclesfield
Huddersfield
Oldham
Barnsley
Doncaster
Rotherham
Sheffield
Scunthorpe
Humber
Spurn Hd.
Grimsby

EA

Beaumaris
Llandudno
Caernarfon
Denbigh
Rhyl
Ruthin
Mold
Chester
Crewe
Chesterfield
Mansfield
Lincoln
Skegness

1085
Snowdon
Dolgellau
(Dolgelley)
Aberystwyth
Cambrian Mts
Welshpool
Montgomery
Shrewsbury
Stafford
Wrexham
Stoke-on-Trent
Derby
Nottingham
Grantham
Sleaford Boston
The Wash
Kings Lynn
Wentum
Norwich
Gt. Yarmouth
Lowestoft

Rhayader
Llandrindod Wells
Presteign
Kidderminster
Worcester
Warwick
Stratford-on-Avon
Hereford
Birmingham
Walsall
Wolverhampton
Burton-upon-Trent
Leicester
Oakham
Corby
Coventry
Rugby
Leamington
Northampton
Wellingborough
Bedford
Peterborough
The Fens
March
Ely
Ouse
Huntingdon
Cambridge
Bury St. Edmunds
Ipswich

Brecon
Merthyr Tydfil
Cheltenham
Gloucester
Monmouth
Cotswolds
Oxford
Thames
Aylesbury
Buckingham
Luton
Hertford
St. Albans
Watford
Colchester
Harwich
The Naze
Chelmsford

swansea
Port Talbot
Rhondda
Newport
Cardiff
Bristol
Bath
Weston-super-Mare
Wells
Trowbridge
Salisbury Plain
Wilton
Swindon
Reading
Aldershot
Guildford
Chiltern Hills
Slough
Windsor
LONDON
Reigate
Thames
Chatham
Gillingham
Maidstone
Margate
Canterbury
Southend
N. Downs
Dover
Folkestone

hannel
Ilfracombe
Exmoor
Barnstaple
Taunton
Yeovil
Exe
Salisbury
Winchester
Southampton
Chichester
The Weald
Ashford
Hastings
South Downs
Lewes
Brighton
Worthing
Newhaven
Eastbourne

Dartmoor
Plymouth
Exeter
Axminster
Dorchester
Poole
Dartmouth
Torquay
Start Pt.
Weymouth
Bournemouth
Needles
Newport
Isle of Wight
Portsmouth

ENGLISH CHANNEL

Dieppe
50

West from Greenwich 0 East from Greenwich

4
2

Map 21

21

British Isles: North

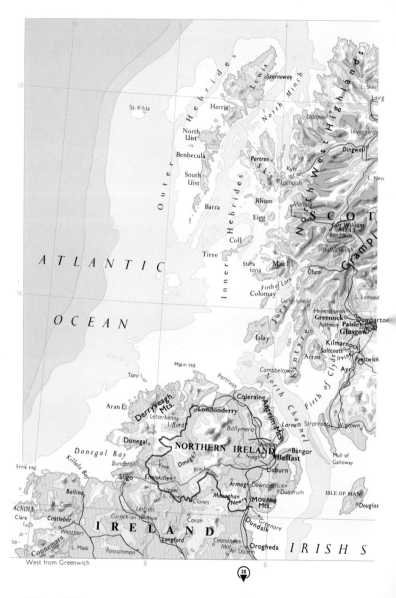

ATLANTIC

OCEAN

Outer Hebrides

Inner Hebrides

St. Kilda

Harris

Lewis

Stornoway

North Uist

Benbecula

Portree

Skye

North Minch

Ullapool

Invergordo

Dingwall

L. Shin

Lairg

L. Ness

North West Highlands

South Uist

Kyle of Lochalsh

Barra

Rhum

Eigg

Mallaig

SCOT

Fort William
1343
Ben Nevis

Coll

Ballachulish

Grampi

Tiree

Staffa
Iona

Mull

Oban

Firth of Lorn

Colonsay

Lochgilphead

L. Lomond

Helensburgh
Greenock
Rothesay Paisley
Glasgow
Dumbarton

Jura

Islay

Kilmarnock
Saltcoats Irvine Prestwick
Arran Ayr

Kintyre

Firth of Clyde

Malin Hd.

Tory I.

Portrush

Coleraine

Campbeltown

North Channel

Stranraer Wigtown

Aran I.

Derryveagh Mts.

Letterkenny
Lifford

Londonderry

Ballymena

Antrim Mts.

Larne

Donegal

NORTHERN IRELAND

L. Neagh

Bangor
Belfast

Mull of Galloway

Donegal Bay

Bundoran

Erne

Omagh

Lisburn

ISLE OF MAN

Erris Hd.

Killala Bay

Sligo

Enniskillen

Blackwater

Armagh Downpatrick

Dundrum

Douglas

Ballina

Upper
L. Erne

Clones

Monaghan

Newry

Mourne Mts.

Achill I.

L. Conn

Leitrim

Cavan

Greenore

Clare I.

Castlebar

Carrick-on-Shannon

Dundalk

Connemara

Westport

L. Mask

IRELAND

Longford

Roscommon

Ceananus Mor
An Uaimh

Drogheda

IRISH S

West from Greenwich

Map 22

1:4 000 000

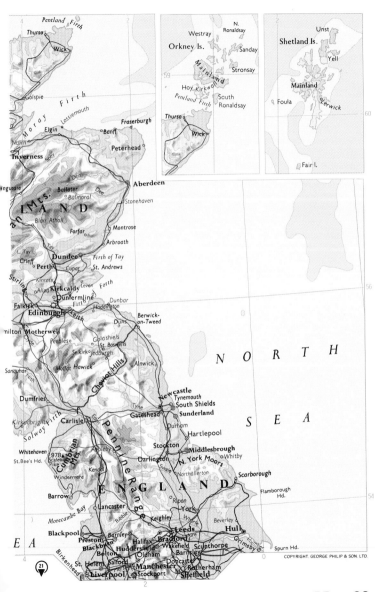

COPYRIGHT. GEORGE PHILIP & SON. LTD.

Map 23

Southern England

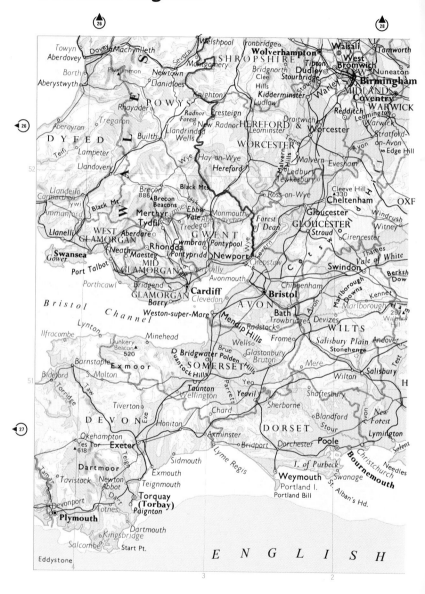

Map 24

1:2 000 000

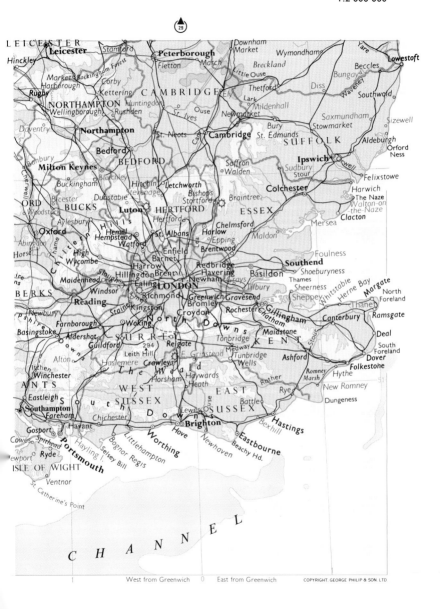

Map 25

Wales and South West England

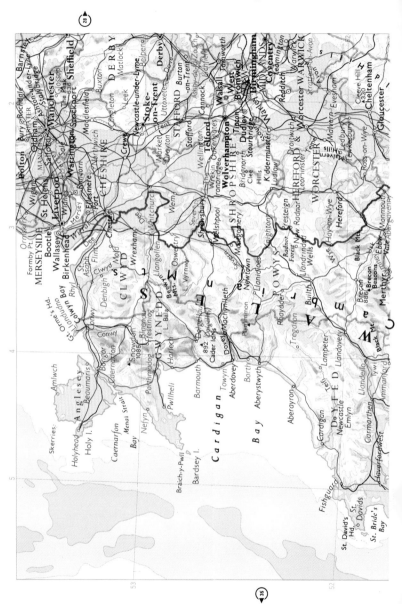

Map 26

1:2 000 000

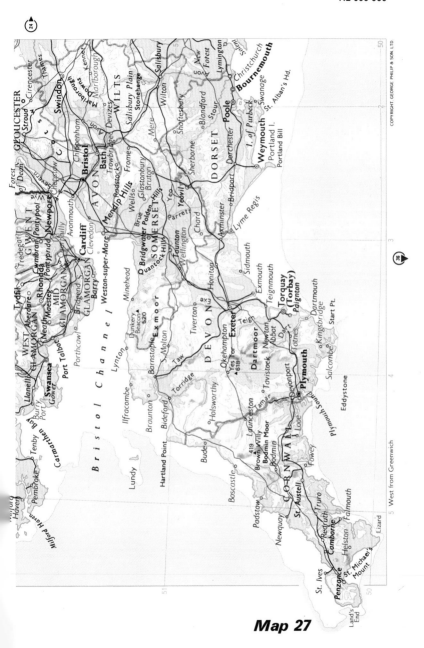

5 West from Greenwich

COPYRIGHT. GEORGE PHILIP & SON LTD.

Map 27

Northern England

Map 28

1:2 000 000

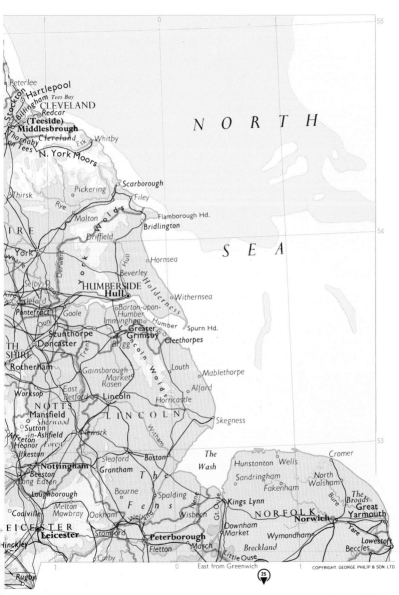

Map 29

Southern Scotland

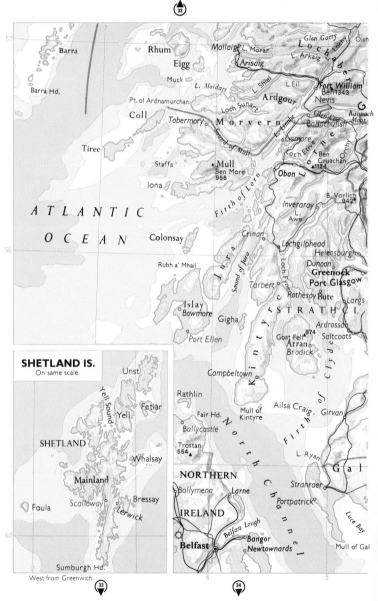

SHETLAND IS.
On same scale

Map 30

1:2 000 000

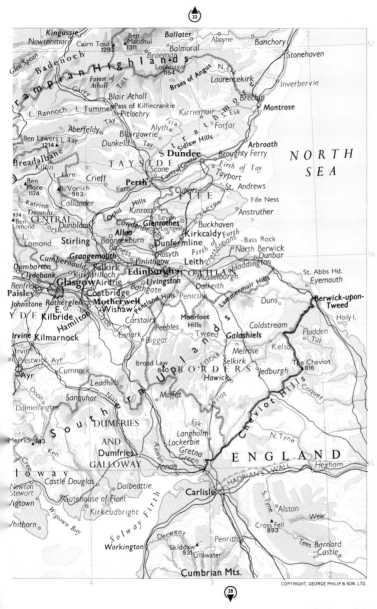

Kingussie
Newtonmore
Cairn Toul
1292
Ben
Macdhui
1311
Ballater
Balmoral
Aboyne
Banchory
Glen Spean
Grampian Highlands
Badenoch
Stonehaven
Braemar
Lochnagar
1154
Forest of
Atholl
N.E.sk
Laurencekirk
Inverbervie
Carry
Tilt
Braes of Angus
Brechin
Blair Atholl
Pass of Killiecrankie
Pitlochry
Kirriemuir
S. Esk
Montrose
L. Rannoch
L. Tummel
Aberfeldy
Tay
Blairgowrie
Alyth
Isla
Forfar
Ben Lawers
1214
L. Tay
Dunkeld
Tay
Sidlaw Hills
Arbroath
Breadalbane
Killin
Scone
Dundee
Broughty Ferry
Firth of Tay
NORTH
SEA
Ben
More
1174
L. Earn
Crieff
Perth
Earn
Carse o'Gowrie
Tayport
St. Andrews
Katrine
B. Vorlich
983
Callander
TAYSIDE
STRATHMORE
Cupar
FIFE
Fife Ness
Trossachs
974
Ben
Lomond
CENTRAL
Dunblane
Ochil Hills
Kinross
L. Leven
Anstruther
Cowdenbeath
Glenrothes
Buckhaven
L.
Lomond
Stirling
Bannockburn
Lochgelly
Kirkcaldy
Forth
Bass Rock
Grangemouth
Dunfermline
North Berwick
Cumbernauld
Falkirk
Rosyth
Firth of Forth
Prestonpans
Dunbar
Dumbarton
Linlithgow
Leith
Clydebank
Kirkintilloch
Edinburgh
Haddington
St. Abbs Hd.
Glasgow
Airdrie
Livingston
LOTHIAN
Musselburgh
Eyemouth
Renfrew
Coatbridge
Bathgate
Dalkeith
Lammermuir Hills
Paisley
Rutherglen
Motherwell
Penicuik
Duns
Berwick-upon-
Tweed
Johnstone
E.
Wishaw
Pentland Hills
Holy I.
Kilbride
Hamilton
Moorfoot
Hills
Coldstream
CLYDE
Kilmarnock
Carstairs
Peebles
Tweed
Galashiels
Flodden
Till
Irvine
Lanark
Biggar
Melrose
Kelso
Irvine
Prestwick
Ayr
Broad Law
840
BORDERS
Selkirk
Ettrick
Jedburgh
The Cheviot
816
Ayr
Cumnock
Leadhills
Hawick
Teviot
Coquet
Doon
Sanquhar
Nith
Moffat
Cheviot Hills
Dalmellington
SOUTHERN
UPLANDS
Esk
N. Tyne
Merrick
843
DUMFRIES
Langholm
Lockerbie
ENGLAND
Ken
AND
Dumfries
Gretna
Green
Hexham
Creek
GALLOWAY
Annan
Annan
HADRIAN'S WALL
GALLOWAY
Newton
Stewart
Castle Douglas
Dalbeattie
Carlisle
S. Tyne
Alston
Wear
Wigtown
Gatehouse of Fleet
Kirkcudbright
Cross Fell
893
Tees
Barnard
Castle
Whithorn
Wigtown Bay
Solway Firth
Derwent
Penrith
Workington
Skiddaw
931
Ullswater
Cumbrian Mts.

COPYRIGHT. GEORGE PHILIP & SON. LTD.

Map 31

Northern Scotland

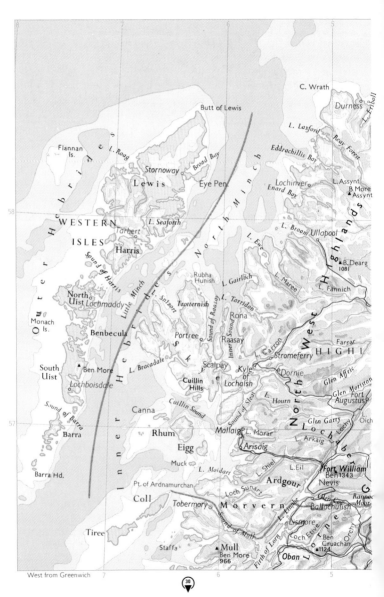

C. Wrath

Durness

L. Laxford

Reay Forest

L. Friboll

Butt of Lewis

Eddrachillis Bay

Flannan Is.

L. Roag

Broad Bay

Lochinver

Enard Bay

L. Assynt

B More Assynt

Stornoway

Lewis

Eye Pen

H i g h l a n d s

North Minch

L. Broom Ullapool

WESTERN

L. Seaforth

Tarbert

ISLES

Harris

L. Ewe

B. Dearg 1081

Sound of Harris

Rubha Hunish

L. Gairloch

L. Fannich

North Uist Lochmaddy

Little Minch

L. Torridon

Trotternish

Monach Is.

Benecula

Snizort

Sound of Raasay

Rona

West Highlands

Portree

Raasay

Farrar

L. Carron

Stromeferry

HIGHL

South Uist

Ben More

L. Bracadale

Scalpay

Kyle of Lochalsh

Dornie

Glen Affric

Lochboisdale

Cuillin Hills

L. Hourn

Glen Moriston

Fort Augustus

Sound of Barra

Canna

Cuillin Sound

Sound of Sleat

Glen Garry

Oich

Barra

Rhum

Mallaig

L. Morar

L. Arkaig

Lochy

Eigg

Arisaig

Muck

L. Moidart

L. Shiel

L. Eil

Fort William

Ben 1343

Barra Hd.

Pt. of Ardnamurchan

Coll

Loch Sunart

Ardgour

Nevis

Rannoc Moor

Tobermory

Morvern

Ballachulish

L. Linnhe

Lismore

Tiree

Sound of Mull

Ben Cruachan 1124

Staffa

Mull Ben More 966

Firth of Lorn

Loch Etive

Orchy

Oban

Map 32

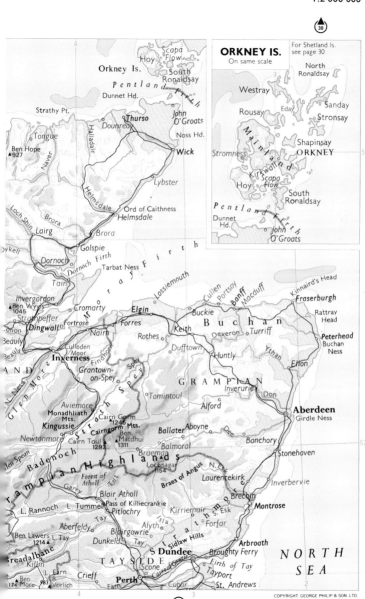

1:2 000 000

ORKNEY IS.
On same scale

For Shetland Is.
see page 30

North
Ronaldsay

Orkney Is.

Scapa Flow

Hoy

South
Ronaldsay

Pentland Firth

Dunnet Hd.

Westray

Rousay

Eday

Sanday

Stronsay

Strathy Pt.

Tongue

Ben Hope
▲927

Dounreay

Thurso

John
O'Groats

Noss Hd.

Wick

Halladale

Naver

Stromness

Shapinsay

ORKNEY
Mainland

Kirkwall

Scapa
Flow

Hoy

South
Ronaldsay

Pentland Firth

Dunnet
Hd.

John
O'Groats

Lybster

Loch Shin

Brora

Lairg

Helmsdale

Ord of Caithness
Helmsdale

Brora

Dykell

Dornoch

Golspie

Dornoch Firth

Tarbat Ness

Tain

Invergordon

Ben Wyvis
▲1045

Cromarty

Strathpeffer

Fortrose

Dingwall

Nairn

Forres

Elgin

Lossiemouth

Cullen

Portsoy

Buckie

Keith

Banff

Macduff

Kinnaird's Head

Fraserburgh

Rattray
Head

B U C H A N

Peterhead
Buchan
Ness

Moray Firth

Conon

Beauly

Beauly

Culloden
Moor

Inverness

Findhorn

Grantown-
on-Spey

Spey

Rothes

Dufftown

Deveron

Turriff

Huntly

Ythan

Elton

Strath Spey

G R A M P I A N

Inverurie

Don

Aviemore

Monadhliath
Mts.

Cairn Gorm
1245

Tomintoul

Alford

Kingussie

Cairngorm Mts.

Newtonmore

Cairn Toul
1293

Ben
Macdhui
1311

Ballater

Aboyne

Dee

Aberdeen

Girdle Ness

Glen Spean

Badenoch

Highlands

Braemar

Balmoral

Lochnagar
1154

Banchory

Stonehaven

Grampian

Garry

Forest of
Atholl

Tilt

Braes of Angus

N. Esk

Laurencekirk

Inverbervie

L. Rannoch

L. Tummel

Blair Atholl

Pass of Killiecrankie

Pitlochry

Kirriemuir

S. Esk

Brechin

Montrose

Aberfeldy

Tay

Blairgowrie

Alyth

Isla

Forfar

Strathmore

Ben Lawers
1214 ▲

L. Tay

Dunkeld

Tay

Sidlaw Hills

Arbroath

Breadalbane

TAYSIDE

Dundee

Broughty Ferry

N O R T H

Killin

Scone

Carse of Gowrie

Firth of Tay

Tayport

S E A

Ben
More
▲1174

983 ▲
Vorlich

L. Earn

Crieff

Earn

Perth

Cupar

St. Andrews

COPYRIGHT GEORGE PHILIP & SON LTD.

Map 33

Ireland

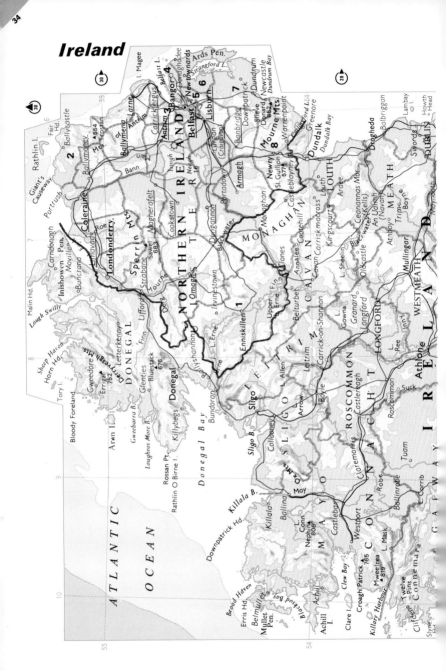

Map 34

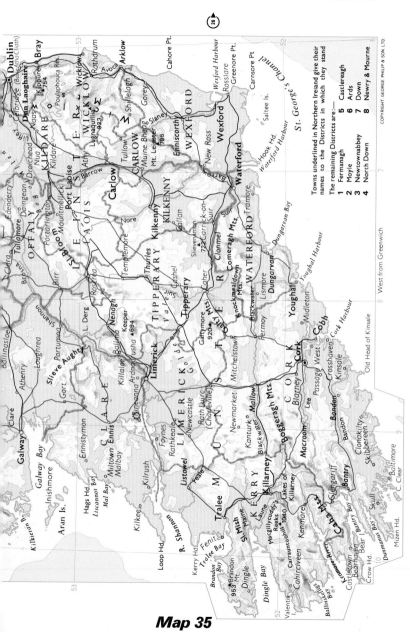

1:2 000 000

Towns underlined in Northern Ireland give their
names to the Districts in which they stand

The remaining Districts are:—

1 Fermanagh	5 Castlereagh
2 Moyle	6 Ards
3 Newtownabbey	7 Down
4 North Down	8 Newry & Mourne

COPYRIGHT GEORGE PHILIP & SON LTD

Map 35

France

Map 36

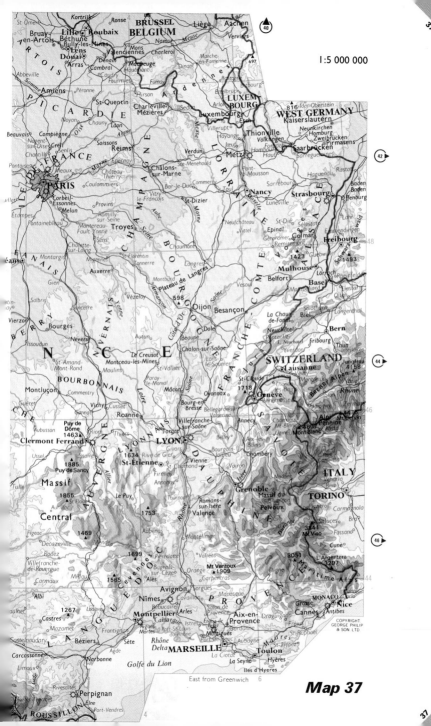

1:5 000 000

Map 37

East from Greenwich 6

COPYRIGHT
GEORGE PHILIP
& SON. LTD

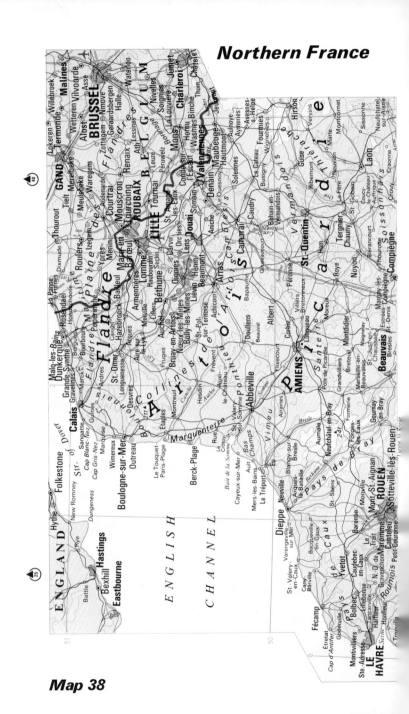

Northern France

Map 38

1:2 000 000

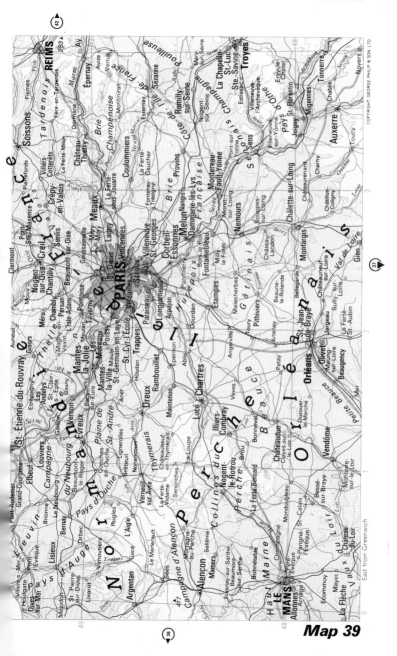

East from Greenwich

Map 39

Netherlands

Map 40

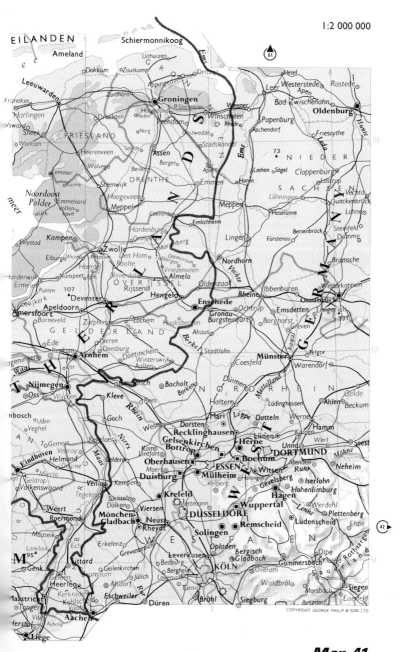

1:2 000 000

61

EILANDEN
Ameland
Schiermonnikoog

Uithuizen
Dokkum   Zoutkamp   Delfzijl
Hesel

Leeuwarden   Zuidhorn   Appingedam   Leer   Westerstede   Rastede
Franeker   Apen
Harlingen   Drachten   Roden   Hoogezand   Groningen   Weener   Bad Zwischenahn   Oldenburg
Olsward   Sneek   Slochteren   Winschoten   Papenburg   Friesoythe
Workum   FRIESLAND   Norg   Veendam   Rhede   Aschendorf
Heerenveen   Smilde   Assen   Stadskanaal   Lathen   Sögel   Cloppenburg   73   N I E D E R
Wolvega   Borger
Lemmer   Beilen   Apen   Haren   S A C H S E N
Kuinre   Steenwijk   DRENTHE   Emmen   Löhningen   Lastrup   Vechta
Noordoost   Emmeloord   Hoogeveen   Quackenbrück
Polder   Vollen-   Meppel   Haselünne   Lohne
meer   Urk   hove   Coevorden   Bersenbrück   Steinfeld
Kampen   Meppen   Lingen   Fürstenau   Damme
Elystad   Hardenberg   Emlichheim   Bramsche
Elburg   Wezep   Zwolle   Den Ham   Ommen   Mariënberg   Nordhorn   Westerkappeln
Harderwijk   Hatten   Daalte   Oatmarsum   Vechte
Ermelo   Heerde   Nijverdal   Tubbergen   Ibbenbüren   Lengerich   331
Nijkerk   Putten   107   OVERIJSSEL   Oldenzaal   Rheine   Osnabrück
Amersfoort   Deventer   Rijssen   Almelo   Ochtrup   Emsdetten   Lengerich   52
Apeldoorn   Lochem   Hengelo   Enschede   Rheine   Greven
Barneveld   Zutphen   Haaksbergen   Gronau   Burgsteinfurt   Borghorst   Telgte
Ede   GELDERLAND   Dieren   Doesburg   Ahaus   Münster   Warendorf
Renkum   Doetinchem   Winterswijk   Stadtlohn   Coesfeld
Wageningen   Arnhem   Elst   Aalten   Berkel   Telgte
Waal   Zevenaar   Bocholt   N O R D R H E I N
Nijmegen   Emmerich   Borken   Dülmen   Mittelland   Oelde
Oss   Wijchen   Kleve   Rees   Haltern   Lüdinghausen   Ahlen   Beckum
nbosch   Uden   Goch   Wesel   Marl   Lippe   Datteln   Werne
Veghel   Kevelaer   Dorsten   Kamen   Hamm
Gemert   Niers   Recklinghausen   Lünen   Werl   Soest
Eindhoven   Venray   Kamp   Gelsenkirchen   Herne   Unna   Möhne
Helmond   Lintfort   Bottrop   Bochum   DORTMUND   Neheim
Mierlo   Geldern   Oberhausen   ESSEN   Witten   Menden   Ruhr
Geldrop   Moers   Duisburg   Mülheim   Hattingen   Gevelsberg   Iserlohn
Volkenswaard   Venlo   Kempen   Velbert   Hohenlimburg
Tegelen   Süchteln   Krefeld   Mettmann   Hagen   Werdohl
Weert   Dülken   Viersen   W E S T F A L E N   Plettenberg
Roermond   Mönchen   Neuss   DÜSSELDORF   Wuppertal   Lüdenscheid   Elspe   42
Gladbach   Rheydt   Remscheid
Maaseik   Erkelenz   Solingen   F A L E N
Lanklaar   Grevenbroich   Opladen   Bergisch   Olpe   51
95   Sittard   Geilenkirchen   Leverkusen   Bedburg   Gladbach   Gummersbach   Rothaarge
M   Genk   Jünssum   Bergheim   KÖLN   Overath   Sieg   Siegen
Geleen   Heerlen   Jülich   Lövenich   Cologne   Waldbröl   Morsbach   Eiserfeld
Kerkrade   Aldorf   Bergisch   Betzdorf
Maastricht   Vaals   Eschweiler   Düren   Brühl   Siegburg   Gladbach
Tongeren   Kohlscheid   Turnich   Aachen   Siegburg
Visé   Aubel   Aachen
erstal   Liège

C O P Y R I G H T   G E O R G E   P H I L I P   &   S O N   L T D

Map 41

Germany and the Low Countries

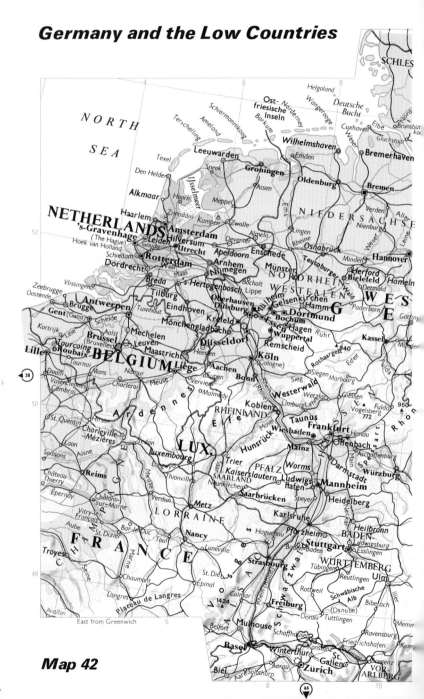

Map 42

1:5 000 000

Map 43

Alpine Lands

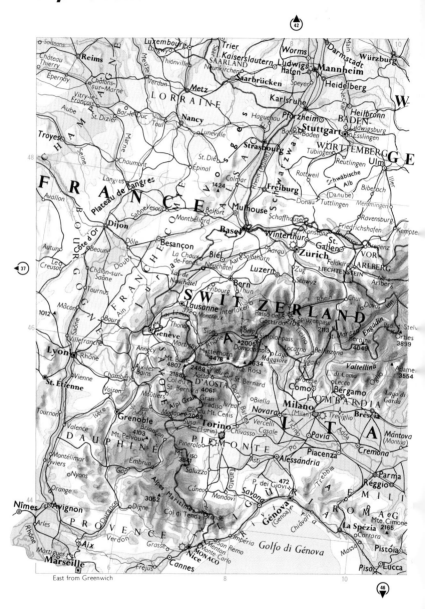

Map 44

1:5 000 000

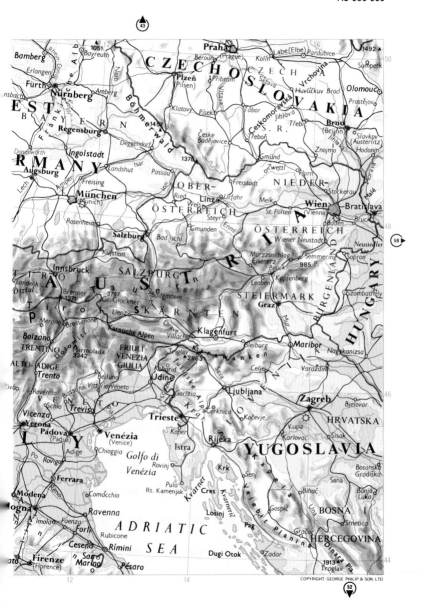

COPYRIGHT GEORGE PHILIP & SON LTD

Map 45

Northern Italy and Corsica

Map 46

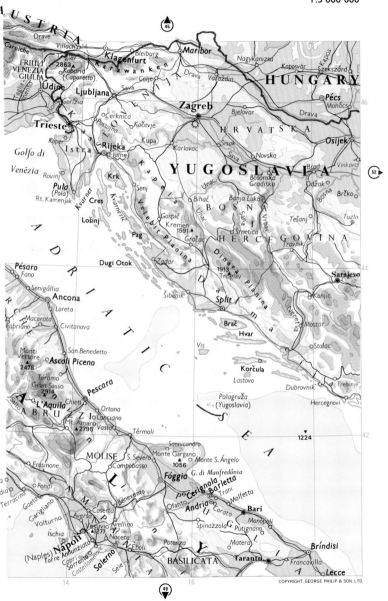

1:5 000 000

AUSTRIA

Carniche
Drave   Villach
Tárvisio   Klagenfurt   Bleiburg   Maribor   Nagykanizsa   Kaposvár   Szekszárd
2863   Karawanken
Triglav   Kobarid
FRIULI   (Caporetto)   Celje   Drava   Varaždin   HUNGARY
VENEZIA
GIULIA   Udine   Ljubljana   Sava   Pécs
Tagliam   Torre   Gorizia   Mohács   46
Isonzo   Zagreb   Bjelovar   Drava
Trieste   Cerknica   Kočevje   HRVATSKA
Karst   Postojna   Kupa   Sisak   Novska   Osijek
Koper   Rijeka   Karlovac   Sava   Vinkovci
Golfo di   Istra   (Fiume)   YUGOSLAVIA   Brod   52
Venézia   Rovinj   Unac   Bosanska   Odžak   Brčko
Pula   Krk   Senj   Gradiška   Bosna
(Pola)   Karner   Bihać   Banja Luka   Tešanj   Tuzla
Rt. Kamenjak   Cres   Sana   BOSNA   Vrbas
Kvarnerić   Gospič   Vrbas   I   Travnik
Lošinj   Kremen   Srnetica   HERCEGOVINA
Pag   1591   Gročac   Dinara   Sarajevo
Dugi Otok   Zadar   1913   Trogiav   Planina
Pésaro   Troglav   Konjic
Fano   Šibenik   Split   Neretva
Senigállia   Ancona   Brač   Mostar
Loreto   Hvar   Stolac
Macerata   Civitanova   Vis
Fabriano   San Benedetto   Korčula
Monti   Lastovo   Dubrovnik   Trebinje
Vettore   Ascoli Piceno   Palagruža   Hercegnovi
2478   (Yugoslavia)
Téramo   1224
Gran Sasso   Pescara
2914   Chieti   Ortona
L'Aquila   Lanciano
ABRUZZI   Mt. Amaro   Vasto   Térmoli
2795   Sannicandro
MOLISE   S. Severo   Monte Gargano
Frosinone   Campobasso   1056   Monte S. Ángelo
Fóggia   G. di Manfredónia
Fondi   Cerignola   Barletta
Terracina   Benevento   Ofanto   Trani   Molfetta
Gaeta   Caserta   Andria   Corato   Bari
Gangliano   Aversa   Avellino   Spinazzola   Putignano   Monopoli
Volturno   Vesuvio   Nocera   Potenza   Matera
Íschia   1277   CAMPANIA   Bríndisi
Napoli   Éboli   BASILICATA   Taranto   Francavilla
(Naples)   Torre Annunziata   Salerno   Lecce
Capri   Sorrento   Sele
Castellommare

ADRIATIC   SEA

PUGLIA

COPYRIGHT. GEORGE PHILIP & SON. LTD.

Map 47

Southern Italy and Sardinia

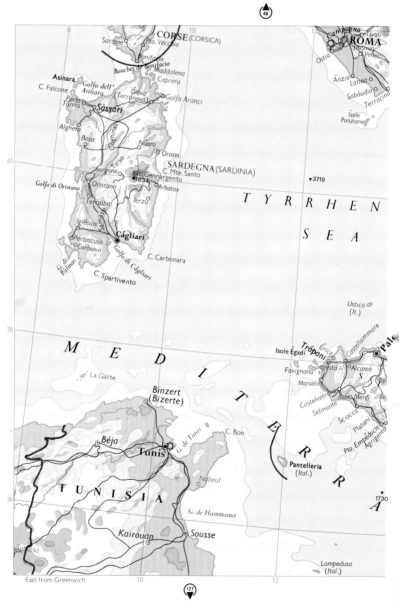

CORSE (CORSICA)
Sartene Pto. Vecchio
Bonifacio
Bouches de Bonifacio
Maddalena
Caprera
Asinara
Golfo dell'
Asinara
C. Falcone
Olbia
(Terranova)
Golfo Aranci
Porto
Torres
Sássari
Alghero
Bosa
Dottmas
Nuoro
Orosei
SARDEGNA (SARDINIA)
▼3719
40
Golfo di Oristano
Gorgono
Tirso
C. Mte. Santo
Gennargentu
★1834
Oristano
Arbatax
Tortolì
Terralba
Samassi
Iglesias
Cágliari
Portoscuso
Carbonia
Golfo di Cágliari
C. Carbonara
G. di
Pàlmas
C. Spartivento

Sábaudia
Terracina
Ísole
Ponziane
Campagna Tivoli
ROMA (Rome)
Velletri
Ostia
Ánzio
Latina

T Y R R H E N
S E A

Ustica
(It.)

38

M E D I T E R R A
Trápani Érice Castellammare
Isole Égadi Pal
Favignana Segesta Alcamó
Marsala Alcamó
Castelvetrano Menfi
Selinunte
Sciacca
Platani
Pto. Empédocle Agrigento

La Galite

Binzert
(Bizerte)

Béja
Tunis
G. de Tunis
C. Bon

Nabeul

Pantelleria
(Ital.)

36
T U N I S I A
1730
G. de Hammamet

Kairouan
Sousse

Lampedusa
(Ital.)

Map 48

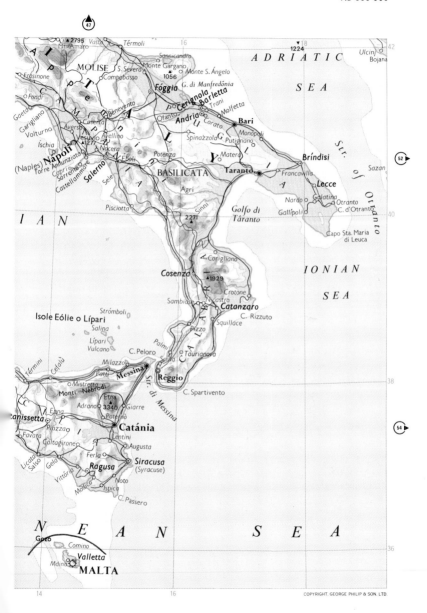

1:5 000 000

47

▲2795
Mt. Amaro
Vasto
Térmoli
16
▼18
1224
Ulcinj
Bojana

ADRIATIC

MOLISE
S. Severo
Monte Gargano
Frosinone
Campobasso
Monte S. Ángelo
1056
SEA

Fondi
CAMPI
Fóggia
G. di Manfredónia

Benevento
Cerignola
Barletta
Andria
Trani
Molfetta

Gaeta
Garigliano
Caserta
Ofanto
Corato
Bari

Volturno
Aversa
Avellino
Spinazzola
Putignano
Monopoli

Ischia
1277
Nocera
Potenza
Matera
PUGLIA
Bríndisi

Nápoli
(Naples)
Torre Annunziato
Salerno
EBOLI
BASILICATA
Taranto
Francavilla
Sazan

Sorrento
Castellammare
Sele
Agri
Lecce

Pisciotta
Agri
Sinni
Golfo di
Táranto
Nardo
Galatina
Otranto
C. d'Otranto

IAN
2271▲
Gallípoli
Capo Sta. Maria
di Leuca

Corigliano
IONIAN

Cosenza
▲1929
SEA

Crotone

Strómboli
Sambiase
Nicastro
Catanzaro

Isole Eólie o Lípari
Salina
Squilláce
C. Rizzuto

Lípari
Vulcano
Pizzo

C. Peloro
Palmi
Tauriánova

Términi
Cefalù
Milazzo
Séilla

Patti
Messina

Mistretta
Réggio

Monti Nebrodi
Str. di Messina
C. Spartivento

Etna
3340▲
Giarre

anissetta
Enna
Adrano
Paternò

Favara
Piazza
Catánia
Lentini

Caltagirone
Augusta

Licato
Ferla
Siracusa
(Syracuse)

Saso
Gela
Ragusa

Vittória
Noto

Módica
Ispica

C. Passero

N
E
A
N
S
E
A

Gozo
Comino

Valletta
Mdina
MALTA

COPYRIGHT. GEORGE PHILIP & SON. LTD.

Map 49

Spain and Portugal

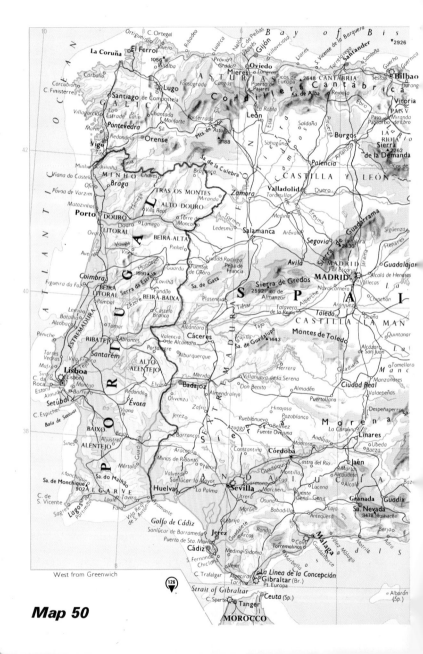

West from Greenwich

Strait of Gibraltar

Map 50

1:6 000 000

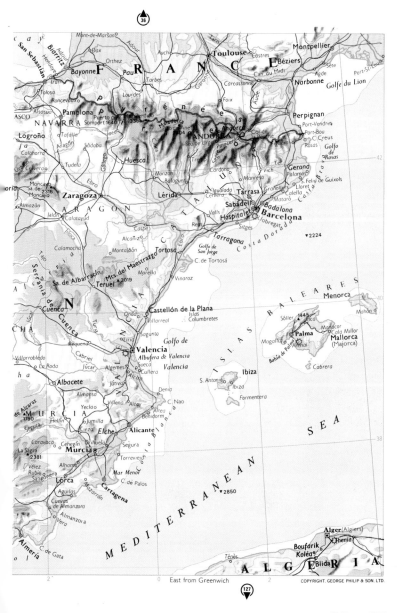

San Sebastián
Biarritz
Hendaye
Bayonne **F** Pau
Adour
Dax
Orthez
Tarbes
Mont-de-Marsan
Adour
Auch
Toulouse
Tarn
Montpellier
Béziers
Costres
F R A N C E
Can. du Midi
Séte
Agde
Port-St-Louis
Narbonne
Golfe du Lion
Irún
Tolosa
Roncevaux
Lourdes
P y r é n é e s
Foix
Carcassonne
Aude
Perpignan
Port-Vendres
C. Creus
ASCO
Alsasua
Pamplona
NAVARRA
Puerto de
Somport 1640
1355
Maladetta
Andorra
Col de
Port-Bou
Rosas
Golfo
de
Rosas
Logroño
Tafalla
Aragón
Sádaba
Sea de Urgel
Puigcerdá
Ter
Gerona
Palamós
Feliu de Guixols
Calahorra
Tudela
Huesca
Monzón
Tremp
Vich
Lloret
Calella
Costa Brava
Almazán
Moncayo
2316
Sa. de
Moncayo
Ebro
Balaguer
Cardona
Manresa
Granollers
Mataró
Zaragoza
A R A G O N
Calatayud
Gállego
Jalón
Iloca
Lérida
Igualada
Cervera
C A T A L U Ñ A
Tárrasa
Sabadell
Hospitalet
Badalona
Barcelona
Calamocha
Montalbán
Caspe
Alcañiz
Valls
Reus
Llobregat
Sitges
Tarragona
Costa Dorada
▼2224
Tajo
Serrania de Albarracín
Mts. del Maestrazgo
Teruel
2019
Morella
Tortosa
C. de Tortosa
Golfo de
San Jorge
Calamocha
Vinaroz
B A L E A R E S
Menorca
Cuenca
N
Cuenca
Turia
Onda
Villarreal
Castellón de la Plana
Islas
Columbretes
Mahón
Sóller
1445
Palma
Manacor
Cala Millor
CHA
Villarrobledo
La Roda
Cabriel
Júcar
Requena
Liria
Sagunto
Golfo de
Valencia
Albufera de Valencia
Valencia
Valencia
Magalluf
Bahía de Palma
Arenal
Mallorca
(Majorca)
a
Albacete
Almansa
Játiva
Algemesí
Sueca
Cullera
Alcira
I S L A S
Cabrera
de Alcaraz
M U R C I A
1790
Yecla
Villena
Alcoy
Denia
C. Nao
Altea
Benidorm
Ibiza
S. Antonio
Ibiza
Formentera
Caravaca
Cehegín
Jumilla
Cieza
Orihuela
Alicante
La Sagra
2381
Murcia
Segura
Torrevieja
Vélez
Rubio
Alhama
Mar Menor
C. de Palos
Sangonera
Lorca
Aguilas
Mazarrón
Cartagena
Cuevas
de Almanzora
Almanzora
Vera
▼2850
Almería
C. de Gata
M E D I T E R R A N E A N
S E A
Ténès
Alger (Algiers)
Thenia
Boufarik
Koléa
Blida
A L G E R I A

East from Greenwich

COPYRIGHT. GEORGE PHILIP & SON, LTD.

Map 51

Danube Lands

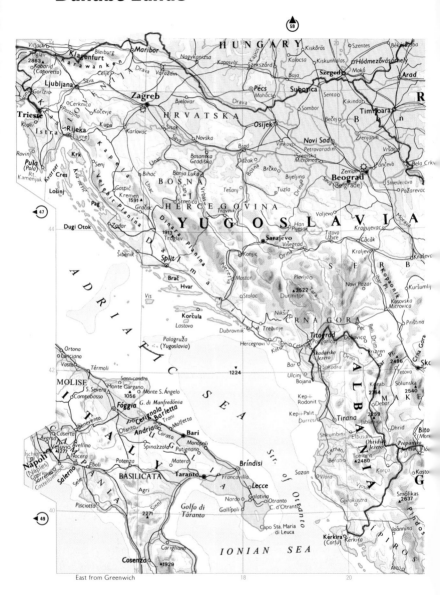

1:6 000 000

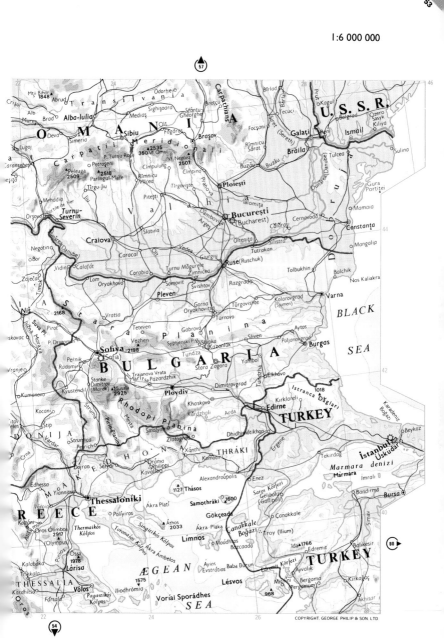

Map 53

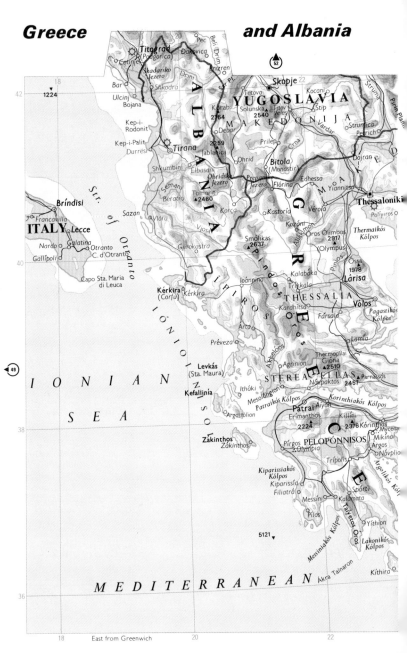

Map 54

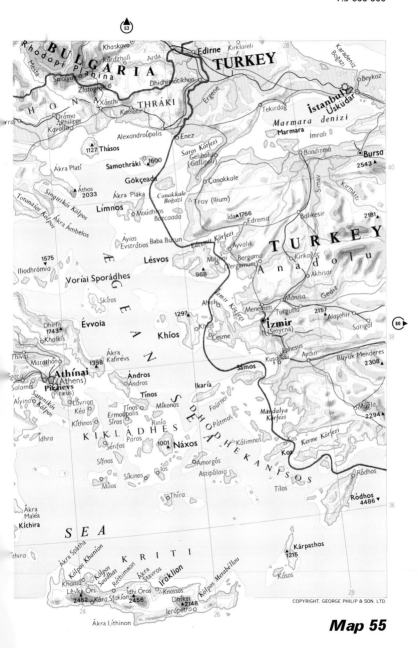

1:5 000 000

Map 55

Romania

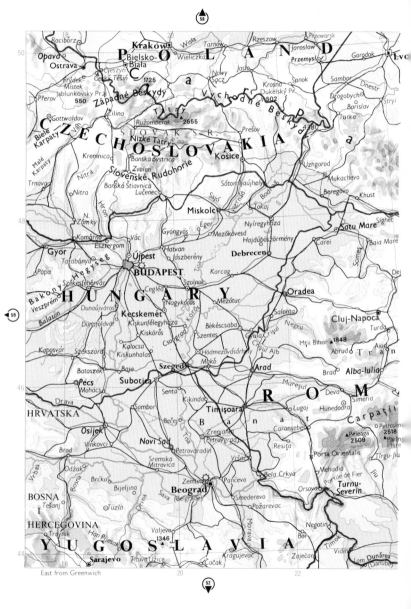

1:5 000 000

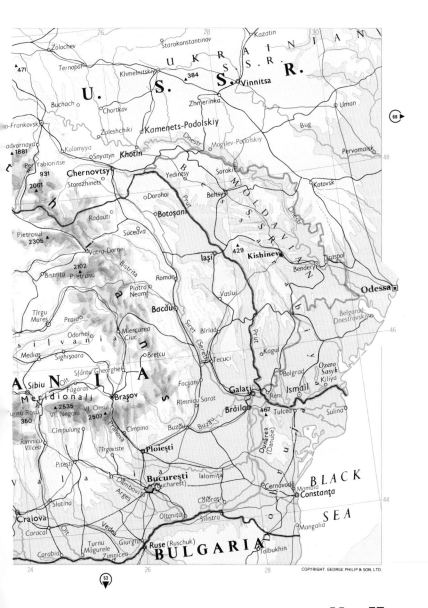

Map 57

Central Europe

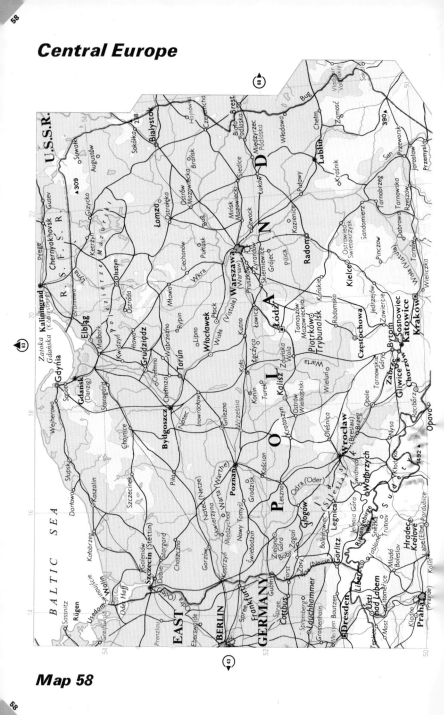

Map 58

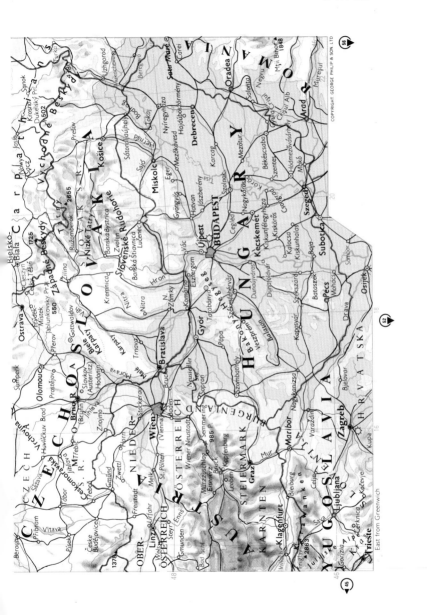

1:5 000 000

Map 59

East from Greenwich

Southern Scandinavia

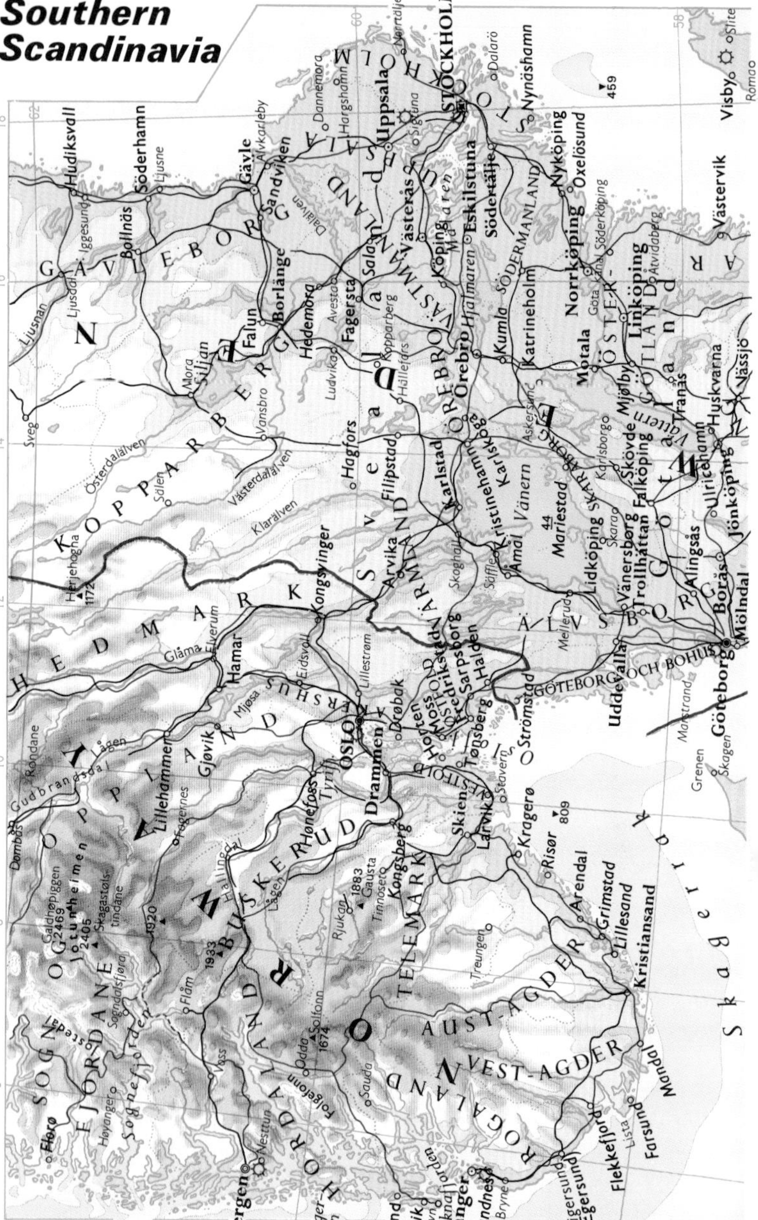

Visby ○ ○Slite
Romao

STOCKHOLM

Nynäshamn
459

Hudiksvall
Söderhamn
Gävle
Sandviken
Bollnäs
Iggesund
Ljusne

GÄVLEBORG

Uppsala
Dannemora
Hargshamn

Nyköping
Oxelösund
Norrköping
Söderköping

Västervik
Ankarsrum
Almvidaberg

Västerås
Köping
Eskilstuna
Sala
Fagersta
Avesta
Hedemora
Ludvika

SÖDERMANLAND

Katrineholm
Kumla
Örebro
Hällefors
Kopparberg

VÄSTMANLAND

Mjölby
Motala
Linköping
Åtvidaberg
Tranås
Nässjö

ÖSTERGÖTLAND

Borlänge
Falun
Mora
Siljan
Vansbro

KOPPARBERG

Hagfors
Filipstad
Karlstad
Kristinehamn
Karlskoga
Askersund
Skövde
Mariestad
Lidköping
Skara
Vänersborg
Trollhättan
Falköping
Alingsås
Borås
Mölndal

ÄLVSBORG

SKARABORG

VÄRMLAND

Göteborg
Uddevalla
Strömstad

GÖTEBORG OCH BOHUS

Vänern
Vättern
Vänersborg

Arvika
Säffle
Åmål
Skoghall
Mellerud

Kongsvinger

HEDMARK

Hamar
Lillehammer
Gjøvik
Elverum
Glåma

OPPLAND

Dombås
Gudbrandsdal
Otta
Fagernes

Gausta
Rjukan
Kongsberg
Notodden
Treungen

TELEMARK

AUST-AGDER
VEST-AGDER

ROGALAND

Galdhøpiggen 2469
Jotunheimen 2405
Skagastøl

OSLO
Drammen
Honefoss
Tyrifj.
Hokksund
Geilo
Hallingdal

BUSKERUD

AKERSHUS
Lillestrøm
Eidsvoll
Drøbak

ØSTFOLD

Moss
Fredrikstad
Sarpsborg
Halden

Oslo
Horten
Tønsberg
Larvik
Sandefjord
Skien
Larvik

VESTFOLD

Kragerø
809
Risør
Arendal
Grimstad
Lillesand
Kristiansand
Mandal

Bergen
Voss
Flåm

SOGN OG FJORDANE

Florø
Måløy
Høyanger
Sognefjord
Sogndal
Lærdal

HORDALAND

Hardangerfjord
Odda
Folgefonn
1674

Haugesund
Kopervik
Skudeneshavn
Stavanger
Sandnes
Bryne
Egersund
(Egersund)
Flekkefjord
Farsund
Lista

Skagerrak

Grenen
Skagen

Moss
Marstrand

Map 60

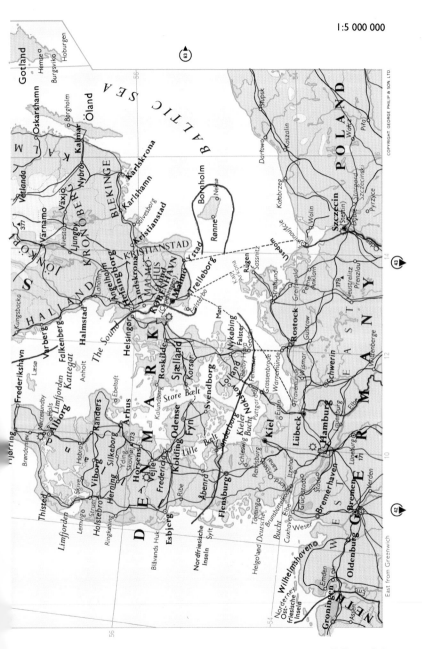

1:5 000 000

Map 61

61

COPYRIGHT GEORGE PHILIP & SON LTD

East from Greenwich

Baltic Lands

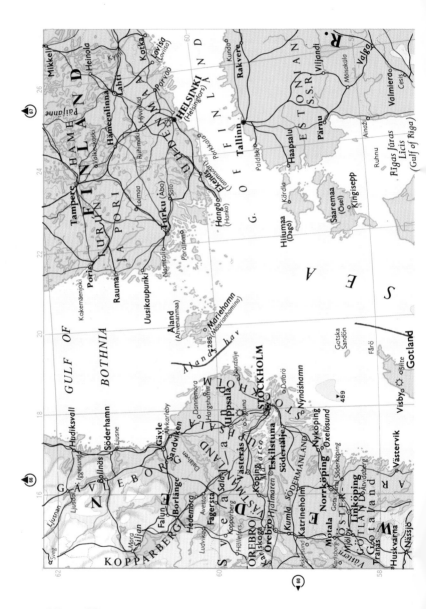

Map 62

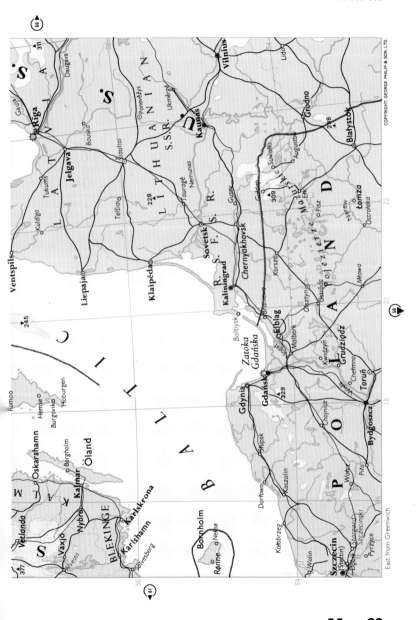

1:5 000 000

Map 63

East from Greenwich

North West Scandinavia and Iceland

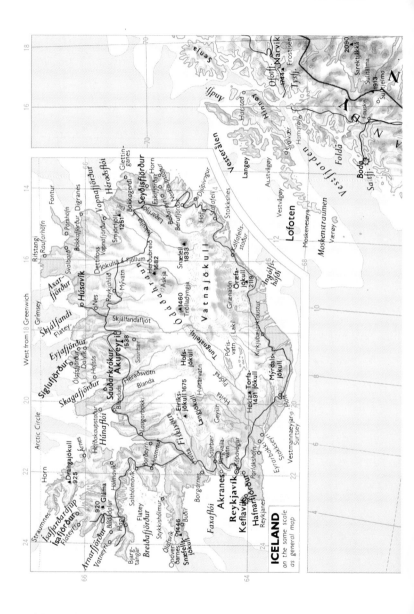

ICELAND
on the same scale
as general map

Map 64

64

1:5 000 000

COPYRIGHT GEORGE PHILIP & SON LTD

East from Greenwich

Map 65

Northern Scandinavia

Map 66

66

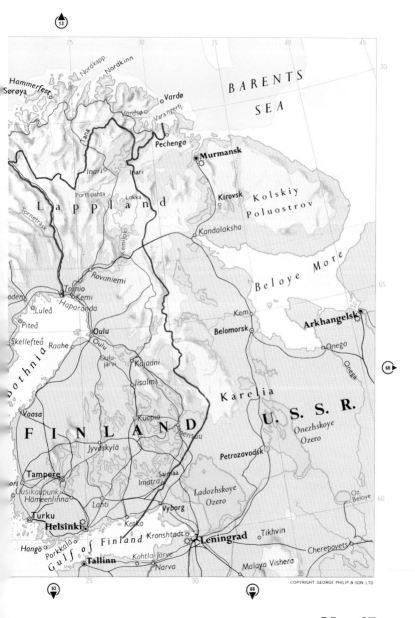

1:10 000 000

BARENTS
SEA

Hammerfest
Sørøya
Nordkapp Nordkinn
Vardø
Vardsø Varangerfj.
Pechenga
Murmansk
Tana
Inari Inari
Porttipahta Lokka
Kirovsk Kolskiy
Poluostrov
L a p p l a n d
Torneträsk Kemijoki
Kandalaksha

Beloye More

Rovaniemi
oden Tornio Kem
Luleå Kemi Haparanda
Piteå Arkhangelsk
Skellefteå Oulu Belomorsk
Raahe Oulu Onega
Oulu- Onega
järvi Kajaani
Iisalmi
K a r e l i a U.S.S.R.
Vaasa Kuopio
F I N L A N D Onezhskoye
Jyväskylä Joensuu Ozero
Tampere Saimaa Petrozavodsk
Imatra
ori Uusikaupunki Ladozhskoye Oz.
Hämeenlinna Lahti Vyborg Ozero Beloye
Turku Kotka
Helsinki Kronshtadt Leningrad Tikhvin
Hangö Porkala Gulf of Finland Cherepovets
Kohtla-Järve Malaya Vishera
Tallinn Narva

COPYRIGHT GEORGE PHILIP & SON LTD

Map 67

U.S.S.R.: West

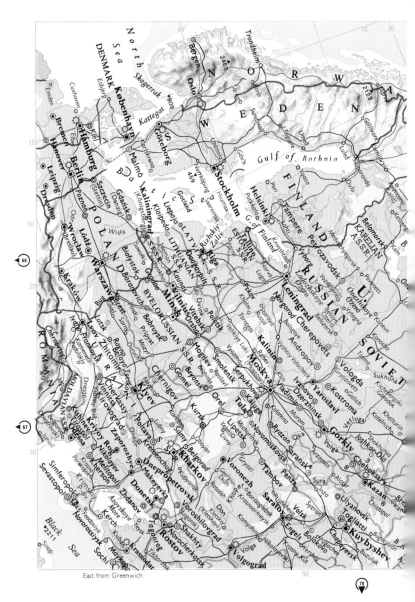

East from Greenwich

Map 68

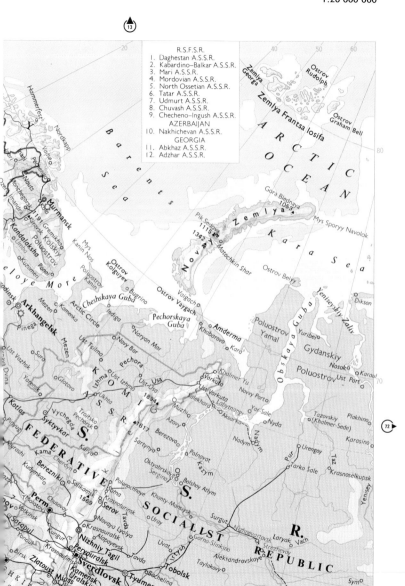

Map 69

U.S.S.R.:
South West

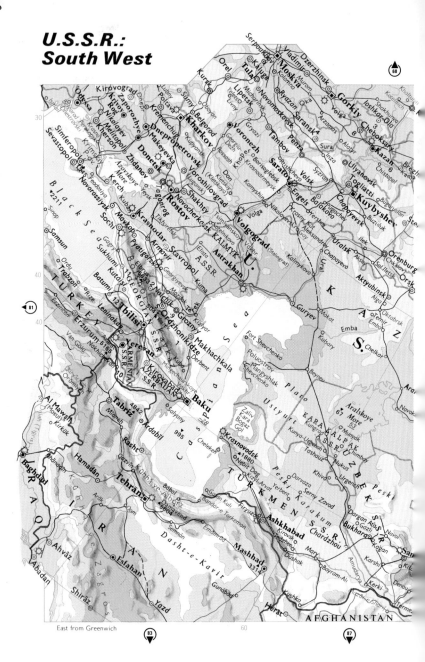

East from Greenwich

Map 70

70

1:20 000 000

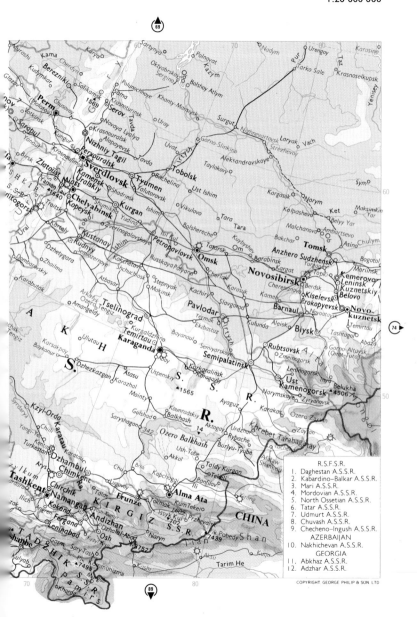

R.S.F.S.R.
1. Daghestan A.S.S.R.
2. Kabardino–Balkar A.S.S.R.
3. Mari A.S.S.R.
4. Mordovian A.S.S.R.
5. North Ossetian A.S.S.R.
6. Tatar A.S.S.R.
7. Udmurt A.S.S.R.
8. Chuvash A.S.S.R.
9. Checheno–Ingush A.S.S.R.
   AZERBAIJAN
10. Nakhichevan A.S.S.R.
    GEORGIA
11. Abkhaz A.S.S.R.
12. Adzhar A.S.S.R.

COPYRIGHT GEORGE PHILIP & SON LTD

Map 71

U.S.S.R.: North East

ARCTIC OCEAN

3800

Ostrov Shmidt
Mys Arkticheskiy
Ostrov Komsomolets
Ostrov Pioner
Ostrov Oktyabrskoy Revolyutsii
965
Severnaya Zemlya
Ostrov Bolshevik
Proliv Vilskutskogo

Ostrov Henrietta
Ostrov Jeanette
Ostrova Delong
Ostrov Znakhoa
Ostrov Bennett
Ostrova Novosibirskiye Ostrova
Ostrov Faddeyevskiy
Ostrov Novaya Sibir
374
Ostrov Molly Lyakhovskiy
Ostrov Bolshoy Lyakhovskiy
Ostrov Belkovskiy
Ostrov Kotelnyy
Lyakhovskiye Ostrova
Ostrov Stolbovoy
Proliv Dmitriya Lapteva

L a p t e v
S e a

Poluostrov Taymyr
Gory Byrranga
1146
Ostrov Bolshoy Begichev
Oz. Taymyr

Nordvik
Ust Olenek
Uryung-Khaya
Saskylakh
Novorybnoye
Popigay
Khatanga
Pyasina
Agapa
Volochanka
Kheta
Chernoye
Koluy
Anabar
Dzhelinde

Mys Buorkhaya
Tiksi
Tit-Ary
Bulun
Kyusyur
Olenek
Kel (Bysyttakh)
Dzhardzhan
Kystatyam

Nizhneyansk
Kazachye
Ust Kuyga
Yana
Deguratskoye
Batagoy

Verkhoyansk
2389
Bilir
Lepikha
Verkhoyanskiy
Batagay
Ust-Ata

Norilsk
Dudinka
Gory Putorana
1701
Igarka
Turukhansk

Yessey
Moyero
Kotuy
Olenek

Zhigansk

962
Arctic Circle
Shologontsy
Ugolyok
Vilyuy

Lena
Kytal ktakh

U.
Vilyuy
Y A S.
Sangar
Atara
Namtsy
S.

Noginsk
Nizhnyaya Tunguska
Tura
Syul'dzhyukyoro
Chernyshovskiy
Nyurba
Pavlovo
Mirnyy
Tuoy-Khaya

Vilyuysk
Vilyuy
Srednevilyuysk
Verkhnevilyuysk
Suntar
A. S.
Yelanskoye
Simskoye
Pokrovsk

Baykit
Podkamennaya Tunguska
Kuyumba
Mutaray
Vanavara
Yukti
Simenga
Yerbogachen
Kurya

Lensk (Mukhtuya)
Nokhtuysk
Roman
Vitim
Krobotkin
Yenyukа

Olekminsk
Buyaga
Dzhikimre
Aldan
Nimmeyr
(Vasleva)

Yartsevo
Severo-Yeniseyskiy
Podkamennaya Tunguska
Verkhneye Kalinino

East from Greenwich

Map 72

1:20 000 000

Mys Dezhneva
(East C.)

Ueleti

Chukotskoye More

Lavrentiya

Provideniya 60

St. Lawrence I.
(U.S.A.)

Anadyrskiy Zaliv

Ostrov Vrangelya

70

Amguema
1843

Chukotskiy Khrebet

Beringovskiy

Egvekinot Iultin

Pevek

Ostrova Medvezhi

Ostrov Ayon

Ust-Chaun

180

Amguema

Anadyr

Anadyr

Ukel'ayo

Koryakskiy Khrebet

East Siberian Sea

Ambarchik

1883

Bilibino

Anadyr

Yeropol

Markovo

Penzhino

2562

Kamenskoye

Korf

170

Ostrov Karaginskiy

Bering Sea

Nizhne Kolymsk

Pohodsk

Srednekolymsk

Kolymskoye

142

Oloy

Penzhinskaya Guba

Rekinniki

Kichiga

Ossora

Kolpakova

Parapol

Iokurdakha

Erchqa

Indigirka

Druzhina

Stolbovaya

Abkit

Omolon

Gizhiga

Ilpi

Tilichiki

Palana

Komandorskiye Ostrova

Uron'gi
Otur-Kyuyel'

Zashiversk

Khonu

Zyryanka

Kolyma

Balygyrchan

Evensk

Nayakhan

Gizhiginskaya Guba

Uka

Ust-Kamchatsk

Nikolskoye

Ostrova

S.
Khrebet

Gora Chen
2682

Pobeda
3147

Taskan

Seymchan
Omsukchan

Viligino

Zaliv Shelikhova

Tigil

Klyuchevskaya
4750

Zhupanova

Cherskogo

Ust-Nera

Kemchua
Orotukan

Yagodnoye

Atka

Tauysk

Tigil

Kozyrevsk

Sobolevo

3456

Petropavlovsk-
Kamchatskiy

Alyaskitovyy

Taskan

Talaya

Iret

Magadan

Ola

Ichinskaya
3621

Pushchino

160

Kyulyunken

2959

Oymyakon

Loshkalakh

Ust-Omchug

Sanga-Toloro

Tompo

Starry Kheydzhan

Palatka

Vorovskoye
Kirovsky

Subotlic

50

Y
Khrebet

Aldan

Khandyga

Okhotskiy
Perevoz

Allakh-Yun

Arka

Okhotsk

Ust-Khayryuzovo

Opala

Ust-Bolsheretsk

Severo
Kuril'sk

130

75

Mayya

Anga

Amga

Ust-Mila

Yakutsk

R.

Mayya

Nyrykchansky

Ulya

Sea of

Okhotsk

1780

Ostrov Paramushir

Ostrov Onekotan

Ostrova

Ust-Maya

Chagda

Uchur

Maya

Nelkan

Chasomya-
Uchurskaya

Ayon

Ostrov Bolshoy
Shantar

Okha

Ostrov Simushir

2246

Kankunskiy

Khrebet Dzhugdzhur

Nemuy

Sakhalinskiy Zaliv

Suputma

Bogorodskoye

Aleksandrovsk-
Sakhalinskiy

Kuril'skiye

2482

Chumikan

Tugur

Nikolayevsk-
na-Am.

Katangli

Sakhalin

1668

Opatina

Ostrov
Simushir

140

COPYRIGHT GEORGE PHILIP & SON. LTD.

Map 73

U.S.S.R.: South East and Mongolia

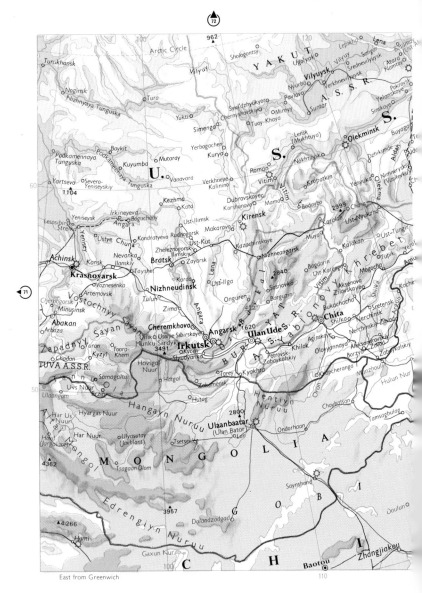

Map 74

1:20 000 000

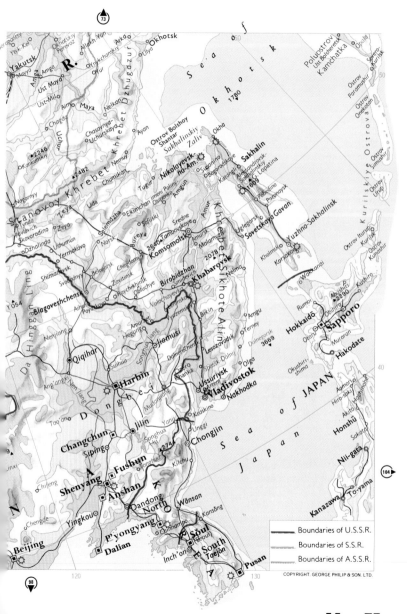

————————	Boundaries of U.S.S.R.
————————	Boundaries of S.S.R.
————————	Boundaries of A.S.S.R.

COPYRIGHT. GEORGE PHILIP & SON. LTD.

Map 75

Asia: Physical

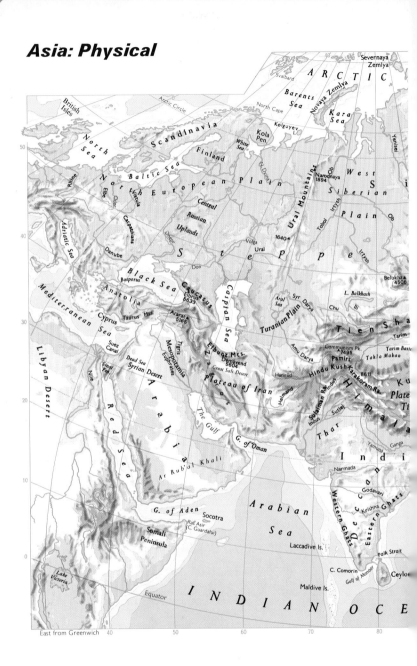

East from Greenwich 40

Map 76

76

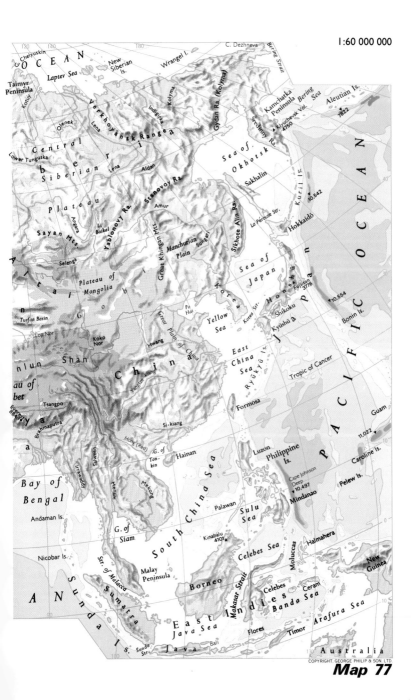

1:60 000 000

C. Dezhneva
Bering Strait

OCEAN
C. Chelyuskin
New Siberian Is.
Wrangel I.
Laptev Sea
Taimyr Peninsula
Kotui
Kamchatka Peninsula
Bering Sea
Aleutian Is.
7822
Olenek
Lena
Verkhoyansk Range
Indigirka
Kolyma
Gydan Ra. (Kolyma)
Sredniny Ra.
Klyuchev Vol. 4750
Lower Tunguska
Central
Siberian
Plateau
Lena
Aldan
Sea of Okhotsk
Sakhalin
Kurils
10,542
PACIFIC OCEAN
Angara
Stanovoy Ra.
Amur
Sayan Mts.
La Baikal
Yablonovoy Ra.
Great Khingan Mts.
Sungari
Manchurian Plain
Sikhote Alin Ra.
La Pérouse Str.
Hokkaidō
Selenga
Altai
Plateau of Mongolia
Gobi
Sea of Japan
Korea
Fujisan 3776
Honshū
10,554
Turfan Basin
Lop Nor
Koko Nor
Hwang
Pei Hai
Yellow Sea
Korea Str.
Shikoku
Kyūshū
Bonin Is.
Plateau of Tibet
nlun Shan
China
Hwang
Great Plain of China
Yangtze-kiang
East China Sea
Ryūkyū Is.
Tropic of Cancer
Tsangpo
Brahmaputra
Si-kiang
Formosa
Guam
11,022
Hong (Red)
G. of Tonkin
Hainan
Luzon
Philippine Is.
Caroline Is.
Bay of Bengal
Irrawaddy
Salween
Menam
Mekong
Cape Johnson Deep 10,497
Mindanao
Pelew Is.
Andaman Is.
G. of Siam
Palawan
Sulu Sea
Nicobar Is.
Str. of Malacca
Malay Peninsula
Kinabalu 4101
Celebes Sea
Halmahera
Moluccas
ANDA
Sunda Is.
Sumatra
Borneo
Makasar Strait
Celebes
Ceram
Banda Sea
Arafura Sea
East Indies
Java Sea
Flores
Timor
Java
Bali
Sundo Str.
New Guinea
Australia

Map 77

Asia: Political

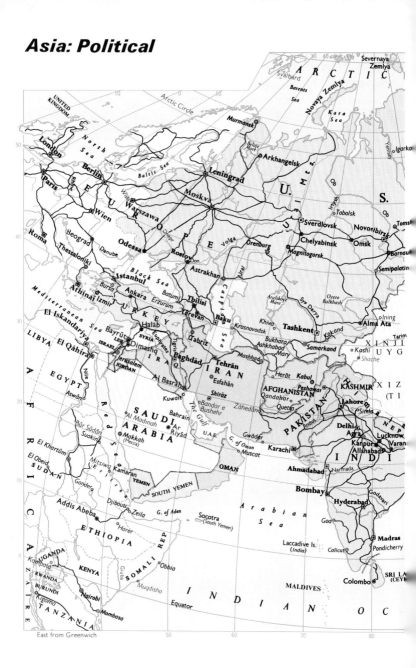

East from Greenwich

Map 78

78

1:60 000 000

OCEAN
Chelyuskin
Novosibirskiye
Ostrova
Ostrova Vrangelya
Laptev Sea
Lena
Nizhnyaya Tunguska
Yakutsk
R.
Aldan
S.
Lena
Okhotsk
Sea of Okhotsk
Bering Sea
Aleutian Is.
Angara
Petropavlovsk-Kamchatskiy
Krasnoyarsk
Ozero Baykal
Chita
Amur
Nikolayevsk
Sakhalin
Irkutsk
Kyakhta
Khabarovsk
Kuril Is.
Manchuria
Harbin
Changchun
Vladivostok
Sapporo
Hokkaidō
Hakodate
Ulaanbaatar (Ulan Bator)
Hovd
MONGOLIA
INNER MONGOLIA
Shenyang (Mukden)
N. KOREA
Sea of Japan
PACIFIC OCEAN
Ürümqi (Urumchi)
Beijing
Tianjin
Dalian
Sŏul
Pusan
Kyōto
Ōsaka
Tōkyō
Yokohama
Kitakyūshū
ANG
UR
S. KOREA
Qingdao
Yellow Sea
Nagasaki
Bonin Is.
ANG
Xi'an
Huang
Nanjing
Shanghai
JAPAN
BET)
CHINA
Chang
Wuhan
Suzhou
East China Sea
Lhasa
Chengdu
Chongqing
Xiangtan
Fuzhou
Ryūkyū-rettō
Tropic of Cancer
BHU.
y
Brahmaputra
Myitkyina
Kunming
Guangzhou
(Taiwan) (Formosa)
PACIFIC
Dhaka
HONG KONG (Br.)
Guam (U.S.)
AL
Bangladesh
Calcutta
BURMA
Mandalay
Hanoi
G. of Tongking
Macau (Port.)
Zhanjiang
Hainan
Luzon
PHILIPPINES
Caroline Is.
Irrawaddy
Bay of Bengal
THAILAND
Hué
VIETNAM
South China Sea
Manila
Andaman Is. (India)
Rangoon (Rangun)
Bangkok
CAMBODIA
Palawan
Davao
Mindanao
Belau
Nicobar Is. (India)
Gulf of Thailand
Thanh Pho Ho Chi Minh
Sulu Sea
Zamboanga
Sabah
Sulu Arch.
Celebes Sea
Halmahera
New Guinea
EAN
George Town
MALAYSIA
BRUNEI
Sarawak
Maluku (Moluccas)
Ceram
Kuala Lumpur
Str. of Malacca
Meloka
Kuching
Borneo
Sulawesi
Banda Sea
Thursday I.
Singapore
Sumatra
INDONESIA
Jakarta
Java Sea
Ujung Pandang
Flores
Timor
Darwin
AUSTRALIA
Selat Sunda
Java

COPYRIGHT, GEORGE PHILIP & SON, LTD.

Map 79

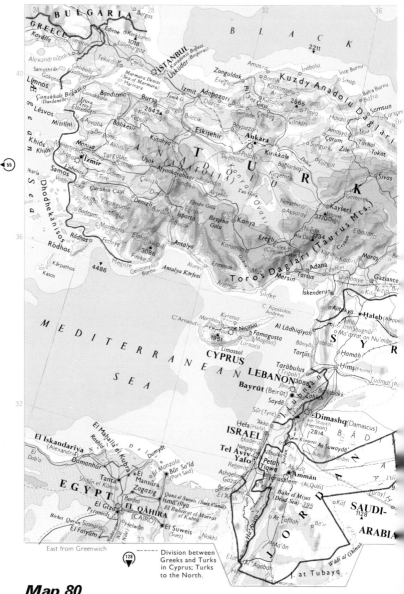

Turkey and the Middle East

Map 80

1:10 000 000

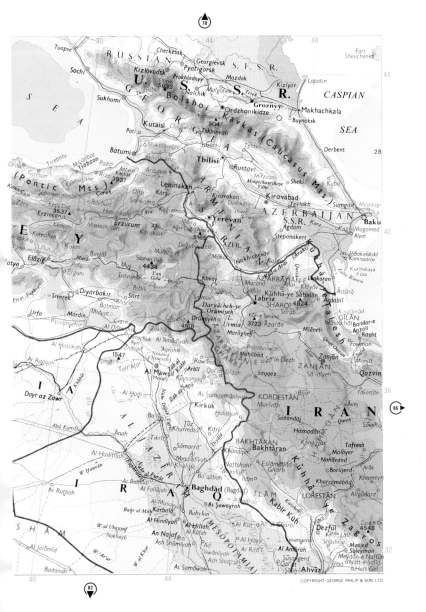

Map 81

Arabian Peninsula

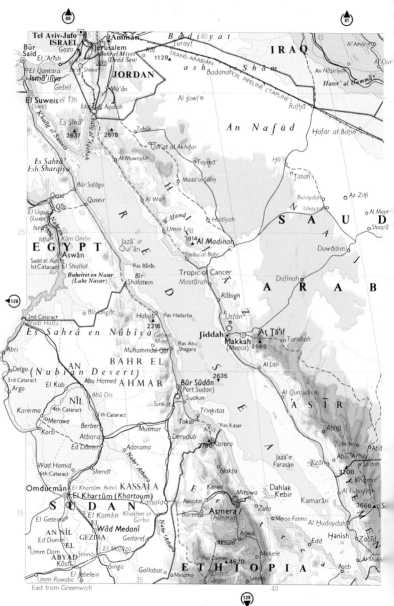

Map 82

1:15 000 000

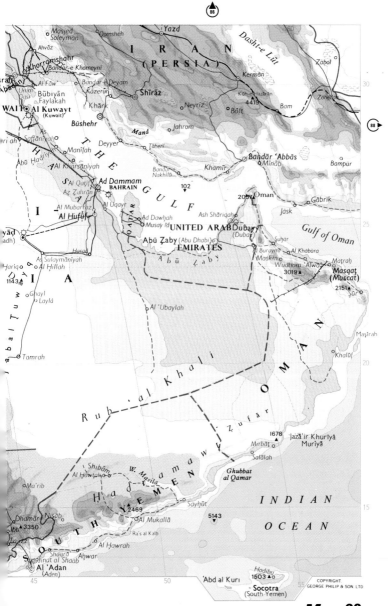

Map 83

The Gulf

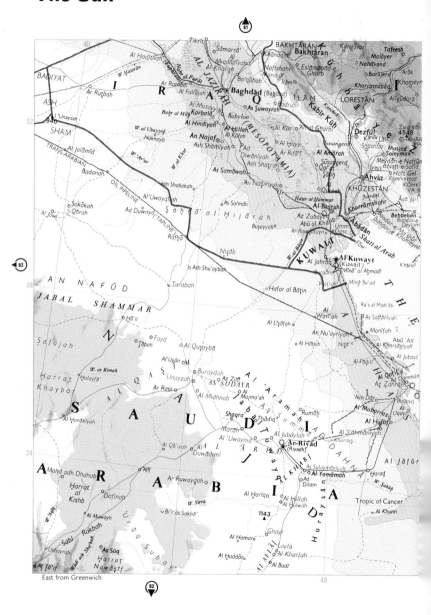

East from Greenwich

Map 84

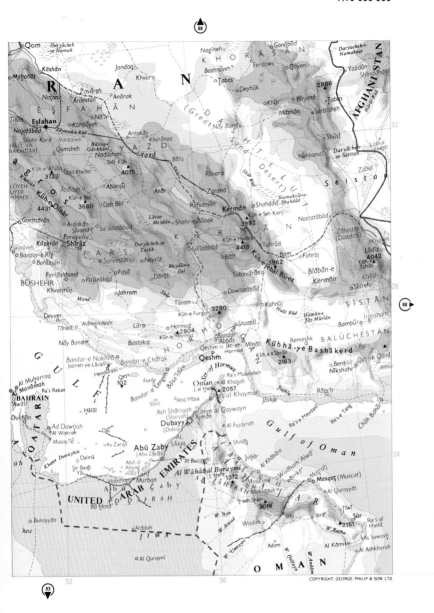

1:10 000 000

Qom · Daryācheh-ye Namak · Naqineh · KHORĀSĀN · Gonābād · Daryācheh-i-Namakzar · AFGHANISTAN · 60

Mahallāt · Kāshān · Jandaq · Khvoro · Boshrūyeh · Ferdows · Qāyen · Yazdān · Shindand

R · Naṭanz · Zavāreh · Anārak · Khvor · Tabas · Deyhūk · Khūr · Bīrjand · 2886 · Tabas · Sarbīsheh

ĒSFAHĀN · Ardestān · Na'īn · Mazhān · Nehbandān · Daryāchen-ye Seistan · Lāsh-e Joveyn

Tirān · Esfahan · Kūnpāyeh · Ardakān · Kharānaq · Nāy Band · Shūsf · 32

Najafābād · Zāyandeh Rūd · Shahr Kord · Varzaneh · YAZD · Daryāchen-ye Seistan · Zābol

HĀLĪ VA BAKHTĪĀRĪ · Qomsheh · Bātlāq-e Gāvkhūni · Nadūshan · Shīr Kūh · Yazd · Bāfq · Seista

Kūh-e Ālījūq 3723 · Ābādeh · Abarqū · 4075 · Lāvar · Rāvaro · Shūr Rūd · Numakzār-e-Shahdād · Zāhedān (Duzdab)

KUHGĪLŪYEH BŪYER AHMADĪ · Kūh-e Dīnār · 4431 · 3660 · Deh Bīd · Anār · Zarand · Shahdād · Kūh-e Seh Konj · Nosratābād · Mināb

Gachsārān · Ardakān · Sīvand · Sa'ādatābād · Saīdābād · KERMĀN · Lādīz · Kūh-e Tāftān 4042

Ganāveh · Kāzerūn · Shīrāz · Persepolis · Daryāchen-ye Tashk · 3992 · Kūh-e Hazārān · Tahrūd · Bam · Fahraj · Bīdbān-e · Khāsh

Bandar-e Rīg · Borāzjān · FARS · Sarvestān · Neyrīz · Saīdābād · 4419 · Kūh-e Jebāl Bārez · 3962 · Kermān · Sīāreh

BŪSHEHR · Farrāshband · Fasā · Dārāb · Meydān-e Gel · Sobzvārān · Dowlatābād · SISTĀN · 28

Khvormūj · Fīrūzābād · Jahrom · Shūr · Tārom · Kahnūj · Halīl Rūd · Hāmūn-e Jāz Mūriān · 88

Deyyer · Tāherī · Alāmarvdasht · Lāro · Kūh-e Furgun · 3280 · Shamīl · Bampūr · Irānshahr

Nāy Band · Bastak · Hormoz · 2804 · Bandar · KŪHHĀ-YE BASHĀKERD · Remeshk · BALŪCHESTĀN

Bandar-e Nakhīlū · Bastako · Qeshm · 'Abbās · Jaz-ye · Kūh-e Kūnrān · 2163 · Bent · Qasr-e Qand

GULF · Jazīreh-ye-Lāvān · Bandar-e Chārak · Qeshm · Strait of Hormuz · Nīkshahr

Al Muharraq · Manāmah · Hendōrābī · Qeys · 102 · Forūr · Bandar-e Lengeh · Bū'sa'īdū · Oman · Ra's Musandam · Ra's-e Meydani · Chāh Bahār

BAHRAIN · 'Awālī · Ra's Rakan · Sirrī · Bandar-e Lengeh · Abū Mūsā · Jal Harm · 2057 · Ra's al Khaymah · Jāsk · Rānch · Ra's-e Tang

Dukhān · Ad Dawhah · Das · As Zarqā' · Ash Shāriqah (Sharjah) · Ajmān · Al Fujayrah · Gulf of Oman · 24

QATAR · Al Wakrah · Dalmā · Abū al Abyad · Shinās · Wudhām 'Alwā · Maṭraḥ (Muscat)

Musay'īd · Khawr Duwayhin · Ṣīr Banī Yās · Tarīf · Abū Zaby (Abu Dhabi) · Al Buraymī · Al Khābūra · 'Ibrā · Barkā' · Masqaţ (Muscat)

UNITED · Bū Ḥasā · Al Wāḥat al Buraymī · Haft · 1372 · Maskin · Al Muladdah · Al Qurayyāt

ARAB EMIRATES · ĀẒ ẒAHĪRAH · ash Shām · 3019 · Izkī · 'Ibrī · Ṣūr · Ra's al Hadd

Bunayyān · JIWA · W. 'Ayn · Wadim · 2151 · W. Bātha

Āziz · Al Quraynī · Habshān · Murbān · Adam · W. Ḥalfayn · Al Kāmil · As Suwayh

OMAN · Al Ashkharah · 60

COPYRIGHT GEORGE PHILIP & SON LTD.

Map 85

Central Asia and Afghanistan

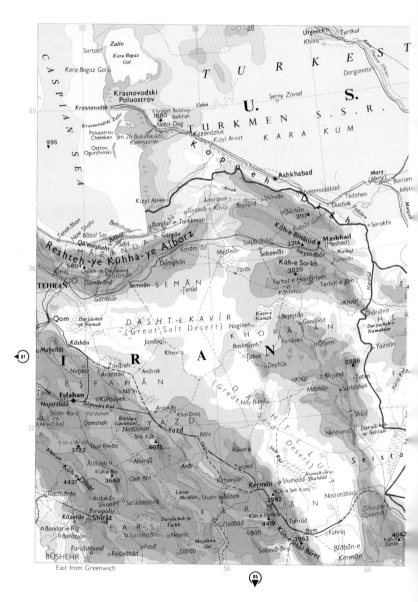

East from Greenwich

Map 86

1:10 000 000

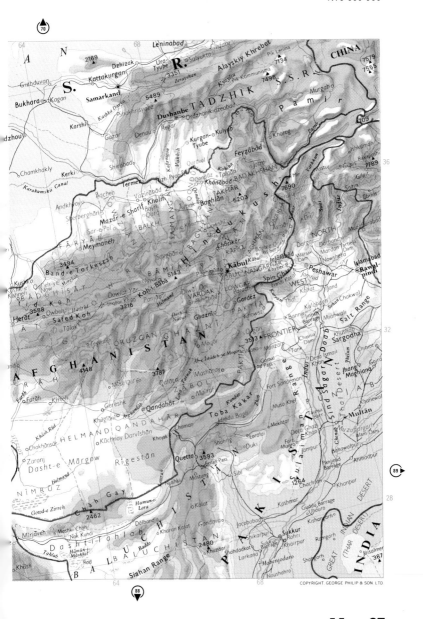

COPYRIGHT GEORGE PHILIP & SON LTD

Map 87

Pakistan and North West India

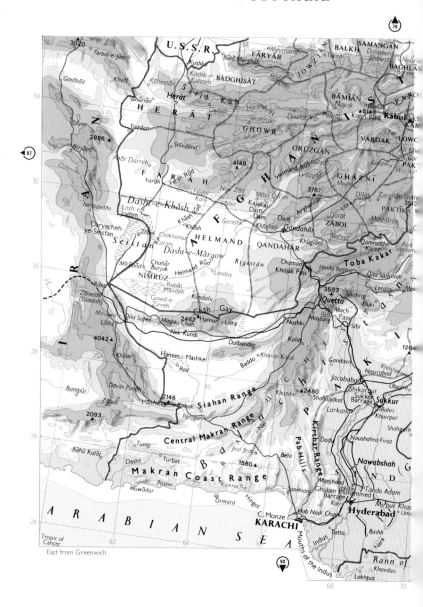

U.S.S.R.

SAMANGAN
FARYAB   BALKH   Dahaneh-ye Nahri
Meymaneh   JOWZJAN   Ghowri   BAGHLAN
Takzar   Brow

Torbat-e Jām   Kushk   Bālā Murghāb
3020   Koshk-e   BĀDGHISĀT   Murghāb
Gonābād   Khvāf   Kūhestān   Kohneh
Ghūrīān   Safīd   Kūh   BĀMIĀN   BAGHLAN
Herāt   Owbeh   Harīrūd   Nayak   5143   Bāmiān   Kabul
HERĀT   Shahrūd   Dowlat Yār   Fayzābād   Koh-i Bābā   KĀB
Qāyen   Yazdan   GHOWR   VARDAK   LOWG
2886   Shīndand   ORŪZGĀN   Top   Ali Khe
Bīrjānd   4148   Gīzāb   Gizhnī   PAK
Anār Darreh   Nili Zād   3787   Dilah   Zarghun Shahr   3513
Dasht-e-Khāsh   Kala   Mūsā Qal'eh   Arghandāb   PAKTĪKA
Nehbandān   Khāsh   Dught   Kajakai   Dām   ZĀBOL   Mashrūgy
Lash-e   Jovayn   Vashir   Dam   Dam   Qal'at   Qamruddīn   Fort
Daryacheh-   Zābol   Chakhansur   Gereshk   Khūgīānī   Qandahār   Kacez   Sandem
ye-Seistan   Zaranj   Khāsh   HELMAND   QANDAHĀR   Khūgīānī   Ma'rūf   X
Seistan   Mīrābād   Dasht-e-Mārgow   Chaman   Hindu Bagh   Toba Kakar
Burjak   Helmand Rūd   Landay   Rigestān   Khojak Pass   Qila Saifullah
IRAN   Rība   Robāt   Kandalu   Hindu Bagh   Loralai   Meh
Zāhedan   Māndeh   3593   Shahrig   Dukī
(Duzdab)   Gowd-e   Quetta   Bolan Pass   Sibi   1264
Mīrjāveh   Zirreh   Chāh   Gay   Mach   Mastung
Qila Safed   2462   Hamūn-i-Lora   Nushki   PAKISTAN
Lādīz   Moshkī Chāh   Kalat   Gandava   Khash
4042   Nok Kundi   Dalbandin   Khuzdar   2480   Jacobabad   Nasirabad   Ubauro
Khāsh   Hamūn-i-Mashkel   Baddo   Kharan Kalat   Shahdadkot   Shikarpur   Sukkur Barrage   Sukkur
Rod   Kharan   Larkana   Rohri   Khairpur
Bampūr   Dāvar Pandū   2146   Siahan Range   Shahbarh
Zāboli   Mashkīa   Kimbak   Panjgūr   Kirthar Range   Nausharo Firoz   Nawabshah
2093   Central Makran Range   Niai   Dadu   SIND
Tump   Bela   Manjhand   Tando Adam
Bāhū Kalāt   Dasht   Turbat   1580   Pab Hills   Ghulam Mohammed   Mirpur Khas   Uma
Makran Coast Range   Barrage   Kotri   Badin
Pasni   Kanracho   Sonmiani   Hab Nadi Chauki   Hyderabad
Gwādar   Ormara   Hingol   C. Monze   KARACHI   Tatta   Nara
A R A B I A N   S E A   Indus   Rann of
Tropic of Cancer   Mouths of the Indus   Khavdao
East from Greenwich   Lakhpat

Map 88

1:10 000 000

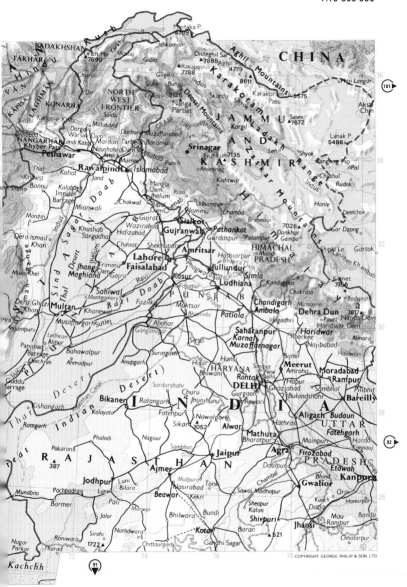

Map 89

Central and Southern India, Sri Lanka

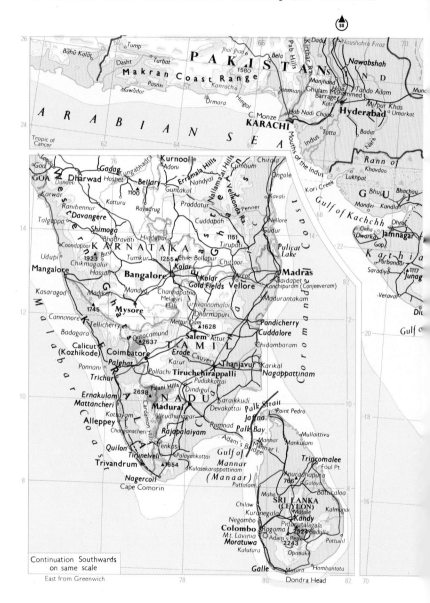

Continuation Southwards
on same scale

East from Greenwich

Map 90

90

1:10 000 000

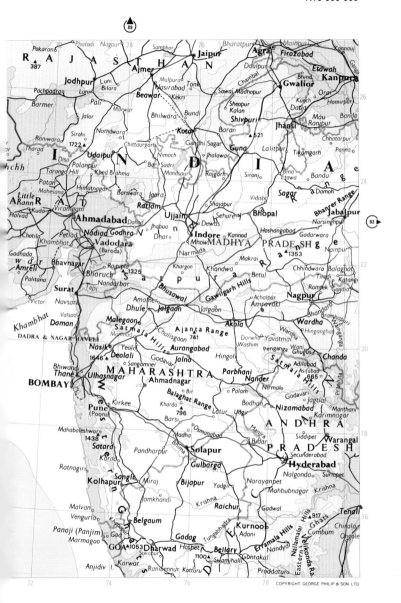

Map 91

COPYRIGHT GEORGE PHILIP & SON LTD

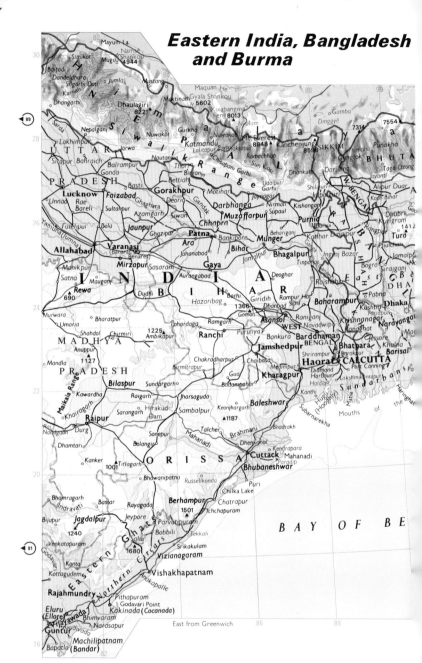

Eastern India, Bangladesh and Burma

Map 92

1:10 000 000

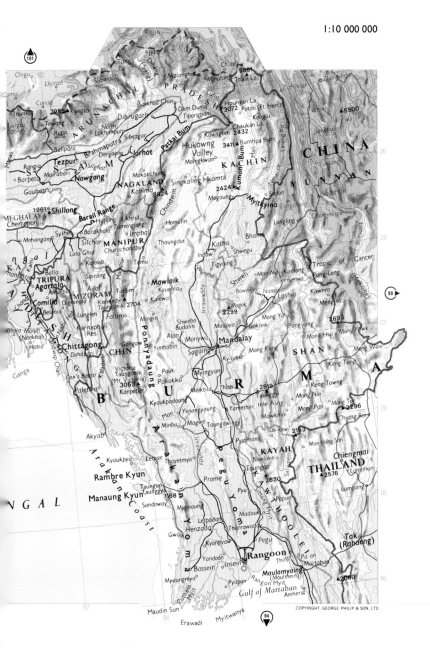

Map 93

Mainland South East Asia

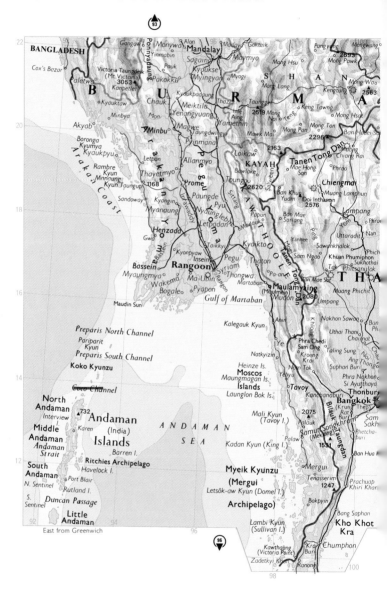

BANGLADESH
Cox's Bazar
Paletwa
Victoria Taungdeik
(Mt. Victoria)
3053
Kanpetlet
Kyauktaw
Chauk
Akyab
Minbya
Mon
Minbu
Boronga
Kyumya
Kyaukpyu
Rambre
Kyun
Manaung
Kyun Taungup
Sandoway
Gwa

Gangaw
Monywa
Alon
Moday
Gokteik
Ponnyadaung
Yinmabin
Pauk
Sagaing
Kyaukse
Pakokku
Myingyan
Myogi
Kyaukpadaung
Meiktila
Thazi
Taungyi
Yenangyaung
Inle
Aing
Taungdwingyi
Mawk Mai
Pyinmana
Loikaw
Thayetmyo
1168
Allanmyo
Prome
Paungde
Kyangin
Pyu
Myanaung
Nyaunglebin
Letpadan
Henzada
Gwa
Kyonpyaw
Taikkyi
Insein
Pegu
Bassein
Rangoon
Syriam
Myaungmya
Ma-Ubin
Thongwa
Wakema
Martaban
Bogale
Pyapon

Monywa
Mandalay
Maymyo
Mong Hsu
Pangyang
Mong Pawk
2693
Mong Wa
Mong Long
Kengtung
2563
Keng Tawng
Mong Hsat
Mong
Nai
Teng
Mong Ton
Mong Pan
2296
Ban Houei
Chiang Rai
2163
KAYAH
TanenTong Dan
Mae Hong
Son
Chiengmai
Bawlake
Muang Lamphun
Toungoo
Ban Khug
Yuam
Doi Inthanon
2576
Lampang
2620
Papun
Ban Mae
Sariang
Yanhee
Ping
Uttaradit
Nan
Phrae
Mudaung
Sawankhalok
Phich
Khuan Phumiphon
Sukhothai
Sam Ngao
Tak
Phitsanulok
Kyaikto
Pa-an
Ban Mae Sot
THA
Thaton
Muang Phichit
Maulamyaing
(Moulmein)
2080
Mudon
Gulf of Martaban
Umpang
Maudin Sun
Kalegauk Kyun
Nakhon Sawan
Ban
Pli
Uthai Thani
Chainat
Ahin
Preparis North Channel
Pariparit
Kyun
Preparis South Channel
Koko Kyunzu
Ye
Phra Chedi
Sam Ong
Taling Sung
Non
Ang Thong
Kroeng
Krai
Natkyizin
Nam Tok
Yebyu
Suphan Buri
Phra Nakhon
Si Ayutthaya
Heinze Is.
Moscos
Maungmagan Is.
Islands
Tavoy
Kanchanaburi
Thonburi
Launglon Bok Is.
Bangkok
(Krung
Thep)
Rat
North
Andaman
Interview
I.
732
Andaman
(India)
Islands
Karen
ANDAMAN
Mali Kyun
(Tavoy I.)
2075
Palauk
Sam
Samut Songkhram
Phetcha-
buri
Middle
Andaman
Andaman
Strait
Barren I.
SEA
Kadan Kyun (King I.)
Palaw
1531
Ban Hua I.
South
Andaman
Ritchies Archipelago
Havelock I.
N. Sentinel
Port Blair
Rutland I.
S.
Sentinel
Duncan Passage
Myeik Kyunzu
(Mergui)
Letsôk-aw Kyun (Domel I.)
Archipelago
Mergui
Tenasserim
1247
Prachuap
Khiri Khan
Bokpyin
Little
Andaman
92
94
96
Lambi Kyun
(Sullivan I.)
Bang Saphan
Kho Khot
Kra
East from Greenwich
96
Kawthaung
(Victoria Point)
Zadetkyi Kyun
Kra
Buri
Ranong
Chumphon
98
100

B U R M A
S H A N
ARAKAN
Arakan Coast
Yoma
Irrawaddy
Pegu Yoma
KAWTHOOLE
Salween
Sittang
Bilauktaung
Tanen Tong Dan

Map 94

1:10 000 000

CHINA

Gejiu • Mengzi
Jinping
2431 • Ha Giang
3076 • Cha Pa • Bac Quang • Longzhou
Yibang • Lai Chau • 3143 **Bac Phan** • Bac Kan **Pingxiang** • Qinzhou **Hepu**
Cao Bang • Ningming
Luan Chau • **(Tongking)** • Thai Nguyen • Beihai
Mengla • Phong Saly • Ngoi Lo • Phu Doan • Loc Binh • Mong Cai • Haikang
Muong Sing • Nam Tha • Dien Bien • Son La • **Hanoi** • Bac Ninh • Quang
Vien Pou Kha • Muong Ngoi • Ha Dong • Leizhou Bandao
Muong • Nam • Sam Neua • Phu Loi • **Hoa Binh** • Phu Ly • **Haiphong**
Pak Beng • Dong • 2257 • Hai • Nam Dinh • **Gulf of**
Muong Soui • Muong Ngoi • Xuan
2061 • Nam Ban Ban • Ninh Binh • **Tongkin**
Luang Prabang • **Cao Nguyen** • Chu • Lingao
Tran Ninh • Thanh Hoa • Xinzhou • Dan Xian
Muong • Xieng • Thai Hoa • Changjiang • **Hainan**
Vieng • Khouang • 2711 • Ban Khe Bo • **Dao**
2820 • Dongfang • Wuzhi Shan ▲
Pak Sane • Kam Keut • **Vinh** • Gancheng • 1867
Theun • Ledong • Yacheng
Nam Cam • Huanglu • Tianpo
Pak • Ha Tinh • Chinmu
Lay • Vientiane • Chiao
Do Luang • Nong Khai • Tuyen Hoa
2300 • Wang Saphung • Loei • Ba Don • Dong Hoi
2320 • Udon Thani • Thakhek
Ubolratna • Nakhon • **VIETNAM**
THAILAND • Phong • Phanom • Dong Hene • Tha Ro
Phetchabun • Nam • Sakon Nakhon • Savannakhet • Sepon • Quang Tri
Phong • Lam • Bang Hieng • **Hué**
Khon Kaen • Kalasin • Pao
Cao Nguyen • Khemmarat • **Da Nang** (Tourane)
Chaiyaphum • Chi • Roi Et • Saravane • Hoi An
Ban Phai • Yasothon • 1572 • Thang Binh
Khorat • Ubon • Thateng • **Cao Nguyen** • Binh Son
Ban Bua • Ratchathani • **Pakse** • 3280 • Quang Ngai
Yai • Buriram • Se Done • **Boloven** • Kontum • Hoai Nhon
Nakhon • Surin • Sisaket • Hat Nhao • Attopeu • (Bong Son)
Ratchasima • **An Nhon**
1328 • **(Khorat)** • **Phanom Dang Rek** • 761 • Khong • Pleiku • (Binh Dinh)
Nong • Prachin Buri • Cheom Ksan • Phnom Tbeng • Khong • San • Gia Lai • **Qui**
Khae • Ban Aranyaprathet • Meanchey • **Nhon**
Chachoengsao • Sisophon • Koulen • Mekong • Srepok • Cheo Reo • Song Cau
Samut Prakan (Paknam) • Angkor • Stung-Treng • Tuy Hoa
Chon Buri • **Battambang** • Siem Reap • **Ba**
Si Racha • Po lin • Tonlé Sap • Sandan (Sunbor) • Buon Me Thuot
Ban Lamung • Pursat • Kratie • Senmonorom • 2405 • Nha
Rayong • Chhlong • **Cao Nguyen** • Trang
Chanthaburi • Tra • 1744 ▲ • **CAMBODIA** • Gia Nghia • Da Lat • Cam Ranh
Ko Chang • 1813 • Kompong • Budop • Di Linh • Phan
Ko Kut • Phnom Kravanh • Chhnang • Kompong • Loc Ninh • Djirlagnear • Rang
Cham • Phan Thiet
Koh Kong • Kong • **Phnom Penh** • Prey-Veng • Tay Ninh • Bien Hoa • Ho Da (Phan Ri)
Prek Thnot • Banam • **Thanh Pho** • Phan Thiet
Kompong Som • Kompong • Svay • My • **Ho Chi Minh** (Saigon)
Sre Umbell • Speu • Rieng • Ba Ria
of Thailand • 1075 • Takeo • Long • Tho • Vung Tau
Kampot • Xuyen • Go Cong
Phu • Hon • Rach Gia • Sa Dec • Can Tho
Quoc • Chong • Khanh Hung
Ca Mau • Bac Lieu • (Soc Trang)
Mui Ca Mau • Can Dao

COPYRIGHT
GEORGE PHILIP & SON LTD.

Map 95

The Malay Peninsula

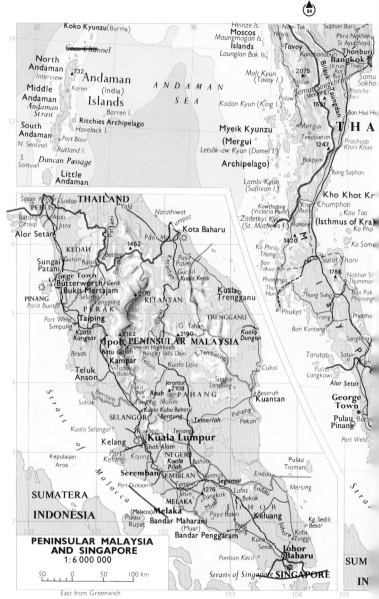

Map 96

1:10 000 000

95

1328
Nong
Khae   Prachin Buri
Phanom Dang Rang R   Kontum
Chachoengsao   Ban   Cheom Ksan   Khong   San   Pleiku   Gia Lai   An Nhon
Samut Prakan(Paknam) Aranyaprathet Sisophon   Preah Vihear   (Binh Dinh)
Chon Buri   Koulen   Srepok   Cheo Reo   Qui
Si Racha   Angkor Siem Reap   Nhon Song
Ban Lamung Battambang Tonlé Sap   Cau
Rayong   Pailin   Buon Me Thuot   Tuy
Chanthaburi   Trat Sre   Pursat   Sandan(Sanbor)   Hoa
ILAND Ko Chang 1744   1813 Kompong Kompong Kratie Senmonorom   Nha
Ko Kut   Phnom Kravanh Chhnang Cham Chhlong   Cao Nguyen   Trang
of Thailand Kas   Phnom Penh   Prey-Veng Budop Gia Nghia Da Lat   Di Linh   Cam Rhan
Kong   Kong Prek Thnot Banam Loc Ninh   Phan
Koh Kohg Sre Umbell Kompong Svay   Tay Ninh Djiringa   Rang
1075 Speu Takeo Rieng   Bien Hoa   Hoa Da Phan Thiet
Koh Rong Kampot   My Tho PC Thanh Pho   Phan Ri
Kompong Soma   Long   So Dec Ho Chi Minh(Saigon)
(Sihanoukville) Ream   Xuyen   Ba Ria   Cu Lao Hon
Phu Quoc   Hon   Rach Gia Can Tho Go Vung Tau
Chong   Cong
Khanh Hung (Soc Trang)
Bac Lieu
Ca Mau
Mui Ca Mau   Côn Dao

S O U T H   C H I N A   S E A

Pattani
Yala   Narathiwat
Tumpat
Beton Kelantan Kota Baharu
Gerik   Kepulauan
Perhentian
Taiping 2170 Kuala Trengganu
2182   PENINSULAR   Laut
Ipoh Gunong Tahan Kuala Dungun   Telukbutun 959
Cameron Highlands 2190   Kepulauan
Kuala Lipis   MALAYSIA   Natuna Besar
Binjai
Raub Pahang Kuantan
Kuala   Matak   Subi
Selangor   Kuantan   Siantan
Port   Kuala Lumpur   Tioman Jemaja Kuala Midai Kepulauan
Kelang Kelong Seremban   Kepulauan   Natuna Selatan
Port Dickson Gemas   Mersing Anambas
Melaka
Bandar   Keluang   Kepulauan
TERA Maharani   Malacca Bandar   Tambelan
ONESIA Penggaram Johor Baharu I N D O N E S I A
SINGAPORE

111

Map 97

China: East

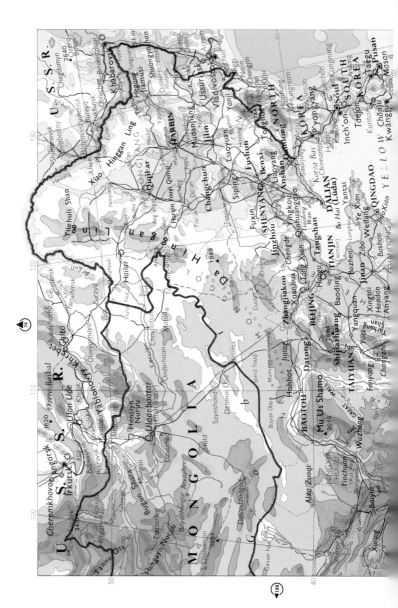

Map 98

1:20 000 000

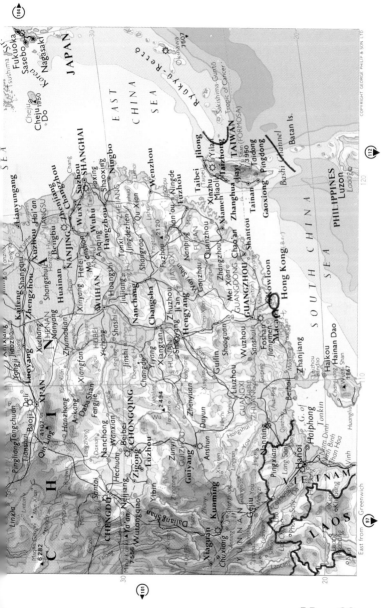

Map 99

China: West

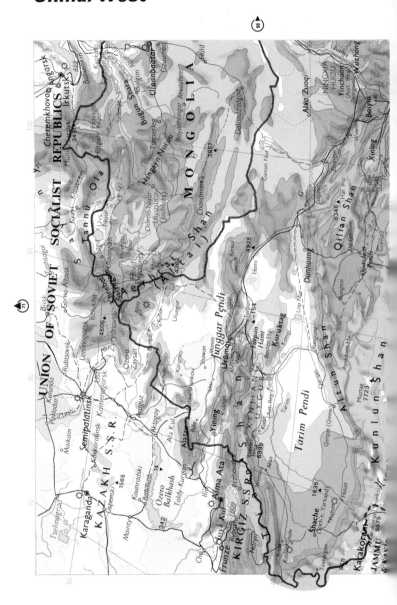

Map 100

100

1:20 000 000

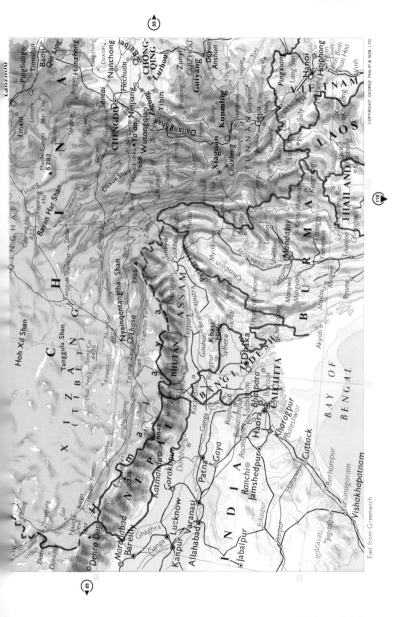

East from Greenwich

Map 101

Japan: North

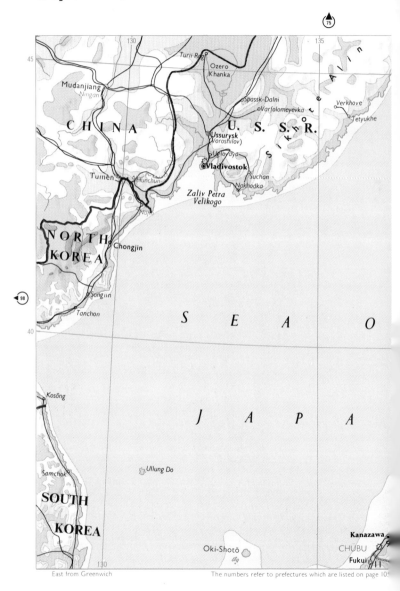

45

130

135

Turii Rog

Ozero
Khanka

Mudanjiang
Ningan

Spassk-Dalni

Varfolomeyevka

Verkhove

Tetyukhe

C H I N A

U. S. S. R.

Ussursk
(Voroshilov)

S
i
k
h
o
t
e
A
l
i
n

Ugloyaya

Vladivostok

Suchan

Tumen

Hunchun

Nakhodka

Zaliv Petra
Velikogo

Naj

98

N O R T H
K O R E A

Chongjin

Songjin

40

Tanchon

S   E   A   O

Kosŏng

J   A   P   A

Samchok

Ullung Do

S O U T H

K O R E A

130

Oki-Shotō

Kanazawa

CHUBU

Fukui

The numbers refer to prefectures which are listed on page 10

Map 102

1:7 500 000

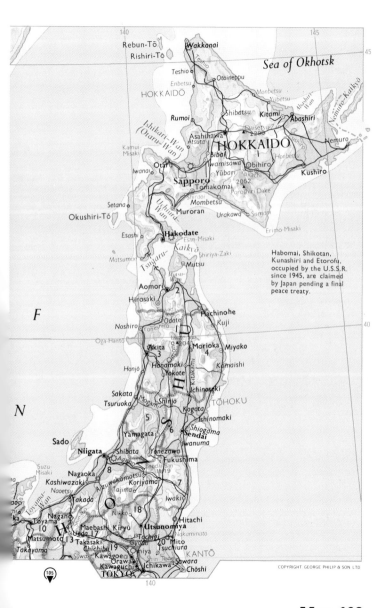

Habomai, Shikotan,
Kunashiri and Etorofu,
occupied by the U.S.S.R.
since 1945, are claimed
by Japan pending a final
peace treaty.

COPYRIGHT GEORGE PHILIP & SON LTD

Map 103

Japan: South

1:7 500 000

HOKKAIDŌ
1 Hokkaidō
TOHŌKU
2 Aomori
3 Akita
4 Iwate
5 Yamagata
6 Miyagi
7 Fukushima
CHŪBU
8 Niigata
9 Ishikawa
10 Toyama
11 Fukui
12 Gifu
13 Nagano
14 Yamanashi
15 Aichi
16 Shizuoka
KANTŌ
17 Gumma
18 Tochigi
19 Saitama
20 Ibaraki
21 Tokyō
22 Chiba
23 Kanagawa

KINKI
24 Hyōgo
25 Kyōto
26 Shiga
27 Ōsaka
28 Nara
29 Mie
30 Wakayama
CHŪGOKU
31 Tottori
32 Okayama
33 Shimane
34 Hiroshima
35 Yamaguchi
SHIKOKU
36 Kagawa
37 Tokushima
38 Ehime
39 Kōchi
KYŪ SHŪ
40 Fukuoka
41 Saga
42 Nagasaki
43 Kumamoto
44 Ōita
45 Miyazaki
46 Kagoshima

Map 105

Japan: Tokyo, Kyoto, Osaka

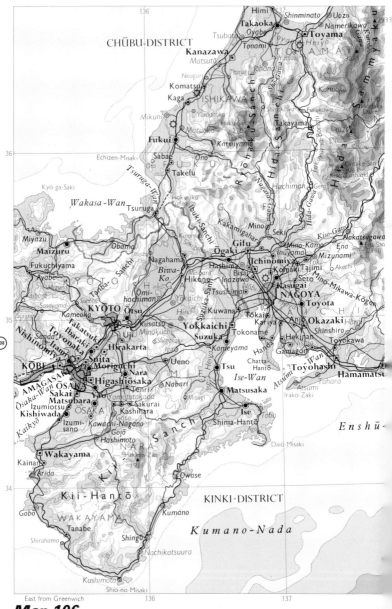

1 : 2 500 000

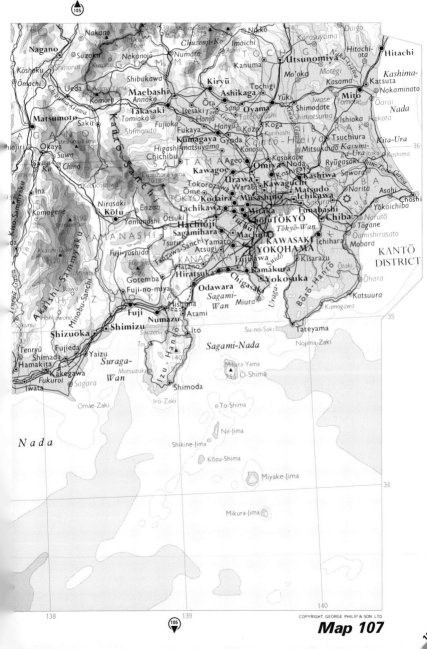

Map 107

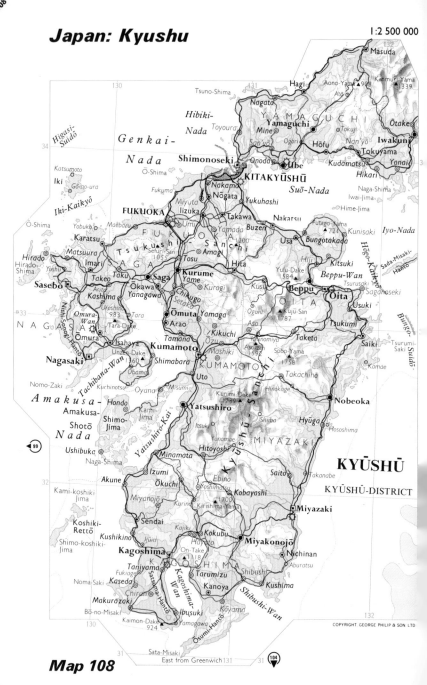

Japan: Kyushu

1:2 500 000

Masuda

Hagi   Aono-Yama ▲908   Kanmuri-Yama ▲1339

Tsuno-Shima
130   131
Nagato

Hibiki-
Nada   Y A M A G U C H I   Ōtake
Toyoura   Yamaguchi   Tokuji   Iwakuni

Higasi-   Mine   San'yō   Hōfu   Nan'yō   Tokuyama
Suidō   Ogōri   Kudamatsu   Yanai
34   *G e n k a i -*   Onoda   Ube   Hikari
Katsumoto   Ō-Shima   *N a d a*   Shimonoseki   3
Iki   Gō-no-ura   Naga-Shima
Fukuma   KITAKYŪSHŪ   *Iwai-Jima*

Iki-Kaikyō   Nakama   *Suō-Nada*   *Hime-Jima*
Ō-Shima   Yobuko   Maēbaru   Nōgata   Yukuhashi   *Iyo-Nada*
Karatsu   FUKUOKA   Iizuka   Takawa   Nakatsu
F U K U O K A   Miyuta   Yamada   Buzen   Kunisaki
Matsuura   Sefuri-San   Amagi   Usa   Bungotakada   ▲721   Futago-Yama
Hirado   Imari   T s u k u s h i - S a n c h i   Hiji   Kitsuki   *Sada-Misaki-*
Hirado-   Aita   Taku   Tosu   Hita   Yufu-Dake   Beppu-Wan   *Hantō*
Shima   Yoshii   SAGA   1055   Kurume   Kusu   1584   Beppu   Saganoseki
Kashima   Okawa   Saga   Yame   Kurogi   Tsurusaki   Ōita
Sasebo   Ureshino   Yanagawa   Chikugo   O I T A   Usuki
983   Tara   Setaka   Yamaga   Oguni   Kujū-San   Tsukumi
Omura-   Tara-Dake   Ōmuta   1787
Wan   N A G A   Arao   Yamaga   Aso   Ōita   Saiki   *Tsurumi-*
N A G A S A   Isahaya   Tamana   Kikuchi   Innomiya   Sobo-Yama   *Saki*   *Bungo-*
Ōmura   Kumamoto   Ōzu   Taketa   1758   *Suidō*
Nagasaki   Unzen-Dake   KUMAMOTO   Ascizan   Kamae
1360   Shimabara   Mashiki   1592   Takachiho
Obama   Uto   Hinokage   Nobeoka

Nomo-Zaki   Kuchinotsu   Oyama   Misumi   Kunimi-Dake
A m a k u s a -   Hondo   Kami-   739   Shiba   Hyūga   Hososhima
Amakusa-   Shimo-   Jima   K y ū s h ū - S a n c h i   M I Y A Z A K I
Shotō   Jima   Itsuki
N a d a   Yatsushiro   Hitoyoshi   KYŪSHŪ

99   Ushibuka   *Yatsushiro-Kai*   Yunomae   KYŪSHŪ-DISTRICT
Naga-Shima   Minamata
Akune   Izumi   Ebino   Takanabe
32   Kami-koshiki   Ōkuchi   Yoshimatsu   Saito
Jima   Miyanojō   Kurino   Kobayashi   Miyazaki
Koshiki-   1700   Kirishima-Yama
Rettō   Kajiki   Kokubu   Miyakonojō
Shimo-koshiki-   Sendai   Hayato   Nichinan
Jima   Kushikino   Iijūin   On-Take   Aburatsu
Kagoshima   1118   Shibushi
K A G O S H I M A   Tarumizu   Kushima
Noma-Saki   Taniyama   *Satsuma-Hantō*   Kanoya   Kōyama   *Shibushi-Wan*
Kaseda   Fukiage   *Kagoshima-*
Makurazaki   Chiran   *Wan*   *Ōsumi-Hantō*
Bō-no-Misaki   Ibusuki   132
Kaimon-Dake   Yamagawa   COPYRIGHT GEORGE PHILIP & SON LTD
924
130   *Sata-Misaki*   31
31   East from Greenwich 131   104

Map 108

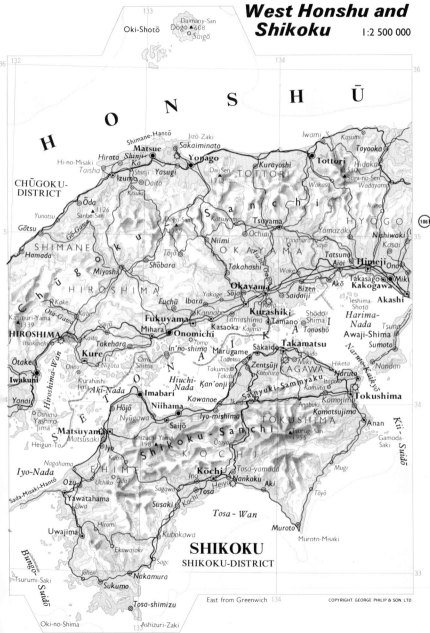

West Honshu and Shikoku

1:2 500 000

Map 109

East from Greenwich 134

COPYRIGHT GEORGE PHILIP & SON. LTD

Indonesia: West

Map 110

1:20 000 000

East from Greenwich

Map 111

Indonesia: East

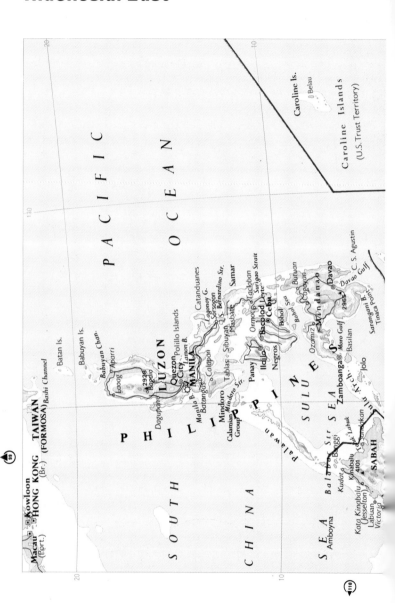

Map 112

1:20 000 000

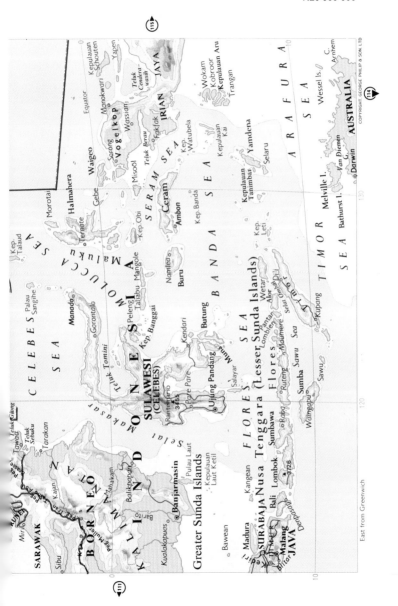

East from Greenwich

Map 113

Australia, New Zealand and Papua New Guinea

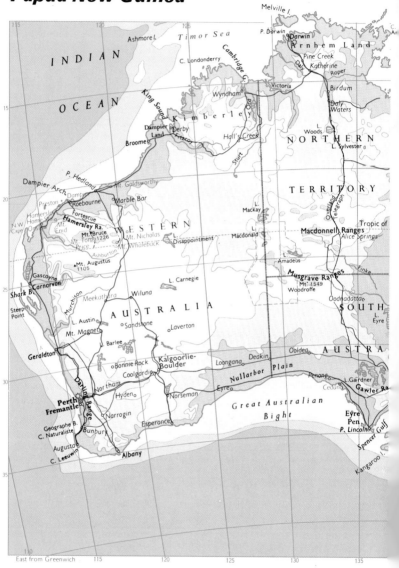

Map 114

114

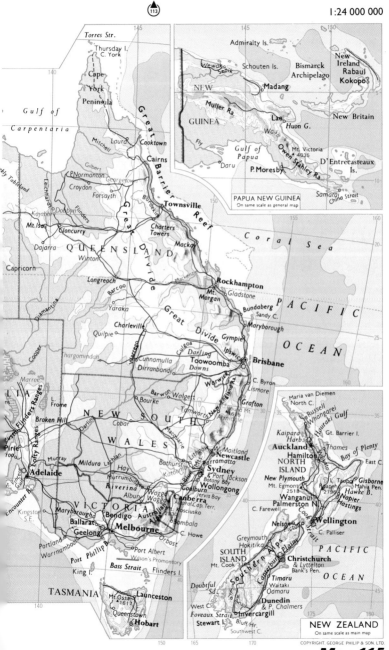

1:24 000 000

Torres Str.

Thursday I.
C. York

Admiralty Is.

New
Ireland
Rabaul
Kokopo

Cape
York
Peninsula

Gulf of
Carpentaria

Wewak
Sepik

Schouten Is.

Bismarck
Archipelago

NEW

Madang

Muller Ra.

Lae
Huon G.
Wau

New Britain

GUINEA

Mitchell

Laura

Cooktown

Gilbert

P.Normanton
Georgetown

Cairns

Croydon
Forsayth

Fly

Daru

Gulf of
Papua

Mt. Victoria
4935

Owen Stanley Ra.

P. Moresby

D'Entrecasteaux
Is.

China Strait

Samarai

PAPUA NEW GUINEA
On same scale as general map

Leichhardt

Kajabbi P.Dobbyn

Flinders

Townsville

Mt.Isa
Cloncurry

Charters
Towers

Great Barrier Reef

Dajarra

QUEENSLAND

Mackay

Coral Sea

Winton

Capricorn

Longreach

Mackenzie

Great Divide

Rockhampton

Mt.
Morgan

Gladstone

Barcoo

PACIFIC

Diamantina

Yaraka

Bundaberg
Sandy C.

Charleville

Maryborough

Quilpie

Gympie

OCEAN

Thargomindah

Cunnamulla
Dirranbandi

Toowoomba
Darling
Downs

Ipswich

Brisbane

Cooper

Warwick

Marree

Barwon

Walgett

C. Byron

Lismore

L.
Frome

Bourke

Tamworth

Grafton

Armidale

NEW SOUTH

Maria van Diemen
North C.

Pirie
roo

Flinders Ranges

Cobar

Macquarie

WALES

C. Russell

Whangarei

Gt. Barrier I.

Broken Hill

Darling

Lachlan

Hay

Mildura

Murrumbidgee

Bathurst

Katoomba

W. Maitland
Parramatta

Newcastle

Sydney

Port Jackson
Botany Bay

Hauraki Gulf

Kaipara

Auckland

Hamilton

Thames

Bay of Plenty

East C.

NORTH
ISLAND

New Plymouth
Mt. Egmont

L. Taupo

Gisborne

Adelaide

Murray

Riverina

Wagga
Albury Wagga

Goulburn

Wollongong

Canberra
Austral.Cap.Terr.

Jervis Bay

Wanganui

Ruapehu
2518

Mahia Pen.

Hawke B.

Palmerston N.
Napier
Hastings

Encounter B.

Kingston
S.E.

VICTORIA

Maryborough

Bendigo

Ballarat
Geelong

Melbourne

Kosciusko
2230

Bombala

C. Howe

C. Farewell

Nelson

Cook Strait

Wellington

C. Palliser

Portland
Warrnambool

Port Albert

Wilson's Promontory

Orbost

Greymouth
Hokitika

SOUTH
ISLAND

Nelson
Picton

Canterbury Plains

PACIFIC

Christchurch
& Lyttelton
Bank's Pen.

King I.

Bass Strait

Flinders I.

Doubtful
Sd.

Mt. Cook 3764

Southern Alps

Timaru
Waitaki
Oamaru

OCEAN

TASMANIA

Launceston

Mt.Ossa
1617

Queenstown

Hobart

West C.

Foveaux Strait

Invercargill

Dunedin
& P. Chalmers

Bluff Hr.

Stewart I.

Southwest C.

NEW ZEALAND
On same scale as main map

COPYRIGHT. GEORGE PHILIP & SON LTD.

Map 115

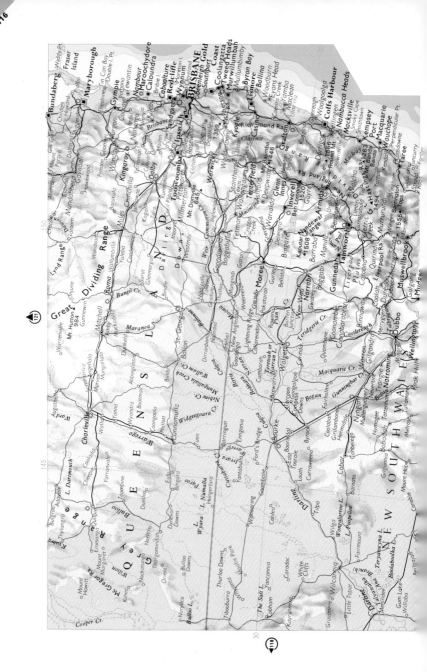

Map 116

116

Australia: Brisbane, Sydney, Melbourne

1:8 000 000

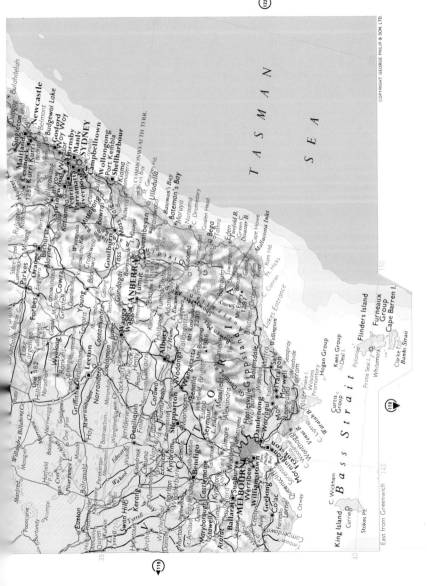

Map 117

Australia: Adelaide, Melbourne, Tasmania

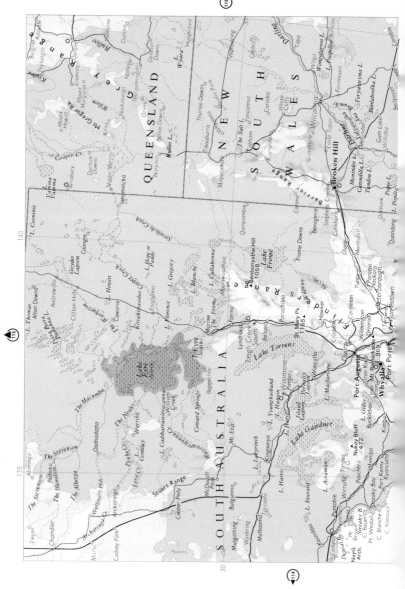

Map 118

118

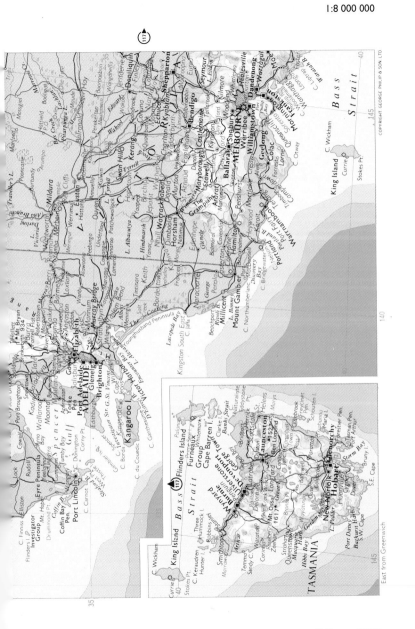

1:8 000 000

Map 119

Australia: Perth

1:8 000 000

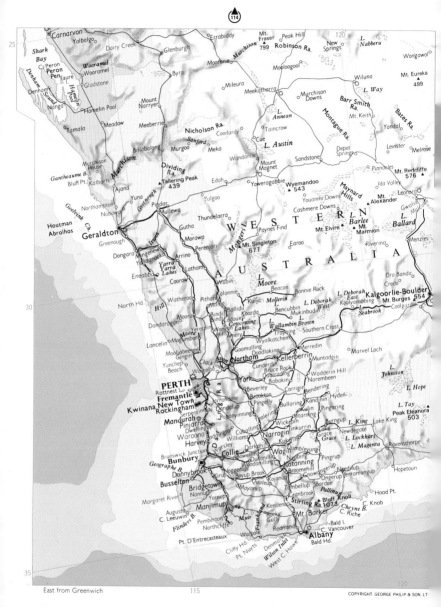

East from Greenwich

115

Map 120

Australia: North East Queensland

1:8 000 000

East from Greenwich

Map 121

New Zealand, Central and South West Pacific

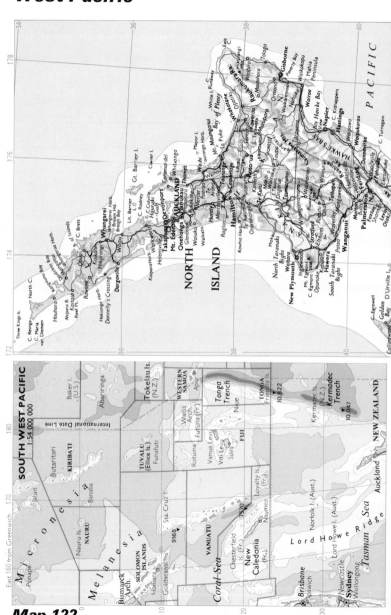

Map 122

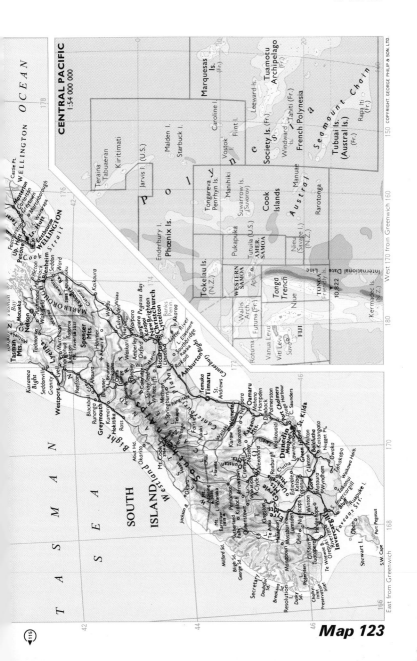

1:7 000 000

CENTRAL PACIFIC
1:54 000 000

Map 123

Africa: Physical

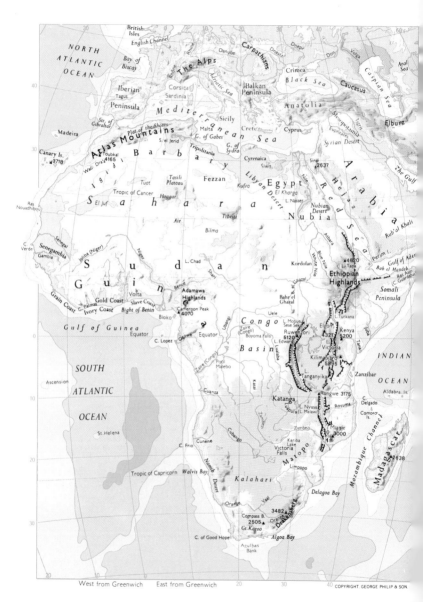

NORTH ATLANTIC OCEAN

British Isles
English Channel
Bay of Biscay
The Alps
Carpathians
Dnepr
Don
Volga
Aral Sea
Crimea
Black Sea
Caucasus
Caspian Sea
Iberian Peninsula
Tagus
Corsica
Sardinia
Balkan Peninsula
Anatolia
Elburz
Mesopotamia
Tigris
Madeira
Str. of Gibraltar
Atlas Mountains
Plat. of the Shotts
Toubkal 4165
Sicily
Malta
Crete
Mediterranean Sea
Cyprus
Euphrates
Syrian Desert
The Gulf
Canary Is. 3718
Wadi Draa
Igidi
Barbary
S/el Jerid
G. of Gabes
Tripolitania
G. of Sydra
Cyrenaica
Siwa
Libyan Desert
Egypt
El Kharga
Sinai 2637
Hejaz
Arabia
Ras Nouadhibou
S el Juf
Sahara
Tuat
Tasili Plateau
Fezzan
Kufra
Hoggar
Tibesti
El Nasser
Nubian Desert
Nubia
Red Sea
Rub'al Khali
Tropic of Cancer
Air
Bilma
White Nile
Gulf of Aden
Bab el Mandeb
C. Verde
Senegal
Senegambia
Gambia
Joliba (Niger)
Sudan
L. Chad
Shari
Kordofan
Blue Nile
Atbara
4620
Ethiopian Highlands
L. Tana
Perim I.
Ras Asir (C. Guardafui)
Grain Coast
Guinea
Niger
Benue
Adamawa Highlands
Bahr el Ghazal
Bahr el Ghazal
Uele
Somali Peninsula
C. Palmas
Gold Coast
Volta
Ivory Coast
Slave Coast
Bight of Benin
Cameroon Peak 4070
Bioko
Ubangi
Congo
L. Mobutu Sese Seko
Elgon
L. Turkana
Kenya 5200
Gulf of Guinea
C. Lopez
Gabwe
Equator
Equator
Zaïre (Congo)
Boyoma Falls
Ruwenzori 5120
L. Edward
L. Victoria
Kilimanjaro 5895
Juba
INDIAN OCEAN
SOUTH ATLANTIC OCEAN
Ascension
Basin
Pool Malebo
Zaïre (Congo)
Lualaba
L. Tanganyika
Zanzibar
Aldabra Is.
St. Helena
Kasai
Katanga
Rungwe 3175
Rovuma
C. Delgado
Comoro Is.
Cuanza
L. Nyasa (L. Malawi)
Lufupa (L. Malawi)
Zambezi
Mlanje 3000
Madagascar 2638
Cunene
Cubango
Zambezi
Kariba Lake
Victoria Falls
Mozambique Channel
Tropic of Capricorn
Walvis Bay
Namib Desert
Kalahari
Matopo
Limpopo
Delagoa Bay
Orange
Vaal
Compass B. 3482
2505
Gt. Karoo
Drakensberg
Algoa Bay
C. of Good Hope
Agulhas Bank

West from Greenwich   East from Greenwich

Map 124

Africa: Political

1:70 000 000

West from Greenwich East from Greenwich

Map 125

Africa: North West

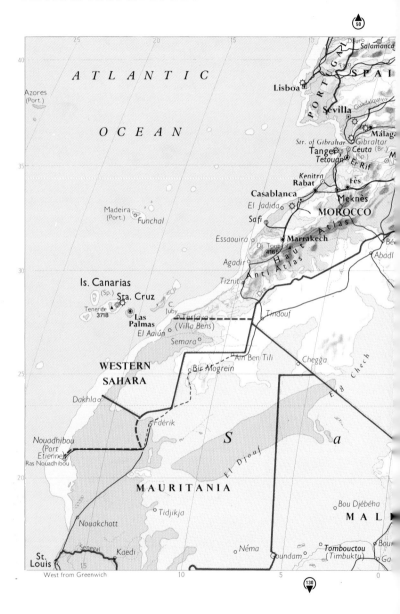

ATLANTIC

Azores
(Port.)

OCEAN

PORTUGAL

SPAI

Lisboa

Douro
Salamanca

Sevilla
Guadalquivir

Str. of Gibraltar
Tanger
Tetouan
El Rif

Málag
Gibraltar
(Br.)
Ceuta
(Sp.)

M

Kenitra
Rabat
Casablanca
El Jadida
Safi

Fès
Meknès
MOROCCO

Madeira
(Port.)
Funchal

Essaouira
Marrakech
Dj. Toubkal
4165
Haut Atlas

Bé
Abadl

Agadir
Anti Atlas

Is. Canarias
(Sp.)
Sta. Cruz
Tenerife ▲
3718
Las
Palmas
El Aaiún

Tiznit

C.
Juby
Tarfaya
(Villa Bens)
Semara

Dra

Tindouf

WESTERN

SAHARA

Aïn Ben Tili

Chegga

El
B
Chech

Dakhla

Bir Mogrein

Fdérik

Nouadhibou
(Port
Etienne)
Ras Noüadhibou

S

El Djouf

a

MAURITANIA

Tidjikja

Bou Djébéha

MAL

Nouakchott

Néma

Tombouctou
(Timbuktu)

Bou
Ga

St.
Louis

Senegal
Kaedi

Goundam

Map 126

1:20 000 000

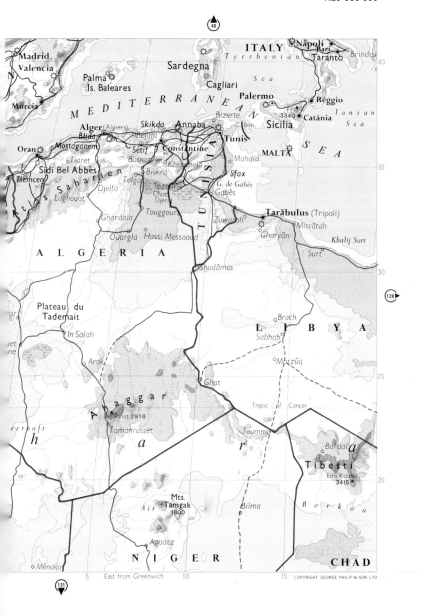

48

ITALY
Madrid
Valencia
Murcia
Palma
Is. Baleares

Sardegna
Tyrrhenian
Sea
Cagliari

Napoli
Bari
Brindisi
Taranto

40

Palermo
Etna
3340
Catánia
Sicilia
Ionian
Sea

Réggio

M E D I T E R R A N E A N   S E A

Alger (Algiers)
Skikda
Annaba
Bizerte
C. Bon

Blida
Béjaïa
Setif
Constantine
Tunis

Oran
Mostaganem
Tiaret
Khenchela
Mahdia

MALTA

Sidi Bel Abbès
Batna
Setif
Biskra
Sfax

Tlemcen
Laghouat
Djelfa
Tolga
Tozeur
Chott
Djerid
G. de Gabès
Gabès

35

Atlas Saharien

Ghardaïa
Touggourt
Zuwārah
Tarābulus (Tripoli)
Misrātah

Ouargla
Hassi Messaoud
Gharyān
Khalij Surt

A L G E R I A
Surt

Ghudāmes
30

128

Plateau du
Tademaït
Brach
L I B Y A
In Salah
Sabhah

Arak
Marzūq

Ghat

Tropic of Cancer
25

H a g g a r
Tahat 2918
Tamanrasset
Toummo
Bardaï
Tibesti
Emi Koussi
3415

ezrouft
h
a
r
20

Mts.
Tamgak
1800
Aïr
Bilma
Borkou

Agadez

N I G E R
CHAD
Ménaka

131

Map 127

Africa: North East

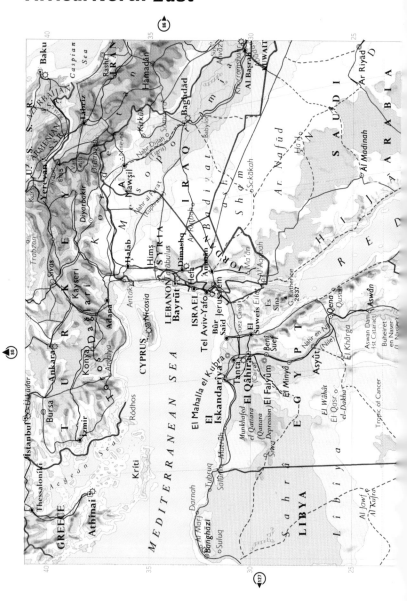

Map 128

128

128

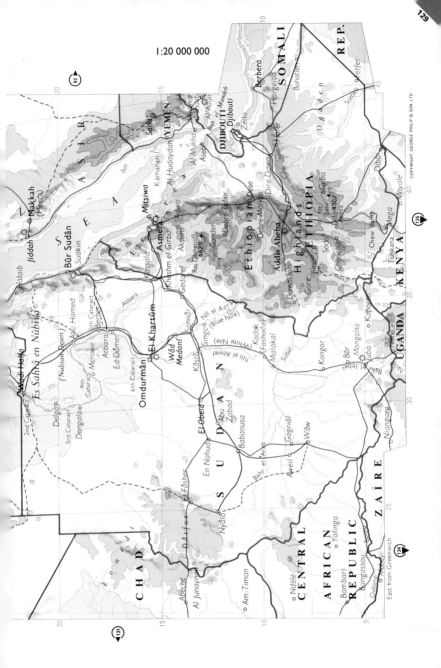

1:20 000 000

COPYRIGHT GEORGE PHILIP & SON LTD

Map 129

Africa: West

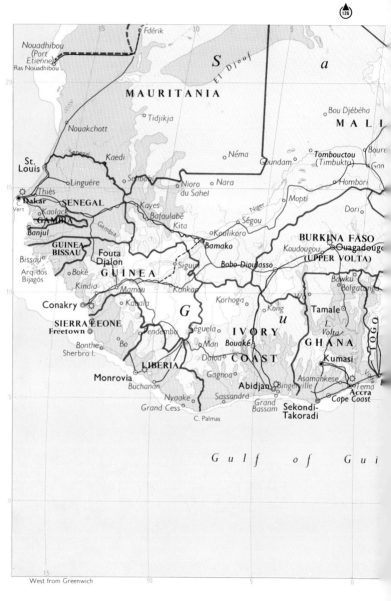

Map 130

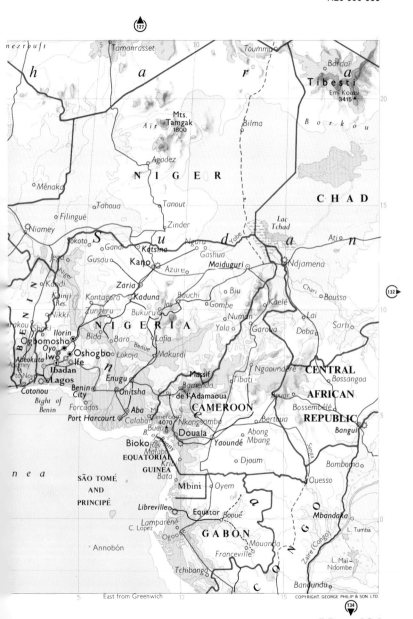

1:20 000 000

nezrouft   Tamanrasset   Toumma   Bardaï
   h   a   r   Tibesti
                                               Emi Koussi
                                                 3415
                                 Bilma   B o r k o u
        Aïr Mts.
            Tamgak
             1800
        Agadez

   Ménaka   N   I   G   E   R   C H A D

           Tahoua   Tanout
   Filingué
       Sokoto S   Zinder   Lac
Niamey   Tchad
      Sokoto o Gandi Katsina Nguru   a
             o Gusau   Tobe   Ati   n
   Jega   Gusau Kano Azare Gashua
                            Maiduguri   Ndjamena
B   Zaria
E   Kainji Kontagora Kaduna Bauchi Biu   Chari Bousso
N   Res.   Jos Gombe Kaelé
I   Nikki Zungeru Bukuru   Numan Lai   Sarh
N   Baro   Yola Garoua Doba
   Shaki Ilorin N I G E R I A
Oshomosho Oyo Bida   Lafia
   Iwo Oshogbo Lokoja Makurdi   Ngaoundéré CENTRAL
Abeokuta Ife n Enugu Massif   Bossangoa
   Ibadan   Enugu Bamenda Tibati   AFRICAN
Lagos Benin Onitsha de l'Adamaoua Bouar
Cotonou City   Bertoua Bossembélé REPUBLIC
Bight of Forcados Aba Cameroon Nkongsamba Abong Bangui
Benin Port Harcourt Calabar 4070 Douala Mbang
             Buea Yaoundé
   Bioko Malabo
   EQUATORIAL Kribi Djoum   Bomboma
   GUINEA Bata
 n e a   SÃO TOMÉ   a   Ouesso
        AND   Mbini Oyem
        PRINCIPE
         Libreville Equator Booué   Mbandaka
        Lamparéné   O   L. Tumba
   Annobón C. Lopez GABON Mouanda Zaïre (Congo)
              Ogooué Franceville   L. Mai-
                                      Ndombe
           Tchibanga   C   Bandundu
   East from Greenwich   COPYRIGHT GEORGE PHILIP & SON LTD

Map 131

Africa: East

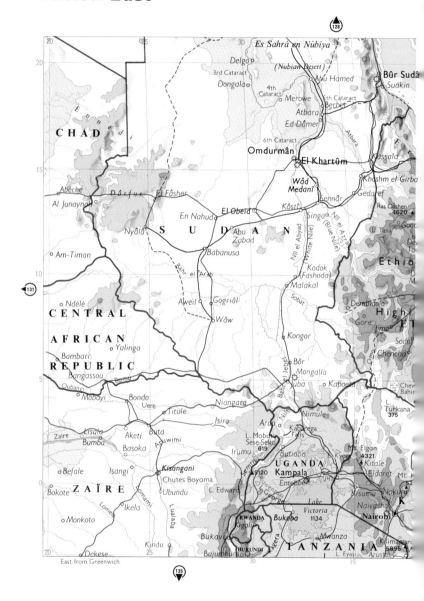

Map 132

1:20 000 000

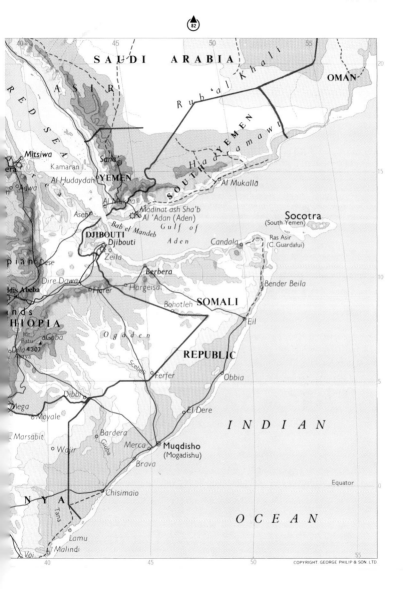

Map 133

Africa: Central

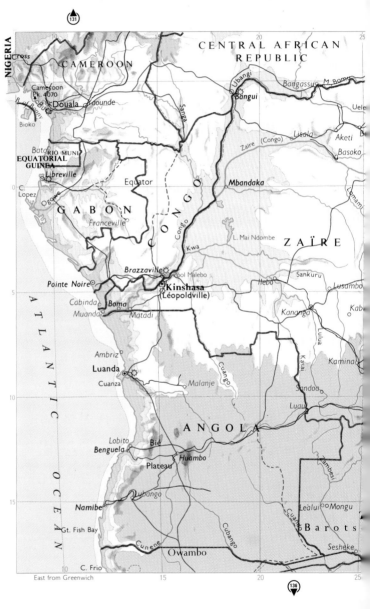

Map 134

134

1:20 000 000

SUDAN

ETHIOPIA

Mongalla
Juba
Bahr el Jebel
Omo
Chew Bahir
(L. Stefanie)

Niangara
Nimule
L. Turkana
Nile

Isiro
Wadelai
KaBarega Falls
Marsabit

Aruwimi
L. Mobutu Sese Seko
Irumu
Buraba
Mt. Elgon 4321
L. Kioga
Kitale
Eldoret
Mt. Kenya 5199

Kisangani
(Stanleyville)
Stanley Falls
Semliki
UGANDA
Kampala
Entebbe
Jinja
Nakuru
KENYA

Ubundi
L. Edward
Rwenzori
George
Kisumu
Naivasha

Lualaba
Kigali
RWANDA
Bukoba
Lake Victoria
Nairobi

Bukavu
(Costermansville)
BURUNDI
Bujumbura
Kagera
Mwanza
Kilimanjaro 5895
Moshi
Voi
Lamu
Malindi

nduo
Kasongo
Kipoma
L. Eyasi
Arusha
L. Manyara
Mombasa
and Kilindini

Kongolo
Tabora
Kongwa
Mpwapwa
Bagamoyo
Pemba
Zanzibar

Kabalo
Lukuga
Kalemie
(Albertville)
Mpanda
Dodoma
Morogoro
Dar-es-Salaam

Luvua
Pangani
Tanga

ha b a
Bukama
L. Mweru
Kasanga
L. Rukwa
Mbala
Iringa
Rufiji
Mafia
Kilwa

Likasi
Lubumbashi
(Elisabethville)
Bangweulu
Chambeshi
Mbeya
Tukuyu
Karonga
Livingstonia
Loangwa
Manda
Ruvuma
Lindi
Mikindani
C. Delgado

Kitwe
Ndola
Chipata
Lilongwe
Salima
MOZAMBIQUE

Kafue
Kabwe
ZAMBIA
Zumbo
Zambezi
Blantyre
Zomba
Shirwa
Nampula
Mozambique

land
Lusaka
Kafue
Cahora Bassa Dam
Tete
Sena
MALAWI
L. Nyasa

Livingstone
L. Kariba
ZIMBABWE
Harare
(Salisbury)
Sena
Shire
Quelimane

SOMALI REP.

Giuba
Kisimayu

Tana

COPYRIGHT GEORGE PHILIP & SON LTD

Map 135

Africa: South

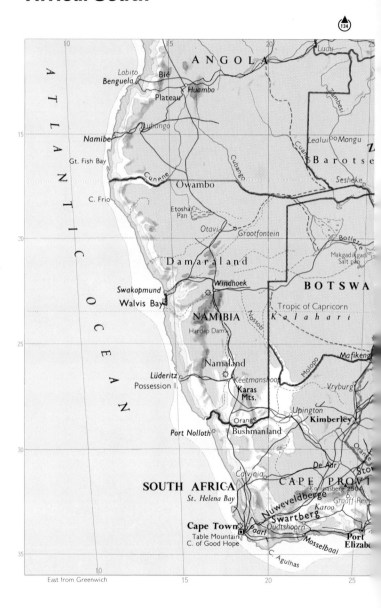

Map 136

136

1:20 000 000

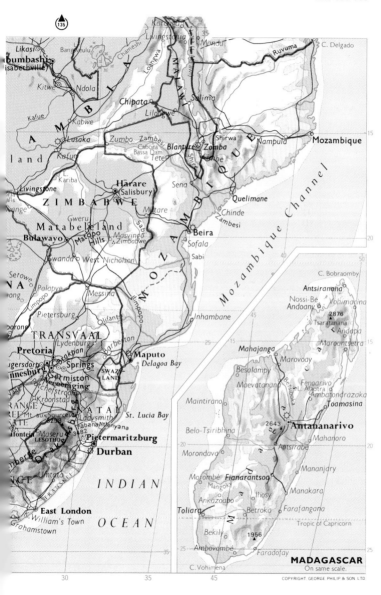

Map 137

North America: Physical

1:60 000 000

Map 138

West from Greenwich

COPYRIGHT. GEORGE PHILIP & SON.

North America: Political

1:60 000 000

ASIA

Bering Sea — *Bering Str.*

ARCTIC OCEAN

Ostrov Vrangelya — Pr. Barrow

Beaufort Sea — Banks I.

Parry Is.

M'Clure Str. — Viscount Melville Sd.

Lancaster Sd.

Ellesmere I.

GREENLAND (Denmark)

ICELAND

Denmark Str.

Upernavik

Baffino Bay

Disko I. — Godthaab

Davis Strait:Limit of pack-ice (Spring)

C. Farewell

ALASKA

Yukon — Fairbanks — Arctic Circle — Dawson — Klondike
Anchorage — Whitehorse — Skagway — Juneau
Mackenzie

Queen Charlotte Is. — Pr. Rupert

Victoria — Baffin Island

Baffin I.

Arctic Circle

Gt. Bear L.
Yellowknife — Gt. Slave L.
Athabasca L.

Chesterfield Inlet — Southampton I.

Hudson Strait

C A N A D A

Hudson Bay

Labrador

Churchill — Nelson
Flin Flon
Dawson Creek — Edmonton — Prince Albert — Saskatoon
Calgary
Lethbridge — Moose Jaw — Regina
Medicine Hat — Winnipeg

James Bay

Sept Iles

Newfoundland — Corner Brook — St. John's

Vancouver — Fraser
Victoria — Vancouver — Seattle — Spokane
Portland — Tacoma

Thunder Bay

Duluth — Sault Ste. Marie — Québec — Montreal

Timmins

Halifax — Nova Scotia — C. Breton I.

Eugene — Snake
Sacramento — Reno — Gt. Salt L.
San Francisco — Oakland — Salt Lake City
Fresno

Billings

Minneapolis — St Paul

Ottawa — Toronto — Boston
Milwaukee — Detroit — Buffalo — New York
Chicago — Cleveland — Philadelphia
Pittsburgh — Baltimore

U N I T E D   S T A T E S

Omaha — Platte
Denver — Kansas City — St. Louis — Cincinnati — Washington
Colorado — Pueblo

C. Hatteras

Los Angeles — San Diego
Phoenix — Amarillo — Red — Memphis — Charlotte
Albuquerque — Dallas — Atlanta — Birmingham — Savannah
Tucson — El Paso — Mississippi
Ciudad Juarez — Baton Rouge — Mobile — Jacksonville
Hermosillo — Houston — New Orleans — Florida
Baja — San Antonio — Galveston — Tampa — Miami

Bermuda (Br.)

ATLANTIC OCEAN

BAHAMAS

California

Tropic of Cancer

Chihuahua — Torreón — Monterrey

Gulf of Mexico

M E X I C O

Mazatlán — La Habana — CUBA

Revilla Gigedo (Mex.) — Guadalajara — S. Luis Potosí — Tampico
León — Mérida — Yucatan Strait
México — Veracruz
Puebla — Coatzacoalcos — BELIZE
Acapulco — Salina Cruz

Santiago de Cuba — HAITI — DOM. REP.
JAMAICA — Kingston — P-au-P. — Prince P. Rico (U.S.)

Caribbean Sea

GUATEMALA — Guatemala — HONDURAS
EL SALVADOR — NICARAGUA
CENTRAL — Managua — Cartagena
AMERICA — COSTA RICA — San José — PANAMA

SOUTH AMERICA

PACIFIC OCEAN

COPYRIGHT. GEORGE PHILIP & SON. LTD

Map 139

Canada: South East

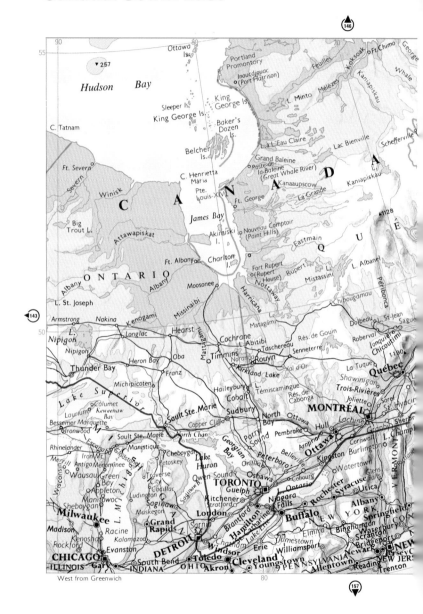

Map 140

1:15 000 000

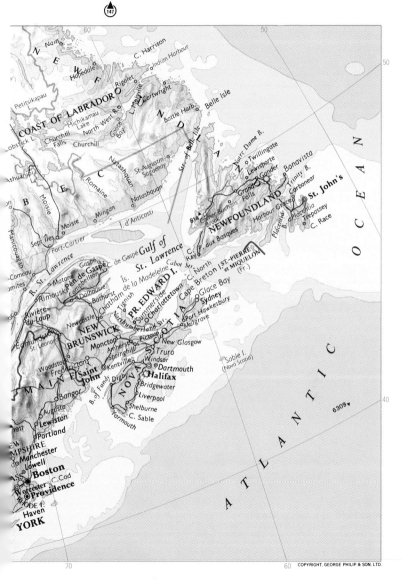

Map 141

Canada: South West and Alaska

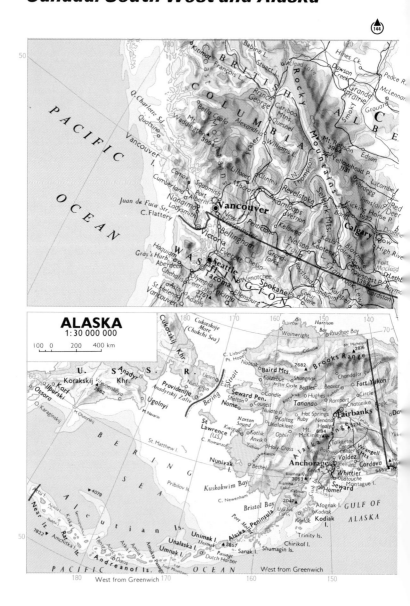

Map 142

1:15 000 000

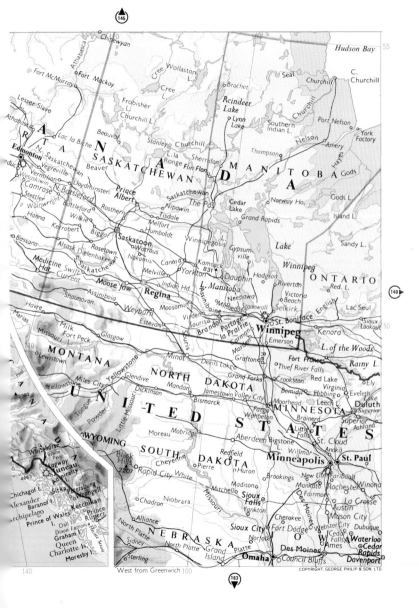

Map 143

Canada: North West

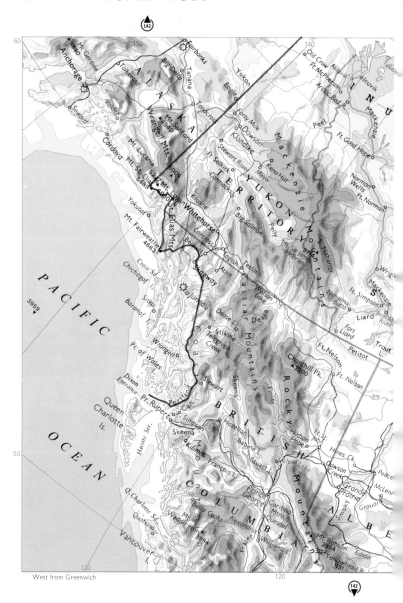

PACIFIC OCEAN

ALASKA

YUKON TERRITORY

BRITISH COLUMBIA

ALBERTA

Mackenzie Mountains

Rocky Mountains

Cassiar Mountains

Cariboo Mtns.

Queen Charlotte Is.

Vancouver I.

Anchorage
Mt. Gerdine 3140
Stalkeasna
Seward
Valdez
Cordova
Mt. St. Elias 5489
Mt. Logan 5960
Mt. Luania 5006
Mt. Fairweather 4663
Mt. Sanford 4940
Wrangell Mts.
Yakutat
Chichagof I.
Sitka
Baranof I.
Pr. of Wales
Wrangell
Dixon Entrance
Pr. Rupert
Hecate Str.
Q. Charlotte Str.
Quatsino

Fairbanks
Big Delta
Tanana
Tanacross
Yukon
Eagle
Forty Mile
Dawson
Klondike
Stewart River
Mayo
Keno Hill
Carmacks
Whitehorse
Kluane
Big Salmon
Pelly
Fort Selkirk
Cordova
Boya
Tagish
Atlin
Teslin
Skagway
Juneau
Stikine
Telegraph Creek
Dease L.
Watson
Nelson
Stewart
Portland Can.
Pt. Simpson
Hazelton
Babine L.
Skeena
Kitimat
François L.
Stuart L.
McLeod Lake
Prince George
Alexandria
Bella Coola
Mt. Waddington 3994
Quesnel
Williams L.
Fraser
Mt. Robson 3954
Yellowhead P. 1131
Edson

Old Crow
Aklavik
Inuvik
Ft. McPherson
Arctic Red R.
Mackenzie
Peel
Ft. Good Hope
Norman Wells
Ft. Norman
Wrigley
Ft. Simpson
Mt. Sir James McBrien
Nahanni Butte
Liard
Ft. Liard
Fort Nelson
Petitot
Trout L.
Churchill Pk. 3200
Ft. Nelson
Finlay
Ft. St. John
Hudson Hope
Hines Ck.
Dawson Creek
Grande Prairie
Grouard
McLennan
Peace
Smoky
Big Delta

Churchill Pk. 3200

3959

3200

West from Greenwich

150   140   120

60   50

Map 144

1:15 000 000

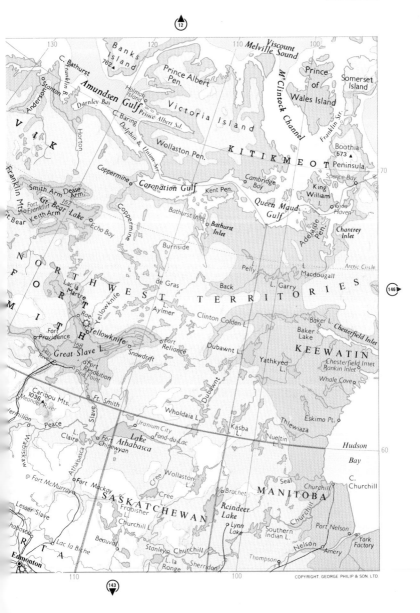

Map 145

Canada: North East

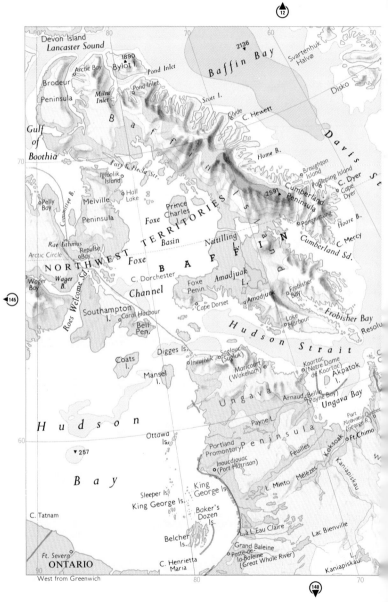

Devon Island
Lancaster Sound
Arctic Bay
Bylot I.
1890
Pond Inlet
Brodeur
Peninsula
Milne
Inlet
Pond Inlet
B
a
f
f
i
n
2136
Baffin Bay
Svartenhuk
Halvø
Scott I.
Clyde
C. Hewett
Disko
D
a
v
i
s
S
t
r

Gulf
of
Boothia
Fury & Hecla Str.
Igloolik
Island
Pelly
Bay
Melville
Hall
Lake
Peninsula
Cumberland B.
Prince
Charles
I.
Foxe
Home B.
Broughton
Island
Padloping Island
C. Dyer
Cape
Dyer
Cumberland
Peninsula
2591
Pangnirtung
Hoare B.

N
O
R
T
H
W
E
S
T
T
E
R
R
I
T
O
R
I
E
S
Rae Isthmus
Arctic Circle
Repulse
Bay
Foxe
Basin
Nettilling
Foxe
C. Dorchester
Nettilling
L.
B
A
F
F
I
N
Cumberland Sd.
C. Mercy

Wager
Bay
Wager
B.
Roes Welcome Sound
Channel
Southampton
I.
Coral Harbour
Bell
Pen.
C. Dorchester
Foxe
Penin.
Cape Dorset
Amadjuak
L.
Amadjuak
Lake
Harbour
Frobisher
Bay
Frobisher Bay
Resolu

Coats
I.
Mansel
I.
Digges Is.
Invujivik
Sagluc
(Sugluk)
Maricourt
(Wakeham)
Koartac
(Notre Dame
de Koartac)
Akpatok
I.

H u d s o n
257
Ungava
Arnaud
Bellin
(Payne Bay)
Ungava Bay
Port
Nouveau-Québec
(George R.)
Ft. Chimo

60
Ottawa
Is.
Payne L.
Portland
Promontory
P e n i n s u l a
Inoucdjouac
(Port Harrison)
Feuilles
Koksoak
Kaniapiskau

B a y
Sleeper Is.
King George Is.
King George Is.
Baker's
Dozen
Is.
L. Minto
Mélèzes
W

C. Tatnam
Belcher
Is.
À L'Eau Claire
Lac Bienville

Ft. Severn
ONTARIO
C. Henrietta
Maria
Grand Baleine
Poste-de-
la-Baleine
(Great Whale River)
Kaniapiskau
L.

90
West from Greenwich
80
70

Map 146

1:15 000 000

Map 147

Canada: Saint Lawrence Estuary

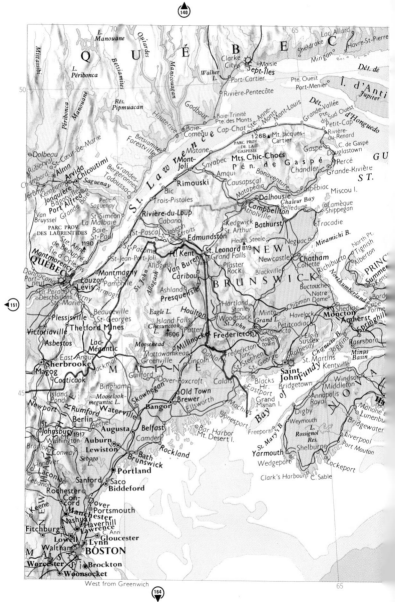

West from Greenwich

Map 148

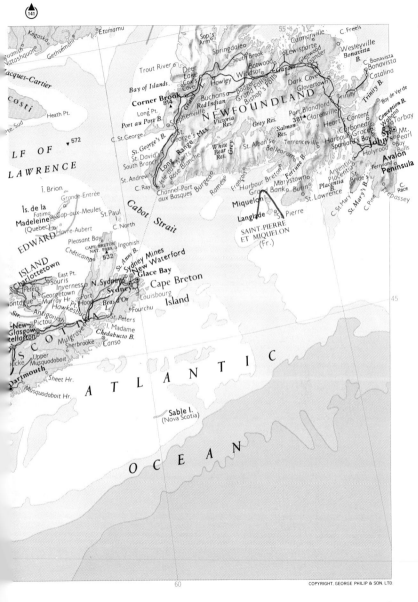

1:7 000 000

Map 149

Canada: The Great Lakes

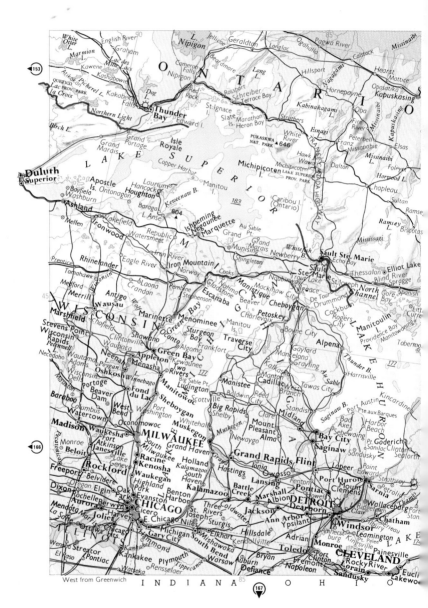

Map 150

1:7 000 000

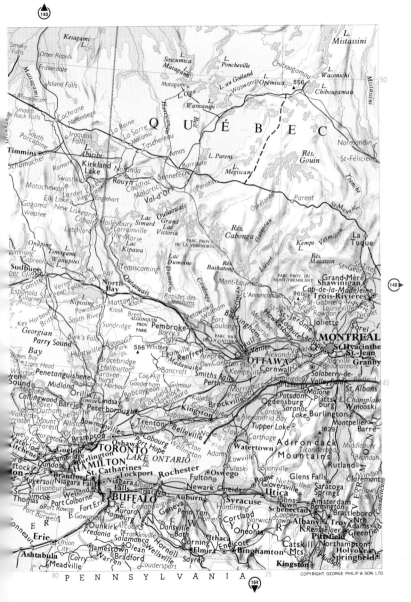

Smoky Falls
Kesagami L.
80
L. Mistassini

Otter Rapids
Soscumica Matagami L.
Poncheville
L. Waconichi

Fraserdale
Matagami
Chibougamau
556
Waswanipi
Opémisca
Chibougamau
50

Island Falls
L. au Goéland
L. Olga

Moonbeam
Cochrane
Norembego
Waswanipi

Smooth Rock Falls
La Reine
L. Parent

South Porcupine
Iroquois Falls
La Sarre
Macamic
Taschereau
QUÉBEC
Normandin

Timmins
Abitibi
Amos
Barraute
L. Parent
St-Félicien

Schumacher
Kirkland Lake
Noranda
Senneterre
L. Mégiscane
Rés. Gouin

Matachewan
Ramore
Swastika
Rouyn
Cadillac
Paradis
Oskélanéo
Parent
St-Maurice

Elk Lake
Larder Lake
Virginiatown
Englehart
Malartic
Val-d'Or

Gogama
New Liskeard
Cobalt
Lac Outaouais
Grand Lac Victoria
Rés. Cabonga
Kempt L.
Vermilion

Westree
Haileybury
Lorrainville
Île-Marie
Lac Kipawa
PARC PROV. DE LA VÉRENDRYE
Rés. Matawin
La Tuque

Onaping
Latchford
Temagami
Wanapitei
Lac Dumoine
Rés. Baskatong
Lièvre
PARC PROV. DU MONT-TREMBLANT
St-Georges

Capreol
Sudbury
per Cliff
Coniston
North Bay
Outaouais
Mont-Laurier
Grand-Mère
Shawinigan
Cap-de-la-Madeleine
Trois-Rivières
St-Gabriel
St-Pie

Espanola
Sturgeon Falls
Verner
Cache Bay
Rapides des Joachims
L'Annonciation
St-Jovite
Rawdon
Louiseville
Nicolet

Killarney
Nipissing
Mattawa
Klock
Petawawa
St-Jérôme
Joliette
Sorel

Key Harbour
Britt
South River
Kiosk
Brent
ALGONQUIN PROV. PARK
Pembroke
Barry's Bay
Wakeham
Fort Coulonge
Buckingham
Hull
Mascouche
Lachute
MONTREAL
St-Hyacinthe

Georgian Bay
Parry Sound
Burk's Falls
Sundridge
Algonquin Park
556 Whitney
PARC NAT. DE LA GATINEAU
Vanier
St-Jean
Granby

Byng Inlet
Huntsville
Eganville
Renfrew
Arnprior
OTTAWA
Alexandria
Bedford

Lions Head
Wiarton
Penetanguishene
Bracebridge
Haliburton
Gravenhurst
Bancroft
Smiths Falls
Perth
Kemptville
Cornwall
Salaberry-de-Valleyfield
St. Albans

Owen Sound
Midland
Victoria Harbour
Coe Hill
Gooderham
Morrisburg
Prescott
Massena
Malone
Platts-burg
L. Champlain
Winooski

Meaford
Collingwood
Orillia
Lindsay
Bobcaygeon
Gilmour
Kaladar
Brockville
Ogdensburg
Saranac
Lake
Burlington
Montpelier

Medford
Barrie
Simcoe L.
Havelock
Marmora
Canton
Alexandria Bay
Barre

Hanover
Durham
Shelburne
Peterborough
Port
Napanee
Kingston
Clayton
Tupper Lake
1629
Middlebury

Walkerton
Mount Forest
Alliston
Bowmanville
Trenton
Brighton
Belleville
Picton
Wellington
Carthage
Adirondack Mountains
Ticonderoga
Rutland

Orangeville
Brampton
Oshawa
Port Hope
Cobourg
Adams
Watertown
Lowville
Boonville
Glens Falls
Brandon

Georgetown
TORONTO
LAKE ONTARIO
Pulaski
Rome
Northville
Saratoga Springs
Claremont

Waterloo
Guelph
Cambridge
Burlington
HAMILTON
St. Catharines
Rochester
Oswego
Fulton
Oneida
Utica
Gloversville
Amsterdam
Bennington
Brattleboro

Stratford
Dundas
Brantford
Niagara Falls
Niagara Falls
Albion
Batavia
Newark
Syracuse
Schenectady
Coopers
Albany
Troy
Adams

Ingersoll
Hillsonburg
Welland
Port Colborne
BUFFALO
Aurora
Geneva
Auburn
Hamilton
Cortland
Norwich
Rensselaer
Pittsfield
Greenfield

Simcoe
Port Rowan
Fort Erie
Hamburg
Dansville
Penn Yan
Homer
Oneonta
Catskill Mts.
Northampton
Holyoke
Springfield

Port Burwell
Gowanda
Arcades
Hornell
Bath
Ithaca
Endicott
Binghamton
Kingston

Erie
Union City
Dunkirk
Fredonia
Salamanca
Olean
Wellsville
Corning
Elmira
Sayre

Ashtabula
Meadville
Jamestown
Bradford
Warren
Coudersport
80
PENNSYLVANIA
75

164

Map 151

Canada: Southern Saskatchewan and Manitoba

Map 152

1:7 000 000

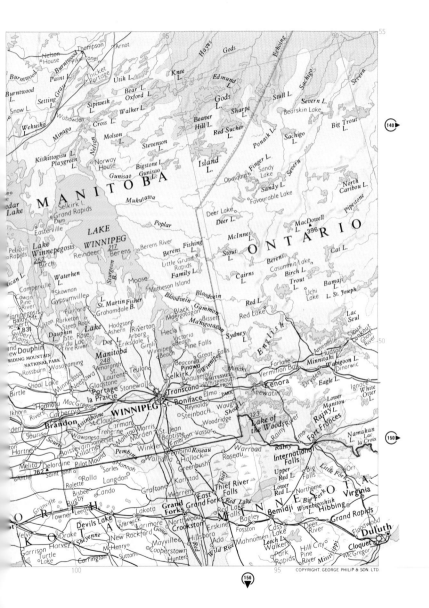

Map 153

Canada: Southern British Columbia and Alberta

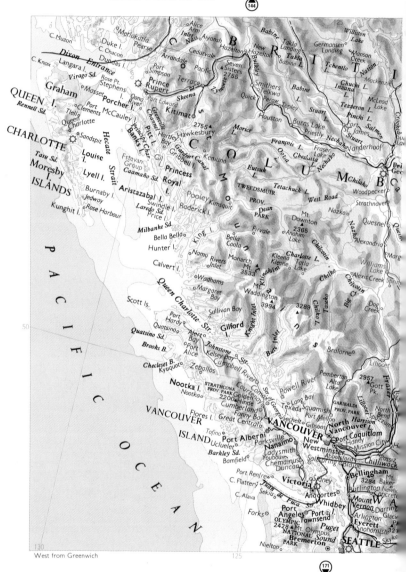

West from Greenwich

Map 154

1:7 000 000

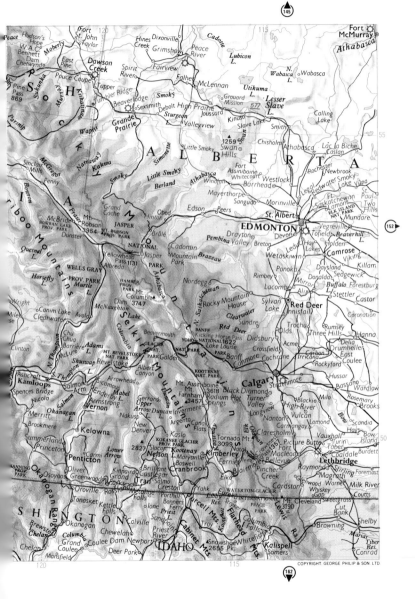

COPYRIGHT GEORGE PHILIP & SON LTD

Map 155

U.S.A.: North East

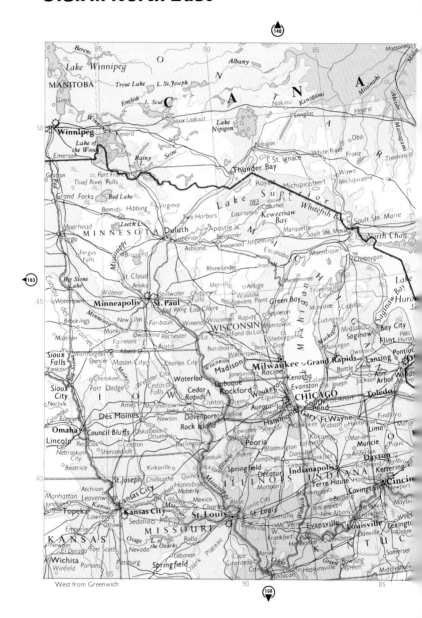

West from Greenwich

Map 156

1:12 000 000

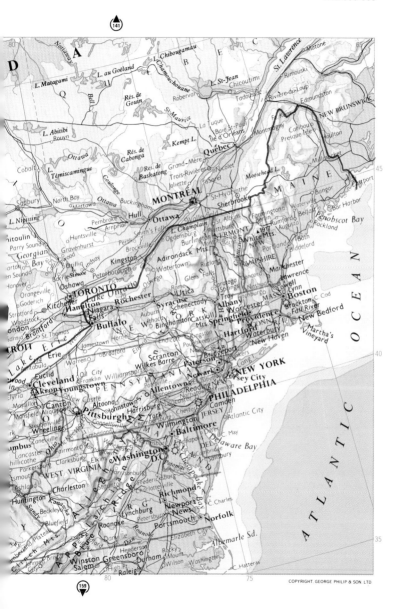

COPYRIGHT GEORGE PHILIP & SON LTD

Map 157

U.S.A.: South East

Map 158

1:12 000 000

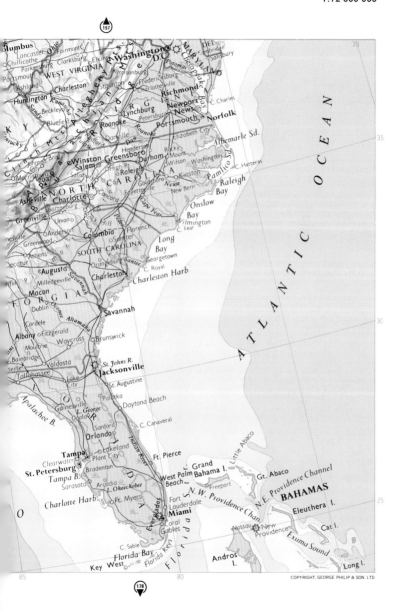

Map 159

U.S.A.: South West and Hawaii

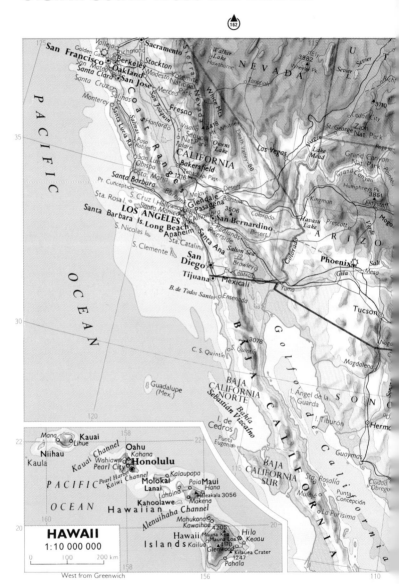

San Francisco
Vallejo
Golden Gate
Richmond
Berkeley
Oakland
San Mateo
Santa Clara·San Jose
Santa Cruz
Monterey
Santa Lucia Ra.
Salinas
Coast Ranges
Sacramento
Stockton
Modesto National
Merced
Fresno
San Joaquin
Visalia
Hanford
Paso Robles
San Luis Obispo
Sta. Maria
Santa Barbara
Sta. Rosa I.
S. Cruz I.
Santa Monica Hollywood
LOS ANGELES
Santa Barbara Is. Long Beach
S. Nicolas I.
S. Clemente I.
Santa Catalina
Sta. Catalina
Anaheim·Santa Ana
San Diego
Tijuana
Ensenada
B. de Todos Santos
Pt. Conception

NEVADA
Walker Lake
Hawthorne
Tonopah
White Mts.
Death Valley
Owens Lake
Las Vegas
Mojave Desert
Barstow
Glendale
Pasadena 3606
Alhambra
San Bernardino
Redlands
Riverside
Colorado Desert
Salton Sea
Brawley
El Centro
Mexicali
Yuma

Wheeler Pk. 3982
Sevier Lake
Sevier
Cedar City
Zion Nat. Park
St. George
Lake Mead
Grand Canyon Nat. Park
Grand Canyon
Humphreys Pk. 3851
Flagstaff
Kingman
Prescott
Havasu Lake
ARIZONA
Phoenix
Mesa
Salt
Gila
Tucson
Nogales

Golfo de California
SONORA
Hermosillo
Guaymas
Sta. Rosalía
Ciudad Obregón
Muleje
Punta Concepción
La Purísima

BAJA CALIFORNIA NORTE
Sebastián Vizcaíno
Bahía Sebastián Vizcaíno
I. de Cedros
Punta Eugenia
C. S. Quintín
S. Quintín
BAJA CALIFORNIA SUR
I. Angel de la Guarda
I. Tiburón
Guadalupe (Mex.)
Magdalena

CALIFORNIA
Yosemite National Park
Sierra Nevada
Mt. Whitney 4418
Sequoia Nat. Park
Tehachapi Pass
Bakersfield
1216
Tejón
Colorado
3078

PACIFIC OCEAN

HAWAII
1:10 000 000
0   100   200 km

Mana
Kauai
Lihue
Niihau
Kaula
Kauai Channel
158
Oahu
Kahana
Wahiawa
Pearl City
Honolulu
Pearl Harbor
Kaiwi Channel
Kalaupapa
Molokai
Lanai
Paia
Maui
Hana
Haleakala 3056
Kahoolawe
Makena
Hawaiian Channel
Alenuihaha Channel
Mahukona
Kawaihae
Mauna Kea 4205
Mauna Loa 4170
Hawaii
Kailua
Hilo
Keaau
Glenwood
Kilauea Crater 1247
Pahala
Islands
158
160
156
West from Greenwich

Map 160

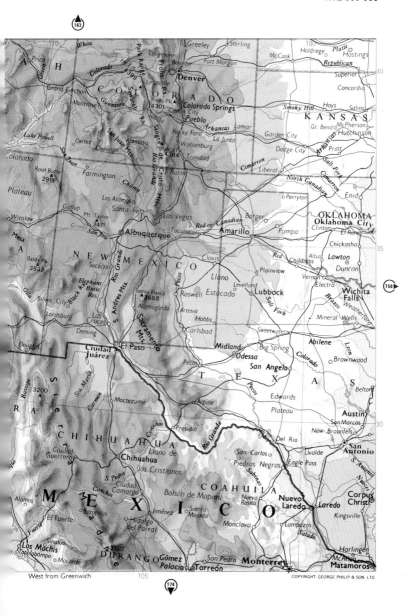

1:12 000 000

Map 161

West from Greenwich

U.S.A.: North West

142

West from Greenwich

160

Map 162

1:12 000 000

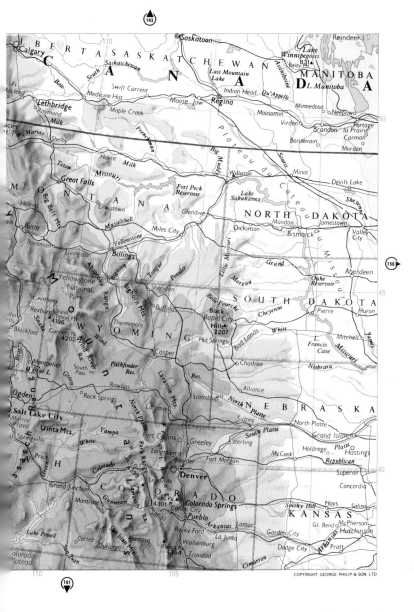

Map 163

U.S.A.: Boston, New York, Washington

1:6 000 000

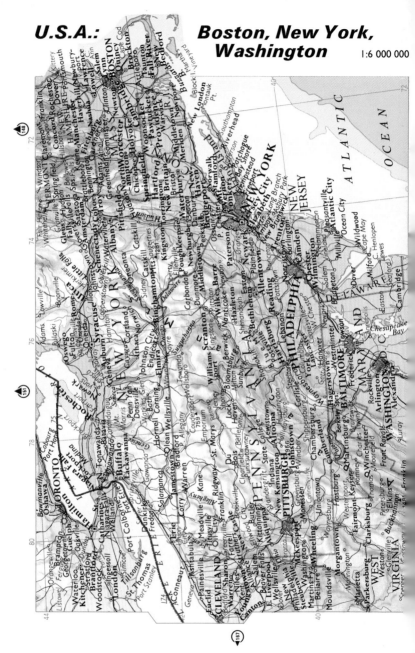

Map 164

U.S.A.: *Washington, Atlanta*

1:6 000 000

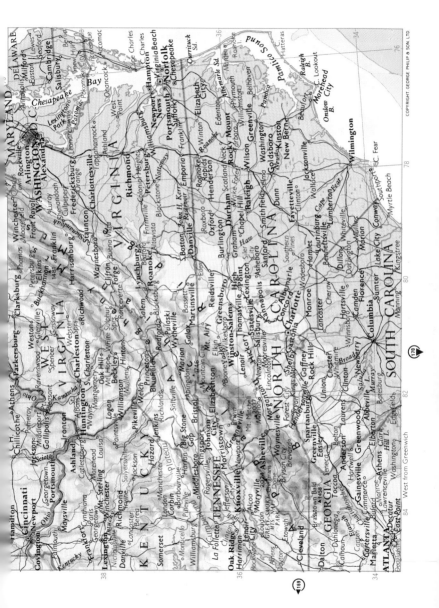

Map 165

U.S.A.: Upper Mississippi

156

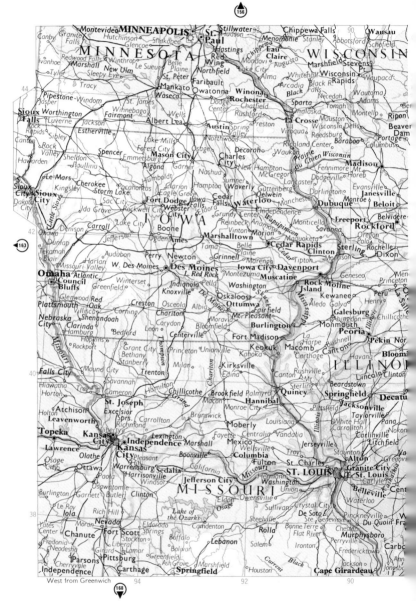

West from Greenwich

Map 166

1:6 000 000

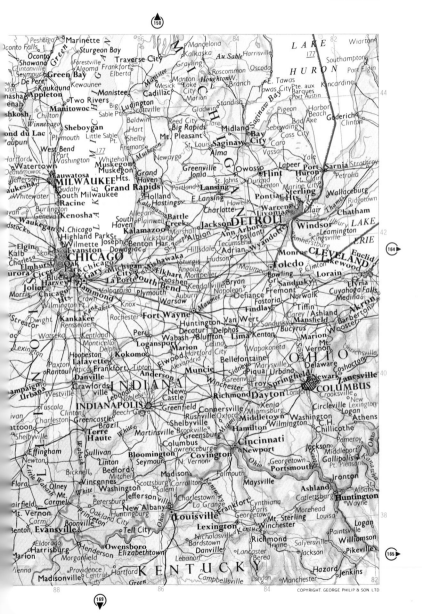

COPYRIGHT GEORGE PHILIP & SON LTD

Map 167

U.S.A.: Lower Mississippi and Gulf Coast

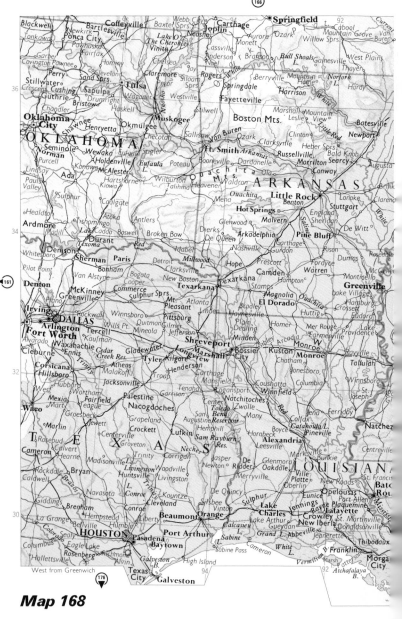

Map 168

1:6 000 000

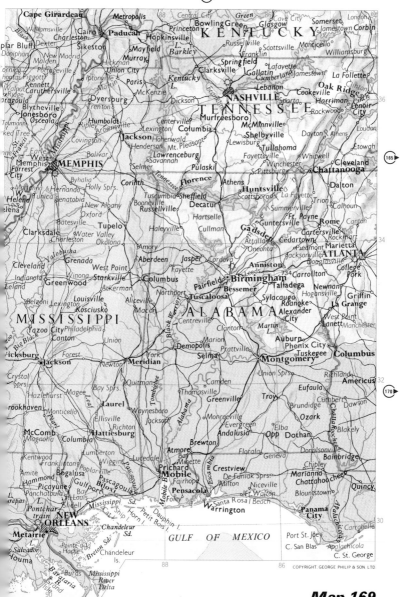

Map 169

U.S.A.: Florida

1:6 000 000

Map 170

U.S.A.: *Columbia Basin*

1:6 000 000

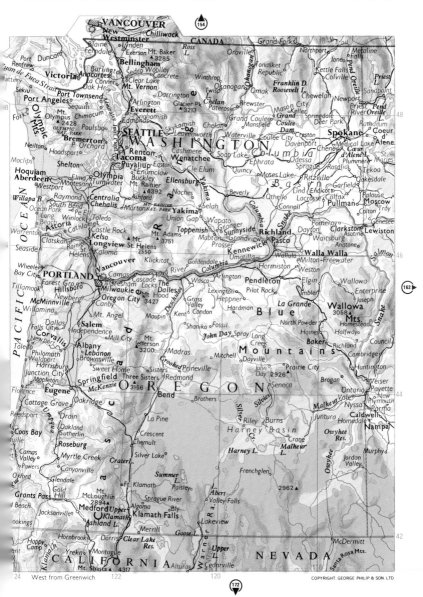

West from Greenwich

Map 171

U.S.A.: California

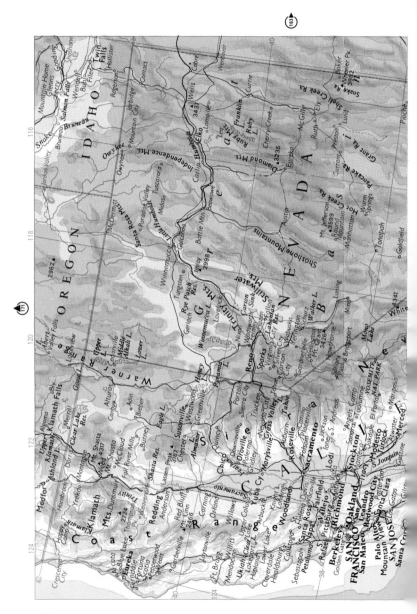

Map 172

1:6 000 000

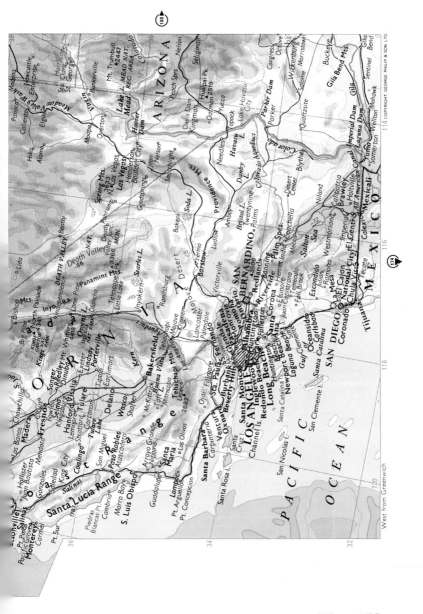

Map 173

Mexico: West

176

161

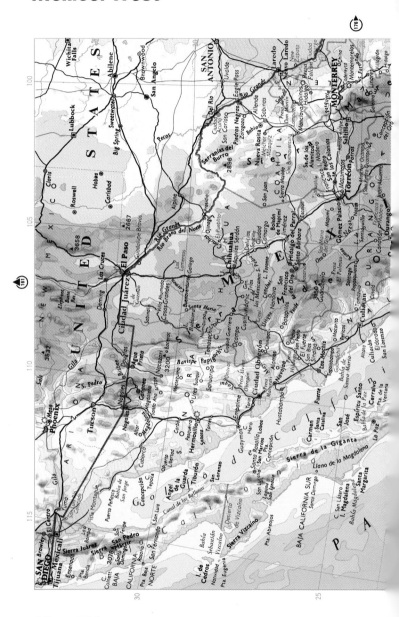

Map 174

1:12 000 000

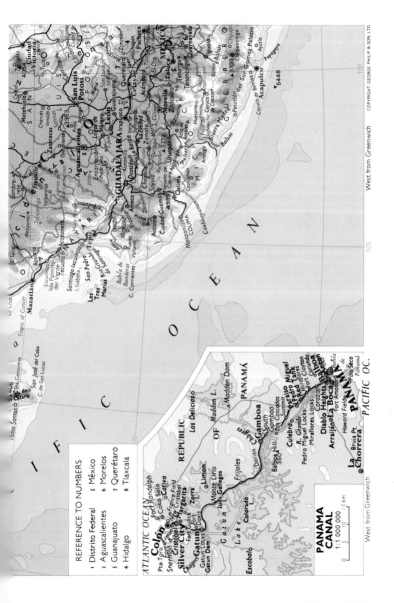

Map 175

Mexico: East

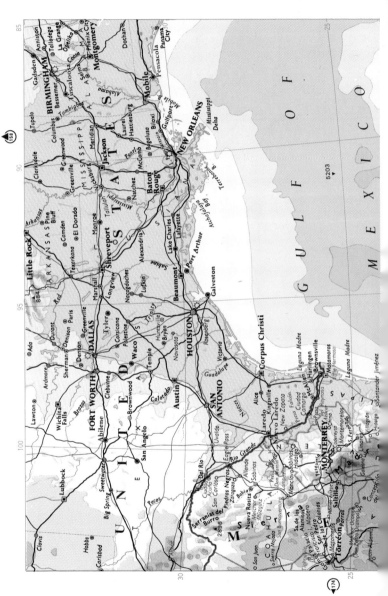

Map 176

1:12 000 000

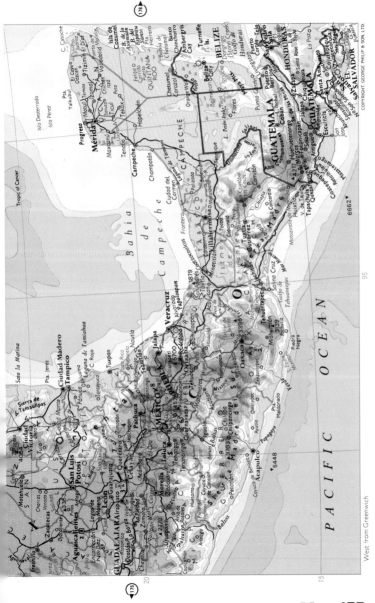

West from Greenwich

Map 177

Caribbean: West

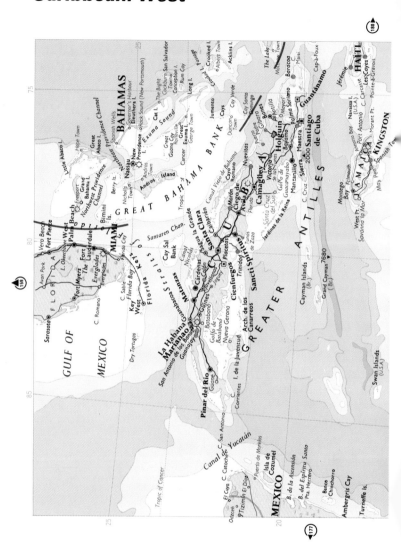

Map 178

1:12 000 000

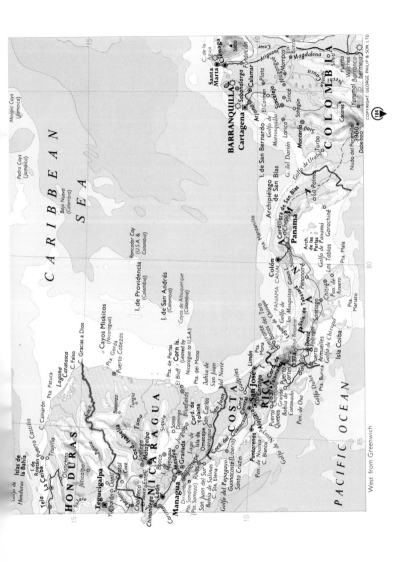

Map 179

Caribbean: East

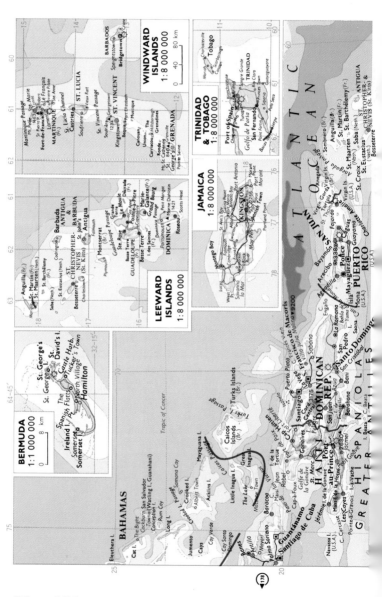

Map 180

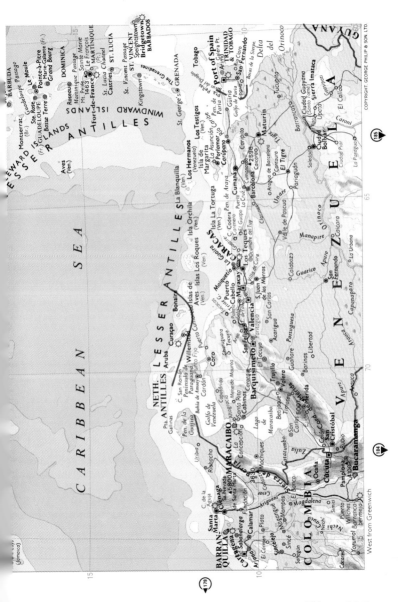

1:12 000 000

Map 181

COPYRIGHT GEORGE PHILIP & SON LTD.

West from Greenwich

South America: Physical

1:50 000 000

Curaçao (Neth.)

Trinidad

G. of Darien
▲5800

10

Cord de Mérida

Orinoco

Kaieteur Falls
Roraima
▲2810
Sa. Pacaraima

Demerara
Courantyne
Surinam

Guiana Highlands

Orinoco

Casiquiare

Llanos

Magdalena

Sa. de Tumucumaque

Amazon
Marajó I.
Pará

Equator

Cotopaxi
▲5897
Chimborazo
▲6267

Putumayo

Japurá

Negro

Amazon

Pta. Parinas

Marañón

Selvas

Tocantins

C. de São Roque

C. Branco

Ucayali

Purus

Madeira

Aripuaná

Xingu

Araguaia

Parnaíba

S. Antônio Falls

Tapajós

▲6768

Guaporé

Plateau of Mato Grosso

São Francisco

L. Titicaca
Illampú Ancohuma
▲6550

Bolivian Plateau

Brazilian Highlands

Andes

Pilcomayo

20

8050
Tropic of Capricorn

Atacama Desert

Gran Chaco

Paraguay

Paraná

Sa. da Mantiqueira ▲2890

C. Frio

Ojos del Salado
▲6863

Iguaçu Falls
Sa. do Mar

Aconcagua
▲6960

PACIFIC OCEAN

Juan Fernández

Pampas

Paraná

Entre Rios

Uruguay

Lagoa dos Patos

30

Colorado

Rio de la Plata

Pta. Mogotes

ATLANTIC

Negro

Chiloé

Patagonia

Chubut

G. of San Matías
Valdés Pen.

40

Chonos Arch.

G. of San Jorge

OCEAN

Andes

▲4058

6212
▼

West from Greenwich

Falkland Is.

50

Magellan's Str.

Tierra del Fuego
Staten I.

C. Froward

C. Horn

COPYRIGHT GEORGE PHILIP & SON LTD

Map 182

South America: 1:50 000 000
Political

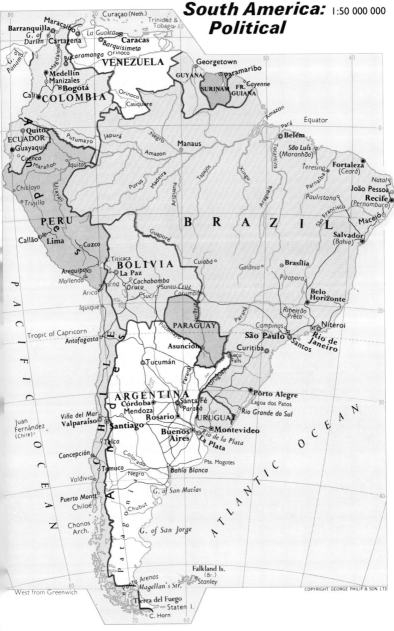

Curaçao (Neth.)
Trinidad & Tobago
Barranquilla
G. of Darien
Maracaibo
Cartagena
La Guaira
Caracas
Bucaramanga
Orinoco
Barquisimeto
VENEZUELA
Georgetown
Paramaribo
GUYANA
SURINAM
FR. Cayenne
GUIANA
Medellín
Manizales
Bogotá
Cali
COLOMBIA
Orinoco
Casiquiare
Amazon
Equator
Quito
ECUADOR
Guayaquil
Cuenca
Marañon
Putumayo
Japurá
Negro
Manaus
Pará
Belém
São Luís (Maranhão)
Tocantins
Teresina
Fortaleza (Ceará)
Natal
João Pessoa
Recife (Pernambuco)
Iquitos
Chiclayo
Trujillo
Ucayali
Purus
Amazon
Madeira
Aripuanã
Tapajós
Xingu
Araguaia
Parnaíba
PERU
Guaporé
Maceió
Salvador (Bahía)
B R A Z I L
São Francisco
Callao
Lima
Cuzco
Titicaca
Cuiabá
Goiânia
Brasília
Paulistana
Arequipa
BOLIVIA
La Paz
Cochabamba
Oruro
Santa Cruz
Corumbá
Piraporá
Belo Horizonte
Mollendo
Tacna
Arica
Sucre
Iquique
PARAGUAY
Paraná
Ribeirão Preto
Campinas
Niterói
Tropic of Capricorn
Antofagasta
Pilcomayo
Asunción
São Paulo
Santos
Rio de Janeiro
Curitiba
Tucumán
Iguaçu Falls
Paraná
Pôrto Alegre
Lagoa dos Patos
Rio Grande do Sul
ARGENTINA
Córdoba
Mendoza
Santa Fé
Paraná
Rosario
URUGUAY
Viña del Mar
Valparaíso
Santiago
Buenos Aires
La Plata
Montevideo
Río de la Plata
Talca
Concepción
Colorado
Pta. Mogotes
Temuco
Valdivia
Negro
Bahía Blanca
Juan Fernández (Chile)
Puerto Montt
Chiloé
Chubut
G. of San Matías
Chonos Arch.
Patagonia
G. of San Jorge
ATLANTIC OCEAN
PACIFIC OCEAN
Falkland Is. (Br.)
Stanley
West from Greenwich
Arenas
Magellan's Str.
Tierra del Fuego
Staten I.
C. Horn

Map 183

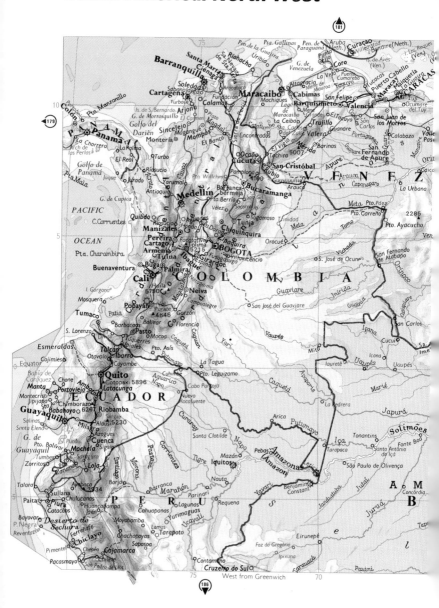

West from Greenwich

Map 184

1:16 000 000

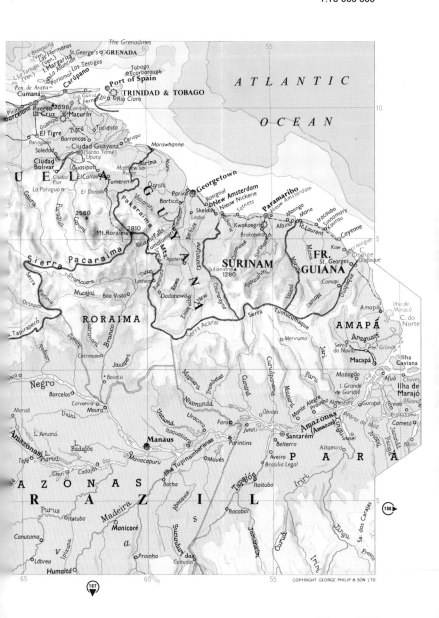

Map 185

South America: West

Salinas
Santa Elena
Milagro **ECUADOR** ▲Alausi 5230
Guayaquil Pto. Bolívar Puná Azogues
G. de Guayaquil **Machala** **Cuenca** Sigsig
Tumbes Saraguro Santa Clotilde
Zorritos Zarumba Napo Pebas
Loja Mazán Iquitos
Macará Morona Nauta
Talara Ayabaca ▲3934 Borja Pastaza Corrientes
Paita **Piura** Chulucanas Barranca Marañón Parinari
Sullana Huancabamba Jaén Requena
Catacaos Cahuapanas Lagunas
Bayovar **Desierto de** Moyobamba Yurimaguas
Pta.Negra **Sechura** Ferreñafe Lamas Tarapoto
Reventazón Chachapoyas Saposoa
Pimentel **Chiclayo**
Chepén **Cajamarca** Contamana
Pacasmayo Chilete **Cruzeiro do Sul**
San Pedro de Lloc Juruá Porto V.
Pto. Chicama Celendín Tayabamba Pucallpa
Salaverry **Trujillo** Masisea
Carás Taumatu
Chimbote ▲Huascarán Pisco Maria
Casma 6768 **Huaraz**
Aija **Huánuco** **P** **E** **R** **U**
Huarmey Chiquián Ambo
Cayllarisquisga Cerro de Pasco Pto. Bermúdez
Barranca Huachón Atalaya Urubamba
6369 **Huacho** Oyón Perené
Chyan Huariloyo
Huntoyoc La **Oroya** Tarma
Ancón Morococha Jauja
Callao **Huancayo**
I. San Lorenzo Motucana Pampas
LIMA Yauyos Quillab
Huancavelica **Ayacucho** Machu
Cañete Uro Cuzco
Chincha Alta Tambo de Mora Huancapi **Cuzco**
Pisco Abancay
Icá Chalhuanca
Paquio Antabamba
Coracora Nudo Coropu
San Juan 6425
Chala Caravelí
Atico Aplao
Camaná
Matarani
6866▼

80   75

PACIFIC

OCEAN

Milne Edwards Trench

Peru

Chile Krümme Tre

Map 186

1:16 000 000

Map 187

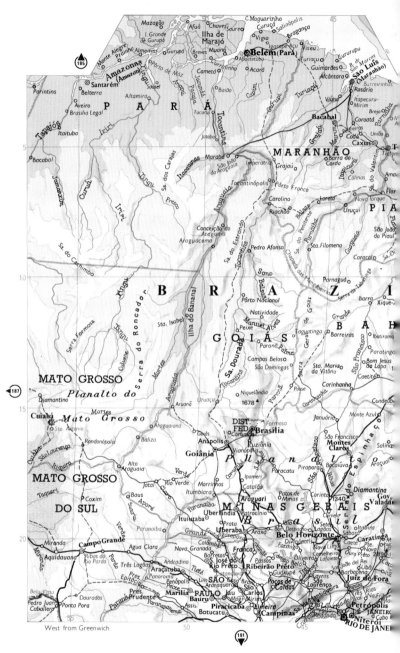

Map 188

West from Greenwich

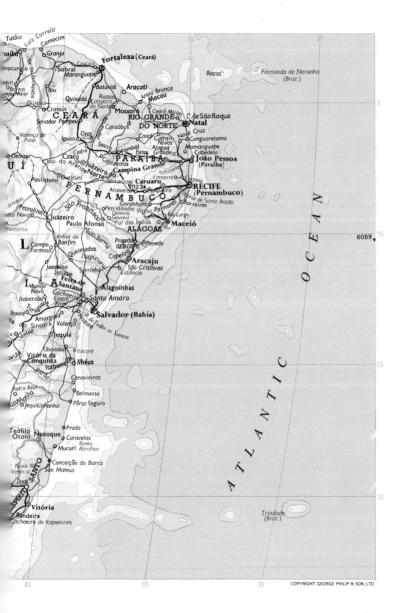

South America: East

1:16 000 000

Map 189

189

South America: Central

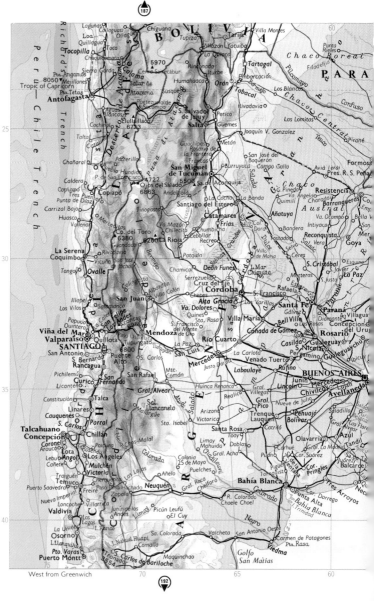

Lagunas o
Colloguasi
Loa
Quillagua
Tocopilla
Pta. Angamos
8050
Meillones
Pta. Tetas
Antofagasta
Chiquicamata
Sierra Gorda
Pedro de Valdivia
Chiguana
Ollagüe
Tupiza
B O L I V I A
Villa Montes
Tarija
Punta
Rieles
Tocopilla
La Quiaca
Rinconada
Iturbe
Yacuiba
P A R A
Calama
5970
C. Sanicaburo
Humahuaca
Orán
Embarcación
Tartagal
Filadelfia
C h a c o   B o r e a l
Portezuelo del Campo
S. Salvador
de Jujuy
Perico
Tabacal
Yuto
Los Blancos
Rivadavia
Confuso
Tropic of Capricorn
Aguas
Blancas
Cochinoca
Susques
Ullaillaco
6723
Salta
Güemes
Las Lomitas
C h a c o   C e n t r a l
25
Taltal
Catai
Patrerillo
Guachipas
Rosario de
la Frontera
Metán
San José del
Boquerón
Joaquín V. Gonzalez
Pirané
Teuco
Chañaral
Pueblo Hundido
P. de San Francisco
4722
San Miguel
de Tucumán
Burruyacú
Campo Gallo
Avia Terai
Formosa
Pres. R. S. Peña
Caldera
Copiapó
5896
Ojos del Salado
6863
Sa. de Azonquija
La Cocha
La Banda
Santiago del Estero
C. G. Pinedo
Va. Angela
Quimili
Charadoy
Resistencia
Barranqueras
Co.
Emp.
Tres Puentes
Andalgalá
Va. Ocampo
Carrizal Bajo
Punta de Díaz
Fiambalá
Catamarca
Añatuya
A u s t r a l
Bell
Huasco
 Va. Mazán
Frías
Intiyaco
Va. Ocampo
Reconquista
Mer.
Vallenar
del Toro
Chumbicha
Chilecito
Col
lo Dara
Bandera
Selva
Vera
Salad
Goya
6380
6250
La Rioja
Ceballar
Recreo
Tostado
S. Cristobal
Esquina
Guandacol
Patquía
Va.
Villa
de Maria
Ceres
S. Javier
S. Justa
La Paz
30
La Serena
Coquimbo
Rivadavia
Dean Funes
L. Mar
Chiquita
Morteros
Javier
Tongoy
Ovalle
Vicuña San José
Jáchal
Chamical
Serrezuela
Cruz del Eje
Rafaela
San Francisco
Santa Fe
Paraná
Illapel
San Juan
Albardón
Villa Colón
Chepes
Va. Dolores
Córdoba
Villaguay
Los Vilos
Salamanca
Alta Gracia
Las Varillas
Concepción
del Uru
Papuoo
Quintero
San Felipe
6800
Aconcagua
Quines
Sta. Rosa
Villa María
Bell Ville
Las Rosas
Rosario
Viña del Mar
Valparaíso
Quillota
San Francisco
del Monte de Oro
Cañada de Gómez
Diamante
SANTIAGO
Tupungato
La Paz
Río Cuarto
Casilda
Gualeguay
Ubicui
San Antonio
Mendoza
San Luis
S. Nicolás
Pergamino
Gualeguay
S. Bernardo
Puente
Alto
S. Carlos
La Carlota
Venado Tuerto
Rancagua
Pichilemú
Mte.
Comán
Mercedes
Justo Daract
Rufino
BUENOS AIRES
San Fernando
San Rafael
Labodaye
Junín
Mercedes
Lujan
Avellaneda
San
Curicó
Fernando
Huinca Renancó
Gral.
Villegas
Lincoln
Chivilcoy
35
Licantén
Gral. Alvear
Realicó
Nueve de Julio
Saladillo
Constitución
Talca
Sal.
Llancanelo
Gral.
Pico
Trenque
Lauquen
Pehuajó
Bolivar
Grat. Flores
Linares
Malargüe
Arizona
Victorica
Catriló
Olavarría
Azul
Cauquenes
S. Carlos
Porral
Sta. Isabel
Santa Rosa
Toay
Doblas
Carhué
Guaminí
Cor. Pringles
Tandil
Talcahuano
Concepción
Chillán
Ñuble
Limay
Mahuida
Gral. Acha
Puán
Cor. Suárez
Sa. de la
Ventana
Balcarce
Coronel
Lota
Arauco
Los Angeles
Colorada
Colonia
25 de Mayo
Puelches
Pigüé
Tres
Arroyos
Lebú
Angol
Mulchén
Añelo
Bahía Blanca
Cañete
Victoria
Los Lagos
Chelforó
Tornquist
Punta Alta
Bahía Blanca
Traiguén
Chos-Malal
Río Colorado
Cor.
Dorrego
Tres Arroyos
Temuco
Freire
Zapala
Neuquén
Choele Choel
Valdivia
Villarrica
Junín de las
Andes
Picún Leufú
El Cuy
Negro
Carmen de Patagones
Pta. Rasa
Osorno
La Unión
Los
Lagos
L. Ranco
Sa. Colorada
Comallo
Valcheta
San Antonio Oeste
Viedma
Pto. Varas
Puerto Montt
L. Llanquihue
Tronador
3554
S. Carlos de Bariloche
Maquinchao
Golfo
San Matías
60
40

West from Greenwich   70   65   60

Map 190

1:16 000 000

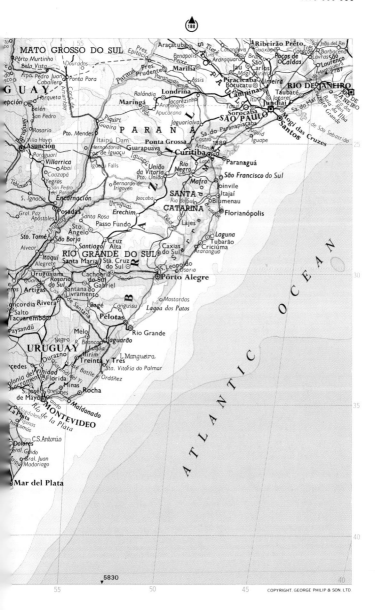

Map 191

COPYRIGHT. GEORGE PHILIP & SON. LTD

South America: South

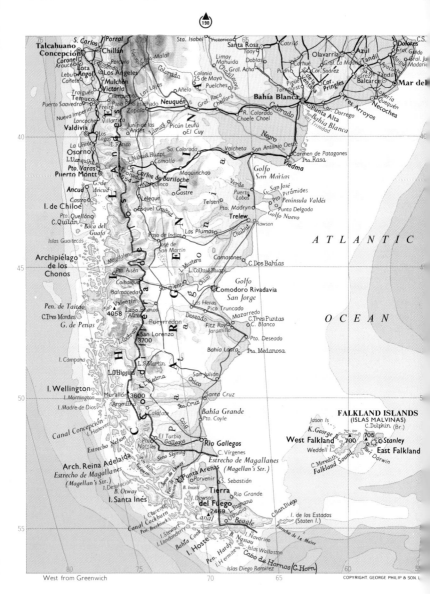

ATLANTIC

OCEAN

FALKLAND ISLANDS
(ISLAS MALVINAS)
C. Dolphin (Br.)
Jason Is.
K. George B.
West Falkland
Weddell
C. Meredith
C. Meredith
Falkland Sound
705
Stanley
East Falkland
Port Darwin

West from Greenwich

Map 192

192

Index

Introduction to Index

The number printed in bold type against each entry indicates the map page where the feature can be found. This is followed by its geographical coordinates. The first coordinate indicates latitude, i.e. distance north or south of the Equator. The second coordinate indicates longitude, i.e. distance east or west of the meridian of Greenwich in England (shown as 0° longitude). Both latitude and longitude are measured in degrees and minutes (with 60 minutes in a degree), and appear on the map as horizontal and vertical gridlines respectively. Thus the entry for Paris in France reads.

Paris, France........**39**   48 50N   2 20 E

This entry indicates that Paris is on page **39,** at latitude 48 degrees 50 minutes north (approximately five-sixths of the distance between horizontal gridlines 48 and 49 , marked on either side of the page) and at longitude 2 degrees 20 minutes east (approximately one-third of the distance between vertical gridlines 2 and 3, marked at top and bottom of the page). Paris can be found where lines extended from these two points cross on the page. The geographical coordinates are sometimes only approximate but are close enough for the place to be located. Rivers have been indexed to their mouth or confluence.

An open square □ signifies that the name refers to an administrative subdivision of a country while a solid square ■ follows the name of a country. An arrow ~► follows the name of a river.

The alphabetical order of names composed of two or more words is governed primarily by the first word and then by the second. This rule applies even if the second word is a description or its abbreviation, R., L., I. for example.

North Walsham
Northallerton
Northampton
Northern Circars
Northumberland Is.
Northumberland Str.

Names composed of a proper name (Gibraltar) and a description (Strait of) are positioned alphabetically by the proper name. This is the case where the definite article follows a proper name (Mans, Le). If the same word occurs in the name of a town and a geographical feature, the town name is listed first followed by the name or names of the geographical features.

Names beginning with M', Mc are all indexed as if they were spelled Mac. All names beginning St. are alphabetised under Saint, but Sankt, Sint, Santa and San are all spelt in full and are alphabetised accordingly.

If the same place name occurs twice or more times in the index and all are in the same country, each is followed by the name of the administrative subdivision in which it is located. The names are placed in the alphabetical order of the subdivisions. If the same place name occurs twice or more in the index and the places are in different countries they will be followed by their country names, the latter governing the alphabetical order. In a mixture of these situations the primary order is fixed by the alphabetical sequence of the countries and the secondary order by that of the country subdivisions.

Abbreviations used

A.S.S.R. – *Autonomous Soviet Socialist Republic*
Ala. – *Alabama*
Arch. – *Archipelago*
Ark. – *Arkansas*
Austral. – *Australia*
B. – *Baie, Bahia, Bay, Boca, Bucht, Bugt*
B.C. – *British Columbia*
Bangla. – *Bangladesh*
Br. – *British*
C. – *Cabo, Cap, Cape, Coast, Costa*
C. Rica – *Costa Rica*
Calif. – *California*
Cap. Terr. – *Capital Territory*
Cat. – *Cataract*
Cent. – *Central*
Chan. – *Channel*
Colo. – *Colorado*
Conn. – *Connecticut*
Cord. – *Cordillera*
D.C. – *District of Columbia*
Del. – *Delaware*
Dét. – *Détroit*
Dom. Rep. – *Dominican Republic*
Domin. – *Dominica*
E. – *East, Eastern*
Est. – *Estrecho*
Falk. Is. – *Falkland Is.*
Fla. – *Florida*
Fr. Gui. – *French Guiana*
G. – *Golfe, Golfo, Gulf, Guba, Gebel*
Ga. – *Georgia*
Gt. – *Great*
Guat. – *Guatemala*
Hants. – *Hampshire*
Hd. – *Head*
Hond. – *Honduras*
Hts. – *Heights*
I.(s) – *Ile, Ilha, Insel, Isla, Island(s)*
I. of W. – *Isle of Wight*
Ill. – *Illinois*
Ind. – *Indiana*
Ind. Oc. – *Indian Ocean*
J. – *Jabal, Jazira*
K. – *Kap. Kapp*
Kans. – *Kansas*

Ky. – *Kentucky*
L. – *Lac, Lacul, Lago, Lagoa, Lake, Limni, Loch, Lough*
La. – *Louisiana*
Lag. – *Laguna*
Lancs. – *Lancashire*
Man. – *Manitoba*
Mass. – *Massachusetts*
Md. – *Maryland*
Mich. – *Michigan*
Minn. – *Minnesota*
Miss. – *Mississippi*
Mo. – *Missouri*
Mont. – *Montana*
Mt.(s) – *Mont, Monta, Monti, Muntii, Montaña, Mount, Mountain(s)*
N. – *North, Northern*
N.B. – *New Brunswick*
N.C. – *North Carolina*
N. Dak. – *North Dakota*
N.H. – *New Hampshire*
N.J. – *New Jersey*
N. Mex. – *New Mexico*
N.S.W. – *New South Wales*
N.W.T. – *North West Territories*
N.Y. – *New York*
N.Z. – *New Zealand*
Nebr. – *Nebraska*
Neth. – *Netherlands*
Nev. – *Nevada*
Nfld. – *Newfoundland*
Nic. – *Nicaragua*
Okla. – *Oklahoma*
Ont. – *Ontario*
Oreg. – *Oregon*
Os. – *Ostrov*
Oz. – *Ozero*
P. – *Pass, Passo, Pasul, Pulau*
P.E.I. – *Prince Edward Island*
Pa. – *Pennsylvania*
Pac. Oc. – *Pacific Ocean*
Papua N.G. – *Papua New Guinea*
Pen. – *Peninsula*
Pk. – *Peak*
Plat. – *Plateau*
P-ov. – *Poluostrov*
Pt. – *Point*
Pta. – *Ponta, Punta*
Queens. – *Queensland*

R. – *Rio, River, Rivière*
R.I. – *Rhode Island*
R.S.F.S.R. – *Russian Soviet Federative Socialist Republic*
Ra.(s) – *Range(s)*
Raj. – *Rajasthan*
Rep. – *Republic*
Res. – *Reserve, Reservoir*
S. – *South, Southern, Sea, Sur*
S.C. – *South Carolina*
S.S.R. – *Soviet Socialist Republic*
S. Africa – *South Africa*
S. Dak. – *South Dakota*
Sa. – *Serra, Sierra*
Salop. – *Shropshire*
Sard. – *Sardinia*
Sask. – *Saskatchewan*
Sd. – *Sound*
Sev. – *Severnaya*
Si. Arabia – *Saudi Arabia*
St. – *Saint*
Sta. – *Santa*
Ste. – *Sainte*
Str. – *Strait, Stretto*
Switz. – *Switzerland*
Tas. – *Tasmania*
Tenn. – *Tennessee*
Terr. – *Territory*
Tex. – *Texas*
Tipp. – *Tipperary*
Trin. & Tob. – *Trinidad and Tobago*
U.K. – *United Kingdom*
U.S.A. – *United States of America*
U.S.S.R. – *Union of Soviet Socialist Republics*
Ut. P. – *Uttar Pradesh*
Va. – *Virginia*
Vic. – *Victoria*
Vol. – *Volcano*
Vt. – *Vermont*
Wash. – *Washington*
W. – *West, Western, Wadi*
W. Va. – *West Virginia*
Wis. – *Wisconsin*
Worcs. – *Worcestershire*
Yorks. – *Yorkshire*

Name	Page	Lat	N/S	Long	E/W
Aachen	42	50	47N	6	4 E
Aalborg = Ålborg	61	57	2N	9	54 E
Aalsmeer	40	52	17N	4	43 E
Aalst	42	50	56N	4	2 E
Aalten	41	51	56N	6	35 E
Aarhus = Århus	61	56	8N	10	11 E
Aba	131	5	10N	7	19 E
Ābādān	84	30	22N	48	20 E
Ābādeh	85	31	8N	52	40 E
Abadla	126	31	2N	2	45W
Abai	191	25	58S	55	54W
Abakan	74	53	40N	91	10 E
Abancay	186	13	35S	72	55W
Abariringa I.	122	2	50S	171	40W
Abashiri	103	44	0N	144	15 E
Abashiri-Wan	103	44	0N	144	30 E
Abaya, L.	133	6	30N	37	50 E
Abbay = Nîl el Azraq →	129	15	38N	32	31 E
Abbeville, France	38	50	6N	1	49 E
Abbeville, U.S.A.	165	34	12N	82	21W
Abéché	129	13	50N	20	35 E
Abeokuta	131	7	3N	3	19 E
Aberaeron	26	52	15N	4	16W
Aberayron = Aberaeron	26	52	15N	4	16W
Aberdare	27	51	43N	3	27W
Aberdeen, U.K.	33	57	9N	2	6W
Aberdeen, S. Dak., U.S.A.	163	45	30N	98	30W
Aberdeen, Wash., U.S.A.	171	47	0N	123	50W
Aberdovey	26	52	33N	4	3W
Aberfeldy	33	56	37N	3	50W
Abergavenny	26	51	49N	3	1W
Aberystwyth	26	52	25N	4	6W
Abha	82	18	0N	42	34 E
Abidjan	130	5	26N	3	58W
Abilene	161	32	22N	99	40W
Abington	25	55	30N	3	42W
Abkhaz A.S.S.R. □	70	43	0N	41	0 E
Abohar	89	30	10N	74	10 E
Aboméy	131	7	10N	2	5 E
Abong-Mbang	131	4	0N	13	8 E
Abrud	56	46	19N	23	5 E
Abruzzi □	47	42	15N	14	0 E
Absaroka Ra.	163	44	40N	110	0W
Abū al Khaşīb	84	30	25N	48	0 E
Abū 'Alī	84	27	20N	49	27 E
Abū 'Arīsh	82	16	58N	45	20 E
Abu Dhabi = Abū Ẕāby	85	24	28N	54	22 E
Abu Hamed	129	19	32N	33	13 E
Abū Ẕāby	85	24	28N	54	22 E
Abunã	187	9	40S	65	20W
Abunã →	187	9	41S	65	20W
Abut Hd.	123	43	7S	170	15 E
Acámbaro	177	20	2N	100	44W
Acaponeta	175	22	30N	105	22W
Acapulco	177	16	51N	99	56W
Acatlán	177	18	10N	98	3W
Acayucan	177	17	57N	94	55W
Accra	130	5	35N	0	6W
Accrington	28	53	46N	2	22W
Achill I.	34	53	58N	10	5W
Achinsk	74	56	20N	90	20 E
Aconcagua, Cerro	190	32	39S	70	0W
Aconquija, Mt.	190	27	0S	66	0W
Açores, Is. dos = Azores	126	38	44N	29	0W
Acre = 'Akko	80	32	55N	35	4 E
Acre □	187	9	1S	71	0W
Ad Dawhah	85	25	15N	51	35 E
Ada	168	34	50N	96	45W
Adamaoua, Massif de l'	131	7	20N	12	20 E
Adamawa Highlands = Adamaoua, Massif de l'	131	7	20N	12	20 E
Adaminaby	117	36	0S	148	45 E
Adams, Mt.	171	46	10N	121	28W
Adam's Bridge	90	9	15N	79	40 E
Adana	80	37	0N	35	16 E
Adapazarı	80	40	48N	30	25 E
Adare, C.	15	71	0S	171	0 E
Addis Ababa = Addis Abeba	133	9	2N	38	42 E
Addis Abeba	133	9	2N	38	42 E
Adelaide	119	34	52S	138	30 E
Adelaide Pen.	145	68	15N	97	30W
Adélie, Terre	15	68	0S	140	0 E
Aden = Al 'Adan	83	12	45N	45	0 E
Aden, G. of	133	13	0N	50	0 E
Adige →	47	45	9N	12	20 E
Adirondack Mts.	151	44	0N	74	15W
Admiralty Is.	115	2	0S	147	0 E
Adoni	90	15	33N	77	18W
Adrian	167	41	55N	84	0W
Adriatic Sea	52	43	0N	16	0 E
Adwa	132	14	15N	38	52 E
Adzhar A.S.S.R. □	70	42	0N	42	0 E
Ægean Sea	55	37	0N	25	0 E
Æolian Is. = Eólie, I.	49	38	30N	14	50 E
Aerht'ai Shan	100	46	40N	92	45 E
Afars & Issas, Terr. of = Djibouti ■	133	12	0N	43	0 E
Afghanistan ■	87	33	0N	65	0 E
Afuá	188	0	15S	50	20W
Afyonkarahisar	80	38	45N	30	33 E
Agadir	126	30	28N	9	35W
Agano →	103	37	57N	139	8 E
Agartala	93	23	50N	91	23 E
Agen	36	44	12N	0	38 E
Agno	107	35	58N	139	36 E
Aghil Pass	89	36	15N	76	35 E
Agra	89	27	17N	77	58 E
Ağri Daği	81	39	50N	44	15 E
Água Clara	188	20	25S	52	45W
Agua Prieta	174	31	18N	109	34W
Aguadas	184	5	40N	75	38W
Aguadilla	180	18	27N	67	10W
Aguas Blancas	190	24	15S	69	55W
Aguascalientes	175	21	53N	102	18W
Aguascalientes □	175	22	0N	102	30W
Agulhas, Kaap	136	34	52S	20	0 E
Ahaggar	127	23	0N	6	30 E
Ahaura →	123	42	21S	171	34 E
Ahmadabad	91	23	0N	72	40 E
Ahmadnagar	91	19	7N	74	46 E
Ahmedabad = Ahmadabad	91	23	0N	72	40 E
Ahmednagar = Ahmadnagar	91	19	7N	74	46 E
Ahvāz	84	31	20N	48	40 E
Ahvenanmaa = Åland	66	60	15N	20	0 E
Ahwar	83	13	30N	46	40 E
Aigle, L'	39	48	46N	0	38 E
Aigues-Mortes	37	43	35N	4	12 E
Aiken	170	33	34N	81	50W
Ailsa Craig	30	55	15N	5	7W
Aimorés	189	19	30S	41	4W
Aïn Ben Tili	126	25	59N	9	27W
Aioi	109	34	48N	134	28 E
Aïr	127	18	30N	8	0 E
Airdrie	31	55	53N	3	57W
Aire →	29	53	42N	0	55W
Airlie Beach	121	20	16S	148	43 E
Aisne →	37	49	26N	2	50 E
Aix-en-Provence	37	43	32N	5	27 E
Aix-la-Chapelle = Aachen	42	50	47N	6	4 E
Aix-les-Bains	37	45	41N	5	53 E
Aizuwakamatsu	105	37	30N	139	56 E
Ajaccio	36	41	55N	8	40 E
Ajanta Ra.	91	20	28N	75	50 E
Ajmer	91	26	28N	74	37 E
Akaishi-Dake	107	35	27N	138	9 E
Akaishi-Sammyaku	107	35	25N	138	10 E
Akashi	109	34	45N	135	0 E
Akershus fylke □	60	60	0N	11	10 E
Akhelóös →	54	38	36N	21	14 E
Akhisar	80	38	56N	27	48 E
Aki	109	33	30N	133	54 E
Aki-Nada	109	34	5S	132	40 E
Akita	103	39	45N	140	7 E
'Akko	80	32	55N	35	4 E
Aklavik	144	68	12N	135	0W
Akō	109	34	45N	134	24 E
Akola	91	20	42N	77	2 E
Akranes	64	64	19N	21	58W
Akron	167	41	7N	81	31W
Aksaray	80	38	25N	34	2 E
Aksarka	69	66	31N	67	50 E
Akşehir	80	38	18N	31	30 E

Name	Page	Lat °	Lat ′	N/S	Long °	Long ′	E/W
Aksum	132	14	5	N	38	40	E
Aktyubinsk	70	50	17	N	57	10	E
Akune	108	32	1	N	130	12	E
Akureyri	64	65	40	N	18	6	W
Al 'Adan	83	12	45	N	45	0	E
Al Amādīyah	81	37	5	N	43	30	E
Al Amārah	84	31	55	N	47	15	E
Al 'Aqabah	80	29	31	N	35	0	E
Al Başrah	84	30	30	N	47	50	E
Al Ḥadīthah	81	31	28	N	37	8	E
Al Ḥāmad	80	31	30	N	39	30	E
Al Ḥasakah	81	36	35	N	40	45	E
Al Ḥawrah	83	13	50	N	47	35	E
Al Ḥayy	84	32	5	N	46	5	E
Al Ḥillah, Iraq	84	32	30	N	44	25	E
Al Ḥillah, Si. Arabia	83	23	35	N	46	50	E
Al Hindīyah	84	32	30	N	44	10	E
Al Ḥudaydah	82	14	50	N	43	0	E
Al Ḥūfuf	84	25	25	N	49	45	E
Al Jāfūrah	84	25	0	N	50	15	E
Al Jawf, Libya	128	24	10	N	23	24	E
Al Jawf, Si. Arabia	82	29	55	N	39	40	E
Al Jazirah	81	33	30	N	44	0	E
Al Khafjī	80	31	32	N	35	6	E
Al Kūt	84	32	30	N	46	0	E
Al Kuwayt	84	29	30	N	47	30	E
Al Lādhiqīyah	80	35	30	N	35	45	E
Al Lidām	82	20	33	N	44	45	E
Al Luḥayyah	82	15	45	N	42	40	E
Al Madīnah	82	24	35	N	39	52	E
Al Manāmāh	85	26	10	N	50	30	E
Al Marj	128	32	25	N	20	30	E
Al Mawşil	81	36	15	N	43	5	E
Al Mubarraz	84	25	30	N	49	40	E
Al Muharraq	85	26	15	N	50	40	E
Al Mukallā	83	14	33	N	49	2	E
Al Qafī	84	26	35	N	50	0	E
Al Quds = Jerusalem	80	31	47	N	35	10	E
Al Qunfudhah	82	19	3	N	41	4	E
Al Qurnah	84	31	1	N	47	25	E
Al 'Ubaylah	83	21	59	N	50	57	E
Al 'Uthmānīyah	84	25	5	N	49	22	E
Al Wajh	82	26	10	N	36	30	E
Alabama □	169	33	0	N	87	0	W
Alabama ~→	169	31	8	N	87	57	W
Alagoas □	189	9	0	S	36	0	W
Alagoinhas	189	12	7	S	38	20	W
Alajuela	179	10	2	N	84	8	W
Alamogordo	161	32	59	N	106	0	W
Álamos	174	27	1	N	108	56	W
Alamosa	163	37	30	N	106	0	W
Åland	66	60	15	N	20	0	E
Alaska □	142	65	0	N	150	0	W
Alaska, G. of	142	58	0	N	145	0	W
Alaska Pen.	142	56	0	N	160	0	W
Alaska Range	142	62	50	N	151	0	W
Alba Iulia	56	46	8	N	23	39	E
Albacete	51	39	0	N	1	50	W
Albania ■	52	41	0	N	20	0	E
Albany, Australia	120	35	1	S	117	58	E
Albany, Ga., U.S.A.	170	31	40	N	84	10	W
Albany, N.Y., U.S.A.	164	42	35	N	73	47	W
Albany, Oreg., U.S.A.	171	44	41	N	123	0	W
Albany ~→	140	52	17	N	81	31	W
Albemarle	165	35	27	N	80	15	W
Albemarle Sd.	165	36	0	N	76	30	W
Albert	38	50	0	N	2	38	E
Albert, L. = Mobutu Sese Seko, L.	132	1	30	N	31	0	E
Albert Lea	166	43	32	N	93	20	W
Alberta □	155	54	40	N	115	0	W
Albertville = Kalemie	135	5	55	S	29	9	E
Albi	37	43	56	N	2	9	E
Albion	167	42	15	N	84	45	W
Ålborg	61	57	2	N	9	54	E
Ålborz, Reshteh-ye Kūhhā-ye	86	36	0	N	52	0	E
Albuquerque	161	35	5	N	106	47	W
Alburquerque	50	39	15	N	6	59	W
Albury	117	36	3	S	146	56	E
Alcântara	188	2	20	S	44	30	W
Alcázar de San Juan	50	39	24	N	3	12	W
Alcira	51	39	9	N	0	30	W
Aldan ~→	75	63	28	N	129	35	E
Aldeburgh	25	52	9	N	1	35	E
Alderney	36	49	42	N	2	12	W
Aldershot	25	51	15	N	0	43	W
Alençon	39	48	27	N	0	4	E
Aleppo = Ḥalab	80	36	10	N	37	15	E
Alès	37	44	9	N	4	5	E
Alessándria	46	44	54	N	8	37	E
Ålesund	65	62	28	N	6	12	E
Aleutian Is.	142	52	0	N	175	0	W
Alexander Arch.	143	57	0	N	135	0	W
Alexander City	169	32	58	N	85	57	W
Alexandra, Australia	117	37	8	S	145	40	E
Alexandra, N.Z.	123	45	14	S	169	25	E
Alexandretta = Iskenderun	80	36	32	N	36	10	E
Alexandria = El Iskandarîya	128	31	0	N	30	0	E
Alexandria, La., U.S.A.	168	31	20	N	92	30	W
Alexandria, Va., U.S.A.	164	38	47	N	77	1	W
Alexandrina, L.	119	35	25	S	139	10	E
Alexandroúpolis	55	40	50	N	25	54	E
Alexis Creek	154	52	10	N	123	20	W
Alfreton	29	53	6	N	1	22	W
Algarve	50	36	58	N	8	20	W
Alger	127	36	42	N	3	8	E
Algeria ■	127	35	10	N	3	11	E
Algiers = Alger	127	36	42	N	3	8	E
Algoa B.	136	33	50	S	25	45	E
Alhambra	173	34	2	N	118	10	W
Alicante	51	38	23	N	0	30	W
Alice Springs	114	23	40	S	133	50	E
Aligarh	89	27	55	N	78	10	E
Alipur Duar	92	26	30	N	89	35	E
Aliquippa	164	40	38	N	80	18	W
Alkmaar	40	52	37	N	4	45	E
Allahabad	92	25	25	N	81	58	E
Allegheny Mts.	165	38	0	N	80	0	W
Allen, Bog of	35	53	15	N	7	0	W
Allende	174	28	20	N	100	51	W
Allentown	164	40	36	N	75	30	W
Alleppey	90	9	30	N	76	28	E
Aller ~→	42	52	57	N	9	10	E
Allier ~→	37	46	57	N	3	4	E
Alloa	31	56	7	N	3	49	W
Alma, Canada	148	48	35	N	71	40	W
Alma, U.S.A.	167	43	25	N	84	40	W
Alma Ata	71	43	15	N	76	57	E
Almada	50	38	40	N	9	9	W
Almelo	41	52	22	N	6	42	E
Almería	51	36	52	N	2	27	W
Almirante	179	9	10	N	82	30	W
Alor	113	8	15	S	124	30	E
Alor Setar	96	6	7	N	100	22	E
Alpena	150	45	6	N	83	24	W
Alphen	40	51	29	N	4	58	E
Alpine	161	30	25	N	103	35	W
Alps	16	47	0	N	8	0	E
Alsace	37	48	15	N	7	25	E
Alsask	152	51	21	N	109	59	W
Alston	28	54	48	N	2	26	W
Alta Gracia	190	31	40	S	64	30	W
Altagracia	184	10	45	N	71	30	W
Altai = Aerht'ai Shan	100	46	40	N	92	45	E
Altamaha ~→	170	31	19	N	81	17	W
Altamira	188	3	12	S	52	10	W
Alto Adige = Trentino-Alto Adige □	47	46	30	N	11	0	E
Alton	166	38	55	N	90	5	W
Altona	43	53	32	N	9	56	E
Altoona	164	40	32	N	78	24	W
Altun Shan	100	38	30	N	88	0	E
Alvarado	177	18	46	N	95	46	W
Alvsborgs län □	60	58	30	N	12	30	E
Alwar	89	27	38	N	76	34	E
Alxa Zuoqi	98	38	50	N	105	40	E
Am-Timan	129	11	0	N	20	10	E
Amadjuak	146	64	0	N	72	39	W
Amadjuak L.	146	65	0	N	71	8	W
Amagasaki	106	34	42	N	135	20	E
Amagi	108	33	25	N	130	39	E
Amakusa-Nada	108	32	35	N	130	5	E

Name	Page	Lat	Long
Amalner	**91**	21 5N	75 5 E
Amapá	**185**	2 5N	50 50W
Amapá □	**185**	1 40N	52 0W
Amarillo	**161**	35 14N	101 46W
Amasya	**80**	40 40N	35 50 E
Amatitlán	**177**	14 29N	90 38W
Amazon = Amazonas →	**185**	0 5S	50 0W
Amazonas □	**185**	4 0S	62 0W
Amazonas →	**185**	0 5S	50 0W
Ambala	**89**	30 23N	76 56 E
Ambato	**184**	1 5S	78 42W
Ambikapur	**92**	23 15N	83 15 E
Ambleside	**28**	54 26N	2 58W
Ambo	**186**	10 5S	76 10W
Ambon	**113**	3 35S	128 20 E
Amboyna I.	**112**	7 50N	112 50 E
Amderma	**69**	69 45N	61 30 E
Ameca	**175**	20 33N	104 2W
Ameca, R. →	**175**	20 41N	105 18W
Ameland	**41**	53 27N	5 45 E
American Highland	**14**	73 0S	75 0 E
American Samoa ■	**123**	14 20S	170 40W
Americus	**170**	32 0N	84 10W
Amersfoort	**40**	52 9N	5 23 E
Amery	**143**	56 34N	94 3W
Ames	**166**	42 0N	93 40W
Amga →	**75**	62 38N	134 32 E
Amgu	**75**	45 45N	137 15 E
Amgun →	**75**	52 56N	139 38 E
Amherst	**148**	45 48N	64 8W
Amherstburg	**150**	42 6N	83 6W
Amiens	**38**	49 54N	2 16 E
Amlwch	**26**	53 24N	4 21W
'Ammān	**80**	31 57N	35 52 E
Amorgós	**55**	36 50N	25 57 E
Amos	**151**	48 35N	78 5W
Amoy = Xiamen	**99**	24 25N	118 4 E
Amravati	**91**	20 55N	77 45 E
Amreli	**91**	21 35N	71 17 E
Amritsar	**89**	31 35N	74 57 E
Amsterdam, Neth.	**40**	52 23N	4 54 E
Amsterdam, U.S.A.	**164**	42 58N	74 10W
Amudarya →	**70**	43 40N	59 0 E
Amundsen Gulf	**145**	71 0N	124 0W
Amundsen Sea	**15**	72 0S	115 0W
Amur →	**75**	52 56N	141 10 E
An Nafūd	**82**	28 15N	41 0 E
An Najaf	**84**	32 3N	44 15 E
An Nāşirīyah	**84**	31 0N	46 15 E
An Nhon	**95**	13 55N	109 7 E
An Nu'ayrīyah	**84**	27 30N	48 30 E
An Uaimh	**34**	53 39N	6 40W
Anabar →	**72**	73 8N	113 36 E
Anaconda	**163**	46 7N	113 0W
Anacortes	**171**	48 30N	122 40W
Anadolu	**80**	38 0N	30 0 E
Anadyr →	**73**	64 55N	176 5 E
Anadyrskiy Zaliv	**73**	64 0N	180 0 E
Anaheim	**173**	33 50N	118 0W
Anambas Is.	**111**	3 20N	106 30 E
Anamur	**80**	36 8N	32 58 E
Anan	**109**	33 54N	134 40 E
Anápolis	**188**	16 15S	48 50W
Anārak	**85**	33 25N	53 40 E
Anatolia = Anadolu	**80**	38 0N	30 0 E
Añatuya	**190**	28 20S	62 50W
Anchorage	**142**	61 10N	149 50W
Ancohuma, Nevada	**187**	16 0S	68 50W
Ancona	**47**	43 37N	13 30 E
Ancud	**192**	42 0S	73 50W
Ancud, G. de	**192**	42 0S	73 0W
Ándalsnes	**65**	62 35N	7 43 E
Andalucía □	**50**	37 35N	5 0W
Andalusia	**169**	31 19N	86 30W
Andalusia □ = Andalucía □	**50**	37 35N	5 0W
Andaman Is.	**94**	12 30N	92 30 E
Andaman Sea	**94**	13 0N	96 0 E
Andaman Str.	**94**	12 15N	92 20 E
Andelys, Les	**39**	49 15N	1 25 E
Anderson, Ind., U.S.A.	**167**	40 5N	85 40W
Anderson, S.C., U.S.A.	**165**	34 32N	82 40W
Andes, Cord. de los	**182**	20 0S	68 0W
Andhra Pradesh □	**91**	16 0N	79 0 E
Andikíthira	**55**	35 52N	23 15 E
Andizhan	**71**	41 10N	72 0 E
Andorra ■	**36**	42 30N	1 30 E
Andover	**24**	51 13N	1 29W
Andreanof Is.	**142**	52 0N	178 0W
Andrewilla	**118**	26 31S	139 17 E
Ándria	**49**	41 13N	16 17 E
Andropov	**68**	58 5N	38 50 E
Ándros	**55**	37 50N	24 57 E
Andros I.	**178**	24 30N	78 0W
Angara →	**74**	58 30N	97 0 E
Angarsk	**74**	52 30N	104 0 E
Angaston	**119**	34 30S	139 8 E
Ånge	**66**	62 31N	15 35 E
Ängelholm	**61**	56 15N	12 58 E
Angels Camp	**172**	38 8N	120 30W
Ångerman →	**66**	64 0N	17 20 E
Angers	**36**	47 30N	0 35W
Angkor	**95**	13 22N	103 50 E
Anglesey	**26**	53 17N	4 20W
Angmagssalik	**147**	65 40N	37 20W
Angol	**190**	37 56S	72 45W
Angola ■	**134**	12 0S	18 0 E
Angoulême	**36**	45 39N	0 10 E
Angoumois	**36**	45 50N	0 25 E
Anguilla	**180**	18 14N	63 5W
Angus, Braes of	**33**	56 51N	3 10W
Anhui □	**99**	32 0N	117 0 E
Anhwei □ = Anhui □	**99**	32 0N	117 0 E
Anin	**94**	15 36N	97 50 E
Anjō	**106**	34 57N	137 5 E
Anjou	**36**	47 20N	0 15W
Anju	**98**	39 36N	125 40 E
Ankang	**99**	32 40N	109 1 E
Ankara	**80**	40 0N	32 54 E
Ann Arbor	**167**	42 17N	83 45W
Annaba	**127**	36 50N	7 46 E
Annam = Trung-Phan	**95**	16 0N	108 0 E
Annamitique, Chaîne	**95**	17 0N	106 0 E
Annan	**31**	55 0N	3 17W
Annapolis	**164**	39 0N	76 30W
Annecy	**37**	45 55N	6 8 E
Anniston	**169**	33 45N	85 50W
Annobón	**131**	1 25S	5 36 E
Annonay	**37**	45 15N	4 40 E
Annotto Bay	**180**	18 17N	77 3W
Anqing	**99**	30 30N	117 3 E
Anse, L'	**150**	46 47N	88 28W
Anshan	**98**	41 3N	122 58 E
Anshun	**99**	26 18N	105 57 E
Anstruther	**31**	56 14N	2 40W
Antabamba	**186**	14 40S	73 0W
Antakya	**80**	36 14N	36 10 E
Antalya	**80**	36 52N	30 45 E
Antalya Körfezi	**80**	36 15N	31 30 E
Antananarivo	**137**	18 55S	47 31 E
Antarctic Pen.	**14**	67 0S	60 0W
Antarctica	**14**	90 0S	0 0 E
Anti Atlas	**126**	30 0N	8 30W
Antibes	**37**	43 34N	7 6 E
Anticosti, Î. d'	**148**	49 30N	63 0W
Antigo	**150**	45 8N	89 5W
Antigua, Guat.	**177**	14 34N	90 41W
Antigua, W. Indies	**180**	17 0N	61 50W
Antigua and Barbuda ■	**180**	17 20N	61 48W
Antilla	**178**	20 40N	75 50W
Antioch	**172**	38 7N	121 45W
Antioquia	**184**	6 40N	75 55W
Antipodes Is.	**11**	49 45S	178 40 E
Antofagasta	**190**	23 50S	70 30W
Antrim	**34**	54 43N	6 13W
Antrim, Mts. of	**34**	54 57N	6 8W
Antsiranana	**137**	12 25S	49 20 E
Antwerp = Antwerpen	**42**	51 13N	4 25 E
Antwerpen	**42**	51 13N	4 25 E
Anvers = Antwerpen	**42**	51 13N	4 25 E
Anvik	**142**	62 37N	160 20W
Anxious B.	**119**	33 24S	134 45 E
Anyang	**98**	36 5N	114 21 E

Name	Page	Lat	Long
Anzhero-Sudzhensk	71	56 10N	86 0 E
Ánzio	46	41 28N	12 37 E
Aoga-Shima	105	32 28N	139 46 E
Aomori	103	40 45N	140 45 E
Apalachee B.	170	30 0N	84 0W
Apalachicola	170	29 40N	85 0W
Apalachicola —►	170	29 40N	85 0W
Aparri	112	18 22N	121 38 E
Apatzingan	175	19 5N	102 21W
Apeldoorn	41	52 13N	5 57 E
Apennines	16	44 20N	10 20 E
Apizaco	177	19 25N	98 9W
Aplao	186	16 0S	72 40W
Apolo	187	14 30S	68 30W
Apostle Is.	150	47 0N	90 30W
Apostolos Andreas, C.	80	35 42N	34 35 E
Appalachian Mts.	138	38 0N	80 0W
Appingedam	41	53 19N	6 51 E
Appleby	28	54 35N	2 29W
Appleton	167	44 17N	88 25W
Apulia = Púglia □	49	41 0N	16 30 E
Apure —►	184	7 37N	66 25W
Aqabah = Al 'Aqabah	80	29 31N	35 0 E
Aquidauana	188	20 30S	55 50W
Áquila, L'	47	42 21N	13 24 E
Aquiles Serdán	174	28 36N	105 53W
Ar Riyāḍ	83	24 41N	46 42 E
Ar Ruṭbah	81	33 0N	40 15 E
Ara	92	25 35N	84 32 E
Arab, Bahr el —►	129	9 50N	29 0 E
Arab, Shatt al	84	30 0N	48 31 E
Arabia	76	25 0N	45 0 E
Arabian Gulf = Gulf, The	85	27 0N	50 0 E
Arabian Sea	76	16 0N	65 0 E
Aracaju	189	10 55S	37 4W
Aracati	189	4 30S	37 44W
Araçatuba	188	21 10S	50 30W
Arad	56	46 10N	21 20 E
Arafura Sea	113	9 0S	135 0 E
Aragón □	51	41 25N	1 0W
Araguacema	188	8 50S	49 20W
Araguaia —►	188	5 21S	48 41W
Araguari	188	18 38S	48 11W
Arāk	84	34 0N	49 40 E
Arakan Coast	93	19 0N	94 0 E
Arakan Yoma	93	20 0N	94 40 E
Araks = Aras, Rūd-e —►	81	39 10N	47 10 E
Aral Sea = Aralskoye More	70	44 30N	60 0 E
Aralsk	70	46 50N	61 20 E
Aralskoye More	70	44 30N	60 0 E
Aran I.	34	55 0N	8 30W
Aran Is.	35	53 5N	9 42W
Aranjuez	50	40 1N	3 40W
Aransas Pass	158	27 55N	97 9W
Arao	108	32 59N	130 25 E
Araraquara	188	21 50S	48 0W
Ararat	119	37 16S	143 0 E
Ararat, Mt. = Ağri Daği	81	39 50N	44 15 E
Aras, Rūd-e —►	81	39 10N	47 10 E
Araya, Pen. de	185	10 40N	64 0W
Arbil	81	36 15N	44 5 E
Arbroath	31	56 34N	2 35W
Arcachon	36	44 40N	1 10W
Arcadia	170	27 20N	81 50W
Archangel = Arkhangelsk	69	64 40N	41 0 E
Arcot	90	12 53N	79 20 E
Arctic Bay	146	73 1N	85 7W
Arctic Ocean	12	78 0N	160 0 W
Arctic Red River	144	67 15N	134 0W
Ardabīl	81	38 15N	48 18 E
Ardennes	42	50 0N	5 10 E
Ardgour	32	56 45N	5 25W
Ardlethan	117	34 22S	146 53 E
Ardmore	168	34 10N	97 5W
Ardnacrusha	35	52 43N	8 38W
Ardnamurchan, Pt. of	32	56 44N	6 14W
Ards Pen.	34	54 30N	5 25W
Arecibo	180	18 29N	66 42W
Arequipa	187	16 20S	71 30W
Arezzo	46	43 28N	11 50 E
Argentan	39	48 45N	0 1W
Argentário, Mte.	46	42 23N	11 11 E
Argentina ■	190	35 0S	66 0W
Argentino, L.	192	50 10S	73 0W
Árgos	54	37 40N	22 43 E
Argostólion	54	38 12N	20 33 E
Argun —►	74	53 20N	121 28 E
Árhus	61	56 8N	10 11 E
Arica, Chile	187	18 32S	70 20W
Arica, Colombia	184	2 0S	71 50W
Arida	106	34 5N	135 8 E
Arima	180	10 38N	61 17W
Ario de Rosales	175	19 12N	101 43W
Aripuanã	187	9 25S	60 30W
Aripuanã —►	187	5 7S	60 25W
Ariquemes	187	9 55S	63 6W
Arisaig	32	56 55N	5 50W
Aristazabal I.	154	52 40N	129 10W
Arizona □	160	34 20N	111 30W
Arjona	184	10 14N	75 22W
Arkadelphia	168	34 5N	93 0W
Arkansas □	168	35 0N	92 30W
Arkansas —►	168	33 48N	91 4W
Arkansas City	158	37 4N	97 3W
Arkhangelsk	69	64 40N	41 0 E
Arklow	35	52 48N	6 10W
Arkticheskiy, Mys	72	81 10N	95 0 E
Arles	37	43 41N	4 40 E
Arlington	164	38 52N	77 5W
Armagh	34	54 22N	6 40W
Armavir	70	45 2N	41 7 E
Armenia	184	4 35N	75 45W
Armenia S.S.R. □	70	40 0N	41 0 E
Armentières	38	50 40N	2 50 E
Armidale	116	30 30S	151 40 E
Armstrong	155	50 25N	119 10W
Arnaouti, C.	80	35 6N	32 17 E
Arnaud —►	146	59 59N	69 46W
Arnhem	41	51 58N	5 55 E
Arnhem, C.	115	12 20S	137 30 E
Arnhem Land	114	13 10S	134 30 E
Arnprior	151	45 26N	76 21W
Arran	30	55 34N	5 12W
Arras	38	50 17N	2 46 E
Arriaga	177	16 14N	93 54W
Árta	54	39 8N	21 2 E
Artigas	191	30 20S	56 30W
Artois	38	50 20N	2 30 E
Aru, Kepulauan	113	6 0S	134 30 E
Arua	132	3 1N	30 58 E
Aruanã	188	14 54S	51 10W
Aruba	181	12 30N	70 0W
Arusha	135	3 20S	36 40 E
Arvida	148	48 25N	71 14W
Arys	71	42 26N	68 48 E
'As Saffānīyah	84	28 5N	48 50 E
As Samāwah	84	31 15N	45 15 E
As Sulaymānīyah	83	24 9N	47 18 E
As Sumaymānīyah	81	35 35N	45 29 E
As Suwaydā'	80	32 40N	36 30 E
As Şuwayrah	84	32 55N	45 0 E
Asahi	107	35 43N	140 39 E
Asahi-Gawa —►	109	34 36N	133 58 E
Asahigawa	103	43 46N	142 22 E
Asama-Yama	107	36 24N	138 31 E
Asamankese	130	5 50N	0 40W
Asansol	92	23 40N	87 1 E
Asbestos	148	45 47N	71 58W
Ascension I.	125	8 0S	14 15W
Áscoli Piceno	47	42 51N	13 34 E
Aseb	133	13 0N	42 40 E
Ash Shām, Bādiyat	80	32 0N	40 0 E
Ash Shāmīyah	84	31 55N	44 35 E
Ash Shāriqah	85	25 23N	55 26 E
Ash Shaṭrah	84	31 30N	46 10 E
Ashburton	123	43 53S	171 48 E
Ashby-de-la-Zouch	28	52 45N	1 29W
Ashcroft	155	50 40N	121 20W
Asheboro	165	35 43N	79 46W
Asheville	165	35 39N	82 30W
Ashford, Australia	116	29 15S	151 3 E
Ashford, U.K.	25	51 8N	0 53 E

Name	Page	Lat	Long
Ashikaga	107	36 28N	139 29 E
Ashizuri-Zaki	109	32 44N	133 0 E
Ashkhabad	70	38 0N	57 50 E
Ashland, Kans., U.S.A.	156	37 13N	99 43W
Ashland, Ky., U.S.A.	165	38 25N	82 40W
Ashland, Oreg., U.S.A.	171	42 10N	122 38W
Ashland, Wis. U.S.A.	150	46 40N	90 52W
Ashq'elon	80	31 42N	34 35 E
Ashtabula	164	41 52N	80 50W
Ashton-under-Lyne	28	53 30N	2 8W
Ashuanipi, L.	147	52 45N	66 15W
Asinara I.	48	41 5N	8 15 E
'Asīr □	82	18 40N	42 30 E
Asir, Ras.	133	11 55N	51 10 E
Asmara = Asmera	132	15 19N	38 55 E
Asmera.	132	15 19N	38 55 E
Aso	108	33 0N	131 5 E
Aso-Zan	108	32 53N	131 6 E
Aspiring, Mt.	123	44 23S	168 46 E
Assam □	93	26 0N	93 0 E
Assen	41	53 0N	6 35 E
Assiniboia	152	49 40N	105 59W
Assiniboine →	153	49 53N	97 8W
Assisi	46	43 4N	12 36 E
Asti	46	44 54N	8 11 E
Astipálaia	55	36 32N	26 22 E
Astoria	171	46 16N	123 50W
Astrakhan	70	46 25N	48 5 E
Asturias □	50	43 15N	6 0W
Asunción	191	25 10S	57 30W
Aswân	128	24 4N	32 57 E
Asyût	128	27 11N	31 4 E
At Ṭafīlah	80	30 45N	35 30 E
At Ta'if	82	21 5N	40 27 E
Atacama, Desierto de	190	24 0S	69 20W
Atacama, Salar de	190	23 30S	68 20W
Atalaya	186	10 45S	73 50W
Atami	107	35 5N	139 4 E
Atbara	129	17 42N	33 59 E
'Atbara →	129	17 40N	33 56 E
Atchafalaya B.	168	29 30N	91 20W
Atchison	166	39 40N	95 10W
Athabasca	155	54 45N	113 20W
Athabasca →	145	58 40N	110 50W
Athabasca, L.	145	59 15N	109 15W
Athenry	35	53 18N	8 45W
Athens = Athínai	55	37 58N	23 46 E
Athens, Ala., U.S.A.	169	34 49N	86 58W
Athens, Ga., U.S.A.	165	33 56N	83 24W
Athens, Ohio, U.S.A.	167	39 25N	82 6W
Athens, Tenn., U.S.A.	169	35 45N	84 38W
Athens, Tex., U.S.A.	168	32 11N	95 48W
Atherton	121	17 17S	145 30 E
Athínai	55	37 58N	23 46 E
Athlone	34	53 26N	7 57W
Atholl, Forest of	33	56 51N	3 50W
Áthos	55	40 9N	24 22 E
Athy	35	53 0N	7 0W
Atico	186	16 14S	73 40W
Atlanta	170	33 50N	84 24W
Atlantic	166	41 25N	95 0W
Atlantic City	164	39 25N	74 25W
Atlantic Ocean	9	0 0	20 0W
Atlas Mts. = Haut Atlas	126	32 30N	5 0W
Atmore	169	31 2N	87 30W
Atsugi	107	35 25N	139 21 E
Atsumi	106	34 35N	137 4 E
Atsumi-Wan	106	34 44N	137 13 E
Attawapiskat →	140	52 57N	82 18W
Attleboro	164	41 56N	71 18W
Aubagne	37	43 17N	5 37 E
Aube →	37	48 34N	3 43 E
Aubenas	37	44 37N	4 24 E
Auburn, Ala., U.S.A.	169	32 37N	85 30W
Auburn, N.Y., U.S.A.	164	42 57N	76 39W
Auckland	122	36 52S	174 46 E
Auckland Is.	15	50 40S	166 5 E
Aude →	37	43 13N	3 14 E
Augsburg	43	48 22N	10 54 E
Augusta, Ga., U.S.A.	170	33 29N	81 59W
Augusta, Maine, U.S.A.	148	44 20N	69 46W
Aunis	36	46 5N	0 50W
Aurangabad	91	19 50N	75 23 E
Aurillac	37	44 55N	2 26 E
Aurora	167	41 42N	88 12W
Aust-Agder fylke □	60	58 55N	7 40 E
Austin, Minn., U.S.A.	166	43 37N	92 59W
Austin, Tex., U.S.A.	161	30 20N	97 45W
Austral Is. = Tubuai Is.	123	25 0S	150 0W
Australia ■	114	23 0S	135 0 E
Australian Alps	117	36 30S	148 30 E
Australian Cap. Terr. □	117	35 30S	149 0 E
Austria ■	45	47 0N	14 0 E
Autlán	175	19 40N	104 30W
Auvergne	37	45 20N	3 15 E
Auxerre	39	47 48N	3 32 E
Avalon Pen.	149	47 30N	53 20W
Aveiro	185	3 10S	55 5W
Avellaneda	190	34 50S	58 10W
Aves, I. de	181	15 45N	63 55W
Avesnes-sur-Helpe	38	50 8N	3 55 E
Aveyron →	36	44 7N	1 5 E
Aviemore	33	57 11N	3 50W
Avignon	37	43 57N	4 50 E
Ávila	50	40 39N	4 43W
Avon □	27	51 30N	2 40W
Avon →, Avon, U.K.	24	51 30N	2 43W
Avon →, Hants., U.K.	24	50 44N	1 45W
Avonmouth	27	51 30N	2 42W
Avranches	36	48 40N	1 20W
Awaji-Shima	109	34 30N	134 50 E
Aweil	129	8 42N	27 20 E
Axel Heiberg I.	12	80 0N	90 0W
Axminster	27	50 47N	3 1W
Ayabe	106	35 20N	135 20 E
Ayacucho	186	13 0S	74 0W
Aylos Evstrátios	55	39 34N	24 58 E
Ayon, Ostrov	73	69 50N	169 0 E
Ayr, Australia	121	19 35S	147 25 E
Ayr, U.K.	31	55 28N	4 37W
Ayre, Pt. of	28	54 27N	4 21W
Aytos	53	42 42N	27 16 E
Ayutla	177	16 58N	99 17W
Aẓ Ẓahrān	84	26 10N	50 7 E
Az Zubayr	84	30 20N	47 50 E
Azamgarh	92	26 5N	83 13 E
Azbine = Aïr	127	18 30N	8 0 E
Azerbaijan S.S.R. □	70	40 20N	48 0 E
Azores	126	38 44N	29 0W
Azov Sea = Azovskoye More.	68	46 0N	36 30 E
Azovskoye More	68	46 0N	36 30 E
Azúa de Compostela	180	18 25N	70 44W
Azuero, Pen. de	179	7 30N	80 30W
Azul.	190	36 42S	59 43W
Ba Ngoi = Cam Lam	95	11 54N	109 10 E
Baarn	40	52 12N	5 17 E
Bāb el Māndeb	133	12 35N	43 25 E
Babahoyo	184	1 40S	79 30W
Babinda	121	17 20S	145 56 E
Babine L.	154	54 48N	126 0W
Bābol	86	36 40N	52 50 E
Babuyan Is.	112	19 10N	121 40 E
Babylon	84	32 40N	44 30 E
Bac Ninh	95	21 13N	106 4 E
Bac Phan	95	22 0N	105 0 E
Bac Quang	95	22 30N	104 48 E
Bacabal	188	4 15S	44 45W
Bacău	57	46 35N	26 55 E
Back →	145	65 10N	104 0W
Bacolod	112	10 40N	122 57 E
Bad Lands	163	43 40N	102 10W
Badajoz	50	38 50N	6 59W
Badakhshān □	87	36 30N	71 0 E
Badalona	51	41 26N	2 15 E
Badanah	82	30 58N	41 30 E
Baden-Baden	42	48 45N	8 15 E
Baden-Württemberg □	42	48 40N	9 0 E
Bādghīsāt □	87	35 0N	63 0 E
Badin	88	24 38N	68 54 E

Baffin □	146	70	0N	80	0W
Baffin B.	13	72	0N	64	0W
Baffin I.	146	68	0N	75	0W
Bafra	80	41	34N	35	54 E
Bāft	85	29	15N	56	38 E
Bagé	191	31	20S	54	15W
Baghdād	84	33	20N	44	30 E
Baghlān	87	36	12N	69	0 E
Baghlān □	87	36	0N	68	30 E
Bahamas ■	178	24	0N	75	0W
Baharampur	92	24	2N	88	27 E
Bahawalpur	89	29	24N	71	40 E
Bahia = Salvador	189	13	0S	38	30W
Bahía □	189	12	0S	42	0W
Bahía Blanca	190	38	35S	62	13W
Bahr el Jebel ⟶	129	7	30N	30	30 E
Bahraich	92	27	38N	81	37 E
Bahrain ■	85	26	0N	50	35 E
Baia Mare	56	47	40N	23	35 E
Baie Comeau	148	49	12N	68	10W
Baie-St-Paul	148	47	28N	70	32W
Ba'iji	81	35	0N	43	30 E
Baikal, L. = Baykal, Oz.	74	53	0N	108	0 E
Baile Atha Cliath = Dublin	35	53	20N	6	18W
Bailleul	38	50	44N	2	41 E
Bainbridge	170	30	53N	84	34W
Baird Mts.	142	67	10N	160	15W
Bairnsdale	117	37	48S	147	36 E
Baiyin	98	36	45N	104	14 E
Baja	59	46	12N	18	59 E
Baja California	174	31	10N	115	12W
Baja California Norte □	174	30	0N	115	0W
Baja California Sur □	174	25	50N	111	50W
Bajimba, Mt.	116	29	17S	152	6 E
Baker	171	44	50N	117	55W
Baker I.	122	0	10N	176	35W
Baker Lake	145	64	20N	96	3W
Bakersfield	173	35	25N	119	0W
Bākhtarān	84	34	23N	47	0 E
Bakony Forest = Bakony Hegység	59	47	10N	17	30 E
Bakony Hegység	59	47	10N	17	30 E
Baku	70	40	25N	49	45 E
Bala	26	52	54N	3	36W
Balabac, Str.	112	7	53N	117	5 E
Balabakk	80	34	0N	36	10 E
Balaghat	91	21	49N	80	12 E
Balaghat Ra.	91	18	50N	76	30 E
Balaklava	119	34	7S	138	22 E
Balakovo	68	52	4N	47	55 E
Balaton	59	46	50N	17	40 E
Balboa	179	9	0N	79	30W
Balbriggan	34	53	35N	6	10W
Balcarce	190	38	0S	58	10W
Balclutha	123	46	15S	169	45 E
Baldy Peak	161	33	50N	109	30W
Baleares, Islas	51	39	30N	3	0 E
Balearic Is. = Baleares, Islas	51	39	30N	3	0 E
Bali	111	8	20S	115	0 E
Balikesir	80	39	35N	27	58 E
Balikpapan	111	1	10S	116	55 E
Balkan Mts. = Stara Planina	53	43	15N	23	0 E
Balkan Pen.	17	42	0N	22	0 E
Balkh □	87	36	30N	67	0 E
Balkhash	71	46	50N	74	50 E
Balkhash, Ozero	71	46	0N	74	50 E
Ballachulish	32	56	40N	5	10W
Ballarat	117	37	33S	143	50 E
Ballard, L.	120	29	20S	120	10 E
Ballater	33	57	2N	3	2W
Ballina, Australia	116	28	50S	153	31 E
Ballina, Mayo, Ireland	34	54	7N	9	10W
Ballina, Tipp., Ireland	35	52	49N	8	27W
Ballinasloe	35	53	20N	8	12W
Ballinrobe	34	53	36N	9	13W
Ballycastle	34	55	12N	6	15W
Ballymena	34	54	53N	6	18W
Ballymoney	34	55	5N	6	30W
Ballyshannon	34	54	30N	8	10W
Balmaceda	192	46	0S	71	50W
Balmoral	33	57	3N	3	13W
Balrampur	92	27	30N	82	20 E
Balranald	117	34	38S	143	33 E
Balsas, R. ⟶	177	17	55N	102	10W
Baltic Sea	16	56	0N	20	0 E
Baltimore	164	39	18N	76	37W
Baluchistan □	88	27	30N	65	0 E
Bamako	130	12	34N	7	55W
Bambari	129	5	40N	20	35 E
Bamberg	43	49	54N	10	53 E
Bāmiān □	87	35	0N	67	0 E
Ban Aranyaprathet	95	13	41N	102	30 E
Ban Don = Surat Thani	96	9	6N	99	20 E
Ban Houei Sai	95	20	22N	100	32 E
Ban Khe Bo	95	19	10N	104	39 E
Ban Khun Yuam	94	18	49N	97	57 E
Ban Nong Pling	94	15	40N	100	10 E
Ban Phai	95	16	4N	102	44 E
Banaras = Varanasi	92	25	22N	83	0 E
Banbridge	34	54	21N	6	17W
Banbury	25	52	4N	1	21W
Bancroft	151	45	3N	77	51W
Banda	91	25	30N	80	26 E
Banda, Kepulauan	113	4	37S	129	50 E
Banda Aceh	111	5	35N	95	20 E
Banda Banda, Mt.	116	31	10S	152	28 E
Banda Sea	113	6	0S	130	0 E
Bandar = Machilipatnam	92	16	12N	81	8 E
Bandār 'Abbās	85	27	15N	56	15 E
Bandar-e Anzalī	81	37	30N	49	30 E
Bandar-e Khomeyni	84	30	30N	49	5 E
Bandar-e Lengeh	85	26	35N	54	58 E
Bandar-e Nakhīlū	85	26	58N	53	30 E
Bandar-e Torkeman	86	37	0N	54	10 E
Bandar Seri Begawan	112	4	52N	115	0 E
Bandeira, Pico da	188	20	26S	41	47W
Bandirma	80	40	20N	28	0 E
Bandon	35	51	44N	8	45W
Bandung	111	6	54S	107	36 E
Banes	178	21	0N	75	42W
Banff, Canada	155	51	10N	115	34W
Banff, U.K.	33	57	40N	2	32W
Bangalore	90	12	59N	77	40 E
Bangassou	129	4	55N	23	7 E
Banggai	113	1	40S	123	30 E
Banghāzī	128	32	11N	20	3 E
Bangka, Selat	111	2	30S	105	30 E
Bangkok	94	13	45N	100	35 E
Bangladesh ■	92	24	0N	90	0 E
Bangor, N. Ireland, U.K.	34	54	40N	5	40W
Bangor, Wales, U.K.	26	53	13N	4	9W
Bangor, U.S.A.	148	44	48N	68	42W
Bangui	131	4	23N	18	35 E
Bangweulu, L.	135	11	0S	30	0 E
Bani	180	18	16N	70	22W
Banja Luka	52	44	49N	17	11 E
Banjarmasin	111	3	20S	114	35 E
Banjul	130	13	28N	16	40W
Bankipore	92	25	35N	85	10 E
Banks I., B.C., Canada	154	53	20N	130	0W
Banks I., N.W.T., Canada	145	73	15N	121	30W
Banks Pen.	123	43	45S	173	15 E
Banks Str.	119	40	40S	148	10 E
Bann ⟶	34	54	30N	6	31W
Banning	173	33	58N	116	52W
Bannockburn	31	56	5N	3	55W
Bannu	89	33	0N	70	18 E
Bantry	35	51	40N	9	28W
Baoding	98	38	50N	115	28 E
Baoji	99	34	20N	107	5 E
Baotou	98	40	32N	110	2 E
Ba'qūbah	81	33	45N	44	50 E
Bar	52	42	8N	19	8 E
Bar Harbor	148	44	15N	68	20W
Baraboo	166	43	28N	89	46W
Baracoa	178	20	20N	74	30W
Barahona	180	18	13N	71	7W
Barail Range	93	25	15N	93	20 E
Baramula	89	34	15N	74	20 E
Baran	91	25	9N	76	40 E
Baranof I.	143	57	0N	135	10W
Baranovichi	68	53	10N	26	0 E

Name	Page	Lat °	′	N/S	Lon °	′	E/W
Barbacoas	184	1	45	N	78	0	W
Barbados ■	180	13	0	N	59	30	W
Barbuda I.	180	17	30	N	61	40	W
Barca, La	175	20	17	N	102	34	W
Barcaldine	121	23	43	S	145	6	E
Barcelona, Spain	51	41	21	N	2	10	E
Barcelona, Venezuela	185	10	10	N	64	40	W
Barcelos	185	1	0	S	63	0	W
Barddhaman	92	23	14	N	87	39	E
Bardera	133	2	20	N	42	27	E
Bardsey I.	26	52	46	N	4	47	W
Bareilly	89	28	22	N	79	27	E
Barentin	38	49	33	N	0	58	E
Barents Sea	13	73	0	N	39	0	E
Bargara	121	24	50	S	152	25	E
Bari	49	41	6	N	16	52	E
Bari Doab	89	30	20	N	73	0	E
Barīm	82	12	39	N	43	25	E
Barinas	184	8	36	N	70	15	W
Barisal	92	22	45	N	90	20	E
Barito →~	111	4	0	S	114	50	E
Barlee, L.	120	29	15	S	119	30	E
Barletta	49	41	20	N	16	17	E
Barmer	91	25	45	N	71	20	E
Barmera	119	34	15	S	140	28	E
Barmouth	26	52	44	N	4	3	W
Barnard Castle	28	54	33	N	1	55	W
Barnaul	71	53	20	N	83	40	E
Barneveld	41	52	7	N	5	36	E
Barnsley	28	53	33	N	1	29	W
Barnstaple	27	51	5	N	4	3	W
Baro	131	8	35	N	6	18	E
Baroda = Vadodara	91	22	20	N	73	10	E
Barpeta	93	26	20	N	91	10	E
Barquísimeto	184	10	4	N	69	19	W
Barra	32	57	0	N	7	30	W
Barra Hd.	32	56	47	N	7	40	W
Barraba	116	30	21	S	150	35	E
Barranca	186	10	45	S	77	50	W
Barrancabermeja	184	7	0	N	73	50	W
Barrancas	185	8	55	N	62	5	W
Barranqueras	190	27	30	S	59	0	W
Barranquilla	184	11	0	N	74	50	W
Barre	151	44	15	N	72	30	W
Barreiros	188	8	49	S	35	12	W
Barrhead	155	54	10	N	114	24	W
Barrie	151	44	24	N	79	40	W
Barrier Ra.	118	31	0	S	141	30	E
Barrington Tops	116	32	6	S	151	28	E
Barrow →~	35	52	10	N	6	57	W
Barrow, Pt.	138	71	22	N	156	30	W
Barrow-in-Furness	28	54	8	N	3	15	W
Barry	27	51	23	N	3	19	W
Barry's Bay	151	45	29	N	77	41	W
Barsi	91	18	10	N	75	50	E
Barstow	173	34	58	N	117	2	W
Bartica	185	6	25	N	58	40	W
Bartow	170	27	53	N	81	49	W
Basel	44	47	35	N	7	35	E
Bashi Channel	99	21	15	N	122	0	E
Bashkir A.S.S.R. □	69	54	0	N	57	0	E
Basilan	112	6	35	N	122	0	E
Basildon	25	51	34	N	0	29	E
Basilicata □	49	40	30	N	16	0	E
Basim = Washim	91	20	3	N	77	0	E
Basle = Basel	44	47	35	N	7	35	E
Basoka	134	1	16	N	23	40	E
Basque Provinces = Vascongadas	50	42	50	N	2	45	W
Basra = Al Baṣrah	84	30	30	N	47	50	E
Bass Rock	31	56	5	N	2	40	W
Bass Str.	117	39	15	S	146	30	E
Bassano	155	50	48	N	112	20	W
Basse-Terre	180	16	0	N	61	40	W
Bassein	93	16	45	N	94	30	E
Basseterre	180	17	17	N	62	43	W
Basti	92	26	52	N	82	55	E
Bastia	36	42	40	N	9	30	E
Batabanó	178	22	40	N	82	20	W
Batamay	74	63	30	N	129	15	E
Batan Is.	112	20	25	N	121	59	E
Batang	101	30	1	N	99	0	E
Batavia	164	43	0	N	78	10	W
Batemans Bay	117	35	44	S	150	11	E
Batesville	168	35	48	N	91	40	W
Bath, U.K.	27	51	22	N	2	22	W
Bath, Maine, U.S.A.	148	43	50	N	69	49	W
Bath, N.Y., U.S.A.	164	42	20	N	77	17	W
Bathurst = Banjul	130	13	28	N	16	40	W
Bathurst, Australia	117	33	25	S	149	31	E
Bathurst, Canada	148	47	37	N	65	43	W
Bathurst, C.	145	70	34	N	128	0	W
Bathurst Inlet	145	66	50	N	108	1	W
Batlow	117	35	31	S	148	9	E
Batman	81	37	55	N	41	5	E
Batna	127	35	34	N	6	15	E
Baton Rouge	168	30	30	N	91	5	W
Batopilas	174	27	1	N	107	44	W
Battambang	95	13	7	N	103	12	E
Batticaloa	90	7	43	N	81	45	E
Battle	25	50	55	N	0	30	E
Battle Creek	167	42	20	N	85	6	W
Battle Harbour	147	52	16	N	55	35	W
Battleford	152	52	45	N	108	15	W
Batu Gajah	96	4	28	N	101	3	E
Batu Is.	111	0	30	S	98	25	E
Batumi	70	41	30	N	41	30	E
Bauchi	131	10	22	N	9	48	E
Bauru	188	22	10	S	49	0	W
Bavaria = Bayern □	43	49	7	N	11	30	E
Bawdwin	93	23	5	N	97	20	E
Bawean	111	5	46	S	112	35	E
Bawku	130	11	3	N	0	19	W
Bay City	167	43	35	N	83	51	W
Bay Shore	164	40	44	N	73	15	W
Bayamo	178	20	20	N	76	40	W
Bayamón	180	18	24	N	66	10	W
Bayan Har Shan	101	34	0	N	98	0	E
Bayan Hot = Alxa Zuoqi	98	38	50	N	105	40	E
Bayern □	43	49	7	N	11	30	E
Bayeux	36	49	17	N	0	42	W
Bayfield	150	43	34	N	81	42	W
Baykal, Oz.	74	53	0	N	108	0	E
Baykonur	71	47	48	N	65	50	E
Bayonne	36	43	30	N	1	28	W
Bayreuth	43	49	56	N	11	35	E
Bayrūt	80	33	53	N	35	31	E
Baytown	168	29	42	N	94	57	W
Beachy Head	25	50	44	N	0	16	E
Beagle, Canal	192	55	0	S	68	30	W
Béarn	36	43	8	N	0	36	W
Beauce, Plaine de la	37	48	10	N	1	45	E
Beaudesert	116	27	59	S	153	0	E
Beaufort	170	32	25	N	80	40	W
Beaufort Sea	12	72	0	N	140	0	W
Beaugency	39	47	47	N	1	38	E
Beauharnois	151	45	20	N	73	52	W
Beauly	33	57	29	N	4	27	W
Beaumaris	26	53	16	N	4	7	W
Beaumont	168	30	5	N	94	8	W
Beaumont-sur-Oise	39	49	9	N	2	17	E
Beauséjour	153	50	5	N	96	35	W
Beauvais	38	49	25	N	2	8	E
Beauval	152	55	9	N	107	37	W
Beaver	142	66	20	N	147	30	W
Beaver →~	152	55	26	N	107	45	W
Beaver Falls	164	40	44	N	80	20	W
Beaverlodge	155	55	11	N	119	29	W
Beawar	91	26	3	N	74	18	E
Bečej	52	45	36	N	20	3	E
Béchar	127	31	38	N	2	18	W
Beckley	165	37	50	N	81	8	W
Bedford, U.K.	25	52	8	N	0	29	W
Bedford, U.S.A.	167	38	50	N	86	30	W
Bedford □	25	52	4	N	0	28	W
Beenleigh	116	27	43	S	153	10	E
Be'er Sheva'	80	31	15	N	34	48	E
Beersheba = Be'er Sheva'	80	31	15	N	34	48	E
Beeston	29	52	55	N	1	11	W
Bega	117	36	41	S	149	51	E
Behbehān	84	30	30	N	50	15	E
Beibei	99	29	47	N	106	22	E

Name	Page	Lat	Long
Beihai	**99**	21 28N	109 6 E
Beijing	**98**	39 55N	116 20 E
Beira	**137**	19 50S	34 52 E
Beira-Alta	**50**	40 35N	7 35W
Beira-Baixa	**50**	40 2N	7 30W
Beira-Litoral	**50**	40 5N	8 30W
Beirut = Bayrūt	**80**	33 53N	35 31 E
Bejaia	**127**	36 42N	5 2 E
Békéscsaba	**59**	46 40N	21 5 E
Bela	**92**	25 50N	82 0 E
Bela Crkva	**52**	44 55N	21 27 E
Belaya Tserkov	**68**	49 45N	30 10 E
Belcher Is.	**140**	56 15N	78 45W
Belém	**188**	1 20S	48 30W
Belfast, U.K.	**34**	54 35N	5 56W
Belfast, U.S.A.	**148**	44 30N	69 0W
Belfort	**37**	47 38N	6 50 E
Belgaum	**91**	15 55N	74 35 E
Belgium ■	**42**	50 30N	5 0 E
Belgorod	**68**	50 35N	36 35 E
Belgrade = Beograd	**52**	44 50N	20 37 E
Belitung	**111**	3 10S	107 50 E
Belize ■	**177**	17 0N	88 30W
Belize City	**177**	17 25N	88 0W
Bell Peninsula	**146**	63 50N	82 0W
Bell Ville	**190**	32 40S	62 40W
Bella Coola	**154**	52 25N	126 40W
Bellaire	**164**	40 1N	80 46W
Bellary	**90**	15 10N	76 56 E
Belle Fourche →	**163**	44 25N	102 19W
Belle Glade	**170**	26 43N	80 38W
Belle Isle	**147**	51 57N	55 25W
Belle Isle, Str. of	**141**	51 30N	56 30W
Bellefontaine	**167**	40 20N	83 45W
Belleville, Canada	**151**	44 10N	77 23W
Bellevue, U.S.A.	**166**	38 30N	90 0W
Bellevue	**155**	49 35N	114 22W
Bellin	**146**	60 0N	70 0W
Bellingham	**171**	48 45N	122 27W
Bellingshausen Sea	**14**	66 0S	80 0W
Belmont	**117**	33 4S	151 42 E
Belmopan	**177**	17 18N	88 30W
Belo Horizonte	**188**	19 55S	43 56W
Belogorsk	**75**	51 0N	128 20 E
Beloit	**166**	42 35N	89 0W
Belomorsk	**68**	64 35N	34 30 E
Belovo	**71**	54 30N	86 0 E
Beloye More	**69**	66 30N	38 0 E
Beloye Ozero	**68**	45 15N	46 50 E
Belper	**28**	53 2N	1 29W
Belukha	**71**	49 50N	86 50 E
Belyy, Ostrov	**69**	73 30N	71 0 E
Bemidji	**156**	47 30N	94 50W
Ben Lomond, N.S.W., Australia	**116**	30 1S	151 40 E
Ben Lomond, Tas., Australia	**119**	41 38S	147 42 E
Ben Macdhui	**33**	57 4N	3 40W
Ben More, Central, U.K.	**32**	56 23N	4 31W
Ben More, Strathclyde, U.K.	**30**	56 26N	6 2W
Ben More Assynt	**32**	58 7N	4 51W
Ben Nevis	**32**	56 48N	5 0W
Benalla	**117**	36 30S	146 0 E
Benares = Varanasi	**92**	25 22N	83 0 E
Benbecula	**32**	57 26N	7 21W
Benbonyathe, Mt.	**118**	30 25S	139 11 E
Bencubbin	**120**	30 48S	117 52 E
Bend	**171**	44 2N	121 15W
Bendemeer	**116**	30 53S	151 8 E
Bender Beila	**133**	9 30N	50 48 E
Bendigo	**117**	36 40S	144 15 E
Benevento	**49**	41 7N	14 45 E
Bengal, Bay of	**92**	15 0N	90 0 E
Bengbu	**99**	32 58N	117 20 E
Benghazi = Banghāzī	**128**	32 11N	20 3 E
Benguela	**134**	12 37S	13 25 E
Beni →	**187**	10 23S	65 24W
Beni Suef	**128**	29 5N	31 6 E
Benidorm	**51**	38 33N	0 9W
Benin ■	**131**	10 0N	2 0 E
Benin, Bight of	**131**	5 0N	3 0 E
Benin City	**131**	6 20N	5 31 E
Benjamin Constant	**187**	4 40S	70 15W
Bennett	**144**	59 56N	134 53W
Bennettsville	**165**	34 38N	79 39W
Benton	**168**	34 30N	92 35W
Benue →	**131**	7 48N	6 46 E
Benxi	**98**	41 20N	123 48 E
Beograd	**52**	44 50N	20 37 E
Beppu	**108**	33 15N	131 30 E
Berau, Teluk	**113**	2 30S	132 30 E
Berber	**129**	18 0N	34 0 E
Berbera	**133**	10 30N	45 2 E
Berck-sur-Mer	**38**	50 25N	1 36 E
Berezniki	**69**	59 24N	56 46 E
Bérgamo	**46**	45 42N	9 40 E
Bergen, Neth.	**40**	52 40N	4 43 E
Bergen, Norway	**60**	60 23N	5 20 E
Bergen-op-Zoom	**40**	51 30N	4 18 E
Bergerac	**36**	44 51N	0 30 E
Berhala, Selat	**111**	1 0S	104 15 E
Berhampore = Baharampur	**92**	24 2N	88 27 E
Berhampur	**92**	19 15N	84 54 E
Bering Sea	**142**	58 0N	167 0 E
Bering Str.	**142**	66 0N	170 0W
Berkeley	**172**	37 52N	122 20W
Berkshire □	**25**	51 30N	1 20W
Berkshire Downs	**24**	51 30N	1 30W
Berlin, Germany	**43**	52 32N	13 24 E
Berlin, U.S.A.	**148**	44 29N	71 10W
Bermuda ■	**180**	32 45N	65 0W
Bern	**44**	46 57N	7 28 E
Bernay	**39**	49 5N	0 35 E
Berne = Bern	**44**	46 57N	7 28 E
Berri	**119**	34 14S	140 35 E
Berry	**37**	47 0N	2 0 E
Bertoua	**131**	4 30N	13 45 E
Berwick-upon-Tweed	**31**	55 47N	2 0W
Berwyn Mts.	**26**	52 54N	3 26W
Besançon	**37**	47 15N	6 0 E
Bessemer, Ala., U.S.A.	**169**	33 25N	86 57W
Bessemer, Mich., U.S.A.	**156**	46 27N	90 0W
Bethel	**142**	60 50N	161 50W
Bethlehem	**164**	40 39N	75 24W
Béthune	**38**	50 30N	2 38 E
Betsiboka →	**137**	16 3S	46 36 E
Beverley	**29**	53 52N	0 26W
Beverly Hills	**173**	34 4N	118 29W
Beverwijk	**40**	52 28N	4 38 E
Bexhill	**24**	50 51N	0 29 E
Beyneu	**70**	45 10N	55 3 E
Beyşehir Gölü	**80**	37 40N	31 45 E
Béziers	**37**	43 20N	3 12 E
Bezwada = Vijayawada	**92**	16 31N	80 39 E
Bhadravati	**90**	13 49N	75 40 E
Bhagalpur	**92**	25 10N	87 0 E
Bhakra Dam	**89**	31 30N	76 45 E
Bhandara	**91**	21 5N	79 42 E
Bhanrer Ra.	**91**	23 40N	79 45 E
Bharat = India ■	**78**	20 0N	78 0 E
Bharatpur	**89**	27 15N	77 30 E
Bharuch	**91**	21 47N	73 0 E
Bhatpara	**92**	22 50N	88 25 E
Bhaunagar = Bhavnagar	**91**	21 45N	72 10 E
Bhavnagar	**91**	21 45N	72 10 E
Bhilwara	**91**	25 25N	74 38 E
Bhima →	**91**	16 25N	77 17 E
Bhiwandi	**91**	19 20N	73 0 E
Bhiwani	**89**	28 50N	76 9 E
Bhopal	**91**	23 20N	77 30 E
Bhubaneshwar	**92**	20 15N	85 50 E
Bhusaval	**91**	21 3N	75 46 E
Bhutan ■	**92**	27 25N	90 30 E
Biafra, B. of = Bonny, Bight of	**131**	3 30N	9 20 E
Biała Podlaska	**58**	52 4N	23 6 E
Białystok	**58**	53 10N	23 10 E
Biarritz	**36**	43 29N	1 33W
Bibai	**103**	43 19N	141 52 E
Bicester	**25**	51 53N	1 9W
Biche, L. la	**155**	54 50N	112 3W
Bidar	**91**	17 55N	77 35 E
Biddeford	**148**	43 30N	70 28W

Bideford **27** 51 1N 4 13W
Bié, Planalto de . . . . **136** 12 0S 16 0 E
Bieber **172** 41 4N 121 6W
Biel . . . . **44** 47 8N 7 14 E
Bielé Karpaty . . . . **59** 49 5N 18 0 E
Bielefeld . . . . **42** 52 2N 8 31 E
Bielsko-Biała . . . . **59** 49 50N 19 2 E
Bien Hoa . . . . **95** 10 57N 106 49 E
Bienne = Biel . . . . **44** 47 8N 7 14 E
Bienville, L. **146** 55 5N 72 40W
Big Belt Mts. **163** 46 50N 111 30W
Big Cypress Swamp **170** 26 12N 81 10W
Big Horn Mts. = Bighorn Mts. . **163** 44 30N 107 30W
Big Rapids **167** 43 42N 85 27W
Big Sioux → **156** 42 30N 96 25W
Big Spring **161** 32 10N 101 25W
Big Stone Gap **165** 36 52N 82 45W
Big Trout L. **153** 53 40N 90 0W
Biggar, Canada **152** 52 4N 108 0W
Biggar, U.K. **31** 55 38N 3 31W
Bighorn → **163** 46 9N 107 28W
Bighorn Mts. **163** 44 30N 107 30W
Bihar . . . . **92** 25 5N 85 40 E
Bihar □ . . . . **92** 25 0N 86 0 E
Bijagós, Arquipélago dos **130** 11 15N 16 10W
Bijapur . . . . **91** 16 50N 75 55 E
Bijeljina . . . . **52** 44 46N 19 17 E
Bikaner . . . . **89** 28 2N 73 18 E
Bikin . . . . **75** 46 50N 134 20 E
Bilaspur . . . . **92** 22 2N 82 15 E
Bilauk Taungdan . . . . **94** 13 0N 99 0 E
Bilbao **50** 43 16N 2 56W
Billingham **29** 54 36N 1 18W
Billings **163** 45 43N 108 29W
Billiton Is. = Belitung . . . . **111** 3 10S 107 50 E
Bilma . . . . **127** 18 50N 13 30 E
Biloela . . . . **121** 24 24S 150 31 E
Biloxi **169** 30 24N 88 53W
Bina-Etawah . . . . **91** 24 13N 78 14 E
Bīnālūd, Kūh-e . . . . **86** 36 30N 58 30 E
Bindi Bindi . . . . **120** 30 37S 116 22 E
Bingara . . . . **116** 29 52S 150 36 E
Bingerville **130** 5 18N 3 49W
Bingham **148** 45 5N 69 50W
Binghamton **164** 42 9N 75 54W
Binh Dinh = An Nhon . . . . **95** 13 55N 109 7 E
Binnaway . . . . **116** 31 28S 149 24 E
Binzert = Bizerte . . . . **127** 37 15N 9 50 E
Bioko . . . . **131** 3 30N 8 40 E
Bir Mogrein **126** 25 10N 11 25W
Birchip . . . . **119** 35 56S 142 55 E
Bird I. = Aves, I. de **181** 15 45N 63 55W
Birdum . . . . **114** 15 39S 133 13 E
Birkenhead **28** 53 24N 3 1W
Birmingham, U.K. **24** 52 30N 1 55W
Birmingham, U.S.A. **169** 33 31N 86 50W
Birobidzhan . . . . **75** 48 50N 132 50 E
Birr **35** 53 7N 7 55W
Bisai . . . . **106** 35 16N 136 44 E
Biscay, B. of **36** 45 0N 2 0W
Biscostasing **150** 47 18N 82 9W
Bishop Auckland **28** 54 40N 1 40W
Bishop's Stortford . . . . **25** 51 52N 0 11 E
Bismarck **163** 46 49N 100 49W
Bismarck Arch. . . . . **115** 2 30S 150 0 E
Bissagos = Bijagós,
Arquipélago dos **130** 11 15N 16 10W
Bissau **130** 11 45N 15 45W
Bitola . . . . **52** 41 5N 21 10 E
Bitolj = Bitola . . . . **52** 41 5N 21 10 E
Bitterroot Range **162** 46 0N 114 20W
Biu . . . . **131** 10 40N 12 3 E
Biwa-Ko . . . . **106** 35 15N 136 10 E
Biysk . . . . **71** 52 40N 85 0 E
Bizen . . . . **109** 34 43N 134 8 E
Bizerte . . . . **127** 37 15N 9 50 E
Bjørnøya . . . . **13** 74 30N 19 0 E
Black → = Da → . . . . **95** 21 15N 105 20 E
Black Diamond **155** 50 45N 114 14W
Black Forest = Schwarzwald . **42** 48 0N 8 0 E
Black Hills **163** 44 0N 103 50W

Black Mts. **26** 51 52N 3 5W
Black Sea . . . . **17** 43 30N 35 0 E
Blackall . . . . **121** 24 25S 145 45 E
Blackburn **28** 53 44N 2 30W
Blackpool **28** 53 48N 3 3W
Blackwater . . . . **121** 23 35S 148 53 E
Blackwater →, Meath,
Ireland **34** 53 46N 7 0W
Blackwater →, Munster,
Ireland **35** 51 55N 7 50W
Blackwater →, U.K. **34** 54 31N 6 35W
Blackwell **168** 36 55N 97 20W
Blaenau Ffestiniog **26** 53 0N 3 57W
Blagoveshchensk . . . . **75** 50 20N 127 30 E
Blair Atholl **33** 56 46N 3 50W
Blairmore **155** 49 40N 114 25W
Blanc, Mont . . . . **37** 45 48N 6 50 E
Blanca Peak **163** 37 35N 105 29W
Blanche L. . . . . **118** 29 15S 139 40 E
Blanco, C. **171** 42 50N 124 40W
Blandford Forum **24** 50 52N 2 10W
Blantyre . . . . **137** 15 45S 35 0 E
Blarney **35** 51 57N 8 35W
Blaydon **28** 54 56N 1 47W
Blayney . . . . **117** 33 32S 149 14 E
Blekinge län □ . . . . **61** 56 20N 15 20 E
Blenheim . . . . **123** 41 38S 173 57 E
Bletchley **25** 51 59N 0 44W
Blida . . . . **127** 36 30N 2 49 E
Blind River **150** 46 10N 82 58W
Blitar . . . . **111** 8 5S 112 11 E
Bloemfontein . . . . **137** 29 6S 26 14 E
Blois . . . . **36** 47 35N 1 20 E
Bloody Foreland **34** 55 10N 8 18W
Bloomington, Ill., U.S.A. **166** 40 27N 89 0W
Bloomington, Ind., U.S.A. **167** 39 10N 86 30W
Bloomsburg **164** 41 0N 76 30W
Blue Mts., Oreg., U.S.A. **171** 45 15N 119 0W
Blue Mts., Pa., U.S.A. **164** 40 30N 76 30W
Blue Nile = Nîl el Azraq → . . . **129** 15 38N 32 31 E
Blue Ridge Mts. **165** 36 30N 80 15W
Bluefield **165** 37 18N 81 14W
Bluefields **179** 12 20N 83 50W
Bluestack, mt. **34** 54 46N 8 5W
Bluff . . . . **123** 46 37S 168 20 E
Blumenau **191** 27 0S 49 0W
Blyth **28** 55 8N 1 32W
Bo **130** 7 55N 11 50W
Bo Hai . . . . **98** 39 0N 120 0 E
Boa Vista **185** 2 48N 60 30W
Boaco **179** 12 29N 85 35W
Bobadah . . . . **116** 32 19S 146 41 E
Bobcaygeon **151** 44 33N 78 33W
Bobo-Dioulasso **130** 11 8N 4 13W
Bobraomby, Tanjon' i. . . . . **137** 12 40S 49 10 E
Bobruysk . . . . **68** 53 10N 29 15 E
Bôca do Acre **187** 8 50S 67 27W
Boca Raton **170** 26 21N 80 5W
Bocas del Toro **179** 9 15N 82 20W
Bocholt . . . . **42** 51 50N 6 35 E
Bochum . . . . **42** 51 28N 7 12 E
Boden . . . . **67** 65 50N 21 42 E
Bodensee . . . . **44** 47 35N 9 25 E
Bodhan . . . . **91** 18 40N 77 44 E
Bodmin **27** 50 28N 4 44W
Bodmin Moor **27** 50 33N 4 36W
Bodø . . . . **64** 67 17N 14 24 E
Bogalusa **169** 30 50N 89 55W
Boggabilla . . . . **116** 28 36S 150 24 E
Boggabri . . . . **116** 30 45S 150 0 E
Boggeragh Mts. **35** 52 2N 8 55W
Bognor Regis **25** 50 47N 0 40W
Bogong, Mt. . . . . **117** 36 47S 147 17 E
Bogor . . . . **111** 6 36S 106 48 E
Bogota **184** 4 34N 74 0W
Boguchany . . . . **74** 58 40N 97 30 E
Bohain . . . . **38** 49 59N 3 28 E
Bohemian Forest =
Böhmerwald . . . . **43** 49 30N 12 40 E
Böhmerwald . . . . **43** 49 30N 12 40 E
Bohol . . . . **112** 9 50N 124 10 E

Name	Page	Lat°	Lat′	Long°	Long′
Bohol Sea	112	9	0N	124	0 E
Bohotleh	133	8	20N	46	25 E
Boise	162	43	43N	116	9W
Boissevain	153	49	15N	100	5W
Boké	130	10	56N	14	17W
Bolan Pass	88	29	50N	67	20 E
Bolaños, R. →	175	21	12N	104	5W
Bolbec	38	49	30N	0	30 E
Bolgatanga	130	10	44N	0	53W
Bolívar	190	36	15S	60	53W
Bolivia ■	187	17	6S	64	0W
Bollnäs	60	61	21N	16	24 E
Bollon	116	28	2S	147	29 E
Bologna	47	44	30N	11	20 E
Boloven, Cao Nguyen	95	15	10N	106	30 E
Bolsena, L. di	46	42	35N	11	55 E
Bolshevik, Ostrov	72	78	30N	102	0 E
Bolshoi Kavkas	70	42	50N	44	0 E
Bolshoy Begichev, Ostrov	72	74	20N	112	30 E
Bolsward	41	53	3N	5	32 E
Bolton	28	53	35N	2	26W
Bolzano	47	46	30N	11	20 E
Boma	134	5	50S	13	4 E
Bombala	117	36	56S	149	15 E
Bombay	91	18	55N	72	50 E
Bomu →	129	4	40N	23	30 E
Bon, C.	127	37	1N	11	2 E
Bonaire	181	12	10N	68	15W
Bonavista	149	48	40N	53	5W
Bonifacio, Bouches de	48	41	12N	9	15 E
Bonn	42	50	43N	7	6 E
Bonneval	39	48	11N	1	24 E
Bonnie Rock	120	30	29S	118	22 E
Bonny, Bight of	131	3	30N	9	20 E
Bonnyville	152	54	20N	110	45W
Bonthe	130	7	30N	12	33W
Boonah	116	27	58S	152	41 E
Boone	166	42	5N	93	53W
Boonville	167	38	3N	87	13W
Boorowa	117	34	28S	148	44 E
Boothia, Gulf of	146	71	0N	90	0W
Boothia Pen.	145	71	0N	94	0W
Bootle	28	53	28N	3	1W
Bôr	129	6	10N	31	40 E
Borås	60	57	43N	12	56 E
Borāzjān	85	29	22N	51	10 E
Bordeaux	36	44	50N	0	36W
Borders □	31	55	35N	2	50W
Bordertown	119	36	19S	140	45 E
Bordj Omar Driss	127	28	10N	6	40 E
Borger	161	35	40N	101	20W
Borja	186	4	20S	77	40W
Borlänge	60	60	29N	15	26 E
Borneo	111	1	0N	115	0 E
Bornholm	61	55	10N	15	0 E
Borujerd	84	33	55N	48	50 E
Borzya	74	50	24N	116	31 E
Boscastle	27	50	42N	4	42W
Boshan	98	36	28N	117	49 E
Bosna →	52	45	4N	18	29 E
Bosna i Hercegovina □	52	44	0N	18	0 E
Bosnia = Bosna i Hercegovina □	52	44	0N	18	0 E
Bōsō-Hantō	107	35	20N	140	20 E
Bosporus = Karadeniz Boğazı	80	41	10N	29	10 E
Bossangoa	131	6	35N	17	30 E
Bossembélé	131	5	25N	17	40 E
Bossier City	168	32	28N	93	48W
Bosten Hu	100	41	55N	87	40 E
Boston, U.K.	29	52	59N	0	2W
Boston, U.S.A.	164	42	20N	71	0W
Bothnia, G. of	67	63	0N	20	0 E
Botletle →	136	20	10S	23	15 E
Botoşani	57	47	42N	26	41 E
Botswana ■	136	22	0S	24	0 E
Botucatu	188	22	55S	48	30W
Bou Djébéha	126	18	25N	2	45W
Bouaké	130	7	40N	5	2W
Bougie = Bejaia	127	36	42N	5	2 E
Boulogne-sur-Mer	38	50	42N	1	36 E
Bourbonnais	37	46	28N	3	0 E
Bourem	130	17	0N	0	24W
Bourg-en-Bresse	37	46	13N	5	12 E
Bourges	37	47	9N	2	25 E
Bourgogne	37	47	0N	4	30 E
Bourke	116	30	8S	145	55 E
Bournemouth	24	50	43N	1	53W
Bousso	131	10	34N	16	52 E
Bouvet I. = Bouvetøya	14	54	26S	3	24 E
Bouvetøya	14	54	26S	3	24 E
Bowen	121	20	0S	148	16 E
Bowland, Forest of	28	54	0N	2	30W
Bowling Green, Ky., U.S.A.	169	37	0N	86	25W
Bowling Green, Ohio, U.S.A.	167	41	22N	83	40W
Bowling Green, C.	121	19	19S	147	25 E
Bowmanville	151	43	55N	78	41W
Bowral	117	34	26S	150	27 E
Boyle	34	53	58N	8	19W
Boyne →	34	53	43N	6	15W
Boyne City	150	45	13N	85	1W
Boyup Brook	120	33	50S	116	23 E
Bozeman	163	45	40N	111	0W
Bozen = Bolzano	47	46	30N	11	20 E
Brač	52	43	20N	16	40 E
Bracciano, L. di	46	42	8N	12	11 E
Bracebridge	151	45	2N	79	19W
Bräcke	66	62	45N	15	26 E
Brad	56	46	10N	22	50 E
Bradenton	170	27	25N	82	35W
Bradford, U.K.	28	53	47N	1	45W
Bradford, U.S.A.	164	41	58N	78	41W
Braemar	33	57	2N	3	20W
Braga	50	41	35N	8	25W
Bragança, Brazil	188	1	0S	47	2W
Bragança, Portugal	50	41	48N	6	50W
Brahmanbaria	93	23	58N	91	15 E
Brahmani →	92	20	39N	86	46 E
Brahmaputra →	93	24	2N	90	59 E
Braidwood	117	35	27S	149	49 E
Bräila	57	45	19N	27	59 E
Brainerd	156	46	20N	94	10W
Braintree	25	51	53N	0	34 E
Brampton	151	43	45N	79	45W
Branco →	185	1	20S	61	50W
Branco, Cabo	182	7	9S	34	47W
Brandenburg	43	52	24N	12	33 E
Brandon	153	49	50N	99	57W
Brantford	151	43	10N	80	15W
Brasil, Planalto	188	18	0S	46	30W
Brasília	188	15	47S	47	55 E
Braşov	57	45	38N	25	35 E
Brassey, Banjaran	111	5	0N	117	15 E
Brasstown Bald, Mt.	165	34	54N	83	45W
Bratislava	59	48	10N	17	7 E
Bratsk	74	56	10N	101	30 E
Brattleboro	164	42	53N	72	37W
Braunschweig	43	52	17N	10	28 E
Brava	133	1	20N	44	8 E
Bravo del Norte →	174	25	57N	97	9W
Brawley	173	32	58N	115	30W
Bray	35	53	12N	6	6W
Brazil	167	39	32N	87	8W
Brazil ■	188	10	0S	50	0W
Brazilian Highlands = Brasil, Planalto	188	18	0S	46	30W
Brazos →	168	28	53N	95	23W
Brazzaville	134	4	9S	15	12 E
Brčko	52	44	54N	18	46 E
Breadalbane	31	56	30N	4	15W
Bream Bay	122	35	56S	174	28 E
Brecon	26	51	57N	3	23W
Brecon Beacons	26	51	53N	3	27W
Breda	40	51	35N	4	45 E
Breiðafjörður →	64	65	15N	23	15W
Bremen	42	53	4N	8	47 E
Bremerhaven	42	53	34N	8	35 E
Bremerton	171	47	30N	122	38W
Brenham	168	30	5N	96	27W
Brentwood	25	51	37N	0	19 E
Bréscia	46	45	33N	10	13 E
Breslau = Wrocław	58	51	5N	17	5 E

Name	Page	Latitude	Longitude
Brest, France	**36**	48 24N	4 31W
Brest, U.S.S.R.	**68**	52 10N	23 40 E
Bretagne	**36**	48 0N	3 0W
Bretçu	**57**	46 7N	26 18 E
Breton Sd.	**169**	29 40N	89 12W
Brett, C.	**122**	35 10S	174 20 E
Brewer	**148**	44 43N	68 50W
Brewster	**171**	48 10N	119 51W
Brewton	**169**	31 9N	87 2W
Brezhnev	**68**	55 42N	52 19 E
Briançon	**37**	44 54N	6 39 E
Bridgend	**27**	51 30N	3 35W
Bridgeport	**164**	41 12N	73 12W
Bridgeton	**164**	39 29N	75 10W
Bridgetown, Australia	**120**	33 58S	116 7 E
Bridgetown, Barbados	**180**	13 0N	59 30W
Bridgnorth	**24**	52 33N	2 25W
Bridgwater	**27**	51 7N	3 0W
Bridlington	**29**	54 6N	0 11W
Bridport	**27**	50 43N	2 45W
Brigham City	**163**	41 30N	112 1W
Bright	**117**	36 42S	146 56 E
Brighton, Australia	**119**	42 42S	147 16 E
Brighton, U K	**25**	50 50N	0 9W
Brindisi	**49**	40 39N	17 55 E
Brisbane	**116**	27 25S	153 2 E
Bristol, U.K.	**27**	51 26N	2 35W
Bristol, Conn., U.S.A.	**164**	41 44N	72 57W
Bristol, Tenn., U.S.A.	**165**	36 36N	82 11W
Bristol B.	**142**	58 0N	160 0W
Bristol Channel	**27**	51 18N	4 30W
Bristow	**168**	35 55N	96 28W
British Columbia □	**154**	55 0N	125 15W
British Guiana = Guyana ■	**185**	5 0N	59 0W
British Honduras = Belize ■	**177**	17 0N	88 30W
British Isles	**18**	55 0N	4 0W
Brittany = Bretagne	**36**	48 0N	3 0W
Brive-la-Gaillarde	**36**	45 10N	1 32 E
Brlik	**71**	44 0N	74 5 E
Brno	**59**	49 10N	16 35 E
Broach = Bharuch	**91**	21 47N	73 0 E
Broad Law	**31**	55 30N	3 22W
Broad Sd.	**121**	22 0S	149 45 E
Broads, The	**29**	52 45N	1 30 E
Brochet	**145**	57 53N	101 40W
Brockton	**164**	42 8N	71 2W
Brockville	**151**	44 35N	75 41W
Brod	**52**	41 35N	21 17 E
Brodeur Pen.	**146**	72 30N	88 10W
Broken Hill = Kabwe	**135**	14 30S	28 29 E
Broken Hill	**118**	31 58S	141 29 E
Bromley	**25**	51 20N	0 5 E
Brookhaven	**169**	31 40N	90 25W
Brooks	**155**	50 35N	111 55W
Brooks Ra.	**142**	68 40N	147 0W
Brosna ~→	**35**	53 8N	8 0W
Brough	**28**	54 32N	2 19W
Broughty Ferry	**31**	56 29N	2 50W
Brouwershaven	**40**	51 45N	3 55 E
Brownsville	**158**	25 56N	97 25W
Brownwood	**161**	31 45N	99 0W
Bruay-en-Artois	**38**	50 29N	2 33 E
Bruce, Mt.	**114**	22 37S	118 8 E
Bruce Rock	**120**	31 52S	118 8 E
Bruck an der Leitha	**45**	48 1N	16 47 E
Bruges = Brugge	**42**	51 13N	3 13 E
Brugge	**42**	51 13N	3 13 E
Brunei = Bandar Seri Begawan	**112**	4 52N	115 0 E
Brunei ■	**111**	4 50N	115 0 E
Bruno	**152**	52 20N	105 30W
Brunswick = Braunschweig	**43**	52 17N	10 28 E
Brunswick, Ga., U.S.A.	**170**	31 10N	81 30W
Brunswick, Maine, U.S.A.	**148**	43 53N	69 50W
Bruny I.	**119**	43 20S	147 15 E
Brussel	**42**	50 51N	4 21 E
Bruthen	**117**	37 42S	147 50 E
Bruton	**27**	51 6N	2 28W
Bryan, Ohio, U.S.A.	**167**	41 30N	84 30W
Bryan, Tex., U.S.A.	**168**	30 40N	96 27W
Bryan, Mt.	**119**	33 30S	139 0 E
Bryansk	**68**	53 13N	34 25 E
Brzeg	**58**	50 52N	17 30 E
Bucaramanga	**184**	7 0N	73 0W
Buchan	**33**	57 32N	2 8W
Buchan Ness	**33**	57 29N	1 48W
Buchanan	**130**	5 57N	10 2W
Buchans	**149**	48 50N	56 52W
Bucharest = Bucureşti	**57**	44 27N	26 10 E
Buckhannon	**165**	39 2N	80 10W
Buckhaven	**31**	56 10N	3 2W
Buckingham, Canada	**151**	45 37N	75 24W
Buckingham, U.K.	**25**	52 0N	0 59W
Buckingham □	**25**	51 50N	0 55W
Buckleboo	**118**	32 54S	136 12 E
Bucureşti	**57**	44 27N	26 10 E
Bucyrus	**167**	40 48N	83 0W
Budalin	**93**	22 20N	95 10 E
Budapest	**59**	47 29N	19 5 E
Budaun	**89**	28 5N	79 10 E
Bude	**27**	50 49N	4 33W
Budgewoi Lake	**117**	33 13S	151 34 E
Buenaventura, Colombia	**184**	3 53N	77 4W
Buenaventura, Mexico	**174**	29 51N	107 29W
Buenos Aires	**190**	34 30S	58 20W
Buffalo	**164**	42 55N	78 50W
Bug ~→	**58**	52 31N	21 5 E
Buga	**184**	4 0N	76 15W
Bugun Shara	**100**	49 0N	104 0 E
Builth Wells	**26**	52 10N	3 26W
Buir Nur	**98**	47 50N	117 42 E
Bujumbura	**135**	3 16S	29 18 E
Bukachacha	**74**	52 55N	116 50 E
Bukavu	**23**	2 20S	28 52 E
Bukhara	**70**	39 48N	64 25 E
Bukit Mertajam	**96**	5 22N	100 28 E
Bukittinggi	**111**	0 20S	100 20 E
Bukoba	**135**	1 20S	31 49 E
Bukuru	**131**	9 42N	8 48 E
Bulahdelah	**117**	32 23S	152 13 E
Bulandshahr	**89**	28 28N	77 51 E
Bulawayo	**137**	20 7S	28 32 E
Bulgaria ■	**53**	42 35N	25 30 E
Bull Shoals L.	**168**	36 40N	93 5W
Bully-les-Mines	**38**	50 27N	2 44 E
Bulsar = Valsad	**91**	20 40N	72 58 E
Bulun	**72**	70 37N	127 30 E
Bunbury	**120**	33 20S	115 35 E
Buncrana	**34**	55 8N	7 28W
Bundaberg	**116**	24 54S	152 22 E
Bundi	**91**	25 30N	75 35 E
Bundoran	**34**	54 24N	8 17W
Bungo-Suidō	**109**	33 0N	132 15 E
Buorkhaya, Mys	**72**	71 50N	132 40 E
Bûr Sa'îd	**128**	31 16N	32 18 E
Bûr Sûdân	**129**	19 32N	37 9 E
Buraymī, Al Wāḥāt al	**83**	24 10N	55 43 E
Burbank	**173**	34 9N	118 23W
Burdur	**80**	37 45N	30 22 E
Burdwan = Barddhaman	**92**	23 14N	87 39 E
Burgas	**53**	42 33N	27 29 E
Burgenland □	**45**	47 20N	16 20 E
Burgos	**50**	42 21N	3 41W
Burgundy = Bourgogne	**37**	47 0N	4 30 E
Burin	**149**	47 1N	55 14W
Burkina Faso ■	**130**	12 0N	1 0W
Burlington, Canada	**151**	43 18N	79 45W
Burlington, Iowa, U.S.A.	**166**	40 50N	91 5W
Burlington, N.C., U.S.A.	**165**	36 7N	79 27W
Burlington, N.J., U.S.A.	**164**	40 5N	74 50W
Burlington, Vt., U.S.A.	**151**	44 27N	73 14W
Burma ■	**93**	21 0N	96 30 E
Burnie	**119**	41 4S	145 56 E
Burnley	**28**	53 47N	2 15W
Burns	**171**	43 40N	119 4W
Burns Lake	**154**	54 20N	125 45W
Burra	**119**	33 40S	138 55 E
Bursa	**80**	40 15N	29 5 E
Burton-upon-Trent	**28**	52 48N	1 39W
Buru	**113**	3 30S	126 30 E
Burundi ■	**135**	3 15S	30 0 E
Bury	**28**	53 36N	2 19W

Name	Page	Latitude	Longitude
Bury St. Edmunds	25	52 15N	0 42 E
Buryat A.S.S.R. □	74	53 0N	110 0 E
Buskerud fylke □	60	60 13N	9 0 E
Busselton	120	33 42S	115 15 E
Bussum	40	52 16N	5 10 E
Bute	30	55 48N	5 2W
Butiaba	132	1 50N	31 20 E
Butler	164	40 52N	79 52W
Butte	163	46 0N	112 31W
Butterworth	96	5 24N	100 23 E
Butuan	112	8 57N	125 33 E
Butung	113	5 0S	122 45 E
Buxton	28	53 16N	1 54W
Buyaga	74	59 50N	127 0 E
Buzău	57	45 10N	26 50 E
Buzen	108	33 35N	131 5 E
Buzzards Bay	164	41 45N	70 38W
Bydgoszcz	58	53 10N	18 0 E
Byelorussian S.S.R. □	68	53 30N	27 0 E
Bylot I.	146	73 13N	78 34W
Byrd Land	15	79 30S	125 0W
Byron Bay	116	28 43S	153 37 E
Byrranga, Gory	72	75 0N	100 0 E
Bytom	58	50 25N	18 54 E
Cabimas	184	10 23N	71 25W
Cabinda	134	5 33S	12 11 E
Cabinda □	134	5 0S	12 30 E
Cabo Pantoja	184	1 0S	75 10W
Cabonga, Réservoir	151	47 20N	76 40W
Caboolture	116	27 5S	152 58 E
Cabora Bassa Dam	137	15 20S	32 50 E
Caborca	174	30 40N	112 10W
Cabot Strait	149	47 15N	59 40W
Cabrera, I.	51	39 8N	2 57 E
Cabri	152	50 35N	108 25W
Čačak	52	43 54N	20 20 E
Cáceres	50	39 26N	6 23W
Cache Bay	151	46 22N	80 0W
Cachoeira	189	12 30S	39 0W
Cachoeira de Itapemirim	189	20 51S	41 7W
Cachoeira do Sul	191	30 3S	52 53W
Cader Idris	26	52 43N	3 56W
Cadibarrawirracanna, L.	118	28 52S	135 27 E
Cadillac, Canada	151	48 14N	78 23W
Cadillac, U.S.A.	167	44 16N	85 25W
Cádiz	50	36 30N	6 20W
Cádiz, G. de	50	36 40N	7 0W
Caen	36	49 10N	0 22W
Caernarfon	26	53 8N	4 17W
Caernarfon B.	26	53 4N	4 40W
Caernarvon = Caernarfon	26	53 8N	4 17W
Caerphilly	27	51 34N	3 13W
Cagayan de Oro	112	8 30N	124 40 E
Cágliari	48	39 15N	9 6 E
Caguas	180	18 14N	66 4W
Caha Mts.	35	51 45N	9 40W
Caher	35	52 23N	7 56W
Cahors	36	44 27N	1 27 E
Cahuapanas	186	5 15S	77 0W
Caibarién	178	22 30N	79 30W
Caicos Is.	180	21 40N	71 40W
Cairngorm Mts.	33	57 6N	3 42W
Cairns	121	16 57S	145 45 E
Cairo = El Qâhira	128	30 1N	31 14 E
Cairo	169	37 0N	89 10W
Cajamarca	186	7 5S	78 28W
Calabar	131	4 57N	8 20 E
Calabozo	184	9 0N	67 28W
Calàbria □	49	39 24N	16 30 E
Calais, France	38	50 57N	1 56 E
Calais, U.S.A.	148	45 11N	67 20W
Calama, Brazil	187	8 0S	62 50W
Calama, Chile	190	22 30S	68 55W
Calamar	184	10 15N	74 55W
Calamian Group	112	11 50N	119 55 E
Calca	187	13 22S	72 0W
Calcutta	92	22 36N	88 24 E
Caldwell	171	43 45N	116 42W
Calgary	155	51 0N	114 10W
Cali	184	3 25N	76 35W
Calicut	90	11 15N	75 43 E
California □	172	37 25N	120 0W
California, Golfo de	174	28 0N	112 0W
Callander	31	56 15N	4 14W
Callao	186	12 0S	77 0W
Caloundra	116	26 45S	153 10 E
Caltanissetta	49	37 30N	14 3 E
Cam Lam	95	11 54N	109 10 E
Cam Ranh	95	11 54N	109 12 E
Camagüey	178	21 20N	78 0W
Camaná	186	16 30S	72 50W
Camargue	37	43 34N	4 34 E
Camarones	192	44 50S	65 40W
Cambay = Khambhat	91	22 23N	72 33 E
Cambodia ■	95	12 15N	105 0 E
Camborne	27	50 13N	5 18W
Cambrai	38	50 11N	3 14 E
Cambrian Mts.	26	52 25N	3 52W
Cambridge, Canada	151	43 23N	80 15W
Cambridge, N.Z.	122	37 54S	175 29 E
Cambridge, U.K.	25	52 13N	0 8 E
Cambridge, Mass., U.S.A.	164	42 20N	71 8W
Cambridge, Md., U.S.A.	164	38 33N	76 2W
Cambridge, Ohio, U.S.A.	167	40 1N	81 35W
Cambridge Bay	145	69 10N	105 0W
Cambridge Gulf	114	14 55S	128 15 E
Cambridgeshire □	25	52 12N	0 7 E
Camden, Ark., U.S.A.	168	33 40N	92 50W
Camden, N.J., U.S.A.	164	39 57N	75 7W
Camden, S.C., U.S.A.	165	34 17N	80 34W
Cameroon ■	131	6 0N	12 30 E
Cameroun, Mt.	131	4 13N	9 10 E
Cametá	188	2 12S	49 30W
Camiri	187	20 3S	63 31W
Camocim	189	2 55S	40 50W
Campagna	46	40 40N	15 5 E
Campania □	49	40 50N	14 45 E
Campbell I.	15	52 30S	169 0 E
Campbell River	154	50 5N	125 20W
Campbellton	148	47 57N	66 43W
Campbelltown, Australia	117	34 4S	150 49 E
Campbeltown, U.K.	30	57 34N	4 2W
Campeche	177	19 51N	90 32W
Campeche □	177	19 0N	90 30W
Campeche, B. de	177	20 0N	94 0W
Camperdown	119	38 14S	143 9 E
Camperville	153	51 59N	100 9W
Campina Grande	189	7 20S	35 47W
Campinas	188	22 50S	47 0W
Campo Grande	188	20 25S	54 40W
Campos	188	21 50S	41 20W
Camrose	155	53 0N	112 50W
Can Tho	95	10 2N	105 46 E
Canada ■	139	60 0N	100 0W
Cañada de Gómez	190	32 40S	61 30W
Canadian →	158	35 27N	95 3W
Çanakkale Boğazı	80	40 0N	26 0 E
Cananea	174	30 57N	110 18W
Canarias, Islas	126	28 30N	16 0W
Canary Is. = Canarias, Islas	126	28 30N	16 0W
Canaveral, C.	170	28 28N	80 31W
Canberra	117	35 15S	149 8 E
Candala	133	11 30N	49 58 E
Candia = Iráklion	55	35 20N	25 12 E
Canea = Khaniá	55	35 30N	24 4 E
Çankırı	80	40 40N	33 37 E
Canmore	155	51 7N	115 18W
Canna	32	57 3N	6 33W
Cannanore	90	11 53N	75 27 E
Cannes	37	43 32N	7 0 E
Cannock	28	52 42N	2 2W
Canora	152	51 40N	102 30W
Canowindra	117	33 35S	148 38 E
Canso	149	45 20N	61 0W
Cantabrian Mts. = Cantábrica, Cordillera	50	43 0N	5 10W
Cantábrica, Cordillera	50	43 0N	5 10W
Canterbury	25	51 17N	1 5 E
Canterbury □	123	43 45S	171 19 E

Name	Page	Lat°	Lat′	N/S	Lon°	Lon′	E/W
Canterbury Bight	123	44	16S	171	55 E
Canterbury Plains	123	43	55S	171	22 E
Canton = Guangzhou	99	23	5N	113	10 E
Canton, Ill., U.S.A.	166	40	32N	90	0W
Canton, Miss., U.S.A.	169	32	40N	90	1W
Canton, Ohio, U.S.A.	167	40	47N	81	22W
Canutama	185	6	30S	64	20W
Cap-Chat	148	49	6N	66	40W
Cap-de-la-Madeleine	151	46	22N	72	31W
Cap-Haïtien	180	19	40N	72	20W
Cape Barren I.	119	40	25S	148	15 E
Cape Breton I.	149	46	0N	60	30W
Cape Coast	130	5	5N	1	15W
Cape Dorset	146	64	14N	76	32W
Cape Fear →	165	34	30N	78	25W
Cape Girardeau	169	37	20N	89	30W
Cape May	164	39	1N	74	53W
Cape Montague	149	46	5N	62	25W
Cape Province □	136	32	0S	23	0 E
Cape Town	136	33	55S	18	22 E
Cape Verde Is. ■	9	17	10N	25	20W
Cape York Peninsula	115	12	0S	142	30 E
Caquetá →	184	1	15S	69	15W
Caracal	57	44	8N	24	22 E
Caracas	184	10	30N	66	55W
Caratinga	188	19	50S	42	10W
Carberry	153	49	50N	99	25W
Carbonara, C.	48	39	8N	9	30 E
Carbondale	166	37	45N	89	10W
Carbonear	149	47	42N	53	13W
Carcassonne	37	43	13N	2	20 E
Carcross	144	60	13N	134	45W
Cárdenas, Cuba	178	23	0N	81	30W
Cárdenas, Mexico	177	21	0N	99	40W
Cardiff	27	51	28N	3	11W
Cardigan	26	52	6N	4	41W
Cardigan B.	26	52	30N	4	30W
Cardston	155	49	15N	113	20W
Cardwell	121	18	14S	146	2 E
Caribbean Sea	181	15	0N	75	0W
Cariboo Mts.	155	53	0N	121	0W
Caribou	148	46	55N	68	0W
Caribou Mts.	145	59	12N	115	40W
Carinhanha	188	14	15S	44	46W
Carinthia □ = Kärnten □ ...	45	46	52N	13	30 E
Carlisle, U.K.	28	54	54N	2	55W
Carlisle, U.S.A.	164	40	12N	77	10W
Carlow	35	52	50N	6	58W
Carlow □	35	52	43N	6	50W
Carlsbad, Calif., U.S.A.	173	33	11N	117	25W
Carlsbad, N. Mex., U.S.A.	161	32	20N	104	14W
Carlyle	152	49	40N	102	20W
Carmacks	144	62	5N	136	16W
Carman	153	49	30N	98	0W
Carmarthen	26	51	52N	4	20W
Carmarthen B.	27	51	40N	4	30W
Carnarvon	120	24	51S	113	42 E
Carnegie, L.	114	26	5S	122	30 E
Carniche, Alpi	47	46	36N	13	0 E
Carnsore Pt.	35	52	10N	6	20W
Caroline Is.	122	8	0N	150	0 E
Caroona	116	31	24S	150	26 E
Carpathians, Mts.	17	49	50N	21	0 E
Carpații Meridionali	57	45	30N	25	0 E
Carpentaria, G. of	115	14	0S	139	0 E
Carrara	46	44	5N	10	7 E
Carrick-on-Shannon	34	53	57N	8	7W
Carrick-on-Suir	35	52	22N	7	30W
Carrickfergus	34	54	43N	5	50W
Carrickmacross	34	54	0N	6	43W
Carroll	166	42	2N	94	55W
Carrollton	170	33	36N	85	5W
Carse of Gowrie	31	56	30N	3	10W
Carson City	172	39	12N	119	46W
Carstairs	31	55	42N	3	41W
Cartagena, Colombia	184	10	25N	75	33W
Cartagena, Spain	51	37	38N	0	59W
Cartago, Colombia	184	4	45N	75	55W
Cartago, C. Rica	179	9	50N	85	52W
Cartersville	169	34	11N	84	48W
Carthage	168	37	10N	94	20W
Cartwright	147	53	41N	56	58W
Caruaru	189	8	15S	35	55W
Carúpano	185	10	39N	63	15W
Caruthersville	169	36	10N	89	40W
Carvin	38	50	30N	2	57 E
Casablanca	126	33	36N	7	36W
Casas Grandes	174	30	22N	107	57W
Cascade Ra.	171	47	0N	121	30W
Casilda	190	33	10S	61	10W
Casino	116	28	52S	153	3 E
Casiquiare →	184	2	1N	67	7W
Casma	186	9	30S	78	20W
Casper	163	42	52N	106	20W
Caspian Sea	70	43	0N	50	0 E
Cassiar Mts.	144	59	30N	130	30W
Castellón de la Plana	51	39	58N	0	3W
Castelsarrasin	36	44	2N	1	7 E
Casterton	119	37	30S	141	30 E
Castilla La Nueva	50	39	45N	3	20W
Castilla La Vieja	50	41	55N	4	0W
Castle Douglas	31	54	57N	3	57W
Castlebar	34	53	52N	9	17W
Castleblaney	34	54	7N	6	44W
Castlegar	155	49	20N	117	40W
Castlemaine	117	37	2S	144	12 E
Castlereagh →	34	53	47N	8	30W
Castleton	28	58	35N	3	22W
Castletown Bearhaven	35	51	40N	9	54W
Castor	155	52	15N	111	50W
Castres	37	43	37N	2	13 E
Castricum	40	52	33N	4	40 E
Castries	180	14	0N	60	50W
Castro	192	42	30S	73	50W
Cat I.	178	24	30N	75	30W
Catacáos	186	5	20S	80	45W
Catalonia = Cataluña □	51	41	40N	1	15 E
Cataluña □	51	41	40N	1	15 E
Catamarca	190	28	30S	65	50W
Catanduanes	112	13	50N	124	20 E
Catánia	49	37	31N	15	4 E
Catanzaro	49	38	54N	16	38 E
Catoche, C.	177	21	35N	87	5W
Catskill Mts.	164	42	15N	74	15W
Cauca →	184	8	54N	74	28W
Caucasus Mts. = Bolshoi Kavkas	70	42	50N	44	0 E
Caudry	38	50	7N	3	22 E
Cauquenes	190	36	0S	72	22W
Cavaillon	37	43	50N	5	2 E
Cavan	34	54	0N	7	22W
Cawnpore = Kanpur	91	26	28N	80	20 E
Caxias	188	4	55S	43	20W
Caxias do Sul	191	29	10S	51	10W
Cayenne	185	5	0N	52	18W
Cayes, Les	180	18	15N	73	46W
Cayman Is.	178	19	40N	80	30W
Ceanannus Mor	34	53	42N	6	53W
Ceará = Fortaleza	189	3	45S	38	35W
Ceará □	189	5	0S	40	0W
Cebu	112	10	18N	123	54 E
Cedar →	166	41	17N	91	21W
Cedar City	162	37	41N	113	3W
Cedar Falls	166	42	39N	92	29W
Cedar L.	152	53	10N	100	0W
Cedar Rapids	166	42	0N	91	38W
Cedartown	169	34	1N	85	15W
Ceduna	118	32	7S	133	46 E
Cegléd	59	47	11N	19	47 E
Ceiba, La	179	15	40N	86	50W
Celaya	177	20	31N	100	37W
Celebes = Sulawesi □	113	2	0S	120	0 E
Celebes Sea	113	3	0N	123	0 E
Center	168	31	50N	94	10W
Centerville	166	40	45N	92	57W
Central □	31	56	10N	4	30W
Central, Cordillera	184	5	0N	75	0W
Central African Republic ■	129	7	0N	20	0 E
Central Auckland □	122	37	30S	175	30 E
Central Makran Range	88	26	30N	64	15 E
Central Russian Uplands	17	54	0N	36	0 E
Central Siberian Plateau	77	65	0N	105	0 E

Name	Page	Lat	Long
Centralia	166	38 32N	89 5W
Cephalonia = Kefallinía	54	38 20N	20 30 E
Ceram = Seram	113	3 10S	129 0 E
Ceram Sea = Seram Sea	113	2 30S	128 30 E
Cerignola	49	41 17N	15 53 E
Cerigo = Kíthira	55	36 9N	23 0 E
Cerritos	177	22 26N	100 17W
Cesena	47	44 9N	12 14 E
Ceskomoravská Vrchovina	59	49 30N	15 40 E
Cesky Těšin	59	49 45N	18 39 E
Cessnock	117	32 50S	151 21 E
Cetinje	52	42 23N	18 59 E
Ceuta	126	35 52N	5 18W
Cévennes	37	44 10N	3 50 E
Ceylon = Sri Lanka ■	90	7 30N	80 50 E
Chachapoyas	186	6 15S	77 50W
Chachoengsao	95	13 42N	101 5 E
Chad ■	131	15 0N	17 15 E
Chad, L. = Tchad, L.	131	13 30N	14 30 E
Chadron	163	42 50N	103 0W
Chagos Arch.	76	6 0S	72 0 E
Chāh Bahār	85	25 20N	60 40 E
Chakradharpur	92	22 45N	85 40 E
Chala	186	15 48S	74 20W
Chalcis = Khalkís	55	38 27N	23 42 E
Chalhuanca	186	14 15S	73 15W
Chalisgaon	91	20 30N	75 10 E
Challapata	187	18 53S	66 50W
Chalon-sur-Saône	37	46 48N	4 50 E
Châlons-sur-Marne	37	48 58N	4 20 E
Chambal —►	91	26 29N	79 15 E
Chambersburg	164	39 53N	77 41W
Chambéry	37	45 34N	5 55 E
Chamonix	37	45 55N	6 51 E
Champagne	37	49 0N	4 40 E
Champaign	167	40 8N	88 14W
Champlain, L.	151	44 30N	73 20W
Chañaral	190	26 23S	70 40W
Chandigarh	89	30 43N	76 47 E
Chandler	118	27 0S	133 19 E
Chang Jiang —►	99	31 48N	121 10 E
Changchiak'ou = Zhangjiakou	98	40 48N	114 55 E
Ch'angchou = Changzhou	99	31 47N	119 58 E
Changchun	98	43 57N	125 17 E
Changde	99	29 4N	111 35 E
Shanghai = Shanghai	99	31 15N	121 26 E
Changsha	99	28 12N	113 0 E
Changzhi	98	36 10N	113 6 E
Changzhou	99	31 47N	119 58 E
Channel Is.	36	49 30N	2 40W
Channel-Port aux Basques	149	47 30N	59 9W
Chanthaburi	95	12 38N	102 12 E
Chantilly	39	49 12N	2 29 E
Chanute	166	37 45N	95 25W
Chao Phraya —►	94	13 32N	100 36 E
Ch'aoan	99	23 41N	116 33 E
Chapala, L. de	175	20 15N	103 0W
Chapayevsk	68	53 0N	49 40 E
Chapel Hill	165	35 53N	79 3W
Chapleau	150	47 50N	83 24W
Charagua	187	19 45S	63 10W
Charaña	187	17 30S	69 25W
Chard	27	50 52N	2 59W
Chardzhou	70	39 6N	63 34 E
Chari —►	131	12 58N	14 31 E
Chārīkār	87	35 0N	69 10 E
Charleroi	42	50 24N	4 27 E
Charles, C.	165	37 10N	75 59W
Charles City	166	43 2N	92 41W
Charleston, S.C., U.S.A.	170	32 47N	79 56W
Charleston, W. Va., U.S.A.	165	38 24N	81 36W
Charleville = Rath Luirc	35	52 21N	8 40W
Charleville	116	26 24S	146 15 E
Charleville-Mézières	37	49 44N	4 40 E
Charlotte, Mich., U.S.A.	167	42 36N	84 48W
Charlotte, N.C., U.S.A.	165	35 16N	80 46W
Charlotte Amalie	180	18 22N	64 56W
Charlotte Harbor	170	26 58N	82 4W
Charlottenburg	43	52 31N	13 15 E
Charlottesville	165	38 1N	78 30W
Charlottetown	149	46 14N	63 8W
Charlton, Australia	117	36 16S	143 24 E
Charlton, U.S.A.	166	40 59N	93 20W
Charters Towers	121	20 5S	146 13 E
Chartres	39	48 29N	1 30 E
Chascomús	191	35 30S	58 0W
Château-du-Loir	39	47 40N	0 25 E
Château-Thierry	39	49 3N	3 20 E
Châteaubriant	36	47 43N	1 23W
Châteaudun	39	48 3N	1 20 E
Châteauroux	37	46 50N	1 40 E
Châtellerault	36	46 50N	0 30 E
Chatham, N.B., Canada	148	47 2N	65 28W
Chatham, Ont., Canada	141	42 24N	82 11W
Chatham, U.K.	25	51 22N	0 32 E
Chatta-Hantō	106	34 45N	136 55 E
Chattahoochee —►	170	30 43N	84 51W
Chattanooga	169	35 2N	85 17W
Chaumont	37	48 7N	5 8 E
Chauny	38	49 37N	3 12 E
Cheboksary	68	56 8N	47 12 E
Cheboygan	150	45 38N	84 29W
Checheno-Ingush A.S.S.R. □	70	43 30N	45 29 E
Chegdomyn	75	51 7N	133 1 E
Chegga	126	25 27N	5 40W
Chehalis	171	46 44N	122 59W
Cheju Do	99	33 29N	126 34 E
Chekiang = Zhejiang □	99	29 0N	120 0 E
Chelforó	190	39 0S	66 33W
Chelkar Tengiz, Solonchak	70	48 0N	62 30 E
Chełm	58	51 8N	23 30 E
Chełmża	58	53 10N	18 39 E
Cheltenham	24	51 55N	2 5W
Chelyabinsk	71	55 10N	61 24 E
Chemainus	154	48 55N	123 42W
Chemnitz = Karl-Marx-Stadt	43	50 50N	12 55 E
Chemult	171	43 14N	121 47W
Chen, Gora	73	65 16N	141 50 E
Chencha	132	6 15N	37 32 E
Chenchiang = Zhenjiang	99	32 11N	119 26 E
Chengchou = Zhengzhou	99	34 45N	113 34 E
Chengde	98	40 59N	117 58 E
Chengdu	99	30 38N	104 2 E
Ch'engtu = Chengdu	99	30 38N	104 2 E
Cheo Reo	95	13 25N	108 28 E
Chepstow	27	51 38N	2 40W
Cher —►	36	47 21N	0 29 E
Cherbourg	36	49 39N	1 40W
Cheremkhovo	74	53 8N	103 1 E
Cherepovets	68	59 5N	37 55 E
Cherkassy	68	49 27N	32 4 E
Chernigov	68	51 28N	31 20 E
Chernovtsy	68	48 15N	25 52 E
Chernoye	72	70 30N	89 10 E
Cherokee	166	42 40N	95 30W
Cherrapunji	93	25 17N	91 47 E
Cherskiy	73	68 45N	161 18 E
Cherskogo Khrebet	73	65 0N	143 0 E
Cherwell —►	25	51 46N	1 18W
Chesapeake	165	36 43N	76 15W
Chesapeake Bay	165	38 0N	76 12W
Cheshire □	28	53 14N	2 30W
Cheshskaya Guba	69	67 20N	47 0 E
Chester, U.K.	28	53 12N	2 53W
Chester, Pa., U.S.A.	164	39 54N	75 20W
Chester, S.C., U.S.A.	165	34 44N	81 13W
Chesterfield	28	53 14N	1 26W
Chesterfield Inlet	145	63 30N	90 45W
Chetumal	177	18 30N	88 18W
Cheviot, The	31	55 29N	2 8W
Cheviot Hills	31	55 20N	2 30W
Chew Bahir	132	4 40N	36 50 E
Cheyenne	163	41 9N	104 49W
Cheyenne —►	163	44 40N	101 15W
Chhapra	92	25 48N	84 44 E
Chiamussu = Jiamusi	98	46 40N	130 26 E
Chiang Mai	94	18 47N	98 59 E
Chiapa —►	177	16 42N	93 0W
Chiapas □	177	16 30N	92 30W
Chiba	107	35 30N	140 7 E
Chibougamau	151	49 56N	74 24W

Place	Map	Lat	Long
Chicago	167	41 53N	87 40W
Chicago Heights	167	41 29N	87 37W
Chichagof I.	143	58 0N	136 0W
Chichester	25	50 50N	0 47W
Chichibu	107	36 5N	139 10 E
Ch'ich'ihaerh = Qiqihar	98	47 26N	124 0 E
Chiclayo	186	6 42S	79 50W
Chico	172	39 45N	121 54W
Chicopee	164	42 6N	72 37W
Chicoutimi	148	48 28N	71 5W
Chidambaram	90	11 20N	79 45 E
Chidley C.	146	60 23N	64 26W
Chigasaki	107	35 19N	139 24 E
Chihli, G. of = Bo Hai	98	39 0N	120 0 E
Chihuahua	174	28 38N	106 5W
Chihuahua □	174	28 30N	106 0W
Chikugo	108	33 14N	130 28 E
Chilapa	177	17 40N	99 11W
Childress	161	34 30N	100 15W
Chile ■	190	35 0S	72 0W
Chilin = Jilin	98	43 44N	126 30 E
Chilka L.	92	19 40N	85 25 E
Chillán	190	36 40S	72 10W
Chillicothe, Mo., U.S.A.	166	30 46N	93 30W
Chillicothe, Ohio, U.S.A.	167	39 20N	82 58W
Chilliwack	154	49 10N	121 54W
Chiloé, I. de	192	42 30S	73 50W
Chilpancingo	177	17 30N	99 30W
Chiltern Hills	25	51 44N	0 42W
Chimborazo	184	1 29S	78 55W
Chimbote	186	9 0S	78 35W
Chimkent	71	42 18N	69 36 E
Chin □	93	22 0N	93 0 E
China ■	79	30 0N	110 0 E
Chinan = Jinan	98	36 38N	117 1 E
Chinandega	179	12 35N	87 12W
Chincha Alta	186	13 25S	76 7W
Chinchilla	116	26 45S	150 38 E
Chinchou = Jinzhou	98	41 5N	121 3 E
Chindwin →	93	21 26N	95 15 E
Ch'ingtao = Qingdao	98	36 5N	120 20 E
Chinju	98	35 12N	128 2 E
Chinnampo	98	38 52N	125 10 E
Chino	107	35 59N	138 9 E
Chinon	36	47 10N	0 15 E
Chippenham	24	51 27N	2 7W
Chippewa Falls	166	44 55N	91 22W
Chiquián	186	10 10S	77 0W
Chiquimula	177	14 51N	89 37W
Chiquinquira	184	5 37N	73 50W
Chirala	90	15 50N	80 26 E
Chirchik	71	41 29N	69 35 E
Chita	74	52 0N	113 35 E
Chitral	89	35 50N	71 56 E
Chitré	179	7 59N	80 27W
Chittagong	93	22 19N	91 48 E
Chittagong □	93	24 5N	91 0 E
Chivilcoy	190	34 55S	60 0W
Chkalov = Orenburg	70	51 45N	55 6 E
Chōfu	107	35 39N	139 33 E
Choix	174	26 43N	108 17W
Chojnice	58	53 42N	17 32 E
Cholet	36	47 4N	0 52W
Choluteca	179	13 20N	87 14W
Chon Buri	95	13 21N	101 1 E
Chongjin	98	41 47N	129 50 E
Chŏngju	98	36 39N	127 27 E
Chongqing	99	29 35N	106 25 E
Chŏnju	98	35 50N	127 4 E
Chonos, Arch. de los	192	45 0S	75 0W
Chorley	28	53 39N	2 39W
Chorzów	58	50 18N	18 57 E
Chōshi	107	35 45N	140 51 E
Christchurch, N.Z.	123	43 33S	172 47 E
Christchurch, U.K.	24	50 44N	1 33W
Christianshåb	147	68 50N	51 18W
Christmas I. = Kiritimati	123	1 58N	157 27W
Christmas I.	111	10 30S	105 40 E
Ch'uanchou = Quanzhou	99	24 55N	118 34 E
Chūbu □	106	36 45N	137 30 E
Chubut →	192	43 20S	65 5W
Chūgoku □	109	35 0N	133 0 E
Chūgoku-Sanchi	109	35 0N	133 0 E
Chukotskiy Khrebet	73	68 0N	175 0 E
Chukotskoye More	73	68 0N	175 0W
Chula Vista	173	32 39N	117 8W
Chulman	74	56 52N	124 52 E
Chulucanas	186	5 8S	80 10W
Chumikan	75	54 40N	135 10 E
Chumphon	94	10 35N	99 14 E
Chunchŏn	98	37 58N	127 44 E
Chungking = Chongqing	99	29 35N	106 25 E
Chuquibamba	186	15 47S	72 44W
Chur	44	46 52N	9 32 E
Churchill →, Man., Canada	143	58 47N	94 12W
Churchill →, Nfld., Canada	147	53 19N	60 10W
Churchill, C.	143	58 46N	93 12W
Churchill Falls	147	53 36N	64 19W
Churchill Pk.	144	58 10N	125 10W
Churu	89	28 20N	74 50 E
Chuvash A.S.S.R. □	68	55 30N	47 0 E
Chuxiong	101	25 2N	101 28 E
Cicero	167	41 48N	87 48W
Ciego de Avila	178	21 50N	78 50W
Ciénaga	184	11 1N	74 15W
Cienfuegos	178	22 10N	80 30W
Cimarron →	161	36 10N	96 17W
Cincinnati	167	39 10N	84 26W
Cinto, Mt.	36	42 24N	8 54 E
Ciotat, La	37	43 12N	5 36 E
Circle	142	65 50N	144 10W
Circleville	167	39 35N	82 57W
Cirebon	111	6 45S	108 32 E
Cirencester	24	51 43N	1 59W
Citlaltépetl, Volcán	177	19 1N	97 16W
Ciudad Acuña	174	29 20N	100 58W
Ciudad Bolívar	185	8 5N	63 36W
Ciudad Camargo, Chihuahua, Mexico	174	27 40N	105 10W
Ciudad Camargo, Tamaulipas, Mexico	176	26 19N	98 50W
Ciudad de Valles	177	21 59N	99 1W
Ciudad del Carmen	177	18 38N	91 50W
Ciudad Guayana	185	8 0N	62 30W
Ciudad Guzmán	175	19 41N	103 29W
Ciudad Juárez	174	31 44N	106 29W
Ciudad Madero	177	22 16N	97 50W
Ciudad Mante	177	22 44N	98 57W
Ciudad Obregón	174	27 29N	109 56W
Ciudad Real	50	38 59N	3 55W
Ciudad Rodrigo	50	40 35N	6 32W
Ciudad Trujillo = Santo Domingo	180	18 30N	64 54W
Ciudad Victoria	177	23 44N	99 8W
Civril	80	38 20N	29 43 E
Cizre	81	37 19N	42 10 E
Clare	119	33 50S	138 37 E
Clare □	35	52 20N	9 0W
Clare →	35	53 22N	9 5W
Clare I.	34	53 48N	10 0W
Claremont	164	43 23N	72 20W
Claremore	168	36 40N	95 37W
Claremorris	34	53 45N	9 0W
Claresholm	155	50 0N	113 33W
Clark Fork →	162	48 9N	116 15W
Clarksburg	164	39 18N	80 21W
Clarksdale	169	34 12N	90 33W
Clarkston	171	46 28N	117 2W
Clarksville	169	36 32N	87 20W
Clear, C.	20	51 26N	9 30W
Clearwater, Canada	155	51 38N	120 2W
Clearwater, U.S.A.	170	27 58N	82 45W
Cleburne	168	32 18N	97 25W
Clee Hills	24	52 26N	2 35W
Cleethorpes	29	53 33N	0 2W
Cleeve Hill	24	51 54N	2 0W
Clermont, Australia	121	22 49S	147 39 E
Clermont, France	39	49 23N	2 24 E
Clermont-Ferrand	37	45 46N	3 4 E
Clevedon	27	51 26N	2 52W
Cleveland, Miss., U.S.A.	169	33 43N	90 43W
Cleveland, Ohio, U.S.A.	167	41 28N	81 43W

Cleveland, Tenn., U.S.A.	**169**	35	9N	84 52W
Cleveland, Tex., U.S.A.	**169**	30	18N	95 0W
Cleveland □	**29**	54	35N	1 8 E
Cleveleys	**28**	53	52N	3 3W
Clew B.	**34**	53	54N	9 50W
Clifton Beach	**121**	16	46S	145 39 E
Clifton Forge	**165**	37	49N	79 51W
Clinton, Canada	**150**	43	37N	81 32W
Clinton, Iowa, U.S.A.	**166**	41	50N	90 12W
Clinton, Mass., U.S.A.	**164**	42	26N	71 40W
Clinton, Mo., U.S.A.	**166**	38	20N	93 46W
Clinton, Okla., U.S.A.	**161**	35	30N	99 0W
Clinton, S.C., U.S.A.	**165**	34	30N	81 54W
Clinton Colden L.	**145**	63	58N	107 27W
Clonakilty	**35**	51	37N	8 53W
Cloncurry	**115**	20	40S	140 28 E
Clones	**34**	54	10N	7 13W
Clonmel	**35**	52	22N	7 42W
Clovis	**161**	34	20N	103 10W
Cluj-Napoca	**56**	46	47N	23 38 E
Clunes	**117**	37	20S	143 45 E
Clwyd □	**26**	53	5N	3 20W
Clyde ⟶	**31**	55	56N	4 29W
Clyde, Firth of	**30**	55	20N	5 0W
Clydebank	**31**	55	54N	4 25W
Coahuila □	**174**	27	20N	102 0W
Coaldale	**155**	49	45N	112 35W
Coalinga	**173**	36	10N	120 21W
Coalville	**29**	52	43N	1 21W
Coast Mts.	**144**	55	0N	129 0W
Coast Ranges	**173**	41	0N	123 0W
Coatbridge	**31**	55	52N	4 2W
Coatepeque	**177**	14	46N	91 55W
Coats I.	**146**	62	30N	83 0W
Coats Land	**14**	77	0S	25 0W
Coatzacoalcos	**177**	18	9N	94 25W
Cobalt	**151**	47	25N	79 42W
Cobán	**177**	15	30N	90 21W
Cobar	**116**	31	27S	145 48 E
Cóbh	**35**	51	50N	8 18W
Cobham	**118**	30	18S	142 7 E
Cobourg	**151**	43	58N	78 10W
Cobram	**117**	35	54S	145 40 E
Cocanada = Kakinada	**92**	16	57N	82 11 E
Cochabamba	**187**	17	26S	66 10W
Cochin China = Nam-Phan	**95**	10	30N	106 0 E
Cochran	**170**	32	25N	83 23W
Cochrane	**151**	49	0N	81 0W
Cockburn, Canal	**192**	54	30S	72 0W
Coco ⟶	**179**	15	0N	83 8W
Coco Chan.	**94**	13	50N	93 25 E
Cocos Is.	**111**	12	10S	96 55 E
Cod, C.	**164**	42	8N	70 10W
Codajás	**185**	3	55S	62 0W
Codó	**185**	4	30S	43 55W
Cœur d'Alene	**171**	47	45N	116 51W
Coffs Harbour	**116**	30	16S	153 5 E
Cohoes	**164**	42	47N	73 42W
Cohuna	**117**	35	45S	144 15 E
Coiba, I.	**179**	7	30N	81 40W
Coihaique	**192**	45	30S	71 45W
Coimbatore	**90**	11	2N	76 59 E
Coimbra	**50**	40	15N	8 27W
Cojimies	**184**	0	20N	80 0W
Cojutepeque	**177**	13	41N	88 54W
Colac	**117**	38	21S	143 35 E
Colchester	**25**	51	54N	0 55 E
Coldstream	**31**	55	39N	2 14W
Coleman	**155**	49	40N	114 30W
Coleraine, Australia	**119**	37	36S	141 40 E
Coleraine, U.K.	**34**	55	8N	6 40W
Colima	**175**	19	14N	103 43W
Colima □	**175**	19	10N	104 0W
Coll	**30**	56	40N	6 35W
College Park	**170**	33	42N	84 27W
Collie	**120**	33	22S	116 8 E
Collingwood	**151**	44	29N	80 13W
Collinsville	**121**	20	30S	147 56 E
Collooney	**34**	54	11N	8 28W
Colmar	**37**	48	5N	7 20 E
Colne	**28**	53	51N	2 11W
Cologne = Köln	**42**	50	56N	6 58 E
Colomb-Béchar = Béchar	**127**	31	38N	2 18W
Colômbia	**188**	20	10S	48 40W
Colombia ■	**184**	3	45N	73 0W
Colombo	**90**	6	56N	79 58 E
Colón, Cuba	**178**	22	42N	80 54W
Colón, Panama	**179**	9	20N	79 54W
Colonia	**191**	34	25S	57 50W
Colonsay	**30**	56	4N	6 12W
Colorado □	**163**	37	40N	106 0W
Colorado ⟶, Argentina	**190**	39	50S	62 8W
Colorado ⟶, Calif., U.S.A.	**173**	34	45N	114 40W
Colorado ⟶, Tex., U.S.A.	**161**	28	36N	95 58W
Colorado Desert	**160**	34	20N	116 0W
Colorado Plateau	**161**	36	40N	110 30W
Colorado Springs	**163**	38	55N	104 50W
Columbia, Miss., U.S.A.	**169**	31	16N	89 50W
Columbia, Mo., U.S.A.	**166**	38	58N	92 20W
Columbia, S.C., U.S.A.	**165**	34	0N	81 0W
Columbia, Tenn., U.S.A.	**169**	35	40N	87 0W
Columbia ⟶	**171**	46	15N	124 5W
Columbia Basin	**171**	47	30N	118 30W
Columbretes, Is.	**51**	39	50N	0 50 E
Columbus, Ga., U.S.A.	**170**	32	30N	84 58W
Columbus, Ind., U.S.A.	**167**	39	14N	85 55W
Columbus, Miss., U.S.A.	**169**	33	30N	88 26W
Columbus, Ohio, U.S.A.	**167**	39	57N	83 1W
Colwyn Bay	**26**	53	17N	3 44W
Comeragh Mts.	**35**	52	17N	7 35W
Comilla	**93**	23	28N	91 10 E
Comitán	**177**	16	18N	92 9W
Committee B.	**146**	68	30N	86 30W
Communism Pk. = Kommunizma, Pik.	**71**	39	0N	72 2 E
Como	**46**	45	48N	9 5 E
Como, L. di	**46**	46	5N	9 17 E
Comodoro Rivadavia	**192**	45	50S	67 40W
Comorin, C.	**90**	8	3N	77 40 E
Comoro Is. ■	**125**	12	10S	44 15 E
Comox	**154**	49	42N	124 55W
Compiègne	**38**	49	24N	2 50 E
Côn Dao	**95**	8	45N	106 45 E
Conakry	**130**	9	29N	13 49W
Conceição da Barra	**189**	18	35S	39 45W
Concepción, Argentina	**191**	27	20S	65 35W
Concepción, Chile	**190**	36	50S	73 0W
Concepción, Est. de	**192**	50	30S	74 55W
Concepción del Oro	**174**	24	38N	101 25W
Concepción del Uruguay	**190**	32	35S	58 20W
Conchos, R. ⟶	**174**	29	35N	104 25W
Concord, Calif., U.S.A.	**172**	37	59N	122 2W
Concord, N.C., U.S.A.	**165**	35	28N	80 35W
Concord, N.H., U.S.A.	**164**	43	12N	71 30W
Concordia, Argentina	**190**	31	20S	58 2W
Concordia, U.S.A.	**161**	39	35N	97 40W
Condamine	**155**	26	56S	150 9 E
Condé	**38**	50	26N	3 34 E
Condobolin	**117**	33	4S	147 6 E
Congleton	**28**	53	10N	2 12W
Congo = Zaïre ⟶	**134**	6	4S	12 24 E
Congo (Kinshasa) ■ = Zaïre ■	**134**	3	0S	23 0 E
Congo ■	**134**	1	0S	16 0 E
Congo Basin	**124**	0	10S	24 30 E
Conjeeveram = Kanchipuram	**90**	12	52N	79 45 E
Connacht	**34**	53	23N	8 40W
Conneaut	**164**	41	55N	80 32W
Connecticut □	**164**	41	40N	72 40W
Connecticut ⟶	**157**	41	17N	72 21W
Connemara	**34**	53	29N	9 45W
Connors Ra.	**121**	21	40S	149 10 E
Consett	**28**	54	52N	1 50W
Constance = Konstanz	**44**	47	39N	9 10 E
Constance, L. = Bodensee	**44**	47	35N	9 25 E
Constanța	**57**	44	14N	28 38 E
Constantine	**127**	36	25N	6 42 E
Contamana	**186**	7	19S	74 55W
Conway = Conwy	**26**	53	17N	3 50W
Conway = Conwy ⟶	**26**	53	18N	3 50W
Conway, N.H., U.S.A.	**148**	43	58N	71 8W
Conway, S.C., U.S.A.	**165**	33	49N	79 2W

Conwy **26** 53 17N 3 50W
Conwy —► **26** 53 18N 3 50W
Cook, Mt. .... **123** 43 36S 170 9 E
Cook Inlet................. **142** 59 0N 151 0W
Cook Is. **123** 17 0S 160 0W
Cook Strait .... **123** 41 15S 174 29 E
Cookeville **169** 36 12N 85 30W
Cookstown................ **34** 54 40N   6 43W
Coolah .... **116** 31 48S 149 41 E
Coolamon .... **117** 34 46S 147 8 E
Coolangatta.............. **116** 28 11S 153 29 E
Coolgardie................ **120** 30 55S 121 8 E
Cooma .... **117** 36 12S 149 8 E
Coonabarabran .... **116** 31 14S 149 18 E
Coonamble .... **116** 30 56S 148 27 E
Cooper Cr. —► .... **118** 12 7S 132 41 E
Coorong, The .... **119** 35 50S 139 20 E
Coorow.................. **120** 29 53S 116 2 E
Coos Bay **171** 43 26N 124 7W
Cootamundra .... **117** 34 36S 148 1 E
Copenhagen = København . . . **61** 55 41N 12 34 E
Copiapó.................. **190** 27 30S 70 20W
Copper Center **142** 62 10N 145 25W
Coppermine **145** 67 50N 115 5W
Coppermine —► **145** 67 49N 116 4W
Coquilhatville = Mbandaka . **134** 0 1N 18 18 E
Coquimbo **190** 30 0S 71 20W
Coracora **186** 15 5S 73 45W
Coral Gables.............. **170** 25 45N 80 16W
Coral Harbour **146** 64 8N 83 10W
Coral Sea .... **121** 15 0S 150 0 E
Corbeil-Essonnes.......... **39** 48 36N   2 26 E
Corbin **165** 37 0N 84 3W
Corby **25** 52 29N   0 41W
Cordele **170** 31 55N 83 49W
Córdoba, Argentina **190** 31 20S 64 10W
Córdoba, Mexico **177** 18 53N 96 56W
Córdoba, Spain **50** 37 50N   4 50W
Córdoba, Sierra de......... **190** 31 10S 64 25W
Cordova **142** 60 36N 145 45W
Corfu = Kérkira........... **54** 39 38N 19 50 E
Corinth = Kórinthos ...... **54** 37 56N 22 55 E
Corinth **169** 34 54N 88 30W
Corinth, G. of = Korinthiakós
  Kólpos .... **54** 38 16N 22 30 E
Corinto, Brazil **188** 18 20S 44 30W
Corinto, Nic. **179** 12 30N 87 10W
Cork **35** 51 54N   8 30W
Cork □ **35** 51 50N   8 50W
Corlu .... **80** 41 11N 27 49 E
Corn Is. = Maíz, Islas del .. **179** 12 15N 83 4W
Corner Brook.............. **140** 48 57N 57 58W
Cornwall **151** 45 2N 74 44W
Cornwall □............... **27** 50 26N   4 40W
Coro **184** 11 25N 69 41W
Coroatá **188** 4 8S 44 0W
Corocoro **187** 17 15S 68 28W
Coroico **187** 16 0S 67 50W
Coromandel Coast .... **90** 12 30N 81 0 E
Corona **173** 33 49N 117 36W
Coronado **173** 32 45N 117 9W
Coronation Gulf........... **145** 68 25N 110 0W
Coronel **190** 37 0S 73 10W
Coronel Pringles.......... **190** 38 0S 61 30W
Corowa.................. **117** 35 58S 146 21 E
Corozal.................. **177** 9 19N 75 18W
Corpus Christi............ **161** 27 50N 97 28W
Corrib, L. **34** 53 5N   9 10W
Corrientes **190** 27 30S 58 45W
Corrientes, C., Colombia **184** 5 30N 77 34W
Corrientes, C., Cuba **178** 21 43N 84 30W
Corrientes, C., Mexico **175** 20 25N 105 42W
Corrigin .... **120** 32 20S 117 53 E
Corse .... **36** 42 0N   9 0 E
Corsica = Corse.......... **36** 42 0N   9 0 E
Corsicana **168** 32 5N 96 30W
Cortez.................. **163** 37 24N 108 35W
Cortland................ **164** 42 35N 76 11W
Corum .... **80** 40 30N 34 57 E
Corumbá **187** 19 0S 57 30W
Coruña, La................ **50** 43 20N   8 25W

Corunna = Coruña, La **50** 43 20N   8 25W
Corvallis **171** 44 36N 123 15W
Cosamaloapan **177** 18 23N 95 50W
Cosenza.................. **49** 39 17N 16 14 E
Coshocton **167** 40 17N 81 51W
Costa Blanca.............. **51** 38 25N   0 10W
Costa Brava .... **51** 41 30N   3 0 E
Costa del Sol **50** 36 30N   4 30W
Costa Dorada .... **51** 40 45N   1 15 E
Costa Rica ■.............. **179** 10 0N 84 0W
Cotagaita **187** 20 45S 65 40W
Côte d'Or .... **37** 47 10N   4 50 E
Coteau des Prairies **156** 44 30N 97 0W
Cotonou .... **131** 6 20N   2 25 E
Cotopaxi, Vol. **184** 0 40S 78 30W
Cotswold Hills **24** 51 42N   2 10W
Cottbus .... **43** 51 44N 14 20 E
Coulommiers.............. **39** 48 50N   3 3 E
Council **142** 64 55N 163 45W
Council Bluffs **166** 41 20N 95 50W
Courantyne —► **185** 5 55N 57 5W
Courtrai = Kortrijk.......... **42** 50 50N   3 17 E
Coventry **24** 52 25N   1 31W
Cuvirigtun, Ga., U.S.A. **170** 33 30N 83 50W
Covington, Ky., U.S.A. **167** 39 5N 84 30W
Cowdenbeath **31** 56 7N   3 20W
Cowes **25** 50 45N   1 18W
Cowra.................. **117** 33 49S 148 42 E
Coxim **188** 18 30S 54 55W
Cracow = Kraków .... **58** 50 4N 19 57 E
Craigavon = Lurgan **34** 54 28N   6 20W
Craiova.................. **57** 44 21N 23 48 E
Cranbrook, Australia ...... **120** 34 18S 117 33 E
Cranbrook, Canada **155** 49 30N 115 46W
Crateús **189** 5 10S 40 39W
Crato.................. **189** 7 10S 39 25W
Crawfordsville **167** 40 2N 86 51W
Crawley **24** 51 7N   0 10W
Creil .... **39** 49 15N   2 34 E
Cremona .... **46** 45 8N 10 2 E
Crépy-en-Valois .... **39** 49 14N   2 54 E
Cres .... **52** 44 58N 14 25 E
Crescent City **172** 41 45N 124 12W
Creston, Canada **155** 49 10N 116 31W
Creston, U.S.A............ **166** 41 0N 94 20W
Crestview **169** 30 45N 86 35W
Crete = Kríti.............. **55** 35 15N 25 0 E
Creuse —► .... **36** 47 0N   0 34 E
Creusot, Le .... **37** 46 50N   4 24 E
Crewe **28** 53 6N   2 28W
Criciúma **191** 28 40S 49 23W
Crieff.................... **31** 56 22N   3 50W
Crimea = Krymskiy P-ov. .... **68** 45 0N 34 0 E
Crişul Alb —► .... **56** 46 42N 21 17 E
Crişul Negru —► .... **56** 46 38N 22 26 E
Crna Gora .... **52** 42 10N 21 30 E
Crna Gora □ .... **52** 42 40N 19 20 E
Croatia = Hrvatska □ ...... **52** 45 20N 18 0 E
Crockett **168** 31 20N 95 30W
Cromarty **33** 57 40N   4 2W
Cromer.................. **29** 52 56N   1 18 E
Crooked I. **180** 22 50N 74 10W
Crookwell................ **117** 34 28S 149 24 E
Cross Fell **28** 54 44N   2 29W
Cross L. **153** 54 45N 97 30W
Crosse, La **166** 43 48N 91 13W
Crowley **168** 30 15N 92 20W
Crowsnest Pass **155** 49 40N 114 40W
Cruz, C. **178** 19 50N 77 50W
Cruz Alta **191** 28 45S 53 40W
Cruz del Eje.............. **190** 30 45S 64 50W
Cruzeiro do Sul **186** 7 35S 72 35W
Crystal Brook............ **119** 33 21S 138 12 E
Cu Lao Hon .... **95** 10 54N 108 18 E
Cuando —► .... **134** 14 0S 19 30 E
Cuanza —► .... **134** 9 2S 13 30 E
Cuba ■.................. **178** 22 0N 79 0W
Cubango —► .... **134** 18 50S 22 25 E
Cucuí **184** 1 12N 66 50W
Cúcuta.................. **184** 7 54N 72 31W
Cuddalore .... **90** 11 46N 79 45 E

Name		Lat			Long		
Cuddapah	90	14	30N	78	47	E
Cue	120	27	25S	117	54	E
Cuenca, Ecuador	184	2	50S	79	9	W
Cuenca, Spain	51	40	5N	2	10	W
Cuenca, Serranía de	51	39	55N	1	50	W
Cuernavaca	177	18	55N	99	15	W
Cuevo	187	20	15S	63	30	W
Cuiabá	188	15	30S	56	0	W
Cuillin Hills	32	57	14N	6	15	W
Cuitzeo, L. de	175	19	55N	101	5	W
Culcairn	117	35	41S	147	3	E
Culiacán	174	24	48N	107	24	W
Cullarin Range	117	34	30S	149	30	E
Culloden Moor	33	57	29N	4	7	W
Culverden	123	42	47S	172	49	E
Cumaná	185	10	30N	64	5	W
Cumberland	164	39	40N	78	43	W
Cumberland —►	169	36	15N	87	0	W
Cumberland Is.	121	20	35S	149	10	E
Cumberland Pen.	146	67	0N	64	0	W
Cumberland Plat.	169	36	0N	84	30	W
Cumberland Sd.	146	65	30N	66	0	W
Cumbria □	28	54	35N	2	55	W
Cumbrian Mts.	28	54	30N	3	0	W
Cumbum	90	15	40N	79	10	E
Cummins	119	34	16S	135	43	E
Cumnock	31	55	27N	4	18	W
Cunene —►	134	17	20S	11	50	E
Cunnamulla	116	28	2S	145	38	E
Curaçao	181	12	10N	69	0	W
Curaray —►	184	2	20S	74	5	W
Curiapo	185	8	33N	61	5	W
Curicó	190	34	55S	71	20	W
Curitiba	191	25	20S	49	10	W
Curtis Group	117	39	30S	146	37	E
Curuá —►	99	5	23S	54	22	W
Curuçá	188	0	43S	47	50	W
Curuzú Cuatiá	191	29	50S	58	5	W
Cushing	168	35	59N	96	46	W
Cusihuiriáchic	174	28	14N	106	50	W
Cuthbert	170	31	47N	84	47	W
Cuttack	92	20	25N	85	57	E
Cuxhaven	42	53	51N	8	41	E
Cuyahoga Falls	167	41	8N	81	30	W
Cuzco, Bolivia	187	20	0S	66	50	W
Cuzco, Peru	186	13	32S	72	0	W
Cwmbran	27	51	39N	3	0	W
Cypress Hills	152	49	40N	109	30	W
Cyprus ■	80	35	0N	33	0	E
Cyrenaica	124	27	0N	23	0	E
Czechoslovakia ■	59	49	0N	17	0	E
Czeremcha	58	52	31N	23	21	E
Częstochowa	58	50	49N	19	7	E
Da —►	95	21	15N	105	20	E
Da Hinggan Ling	98	48	0N	121	0	E
Da Nang	95	16	4N	108	13	E
Da Yunhe —►	99	34	25N	120	5	E
Daba Shan	99	32	0N	109	0	E
Dacca = Dhaka	92	23	43N	90	26	E
Dacca □ = Dhaka □	93	24	25N	90	25	E
Dadanawa	185	2	50N	59	30	W
Dadra and Nagar Haveli □	91	20	5N	73	0	E
Daghestan A.S.S.R. □	70	42	30N	47	0	E
Dahomey = Benin ■	131	10	0N	2	0	E
Dai-Sen	109	35	22N	133	32	E
Daiō-Misaki	106	34	15N	136	45	E
Daisetsu-Zan	103	43	30N	142	57	E
Daito	109	35	19N	132	58	E
Dajarra	115	21	42S	139	30	E
Dakar	130	14	34N	17	29	W
Dakhla	126	23	50N	15	53	W
Dakhla, El Wâhât el-	128	25	30N	28	50	E
Ðakovica	52	42	22N	20	26	E
Dalandzadgad	98	43	27N	104	30	E
Dalbeattie	31	54	55N	3	50	W
Dalby	116	27	10S	151	17	E
Dalhousie	148	48	5N	66	26	W
Dali	99	25	40N	100	10	E
Dalian	98	38	50N	121	40	E
Daliang Shan	99	28	0N	102	45	E
Dallas, Oreg., U.S.A.	171	45	0N	123	15	W
Dallas, Tex., U.S.A.	168	32	50N	96	50	W
Dalmacija □	52	43	20N	17	0	E
Dalmatia = Dalmacija □	52	43	20N	17	0	E
Daloa	130	7	0N	6	30	W
Dalton	169	34	47N	84	58	W
Daly Waters	114	16	15S	133	24	E
Daman	91	20	25N	72	57	E
Damaraland	136	21	0S	17	0	E
Damascus = Dimashq	80	33	30N	36	18	E
Damāvand	86	35	47N	52	0	E
Damāvand, Qolleh-ye	86	35	56N	52	10	E
Dampier	114	20	41S	116	42	E
Dampier Arch.	114	20	38S	116	32	E
Danbury	164	41	23N	73	29	W
Dandenong	117	38	0S	145	15	E
Dandong	98	40	10N	124	20	E
Dangriga	177	17	0N	88	13	W
Dannevirke	122	40	12S	176	8	E
Dansville	164	42	32N	77	41	W
Danville, Ill., U.S.A.	167	40	10N	87	40	W
Danville, Ky., U.S.A.	167	37	40N	84	45	W
Danville, Va., U.S.A.	165	36	40N	79	20	W
Danzig = Gdańsk	58	54	22N	18	40	E
Dar es Salaam	135	6	50S	39	12	E
Darbhanga	92	26	15N	85	55	E
Dardanelles = Çanakkale Boğazi	80	40	0N	26	0	E
Dârfûr	129	13	40N	24	0	E
Dargan Ata	70	40	29N	62	10	E
Dargaville	122	35	57S	173	52	E
Darién, G. del	184	9	0N	77	0	W
Darjeeling = Darjiling	92	27	3N	88	18	E
Darjiling	92	27	3N	88	18	E
Darling —►	119	34	4S	141	54	E
Darling Downs	116	27	30S	150	30	E
Darling Ra.	120	32	30S	116	0	E
Darlington	28	54	33N	1	33	W
Darmstadt	42	49	51N	8	40	E
Darnley, C.	14	68	0S	69	0	E
Dart —►	27	50	24N	3	36	W
Dartmoor	27	50	36N	4	0	W
Dartmouth, Canada	149	44	40N	63	30	W
Dartmouth, U.K.	27	50	21N	3	35	W
Darwin	114	12	25S	130	51	E
Dasht-e Kavīr	86	34	30N	55	0	E
Dasht-e Lūt	85	31	30N	58	0	E
Dasht-e Mārgow	87	30	40N	62	30	E
Datia	91	25	39N	78	27	E
Datong	98	40	6N	113	18	E
Daugavpils	68	55	53N	26	32	E
Dauphin	153	51	9N	100	5	W
Dauphiné	37	45	15N	5	25	E
Davangere	90	14	25N	75	55	E
Davao	112	7	0N	125	40	E
Davenport	166	41	30N	90	40	W
Daventry	24	52	16N	1	10	W
David	179	8	30N	82	30	W
Davis Sea	15	66	0S	92	0	E
Davis Str.	146	65	0N	58	0	W
Davos	44	46	48N	9	49	E
Dawson	144	64	10N	139	30	W
Dawson Creek	155	55	45N	120	15	W
Dawson Range	121	24	30S	149	48	E
Daylesford	117	37	21S	144	9	E
Dayr az Zawr	81	35	20N	40	5	E
Dayton, Ohio, U.S.A.	167	39	45N	84	10	W
Dayton, Wash., U.S.A.	171	46	20N	118	10	W
Daytona Beach	170	29	14N	81	0	W
De Aar	136	30	39S	24	0	E
De Land	170	29	1N	81	19	W
De Ridder	168	30	48N	93	15	W
De Soto	166	38	7N	90	33	W
Deakin	114	30	46S	128	0	E
Deal	25	51	13N	1	25	E
Dean, Forest of	24	51	50N	2	35	W
Deán Funes	190	30	20S	64	20	W
Dease —►	144	59	56N	128	32	W
Dease Lake	144	58	25N	130	6	W

Death Valley	**173**	36 19N	116 52W
Deauville	**38**	49 23N	0 2 E
Debar	**52**	41 31N	20 30 E
Debre Markos	**132**	10 20N	37 40 E
Debre Tabor	**132**	11 50N	38 26 E
Debrecen	**59**	47 33N	21 42 E
Decatur, Ala., U.S.A.	**169**	34 35N	87 0W
Decatur, Ga., U.S.A.	**170**	33 47N	84 17W
Decatur, Ill., U.S.A.	**166**	39 50N	89 0W
Deccan	**76**	18 0N	79 0 E
Dedéagach = Alexandroúpolis	**55**	40 50N	25 54 E
Dee →, Scotland, U.K.	**33**	57 4N	2 7W
Dee →, Wales, U.K.	**26**	53 15N	3 7W
Deepwater	**116**	29 25S	151 51 E
Deer Lake	**149**	49 11N	57 27W
Defiance	**167**	41 20N	84 20W
Deh Bīd	**85**	30 39N	53 11 E
Dehra Dun	**89**	30 20N	78 4 E
Dej	**56**	47 10N	23 52 E
Del Rio	**161**	29 23N	100 50W
Delano	**173**	35 48N	119 13W
Delaware □	**164**	39 0N	75 40W
Delaware →	**164**	39 20N	75 25W
Delaware B.	**157**	38 50N	75 0W
Delft	**40**	52 1N	4 22 E
Delfzijl	**41**	53 20N	6 55 E
Delgado, C.	**137**	10 45S	40 40 E
Delgo	**129**	20 6N	30 40 E
Delhi	**89**	28 38N	77 17 E
Delice →	**80**	39 45N	34 15 E
Delicias	**174**	28 13N	105 28W
Delong, Ostrova	**72**	76 40N	149 20 E
Deloraine	**119**	41 30S	146 40 E
Delray Beach	**170**	26 27N	80 4W
Demanda, Sierra de la	**50**	42 15N	3 0W
Dembidolo	**132**	8 34N	34 50 E
Deming	**161**	32 10N	107 50W
Demopolis	**169**	32 30N	87 48W
Den Burg	**40**	53 3N	4 47 E
Den Haag = 's-Gravenhage	**40**	52 7N	4 17 E
Den Helder	**40**	52 57N	4 45 E
Den Oever	**40**	52 56N	5 2 E
Denain	**38**	50 20N	3 22 E
Denbigh	**26**	53 12N	3 26W
Denham	**120**	25 56S	113 31 E
Deniliquin	**117**	35 30S	144 58 E
Denison	**168**	33 50N	96 40W
Denizli	**80**	37 42N	29 2 E
Denmark	**120**	34 59S	117 25 E
Denmark ■	**61**	55 30N	9 0 E
Denmark Str.	**13**	66 0N	30 0W
Denton	**168**	33 12N	97 10W
D'Entrecasteaux Is.	**115**	9 0S	151 0 E
Denver	**163**	39 45N	105 0W
Deolali	**91**	19 58N	73 50 E
Deoria	**92**	26 31N	83 48 E
Deosai Mts.	**89**	35 40N	75 0 E
Dera Ghazi Khan	**89**	30 5N	70 43 E
Dera Ismail Khan	**89**	31 50N	70 50 E
Derby	**28**	52 55N	1 28W
Derby □	**28**	52 55N	1 28W
Derg, L.	**35**	53 0N	8 20W
Derry = Londonderry	**34**	55 0N	7 20W
Derryveagh Mts.	**34**	55 0N	8 40W
Derwent →, Cumbria, U.K.	**28**	54 42N	3 22W
Derwent →, Derby, U.K.	**29**	52 53N	1 17W
Derwent →, N. Yorks., U.K.	**29**	53 45N	0 57W
Derwent Water, L.	**28**	54 35N	3 9W
Des Moines	**166**	41 35N	93 37W
Des Moines →	**166**	40 23N	91 25W
Deschutes →	**171**	45 30N	121 0W
Dese	**133**	11 5N	39 40 E
Despeñaperros, Paso	**50**	38 24N	3 30W
Dessau	**43**	51 49N	12 15 E
Dessye = Dese	**133**	11 5N	39 40 E
Desvrès	**38**	50 40N	1 48 E
Detroit	**167**	42 23N	83 5W
Deurne	**41**	51 27N	5 49 E
Deutsche Bucht	**42**	54 10N	7 51 E
Devakottai	**90**	9 55N	78 45 E

Deventer	**41**	52 15N	6 10 E
Devizes	**24**	51 21N	2 0W
Devon I.	**13**	75 10N	85 0W
Devonport, Australia	**119**	41 10S	146 22 E
Devonport, N.Z.	**122**	36 49S	174 49 E
Devonport, U.K.	**27**	50 23N	4 11W
Devonshire □	**27**	50 50N	3 40W
Dewsbury	**28**	53 42N	1 38W
Dezfūl	**84**	32 20N	48 30 E
Dezhneva, Mys	**73**	66 5N	169 40W
Dhahran = Az̧ Z̧ahrān	**84**	26 10N	50 7 E
Dhaka	**92**	23 43N	90 26 E
Dhaka □	**93**	24 25N	90 25 E
Dhamar	**83**	14 30N	44 20 E
Dhar	**91**	22 35N	75 26 E
Dharmapuri	**90**	12 10N	78 10 E
Dharwad	**90**	15 22N	75 15 E
Dhidhimótikhon	**55**	41 22N	26 29 E
Dhikti	**55**	35 8N	25 22 E
Dhodhekánisos	**55**	36 35N	27 0 E
Dhuburi	**92**	26 2N	89 59 E
Dhule	**91**	20 58N	74 50 E
Di Linh, Cao Nguyen	**95**	11 30N	108 0 E
Diamantina	**188**	18 17S	43 40W
Diamantina →	**115**	26 45S	139 10 E
Diamantino	**188**	14 30S	56 30W
Dibrugarh	**93**	27 29N	94 55 E
Dickinson	**163**	46 50N	102 48W
Didsbury	**155**	51 35N	114 10W
Diefenbaker L.	**152**	51 0N	106 55W
Dieppe	**38**	49 54N	1 4 E
Dieren	**41**	52 3N	6 6 E
Digby	**148**	44 38N	65 50W
Digne	**37**	44 5N	6 12 E
Dijlah, Nahr →	**81**	31 0N	47 25 E
Dijon	**37**	47 20N	5 0 E
Dila	**133**	6 21N	38 22 E
Dillon	**165**	34 26N	79 20W
Dimashq	**80**	33 30N	36 18 E
Dimboola	**119**	36 28S	142 7 E
Dîmbovita →	**57**	44 14N	26 13 E
Dimitrovgrad	**53**	42 5N	25 35 E
Dimitrovo = Pernik	**53**	42 35N	23 2 E
Dinan	**36**	48 28N	2 2W
Dinara Planina	**52**	44 0N	16 30 E
Dinaric Alps = Dinara Planina	**52**	44 0N	16 30 E
Dindigul	**90**	10 25N	78 0 E
Dingle	**35**	52 9N	10 17W
Dingle B.	**35**	52 3N	10 20W
Dingwall	**33**	57 36N	4 26W
Dinuba	**173**	36 31N	119 22W
Dire Dawa	**133**	9 35N	41 45 E
Diriamba	**179**	11 51N	86 19W
Dirranbandi	**116**	28 33S	148 17 E
Disappointment L.	**114**	23 20S	122 40 E
Discovery B.	**119**	38 10S	140 40 E
Disko	**146**	69 45N	53 30W
Diss	**25**	52 23N	1 6 E
District of Columbia □	**164**	38 55N	77 0W
Diu	**91**	20 45N	70 58 E
Dives-sur-Mer	**39**	49 18N	0 8W
Dixon	**166**	41 50N	89 30W
Dixon Entrance	**154**	54 30N	132 0W
Diyarbakir	**81**	37 55N	40 18 E
Djakarta = Jakarta	**111**	6 9S	106 49 E
Djelfa	**130**	34 40N	3 15 E
Djerid, Chott	**127**	33 42N	8 30 E
Djibouti	**133**	11 30N	43 5 E
Djibouti ■	**133**	12 0N	43 0 E
Djoum	**131**	2 41N	12 35 E
Dmitriya Lapteva, Proliv	**72**	73 0N	140 0 E
Dnepr →	**68**	46 30N	32 18 E
Dnepropetrovsk	**68**	48 30N	35 0 E
Dnestr →	**68**	46 18N	30 17 E
Dnestrovski = Belgorod	**68**	50 35N	36 35 E
Dnieper = Dnepr →	**68**	46 30N	32 18 E
Dniester = Dnestr →	**68**	46 18N	30 17 E
Dobruja	**57**	44 30N	28 15 E
Dodecanese = Dhodhekánisos	**55**	36 35N	27 0 E
Dodge City	**161**	37 42N	100 0W

Name	Page	Lat	Long
Dodoma	**135**	6 8S	35 45 E
Doesburg	**41**	52 1N	6 9 E
Doetinchem	**41**	51 59N	6 18 E
Dogger Bank	**124**	54 50N	2 0 E
Doi Luang	**95**	18 30N	101 0 E
Dojran	**54**	41 10N	22 45 E
Dokkum	**41**	53 20N	5 59 E
Dolbeau	**148**	48 53N	72 18W
Dole	**37**	47 7N	5 31 E
Dolgellau	**26**	52 44N	3 53W
Dolgelley = Dolgellau	**26**	52 44N	3 53W
Dolomites = Dolomiti	**47**	46 30N	11 40 E
Dolomiti	**47**	46 30N	11 40 E
Dolores	**191**	36 20S	57 40W
Dolphin and Union Str.	**145**	69 5N	114 45W
Domel I. = Letsôk-aw Kyun	**94**	11 30N	98 25 E
Dominica ■	**180**	15 20N	61 20W
Dominican Rep. ■	**180**	19 0N	70 30W
Don →, U.K.	**33**	57 14N	2 5W
Don →, U.S.S.R.	**68**	47 4N	39 18 E
Donaghadee	**34**	54 38N	5 32W
Donau →	**42**	48 10N	17 0 E
Doncaster	**29**	53 31N	1 9W
Dondra Head	**90**	5 55N	80 40 E
Donegal	**34**	54 39N	8 8W
Donegal □	**34**	54 53N	8 0W
Donegal B.	**34**	54 30N	8 35W
Donetsk	**68**	48 0N	37 45 E
Dongara	**120**	29 14S	114 57 E
Dongen	**40**	51 38N	4 56 E
Dongting Hu	**99**	29 18N	112 45 E
Donnelly's Crossing	**122**	35 42S	173 38 E
Donnybrook	**120**	33 34S	115 48 E
Doon →	**31**	55 26N	4 41W
Dorada, La	**184**	5 30N	74 40W
Dorchester	**27**	50 42N	2 28W
Dorchester, C.	**146**	65 27N	77 27W
Dordogne □	**36**	45 5N	0 40 E
Dordrecht	**40**	51 48N	4 39 E
Dornoch	**33**	57 52N	4 0W
Dorrigo	**116**	30 20S	152 44 E
Dorris	**172**	41 59N	121 58W
Dorset □	**27**	50 48N	2 25W
Dortmund	**42**	51 32N	7 28 E
Dothan	**169**	31 10N	85 25W
Douai	**38**	50 21N	3 4 E
Douala	**131**	4 0N	9 45 E
Douarnenez	**36**	48 6N	4 21W
Douglas, U.K.	**28**	54 9N	4 29W
Douglas, U.S.A.	**170**	31 32N	82 52W
Doullens	**38**	50 10N	2 20 E
Dounreay	**33**	58 34N	3 44W
Dourados	**188**	22 9S	54 50W
Douro →	**50**	41 8N	8 40W
Douro Litoral □	**50**	41 10N	8 20W
Dove →	**28**	52 51N	1 36W
Dover, U.K.	**25**	51 7N	1 19 E
Dover, Del., U.S.A.	**164**	39 10N	75 31W
Dover, N.H., U.S.A.	**164**	43 12N	70 51W
Dover, Str. of	**38**	51 0N	1 30 E
Dovey →	**26**	52 32N	4 0W
Downham Market	**25**	52 36N	0 22 E
Downpatrick	**34**	54 20N	5 43W
Drachten	**41**	53 7N	6 5 E
Dragoman, Prokhod	**53**	43 0N	22 53 E
Draguignan	**37**	43 30N	6 27 E
Drakensberg	**137**	31 0S	28 0 E
Dráma	**55**	41 9N	24 10 E
Drammen	**60**	59 42N	10 12 E
Drau = Drava →	**59**	45 33N	18 55 E
Drava →	**59**	45 33N	18 55 E
Drayton Valley	**155**	53 12N	114 58W
Drenthe □	**41**	52 52N	6 40 E
Dresden	**43**	51 2N	13 45 E
Dreux	**39**	48 44N	1 23 E
Driffield	**29**	54 0N	0 25W
Drin i zi →	**52**	41 37N	20 28 E
Drina →	**52**	44 53N	19 21 E
Drogheda	**34**	53 45N	6 20W
Droitwich	**24**	52 16N	2 10W
Dronne →	**36**	45 2N	0 9W
Dronning Maud Land	**14**	72 30S	12 0 E
Drumheller	**155**	51 25N	112 40W
Drummond Ra.	**121**	23 45S	147 10 E
Drummondville	**151**	45 55N	72 25W
Dryden	**153**	49 47N	92 50W
Du Bois	**164**	41 8N	78 46W
Du Quoin	**166**	38 0N	89 10W
Dubai = Dubayy	**85**	25 18N	55 20 E
Dubawnt →	**145**	64 33N	100 6W
Dubawnt, L.	**143**	63 4N	101 42W
Dubayy	**85**	25 18N	55 20 E
Dubbo	**116**	32 11S	148 35 E
Dublin, Ireland	**35**	53 20N	6 18W
Dublin, U.S.A.	**170**	32 30N	82 34W
Dublin □	**34**	53 24N	6 20W
Dubrovnik	**52**	42 39N	18 6 E
Dubuque	**166**	42 30N	90 41W
Dudley	**24**	52 30N	2 5W
Dugi Otok	**52**	44 0N	15 0 E
Duisburg	**42**	51 27N	6 42 E
Duluth	**150**	46 48N	92 10W
Dumbarton	**31**	55 58N	4 35W
Dumfries	**31**	55 4N	3 37W
Dumfries & Galloway □	**31**	55 0N	4 0W
Dun Laoghaire	**35**	53 17N	6 9W
Dunărea →	**57**	45 30N	8 15 E
Dunaújváros	**59**	47 0N	18 57 E
Dunbar	**31**	56 0N	2 32W
Dunblane	**31**	56 10N	3 58W
Duncan, Canada	**154**	48 45N	123 40W
Duncan, U.S.A.	**161**	34 25N	98 0W
Duncan Pass.	**94**	11 0N	92 30 E
Dundalk	**34**	54 1N	6 25W
Dundas, Canada	**151**	43 17N	79 59W
Dundas, Greenland	**13**	77 0N	69 0W
Dundee	**31**	56 29N	3 0W
Dundrum	**34**	54 17N	5 50W
Dunedin	**123**	45 50S	170 33 E
Dunedoo	**116**	32 0S	149 25 E
Dunfermline	**31**	56 5N	3 28W
Dungannon	**34**	54 30N	6 47W
Dungarvan	**35**	52 6N	7 40W
Dungeness	**25**	50 54N	0 59 E
Dungog	**117**	32 22S	151 46 E
Dunhuang	**100**	40 8N	94 36 E
Dunkeld	**33**	56 34N	3 36W
Dunkerque	**38**	51 2N	2 20 E
Dunkery Beacon	**27**	51 15N	3 37W
Dunkirk = Dunkerque	**38**	51 2N	2 20 E
Dunkirk	**164**	42 30N	79 18W
Dúnleary = Dun Laoghaire	**35**	53 17N	6 9W
Dunmore	**164**	41 27N	75 38W
Dunn	**165**	35 18N	78 36W
Dunnet Hd.	**33**	58 38N	3 22W
Duns	**31**	55 47N	2 20W
Dunsmuir	**172**	41 10N	122 18W
Dunstan Mts.	**123**	44 53S	169 35 E
Durance →	**37**	43 55N	4 45 E
Durango, Mexico	**174**	24 3N	104 39W
Durango, U.S.A.	**163**	37 16N	107 50W
Durango □	**174**	24 50N	104 50W
Durant	**168**	34 0N	96 25W
Durazno	**191**	33 25S	56 31W
Durban	**137**	29 49S	31 1 E
Durg	**92**	21 15N	81 22 E
Durham, U.K.	**28**	54 47N	1 34W
Durham, U.S.A.	**165**	36 0N	78 55W
Durham □	**28**	54 42N	1 45W
Durmitor	**52**	43 10N	19 0 E
Durness	**32**	58 34N	4 45W
D'Urville I.	**122**	40 50S	173 55 E
Dushanbe	**71**	38 33N	68 48 E
Düsseldorf	**42**	51 15N	6 46 E
Duwādimi	**82**	24 35N	44 15 E
Duyun	**99**	26 18N	107 29 E
Duzce	**80**	40 50N	31 10 E
Duzdab = Zāhedān	**86**	29 30N	60 50 E
Dvina, Sev. →	**69**	64 32N	40 30 E
Dvinsk = Daugavpils	**68**	55 53N	26 32 E
Dyer, C.	**146**	66 40N	61 0W
Dyersburg	**169**	36 2N	89 20W

Name	Page	Lat °	Lat ′	N/S	Long °	Long ′	E/W
Dyfed □	26	52	0	N	4	30	W
Dysart	121	22	32	S	148	23	E
Dzamin Üüd	98	43	50	N	111	58	E
Dzerzhinsk	68	53	40	N	27	1	E
Dzhalal-Abad	71	40	56	N	73	0	E
Dzhalinda	75	53	26	N	124	0	E
Dzhambul	71	42	54	N	71	22	E
Dzhardzhan	72	68	10	N	124	10	E
Dzhetygara	71	52	11	N	61	12	E
Dzhezkazgan	71	47	44	N	67	40	E
Dzhugdzur, Khrebet	75	57	30	N	138	0	E
Dzuumod	98	47	45	N	106	58	E
Eagle	142	64	44	N	141	7	W
Eagle Pass	161	28	45	N	100	35	W
Eagle River	150	45	55	N	89	17	W
Ealing	25	51	30	N	0	19	W
Earn →	31	56	20	N	3	19	W
Easley	165	34	52	N	82	35	W
East Angus	148	45	30	N	71	40	W
East Bengal	92	24	0	N	90	0	E
East Beskids = Vychodné Beskydy	59	49	30	N	22	0	E
East C.	122	37	42	S	178	35	E
East Chicago	167	41	40	N	87	30	W
East China Sea	99	30	5	N	126	0	E
East Falkland	192	51	30	S	58	30	W
East Germany ■	43	52	0	N	12	0	E
East Indies	77	0	0		120	0	E
East Kilbride	31	55	46	N	4	10	W
East Liverpool	164	40	39	N	80	35	W
East London	137	33	0	S	27	55	E
East Main = Eastmain	140	52	10	N	78	30	W
East Pakistan = Bangladesh ■	92	24	0	N	90	0	E
East Point	170	33	40	N	84	28	W
East St. Louis	166	38	37	N	90	4	W
East Schelde → = Oosterschelde →	40	51	33	N	4	0	E
East Siberian Sea	73	73	0	N	160	0	E
East Sussex □	25	51	0	N	0	20	E
Eastbourne, N.Z.	123	41	19	S	174	55	E
Eastbourne, U.K.	25	50	46	N	0	18	E
Eastern Ghats	90	14	0	N	78	50	E
Eastleigh	25	50	58	N	1	21	W
Eastmain	140	52	10	N	78	30	W
Eastmain →	140	52	27	N	78	26	W
Easton	164	40	41	N	75	15	W
Eau Claire	166	44	46	N	91	30	W
Eau Claire, L. à l'	146	56	10	N	74	25	W
Ebbw Vale	26	51	47	N	3	12	W
Eboli	49	40	39	N	15	2	E
Ebro →	51	40	43	N	0	54	E
Echizen-Misaki	106	35	59	N	135	57	E
Echo Bay	145	46	29	N	84	4	W
Echuca	117	36	10	S	144	20	E
Ecuador ■	184	2	0	S	78	0	W
Ed Dâmer	129	17	27	N	34	0	E
Edam	40	52	31	N	5	3	E
Eddystone	27	50	11	N	4	16	W
Ede	41	52	4	N	5	40	E
Eden →	117	37	3	S	149	55	E
Eden →	28	54	57	N	3	2	W
Edenhope	119	37	4	S	141	19	E
Edge Hill	24	52	7	N	1	28	W
Edhessa	54	40	48	N	22	5	E
Edinburgh	31	55	57	N	3	12	W
Edirne	80	41	40	N	26	34	E
Edmonton, Australia	121	17	2	S	145	46	E
Edmonton, Canada	155	53	30	N	113	30	W
Edmundston	148	47	23	N	68	20	W
Edson	155	53	35	N	116	28	W
Edward, L.	132	0	25	S	29	40	E
Edward VII Land	15	80	0	S	150	0	W
Edwards Plat.	161	30	30	N	101	5	W
Effingham	167	39	8	N	88	30	W
Égadi, Isole	48	37	55	N	12	16	E
Eger	59	47	53	N	20	27	E
Egmont, Mt.	122	39	17	S	174	5	E
Eğridir Gölü	80	37	53	N	30	50	E
Egypt ■	128	28	0	N	31	0	E
Eifel	42	50	10	N	6	45	E
Eigg	32	56	54	N	6	10	W
Eil	133	8	0	N	49	50	E
Eindhoven	41	51	26	N	5	30	E
Eirunepé	187	6	35	S	69	53	W
El Aaiún	126	27	9	N	13	12	W
El Cajon	173	32	49	N	117	0	W
El Callao	185	7	18	N	61	50	W
El Centro	173	32	50	N	115	40	W
El Cerro	187	17	30	S	61	40	W
El Dere	133	3	50	N	47	8	E
El Djouf	126	20	0	N	11	30	E
El Dorado	168	33	10	N	92	40	W
El Escorial	50	40	35	N	4	7	W
El Faiyûm	128	29	19	N	30	50	E
El Fâsher	129	13	33	N	25	26	E
El Ferrol	50	43	29	N	8	15	W
El Fuerte	174	26	25	N	108	39	W
El Geteina	129	14	50	N	32	27	E
El Iskandarîya	128	31	0	N	30	0	E
El Jadida	126	33	11	N	8	17	W
El Khârga	128	25	30	N	30	33	E
El Khartûm	129	15	31	N	32	35	E
El Mahalla el Kubra	128	31	0	N	31	0	E
El Minyâ	128	28	7	N	30	33	E
El Obeid	129	13	8	N	30	10	E
El Oro	177	27	15	N	103	30	W
El Paso	161	31	50	N	106	30	W
El Progreso	177	15	26	N	87	51	W
El Qâhira	128	30	1	N	31	14	E
El Qasr	128	25	44	N	28	42	E
El Salvador ■	177	13	50	N	89	0	W
El Suweis	128	29	58	N	32	31	E
El Tigre	185	8	44	N	64	15	W
El Turbio	192	51	45	S	72	5	W
Elat	80	29	30	N	34	56	E
Elâziğ	81	38	37	N	39	14	E
Elba	46	42	48	N	10	15	E
Elbasani	52	41	9	N	20	9	E
Elbe →	42	53	50	N	9	0	E
Elbert, Mt.	163	39	5	N	106	27	W
Elberton	165	34	7	N	82	51	W
Elbeuf	39	49	17	N	1	2	E
Elbing = Elbląg	58	54	10	N	19	25	E
Elbląg	58	54	10	N	19	25	E
Elbrus	70	43	21	N	42	30	E
Elburg	41	52	26	N	5	50	E
Elburz Mts. = Alborz, Reshteh-ye Kūhhā-ye	86	36	0	N	52	0	E
Elche	51	38	15	N	0	42	W
Eldorado	174	24	20	N	107	22	W
Eldorado Springs	166	37	54	N	93	59	W
Eldoret	132	0	30	N	35	17	E
Eleanora, Peak	120	32	57	S	121	9	E
Electra	161	34	0	N	99	0	W
Elephant Butte Res.	161	33	45	N	107	30	W
Eleuthera	178	25	0	N	76	20	W
Elgin, U.K.	33	57	39	N	3	20	W
Elgin, Ill., U.S.A.	167	42	0	N	88	20	W
Elgin, Oreg., U.S.A.	171	45	37	N	118	0	W
Elgon, Mt.	132	1	10	N	34	30	E
Elisabethville = Lubumbashi	135	11	40	S	27	28	E
Elizabeth, Australia	119	34	42	S	138	41	E
Elizabeth, U.S.A.	164	40	37	N	74	12	W
Elizabeth City	165	36	18	N	76	16	W
Elizabethton	165	36	20	N	82	13	W
Elizabethtown	167	37	40	N	85	54	W
Elk Point	152	53	54	N	110	55	W
Elkhart	167	41	42	N	85	55	W
Elkins	165	38	53	N	79	53	W
Elko	172	40	50	N	115	50	W
Ellensburg	171	47	0	N	120	30	W
Ellery, Mt.	117	37	28	S	148	47	E
Ellesmere I.	13	79	30	N	80	0	W
Ellesmere Port	28	53	17	N	2	55	W
Ellice Is. = Tuvalu ■	122	8	0	S	178	0	E
Elliot Lake	150	46	25	N	82	35	W
Ellore = Eluru	92	16	48	N	81	8	E
Ellsworth Land	14	76	0	S	89	0	W

Name	Page	Lat°	Lat′	N/S	Long°	Long′	E/W
Ellsworth Mts.	14	78	30	S	85	0	W
Elmhurst	167	41	52	N	87	58	W
Elmira	164	42	8	N	76	49	W
Elrose	152	51	12	N	108	0	W
Eluru	92	16	48	N	81	8	E
Elvas	50	38	50	N	7	10	W
Elwood	167	40	20	N	85	50	W
Ely	172	39	10	N	114	50	W
Elyria	167	41	22	N	82	8	W
Emāmrūd	86	36	30	N	55	0	E
Emba →	70	46	38	N	53	14	E
Emden	42	53	22	N	7	12	E
Emerald	121	23	32	S	148	10	E
Emilia-Romagna □	46	44	33	N	10	40	E
Emmeloord	41	52	44	N	5	46	E
Emmen	41	52	48	N	6	57	E
Empalme	174	27	58	N	110	51	W
Emporia, Kans., U.S.A.	158	38	25	N	96	10	W
Emporia, Va., U.S.A.	165	36	41	N	77	32	W
Ems →	42	52	37	N	9	26	E
En Nahud	129	12	45	N	28	25	E
Ena	106	35	25	N	137	25	E
Ena-San	106	35	26	N	137	36	E
Encarnación	191	27	15	S	55	50	W
Encarnación de Díaz	175	21	31	N	102	14	W
Encontrados	184	9	3	N	72	14	W
Enderby	155	50	35	N	119	10	W
Enderby Land	14	66	0	S	53	0	E
Endicott	164	42	6	N	76	2	W
Engaño, C.	180	18	30	N	68	20	W
Engels	68	51	28	N	46	6	E
Enggano	111	5	20	S	102	40	E
England □	21	53	0	N	2	0	W
English Bazar = Ingraj Bazar .	92	24	58	N	88	10	E
English Channel	16	50	0	N	2	0	W
Enid	161	36	26	N	97	52	W
Enkhuizen	40	52	42	N	5	17	E
Ennedi	129	17	15	N	22	0	E
Ennis	35	52	51	N	8	59	W
Enniscorthy	35	52	30	N	6	35	W
Enniskillen	34	54	20	N	7	40	W
Enriquillo, L.	180	18	20	N	72	5	W
Enschede	41	52	13	N	6	53	E
Ensenada	174	31	52	N	116	37	W
Enshū-Nada	106	34	27	N	137	38	E
Entebbe	132	0	4	N	32	28	E
Enterprise	171	45	30	N	117	18	W
Entre Ríos □	190	30	30	S	58	30	W
Enugu	131	6	20	N	7	30	E
Enzan	107	35	42	N	138	44	E
Eólie, I.	49	38	30	N	14	50	E
Epe	41	52	21	N	5	59	E
Épernay	39	49	3	N	3	56	E
Ephesus	80	37	50	N	27	33	E
Épinal	37	48	10	N	6	27	E
Epping	25	51	42	N	0	8	E
Equatorial Guinea ■	134	2	0	S	8	0	E
Er Rif	126	35	1	N	4	1	W
Erāwadī Myit → =							
Irrawaddy →	93	15	50	N	95	6	E
Ercha	73	69	45	N	147	20	E
Erciyaş Daği	80	38	30	N	35	30	E
Erebus, Mt.	15	77	35	S	167	0	E
Erechim	191	27	35	S	52	15	W
Ereğli	80	41	15	N	31	30	E
Erfurt	43	50	58	N	11	2	E
Erg Chech	126	50	59	N	11	0	E
Erie	164	42	10	N	80	7	W
Erie, L.	151	42	15	N	81	0	W
Erlmanthos	54	37	57	N	21	50	E
Erimo-misaki	103	41	50	N	143	15	E
Eritrea □	132	14	0	N	41	0	E
Ermoúpolis = Síros	55	37	28	N	24	57	E
Erne, Lough	34	54	26	N	7	46	W
Erode	90	11	24	N	77	45	E
Erramala Hills	90	15	30	N	78	15	E
Erris Hd.	34	54	19	N	10	0	W
Erzgebirge	43	50	25	N	13	0	E
Erzincan	81	39	46	N	39	30	E
Erzurum	81	39	57	N	41	15	E
Es Sînâ'	128	29	0	N	34	0	E
Esan-Misaki	103	41	40	N	141	10	E
Esashi	103	41	52	N	140	7	E
Esbjerg	61	55	29	N	8	29	E
Escanaba	150	45	44	N	87	5	W
Escondido	173	33	9	N	117	4	W
Escuintla	177	14	20	N	90	48	W
Eşfahān	85	33	0	N	53	0	E
Esh Sham = Dimashq	80	33	30	N	36	18	E
Esk →	29	54	27	N	0	36	W
Eskilstuna	60	59	22	N	16	32	E
Eskimo Pt.	145	61	10	N	94	15	W
Eskişehir	80	39	50	N	30	35	E
Eslāmābād-e Gharb	84	34	10	N	46	30	E
Esmeraldas	184	1	0	N	79	40	W
Espanola	151	46	15	N	81	46	W
Esperance	114	33	45	S	121	55	E
Espinazo, Sierra del =							
Espinhaço, Serra do	188	17	30	S	43	30	W
Espinhaço, Serra do	188	17	30	S	43	30	W
Espírito Santo □	189	20	0	S	40	45	W
Essaouira	126	31	32	N	9	42	W
Essen	42	51	28	N	6	59	E
Essequibo →	185	6	50	N	58	30	W
Essex □	25	51	48	N	0	30	E
Estados, I. de los	192	54	40	S	64	30	W
Estelí	179	13	9	N	86	22	W
Estevan	152	49	10	N	102	59	W
Estherville	166	43	25	N	94	50	W
Estonian S.S.R. □	68	58	30	N	25	30	E
Estoril	50	38	42	N	9	23	W
Estrêla, Serra da	50	40	10	N	7	45	W
Estremadura	50	39	0	N	9	0	W
Étampes	39	48	26	N	2	10	E
Étaples	38	50	30	N	1	39	E
Etawah	91	26	48	N	79	6	E
Ethiopia ■	133	8	0	N	40	0	E
Ethiopian Highlands	132	10	0	N	37	0	E
Etna	49	37	45	N	15	0	E
Etosha Pan	136	18	40	S	16	30	E
Etzatlán	175	20	46	N	104	5	W
Euboea = Évvoia	55	38	30	N	24	0	E
Euclid	167	41	32	N	81	31	W
Eucumbene, L.	117	36	2	S	148	40	E
Eufaula	169	35	20	N	95	33	W
Eugene	171	44	0	N	123	8	W
Eupen	42	50	37	N	6	3	E
Euphrates = Furāt, Nahr							
al →	84	31	0	N	47	25	E
Eureka, Calif., U.S.A.	172	40	50	N	124	0	W
Eureka, Nev., U.S.A.	172	39	32	N	116	2	W
Euroa	117	36	44	S	145	35	E
Europa, Pta. de	50	36	3	N	5	21	W
Europa Pt. = Europa, Pta. de .	50	36	3	N	5	21	W
Europoort	40	51	57	N	4	10	E
Euston	119	34	30	S	142	46	E
Eutsuk L.	154	53	20	N	126	45	W
Evans Head	116	29	7	S	153	27	E
Evanston	167	42	0	N	87	40	W
Evansville	167	38	0	N	87	35	W
Everard, L.	118	31	30	S	135	0	E
Everest, Mt.	92	28	5	N	86	58	E
Everett	171	48	0	N	122	10	W
Everglades	170	26	0	N	80	30	W
Evesham	24	52	6	N	1	57	W
Évora	50	38	33	N	7	57	W
Évreux	39	49	0	N	1	8	E
Évvoia	55	38	30	N	24	0	E
Excelsior Springs	166	39	20	N	94	10	W
Exe →	27	50	38	N	3	27	W
Exeter	27	50	43	N	3	31	W
Exmoor	27	51	10	N	3	59	W
Exmouth	27	50	37	N	3	26	W
Extremadura □	50	39	30	N	6	5	W
Eyasi, L.	135	3	30	S	35	0	E
Eye Pen.	32	58	13	N	6	10	W
Eyre, L.	118	29	30	S	137	26	E
Eyre Mts.	123	45	25	S	168	25	E
Eyre Pen.	119	33	30	S	137	17	E

Name				
Facatativá	184	4	49N	74 22W
Faddeyevskiy, Ostrov	72	76	0N	150 0 E
Fair Hd.	34	55	14N	6 10W
Fairbanks	142	64	50N	147 50W
Fairfield, N.Z.	123	45	54S	170 24 E
Fairfield, Ala., U.S.A.	169	33	30N	87 0W
Fairfield, Calif., U.S.A.	172	38	14N	122 1W
Fairfield, Tex., U.S.A.	168	31	40N	96 0W
Fairmont, Minn., U.S.A.	166	43	37N	94 30W
Fairmont, W. Va., U.S.A.	164	39	29N	80 10W
Fairview	155	56	5N	118 25W
Fairweather, Mt.	143	58	55N	137 45W
Faisalabad	89	31	30N	73 5 E
Faizabad	92	26	45N	82 10 E
Fajardo	180	18	20N	65 39W
Fakenham	29	52	50N	0 51 E
Falam	93	23	0N	93 45 E
Falkirk	31	56	0N	3 47W
Falkland Is.	192	51	30S	59 0W
Falköping	60	58	12N	13 33 E
Fall River	164	41	45N	71 5W
Falls City	166	40	0N	95 40W
Falmouth, Jamaica	180	10	30N	77 40W
Falmouth, U.K.	27	50	9N	5 5W
Famagusta	80	35	8N	33 55 E
Farāh	87	32	20N	62 7 E
Farāh □	87	32	25N	62 10 E
Fareham	25	50	52N	1 11W
Farewell, C.	122	40	29S	172 43 E
Farewell C. = Farvel, Kap	147	59	48N	43 55W
Fargo	156	46	52N	96 40W
Farmington, N.H., U.S.A.	157	43	25N	71 3W
Farmington, N. Mex., U.S.A.	161	36	45N	108 28W
Farnborough	25	51	17N	0 46W
Faro	50	37	2N	7 55W
Faroe Is.	16	62	0N	7 0W
Fars □	85	29	30N	55 0 E
Fársala	54	39	17N	22 23 E
Farvel, Kap	147	59	48N	43 55W
Fāryāb □	87	36	0N	65 0 E
Fatehgarh	89	27	25N	79 35 E
Fatehpur, Raj., India	92	28	0N	74 40 E
Fatehpur, Ut. P., India	89	25	56N	81 13 E
Faxaflói	64	64	29N	23 0W
Fayetteville, Ark., U.S.A.	168	36	0N	94 5W
Fayetteville, N.C., U.S.A.	165	35	0N	78 58W
Fazilka	89	30	27N	74 2 E
Fdérik	126	22	40N	12 45W
Fear, C.	165	33	51N	78 0W
Fécamp	38	49	45N	0 22 E
Feilding	122	40	13S	175 35 E
Feira de Santana	189	12	15S	38 57W
Felixstowe	25	51	58N	1 22 E
Fengjie	99	31	5N	109 36 E
Fens, The	29	52	45N	0 2 E
Fenyang	98	37	19N	111 46 E
Ferfer	133	5	4N	45 9 E
Fergana	71	40	23N	71 19 E
Fergus Falls	156	46	18N	96 7W
Fermoy	35	52	4N	8 18W
Fernando de Noronha	189	4	0S	33 10W
Fernando Póo = Bioko	131	3	30N	8 40 E
Fernie	155	49	30N	115 5W
Ferrara	47	44	50N	11 36 E
Ferté-Bernard, La	39	48	10N	0 40 E
Fès	126	34	0N	5 0W
Feuilles ~►	146	58	47N	70 4W
Feyzābād	87	37	7N	70 33 E
Fezzan	124	27	0N	15 0 E
Fianarantsoa	137	21	26S	47 5 E
Fichtelgebirge	43	50	10N	12 0 E
Fife □	31	56	13N	3 2W
Fife Ness	31	56	17N	2 35W
Fiji ■	122	17	20S	179 0 E
Filey	29	54	13N	0 18W
Findlay	167	41	0N	83 41W
Finisterre, C.	50	42	50N	9 19W
Finland ■	67	63	0N	27 0 E
Finland, G. of	67	60	0N	26 0 E
Finlay ~►	144	57	0N	125 10W
Finley	117	35	38S	145 35 E
Firenze	47	43	47N	11 15 E
Firozabad	89	27	10N	78 25 E
Fishguard	26	51	59N	4 59W
Fiskenæsset	147	63	5N	50 45W
Fitchburg	164	42	35N	71 47W
Fitzgerald	170	31	45N	83 16W
Fitzroy ~►	121	23	32S	150 52 E
Fiume = Rijeka	52	45	20N	14 21 E
Flagstaff	160	35	10N	111 40W
Flamborough Hd.	29	54	8N	0 4W
Flannan Is.	32	58	9N	7 52W
Flattery, C.	171	48	21N	124 43W
Flèche, La	39	47	42N	0 4W
Fleetwood	28	53	55N	3 1W
Flekkefjord	60	58	18N	6 39 E
Flensburg	43	54	46N	9 28 E
Flers	36	48	47N	0 33W
Flin Flon	152	54	46N	101 53W
Flinders I.	117	40	0S	148 0 E
Flinders Ranges	118	31	30S	138 30 E
Flinders Reefs	121	17	37S	148 31 E
Flint, U.K.	26	53	15N	3 7W
Flint, U.S.A.	167	43	5N	83 40W
Flint ~►	170	30	52N	84 38W
Flodden	31	55	37N	2 8W
Flora	167	38	40N	88 30W
Florence = Firenze	47	43	47N	11 15 E
Florence, Ala., U.S.A.	169	34	50N	87 40W
Florence, S.C., U.S.A.	165	34	12N	79 44W
Flores, Guat.	177	16	59N	89 50W
Flores, Indonesia	113	8	35S	121 0 E
Flores Sea	113	6	30S	124 0 E
Floriano	188	6	50S	43 0W
Florianópolis	191	27	30S	48 30W
Florida	191	34	7S	56 10W
Florida □	170	28	30N	82 0W
Florida, Straits of	159	25	0N	80 0W
Florida B.	159	25	0N	81 20W
Florida Keys	159	25	0N	80 40W
Flórina	54	40	48N	21 26 E
Flushing = Vlissingen	40	51	26N	3 34 E
Fly ~►	115	8	25S	143 0 E
Foam Lake	152	51	40N	103 32W
Fóggia	49	41	28N	15 31 E
Foix	36	42	58N	1 38 E
Folda	64	64	41N	10 50 E
Folkestone	25	51	5N	1 11 E
Follette, La	169	36	23N	84 9W
Fond-du-Lac, Canada	145	59	19N	107 12W
Fond-du-Lac, U.S.A.	167	43	46N	88 26W
Fontainebleau	39	48	24N	2 40 E
Fonte Boa	184	2	33S	66 0W
Foochow = Fuzhou	99	26	5N	119 16 E
Forbes	117	33	22S	148 0 E
Forestburg	155	52	35N	112 1W
Forestville	148	48	48N	69 2W
Forfar	33	56	40N	2 53W
Forlì	47	44	14N	12 2 E
Formby Pt.	28	53	33N	3 7W
Formentera	51	38	43N	1 27 E
Formosa = Taiwan ■	99	23	30N	121 0 E
Formosa	191	26	15S	58 10W
Forrest City	169	35	0N	90 50W
Fort Albany	140	52	15N	81 35W
Fort Augustus	32	57	9N	4 40W
Fort Chipewyan	145	58	42N	111 8W
Fort Collins	163	40	30N	105 4W
Fort-Coulonge	151	45	50N	76 45W
Fort-de-France	180	14	36N	61 2W
Fort Dodge	166	42	29N	94 10W
Fort Frances	153	48	36N	93 24W
Fort Franklin	145	65	10N	123 30W
Fort George	140	53	50N	79 0W
Fort Good-Hope	144	66	14N	128 40W
Fort Hertz = Putao	93	27	28N	97 30 E
Fort Kent	148	47	12N	68 30W
Fort-Lamy = Ndjamena	131	12	10N	14 59 E
Fort Lauderdale	170	26	10N	80 5W
Fort Liard	144	60	14N	123 30W
Fort Mackay	143	57	12N	111 41W
Fort Macleod	155	49	45N	113 30W

Fort McMurray	**155**	56	44N	111	7W
Fort McPherson	**144**	67	30N	134	55W
Fort Madison	**166**	40	39N	91	20W
Fort Morgan	**163**	40	10N	103	50W
Fort Myers	**170**	26	39N	81	51W
Fort Nelson	**144**	58	50N	122	44W
Fort Nelson →	**144**	59	32N	124	0W
Fort Payne	**169**	34	25N	85	44W
Fort Peck L.	**163**	47	40N	107	0W
Fort Pierce	**170**	27	29N	80	19W
Fort Providence	**145**	61	3N	117	40W
Fort Qu'Appelle	**152**	50	45N	103	50W
Fort Resolution	**145**	61	10N	113	40W
Fort Rupert	**140**	51	30N	78	40W
Fort St. James	**154**	54	30N	124	10W
Fort St. John	**155**	56	15N	120	50W
Fort Sandeman	**88**	31	20N	69	31 E
Fort Saskatchewan	**155**	53	40N	113	15W
Fort Scott	**166**	37	50N	94	40W
Fort Severn	**140**	56	0N	87	40W
Fort Shevchenko	**70**	43	40N	51	20 E
Fort Simpson	**144**	61	45N	121	15W
Fort Smith, Canada	**145**	60	0N	111	51W
Fort Smith, U.S.A.	**168**	35	25N	94	25W
Fort Smith Region □	**145**	63	0N	120	0W
Fort Trinquet = Bir Mogrein	**126**	25	10N	11	25W
Fort Valley	**170**	32	33N	83	52W
Fort Vermilion	**145**	58	24N	116	0W
Fort Wayne	**167**	41	5N	85	10W
Fort William	**32**	56	48N	5	8W
Fort Worth	**168**	32	45N	97	25W
Fort Yukon	**142**	66	35N	145	20W
Fortaleza	**189**	3	45S	38	35W
Forth →	**31**	56	9N	4	18W
Forth, Firth of	**31**	56	5N	2	55W
Fortuna	**172**	40	38N	124	8W
Foshan	**99**	23	4N	113	5 E
Foster	**117**	38	40S	146	15 E
Fougères	**36**	48	21N	1	14W
Foula, I.	**30**	60	10N	2	5W
Foulness I.	**24**	51	36N	0	55 E
Fourmies	**38**	50	1N	4	2 E
Foúrnoi	**55**	37	36N	26	32 E
Fouta Djalon	**130**	11	20N	12	10W
Foveaux Str.	**123**	46	42S	168	10 E
Fowey	**27**	50	20N	4	39W
Foxe Basin	**146**	66	0N	77	0W
Foxe Chan.	**146**	65	0N	80	0W
Foxe Pen.	**146**	65	0N	76	0W
Foxton	**122**	40	29S	175	18 E
Foyle, Lough	**34**	55	6N	7	8W
Foynes	**35**	52	37N	9	5W
Franca	**188**	20	33S	47	30W
France ■	**37**	47	0N	3	0 E
Franche-Comté	**37**	46	30N	5	50 E
François	**180**	14	38N	60	57W
Franeker	**41**	53	12N	5	33 E
Frankfort, Ind., U.S.A.	**167**	40	20N	86	33W
Frankfort, Ky., U.S.A.	**165**	38	12N	84	52W
Frankfurt am Main	**42**	50	7N	8	40 E
Frankfurt an der Oder	**43**	52	50N	14	31 E
Fränkische Alb	**43**	49	20N	11	30 E
Franklin, La., U.S.A.	**168**	29	45N	91	30W
Franklin, N.H., U.S.A.	**164**	43	28N	71	39W
Franklin, W. Va., U.S.A.	**165**	38	38N	79	21W
Franklin D. Roosevelt L.	**162**	48	30N	118	16W
Franklin Mts.	**145**	65	0N	125	0W
Franklin Str.	**145**	72	0N	96	0W
Frankston	**117**	38	8S	145	8 E
Franz	**150**	48	25N	84	30W
Fraser →	**154**	49	7N	123	11W
Fraser, Mt.	**120**	25	35S	118	20 E
Fraser I.	**116**	25	15S	153	10 E
Fraserburgh	**33**	57	41N	2	0W
Fray Bentos	**190**	33	10S	58	15W
Frederick	**164**	39	25N	77	23W
Fredericksburg	**165**	38	16N	77	29W
Fredericton	**148**	45	57N	66	40W
Frederikshavn	**61**	57	28N	10	31 E
Fredrikstad	**60**	59	13N	10	57 E
Freeport, Bahamas	**178**	26	30N	78	47W
Freeport, Ill., U.S.A.	**166**	42	18N	89	40W
Freeport, N.Y., U.S.A.	**164**	40	39N	73	35W
Freeport, Tex., U.S.A.	**158**	28	55N	95	22W
Freetown	**130**	8	30N	13	17W
Freiberg	**42**	50	55N	13	20 E
Freibourg = Fribourg	**44**	46	49N	7	9 E
Fréjus	**37**	43	25N	6	44 E
Fremantle	**120**	32	7S	115	47 E
Fremont, Calif., U.S.A.	**172**	37	32N	122	1W
Fremont, Nebr., U.S.A.	**166**	41	30N	96	30W
French Guiana ■	**185**	4	0N	53	0W
French Pass	**123**	40	55S	173	55 E
French Terr. of Afars & Issas = Djibouti ■	**133**	12	0N	43	0 E
Fresnillo	**175**	23	10N	102	53W
Fresno	**173**	36	47N	119	50W
Fria, C.	**136**	18	0S	12	0 E
Frías	**190**	28	40S	65	5W
Fribourg	**44**	46	49N	7	9 E
Friendly, Is. = Tonga ■	**123**	19	50S	174	30W
Friesland □	**41**	53	5N	5	50 E
Frio, C.	**182**	22	50S	41	50W
Friuli-Venezia Giulia □	**47**	46	0N	13	0 E
Frobisher B.	**146**	62	30N	66	0W
Frobisher Bay	**146**	63	44N	68	31W
Frobisher L.	**152**	56	20N	108	15W
Frome	**27**	51	16N	2	17W
Frome, L.	**118**	30	45S	139	45 E
Frome Downs	**118**	31	13S	139	45 E
Front Range	**163**	40	0N	105	40W
Front Royal	**164**	38	55N	78	10W
Frontera	**177**	18	32N	92	38W
Frostburg	**164**	39	43N	78	57W
Frunze	**71**	42	54N	74	46 E
Frutal	**188**	20	0S	49	0W
Fuchou = Fuzhou	**99**	26	5N	119	16 E
Fuchū, Hiroshima, Japan	**109**	34	34N	133	14 E
Fuchū, Tōkyō, Japan	**107**	35	40N	139	29 E
Fuerte, R. →	**174**	25	54N	109	22W
Fuji	**107**	35	9N	138	39 E
Fuji-no-miya	**107**	35	10N	138	40 E
Fuji-San	**107**	35	22N	138	44 E
Fuji-yoshida	**107**	35	30N	138	46 E
Fujian □	**99**	26	0N	118	0 E
Fujieda	**107**	34	52N	138	16 E
Fujisawa	**107**	35	22N	139	29 E
Fukaya	**107**	36	12N	139	12 E
Fukien = Fujian □	**99**	26	0N	118	0 E
Fukuchiyama	**106**	35	19N	135	9 E
Fukue-Shima	**104**	32	40N	128	45 E
Fukui	**106**	36	0N	136	10 E
Fukuoka	**108**	33	39N	130	21 E
Fukushima	**103**	37	44N	140	28 E
Fukuyama	**109**	34	35N	133	20 E
Fulton, Mo., U.S.A.	**166**	38	50N	91	55W
Fulton, N.Y., U.S.A.	**164**	43	20N	76	22W
Funabashi	**107**	35	45N	140	0 E
Funchal	**126**	32	38N	16	54W
Fundación	**184**	10	31N	74	11W
Fundy, B. of	**148**	45	0N	66	0W
Furāt, Nahr al →	**84**	31	0N	47	25 E
Furneaux Group	**119**	40	10S	147	50 E
Furness	**28**	54	14N	3	8W
Fürth	**43**	49	29N	11	0 E
Fury and Hecla Str.	**146**	69	56N	84	0W
Fushun	**98**	41	50N	123	55 E
Fuxin	**98**	42	5N	121	48 E
Fuzhou	**99**	26	5N	119	16 E
Fylde	**28**	53	50N	2	58W
Fyn	**61**	55	20N	10	30 E
Fyne, L.	**30**	56	0N	5	20W
Gabès, Golfe de	**127**	34	0N	10	30 E
Gabon ■	**134**	0	10S	10	0 E
Gaborone	**137**	24	45S	25	57 E
Gachsārān	**85**	30	15N	50	45 E
Gadag	**90**	15	30N	75	45 E
Gadsden	**169**	34	1N	86	0W
Gaeta	**49**	41	12N	13	35 E

Gaffney **165** 35 3N 81 40W
Gagnon **141** 51 50N 68 5W
Gainesville, Fla., U.S.A. **170** 29 38N 82 20W
Gainesville, Ga., U.S.A. **165** 34 17N 83 47W
Gainesville, Tex., U.S.A. **168** 33 40N 97 10W
Gainsborough **29** 53 23N 0 46W
Gairdner L. .... **118** 31 30S 136 0 E
Galápagos **10** 0 0 89 0W
Galas →– .... **96** 4 55N 101 57 E
Galashiels **31** 55 37N 2 50W
Galaţi .... **57** 45 27N 28 2 E
Galatina .... **49** 40 10N 18 10 E
Galdhøpiggen .... **60** 61 38N 8 18 E
Galesburg **166** 40 57N 90 23W
Galicia □ **50** 42 43N 7 45W
Galilee, L. .... **121** 22 20S 145 50 E
Gallatin **169** 36 24N 86 27W
Galle .... **90** 6 5N 80 10 E
Gallinas, Pta. **184** 12 28N 71 40W
Gallipoli = Gelibolu .... **80** 40 28N 26 43 E
Gallípoli .... **49** 40 8N 18 0 E
Gällivare .... **66** 67 9N 20 40 E
Galloway **31** 55 0N 4 25W
Galloway, Mull of **30** 54 38N 4 50W
Gallup **161** 35 30N 108 45W
Galty Mts. **35** 52 22N 8 10W
Galveston **168** 29 15N 94 48W
Galveston B. **168** 29 30N 94 50W
Galway **35** 53 16N 9 4W
Galway □ **34** 53 16N 9 3W
Gamagori .... **106** 34 50N 137 14 E
Gambia ■ **130** 13 25N 16 0W
Gambia →– **130** 13 28N 16 34W
Gand = Gent .... **42** 51 2N 3 42 E
Gander **149** 48 58N 54 35W
Gandhi Sagar .... **91** 24 40N 75 40 E
Gandi .... **131** 12 55N 5 49 E
Ganga →– .... **92** 23 20N 90 30 E
Ganges = Ganga →– ..... **92** 23 20N 90 30 E
Gangtok .... **92** 27 20N 88 37 E
Gannett Pk. **163** 43 15N 109 38W
Gansu □ .... **98** 36 0N 104 0 E
Ganzhou .... **99** 25 51N 114 56 E
Gao **130** 16 15N 0 5W
Gaoxiong .... **99** 22 38N 120 18 E
Garachiné **179** 8 0N 78 12W
Garanhuns **189** 8 50S 36 30W
Garberville **172** 40 11N 123 50W
Garda, L. di .... **46** 45 40N 10 40 E
Garden City **161** 38 0N 100 45W
Garden Grove **173** 33 47N 117 55W
Gardēz .... **87** 33 37N 69 9 E
Garmsār .... **86** 35 20N 52 25 E
Garonne →– **36** 45 2N 0 36W
Garoua .... **131** 9 19N 13 21 E
Garrison Res. = Sakakawea,
  L. **163** 47 30N 102 0W
Garry L. **145** 65 58N 100 18W
Garvie Mts. .... **123** 45 30S 168 50 E
Garwa = Garoua .... **131** 9 19N 13 21 E
Gary **167** 41 35N 87 20W
Garzón **184** 2 10N 75 40W
Gascogne .... **36** 43 45N 0 20 E
Gascony = Gascogne .... **36** 43 45N 0 20 E
Gaspé **148** 48 52N 64 30W
Gaspé, C. de **148** 48 48N 64 7W
Gaspé, Pén. de **148** 48 45N 65 40W
Gastonia **165** 35 17N 81 10W
Gastre **192** 42 20S 69 15W
Gata, C. de **51** 36 41N 2 13W
Gateshead **28** 54 57N 1 37W
Gauhati .... **93** 26 10N 91 45 E
Gävle .... **60** 60 40N 17 9 E
Gävleborgs län □ .... **60** 61 30N 16 15 E
Gawilgarh Hills .... **91** 21 15N 76 45 E
Gawler .... **119** 34 30S 138 42 E
Gawler Ranges .... **114** 32 30S 135 45 E
Gaxun Nur .... **100** 42 22N 100 30 E
Gaya .... **92** 24 47N 85 4 E
Gaylord **150** 45 1N 84 41W
Gayndah .... **116** 25 35S 151 32 E

Gaza .... **80** 31 30N 34 28 E
Gaziantep .... **80** 37 6N 37 23 E
Gdańsk .... **58** 54 22N 18 40 E
Gdańska, Zatoka .... **58** 54 30N 19 20 E
Gdynia .... **58** 54 35N 18 33 E
Gedaref .... **129** 14 2N 35 28 E
Geelong .... **117** 38 10S 144 22 E
Gejiu .... **99** 23 20N 103 10 E
Gelderland □ .... **41** 52 5N 6 10 E
Geldermalsen .... **40** 51 53N 5 17 E
Geldrop .... **41** 51 25N 5 32 E
Geleen .... **41** 50 57N 5 49 E
Gelibolu .... **80** 40 28N 26 43 E
Gelsenkirchen .... **42** 51 30N 7 5 E
Gemert .... **41** 51 33N 5 41 E
General Alvear **190** 35 0S 67 40W
General Pico **190** 35 45S 63 50W
Geneva = Genève ...... **44** 46 12N 6 9 E
Geneva **164** 42 53N 77 0W
Geneva, L. = Léman, Lac .. **44** 46 26N 6 30 E
Genève .... **44** 46 12N 6 9 E
Genk .... **41** 50 58N 5 32 E
Genkai-Nada .... **108** 34 0N 130 0 E
Gennargentu, Mti. del .... **48** 40 0N 9 10 E
Genoa = Génova .... **46** 44 24N 8 56 E
Génova .... **46** 44 24N 8 56 E
Génova, Golfo di .... **46** 44 0N 9 0 E
Gent .... **42** 51 2N 3 42 E
George, L. .... **132** 0 5N 30 10 E
George River = Port
  Nouveau-Québec **146** 58 30N 65 59W
George Town .... **96** 5 25N 100 15 E
Georgetown, Australia ... **119** 18 17S 143 33 E
Georgetown, Canada **151** 43 40N 79 56W
Georgetown, Guyana **185** 6 50N 58 12W
Georgetown, U.S.A. **170** 33 22N 79 15W
Georgia □ **170** 32 0N 82 0W
Georgian B. **151** 45 15N 81 0W
Georgian S.S.R. □ ..... **70** 42 0N 43 0 E
Gera .... **43** 50 53N 12 11 E
Geraldton, Australia .... **120** 28 48S 114 32 E
Geraldton, Canada **150** 49 44N 86 59W
Gereshk .... **87** 31 47N 64 35 E
Germany, East ■ ...... **18** 52 0N 12 0 E
Germany, West ■ ...... **18** 52 0N 9 0 E
Germiston .... **137** 26 15S 28 10 E
Gerona .... **51** 41 58N 2 46 E
Ghana ■ **130** 6 0N 1 0W
Ghat .... **127** 24 59N 10 11 E
Ghawdex = Gozo .... **49** 36 0N 14 13 E
Ghaziabad .... **89** 28 42N 77 26 E
Ghazipur .... **92** 25 38N 83 35 E
Ghaznī .... **87** 33 30N 68 28 E
Ghaznī □ .... **87** 32 10N 68 20 E
Ghent = Gent .... **42** 51 2N 3 42 E
Ghowr □ .... **87** 34 0N 64 20 E
Ghulam Mohammad Barrage. **88** 25 30N 68 20 E
Giant's Causeway **34** 55 15N 6 30W
Gibara **178** 21 9N 76 11W
Gibraltar **50** 36 7N 5 22W
Gibraltar, Str. of **50** 35 55N 5 40W
Gien .... **39** 47 40N 2 36 E
Gifu .... **106** 35 30N 136 45 E
Gigha **30** 55 42N 5 45W
Gijón **50** 43 32N 5 42W
Gila →– **173** 32 43N 114 33W
Gīlān □ .... **81** 37 0N 50 0 E
Gilbert Is. = Kiribati ■ .. **122** 1 0N 176 0 E
Gilford I. **154** 50 40N 126 30W
Gilgandra .... **116** 31 43S 148 39 E
Gilgit .... **89** 35 50N 74 15 E
Gillingham .... **25** 51 23N 0 34 E
Gingin .... **120** 31 22S 115 54 E
Gippsland .... **117** 37 45S 147 15 E
Girardot **184** 4 18N 74 48W
Giresun .... **81** 40 55N 38 30 E
Gironde →– **36** 45 32N 1 7W
Girvan **30** 55 15N 4 50W
Gisborne .... **122** 38 39S 178 5 E
Gisors .... **39** 49 15N 1 47 E
Gizhiga .... **73** 62 3N 160 30 E

Name	Map	Lat	Long
Gizhiginskaya, Guba	73	61 0N	158 0 E
Giżycko	58	54 2N	21 48 E
Gjoa Haven	145	68 20N	96 8W
Glace Bay	149	46 11N	59 58W
Gladstone, Queens., Australia	121	23 52S	151 16 E
Gladstone, S. Austral., Australia	118	33 15S	138 22 E
Gláma	64	65 48N	23 0W
Glasgow, U.K.	31	55 52N	4 14W
Glasgow, U.S.A.	169	37 2N	85 55W
Glastonbury	27	51 9N	2 42W
Gleiwitz = Gliwice	58	50 22N	18 41 E
Glen Coe	32	56 40N	5 0W
Glen Innes	116	29 44S	151 44 E
Glen Mor	33	57 12N	4 37 E
Glenburgh	120	25 26S	116 6 E
Glendale	173	34 7N	118 18W
Glendive	163	47 7N	104 40W
Glenelg	119	34 58S	138 31 E
Glenns Ferry	172	43 0N	115 15W
Glenorchy	119	42 49S	147 18 E
Glenrothes	31	56 12N	3 11W
Glens Falls	164	43 20N	73 40W
Gliwice	58	50 22N	18 41 E
Głogów	58	51 37N	16 5 E
Glossop	28	53 27N	1 56W
Gloucester	24	51 52N	2 15W
Gloucestershire □	24	51 44N	2 10W
Gloversville	164	43 5N	74 18W
Gniezno	58	52 30N	17 35 E
Go Cong	95	10 22N	106 40 E
Goa	91	15 33N	73 59 E
Goa □	90	15 33N	73 59 E
Goat Fell	30	55 37N	5 11W
Goba	133	7 1N	39 59 E
Gobi	98	44 0N	111 0 E
Gobō	106	33 53N	135 10 E
Godavari →	91	16 25N	82 18 E
Godbout	148	49 20N	67 38W
Goderich	150	43 45N	81 41W
Godhra	91	22 49N	73 40 E
Gods L.	153	54 40N	94 15W
Godthåb	147	64 10N	51 35W
Goeie Hoop, Kaap die	136	34 24S	18 30 E
Goeree	40	51 50N	4 0 E
Goes	40	51 30N	3 55 E
Gogama	151	47 35N	81 43W
Goiânia	188	16 43S	49 20W
Goiás □	188	12 10S	48 0W
Goirle	40	51 31N	5 4 E
Gojō	106	34 21N	135 42 E
Gökçeada	55	40 10N	25 50 E
Gold Coast, Australia	116	28 0S	153 25 E
Gold Coast, W. Afr.	124	4 0N	1 40W
Golden Bay	122	40 40S	172 50 E
Golden Gate	172	37 54N	122 30W
Golden Hinde	154	49 40N	125 44W
Golden Vale	35	52 33N	8 17W
Goldfield	172	37 45N	117 13W
Goldsboro	165	35 24N	77 59W
Goldsworthy	114	20 21S	119 30 E
Golfo Aranci	48	41 0N	9 35 E
Gomel	68	52 28N	31 0 E
Gómez Palacio	174	25 34N	103 30W
Gonābād	86	34 15N	58 45 E
Gonaïves	180	19 20N	72 42W
Gonda	92	27 9N	81 58 E
Gonder	132	12 39N	37 30 E
Good Hope, C. of = Goeie Hoop, Kaap die	136	34 24S	18 30 E
Goole	29	53 42N	0 52W
Goondiwindi	116	28 30S	150 21 E
Goose Bay	147	53 15N	60 20W
Gorakhpur	92	26 47N	83 23 E
Gordonvale	121	17 5S	145 50 E
Gore, Ethiopia	132	8 12N	35 32 E
Gore, N.Z.	123	46 5S	168 58 E
Gorey	35	52 41N	6 18W
Gorinchem	40	51 50N	4 59 E
Gorki = Gorkiy	68	56 20N	44 0 E
Gorkiy	68	56 20N	44 0 E
Görlitz	43	51 10N	14 59 E
Gorna Oryakhovitsa	53	43 7N	25 40 E
Gort	35	53 4N	8 50W
Gorzów Wielkopolski	58	52 43N	15 15 E
Gosford	117	33 23S	151 18 E
Gospič	52	44 35N	15 23 E
Gosport	25	50 48N	1 8W
Göteborg	60	57 43N	11 59 E
Göteborgs och Bohus län □	60	58 30N	11 30 E
Gotemba	107	35 18N	138 56 E
Gotha	43	50 56N	10 42 E
Gotland	60	57 30N	18 33 E
Gōtsu	109	35 0N	132 14 E
Gottwaldov	59	49 14N	17 40 E
Gouda	40	52 1N	4 42 E
Gouin, Rés.	151	48 35N	74 40W
Goulburn	117	34 44S	149 44 E
Goundam	130	16 25N	3 45W
Gournay-en-Bray	38	49 29N	1 44 E
Governador Valadares	188	18 15S	41 57W
Governor's Harbour	178	25 10N	76 14W
Gower, The	27	51 35N	4 10W
Goya	190	29 10S	59 10W
Gozo	49	36 0N	14 13 E
Graaff-Reinet	136	32 13S	24 32 E
Gracias a Dios, C.	179	15 0N	83 10W
Grafton	116	29 38S	152 58 E
Graham	165	36 5N	79 22W
Graham I.	154	53 40N	132 30W
Graham Land	14	65 0S	64 0W
Grahamstown	137	33 19S	26 31 E
Grain Coast	124	4 20N	10 0W
Grampian □	33	57 0N	3 0W
Grampian Mts.	33	56 50N	4 0W
Grampians, The	119	37 0S	142 20 E
Gran Chaco	190	25 0S	61 0W
Gran Sasso d'Italia	47	42 25N	13 30 E
Granada, Nic.	179	11 58N	86 0W
Granada, Spain	50	37 10N	3 35W
Granby	151	45 25N	72 45W
Grand Bank	149	47 6N	55 48W
Grand Bassam	130	5 10N	3 49W
Grand Canyon	160	36 3N	112 9W
Grand Cayman	178	19 20N	81 20W
Grand Cess	130	4 40N	8 12W
Grand Falls	149	48 56N	55 40W
Grand Forks, Canada	155	49 0N	118 30W
Grand Forks, U.S.A.	156	48 0N	97 3W
Grand Island	163	40 59N	98 25W
Grand Junction	163	39 0N	108 30W
Grand Mère	151	46 36N	72 40W
Grand Portage	150	47 58N	89 41W
Grand Rapids, Canada	153	53 12N	99 19W
Grand Rapids, U.S.A.	167	42 57N	86 40W
Grand St.-Bernard, Col. du	44	45 53N	7 11 E
Grand Teton	163	43 54N	111 50W
Grand View	153	51 10N	100 42W
Grande →, Bolivia	187	15 51S	64 39W
Grande →, Brazil	188	20 6S	51 4W
Grande, B.	192	50 30S	68 20W
Grande, La	171	45 15N	118 0W
Grande, La →	140	53 50N	79 0W
Grande Baleine, R. de la →	140	55 16N	77 47W
Grande de Santiago, R. →	175	21 36N	105 26W
Grande Prairie	155	55 10N	118 50W
Grande-Rivière	148	48 26N	64 30W
Grange, La	170	33 4N	85 0W
Grangemouth	31	56 1N	3 43W
Grangeville	162	45 57N	116 4W
Granite City	166	38 45N	90 3W
Grant, Mt.	172	38 34N	118 48W
Grantham	29	52 55N	0 39W
Grantown-on-Spey	33	57 19N	3 36W
Grants Pass	171	42 30N	123 22W
Grass Valley	172	39 18N	121 0W
Grasse	37	43 38N	6 56 E
Gravelbourg	152	49 50N	106 35W
Gravelines	38	51 0N	2 10 E
's-Gravenhage	40	52 7N	4 17 E

Gravesend	**25**	51	25N	0	22 E
Grayling	**167**	44	40N	84	42W
Graz	**45**	47	4N	15	27 E
Great Abaco I.	**178**	26	25N	77	10W
Great Australian Bight	**114**	33	30S	130	0 E
Great Bahama Bank	**178**	23	15N	78	0W
Great Barrier I.	**122**	36	11S	175	25 E
Great Barrier Reef	**121**	18	0S	146	50 E
Great Basin	**172**	40	0N	116	30W
Great Bear L.	**145**	65	30N	120	0W
Great Britain	**16**	54	0N	2	15W
Great Divide, The	**117**	35	0S	149	17 E
Great Dividing Ra.	**121**	23	0S	146	0 E
Great Exuma I.	**178**	23	30N	75	50W
Great Falls	**163**	47	27N	111	12W
Great Inagua I.	**180**	21	0N	73	20W
Great Indian Desert = Thar Desert	**89**	28	0N	72	0 E
Great Orme's Head	**26**	53	20N	3	52W
Great Ouse →	**29**	52	47N	0	22 E
Great Plains	**138**	47	0N	105	0W
Great Salt Lake	**162**	41	0N	112	30W
Great Salt Lake Desert	**162**	40	20N	113	50W
Great Slave L.	**145**	61	23N	115	0W
Great Wall	**98**	38	30N	109	30 E
Great Whernside	**28**	54	9N	1	59W
Great Yarmouth	**29**	52	40N	1	45 E
Greater Antilles	**181**	17	40N	74	0W
Greater Manchester □	**28**	53	30N	2	15W
Greater Sunda Is.	**111**	2	30S	110	0 E
Gredos, Sierra de	**50**	40	20N	5	0W
Greece ■	**54**	40	0N	23	0 E
Greeley	**163**	40	30N	104	40W
Green →, Ky., U.S.A.	**167**	37	54N	87	30W
Green →, Utah, U.S.A.	**163**	38	11N	109	53W
Green Bay	**167**	44	30N	88	0W
Greenfield	**164**	42	38N	72	38W
Greenland □	**147**	66	0N	45	0W
Greenland Sea	**13**	73	0N	10	0W
Greenock	**30**	55	57N	4	46W
Greensboro	**165**	36	7N	79	46W
Greenville, Ala., U.S.A.	**169**	31	50N	86	37W
Greenville, Mich., U.S.A.	**167**	43	12N	85	14W
Greenville, Miss., U.S.A.	**168**	33	25N	91	0W
Greenville, N.C., U.S.A.	**165**	35	37N	77	26W
Greenville, S.C., U.S.A.	**165**	34	54N	82	24W
Greenville, Tenn., U.S.A.	**165**	36	13N	82	51W
Greenwood, Miss., U.S.A.	**169**	33	30N	90	4W
Greenwood, S.C., U.S.A.	**165**	34	13N	82	13W
Grenada	**169**	33	45N	89	50W
Grenada ■	**180**	12	10N	61	40W
Grenoble	**37**	45	12N	5	42 E
Grenville	**117**	37	46S	143	52 E
Gretna Green	**31**	55	0N	3	3W
Grey Range	**116**	27	0S	143	30 E
Grey Res.	**149**	48	20N	56	30W
Greymouth	**123**	42	29S	171	13 E
Griffin	**170**	33	17N	84	14W
Griffith	**117**	34	18S	146	2 E
Grimsby	**29**	53	35N	0	5W
Grimshaw	**155**	56	10N	117	40W
Grinnell	**166**	41	45N	92	43W
Grodno	**68**	53	42N	23	52 E
Groningen	**41**	53	15N	6	35 E
Groningen □	**41**	53	16N	6	40 E
Grootfontein	**136**	19	31S	18	6 E
Groznyy	**70**	43	20N	45	45 E
Grudziądz	**58**	53	30N	18	47 E
Grytviken	**14**	53	50S	37	10W
Gt. Stour = Stour →	**25**	51	15N	1	20 E
Guadalajara, Mexico	**175**	20	40N	103	20W
Guadalajara, Spain	**50**	40	37N	3	12W
Guadalquivir →	**50**	36	47N	6	22W
Guadalupe = Guadeloupe ■	**180**	16	20N	61	40W
Guadalupe Bravos	**174**	31	23N	106	7W
Guadarrama, Sierra de	**50**	41	0N	4	0W
Guadeloupe ■	**180**	16	20N	61	40W
Guadiana →	**50**	37	14N	7	22W
Guadix	**50**	37	18N	3	11W
Guaíra	**191**	24	5S	54	10W

Guajará-Mirim	**187**	10	50S	65	20W
Gualeguay	**190**	33	10S	59	14W
Gualeguaychú	**190**	33	3S	59	31W
Guam	**10**	13	27N	144	45 E
Guanabacoa	**178**	23	8N	82	18W
Guanacaste, Cordillera del	**179**	10	40N	85	4W
Guanahani = San Salvador	**178**	24	0N	74	40W
Guanajay	**178**	22	56N	82	42W
Guanajuato	**177**	21	1N	101	15W
Guanajuato □	**177**	21	0N	101	0W
Guanare	**184**	8	42N	69	12W
Guangdong □	**99**	23	0N	113	0 E
Guangxi Zhuangzu Zizhiqu □	**99**	24	0N	109	0 E
Guangzhou	**99**	23	5N	113	10 E
Guantánamo	**178**	20	10N	75	14W
Guaporé →	**187**	11	55S	65	4W
Guaqui	**187**	16	41S	68	54W
Guarapuava	**191**	25	20S	51	30W
Guarda	**50**	40	32N	7	20W
Guardafui, C. = Asir, Ras	**133**	11	55N	51	10 E
Guatemala	**177**	14	40N	90	22W
Guatemala ■	**177**	15	40N	90	30W
Guaviare →	**184**	4	3N	67	44W
Guayama	**180**	17	59N	66	7W
Guayaquil	**184**	2	15S	79	52W
Guayaquil, G. de	**186**	3	10S	81	0W
Guaymas	**174**	27	56N	110	54W
Guddu Barrage	**89**	28	30N	69	50 E
Gudur	**90**	14	12N	79	55 E
Guelph	**151**	43	35N	80	20W
Guernica	**50**	43	19N	2	40W
Guernsey	**36**	49	30N	2	35W
Guerrero □	**177**	17	40N	100	0W
Guilin	**99**	25	18N	110	15 E
Guimarães	**188**	2	9S	44	42W
Guinea ■	**130**	10	20N	10	0W
Guinea, Gulf of	**130**	3	0N	2	30 E
Guinea-Bissau ■	**130**	12	0N	15	0W
Güines	**178**	22	50N	82	0W
Guiyang	**99**	26	32N	106	40 E
Guizhou □	**99**	27	0N	107	0 E
Gujarat □	**91**	23	20N	71	0 E
Gujranwala	**89**	32	10N	74	12 E
Gujrat	**89**	32	40N	74	2 E
Gulbarga	**91**	17	20N	76	50 E
Gulf, The	**85**	27	0N	50	0 E
Gulfport	**169**	30	21N	89	3W
Gulgong	**116**	32	20S	149	49 E
Gull Lake	**152**	50	10N	108	29W
Gümüsane	**81**	40	30N	39	30 E
Guna	**91**	24	40N	77	19 E
Gundagai	**117**	35	3S	148	6 E
Gunnedah	**116**	30	59S	150	15 E
Gunningbar Cr. →	**116**	31	14S	147	6 E
Guntakal	**90**	15	11N	77	27 E
Guntersville	**169**	34	18N	86	16W
Guntur	**92**	16	23N	80	30 E
Gurdaspur	**89**	32	5N	75	31 E
Gurgaon	**89**	28	27N	77	1 E
Gurkha	**92**	28	5N	84	40 E
Gurupi →	**188**	1	13S	46	6W
Guryev	**70**	47	5N	52	0 E
Gusau	**131**	12	12N	6	40 E
Guthrie	**168**	35	55N	97	30W
Guyana ■	**185**	5	0N	59	0W
Guyenne	**36**	44	30N	0	40 E
Guyra	**116**	30	15S	151	40 E
Gwalior	**91**	26	12N	78	10 E
Gwent □	**27**	51	45N	2	55W
Gweru	**137**	19	28S	29	45 E
Gwynedd □	**26**	53	0N	4	0W
Gyaring Hu	**101**	34	50N	97	40 E
Gydanskiy P-ov.	**69**	70	0N	78	0 E
Gympie	**116**	26	11S	152	38 E
Gyoda	**107**	36	10N	139	30 E
Gyöngyös	**59**	47	48N	20	0 E
Györ	**59**	47	41N	17	40 E
Gypsumville	**153**	51	45N	98	40W

Ha 'Arava	**80**	30 50N	35	20 E
Ha Giang	**95**	22 50N	104	59 E
Haarlem	**40**	52 23N	4	39 E
Habana, La	**178**	23 8N	82	22W
Hachijō-Jima	**105**	33 5N	139	45 E
Hachinohe	**103**	40 30N	141	29 E
Hachiōji	**107**	35 40N	139	20 E
Hadera	**80**	32 27N	34	55 E
Hadhramaut = Hadramawt ..	**83**	15 30N	49	30 E
Hadiya	**82**	25 30N	36	56 E
Hadramawt	**83**	15 30N	49	30 E
Hadrians Wall	**28**	55 0N	2	30W
Haeju	**98**	38 3N	125	45 E
Haerhpin = Harbin	**98**	45 48N	126	40 E
Hafar al Bāṭin	**82**	28 25N	46	0 E
Hafnarfjörður	**64**	64 4N	21	57W
Haft-Gel	**84**	31 30N	49	32 E
Hagen	**42**	51 21N	7	29 E
Hagerstown	**164**	39 39N	77	46W
Hagi	**108**	34 30N	131	22 E
Hags Hd.	**35**	52 57N	9	30W
Hague, The = 's-Gravenhage	**40**	52 7N	4	17 E
Hai'an	**99**	32 37N	120	27 E
Haifa = Hefa	**80**	32 46N	35	0 E
Haikou	**99**	20 1N	110	16 E
Ḥāʾil	**82**	27 28N	41	45 E
Hailar	**98**	49 10N	119	38 E
Hailey	**162**	43 30N	114	15W
Haileybury	**151**	47 30N	79	38W
Hainan	**99**	19 0N	110	0 E
Hainan Dao	**99**	19 0N	109	30 E
Haiphong	**95**	20 47N	106	41 E
Haiti ■	**180**	19 0N	72	30W
Hakken-Zan	**106**	34 10N	135	54 E
Hakodate	**103**	41 45N	140	44 E
Ḥalab	**80**	36 10N	37	15 E
Halaib	**129**	22 12N	36	30 E
Halberstadt	**43**	51 53N	11	2 E
Halfmoon Bay	**123**	46 50S	168	5 E
Halifax, Canada	**148**	44 38N	63	35W
Halifax, U.K.	**28**	53 43N	1	51W
Halifax B.	**121**	18 50S	147	0 E
Hallands län □	**61**	56 50N	12	50 E
Halle	**43**	51 29N	12	0 E
Halls Creek	**114**	18 16S	127	38 E
Halmahera	**113**	0 40N	128	0 E
Halmstad	**61**	56 41N	12	52 E
Hälsingborg = Helsingborg ..	**61**	56 3N	12	42 E
Hamada	**109**	34 56N	132	4 E
Hamadān	**81**	34 52N	48	32 E
Hamadān □	**81**	35 0N	49	0 E
Hamāh	**80**	35 5N	36	40 E
Hamakita	**107**	34 45N	137	47 E
Hamamatsu	**106**	34 45N	137	45 E
Hamar	**60**	60 48N	11	7 E
Hamburg	**43**	53 32N	9	59 E
Hämeenlinna	**67**	61 0N	24	28 E
Hamelin Pool	**120**	26 22S	114	20 E
Hameln	**42**	52 7N	9	24 E
Hamhung	**98**	39 54N	127	30 E
Hamilton, Australia	**119**	37 45S	142	2 E
Hamilton, Bermuda	**180**	32 15N	64	45W
Hamilton, Canada	**151**	43 15N	79	50W
Hamilton, N.Z.	**122**	37 47S	175	19 E
Hamilton, U.K.	**31**	55 47N	4	2W
Hamilton, U.S.A.	**167**	39 20N	84	35W
Hamm	**42**	51 40N	7	49 E
Hammerfest	**67**	70 39N	23	41 E
Hammond, Ind., U.S.A.	**167**	41 40N	87	30W
Hammond, La., U.S.A.	**169**	30 32N	90	30W
Hampshire □	**25**	51 3N	1	20W
Hampshire Downs	**25**	51 10N	1	10W
Hampton	**165**	37 4N	76	18W
Hanamaki	**103**	39 23N	141	7 E
Hancock	**150**	47 10N	88	40W
Handa	**106**	34 53N	137	0 E
Handan	**98**	36 35N	114	28 E
Haney	**154**	49 12N	122	40W
Hanford	**173**	36 23N	119	39W
Hangayn Nuruu	**100**	47 30N	100	0 E
Hangchou = Hangzhou	**99**	30 18N	120	11 E
Hangö	**67**	59 50N	22	57 E
Hangu	**98**	39 18N	117	53 E
Hangzhou	**99**	30 18N	120	11 E
Hanna	**155**	51 40N	111	54W
Hannibal	**166**	39 42N	91	22W
Hannover	**42**	52 23N	9	43 E
Hanoi	**95**	21 5N	105	55 E
Hanover = Hannover	**42**	52 23N	9	43 E
Hanover, N.H., U.S.A.	**148**	43 43N	72	17W
Hanover, Pa., U.S.A.	**164**	39 46N	76	59W
Hansi	**89**	29 10N	75	57 E
Hanyū	**107**	36 10N	139	32 E
Hanzhong	**99**	33 10N	107	1 E
Haora	**92**	22 37N	88	20 E
Haparanda	**67**	65 52N	24	8 E
Haraḍ, Si. Arabia	**83**	24 22N	49	0 E
Haraḍ, Yemen	**83**	16 26N	43	5 E
Harare	**137**	17 43S	31	2 E
Harbin	**98**	45 48N	126	40 E
Harbour Breton	**149**	47 29N	55	50W
Harbour Grace	**149**	47 40N	53	22W
Hardap Dam	**136**	24 32S	17	50 E
Hardenberg	**41**	52 34N	6	37 E
Harderwijk	**41**	52 21N	5	38 E
Hardinxveld	**40**	51 49N	4	53 E
Hardwar = Haridwar	**89**	29 58N	78	9 E
Harer	**133**	9 20N	42	8 E
Harfleur	**38**	49 30N	0	10 E
Hargeisa	**133**	9 30N	44	2 E
Hari →	**111**	1 16S	104	5 E
Haridwar	**89**	29 58N	78	9 E
Harima-Nada	**109**	34 30N	134	35 E
Harīrūd →	**86**	34 20N	62	30 E
Harlech	**26**	52 52N	4	7W
Harlingen, Neth.	**41**	53 11N	5	25 E
Harlingen, U.S.A.	**161**	26 20N	97	50W
Harlow	**25**	51 47N	0	9 E
Harney Basin	**171**	43 30N	119	0W
Härnösand	**66**	62 38N	18	0 E
Harriman	**169**	36 0N	84	35W
Harris	**32**	57 50N	6	55W
Harris L.	**118**	31 10S	135	10 E
Harrisburg, Ill., U.S.A.	**167**	37 42N	88	30W
Harrisburg, Pa., U.S.A.	**164**	40 18N	76	52W
Harrison	**168**	36 10N	93	4W
Harrison, C.	**147**	54 55N	57	55W
Harrison B.	**142**	70 25N	151	30W
Harrisonburg	**165**	38 28N	78	52W
Harrogate	**28**	53 59N	1	32W
Harrow	**25**	51 35N	0	15W
Hartford	**164**	41 47N	72	41W
Hartland Pt.	**27**	51 2N	4	32W
Hartlepool	**29**	54 42N	1	11W
Hartsville	**165**	34 23N	80	2W
Harvey, Australia	**120**	33 5S	115	54 E
Harvey, U.S.A.	**167**	41 40N	87	40W
Harwich	**25**	51 56N	1	18 E
Haryana □	**89**	29 0N	76	10 E
Hashima	**106**	35 20N	136	40 E
Hashimoto	**106**	34 19N	135	37 E
Hastings, N.Z.	**122**	39 39S	176	52 E
Hastings, U.K.	**25**	50 51N	0	36 E
Hastings, U.S.A.	**163**	40 34N	98	22W
Hastings Ra.	**116**	31 15S	152	14 E
Hatano	**107**	35 22N	139	14 E
Hathras	**89**	27 36N	78	6 E
Hatteras, C.	**165**	35 10N	75	30W
Hattiesburg	**169**	31 20N	89	20W
Hatvan	**59**	47 40N	19	45 E
Hau Bon = Cheo Reo	**95**	13 25N	108	28 E
Hauraki Gulf	**122**	36 35S	175	5 E
Haut Atlas	**126**	32 30N	5	0W
Havana = Habana, La	**178**	23 8N	82	22W
Havant	**25**	50 51N	0	59W
Havelock	**151**	44 26N	77	53W
Haverfordwest	**26**	51 48N	4	59W
Haverhill	**164**	42 50N	71	2W
Havre	**163**	48 34N	109	40W
Havre, Le	**38**	49 30N	0	5 E
Hawaii □	**160**	20 30N	157	0W
Hawaiian Is.	**160**	20 30N	156	0W

Name	Page	Lat °	Lat ′	N/S	Long °	Long ′	E/W
Hawea Lake	123	44	28	S	169	19	E
Hawera	122	39	35	S	174	19	E
Hawick	31	55	25	N	2	48	W
Hawke B.	122	39	25	S	177	20	E
Hawke's Bay □	122	39	45	S	176	35	E
Hawkesbury	151	45	37	N	74	37	W
Hawthorne	172	38	31	N	118	37	W
Hay, Australia	117	34	30	S	144	51	E
Hay, U.K.	26	52	4	N	3	9	W
Hay River	145	60	51	N	115	44	W
Hayward's Heath	25	51	0	N	0	5	W
Hazard	165	37	18	N	83	10	W
Hazaribag	92	23	58	N	85	26	E
Hazebrouck	38	50	42	N	2	31	E
Hazelton	154	55	20	N	127	42	W
Hazleton	164	40	58	N	76	0	W
Healdsburg	172	38	33	N	122	51	W
Healesville	117	37	35	S	145	30	E
Heanor	29	53	1	N	1	20	W
Hearst	150	49	40	N	83	41	W
Hebei □	98	39	0	N	116	0	E
Hebel	116	28	58	S	147	47	E
Hebrides	16	57	30	N	7	0	W
Hebron = Al Khalīl	80	31	32	N	35	6	E
Hebron	147	58	5	N	62	30	W
Hecate Str.	154	53	10	N	130	30	W
Hechuan	99	30	2	N	106	12	E
Hedmark fylke □	60	61	17	N	11	40	E
Heemstede	40	52	22	N	4	37	E
Heerenveen	41	52	57	N	5	55	E
Heerlen	41	50	55	N	6	0	E
Hefa	80	32	46	N	35	0	E
Hefei	99	31	52	N	117	18	E
Hegang	98	47	20	N	130	19	E
Heidelberg	42	49	23	N	8	41	E
Heilbronn	42	49	8	N	9	13	E
Heilongjiang □	98	48	0	N	126	0	E
Heilunkiang = Heilongjiang □	98	48	0	N	126	0	E
Heinze Is.	94	14	25	N	97	45	E
Hekimhan	81	38	50	N	38	0	E
Hekinan	106	34	52	N	137	0	E
Hekla	16	63	56	N	19	35	W
Helena, Ark., U.S.A.	169	34	30	N	90	35	W
Helena, Mont., U.S.A.	163	46	40	N	112	0	W
Helensburgh	30	56	0	N	4	44	W
Helmand →	87	31	12	N	61	34	E
Helmond	41	51	29	N	5	41	E
Helmsdale	33	58	7	N	3	40	W
Helsingborg	61	56	3	N	12	42	E
Helsinki	67	60	15	N	25	3	E
Helston	27	50	7	N	5	17	W
Helvellyn	28	54	31	N	3	1	W
Hemel Hempstead	25	51	45	N	0	28	W
Hempstead	164	30	5	N	96	5	W
Henan □	99	34	0	N	114	0	E
Henderson	165	36	20	N	78	25	W
Hendersonville	165	35	21	N	82	28	W
Hengelo	41	52	16	N	6	48	E
Hengyang	99	26	51	N	112	30	E
Hénin-Beaumont	38	50	25	N	2	58	E
Hennebont	36	47	49	N	3	19	W
Henrietta Maria C.	140	55	9	N	82	20	W
Henty	117	35	30	S	147	0	E
Henzada	93	17	38	N	95	26	E
Herāt	87	34	20	N	62	7	E
Herāt □	87	35	0	N	62	0	E
Herbert ~ ►	121	18	31	S	146	17	E
Herbiers, Les	36	46	52	N	1	0	W
Hercegnovi	52	42	30	N	18	33	E
Hercegovina = Bosna i Hercegovina □	52	44	0	N	18	0	E
Hereford	24	52	4	N	2	42	W
Hereford and Worcester □	24	52	10	N	2	30	W
Herford	42	52	7	N	8	40	E
Hermosillo	174	29	4	N	110	58	W
Heroica = Caborca	174	30	40	N	112	10	W
Heroica Nogales = Nogales	174	31	20	N	110	56	W
Heron Bay	150	48	40	N	86	25	W
Herrin	166	37	50	N	89	0	W
Hertford □	25	51	51	N	0	5	W
's-Hertogenbosch	40	51	42	N	5	17	E
Hesse = Hessen □	42	50	40	N	9	20	E
Hessen □	42	50	40	N	9	20	E
Hewett, C.	146	70	16	N	67	45	W
Hexham	28	54	58	N	2	7	W
Heysham	28	54	5	N	2	53	W
Heywood	119	38	8	S	141	37	E
Hi-no-Misaki	109	35	26	N	132	38	E
Hialeach	170	25	49	N	80	17	W
Hibiki-Nada	108	34	0	N	130	0	E
Hickory	165	35	46	N	81	17	W
Hida-Gawa →	106	35	26	N	137	3	E
Hida-Sammyaku	106	36	30	N	137	40	E
Hida-Sanchi	106	36	10	N	137	0	E
Hidaka	109	35	30	N	134	44	E
Hidalgo □	177	20	30	N	99	0	W
Hidalgo del Parral	174	26	56	N	105	40	W
Higashi-matsuyama	107	36	2	N	139	25	E
Higashiōsaka	106	34	40	N	135	37	E
Higasi-Suidō	108	34	0	N	129	30	E
High Atlas = Haut Atlas	126	32	30	N	5	0	W
High Point	165	35	57	N	79	58	W
High Prairie	155	55	30	N	116	30	W
Highland □	32	57	30	N	5	0	W
Highland Park	167	42	10	N	87	50	W
Ḥijārah, Ṣaḥrā' al	84	30	25	N	44	30	E
Hikari	108	33	58	N	131	58	E
Hikone	106	35	15	N	136	10	E
Hildesheim	43	52	9	N	9	55	E
Hillegom	40	52	18	N	4	35	E
Hillsboro	171	45	31	N	123	0	W
Hillston	117	33	30	S	145	31	E
Hilo	160	19	44	N	155	5	W
Hilversum	40	52	14	N	5	10	E
Himachal Pradesh □	89	31	30	N	77	0	E
Himalaya, Mts.	101	29	0	N	84	0	E
Hime-Jima	108	33	43	N	131	40	E
Himeji	109	34	50	N	134	40	E
Himi	106	36	50	N	137	0	E
Ḥimṣ	80	34	40	N	36	45	E
Hinchinbrook I.	121	18	20	S	146	15	E
Hinckley	25	52	33	N	1	21	W
Hindmarsh	119	34	54	S	138	34	E
Hindu Kush	89	36	0	N	71	0	E
Hindupur	90	13	49	N	77	32	E
Hines Creek	155	56	20	N	118	40	W
Hingoli	91	19	41	N	77	15	E
Hinton	165	37	40	N	80	51	W
Hirado	108	33	22	N	129	33	E
Hirakarta	106	34	48	N	135	40	E
Hirakud Dam	92	21	32	N	83	45	E
Hirata	109	35	24	N	132	49	E
Hiratsuka	107	35	19	N	139	21	E
Hirosaki	103	40	34	N	140	28	E
Hiroshima	109	34	24	N	132	30	E
Hirson	38	49	55	N	4	4	E
Hispaniola	180	19	0	N	71	0	W
Hita	108	33	20	N	130	58	E
Hitachi	107	36	36	N	140	39	E
Hitachiota	107	36	30	N	140	30	E
Hitchin	25	51	57	N	0	16	W
Hitoyoshi	108	32	13	N	130	45	E
Hitra	65	63	30	N	8	45	E
Hiuchi-Nada	109	34	5	N	133	20	E
Ho Chi Minh City = Thanh Pho Ho Chi Minh	95	10	58	N	106	40	E
Hoa Binh	95	20	50	N	105	20	E
Hobart	119	42	50	S	147	21	E
Hobbs	161	32	40	N	103	3	W
Hodaka-Dake	106	36	17	N	137	39	E
Hódmezövásárhely	59	46	28	N	20	22	E
Hoek van Holland	40	52	0	N	4	7	E
Hofsjökull	64	64	49	N	18	48	W
Hōfu	108	34	3	N	131	34	E
Hogan Group	117	39	13	S	147	1	E
Hoh Xil Shan	101	35	0	N	89	0	E
Hohhot	98	40	52	N	111	40	E
Hōjō	109	33	58	N	132	46	E
Hokitika	123	42	42	S	171	0	E
Hokkaidō □	103	43	30	N	143	0	E
Holbrook	117	35	42	S	147	18	E
Holderness	29	53	45	N	0	5	W

Name	Map	Lat	Long
Holdrege	163	40 26N	99 22W
Holguín	178	20 50N	76 20W
Holland	167	42 47N	86 7W
Holly Springs	169	34 45N	89 25W
Hollywood, Calif., U.S.A.	173	34 7N	118 25W
Hollywood, Fla., U.S.A.	170	26 0N	80 9W
Holsteinsborg	147	66 40N	53 30W
Holsworthy	27	50 48N	4 21W
Holt	64	63 33N	19 48W
Holy I., Scotland, U.K.	31	55 31N	5 4W
Holy I., Wales, U.K.	26	53 17N	4 37W
Holyhead	26	53 18N	4 38W
Holyoke	164	42 14N	72 37W
Hombori	130	15 20N	1 38W
Home Hill	121	19 43S	147 25 E
Homer	142	59 40N	151 35W
Homs = Ḥimş	80	34 40N	36 45 E
Honan = Henan □	99	34 0N	114 0 E
Hondo	108	32 27N	130 12 E
Honduras ■	179	14 40N	86 30W
Honduras, Golfo de	177	16 50N	87 0W
Hong Kong ■	99	22 11N	114 14 E
Hongha ~>	95	22 0N	104 0 E
Hongshui He ~>	99	23 48N	109 30 E
Honiton	27	50 48N	3 11W
Honolulu	160	21 19N	157 52W
Honshū	106	36 0N	138 0 E
Hoogeveen	41	52 44N	6 30 E
Hook Hd.	35	52 8N	6 57W
Hook of Holland = Hoek van Holland	40	52 0N	4 7 E
Hoorn	40	52 38N	5 4 E
Hope, Canada	154	49 25N	121 25 E
Hope, U.S.A.	168	33 40N	93 36W
Hope Town	178	26 35N	76 57W
Hopedale	147	55 28N	60 13W
Hopei = Hebei □	98	39 0N	116 0 E
Hopelchén	177	19 46N	89 51W
Hopetoun, Vic., Australia	119	35 42S	142 22 E
Hopetoun, W. Austral., Australia	120	33 57S	120 7 E
Hopkinsville	169	36 52N	87 26W
Hoquiam	171	46 50N	123 55W
Hordaland fylke □	60	60 25N	6 15 E
Hormoz	85	27 35N	55 0 E
Hormuz Str.	85	26 30N	56 30 E
Horn, Cape = Hornos, Cabo de	192	55 50S	67 30W
Hornavan	66	66 15N	17 30 E
Hornell	164	42 23N	77 41W
Hornos, Cabo de	192	55 50S	67 30W
Hornsby	117	33 42S	151 2 E
Hornsea	29	53 55N	0 10W
Horqin Youyi Qianqi	98	46 5N	122 3 E
Horsens	61	55 52N	9 51 E
Horsham	119	36 44S	142 13 E
Horton ~>	145	69 56N	126 52W
Hoshiarpur	89	31 30N	75 58 E
Hospet	90	15 15N	76 20 E
Hospitalet de Llobregat	51	41 21N	2 6 E
Hoste, I.	192	55 0S	69 0W
Hot Springs	168	34 30N	93 0W
Houghton	150	47 9N	88 39W
Houghton-le-Spring	28	54 51N	1 28W
Houhora	122	34 49S	173 9 E
Houlton	148	46 5N	67 50W
Houma	169	29 35N	90 44W
Houston, Canada	154	54 25N	126 39W
Houston, U.S.A.	168	29 50N	95 20W
Houtman Abrolhos	120	28 43S	113 48 E
Hovd	100	48 2N	91 37 E
Hove	25	50 50N	0 10W
Howe, C.	117	37 30S	150 0 E
Howrah = Haora	92	22 37N	88 20 E
Hoy I.	33	58 50N	3 15W
Hrádec Králové	58	50 15N	15 50 E
Hrvatska □	52	45 20N	18 0 E
Hsiamen = Xiamen	99	24 25N	118 4 E
Hsian = Xi'an	99	34 15N	109 0 E
Hsinhailien = Lianyungang	99	34 40N	119 11 E
Hsüchou = Xuzhou	99	34 18N	117 10 E
Hua Hin	94	12 34N	99 58 E
Huacho	186	11 10S	77 35W
Huainan	99	32 38N	116 58 E
Huallaga ~>	186	5 0S	75 30W
Huambo	134	12 42S	15 54 E
Huancane	187	15 10S	69 44W
Huancavelica	186	12 50S	75 5W
Huancayo	186	12 5S	75 12W
Huanchaca	187	20 15S	66 40W
Huang Hai = Yellow Sea	99	35 0N	123 0 E
Huang Ho ~>	98	37 30N	118 50 E
Huangshi	99	30 10N	115 3 E
Huánuco	186	9 55S	76 15W
Huaraz	186	9 30S	77 32W
Huascarán	186	9 8S	77 36W
Huasco	190	28 30S	71 15W
Huatabampo	174	26 50N	109 38W
Huautla	177	17 51N	100 5W
Hubei □	99	31 0N	112 0 E
Hubli-Dharwad = Dharwad	90	15 22N	75 15 E
Huddersfield	28	53 38N	1 49W
Hudiksvall	66	61 43N	17 10 E
Hudson	164	42 15N	73 46W
Hudson ~>	164	40 42N	74 2W
Hudson Bay	146	52 51N	102 23W
Hudson Str.	146	62 0N	70 0W
Hudson's Hope	155	56 0N	121 54W
Hue	95	16 30N	107 35 E
Huehuetenango	177	15 20N	91 28W
Huelva	50	37 18N	6 57W
Huesca	51	42 8N	0 25W
Hughenden	121	20 52S	144 10 E
Huila, Nevado del	184	3 0N	76 0W
Huinca Renancó	190	34 51S	64 22W
Huixtla	177	15 9N	92 28W
Huizen	40	52 18N	5 14 E
Hukawng Valley	93	26 30N	96 30 E
Hull, Canada	151	45 25N	75 44W
Hull, U.K.	29	53 45N	0 20W
Hulst	40	51 17N	4 2 E
Hulun Nur	98	49 0N	117 30 E
Humaitá	187	27 2S	58 31W
Humber ~>	29	53 40N	0 10W
Humberside □	29	53 50N	0 30W
Humboldt, Canada	152	52 15N	105 9W
Humboldt, U.S.A.	169	35 50N	88 55W
Humboldt ~>	172	40 2N	118 31W
Hume, L.	117	36 0S	147 0 E
Húnaflói	64	65 50N	20 50W
Hunan □	99	27 30N	111 30 E
Hunedoara	56	45 40N	22 50 E
Hungary ■	59	47 20N	19 20 E
Hungary, Plain of	17	47 0N	20 0 E
Hungnam	98	39 49N	127 45 E
Hunsrück	42	49 30N	7 0 E
Hunstanton	29	52 57N	0 30 E
Hunter Ra.	117	32 45S	150 15 E
Huntingdon	25	52 20N	0 11W
Huntington, Ind., U.S.A.	167	40 52N	85 30W
Huntington, W. Va., U.S.A.	165	38 20N	82 30W
Huntington Beach	173	33 40N	118 0W
Huntly	122	37 34S	175 11 E
Huntsville, Canada	151	45 20N	79 14W
Huntsville, Ala., U.S.A.	169	34 45N	86 35W
Huntsville, Tex., U.S.A.	168	30 45N	95 35W
Huonville	119	43 0S	147 5 E
Hupeh □ = Hubei □	99	31 0N	112 0 E
Huron, L.	150	45 0N	83 0W
Hurricane	173	37 10N	113 12W
Húsavík	64	66 3N	17 21W
Hutchinson	161	38 3N	97 59W
Hvar	52	43 11N	16 28 E
Hwang Ho = Huang Ho ~>	98	37 30N	118 50 E
Hwange	137	18 18S	26 30 E
Hyden	120	32 24S	118 53 E
Hyderabad, India	91	17 22N	78 29 E
Hyderabad, Pakistan	88	25 23N	68 24 E
Hyères	37	43 8N	6 9 E
Hyndman Pk.	162	43 50N	114 10W
Hythe	24	51 4N	1 5 E
Hyūga	108	32 25N	131 35 E

Name	Page	Lat °	′		Long °	′	
Iaşi	57	47	10N		27	40 E	
Ibadan	131	7	22N		3	58 E	
Ibagué	184	4	20N		75	20W	
Ibara	109	34	36N		133	28 E	
Ibaraki	106	34	49N		135	34 E	
Ibarra	184	0	21N		78	7W	
Iberian Peninsula	16	40	0N		5	0W	
Ibiza	51	38	54N		1	26 E	
Ibuki-Sanchi	106	35	25N		136	18 E	
Ibusuki	108	31	12N		130	40 E	
Icá	186	14	0S		75	48W	
Içá ~►	184	2	55S		67	58W	
Iceland ■	64	65	0N		19	0W	
Icha	73	55	30N		156	0 E	
Ich'ang = Yichang	99	30	40N		111	20 E	
Ichchapuram	92	19	10N		84	40 E	
Ichihara	107	35	28N		140	5 E	
Ichikawa	107	35	44N		139	55 E	
Ichinomiya	106	35	18N		136	48 E	
Ichinoseki	103	38	55N		141	8 E	
Idaho □	162	44	10N		114	0W	
Idaho Falls	163	43	30N		112	1W	
Ídhi Óros	55	35	15N		24	45 E	
Ídhra	55	37	20N		23	28 E	
Ierápetra	55	35	0N		25	44 E	
Ife	131	7	30N		4	31 E	
Igloolik	146	69	20N		81	49W	
Iguaçu ~►	191	25	36S		54	36W	
Iguaçu, Cat. del	191	25	41S		54	26W	
Iguaçu Falls = Iguaçu, Cat. del	191	25	41S		54	26W	
Iguala de la Independencia	177	18	21N		99	32W	
Iguassu = Iguaçu ~►	191	25	36S		54	36W	
Iida	107	35	35N		137	50 E	
Iisalmi	67	63	32N		27	10 E	
Iizuka	108	33	38N		130	42 E	
IJmuiden	40	52	28N		4	35 E	
IJsselmeer	40	52	45N		5	20 E	
IJsselstein	40	52	1N		5	2 E	
Ikaría	55	37	35N		26	10 E	
Ikeda	109	34	1N		133	48 E	
Iki	108	33	45N		129	42 E	
Iki-Kaikyō	108	33	40N		129	45 E	
Île-de-France	37	49	0N		2	20 E	
Ilebo	134	4	17S		20	55 E	
Ilfracombe	27	51	13N		4	8W	
Ilhéus	189	14	49S		39	2W	
Ili ~►	71	45	53N		77	10 E	
Iliamna L.	142	59	35N		155	30W	
Iliodhrómia	55	39	12N		23	50 E	
Ilkeston	29	52	59N		1	19W	
Illampu = Ancohuma, Nevada	187	16	0S		68	50W	
Illinois □	166	40	15N		89	30W	
Illinois ~►	166	38	55N		90	28W	
Ilo	187	17	40S		71	20W	
Iloilo	112	10	45N		122	33 E	
Ilorin	131	8	30N		4	35 E	
Imabari	109	34	4N		133	0 E	
Imari	108	33	15N		129	52 E	
Imatra	67	61	12N		28	48 E	
Immingham	29	53	37N		0	12W	
Imperial	152	51	21N		105	28W	
Imphal	92	24	48N		93	56 E	
Imroz = Gökçeada	55	40	10N		25	50 E	
Ina	107	35	50N		138	0 E	
Iñapari	187	11	0S		69	40W	
Inari	67	68	54N		27	5 E	
Inarijärvi	67	69	0N		28	0 E	
Inazawa	106	35	15N		136	47 E	
Inchon	98	37	27N		126	40 E	
Indalsälven ~►	66	62	36N		17	30 E	
Independence, Kans., U.S.A.	166	37	10N		95	43W	
Independence, Mo., U.S.A.	166	39	3N		94	25W	
India ■	78	20	0N		78	0 E	
Indian Head	152	50	30N		103	41W	
Indiana	164	40	38N		79	9W	
Indiana □	167	40	0N		86	0W	
Indianapolis	167	39	42N		86	10W	
Indigirka ~►	73	70	48N		148	54 E	
Indonesia ■	111	5	0S		115	0 E	
Indore	91	22	42N		75	53 E	
Indre ~►	36	47	16N		0	19 E	
Indus ~►	88	24	20N		67	47 E	
Indus, Mouth of the	88	24	0N		68	0 E	
Inebolu	80	41	55N		33	40 E	
Inegöl	80	40	5N		29	31 E	
Ingersoll	151	43	4N		80	55W	
Ingham	121	18	43S		146	10 E	
Ingleborough	28	54	11N		2	23W	
Inglewood, N.Z.	122	39	9S		174	14 E	
Inglewood, U.S.A.	173	33	58N		118	21W	
Ingolstadt	43	48	45N		11	26 E	
Ingraj Bazar	92	24	58N		88	10 E	
Inhambane	137	23	54S		35	30 E	
Ining = Yining	100	43	58N		81	10 E	
Inishmore	35	53	8N		9	45W	
Inishowen	34	55	14N		7	15W	
Inn ~►	43	48	35N		13	28 E	
Innamincka	118	27	44S		140	46 E	
Inner Hebrides	32	57	0N		6	30W	
Inner Mongolia = Nei Monggol Zizhiqu □	98	42	0N		112	0 E	
Innisfail, Australia	121	17	33S		146	5 E	
Innisfail, Canada	155	52	0N		113	57W	
In'no-shima	109	34	19N		133	10 E	
Innsbruck	45	47	16N		11	23 E	
Inoucdjouac	146	58	25N		78	15W	
Inowrocław	58	52	50N		18	12 E	
Inquisivi	187	16	50S		67	10W	
Insein	93	16	50N		96	5 E	
Interlaken	44	46	41N		7	50 E	
Inuvik	144	68	16N		133	40W	
Inuvik □	144	70	0N		130	0W	
Inuyama	106	35	23N		136	56 E	
Inveraray	30	56	13N		5	5W	
Invercargill	123	46	24S		168	24 E	
Inverell	116	29	45S		151	8 E	
Invergordon	33	57	41N		4	10W	
Inverness	33	57	29N		4	12W	
Investigator Group	119	34	45S		134	20 E	
Investigator Str.	119	35	30S		137	0 E	
Ioánnina	54	39	42N		20	47 E	
Iola	166	38	0N		95	20W	
Iona	30	56	20N		6	25W	
Ionian Is. = Iónioi Nísoi	54	38	40N		20	0 E	
Ionian Sea	54	37	30N		17	30 E	
Iónioi Nísoi	54	38	40N		20	0 E	
Íos	55	36	41N		25	20 E	
Iowa □	166	42	18N		93	30W	
Iowa City	166	41	40N		91	35W	
Iowa Falls	166	42	30N		93	15W	
Ipiales	184	0	50N		77	37W	
Ipin = Yibin	99	28	45N		104	32 E	
Ipiros □	54	39	30N		20	30 E	
Ipoh	96	4	35N		101	5 E	
Ipswich, Australia	116	27	35S		152	40 E	
Ipswich, U.K.	25	52	4N		1	9 E	
Iquique	187	20	19S		70	5W	
Iquitos	186	3	45S		73	10W	
Iracoubo	185	5	30N		53	10W	
Iráklion	55	35	20N		25	12 E	
Iran ■	86	33	0N		53	0 E	
Iran Ra.	111	2	20N		114	50 E	
Irapuato	177	20	41N		101	28W	
Iraq ■	81	33	0N		44	0 E	
Irbid	80	32	35N		35	48 E	
Ireland ■	34	53	0N		8	0W	
Irian Jaya □	113	4	0S		137	0 E	
Iriri ~►	188	3	52S		52	37W	
Irish Republic ■	20	53	0N		8	0W	
Irish Sea	20	54	0N		5	0W	
Irkutsk	74	52	18N		104	20 E	
Irō-Zaki	107	34	36N		138	51 E	
Iron Gate = Portile de Fier	56	44	42N		22	30 E	
Iron Knob	118	32	46S		137	8 E	
Iron Mountain	150	45	49N		88	4W	
Ironbridge	24	52	38N		2	29W	
Ironton	167	38	35N		82	40W	
Ironwood	150	46	30N		90	10W	

IAS

34

Place	Pg	Lat°	Lat′		Long°	Long′	
Iroquois Falls	151	48	46N		80	41W	
Irrawaddy →	93	15	50N		95	6 E	
Irtysh →	69	61	4N		68	52 E	
Irumu	135	1	32N		29	53 E	
Irún	51	43	20N		1	52W	
Irvine	31	55	37N		4	40W	
Irvinestown	34	54	28N		7	38W	
Ísafjörður	64	66	5N		23	9W	
Isahaya	108	32	52N		130	2 E	
Ischia	49	40	45N		13	51 E	
Ise	106	34	25N		136	45 E	
Ise-Wan	106	34	43N		136	43 E	
Isère →	37	44	59N		4	51 E	
Isesaki	107	36	19N		139	12 E	
Ishikari-Wan	103	43	25N		141	1 E	
Ishinomaki	103	38	32N		141	20 E	
Ishioka	107	36	11N		140	16 E	
Ishkuman	89	36	30N		73	50 E	
Ishpeming	150	46	30N		87	40W	
Iskenderun	80	36	32N		36	10 E	
Islamabad	89	33	40N		73	10 E	
Island L.	153	53	47N		94	25W	
Island Pond	148	48	25N		56	23W	
Islay	30	55	46N		6	10W	
Isle-Adam, L'	39	49	6N		2	14 E	
Isle Royale	150	48	0N		88	50W	
Isparta	80	37	47N		30	30 E	
Israel ■	80	32	0N		34	50 E	
Issoire	37	45	32N		3	15 E	
Issyk-Kul, Ozero	71	42	25N		77	15 E	
Istanbul	80	41	0N		29	0 E	
Istra	52	45	10N		14	0 E	
Istria = Istra	52	45	10N		14	0 E	
Itabuna	189	14	48S		39	16W	
Itaituba	185	4	10S		65	60W	
Itajaí	191	27	50S		48	39W	
Italy ■	19	42	0N		13	0 E	
Itaquatiara	185	2	58S		58	30W	
Itaquí	191	29	8S		56	30W	
Itchen →	24	50	57N		1	20W	
Ithaca = Itháki	54	38	25N		20	40 E	
Ithaca	164	42	25N		76	30W	
Itháki	54	38	25N		20	40 E	
Ito	107	34	58N		139	5 E	
Ituaçu	189	13	50S		41	18W	
Ituiutaba	188	19	0S		49	25W	
Iturup, Ostrov	75	45	0N		148	0 E	
Ivano-Frankovsk	68	48	40N		24	40 E	
Ivanovo, Byelorussian S.S.R., U.S.S.R.	68	52	7N		25	29 E	
Ivanovo, R.S.F.S.R., U.S.S.R.	68	57	5N		41	0 E	
Ivigtut	147	61	14N		48	12W	
Iviza = Ibiza	51	38	54N		1	26 E	
Ivory Coast ■	130	7	30N		5	0W	
Iwai-Jima	108	33	47N		131	58 E	
Iwaki	105	37	3N		140	55 E	
Iwakuni	109	34	15N		132	8 E	
Iwami	109	35	32N		134	15 E	
Iwamizawa	103	43	12N		141	46 E	
Iwanuma	103	38	7N		140	51 E	
Iwata	107	34	42N		137	51 E	
Iwo	131	7	39N		4	9 E	
Ixiamas	187	13	50S		68	5W	
Ixtepec	177	16	34N		95	6W	
Ixtlán	175	20	11N		102	24W	
Ixtlán de Juárez	177	17	23N		96	28W	
Iyo	109	33	45N		132	45 E	
Iyo-mishima	109	33	58N		133	30 E	
Iyo-Nada	109	33	40N		132	20 E	
Izamal	177	20	56N		89	1W	
Izhevsk = Ustinov	69	56	51N		53	14 E	
Izmir	80	38	25N		27	8 E	
Izmit	80	40	45N		29	50 E	
Izu-Hantō	107	34	45N		139	0 E	
Izumi	108	32	5N		130	22 E	
Izumi-sano	106	34	23N		135	18 E	
Izumiotsu	106	34	30N		135	24 E	
Izumo	109	35	20N		132	46 E	
Jabalpur	91	23	9N		79	58 E	
Jacarèzinho	191	23	5S		50	0W	
Jackson, Mich., U.S.A.	167	42	18N		84	25W	
Jackson, Miss., U.S.A.	169	32	20N		90	10W	
Jackson, Tenn., U.S.A.	169	35	40N		88	50W	
Jacksonville, Fla., U.S.A.	170	30	15N		81	38W	
Jacksonville, Ill., U.S.A.	166	39	42N		90	15W	
Jacksonville, N.C., U.S.A.	165	34	50N		77	29W	
Jacksonville, Tex., U.S.A.	168	31	58N		95	19W	
Jacmel	180	18	14N		72	32W	
Jacobabad	88	28	20N		68	29 E	
Jacques Cartier, Dét. de	149	50	0N		63	30W	
Jadotville = Likasi	135	10	55S		26	48 E	
Jaén, Peru	186	5	25S		78	40W	
Jaén, Spain	50	37	44N		3	43W	
Jaffa = Tel Aviv-Yafo	80	32	4N		34	48 E	
Jaffna	90	9	45N		80	2 E	
Jagdalpur	92	19	3N		82	0 E	
Jaguariaíva	191	24	10S		49	50W	
Jagüey Grande	178	22	35N		81	7W	
Jahrom	85	28	30N		53	31 E	
Jaipur	91	27	0N		75	50 E	
Jakarta	111	6	9S		106	49 E	
Jalalabad	87	34	30N		70	29 E	
Jalapa, Guat.	177	14	39N		89	59W	
Jalapa, Mexico	177	17	43N		92	49W	
Jalgaon	91	21	0N		75	42 E	
Jalisco □	175	20	20N		103	40W	
Jalna	91	19	48N		75	38 E	
Jalón →	51	41	47N		1	4W	
Jalpaiguri	92	26	32N		88	46 E	
Jamaica ■	180	18	10N		77	30W	
Jamalpur, Bangla.	92	24	52N		89	56 E	
Jamalpur, India	92	25	18N		86	28 E	
Jambi	111	1	38S		103	30 E	
James →	163	42	52N		97	18W	
James B.	140	51	30N		80	0W	
Jamestown, Australia	118	33	10S		138	32 E	
Jamestown, N. Dak., U.S.A.	163	46	54N		98	42W	
Jamestown, N.Y., U.S.A.	164	42	5N		79	18W	
Jamkhandi	91	16	30N		75	15 E	
Jammu	89	32	43N		74	54 E	
Jammu & Kashmir □	89	34	25N		77	0 E	
Jamnagar	90	22	30N		70	6 E	
Jamshedpur	92	22	44N		86	12 E	
Jan Mayen Is.	13	71	0N		9	0W	
Janesville	166	42	39N		89	1W	
Januária	188	15	25S		44	25W	
Jaora	91	23	40N		75	10 E	
Japan ■	79	36	0N		136	0 E	
Japan, Sea of	102	40	0N		135	0 E	
Japurá →	185	3	8S		64	46W	
Jargalant = Hovd	100	48	2N		91	37 E	
Jargeau	39	47	50N		2	1 E	
Jarosław	58	50	2N		22	42 E	
Jäsk	85	25	38N		57	45 E	
Jasfo	59	49	45N		21	30 E	
Jasper, Canada	155	52	55N		118	5W	
Jasper, U.S.A.	169	33	48N		87	16W	
Jassy = Iaşi	57	47	10N		27	40 E	
Jataí	188	17	58S		51	48W	
Jaú	188	22	10S		48	30W	
Jaunpur	92	25	46N		82	44 E	
Java, I.	111	7	0S		110	0 E	
Java Sea	111	4	35S		107	15 E	
Javhlant = Ulyasutay	100	47	56N		97	28 E	
Jean Marie River	144	61	32N		120	38W	
Jean Rabel	180	19	50N		73	5W	
Jedburgh	31	55	28N		2	33W	
Jędrzejów	58	50	35N		20	15 E	
Jefferson, Mt.	171	44	45N		121	50W	
Jefferson City	166	38	34N		92	10W	
Jeffersonville	167	38	20N		85	42W	
Jelenia Góra	58	50	50N		15	45 E	
Jena	43	50	56N		11	33 E	
Jenkins	165	37	13N		82	41W	
Jennings	168	30	10N		92	45W	
Jeparit	119	36	8S		142	1 E	
Jequié	189	13	51S		40	5W	
Jequitinhonha	189	16	30S		41	0W	
Jérémie	180	18	40N		74	10W	

Jerez de García Salinas	**175**	22	39N	103	0W
Jerez de la Frontera	**50**	36	41N	6	7W
Jerez de los Caballeros	**50**	38	20N	6	45W
Jericho	**121**	23	38S	146	6 E
Jerilderie	**117**	35	20S	145	41 E
Jerome	**148**	47	37N	82	14W
Jersey, I.	**36**	49	13N	2	7W
Jersey City	**164**	40	41N	74	8W
Jerseyville	**166**	39	5N	90	20W
Jerusalem	**80**	31	47N	35	10 E
Jesselton = Kota Kinabalu	**112**	6	0N	116	4 E
Jhang Maghiana	**89**	31	15N	72	22 E
Jhansi	**91**	25	30N	78	36 E
Jharsuguda	**92**	21	56N	84	5 E
Jhelum →	**89**	31	20N	72	10 E
Jhunjhunu	**89**	28	10N	75	30 E
Jiamusi	**98**	46	40N	130	26 E
Ji'an	**99**	27	6N	114	59 E
Jiangmen	**99**	22	32N	113	0 E
Jiangsu □	**99**	33	0N	120	0 E
Jiangxi □	**99**	27	30N	116	0 E
Jian'ou	**99**	27	3N	118	17 E
Jiao Xian	**98**	36	18N	120	1 E
Jiaozuo	**99**	35	16N	113	12 E
Jiaxing	**99**	30	49N	120	45 E
Jiayi	**99**	23	30N	120	24 E
Jibuti = Djibouti ■	**133**	12	0N	43	0 E
Jiddah	**82**	21	29N	39	10 E
Jido	**93**	29	2N	94	58 E
Jihlava	**59**	49	28N	15	35 E
Jilin	**98**	43	44N	126	30 E
Jilong	**99**	25	8N	121	42 E
Jima	**132**	7	40N	36	47 E
Jiménez	**174**	27	8N	104	54W
Jinan	**98**	36	38N	117	1 E
Jingdezhen	**99**	29	20N	117	11 E
Jining, Nei Mongol Zizhiqu, China	**98**	41	5N	113	0 E
Jining, Shandong, China	**99**	35	22N	116	34 E
Jinja	**132**	0	25N	33	12 E
Jinnah Barrage	**89**	32	58N	71	33 E
Jinotega	**179**	13	6N	85	59W
Jinotepe	**179**	11	50N	86	10W
Jinshi	**99**	29	40N	111	50 E
Jinzhou	**98**	41	5N	121	3 E
Jipijapa	**184**	1	0S	80	40W
Jiquilpan de Juárez	**175**	19	59N	102	43W
Jisr ash Shughūr	**80**	35	49N	36	18 E
Jiujiang	**99**	29	42N	115	58 E
Jixi	**98**	45	20N	130	50 E
João Pessoa	**189**	7	10S	34	52W
Jodhpur	**91**	26	23N	73	8 E
Joensuu	**67**	62	37N	29	49 E
Jogjakarta = Yogyakarta	**111**	7	49S	110	22 E
Jōhana	**106**	36	30N	136	57 E
Johannesburg	**137**	26	10S	28	2 E
John o' Groats	**33**	58	39N	3	3W
Johnson City, N.Y., U.S.A.	**164**	42	7N	75	57W
Johnson City, Tenn., U.S.A.	**165**	36	18N	82	21W
Johnston	**31**	51	45N	5	5W
Johnstown, N.Y., U.S.A.	**164**	43	1N	74	20W
Johnstown, Pa., U.S.A.	**164**	40	19N	78	53W
Johor □	**96**	2	5N	103	20 E
Johor Baharu	**96**	1	28N	103	46 E
Joigny	**39**	48	0N	3	20 E
Joinvile	**191**	26	15S	48	55 E
Joliet	**167**	41	30N	88	0W
Joliette	**151**	46	3N	73	24W
Jolo	**112**	6	0N	121	0 E
Jonesboro	**169**	35	50N	90	45W
Jönköping	**60**	57	45N	14	10 E
Jönköpings län □	**61**	57	30N	14	30 E
Jonquière	**148**	48	27N	71	14W
Joplin	**168**	37	0N	94	31W
Jordan ■	**80**	31	0N	36	0 E
Jordan →	**80**	31	48N	35	32 E
Jorhat	**93**	26	45N	94	12 E
José de San Martín	**192**	44	4S	70	26W
Jowzjān □	**87**	36	10N	66	0 E
Juan de Fuca Str.	**142**	48	15N	124	0W
Juan Fernández, Arch. de	**183**	33	50S	80	0W

Juàzeiro	**189**	9	30S	40	30W
Juàzeiro do Norte	**189**	7	10S	39	18W
Jubbulpore = Jabalpur	**91**	23	9N	79	58 E
Júcar →	**51**	39	5N	0	10W
Juchitán de Zaragoza	**177**	16	26N	95	1W
Jugoslavia = Yugoslavia ■	**52**	44	0N	20	0 E
Juiz de Fora	**188**	21	43S	43	19W
Juli	**187**	16	10S	69	25W
Juliaca	**187**	15	25S	70	10W
Julianehåb	**147**	60	43N	46	0W
Jullundur	**89**	31	20N	75	40 E
Jumla	**92**	29	15N	82	13 E
Jumna = Yamuna →	**92**	25	30N	81	53 E
Junagadh	**91**	21	30N	70	30 E
Jundiaí	**191**	24	30S	47	0W
Juneau	**143**	58	20N	134	20W
Junee	**117**	34	53S	147	35 E
Junggar Pendi	**100**	44	30N	86	0 E
Junín	**190**	34	33S	60	57W
Jura, Europe	**37**	46	35N	6	5 E
Jura, U.K.	**30**	56	0N	5	50W
Jurado	**184**	7	7N	77	46W
Juruá →	**184**	2	37S	65	44W
Juruena	**187**	13	0S	58	10W
Juruena →	**187**	7	20S	58	3W
Juticalpa	**179**	14	40N	86	12W
Jutland = Jylland	**61**	56	25N	9	30 E
Juventud, I. de la	**178**	21	40N	82	40W
Jylland	**61**	56	25N	9	30 E
Jyväskylä	**67**	62	14N	25	50 E

Kaapstad = Cape Town	**136**	33	55S	18	22 E
Kabala	**130**	9	38N	11	37W
Kabardino-Balkar-A.S.S.R. □	**70**	43	30N	43	30 E
Kabarega Falls	**132**	2	15N	31	30 E
Kabīr Kūh	**84**	33	0N	47	30 E
Kābul	**87**	34	28N	69	11 E
Kābul □	**87**	34	30N	69	0 E
Kabwe	**135**	14	30S	28	29 E
Kachin □	**93**	26	0N	97	30 E
Kadan Kyun	**94**	12	30N	98	20 E
Kadina	**119**	34	0S	137	43 E
Kaduna	**131**	10	30N	7	21 E
Kaédi	**126**	16	9N	13	28W
Kāf	**80**	31	25N	37	29 E
Kafirévs, Ákra	**55**	38	9N	24	38 E
Kafue →	**135**	15	30S	26	0 E
Kaga	**106**	36	16N	136	15 E
Kagoshima	**108**	31	35N	130	33 E
Kagoshima-Wan	**108**	31	25N	130	40 E
Kai, Kepulauan	**113**	5	55S	132	45W
Kaieteur Falls	**185**	5	1N	59	10W
Kaifeng	**99**	34	49N	114	30 E
Kaikoura Ra.	**123**	41	59S	173	41 E
Kailua	**160**	19	39N	156	0W
Kaimanawa Mts.	**122**	39	15S	175	56 E
Kainan	**106**	34	9N	135	12 E
Kainji Res.	**131**	10	1N	4	40 E
Kaipara Harbour	**122**	36	25S	174	14 E
Kaiserslautern	**42**	49	30N	7	43 E
Kaitaia	**122**	35	8S	173	17 E
Kajaani	**67**	64	17N	27	46 E
Kajana = Kajaani	**67**	64	17N	27	46 E
Kakabeka Falls	**150**	48	24N	89	37W
Kakamigahara	**106**	35	28N	136	48 E
Kakanui Mts.	**123**	45	10S	170	30 E
Kakegawa	**107**	34	45N	138	1 E
Kakinada	**92**	16	57N	82	11 E
Kakogawa	**109**	34	46N	134	51 E
Kalabáka	**54**	39	42N	21	39 E
Kalahari	**136**	24	0S	21	30 E
Kalamata	**54**	37	3N	22	10 E
Kalamazoo	**167**	42	20N	85	35W
Kalamazoo →	**167**	42	40N	86	12W
Kalat	**88**	29	8N	66	31 E
Kalaupapa	**160**	21	12N	156	59W
Kalemie	**135**	5	55S	29	9 E
Kalgan = Zhangjiakou	**98**	40	48N	114	55 E
Kalgoorlie-Boulder	**120**	30	40S	121	22 E

Kálimnos	**55**	37 0N	27 0 E
Kalinin	**68**	56 55N	35 55 E
Kaliningrad	**68**	54 42N	20 32 E
Kalispell	**162**	48 10N	114 22W
Kalisz	**58**	51 45N	18 8 E
Kalmar	**61**	56 40N	16 20 E
Kalmar län □	**61**	57 25N	16 0 E
Kalmyk A.S.S.R. □	**70**	46 5N	46 1 E
Kalocsa	**59**	46 32N	19 0 E
Kaluga	**68**	54 35N	36 10 E
Kama →	**68**	55 45N	52 0 E
Kamaishi	**103**	39 16N	141 53 E
Kamakura	**107**	35 19N	139 33 E
Kamaran	**82**	15 21N	42 35 E
Kamchatka, P-ov.	**73**	57 0N	160 0 E
Kamenka	**69**	53 10N	44 5 E
Kamensk Uralskiy	**69**	56 25N	62 2 E
Kamenskoye	**73**	62 45N	165 30 E
Kameoka	**106**	35 0N	135 35 E
Kameyama	**106**	34 51N	136 27 E
Kami-koshiki-Jima	**108**	31 50N	129 52 E
Kamioka	**106**	36 25N	137 15 E
Kamloops	**155**	50 40N	120 20W
Kampala	**132**	0 20N	32 30 E
Kampar	**96**	4 18N	101 9 E
Kampen	**41**	52 33N	5 53 E
Kampot	**95**	10 36N	104 10 E
Kampuchea = Cambodia ■	**95**	12 15N	105 0 E
Kamsack	**152**	51 34N	101 54W
Kamui-Misaki	**103**	43 20N	140 21 E
Kamyshin	**68**	50 10N	45 24 E
Kananga	**134**	5 55S	22 18 E
Kanawha →	**165**	38 50N	82 8W
Kanazawa	**106**	36 30N	136 38 E
Kanchenjunga	**92**	27 50N	88 10 E
Kanchipuram	**90**	12 52N	79 45 E
Kandahar = Qandahār	**87**	31 32N	65 30 E
Kandalaksha	**69**	67 9N	32 30 E
Kandi	**131**	11 7N	2 55 E
Kandos	**117**	32 45S	149 58 E
Kandy	**90**	7 18N	80 43 E
Kangar	**97**	6 27N	100 12 E
Kangaroo I.	**119**	35 45S	137 0 E
Kangean Is.	**113**	6 55S	115 23 E
Kangnŭng	**98**	37 45N	128 54 E
Kangto	**93**	27 50N	92 35 E
Kaniapiskau →	**146**	56 40N	69 30W
Kanin, P-ov.	**69**	68 0N	45 0 E
Kaniva	**119**	36 22S	141 18 E
Kankakee	**167**	41 6N	87 50W
Kankakee →	**167**	41 23N	88 16W
Kankan	**130**	10 23N	9 15W
Kanmuri-Yama	**109**	34 30N	132 4 E
Kannapolis	**165**	35 32N	80 37W
Kano	**131**	12 2N	8 30 E
Kan'onji	**109**	34 7N	133 39 E
Kanoya	**108**	31 25N	130 50 E
Kanpur	**91**	26 28N	80 20 E
Kansas □	**161**	38 40N	98 0W
Kansas →	**158**	39 7N	94 36W
Kansas City, Kans., U.S.A.	**166**	39 0N	94 40W
Kansas City, Mo., U.S.A.	**166**	39 3N	94 30W
Kansk	**74**	56 20N	95 37 E
Kansu = Gansu □	**98**	36 0N	104 0 E
Kantō □	**107**	36 15N	139 30 E
Kantō-Sanchi	**107**	35 59N	138 50 E
Kanuma	**107**	36 34N	139 42 E
Kaohsiung = Gaoxiong	**99**	22 38N	120 18 E
Kaolack	**130**	14 5N	16 8W
Kāpīsā □	**87**	35 0N	69 20 E
Kapoeta	**129**	4 50N	33 35 E
Kapuas →	**111**	0 25S	109 20 E
Kapunda	**119**	34 20S	138 56 E
Kapuskasing	**150**	49 25N	82 30W
Kaputar, Mt.	**116**	30 15S	150 10 E
Kara Bogaz Gol, Zaliv	**70**	41 0N	53 30 E
Kara Kalpak A.S.S.R. □	**70**	43 0N	60 0 E
Kara Kum = Karakum, Peski	**70**	39 30N	60 0 E
Kara Sea	**69**	75 0N	70 0 E
Karabük	**80**	41 12N	32 37 E
Karachi	**88**	24 53N	67 0 E
Karad	**91**	17 15N	74 10 E
Karadeniz Boğazı	**80**	41 10N	29 10 E
Karaganda	**71**	49 50N	73 10 E
Karaj	**86**	35 48N	51 0 E
Karakoram Pass	**89**	35 33N	77 50 E
Karakoram Ra.	**89**	35 30N	77 0 E
Karakum, Peski	**70**	39 30N	60 0 E
Karaman	**80**	37 14N	33 13 E
Karamea Bight	**123**	41 22S	171 40 E
Karasuk	**71**	53 44N	78 2 E
Karatau, Khrebet	**71**	43 30N	69 30 E
Karbalā	**84**	32 36N	44 3 E
Karelian A.S.S.R. □	**68**	65 30N	32 30 E
Karen	**94**	12 49N	92 53 E
Kariba Lake	**137**	16 40S	28 25 E
Karimata I.	**111**	1 40S	109 0 E
Karimnagar	**91**	18 26N	79 10 E
Karimunjawa, Kepulauan	**111**	5 50S	110 30 E
Kariya	**106**	34 58N	137 1 E
Karl-Marx-Stadt	**43**	50 50N	12 55 E
Karlskrona	**61**	56 10N	15 35 E
Karlsruhe	**42**	49 3N	8 23 E
Karlstad	**60**	59 23N	13 30 E
Karnal	**89**	29 42N	77 2 E
Karnaphuli Res.	**93**	22 40N	92 20 E
Karnataka □	**90**	13 15N	77 0 E
Kärnten □	**45**	46 52N	13 30 E
Kárpathos	**55**	35 37N	27 10 E
Kars	**81**	40 40N	43 5 E
Karshi	**70**	38 53N	65 48 E
Kasai →	**134**	3 30S	16 10 E
Kasaoka	**109**	34 30N	133 30 E
Kaseda	**108**	31 25N	130 19 E
Kāshān	**86**	34 5N	51 30 E
Kashi	**100**	39 30N	76 2 E
Kashihara	**106**	34 27N	135 46 E
Kashima	**108**	33 7N	130 6 E
Kashima-Nada	**107**	36 0N	140 45 E
Kashiwa	**107**	35 52N	139 59 E
Kāshmar	**86**	35 16N	58 26 E
Kashmir	**78**	34 0N	76 0 E
Kashun Noerh = Gaxun Nur	**100**	42 22N	100 30 E
Kásos	**55**	35 20N	26 55 E
Kassala	**129**	16 0N	36 0 E
Kassel	**42**	51 19N	9 32 E
Kastoría	**54**	40 30N	21 19 E
Kasugai	**106**	35 12N	136 59 E
Kasukabe	**107**	35 58N	139 49 E
Kasumiga-Ura	**107**	36 0N	140 25 E
Kasur	**89**	31 5N	74 25 E
Katanning	**120**	33 40S	117 33 E
Katha	**93**	24 10N	96 30 E
Katherína, Gebel	**128**	28 30N	33 57 E
Katherine	**114**	14 27S	132 20 E
Kathiawar	**91**	22 20N	71 0 E
Katihar	**92**	25 34N	87 36 E
Katmandu	**92**	27 45N	85 20 E
Katoomba	**117**	33 41S	150 19 E
Katowice	**58**	50 17N	19 5 E
Katsuta	**107**	36 25N	140 31 E
Katsuura	**107**	35 10N	140 20 E
Katsuyama	**106**	36 3N	136 30 E
Kattegatt	**61**	57 0N	11 20 E
Katwijk-aan-Zee	**40**	52 12N	4 24 E
Kauai	**160**	22 0N	159 30W
Kaukauna	**167**	44 20N	88 13W
Kaunas	**68**	54 54N	23 54 E
Kawachi-Nagano	**106**	34 28N	135 31 E
Kawagoe	**107**	35 55N	139 29 E
Kawaguchi	**107**	35 52N	139 45 E
Kawanoe	**109**	34 1N	133 34 E
Kawarau	**122**	45 3S	168 45 E
Kawasaki	**107**	35 35N	139 42 E
Kayah □	**93**	19 15N	97 15 E
Kayes	**130**	14 25N	11 30W
Kayseri	**80**	38 45N	35 30 E
Kazachinskoye	**74**	56 16N	107 36 E
Kazachye	**72**	70 52N	135 58 E
Kazakh S.S.R. □	**71**	50 0N	70 0 E
Kazan	**68**	55 48N	49 3 E
Kazanlŭk	**53**	42 38N	25 20 E

Name	Page	Lat	Long
Käzerün	**85**	29 38N	51 40 E
Kazo	**107**	36 7N	139 36 E
Kéa	**55**	37 35N	24 22 E
Keaau	**160**	19 37N	155 3W
Kebnekaise	**66**	67 53N	18 33 E
Kecskemét	**59**	46 57N	19 42 E
Kedah □	**96**	5 50N	100 40 E
Kediri	**111**	7 51S	112 1 E
Keeling Is. = Cocos Is.	**111**	12 10S	96 55 E
Keene	**164**	42 57N	72 17W
Keetmanshoop	**136**	26 35S	18 8 E
Keewatin	**153**	49 46N	94 34W
Keewatin □	**145**	63 20N	95 0W
Kefallinía	**54**	38 20N	20 30 E
Keflavík	**64**	64 2N	22 35W
Keighley	**28**	53 52N	1 54W
Keith, Australia	**119**	36 6S	140 20 E
Keith, U.K.	**33**	57 33N	2 58W
Kelang	**96**	3 2N	101 26 E
Kelantan □	**96**	5 10N	102 0 E
Kelantan ~→	**96**	6 13N	102 14 E
Kellerberrin	**120**	31 36S	117 38 E
Kellogg	**162**	47 30N	116 5W
Kells = Ceanannus Mor	**34**	53 42N	6 53W
Kelowna	**155**	49 50N	119 25W
Kelso, U.K.	**31**	55 36N	2 27W
Kelso, U.S.A.	**171**	46 10N	122 57W
Keluang	**96**	2 3N	103 18 E
Kelvington	**152**	52 10N	103 30W
Kemerovo	**71**	55 20N	86 5 E
Kemi	**67**	65 44N	24 34 E
Kemi ~→	**67**	67 30N	28 30 E
Kempsey	**116**	31 1S	152 50 E
Kendal	**28**	54 19N	2 44W
Keng Tung	**93**	21 0N	99 30 E
Kenitra	**126**	34 15N	6 40W
Kenmare	**35**	51 52N	9 35W
Kennewick	**171**	46 11N	119 2W
Keno Hill	**144**	63 57N	135 18W
Kenora	**153**	49 47N	94 29W
Kenosha	**167**	42 33N	87 48W
Kent	**164**	41 8N	81 20W
Kent □	**25**	51 12N	0 40 E
Kent Group	**117**	39 30S	147 20 E
Kent Pen.	**145**	68 30N	107 0W
Kentucky □	**167**	37 20N	85 0W
Kentucky ~→	**167**	38 41N	85 11W
Kenya ■	**133**	1 0N	38 0 E
Kenya, Mt.	**132**	0 10S	37 18 E
Keokuk	**166**	40 25N	91 24W
Kepsut	**80**	39 40N	28 9 E
Kerala □	**90**	11 0N	76 15 E
Kerang	**117**	35 40S	143 55 E
Kerch	**68**	45 20N	36 20 E
Kerki	**70**	37 50N	65 12 E
Kérkira	**54**	39 38N	19 50 E
Kerkrade	**41**	50 53N	6 4 E
Kermadec Is.	**122**	30 0S	178 15W
Kermän	**85**	30 15N	57 1 E
Kermän □	**85**	30 0N	57 0 E
Kermänshäh = Bäkhtarän	**84**	34 23N	47 0 E
Kerrobert	**152**	52 0N	109 11W
Kerry □	**35**	52 7N	9 35W
Kerulen ~→	**98**	48 48N	117 0 E
Kestenga	**68**	66 0N	31 50 E
Keswick	**28**	54 35N	3 9W
Ketchikan	**143**	55 25N	131 40W
Kettering	**156**	39 41N	84 10W
Kewanee	**166**	41 18N	89 55W
Keweenaw B.	**150**	46 56N	88 23W
Key West	**159**	24 33N	82 0W
Keyser	**164**	39 26N	79 0W
Khabarovsk	**75**	48 30N	135 5 E
Khalkhāl	**81**	37 37N	48 32 E
Khalkís	**55**	38 27N	23 42 E
Khalmer Yu	**69**	67 58N	65 1 E
Khambhat	**91**	22 23N	72 33 E
Khambhat, G. of	**91**	20 45N	72 30 E
Khamir	**82**	16 0N	44 0 E
Khānābād	**87**	36 45N	69 5 E
Khānaqin	**81**	34 23N	45 25 E
Khandwa	**91**	21 49N	76 22 E
Khanewal	**89**	30 20N	71 55 E
Khaniá	**55**	35 30N	24 4 E
Khanka, Ozero	**75**	45 0N	132 24 E
Kharagpur	**92**	22 20N	87 25 E
Kharkov	**68**	49 58N	36 20 E
Khartoum = El Khartûm	**129**	15 31N	32 35 E
Khashm el Girba	**129**	14 59N	35 58 E
Khaskovo	**53**	41 56N	25 30 E
Khatanga	**72**	72 0N	102 20 E
Khatanga ~→	**72**	72 55N	106 0 E
Khenchela	**127**	35 28N	7 11 E
Kherson	**68**	46 35N	32 35 E
Kheta ~→	**72**	71 54N	102 6 E
Khíos, I.	**55**	38 20N	26 0 E
Khmer Rep. = Cambodia ■	**95**	12 15N	105 0 E
Khojak P.	**88**	30 55N	66 30 E
Kholm	**87**	36 45N	67 40 E
Khon Kaen	**95**	16 30N	102 47 E
Khoper ~→	**68**	49 30N	42 20 E
Khorāsān □	**86**	34 0N	58 0 E
Khorat = Nakhon Ratchasima	**95**	14 59N	102 12 E
Khorat, Cao Nguyen	**95**	15 30N	102 50 E
Khorog	**71**	37 30N	71 36 E
Khorramābād	**84**	33 30N	48 25 E
Khorrāmshahr	**84**	30 29N	48 15 E
Khulna	**92**	22 45N	89 34 E
Khulna □	**92**	22 25N	89 35 E
Khushab	**89**	32 20N	72 20 E
Khūzestān □	**84**	31 0N	49 0 E
Khvor	**86**	33 45N	55 0 E
Khvoy	**81**	38 35N	45 0 E
Khyber Pass	**89**	34 10N	71 8 E
Kiama	**117**	34 40S	150 50 E
Kiangsi = Jiangxi □	**99**	27 30N	116 0 E
Kiangsu = Jiangsu □	**99**	33 0N	120 0 E
Kichiga	**73**	59 50N	163 5 E
Kicking Horse Pass	**155**	51 28N	116 16W
Kidderminster	**24**	52 24N	2 13W
Kidnappers, C.	**122**	39 38S	177 5 E
Kiel	**43**	54 16N	10 8 E
Kielce	**58**	50 52N	20 42 E
Kieler Bucht	**42**	54 30N	10 30 E
Kiev = Kiyev	**68**	50 30N	30 28 E
Kigali	**135**	1 59S	30 4 E
Kii-Hantō	**106**	34 0N	135 45 E
Kii-Sanchi	**106**	34 20N	136 0 E
Kii-Suidō	**109**	33 40N	135 0 E
Kikládhes □	**55**	37 0N	25 0 E
Kikuchi	**108**	32 59N	130 47 E
Kilcoy	**116**	26 59S	152 30 E
Kildare	**35**	53 10N	6 50W
Kildare □	**35**	53 10N	6 50W
Kilimanjaro	**132**	3 7S	37 20 E
Kilis	**80**	36 50N	37 10 E
Kilkenny	**35**	52 40N	7 17W
Kilkenny □	**35**	52 35N	7 15W
Killala B.	**34**	54 20N	9 12W
Killarney, Canada	**153**	49 10N	99 40W
Killarney, Ireland	**35**	52 2N	9 30W
Killary Harbour	**34**	53 38N	9 52W
Killiecrankie, Pass of	**33**	56 44N	3 46W
Kilmarnock	**31**	55 36N	4 30W
Kilmore	**117**	37 25S	144 53 E
Kilrush	**35**	52 39N	9 30W
Kimba	**118**	33 8S	136 23 E
Kimberley, Australia	**114**	16 20S	127 0 E
Kimberley, Canada	**155**	49 40N	115 59W
Kimberley, S. Africa	**136**	28 43S	24 46 E
Kinabalu	**112**	6 3N	116 14 E
Kincardine	**150**	44 10N	81 40W
Kindersley	**152**	51 30N	109 10W
Kindia	**130**	10 0N	12 52W
King Frederick VI Land = Kong Frederik VI.s Kyst	**147**	63 0N	43 0W
King George Is.	**140**	57 20N	80 30W
King I. = Kadan Kyun	**94**	12 30N	98 20 E
King I., Australia	**119**	39 50S	144 0 E
King I., Canada	**154**	52 10N	127 40W
King Sd.	**114**	16 50S	123 20 E
King William I.	**145**	69 10N	97 25W
Kingaroy	**116**	26 32S	151 51 E

Name	Map	Lat	Long
Kingman	**173**	35 12N	114 2W
King's Lynn	**29**	52 45N	0 25 E
Kingscote	**119**	35 40S	137 38 E
Kingsport	**165**	36 33N	82 36W
Kingston, Canada	**151**	44 14N	76 30W
Kingston, Jamaica	**180**	18 0N	76 50W
Kingston, N.Z.	**123**	45 20S	168 43 E
Kingston, U.S.A.	**164**	41 55N	74 0W
Kingston South East	**119**	36 51S	139 55 E
Kingstown	**180**	13 10N	61 10W
Kingsville	**150**	42 2N	82 45W
Kingussie	**33**	57 5N	4 2W
Kinistino	**152**	52 57N	105 2W
Kinki □	**106**	33 30N	136 0 E
Kinnairds Hd.	**33**	57 40N	2 0W
Kinsale, Old Hd. of	**35**	51 37N	8 32W
Kinshasa	**134**	4 20S	15 15 E
Kinston	**165**	35 18N	77 35W
Kintyre	**30**	55 30N	5 35W
Kintyre, Mull of	**30**	55 17N	5 55W
Kinu-Gawa →	**107**	35 36N	139 57 E
Kiparissía	**54**	37 15N	21 40 E
Kirensk	**74**	57 50N	107 55 E
Kirgiz S.S.R. □	**71**	42 0N	75 0 E
Kiribati ■	**122**	1 0N	176 0 E
Kirikkale	**80**	39 51N	33 32 E
Kirin = Jilin	**98**	43 44N	126 30 E
Kiritimati	**123**	1 58N	157 27W
Kirkcaldy	**31**	56 7N	3 10W
Kirkcudbright	**31**	54 50N	4 3W
Kirkee	**91**	18 34N	73 56 E
Kirkintilloch	**31**	55 57N	4 10W
Kirkland Lake	**151**	48 9N	80 2W
Kirksville	**166**	40 8N	92 35W
Kirkūk	**81**	35 30N	44 21 E
Kirkwall	**33**	58 59N	2 59W
Kirov	**69**	58 35N	49 40 E
Kirovabad	**70**	40 45N	46 20 E
Kirovograd	**68**	48 35N	32 20 E
Kirthar Range	**88**	27 0N	67 0 E
Kiruna	**66**	67 52N	20 15 E
Kiryū	**107**	36 24N	139 20 E
Kisangani	**135**	0 35N	25 15 E
Kisarazu	**107**	35 23N	139 55 E
Kiselevsk	**71**	54 5N	86 39 E
Kishangarh	**89**	27 50N	70 30 E
Kishinev	**68**	47 0N	28 50 E
Kishiwada	**106**	34 28N	135 22 E
Kiskunfélégyháza	**59**	46 42N	19 53 E
Kiso-Gawa →	**106**	35 20N	136 45 E
Kisumu	**132**	0 3S	34 45 E
Kita	**130**	13 5N	9 25W
Kita-Ura	**107**	36 0N	140 34 E
Kitakami-Gawa →	**103**	38 25N	141 19 E
Kitakyūshū	**108**	33 50N	130 50 E
Kitale	**132**	1 0N	35 0 E
Kitami	**103**	43 48N	143 54 E
Kitchener	**151**	43 27N	80 29W
Kíthira	**55**	36 9N	23 0 E
Kíthnos	**55**	37 26N	24 27 E
Kitikmeot □	**145**	70 0N	110 0W
Kitimat	**154**	54 3N	128 38W
Kitsuki	**108**	33 25N	131 37 E
Kittakittaooloo, L.	**118**	28 3S	138 14 E
Kitwe	**135**	12 54S	28 13 E
Kiyev	**68**	50 30N	30 28 E
Klagenfurt	**45**	46 38N	14 20 E
Klaipeda	**68**	55 43N	21 10 E
Klamath →	**172**	41 40N	124 4W
Klamath Falls	**171**	42 20N	121 50W
Klamath Mts.	**172**	41 20N	123 0W
Kleena Kleene	**154**	52 0N	124 59W
Klondike	**144**	64 0N	139 26W
Kluane L.	**144**	61 15N	138 40W
Klyuchevsk, mt.	**73**	55 50N	160 30 E
Knaresborough	**28**	54 1N	1 29W
Knockmealdown Mts.	**35**	52 16N	8 0W
Knossos	**55**	35 16N	25 10 E
Knoxville, Iowa, U.S.A.	**166**	41 20N	93 5W
Knoxville, Tenn., U.S.A.	**165**	35 58N	83 57W
Ko Chang	**95**	12 0N	102 20 E
Ko Kut	**95**	11 40N	102 32 E
Koartac	**146**	60 55N	69 40W
Kobarid	**52**	46 15N	13 30 E
Kobayashi	**108**	31 56N	130 59 E
Kobdo = Hovd	**100**	48 2N	91 37 E
Kōbe	**106**	34 45N	135 10 E
København	**61**	55 41N	12 34 E
Koblenz	**42**	50 21N	7 36 E
Kobroor, Kepulauan	**113**	6 10S	134 30 E
Kočani	**53**	41 55N	22 25 E
Kōchi	**109**	33 30N	133 35 E
Kochiu = Gejiu	**99**	23 20N	103 10 E
Kodaira	**107**	35 44N	139 29 E
Kodiak I.	**142**	57 30N	152 45W
Kōfu	**107**	35 40N	138 30 E
Koga	**107**	36 11N	139 43 E
Kogota	**103**	38 33N	141 3 E
Koh-i-Bābā	**87**	34 30N	67 0 E
Kohat	**89**	33 40N	71 29 E
Kokand	**71**	40 30N	70 57 E
Kokchetav	**71**	53 20N	69 25 E
Koko Kyunzu	**94**	14 10N	93 25 E
Kokomo	**167**	40 30N	86 6W
Kokopo	**115**	4 22S	152 19 E
Koksoak →	**146**	58 30N	68 10W
Kokubu	**108**	31 44N	130 46 E
Kola Pen. = Kolskiy Poluostrov	**69**	67 30N	38 0 E
Kolar	**90**	13 12N	78 15 E
Kolar Gold Fields	**90**	12 58N	78 16 E
Kolarovgrad	**53**	43 18N	26 55 E
Kolding	**61**	55 30N	9 29 E
Kolguyev, Ostrov	**69**	69 20N	48 30 E
Kolhapur	**91**	16 43N	74 15 E
Köln	**42**	50 56N	6 58 E
Kofo	**58**	52 14N	18 40 E
Kolomna	**68**	55 8N	38 45 E
Kolskiy Poluostrov	**69**	67 30N	38 0 E
Kolyma →	**73**	69 30N	161 0 E
Komagene	**107**	35 44N	137 58 E
Komaki	**106**	35 17N	136 55 E
Komandorskiye, Is.	**73**	55 0N	167 0 E
Komárno	**59**	47 49N	18 5 E
Komatsu	**106**	36 25N	136 30 E
Komatsujima	**109**	34 0N	134 35 E
Komi A.S.S.R. □	**69**	64 0N	55 0 E
Kommunizma, Pik	**71**	39 0N	72 2 E
Komoro	**107**	36 19N	138 26 E
Kompong Cham	**95**	12 0N	105 30 E
Kompong Chhnang	**95**	12 20N	104 35 E
Kompong Som	**95**	10 38N	103 30 E
Komsomolets, Ostrov	**72**	80 30N	95 0 E
Komsomolsk	**75**	50 30N	137 0 E
Konarhá □	**87**	35 30N	71 3 E
Kong	**130**	8 54N	4 36W
Kong, Koh	**95**	11 20N	103 0 E
Kong Christian X.s Land	**13**	74 0N	29 0W
Kong Frederik VI.s Kyst	**147**	63 0N	43 0W
Kong Frederik VIII.s Land	**13**	78 30N	26 0W
Kongor	**129**	7 1N	31 27 E
Königsberg = Kaliningrad	**68**	54 42N	20 32 E
Konin	**58**	52 12N	18 15 E
Konjic	**52**	43 42N	17 58 E
Konosha	**68**	61 0N	40 5 E
Konstanz	**44**	47 39N	9 10 E
Kontagora	**131**	10 23N	5 27 E
Konya	**80**	37 52N	32 35 E
Konya Ovasi	**80**	38 30N	33 0 E
Koolyanobbing	**120**	30 48S	119 36 E
Kopaonik Planina	**52**	43 10N	21 50 E
Kopeysk	**71**	55 7N	61 37 E
Kopparberg	**60**	59 52N	15 0 E
Koppeh Dāgh	**86**	38 0N	58 0 E
Korab	**52**	41 44N	20 40 E
Korça	**52**	40 37N	20 50 E
Korčula	**52**	42 57N	17 8 E
Kordestān □	**81**	36 0N	47 0 E
Korea Bay	**98**	39 0N	124 0 E
Korea Strait	**104**	34 0N	129 30 E
Korhogo	**130**	9 29N	5 28W
Korinthiakós Kólpos	**54**	38 16N	22 30 E

Kórinthos . . . . **54** 37 56N 22 55 E
Kōriyama . . . . **105** 37 24N 140 23 E
Koroit . . . . **119** 38 18S 142 24 E
Kortrijk . . . . **42** 50 50N 3 17 E
Koryakskiy Khrebet . . . . **73** 61 0N 171 0 E
Kos . . . . **55** 36 50N 27 15 E
Kosciusko **169** 33 3N 89 34W
Kosciusko, Mt. . . . . **117** 36 27S 148 16 E
Koshigaya . . . . **107** 35 54N 139 48 E
K'oshih = Kashi . . . . **100** 39 30N 76 2 E
Koshiki-Rettō . . . . **108** 31 45N 129 49 E
Kōshoku . . . . **107** 36 38N 138 6 E
Košice . . . . **59** 48 42N 21 15 E
Kosovska-Mitrovica . . . . **52** 42 54N 20 52 E
Kôstî . . . . **129** 13 8N 32 43 E
Kostroma . . . . **68** 57 50N 40 58 E
Koszalin . . . . **58** 53 50N 16 8 E
Kota . . . . **91** 25 14N 75 49 E
Kota Baharu . . . . **96** 6 7N 102 14 E
Kota Kinabalu . . . . **112** 6 0N 116 4 E
Kotelnich . . . . **68** 58 20N 48 10 E
Kotka . . . . **67** 60 28N 26 58 E
Kotlas . . . . **69** 61 15N 47 0 E
Kotor . . . . **52** 42 25N 18 47 E
Kotuy →→ . . . . **77** 71 54N 102 6 E
Kotzebue **142** 66 50N 162 40W
Kowloon . . . . **99** 22 20N 114 15 E
Kōyama . . . . **108** 31 20N 130 56 E
Koyukuk →→ **142** 64 56N 157 30W
Kozáni . . . . **55** 40 19N 21 47 E
Kozhikode = Calicut . . . . **90** 11 15N 75 43 E
Kōzu-Shima . . . . **107** 34 13N 139 10 E
Kra, Isthmus of = Kra, Kho
  Khot . . . . **94** 10 15N 99 30 E
Kra, Kho Khot . . . . **94** 10 15N 99 30 E
Kragujevac . . . . **52** 44 2N 20 56 E
Kraków . . . . **58** 50 4N 19 57 E
Kraljevo . . . . **52** 43 44N 20 41 E
Krasnodar . . . . **68** 45 5N 39 0 E
Krasnovodsk . . . . **70** 40 0N 52 52 E
Krasnoyarsk . . . . **74** 56 8N 93 0 E
Krasnyy Kut . . . . **68** 50 50N 47 0 E
Kratie . . . . **95** 12 32N 106 10 E
Kravanh, Chuor Phnum . . . . . **95** 12 0N 103 32 E
Krefeld . . . . **42** 51 20N 6 32 E
Kremenchug . . . . **68** 49 5N 33 25 E
Krishna →→ . . . . **91** 15 57N 80 59 E
Krishnanagar . . . . **92** 23 24N 88 33 E
Kristiansand . . . . **60** 58 9N 8 1 E
Kristianstad . . . . **61** 56 2N 14 9 E
Kristianstads län □ . . . . **61** 56 15N 14 0 E
Kristiansund . . . . **65** 63 7N 7 45 E
Krlti . . . . **55** 35 15N 25 0 E
Krivoy Rog . . . . **68** 47 51N 33 20 E
Krk . . . . **52** 45 8N 14 40 E
Kronobergs län □ . . . . **61** 56 45N 14 30 E
Kronshtadt . . . . **68** 60 5N 29 45 E
Krotoszyn . . . . **58** 51 42N 17 23 E
Krugersdorp . . . . **137** 26 5S 27 46 E
Krung Thep = Bangkok . . . . . **94** 13 45N 100 35 E
Kruševac . . . . **52** 43 35N 21 28 E
Krymskiy P-ov. . . . . **68** 45 0N 34 0 E
Kuala Dungun . . . . **96** 4 45N 103 25 E
Kuala Kangsar . . . . **96** 4 46N 100 56 E
Kuala Lipis . . . . **96** 4 10N 102 3 E
Kuala Lumpur . . . . **96** 3 9N 101 41 E
Kuala Pilah . . . . **96** 2 45N 102 15 E
Kuala Trengganu . . . . **96** 5 20N 103 8 E
Kuangchou = Guangzhou . . . **99** 23 5N 113 10 E
Kuantan . . . . **96** 3 49N 103 20 E
Kubak . . . . **88** 27 10N 63 10 E
Kuban →→ . . . . **68** 45 20N 37 30 E
Kubokawa . . . . **109** 33 12N 133 8 E
Kuchinoerabu-Jima . . . . **104** 30 28N 130 11 E
Kucing . . . . **111** 1 33N 110 25 E
Kudamatsu . . . . **108** 34 0N 131 52 E
Kueiyang = Guiyang . . . . **99** 26 32N 106 40 E
Kūh-e-Jebāl Bārez . . . . **85** 29 0N 58 0 E
Kūh-e Sorkh . . . . **86** 35 30N 58 45 E
Kūhhā-ye-Bashākerd . . . . **85** 26 45N 59 0 E
Kūhhā-ye Sabalān . . . . **81** 38 15N 47 45 E

Kuji . . . . **103** 40 11N 141 46 E
Kuldja = Yining . . . . **100** 43 58N 81 10 E
Kulunda . . . . **71** 52 35N 78 57 E
Kumagaya . . . . **107** 36 9N 139 22 E
Kumamoto . . . . **108** 32 45N 130 45 E
Kumano . . . . **106** 33 54N 136 5 E
Kumano-Nada . . . . **106** 33 47N 136 20 E
Kumasi **130** 6 41N 1 38W
Kumon Bum . . . . **93** 26 30N 97 15 E
Kunashir, Ostrov . . . . **75** 44 0N 146 0 E
Kunimi-Dake . . . . **109** 32 33N 131 1 E
Kunlun Shan . . . . **100** 36 0N 86 30 E
Kunming . . . . **101** 25 1N 102 41 E
Kunsan . . . . **98** 35 59N 126 45 E
Kuopio . . . . **67** 62 53N 27 35 E
Kupang . . . . **113** 10 19S 123 39 E
Kurashiki . . . . **109** 34 40N 133 50 E
Kurayoshi . . . . **109** 35 26N 133 50 E
Kure . . . . **109** 34 14N 132 32 E
Kurgan . . . . **71** 55 26N 65 18 E
Kuril Is. = Kurilskiye Ostrova . **75** 45 0N 150 0 E
Kurilskiye Ostrova . . . . **75** 45 0N 150 0 E
Kurnool . . . . **90** 15 45N 78 0 E
Kurobe-Gawe →→ . . . . **106** 36 55N 137 25 E
Kurri Kurri . . . . **117** 32 50S 151 28 E
Kursk . . . . **68** 51 42N 36 11 E
Kuršumlija . . . . **52** 43 9N 21 19 E
Kurume . . . . **108** 33 15N 130 30 E
Kurunegala . . . . **90** 7 30N 80 23 E
Kusatsu . . . . **106** 34 58N 135 57 E
Kushikino . . . . **108** 31 44N 130 16 E
Kushima . . . . **108** 31 29N 131 14 E
Kushimoto . . . . **106** 33 28N 135 47 E
Kushiro . . . . **103** 43 0N 144 25 E
Kushka . . . . **70** 35 20N 62 18 E
Kushtia . . . . **92** 23 55N 89 5 E
Kuskokwim Bay **142** 59 50N 162 56W
Kustanay . . . . **71** 53 10N 63 35 E
Kusu . . . . **108** 33 16N 131 9 E
Kütahya . . . . **80** 39 30N 30 2 E
Kutaisi . . . . **70** 42 19N 42 40 E
Kutaraja = Banda Aceh . . . . **111** 5 35N 95 20 E
Kutno . . . . **58** 52 15N 19 23 E
Kuujjuaq **146** 58 6N 68 15W
Kuwait = Al Kuwayt . . . . **84** 29 30N 47 30 E
Kuwait ■ . . . . **84** 29 30N 47 30 E
Kuwana . . . . **106** 35 0N 136 43 E
Kuybyshev . . . . **68** 53 8N 50 6 E
Kwakoegron **185** 5 12N 55 25W
Kwangju . . . . **98** 35 9N 126 54 E
Kwangsi-Chuang = Guangxi
  Zhuangzu Zizhiqu □ . . . . . **99** 24 0N 109 0 E
Kwangtung = Guangdong □ . . **99** 23 0N 113 0 E
Kweichow = Guizhou □ . . . . . **99** 27 0N 107 0 E
Kwinana New Town . . . . **120** 32 15S 115 47 E
Kyabram . . . . **117** 36 19S 145 4 E
Kyaukpadaung . . . . **93** 20 52N 95 8 E
Kyle of Lochalsh **32** 57 17N 5 43W
Kyneton . . . . **117** 37 10S 144 29 E
Kyō-ga-Saki . . . . **106** 35 45N 135 15 E
Kyoga, L. . . . . **132** 1 35N 33 0 E
Kyogle . . . . **116** 28 40S 153 0 E
Kyōto . . . . **106** 35 0N 135 45 E
Kyrenia . . . . **80** 35 20N 33 20 E
Kyūshū . . . . **108** 33 0N 131 0 E
Kyūshū □ . . . . **108** 33 0N 131 0 E
Kyūshū-Sanchi . . . . **108** 32 35N 131 17 E
Kyustendil . . . . **53** 42 16N 22 41 E
Kyzyl . . . . **74** 51 50N 94 30 E
Kyzylkum, Peski . . . . **70** 42 30N 65 0 E
Kzyl-Orda . . . . **71** 44 48N 65 28 E

Labe = Elbe →→ . . . . **42** 53 50N 9 0 E
Laboulaye **190** 34 10S 63 30W
Labrador, Coast of □ **147** 53 20N 61 0W
Lábrea **187** 7 15S 64 51W
Lac la Martre **145** 63 8N 117 16W
Laccadive Is. =
  Lakshadweep Is. . . . . **78** 10 0N 72 30 E

Lachine	**151** 45 30N	73 40W
Lachute	**151** 45 39N	74 21W
Lackawanna	**164** 42 49N	78 50W
Lacombe	**155** 52 30N	113 44W
Laconia	**148** 43 32N	71 30W
Ladakh Ra.	**89** 34 0N	78 0 E
Ladoga, L. = Ladozhskoye		
Ozero	**68** 61 15N	30 30 E
Ladozhskoye Ozero	**68** 61 15N	30 30 E
Ladysmith	**154** 49 0N	123 49W
Lae	**115** 6 40S	147 2 E
Lafayette, Ind., U.S.A.	**167** 40 25N	86 54W
Lafayette, La., U.S.A.	**168** 30 18N	92 0W
Laghmān □	**87** 34 20N	70 0 E
Laghouat	**127** 33 50N	2 59 E
Lagny	**39** 48 52N	2 40 E
Lagos, Nigeria	**131** 6 25N	3 27 E
Lagos, Portugal	**50** 37 5N	8 41W
Lagos de Moreno	**175** 21 21N	101 55W
Laguna	**191** 28 30S	48 50W
Laguna Beach	**173** 33 31N	117 52W
Laguna Madre	**158** 27 0N	97 20W
Lagunas, Chile	**187** 21 0S	69 45W
Lagunas, Peru	**186** 5 10S	75 35W
Lahore	**89** 31 32N	74 22 E
Lahti	**67** 60 58N	25 40 E
Lahtis = Lahti	**67** 60 58N	25 40 E
Laï	**131** 9 25N	16 18 E
Laidley	**116** 27 39S	152 20 E
Lairg	**33** 58 1N	4 24W
Laja, R. de la ⟶	**177** 20 55N	100 46W
Lajes	**191** 27 48S	50 20W
Lake Cargelligo	**117** 33 15S	146 22 E
Lake Charles	**168** 30 15N	93 10W
Lake City, Fla., U.S.A.	**170** 30 10N	82 40W
Lake City, S.C., U.S.A.	**165** 33 51N	79 44W
Lake Grace	**120** 33 7S	118 28 E
Lake Harbour	**146** 62 50N	69 50W
Lake Worth	**170** 26 36N	80 3W
Lakeland	**170** 28 0N	82 0W
Lakes Entrance	**117** 37 50S	148 0 E
Lakewood	**167** 41 28N	81 50W
Lakshadweep Is.	**78** 10 0N	72 30 E
Lala Ghat	**93** 24 30N	92 40 E
Lalitpur	**91** 24 42N	78 28 E
Lamar	**163** 38 9N	102 35W
Lambi Kyun	**96** 10 50N	98 20 E
Lameroo	**119** 35 19S	140 33 E
Lamía	**54** 38 55N	22 26 E
Lammermuir Hills	**31** 55 50N	2 40W
Lamon Bay	**112** 14 30N	122 20 E
Lampa	**187** 15 22S	70 22W
Lampang	**94** 18 16N	99 32 E
Lampeter	**26** 52 6N	4 6W
Lamu	**133** 2 16S	40 55 E
Lanark	**31** 55 40N	3 48W
Lancang Jiang ⟶	**101** 21 40N	101 10 E
Lancashire □	**28** 53 40N	2 30W
Lancaster, U.K.	**28** 54 3N	2 48W
Lancaster, U.S.A.	**164** 40 4N	76 19W
Lancaster Sd.	**146** 74 13N	84 0W
Lanchow = Lanzhou	**99** 36 1N	103 52 E
Landes, Les	**36** 44 20N	1 0W
Land's End	**27** 50 4N	5 43W
Landskrona	**61** 55 53N	12 50 E
Lanett	**169** 33 0N	85 15W
Langjökull	**64** 64 39N	20 12W
Langlade	**149** 46 50N	56 20W
Langøya	**64** 68 45N	14 50 E
Langres, Plateau de	**37** 47 45N	5 3 E
Languedoc	**37** 43 58N	4 0 E
Lannion	**36** 48 46N	3 29W
Lansing	**167** 42 47N	84 40W
Lanzhou	**99** 36 1N	103 52 E
Laois □	**35** 53 0N	7 20W
Laon	**38** 49 33N	3 35 E
Laona	**150** 45 32N	88 41W
Laos ■	**95** 17 45N	105 0 E
Lapeer	**167** 43 3N	83 20W
Lapland = Lappland	**67** 68 7N	24 0 E
Lappland	**67** 68 7N	24 0 E
Laptev Sea	**72** 76 0N	125 0 E
Laramie	**163** 41 20N	105 38W
Laramie Mts.	**163** 42 0N	105 30W
Laredo	**161** 27 34N	99 29W
Laren	**40** 52 16N	5 14 E
Largs	**30** 55 48N	4 51W
Lárisa	**54** 39 49N	22 28 E
Larkana	**88** 27 32N	68 18 E
Larnaca	**80** 35 0N	33 35 E
Larne	**34** 54 52N	5 50W
Laryak	**69** 61 15N	80 0 E
Las Cruces	**161** 32 18N	106 50W
Las Lajas	**190** 38 30S	70 25W
Las Palmas	**126** 28 7N	15 26W
Las Vegas, N. Mex., U.S.A.	**161** 35 35N	105 10W
Las Vegas, Nev., U.S.A.	**173** 36 10N	115 5W
Lashio	**93** 22 56N	97 45 E
Latacunga	**184** 0 50S	78 35W
Latakia = Al Lādhiqīyah	**80** 35 30N	35 45 E
Latium = Lazio □	**46** 42 10N	12 30 E
Latrobe	**119** 41 14S	146 30 E
Latur	**91** 18 25N	76 40 E
Latvian S.S.R. □	**68** 56 50N	24 0 E
Lauchhammer	**43** 51 35N	13 48 E
Launceston, Australia	**119** 41 24S	147 8 E
Launceston, U.K.	**27** 50 38N	4 21W
Launglon Bok	**94** 13 50N	97 54 E
Laurel	**169** 31 41N	89 9W
Laurens	**165** 34 32N	82 2W
Laurentian Plat.	**138** 52 0N	70 0W
Laurinburg	**165** 34 50N	79 25W
Lausanne	**44** 46 32N	6 38 E
Laut, Pulau	**111** 3 40S	116 10 E
Laut Ketil, Kepulauan	**113** 4 45S	115 40 E
Lauzon	**148** 46 48N	71 10W
Laval	**36** 48 4N	0 48W
Lávrion	**55** 37 40N	24 4 E
Lawrence, Kans., U.S.A.	**166** 39 0N	95 10W
Lawrence, Mass., U.S.A.	**164** 42 40N	71 9W
Lawrenceburg	**169** 35 12N	87 19W
Lawton	**161** 34 33N	98 25W
Lazio □	**46** 42 10N	12 30 E
Lea ⟶	**25** 51 30N	0 10 E
Leader	**152** 50 50N	109 30W
Leadhills	**31** 55 25N	3 47W
Leadville	**163** 39 17N	106 23W
Leamington, Canada	**150** 42 3N	82 36W
Leamington, U.K.	**24** 52 18N	1 32W
Leavenworth	**166** 39 25N	95 0W
Lebanon, Mo., U.S.A.	**166** 37 40N	92 40W
Lebanon, Oreg., U.S.A.	**171** 44 31N	122 57W
Lebanon, Pa., U.S.A.	**164** 40 20N	76 28W
Lebanon, Tenn., U.S.A.	**169** 36 15N	86 20W
Lebanon ■	**80** 34 0N	36 0 E
Lecce	**49** 40 20N	18 10 E
Ledbury	**24** 52 3N	2 25W
Leduc	**155** 53 15N	113 30W
Leeds	**28** 53 48N	1 34W
Leek	**28** 53 7N	2 2W
Leerdam	**40** 51 54N	5 6 E
Leesburg	**170** 28 47N	81 52W
Leeton	**117** 34 33S	146 23 E
Leeuwarden	**41** 53 15N	5 48 E
Leeuwin, C.	**120** 34 20S	115 9 E
Leeward Is.	**181** 16 30N	63 30W
Leghorn = Livorno	**46** 43 32N	10 18 E
Legnica	**58** 51 12N	16 10 E
Leicester	**25** 52 39N	1 9W
Leicester □	**25** 52 40N	1 10W
Leichhardt	**121** 33 53S	151 9 E
Leiden	**40** 52 9N	4 30 E
Leigh Creek South	**118** 30 38S	138 26 E
Leinster	**120** 27 51S	120 36 E
Leinster □	**35** 53 0N	7 10W
Leinster, Mt.	**35** 52 38N	6 47W
Leipzig	**43** 51 20N	12 23 E
Leith	**31** 55 59N	3 10W
Leith Hill	**24** 51 10N	0 23W
Leitrim	**34** 54 0N	8 5W
Lek ⟶	**40** 51 54N	4 35 E
Leleque	**192** 42 28S	71 0W

Léman, Lac	44	46 26N	6	30 E
Lemmer	41	52 51N	5	43 E
Lena →	72	72 52N	126	40 E
Leninabad	71	40 17N	69	37 E
Leninakan	70	40 47N	43	50 E
Leningrad	68	59 55N	30	20 E
Leninsk-Kuznetskiy	71	54 44N	86	10 E
Leninskoye	75	47 56N	132	38 E
Lenoir City	165	35 40N	84	20W
Lens, Belgium	38	50 33N	3	54 E
Lens, France	37	50 26N	2	50 E
Lensk	74	60 48N	114	55 E
Leominster, U.K.	24	52 15N	2	43W
Leominster, U.S.A.	164	42 32N	71	45W
León, Mexico	177	21 7N	101	40W
León, Nic.	179	12 20N	86	51W
León, Spain	50	42 38N	5	34W
León □	50	42 40N	5	55W
Leongatha	117	38 30S	145	58 E
Léopold II, Lac = Mai-				
Ndombe, L.	134	2 0S	18	20 E
Léopoldville = Kinshasa	134	4 20S	15	15 E
Lérida	51	41 37N	0	39 E
Lerwick	30	60 10N	1	10W
Lesbos, I. = Lésvos	55	39 10N	26	20 E
Lesotho ■	137	29 40S	28	0 E
Lesozavodsk	75	45 30N	133	29 E
Lesser Antilles	181	15 0N	61	0W
Lesser Slave L.	155	55 30N	115	25W
Lésvos	55	39 10N	26	20 E
Letchworth	25	51 58N	0	13W
Lethbridge	155	49 45N	112	45W
Leti, Kepulauan	113	8 10S	128	0 E
Leticia	184	4 9S	70	0W
Letsôk-aw Kyun	94	11 30N	98	25 E
Letterkenny	34	54 57N	7	42W
Leuven	42	50 52N	4	42 E
Levanger	65	63 45N	11	19 E
Levin	122	40 37S	175	18 E
Lévis	148	46 48N	71	9W
Levkás	54	38 40N	20	43 E
Levkôsia = Nicosia	80	35 10N	33	25 E
Lewes	25	50 53N	0	2 E
Lewis	32	58 10N	6	40W
Lewis, Butt of	32	58 30N	6	12W
Lewis Ra.	162	48 0N	113	15W
Lewisporte	149	49 15N	55	3W
Lewiston	148	44 3N	70	10 E
Lexington, Ky., U.S.A.	165	38 6N	84	30W
Lexington, Mo., U.S.A.	166	39 7N	93	55W
Lexington, N.C., U.S.A.	165	35 50N	80	13W
Lexington, Oreg., U.S.A.	171	45 29N	119	46W
Lexington Park	165	38 16N	76	27W
Leyte	112	11 0N	125	0 E
Lhasa	101	29 50N	91	3 E
Lhazê	101	29 5N	87	38 E
Lianyungang	99	34 40N	119	11 E
Liaoning □	98	41 40N	122	30 E
Liaoyuan	98	42 58N	125	2 E
Liard →	144	61 51N	121	18W
Libau = Liepaja	68	56 30N	21	0 E
Liberec	58	50 47N	15	7 E
Liberia ■	130	6 30N	9	30W
Lîbiya, Sahrâ'	128	27 35N	25	0 E
Libreville	134	0 25N	9	26 E
Libya ■	127	27 0N	17	0 E
Lichfield	28	52 40N	1	50W
Liechtenstein ■	44	47 8N	9	35 E
Liège	42	50 38N	5	35 E
Liegnitz = Legnica	58	51 12N	16	10 E
Lienyünchiangshih =				
Lianyungang	99	34 40N	119	11 E
Liepaja	68	56 30N	21	0 E
Liévin	38	50 24N	2	47 E
Liffey →	35	53 21N	6	20W
Lifford	34	54 50N	7	30W
Liguria □	46	44 30N	9	0 E
Ligurian Sea	46	43 20N	9	0 E
Lihou Reefs and Cays	121	17 25S	151	40 E
Lihue	160	21 59N	159	24W
Likasi	135	10 55S	26	48 E

Lille, Belgium	38	51 15N	4	50 E
Lille, France	37	50 38N	3	3 E
Lille Bœlt	61	55 20N	9	45 E
Lillehammer	60	61 8N	10	30 E
Lillers	38	50 35N	2	28 E
Lillooet	154	50 44N	121	57W
Lilongwe	137	14 0S	33	48 E
Lima, Peru	186	12 0S	77	0W
Lima, U.S.A.	167	40 42N	84	5W
Limassol	80	34 42N	33	1 E
Limavady	34	55 3N	6	58W
Limbe	137	15 55S	35	2 E
Limburg □	41	51 20N	5	55 E
Limeira	188	22 35S	47	28W
Limerick	35	52 40N	8	38W
Limerick □	35	52 30N	8	50W
Limfjorden	61	56 55N	9	0 E
Límnos	55	39 50N	25	5 E
Limoges	36	45 50N	1	15 E
Limón	179	10 0N	83	2W
Limousin	36	46 0N	1	0 E
Limpopo →	137	25 15S	33	30 E
Linares, Chile	190	35 50S	71	40W
Linares, Mexico	176	24 50N	99	40W
Linares, Spain	50	38 10N	3	40W
Lincoln, Argentina	190	34 55S	61	30W
Lincoln, U.K.	29	53 14N	0	32W
Lincoln, Ill., U.S.A.	166	40 10N	89	20W
Lincoln, Maine, U.S.A.	148	45 27N	68	29W
Lincoln, Nebr., U.S.A.	156	40 50N	96	42W
Lincoln □	29	53 14N	0	32W
Lincoln Sea	12	84 0N	55	0W
Lincoln Wolds	29	53 20N	0	5W
Lindsay, Canada	151	44 22N	78	43W
Lindsay, U.S.A.	173	36 14N	119	6W
Línea de la Concepción, La	50	36 15N	5	23W
Lingga, Kepulauan	111	0 10S	104	30 E
Linguéré	130	15 25N	15	5W
Linköping	60	58 28N	15	36 E
Linlithgow	31	55 58N	3	38W
Linxia	99	35 36N	103	10 E
Linz	45	48 18N	14	18 E
Lion, G. du	37	43 0N	4	0 E
Lípari, Is.	49	38 30N	14	50 E
Lipetsk	68	52 37N	39	35 E
Lippe →	42	51 39N	6	38 E
Lisboa	50	38 42N	9	10W
Lisbon = Lisboa	50	38 42N	9	10W
Lisburn	34	54 30N	6	9W
Lisburne, C.	142	68 50N	166	0W
Lisieux	39	49 10N	0	12 E
Lismore	116	28 44S	153	21 E
Lister, Mt.	15	78 0S	162	0 E
Listowel	35	52 27N	9	30W
Litchfield	166	39 10N	89	40W
Lithgow	117	33 25S	150	8 E
Lithuanian S.S.R. □	68	55 30N	24	0 E
Little Andaman I.	94	10 40N	92	15 E
Little Barrier I.	122	36 12S	175	8 E
Little Current	150	45 55N	82	0W
Little Falls	164	43 3N	74	50W
Little Minch	32	57 35N	6	45W
Little Rann	91	23 25N	71	25 E
Little Rock	168	34 41N	92	10W
Littlehampton	25	50 48N	0	32W
Liuzhou	99	24 22N	109	22 E
Liverpool, Australia	117	33 54S	150	58 E
Liverpool, Canada	148	44 5N	64	41W
Liverpool, U.K.	28	53 25N	3	0W
Liverpool Plains	116	31 15S	150	15 E
Livingston, Guat.	177	15 50N	88	50W
Livingston, U.K.	31	55 52N	3	33W
Livingston, Mont., U.S.A.	163	45 40N	110	40W
Livingston, Tex., U.S.A.	168	30 44N	94	54W
Livingstone	135	17 46S	25	52 E
Livonia	167	42 25N	83	23W
Livorno	46	43 32N	10	18 E
Lizard Pt.	27	49 57N	5	11W
Ljubljana	52	46 4N	14	33 E
Ljusnan →	66	61 12N	17	8 E
Llandeilo	26	51 53N	4	0W

Llandovery	**26**	51 59N	3 49W
Llandrindod Wells	**26**	52 15N	3 23W
Llandudno	**26**	53 19N	3 51W
Llanelli	**27**	51 41N	4 11W
Llanes	**50**	43 25N	4 50W
Llangollen	**26**	52 58N	3 10W
Llanidloes	**26**	52 28N	3 31W
Llano Estacado	**161**	34 0N	103 0W
Llanos	**184**	5 0N	71 35W
Lloydminster	**152**	53 17N	110 0W
Loc Ninh	**95**	11 50N	106 34 E
Lochaber	**32**	56 55N	5 0W
Lochboisdale	**32**	57 10N	7 20W
Lochem	**41**	52 9N	6 26 E
Lochgilphead	**30**	56 2N	5 37W
Lochinver	**32**	58 9N	5 15W
Lochmaddy	**32**	57 36N	7 10W
Lochy, L.	**32**	56 58N	4 55W
Lock Haven	**164**	41 7N	77 31W
Lockhart	**117**	35 14S	146 40 E
Lockport	**164**	43 12N	78 42W
Lodi	**172**	38 12N	121 16W
Łódź	**58**	51 45N	19 27 E
Lofoten	**64**	68 30N	15 0 E
Logan, Utah, U.S.A.	**163**	41 45N	111 50W
Logan, W. Va., U.S.A.	**165**	37 51N	81 59W
Logan, Mt	**144**	60 31N	140 22W
Logansport	**167**	40 45N	86 21W
Logroño	**51**	42 28N	2 27W
Loire →	**36**	47 16N	2 10W
Loja	**184**	3 59S	79 16W
Lokka	**67**	67 55N	27 35 E
Lolland	**61**	54 45N	11 30 E
Lom	**53**	43 48N	23 12 E
Lomami →	**134**	0 46N	24 16 E
Lombardia □	**46**	45 35N	9 45 E
Lombardy = Lombardia □	**46**	45 35N	9 45 E
Lombok	**113**	8 45S	116 30 E
Lomé	**130**	6 9N	1 20 E
Lomond, L.	**31**	56 8N	4 38W
Lompoc	**173**	34 41N	120 32W
Łomza	**58**	53 10N	22 2 E
London, Canada	**150**	42 59N	81 15W
London, U.K.	**25**	51 30N	0 5W
Londonderry	**34**	55 0N	7 20W
Londrina	**191**	23 18S	51 10W
Long Beach	**173**	33 46N	118 12W
Long I., Bahamas	**178**	23 20N	75 10W
Long I., U.S.A.	**164**	40 50N	73 20W
Long Range Mts.	**149**	49 30N	57 30W
Long Xuyen	**95**	10 19N	105 28 E
Longford, Australia	**119**	41 32S	147 3 E
Longford, Ireland	**34**	53 43N	7 50W
Longford □	**34**	53 42N	7 45W
Longlac	**150**	49 45N	86 25W
Longmont	**163**	40 10N	105 4W
Longreach	**121**	23 28S	144 14 E
Longview, Tex., U.S.A.	**168**	32 30N	94 45W
Longview, Wash., U.S.A.	**171**	46 9N	122 58W
Looe	**27**	50 24N	4 25W
Loop Hd.	**35**	52 34N	9 55W
Lop Nor	**100**	40 20N	90 10 E
Lopez, C.	**134**	0 47S	8 40 E
Lorain	**167**	41 28N	82 55W
Lorca	**51**	37 41N	1 42W
Lord Howe I.	**122**	31 33S	159 6 E
Lordsburg	**161**	32 22N	108 45W
Lorient	**36**	47 45N	3 23W
Lorn	**30**	56 26N	5 10W
Lorn, Firth of	**30**	56 20N	5 40W
Lorraine	**37**	49 0N	6 0 E
Los Alamos	**161**	35 57N	106 17W
Los Andes	**190**	32 50S	70 40W
Los Angeles, Chile	**190**	37 28S	72 23W
Los Angeles, U.S.A.	**173**	34 0N	118 10W
Los Angeles Aqueduct	**173**	35 25N	118 0W
Los Hermanos	**181**	11 45N	84 25W
Los Mochis	**174**	25 45N	108 57W
Los Testigos	**181**	11 23N	63 6W
Lošinj	**52**	44 30N	14 30 E
Lossiemouth	**33**	57 43N	3 17W
Lot →	**36**	44 18N	0 20 E
Lota	**190**	37 5S	73 10W
Lothian □	**31**	55 50N	3 0W
Loughborough	**29**	52 46N	1 11W
Loughrea	**35**	53 11N	8 33W
Louisbourg	**149**	45 55N	60 0W
Louise I.	**154**	52 55N	131 50W
Louisiana □	**168**	30 50N	92 0W
Louisville, Ky., U.S.A.	**167**	38 15N	85 45W
Louisville, Miss., U.S.A.	**169**	33 7N	89 3W
Lourdes	**36**	43 6N	0 3W
Lourenço-Marques = Maputo	**137**	25 58S	32 32 E
Louth	**29**	53 23N	0 0 E
Louth □	**34**	53 55N	6 30W
Louvain = Leuven	**42**	50 52N	4 42 E
Louviers	**39**	49 12N	1 10 E
Lowell	**164**	42 38N	71 19W
Lower Austria = Niederösterreich □	**45**	48 25N	15 40 E
Lower California = Baja California	**174**	31 10N	115 12W
Lower Hutt	**123**	41 10S	174 55 E
Lower Saxony = Niedersachsen □	**42**	52 45N	9 0 E
Lowestoft	**25**	52 29N	1 44 E
Łowicz	**58**	52 6N	19 55 E
Loxton	**119**	34 28S	140 31 E
Loyalty Is. = Loyauté, Is.	**122**	21 0S	167 30 E
Loyang = Luoyang	**99**	34 40N	112 26 E
Loyauté, Is.	**122**	21 0S	167 30 E
Lualaba →	**135**	0 26N	25 20 E
Luan Chau	**95**	21 38N	103 24 E
Luanda	**134**	8 50S	13 15 E
Luang Prabang	**95**	19 52N	102 10 E
Luarca	**50**	43 32N	6 32W
Lubbock	**161**	33 40N	101 53W
Lübeck	**43**	53 52N	10 41 E
Lublin	**58**	51 12N	22 38 E
Lubnān, J.	**80**	33 50N	35 45 E
Lubumbashi	**135**	11 40S	27 28 E
Lucca	**46**	43 50N	10 30 E
Luce Bay	**30**	54 45N	4 48W
Lučenec	**59**	48 18N	19 42 E
Lucerne = Luzern	**44**	47 3N	8 18 E
Lucknow	**92**	26 50N	81 0 E
Lüda = Dalian	**98**	38 50N	121 40 E
Lüderitz	**136**	26 41S	15 8 E
Ludhiana	**89**	30 57N	75 56 E
Ludington	**167**	43 58N	86 27W
Ludlow	**24**	52 23N	2 42W
Ludwigshafen	**42**	49 27N	8 27 E
Lufkin	**168**	31 25N	94 40W
Lugano	**44**	46 0N	8 57 E
Lugansk = Voroshilovgrad	**68**	48 38N	39 15 E
Lugo	**50**	43 2N	7 35W
Lugovoye	**71**	42 55N	72 43 E
Luján	**190**	34 45S	59 5W
Łuków	**58**	51 55N	22 23 E
Lule älv →	**67**	65 35N	22 10 E
Luleå	**67**	65 35N	22 10 E
Lüleburgaz	**80**	41 23N	27 22 E
Lulua →	**134**	6 30S	22 50 E
Luluabourg = Kananga	**134**	5 55S	22 18 E
Lumberton	**165**	34 37N	78 59W
Lundy	**27**	51 10N	4 41W
Lune →	**28**	54 0N	2 51W
Lüneburg	**43**	53 15N	10 23 E
Lüneburg Heath = Lüneburger Heide	**43**	53 0N	10 0 E
Lüneburger Heide	**43**	53 0N	10 0 E
Lüni →	**91**	24 41N	71 14 E
Luoyang	**99**	34 40N	112 26 E
Lurgan	**34**	54 28N	6 20W
Lusaka	**135**	15 28S	28 16 E
Luta = Dalian	**98**	38 50N	121 40 E
Luton	**25**	51 53N	0 24W
Lutsk	**68**	50 50N	25 15 E
Luvua →	**135**	6 50S	27 30 E
Luxembourg	**42**	49 37N	6 9 E
Luxembourg ■	**42**	50 0N	6 0 E
Luzern	**44**	47 3N	8 18 E

Luzhou	**99**	28 52N	105	20 E
Luziânia	**188**	16 20S	48	0W
Luzon	**112**	16 0N	121	0 E
Lvov	**68**	49 50N	24	0 E
Lyakhovskiye, Ostrova	**72**	73 40N	141	0 E
Lyallpur = Faisalabad	**89**	31 30N	73	5 E
Lyell I.	**154**	52 40N	131	35W
Lyell Range	**123**	41 38S	172	20 E
Lyme Regis	**27**	50 44N	2	57W
Lymington	**24**	50 46N	1	32W
Lynchburg	**165**	37 23N	79	10W
Lynn	**164**	42 28N	70	57W
Lynn Lake	**152**	56 51N	101	3W
Lynton	**27**	51 14N	3	50W
Lyon	**37**	45 46N	4	50 E
Lyons = Lyon	**37**	45 46N	4	50 E
Lytham St. Anne's	**28**	53 45N	2	58W
Lyttelton	**122**	43 35S	172	44 E
Ma'ān	**80**	30 12N	35	44 E
Ma'anshan	**99**	31 44N	118	29 E
Ma'arrat an Nu'mān	**80**	35 43N	36	43 E
Maas →	**40**	51 45N	4	32 E
Maaseik	**41**	51 6N	5	45 E
Maastricht	**41**	50 50N	5	40 E
Mablethorpe	**29**	53 21N	0	14 E
McAlester	**168**	34 57N	95	46W
Macao = Macau ■	**99**	22 16N	113	35 E
Macapá	**185**	0 5N	51	4W
Macau	**189**	5 0S	36	40W
Macau ■	**99**	22 16N	113	35 E
McBride	**155**	53 20N	120	19W
Macclesfield	**28**	53 16N	2	9W
McClure Str.	**12**	75 0N	119	0W
McComb	**169**	31 13N	90	30W
McCook	**163**	40 15N	100	35W
McDermitt	**172**	42 0N	117	45W
Macdonald L.	**114**	23 30S	129	0 E
Macdonnell Ranges	**114**	23 40S	133	0 E
McDouall Peak	**118**	29 51S	134	55 E
Macduff	**33**	57 40N	2	30W
Macedonia = Makedhonía □	**55**	40 39N	22	0 E
Maceió	**189**	9 40S	35	41W
Macfarlane, L.	**118**	32 0S	136	40 E
Macgillycuddy's Reeks	**35**	52 2N	9	45W
Machala	**184**	3 20S	79	57W
Machida	**107**	35 28N	139	23 E
Machilipatnam	**92**	16 12N	81	8 E
Machiques	**184**	10 4N	72	34W
Machynlleth	**26**	52 36N	3	51W
Mackay	**121**	21 8S	149	11 E
Mackay, L.	**114**	22 30S	129	0 E
McKeesport	**164**	40 21N	79	50W
Mackenzie →	**144**	69 10N	134	20W
Mackenzie Bay	**12**	69 0N	137	30W
Mackenzie Mts.	**144**	64 0N	130	0W
McKinley, Mt.	**142**	63 2N	151	0W
McKinley Sea	**13**	84 0N	10	0W
McKinney	**168**	33 10N	96	40W
Macksville	**116**	30 40S	152	56 E
Maclean	**116**	29 26S	153	16 E
McLennan	**155**	55 42N	116	50W
MacLeod Lake	**154**	54 58N	123	0W
M'Clintock Chan.	**145**	72 0N	102	0W
McMinnville, Oreg., U.S.A.	**171**	45 16N	123	11W
McMinnville, Tenn., U.S.A.	**169**	35 43N	85	45W
McMurdo Sd.	**15**	77 0S	170	0 E
McMurray = Fort McMurray	**155**	56 44N	111	7W
McNaughton L.	**155**	52 0N	118	10W
Macomb	**166**	40 25N	90	40W
Mâcon, France	**37**	46 19N	4	50 E
Mâcon, U.S.A.	**170**	32 50N	83	37W
McPherson	**161**	38 25N	97	40W
Macpherson Ra.	**116**	28 15S	153	15 E
Macquarie →	**116**	30 5S	147	30 E
Macquarie Is.	**15**	54 36S	158	55 E
MacRobertson Land	**14**	71 0S	64	0 E
Macroom	**35**	51 54N	8	57W
Madagascar ■	**137**	20 0S	47	0 E
Madang	**115**	5 12S	145	49 E
Madaripur	**93**	23 19N	90	15 E
Made	**40**	51 41N	4	49 E
Madeira	**126**	32 50N	17	0W
Madeira →	**185**	3 22S	58	45W
Madeleine, Ìs. de la	**149**	47 30N	61	40W
Madera	**173**	37 0N	120	1W
Madhya Pradesh □	**91**	21 50N	81	0 E
Madison, Fla., U.S.A.	**170**	30 29N	83	39W
Madison, Ind., U.S.A.	**167**	38 42N	85	20W
Madison, Wis., U.S.A.	**166**	43 5N	89	25W
Madisonville	**167**	37 20N	87	30W
Madiun	**111**	7 38S	111	32 E
Madras = Tamil Nadu □	**90**	11 0N	77	0 E
Madras, India	**90**	13 8N	80	19 E
Madras, U.S.A.	**171**	44 40N	121	10W
Madre, Laguna	**176**	25 0N	97	30W
Madre de Dios →	**187**	10 59S	66	8W
Madre del Sur, Sa.	**177**	17 0N	100	0W
Madre Occidental, Sa.	**174**	25 0N	105	0W
Madre Oriental, Sa.	**177**	22 0N	99	30W
Madrid	**50**	40 25N	3	45W
Madura, Selat	**111**	7 30S	113	20 E
Madurai	**90**	9 55N	78	10 E
Madurantakam	**90**	12 30N	79	50 E
Mae Rim	**94**	18 54N	98	57 E
Maebashi	**107**	36 24N	139	4 E
Maesteg	**27**	51 36N	3	40W
Maestra, Sierra	**178**	20 15N	77	0W
Mafeking	**152**	52 40N	101	10W
Maffra	**117**	37 53S	146	58 E
Mafia	**135**	7 45S	39	50 E
Mafikeng	**136**	25 50S	25	38 E
Mafra	**191**	26 10S	50	0W
Magadan	**73**	59 38N	150	50 E
Magallanes, Estrecho de	**192**	52 30S	75	0W
Magangué	**184**	9 14N	74	45W
Magdalena, Bolivia	**187**	13 13S	63	57W
Magdalena, Mexico	**174**	30 38N	110	57W
Magdalena →	**184**	11 6N	74	51W
Magdeburg	**43**	52 8N	11	36 E
Magelang	**111**	7 29S	110	13 E
Magellan's Str. = Magallanes, Estrecho de	**192**	52 30S	75	0W
Magherafelt	**34**	54 44N	6	37W
Magnitogorsk	**71**	53 27N	59	4 E
Magog	**148**	45 18N	72	9W
Magosa = Famagusta	**80**	35 8N	33	55 E
Magrath	**155**	49 25N	112	50W
Mahābād	**81**	36 50N	45	45 E
Mahajanga □	**137**	17 0S	47	0 E
Mahakam →	**111**	0 35S	117	17 E
Maḥallāt	**86**	33 55N	50	30 E
Mahanadi →	**92**	20 20N	86	25 E
Maharashtra □	**91**	20 30N	75	30 E
Mahbubnagar	**91**	16 45N	77	59 E
Mahia Pen.	**122**	39 9S	177	55 E
Mahón	**51**	39 53N	4	16 E
Mahone Bay	**148**	44 30N	64	20W
Mahukona	**160**	20 11N	155	52W
Mai-Ndombe, L.	**134**	2 0S	18	20 E
Maidenhead	**25**	51 31N	0	42W
Maiduguri	**131**	12 0N	13	20 E
Maikala Ra.	**92**	22 0N	81	0 E
Main →	**42**	50 0N	8	18 E
Maine	**36**	48 0N	0	0 E
Maine □	**148**	45 20N	69	0W
Mainland, Orkney, U.K.	**33**	59 0N	3	10W
Mainland, Shetland, U.K.	**30**	60 15N	1	22W
Mainpuri	**89**	27 18N	79	4 E
Mainz	**42**	50 0N	8	17 E
Maiquetía	**184**	10 36N	66	57W
Maisí, Pta. de	**178**	20 10N	74	10W
Maitland, N.S.W., Australia	**117**	32 33S	151	36 E
Maitland, S. Austral., Australia	**119**	34 23S	137	40 E
Maiz, Islas del	**179**	12 15N	83	4W
Maizuru	**106**	35 25N	135	22 E
Majorca, I. = Mallorca	**51**	39 30N	3	0 E
Makarikari = Makgadikgadi Salt Pans	**136**	20 40S	25	45 E
Makasar = Ujung Pandang	**113**	5 10S	119	20 E

Name	Page	°	′		°	′	
Makasar, Selat	113	1	0	S	118	20	E
Makedhonía □	55	40	39	N	22	0	E
Makena	160	20	39	N	156	27	W
Makeyevka	68	48	0	N	38	0	E
Makgadikgadi Salt Pans	136	20	40	S	25	45	E
Makhachkala	70	43	0	N	47	30	E
Makkah	82	21	30	N	39	54	E
Makó	59	46	14	N	20	33	E
Makran Coast Range	88	25	40	N	64	0	E
Makurazaki	108	31	15	N	130	20	E
Makurdi	131	7	43	N	8	35	E
Malabar Coast	90	11	0	N	75	0	E
Malacca, Str. of	111	3	0	N	101	0	E
Malad City	162	42	10	N	112	20	E
Málaga	50	36	43	N	4	23	W
Malakal	129	9	33	N	31	50	E
Malang	111	7	59	S	112	45	E
Mälaren	60	59	30	N	17	10	E
Malatya	81	38	25	N	38	20	E
Malawi ■	137	13	0	S	34	0	E
Malawi, L.	137	12	30	S	34	30	E
Malay Pen.	97	7	25	N	100	0	E
Malåyer	84	34	19	N	48	51	E
Malaysia ■	111	5	0	N	110	0	E
Malbaie, La	148	47	40	N	70	10	W
Malbork	58	54	3	N	19	1	E
Malcolm	120	28	51	S	121	25	E
Maldives ■	78	7	0	N	73	0	E
Maldonado	191	35	0	S	55	0	W
Malebo, Pool	134	4	17	S	15	20	E
Malegaon	91	20	30	N	74	38	E
Mali ■	130	15	0	N	2	0	W
Mali Kyun	94	13	0	N	98	20	E
Malin Hd.	34	55	18	N	7	24	W
Malindi	133	3	12	S	40	5	E
Malines = Mechelen	42	51	2	N	4	29	E
Mallaig	32	57	0	N	5	50	W
Mallorca	51	39	30	N	3	0	E
Mallow	35	52	8	N	8	40	W
Malmédy	42	50	25	N	6	2	E
Malmö	61	55	36	N	12	59	E
Malmöhus län □	61	55	45	N	13	30	E
Malone	151	44	50	N	74	19	W
Malta ■	49	35	50	N	14	30	E
Malton	29	54	9	N	0	48	W
Maluku	113	1	0	S	127	0	E
Malvern, U.K.	24	52	7	N	2	19	W
Malvern, U.S.A.	168	34	22	N	92	50	W
Malvern Hills	24	52	0	N	2	19	W
Malvinas, Is. = Falkland Is.	192	51	30	S	59	0	W
Mamers	39	48	21	N	0	22	E
Mamoré →	187	10	23	S	65	53	W
Mamou	130	10	15	N	12	0	W
Man	130	7	30	N	7	40	W
Man, I. of	28	54	15	N	4	30	W
Mana, Fr. Gui.	185	5	45	N	53	55	W
Mana, U.S.A.	160	22	3	N	159	45	W
Manaar, Gulf of = Mannar, G. of	90	8	30	N	79	0	E
Manacapuru	185	3	16	S	60	37	W
Manado	113	1	29	N	124	51	E
Managua	179	12	6	N	86	20	W
Manaos = Manaus	185	3	0	S	60	0	W
Manapouri	123	45	34	S	167	39	E
Manaung	93	18	45	N	93	40	E
Manaus	185	3	0	S	60	0	W
Mancha, La	50	39	10	N	2	54	W
Manchester, U.K.	28	53	30	N	2	15	W
Manchester, U.S.A.	164	42	58	N	71	29	W
Mandalay	93	22	0	N	96	4	E
Mandale = Mandalay	93	22	0	N	96	4	E
Mandurah	120	32	36	S	115	48	E
Manfredónia, G. di	49	41	30	N	16	10	E
Mangalore	90	12	55	N	74	47	E
Mangla Dam	89	33	9	N	73	44	E
Mangole	113	1	50	S	125	55	E
Mangonui	122	35	1	S	173	32	E
Mangyshlak P-ov.	70	44	30	N	52	30	E
Manhattan	158	39	10	N	96	40	W
Manicoré	185	5	48	S	61	16	W
Manicouagan →	148	49	30	N	68	30	W
Manila	112	14	40	N	121	3	E
Manilla	116	30	45	S	150	43	E
Manipur □	93	25	0	N	94	0	E
Manisa	80	38	38	N	27	30	E
Manistee	167	44	15	N	86	20	W
Manistique	150	45	59	N	86	18	W
Manitoba □	153	55	30	N	97	0	W
Manitoba, L.	153	51	0	N	98	45	W
Manitoulin I.	150	45	40	N	82	30	W
Manitowoc	167	44	8	N	87	40	W
Manizales	184	5	5	N	75	32	W
Manjil	81	36	46	N	49	30	E
Manjimup	120	34	15	S	116	6	E
Mankato	166	44	8	N	93	59	W
Manly	117	33	48	S	151	17	E
Mannar, G. of	90	8	30	N	79	0	E
Mannar I.	90	9	5	N	79	45	E
Mannheim	42	49	28	N	8	29	E
Mannum	119	34	50	S	139	20	E
Manosque	37	43	49	N	5	47	E
Manouane, L.	148	50	45	N	70	45	W
Mans, Le	39	48	0	N	0	10	E
Mansel I.	146	62	0	N	80	0	W
Mansfield, Australia	117	37	4	S	146	6	E
Mansfield, U.K.	29	53	8	N	1	12	W
Mansfield, U.S.A.	167	40	45	N	82	30	W
Manta	184	1	0	S	80	40	W
Mantes-la-Jolie	39	49	0	N	1	41	E
Mantiqueira, Serra da	188	22	0	S	44	0	W
Mántova	46	45	20	N	10	42	E
Mantua = Mántova	46	45	20	N	10	42	E
Manu	187	12	10	S	70	51	W
Manukau	122	35	14	S	173	13	E
Manyara, L.	135	3	40	S	35	50	E
Manzanillo, Cuba	178	20	20	N	77	31	W
Manzanillo, Mexico	175	19	3	N	104	20	W
Manzhouli	98	49	35	N	117	25	E
Mapimí	174	25	49	N	103	51	W
Maple	152	43	51	N	79	31	W
Maputo	137	25	58	S	32	32	E
Maquinchao	192	41	15	S	68	50	W
Mar, Serra do	191	25	30	S	49	0	W
Mar Chiquita, L.	190	30	40	S	62	50	W
Mar del Plata	191	38	0	S	57	30	W
Mar Menor, L.	51	37	40	N	0	45	W
Marabá	188	5	20	S	49	5	W
Maracaibo	184	10	40	N	71	37	W
Maracaibo, Lago de	184	9	40	N	71	30	W
Maracay	184	10	15	N	67	28	W
Marajó, Ilha de	188	1	0	S	49	30	W
Maranhão = São Luís	188	2	39	S	44	15	W
Maranhão □	188	5	0	S	46	0	W
Marañón →	186	4	30	S	73	35	W
Maraş	80	37	37	N	36	53	E
Marathón	55	38	11	N	23	58	E
Marbella	50	36	30	N	4	57	W
Marble Bar	114	21	9	S	119	44	E
March	25	52	33	N	0	5	E
Marché	36	46	0	N	1	20	E
Marche □	47	43	22	N	13	10	E
Marchena	50	37	18	N	5	23	W
Marches = Marche □	47	43	22	N	13	10	E
Mardan	89	34	20	N	72	0	E
Mardin	81	37	20	N	40	43	E
Mareeba	121	16	59	S	145	28	E
Margarita	175	9	20	N	79	55	W
Margarita I.	185	11	0	N	64	0	W
Margate	25	51	23	N	1	24	E
Mari, A.S.S.R. □	68	56	30	N	48	0	E
Maria van Diemen, C.	122	34	29	S	172	40	E
Marianao	178	23	8	N	82	24	W
Marianna	169	30	45	N	85	15	W
Maribor	52	46	36	N	15	40	E
Maricourt	146	61	30	N	72	0	W
Marie-Galante	180	15	56	N	61	16	W
Marienberg	41	52	30	N	6	35	E
Marietta, Ga., U.S.A.	169	34	0	N	84	30	W
Marietta, Ohio, U.S.A.	164	39	27	N	81	27	W
Marília	188	22	13	S	50	0	W
Marín	50	42	23	N	8	42	W
Marinette	167	45	4	N	87	40	W

Name							
Maringá	191	23	26S		52		2W
Marion, Ill., U.S.A.	166	37	45N		88		55W
Marion, Ind., U.S.A.	167	40	35N		85		40W
Marion, Ohio, U.S.A.	167	40	38N		83		8W
Marken	40	52	26N		5	12	E
Market Drayton	28	52	55N		2		30W
Market Harborough	25	52	29N		0		55W
Market Rasen	29	53	24N		0		20W
Markham Mt.	15	83	0S		164		0 E
Marlborough	24	51	26N		1		44W
Marlborough □	123	41	45S		173	33	E
Marlborough Downs	24	51	25N		1		55W
Marlin	168	31	25N		96		50W
Marmagao	91	15	25N		73	56	E
Marmara, Sea of = Marmara Denizi	80	40	45N		28	15	E
Marmara Denizi	80	40	45N		28	15	E
Marmaris	80	36	50N		28	14	E
Marne ~→	39	8	23N		18	36	E
Maroochydore	116	26	29S		153	5	E
Marquesas Is.	123	9	30S		140		0W
Marquette	150	46	30N		87		21W
Marrakech	126	31	9N		8		0W
Marree	118	29	39S		138	1	E
Marsabit	133	2	18N		38		0 E
Marseille	37	43	18N		5	23	E
Marseilles = Marseille	37	43	18N		5	23	E
Marshall, Minn., U.S.A.	166	44	25N		95		45W
Marshall, Mo., U.S.A.	166	39	8N		93		15W
Marshall, Tex., U.S.A.	168	32	29N		94		20W
Marshalltown	166	42	5N		92		56W
Marshfield	166	44	42N		90		10W
Martaban, G. of	93	16	5N		96	30	E
Martha's Vineyard	164	41	25N		70		35W
Martigues	37	43	24N		5	4	E
Martinique	180	14	40N		61		0W
Martinsburg	164	39	30N		77		57W
Martinsville, Ind., U.S.A.	167	39	29N		86		23W
Martinsville, Va., U.S.A.	165	36	41N		79		52W
Marton	122	40	4S		175	23	E
Marugame	109	34	15N		133	40	E
Maruoka	106	36	9N		136	16	E
Marwar	91	25	43N		73	45	E
Mary	70	37	40N		61	50	E
Maryborough = Port Laoise ..	35	53	2N		7		20W
Maryborough, Queens., Australia	116	25	31S		152	37	E
Maryborough, Vic., Australia	117	37	0S		143	44	E
Maryland □	164	39	10N		76		40W
Maryport	28	54	43N		3		30W
Marysville	172	39	14N		121		40W
Maryville	165	35	50N		84		0W
Marzūq	127	25	53N		13	57	E
Masan	98	35	11N		128	32	E
Masaya	179	12	0N		86		7W
Masbate, I.	112	12	21N		123	36	E
Mascota	175	20	32N		104		49W
Maseru	137	29	18S		27	30	E
Mashhad	86	36	20N		59	35	E
Masisea	186	8	35S		74		22W
Masjed Soleyman	84	31	55N		49	18	E
Mask, L.	34	53	36N		9		24W
Mason City	166	43	9N		93		12W
Masqat	83	23	37N		58	36	E
Massachusetts □	164	42	25N		72		0W
Massawa = Mitsiwa	132	15	35N		39	25	E
Massena	151	44	52N		74		55W
Massif Central	37	45	30N		2	21	E
Massillon	167	40	47N		81		30W
Mastanli = Momchilgrad	53	41	33N		25	23	E
Masterton	123	40	56S		175	39	E
Mastūrah	82	23	7N		38	52	E
Masuda	108	34	40N		131	51	E
Matachewan	151	47	56N		80		39W
Matadi	134	5	52S		13	31	E
Matagalpa	179	13	0N		85		58W
Matamoros, Coahuila, Mexico	174	25	32N		103		15W
Matamoros, Puebla, Mexico ..	177	18	2N		98		17W
Matane	148	48	50N		67		33W
Matanzas	178	23	0N		81		40W
Matapan, C. = Taínaron, Ákra	54	36	22N		22	27	E
Matarani	186	77	0S		72		10W
Matehuala	177	23	39N		100		39W
Mathura	89	27	30N		77	40	E
Matlock	28	53	8N		1		32W
Mato Grosso □	188	14	0S		55		0W
Mato Grosso, Planalto do	188	15	0S		59		57W
Matopo Hills	137	20	36S		28	20	E
Matrah	83	23	37N		58	30	E
Matsubara	106	34	33N		135	34	E
Matsudo	107	35	47N		139	54	E
Matsue	109	35	25N		133	10	E
Matsumoto	107	36	15N		138		0 E
Matsusaka	106	34	34N		136	32	E
Matsutō	106	36	31N		136	34	E
Matsuura	108	33	20N		129	49	E
Matsuyama	109	33	45N		132	45	E
Mattancheri	90	9	50N		76	15	E
Mattawa	151	46	20N		78		45W
Matterhorn	44	45	58N		7	39	E
Matucana	186	11	55S		76		25W
Maturín	185	9	45N		63		11W
Mau Ranipur	91	25	16N		79	8	E
Maubeuge	38	50	17N		3	57	F
Maudin Sun	93	16	0N		94	30	E
Maui	160	20	45N		156	20	E
Maulamyaing	93	16	30N		97	40	E
Mauna Kea	160	19	50N		155		28W
Mauna Loa	160	21	8N		157		10W
Maungmagan Kyunzu	94	14	0N		97	48	E
Mauritania ■	126	20	50N		10		0W
Mauritius ■	9	20	0S		57		0 E
Mawlaik	93	23	40N		94	26	E
May Pen	180	17	58N		77		15W
Maya ~→	75	54	31N		134	41	E
Mayagüez	180	18	12N		67		9W
Mayerthorpe	155	53	57N		115		8W
Mayfield	169	36	45N		88		40W
Maykop	70	44	35N		40	25	E
Maynooth	34	53	22N		6		38W
Mayo	144	63	38N		135		57W
Mayo □	34	53	47N		9		7W
Mayor I.	122	37	16S		176	17	E
Maysville	167	38	39N		83		46W
Mazagán = El Jadida	126	33	11N		8		17W
Mazán	186	3	30S		73		0W
Mazar-e Sharīf	87	36	41N		67		0 E
Mazarredo	192	47	10S		66		50W
Mazatenango	177	14	35N		91		30W
Mazatlán	175	23	13N		106		25W
Mbandaka	134	0	1N		18	18	E
Mdina	49	35	51N		14	25	E
Mead, L.	173	36	1N		114		44W
Meadville	164	41	39N		80		9W
Meander River	145	59	2N		117		42W
Meath □	34	53	32N		6		40W
Meaux	39	48	58N		2	50	E
Mecca = Makkah	82	21	30N		39	54	E
Mechelen	42	51	2N		4	29	E
Mecklenburger Bucht	42	54	20N		11	40	E
Medan	111	3	40N		98	38	E
Medellín	184	6	15N		75		35W
Medford	171	42	20N		122		52W
Mediaş	57	46	9N		24	22	E
Medicine Hat	152	50	0N		110		45W
Medina = Al Madīnah	82	24	35N		39	52	E
Medina	167	41	9N		81		50W
Medina del Campo	50	41	18N		4		55W
Mediterranean Sea	124	35	0N		15		0 E
Medley	152	54	25N		110		16W
Médoc	36	45	10N		0		56W
Medvezhi, Ostrava	73	71	0N		161		0 E
Medway ~→	25	51	28N		0	45	E
Meekatharra	120	26	32S		118	29	E
Meerut	89	29	1N		77	42	E
Mega	133	3	57N		38	19	E
Mégantic, L.	148	45	32N		70		53W
Mégara	55	37	58N		23	22	E
Meghalaya □	93	25	50N		91		0 E
Mei Xian	99	24	16N		116	6	E
Meknès	126	33	57N		5		33W
Mekong ~→	95	9	30N		106	15	E

Melaka	**96**	2 15N	102 15 E
Melaka □	**96**	2 15N	102 15 E
Melanesia	**122**	4 0S	155 0 E
Melbourne	**117**	37 50S	145 0 E
Melchor Muzquiz	**174**	27 53N	101 31W
Melfort	**152**	52 50N	104 37W
Melilla	**126**	35 21N	2 57W
Melitopol	**68**	46 50N	35 22 E
Melo	**191**	32 20S	54 10W
Melrose	**31**	53 35N	2 44W
Melton Mowbray	**29**	52 46N	0 52W
Melun	**39**	48 32N	2 39 E
Melville	**152**	50 55N	102 50W
Melville, L.	**147**	53 30N	60 0W
Melville I., Australia	**114**	11 30S	131 0 E
Melville I., Canada	**12**	75 30N	112 0W
Melville Pen.	**146**	68 0N	84 0W
Memel = Klaipeda	**68**	55 43N	21 10 E
Memphis	**169**	35 7N	90 0W
Menai Strait	**26**	53 14N	4 10W
Ménaka	**131**	15 59N	2 18 E
Menan = Chao Phraya →	**94**	13 32N	100 36 E
Menasha	**167**	44 13N	88 27W
Mende	**37**	44 31N	3 30 E
Mendip Hills	**27**	51 17N	2 40W
Mendocino	**172**	39 26N	123 50W
Mendoza	**190**	32 50S	68 52W
Menindee	**118**	32 20S	142 25 E
Menindee, L.	**118**	32 20S	142 25 E
Menominee	**150**	45 9N	87 39W
Menorca	**51**	40 0N	4 0 E
Mentawai, Kepulauan	**111**	2 0S	99 0 E
Menzies	**120**	29 40S	120 58 E
Meppel	**41**	52 42N	6 12 E
Merbein	**119**	34 10S	142 2 E
Merca	**133**	1 48N	44 50 E
Merced	**172**	37 18N	120 30W
Mercedes, Buenos Aires, Argentina	**190**	34 40S	59 30W
Mercedes, Corrientes, Argentina	**191**	29 10S	58 5W
Mercedes, San Luis, Argentina	**190**	33 40S	65 21W
Mercedes, Uruguay	**191**	33 12S	58 0W
Mere	**24**	51 5N	2 16W
Mergui Arch. = Myeik Kyunzu	**94**	11 30N	97 30 E
Mérida, Mexico	**177**	20 58N	89 37W
Mérida, Spain	**50**	38 55N	6 25W
Mérida, Venezuela	**184**	8 24N	71 8W
Mérida, Cord. de	**182**	9 0N	71 0W
Meriden	**164**	41 33N	72 47W
Meridian	**169**	32 20N	88 42W
Merowe	**129**	18 29N	31 46 E
Merredin	**120**	31 28S	118 18 E
Merrill	**156**	45 11N	89 41W
Merritt	**155**	50 10N	120 45W
Merriwa	**116**	32 6S	150 22 E
Mersey →	**28**	53 20N	2 56W
Merseyside □	**28**	53 25N	2 55W
Mersin	**80**	36 51N	34 36 E
Merthyr Tydfil	**27**	51 45N	3 23W
Méru	**39**	49 13N	2 8 E
Merville	**38**	50 38N	2 38 E
Mesa	**160**	33 20N	111 56W
Mesa, La	**173**	32 48N	117 5W
Meshed = Mashhad	**86**	36 20N	59 35 E
Mesolóngion	**54**	38 21N	21 28 E
Mesopotamia = Al Jazirah	**81**	33 30N	44 0 E
Mesquite	**173**	36 47N	114 6W
Messina, Italy	**49**	38 10N	15 32 E
Messina, S. Africa	**137**	22 20S	30 0 E
Messina, Str. di	**49**	38 5N	15 35 E
Messíni	**54**	37 4N	22 1 E
Meta →	**184**	6 12N	67 28W
Metairie	**169**	29 59N	90 9W
Metán	**190**	25 30S	65 0W
Metropolis	**169**	37 10N	88 47W
Metz	**37**	49 8N	6 10 E
Meuse →	**42**	50 45N	5 41 E
Mexia	**168**	31 38N	96 32W
Mexicali	**174**	32 40N	115 29W
México, Mexico	**177**	19 20N	99 10W
México, U.S.A.	**166**	39 10N	91 55W
México □	**177**	19 20N	99 30W
Mexico ■	**174**	20 0N	100 0W
Mexico, G. of	**138**	25 0N	90 0W
Mezen →	**69**	66 11N	43 59 E
Mhow	**91**	22 33N	75 50 E
Miahuatlán	**177**	16 21N	96 36W
Miami	**170**	25 45N	80 15W
Miami Beach	**170**	25 49N	80 6W
Mīāneh	**81**	37 30N	47 40 E
Mianwali	**89**	32 38N	71 28 E
Miaoli	**99**	24 37N	120 49 E
Miass	**69**	54 59N	60 6 E
Michigan □	**167**	44 40N	85 40W
Michigan, L.	**150**	44 0N	87 0W
Michigan City	**167**	41 42N	86 56W
Michikamau L.	**147**	54 20N	63 10W
Michipicoten	**150**	47 55N	84 55W
Michoacán □	**175**	19 10N	101 50W
Michurinsk	**68**	52 58N	40 27 E
Micronesia	**122**	11 0N	160 0 E
Mid Glamorgan □	**27**	51 40N	3 25W
Middelburg	**40**	51 30N	3 36 E
Middle Andaman I.	**94**	12 30N	92 30 E
Middlesboro	**165**	36 36N	83 43W
Middlesbrough	**29**	54 35N	1 14W
Middleton	**148**	44 57N	65 4W
Middletown, Conn., U.S.A.	**164**	41 37N	72 40W
Middletown, N.Y., U.S.A.	**164**	41 28N	74 28W
Middletown, Ohio, U.S.A.	**167**	39 29N	84 25W
Midland, Canada	**151**	44 45N	79 50W
Midland, Mich., U.S.A.	**167**	43 37N	84 17W
Midland, Tex., U.S.A.	**161**	32 0N	102 3W
Międzyrzec Podlaski	**58**	51 58N	22 45 E
Miercurea Ciuc	**57**	46 21N	25 48 E
Mieres	**50**	43 18N	5 48W
Migennes	**39**	47 58N	3 31 E
Mihara	**109**	34 24N	133 5 E
Miki	**109**	34 48N	134 59 E
Mikonos	**55**	37 30N	25 25 E
Mikuni-Tōge	**107**	36 50N	138 50 E
Mikura-Jima	**107**	33 52N	139 36 E
Milagro	**184**	2 11S	79 36W
Milan = Milano	**46**	45 28N	9 10 E
Milano	**46**	45 28N	9 10 E
Milâs	**80**	37 20N	27 50 E
Mildura	**119**	34 13S	142 9 E
Miles	**116**	26 40S	150 9 E
Miles City	**163**	46 24N	105 50W
Milford	**164**	38 52N	75 27W
Milford Haven	**27**	51 43N	5 2W
Milk →	**163**	48 5N	106 15W
Millau	**37**	44 8N	3 4 E
Millicent	**119**	37 34S	140 21 E
Millinocket	**148**	45 45N	68 45W
Millmerran	**116**	27 53S	151 16 E
Millom	**28**	54 13N	3 16W
Millville	**164**	39 22N	75 0W
Milne Inlet	**146**	72 30N	80 0W
Mílos	**55**	36 44N	24 25 E
Milton Keynes	**25**	52 3N	0 42W
Milwaukee	**167**	43 9N	87 58W
Milwaukie	**171**	45 27N	122 39W
Minamata	**108**	32 10N	130 30 E
Minas	**191**	34 20S	55 10W
Minas Gerais □	**188**	18 50S	46 0W
Minatitlán	**177**	17 59N	94 31W
Mindanao	**112**	8 0N	125 0 E
Mindanao Sea = Bohol Sea	**112**	9 0N	124 0 E
Minden	**168**	32 40N	93 20W
Mindoro	**112**	13 0N	121 0 E
Mindoro Strait	**112**	12 30N	120 30 E
Mine	**108**	34 12N	131 7 E
Minehead	**27**	51 12N	3 29W
Mineral Wells	**161**	32 50N	98 5W
Mingan	**148**	50 20N	64 0W
Mingenew	**120**	29 12S	115 21 E
Minho □	**50**	41 25N	8 20W
Minneapolis	**166**	44 58N	93 20W
Minnedosa	**153**	50 14N	99 50W

47

Minnesota □	156	46	40N	94	0W
Mino	106	35	32N	136	55 E
Mino-Kamo	106	35	23N	137	2 E
Mino-Mikawa-Kōgen	106	35	10N	137	23 E
Minorca = Menorca	51	40	0N	4	0 E
Minot	163	48	10N	101	15W
Minsk	68	53	52N	27	30 E
Mintaka Pass	89	37	0N	74	58 E
Miquelon, I.	149	47	2N	56	20W
Miraj	91	16	50N	74	45 E
Miranda do Douro	50	41	30N	6	16W
Mirpur Khas	88	25	30N	69	0 E
Mirzapur	92	25	10N	82	34 E
Mirzapur-cum-Vindhyachal =					
Mirzapur	92	25	10N	82	34 E
Miscou I.	148	47	57N	64	31W
Mishawaka	167	41	40N	86	8W
Mishima	107	35	10N	138	52 E
Miskitos, Cayos	179	14	26N	82	50W
Miskolc	59	48	7N	20	50 E
Misool	113	1	52S	130	10 E
Misrātah	127	32	24N	15	3 E
Mission City	154	49	10N	122	15W
Mississippi □	169	33	0N	90	0W
Mississippi →	169	29	0N	89	15W
Mississippi, Delta of the	169	29	15N	90	30W
Missoula	162	46	52N	114	0W
Missouri □	166	38	25N	92	30W
Missouri →	166	38	50N	90	8W
Mistassini L.	151	51	0N	73	30W
Mitaka	107	35	40N	139	33 E
Mitchell, Australia	116	26	29S	147	58 E
Mitchell, U.S.A.	163	43	40N	98	0W
Mitchell →	115	15	12S	141	35 E
Mitilíni	55	39	6N	26	35 E
Mito	107	36	20N	140	30 E
Mitsiwa	132	15	35N	39	25 E
Mitsukaidō	107	36	1N	139	59 E
Mittagong	117	34	28S	150	29 E
Mitú	184	1	8N	70	3W
Miura	107	35	12N	139	40 E
Miyake-Jima	107	34	0N	139	30 E
Miyako	103	39	40N	141	59 E
Miyakonojō	108	31	40N	131	5 E
Miyanojō	108	31	54N	130	27 E
Miyazaki	108	31	56N	131	30 E
Miyazu	106	35	35N	135	10 E
Miyoshi	109	34	48N	132	51 E
Mizamis = Ozamis	112	8	15N	123	50 E
Mizen Hd.	35	51	27N	9	50W
Mizoram □	93	23	30N	92	40 E
Mizunami	106	35	22N	137	15 E
Mława	58	53	9N	20	25 E
Mobara	107	35	25N	140	18 E
Moberley	166	39	25N	92	25W
Mobile	169	30	41N	88	3W
Mobutu Sese Seko, L.	132	1	30N	31	0 E
Moçâmedes = Namibe	134	15	7S	12	11 E
Moctezuma, R. →	177	21	59N	98	34W
Módena	46	44	39N	10	55 E
Modesto	172	37	43N	121	0W
Moe	117	38	12S	146	19 E
Moei →	94	17	25N	98	10 E
Moengo	185	5	45N	54	20W
Moffat	31	55	20N	3	27W
Mogadishu = Muqdisho	133	2	2N	45	25 E
Mogador = Essaouira	126	31	32N	9	42W
Mogami →	103	38	45N	140	0 E
Mogi das Cruzes	191	23	31S	46	11W
Mogilev	68	53	55N	30	18 E
Mointy	71	47	10N	73	18 E
Moisie →	148	50	12N	66	1W
Mojave Desert	173	35	0N	116	30W
Mold	26	53	10N	3	10W
Moldavian S.S.R. □	68	47	0N	28	0 E
Molde	65	62	45N	7	9 E
Molfetta	49	41	12N	16	35 E
Moline	166	41	30N	90	30W
Molise □	49	41	45N	14	30 E
Mollendo	187	17	0S	72	0W
Mölndal	60	57	40N	12	3 E

Molong	117	33	5S	148	54 E
Molopo →	136	28	30S	20	13 E
Molotov = Perm	69	58	0N	57	10 E
Molucca Sea	113	4	0S	124	0 E
Moluccas = Maluku	113	1	0S	127	0 E
Mombasa	135	4	2S	39	43 E
Mombetsu	103	42	27N	142	4 E
Momchilgrad	53	41	33N	25	23 E
Mompós	184	9	14N	74	26W
Møn	61	54	57N	12	15 E
Mona, Canal de la	180	18	30N	67	45W
Monach Is.	32	57	32N	7	40W
Monaco ■	37	43	46N	7	23 E
Monaghan	34	54	15N	6	58W
Monaghan □	34	54	10N	7	0W
Monastir = Bitola	52	41	5N	21	10 E
Mönchengladbach	42	51	12N	6	23 E
Monchique	50	37	19N	8	38W
Monclova	174	26	50N	101	30W
Moncton	148	46	7N	64	51W
Monessen	164	40	9N	79	50W
Monforte	50	39	6N	7	25W
Mongalla	129	5	8N	31	42 E
Monghyr = Munger	92	25	23N	86	30 E
Mongolia ■	98	47	0N	103	0 E
Monmouth, U.K.	26	51	48N	2	43W
Monmouth, U.S.A.	166	40	50N	90	40W
Monroe, La., U.S.A.	168	32	32N	92	4W
Monroe, Mich., U.S.A.	167	41	55N	83	26W
Monroe, N.C., U.S.A.	165	35	2N	80	37W
Monrovia, Liberia	130	6	18N	10	47W
Monrovia, U.S.A.	173	34	7N	118	1W
Mons	42	50	27N	3	58 E
Mont-de-Marsan	36	43	54N	0	31W
Mont Laurier	151	46	35N	75	30W
Montague	172	41	47N	122	30W
Montana □	163	47	0N	110	0W
Montargis	39	48	0N	2	43 E
Montauban	36	44	0N	1	21 E
Montbéliard	37	47	31N	6	48 E
Montceau-les-Mines	37	46	40N	4	23 E
Montdidier	38	49	38N	2	35 E
Monte-Carlo	37	43	46N	7	23 E
Monte Caseros	191	30	10S	57	50W
Montego Bay	180	18	30N	78	0W
Montélimar	37	44	33N	4	45 E
Montemorelos	176	25	11N	99	42W
Montenegro = Crna Gora □	52	42	40N	19	20 E
Monterey	173	36	35N	121	57W
Montería	184	8	46N	75	53W
Monterrey	176	25	40N	100	30W
Montes Claros	188	16	30S	43	50W
Montevideo, Uruguay	191	34	50S	56	11W
Montevideo, U.S.A.	166	44	55N	95	40W
Montgomery = Sahiwal	89	30	45N	73	8 E
Montgomery, U.K.	26	52	34N	3	9W
Montgomery, U.S.A.	169	32	20N	86	20W
Montluçon	37	46	22N	2	36 E
Montmagny	148	46	58N	70	34W
Montmorency	148	46	53N	71	11W
Montpelier, Idaho, U.S.A.	163	42	15N	111	20W
Montpelier, Vt., U.S.A.	151	44	15N	72	38W
Montpellier	37	43	37N	3	52 E
Montréal	151	45	31N	73	34W
Montrose, U.K.	33	56	43N	2	28W
Montrose, U.S.A.	163	38	30N	107	52W
Montserrat	180	16	40N	62	10W
Monywa	93	22	7N	95	11 E
Monze, C.	88	24	47N	66	37 E
Mo'oka	107	36	26N	140	1 E
Moonta	119	34	6S	137	32 E
Moora	120	30	37S	115	58 E
Moorfoot Hills	31	55	44N	3	8W
Moorhead	156	46	51N	96	44W
Mooroopna	117	36	25S	145	22 E
Moose Jaw	152	50	24N	105	30W
Moosehead L.	148	45	34N	69	40W
Moosomin	152	50	9N	101	40W
Moosonee	140	51	17N	80	39W
Mopti	130	14	30N	4	0W
Moradabad	89	28	50N	78	50 E

Name	Page	Lat °	'	N/S	Long °	'	E/W
Moranbah	121	22	1	S	148	6	E
Moratuwa	90	6	45	N	79	55	E
Morava →	59	48	10	N	16	59	E
Moravian Hts. =							
Ceskomoravská Vrchovina.	59	49	30	N	15	40	E
Morawa	120	29	13	S	116	0	E
Morawhanna	185	8	30	N	59	40	W
Moray Firth	33	57	50	N	3	30	W
Morden	153	49	15	N	98	10	W
Mordovian A.S.S.R.□	68	54	20	N	44	30	E
Møre og Romsdal fylke □	65	62	30	N	8	0	E
Morecambe	28	54	5	N	2	52	W
Morecambe B.	28	54	7	N	3	0	W
Moree	116	29	28	S	149	54	E
Morehead City	165	34	46	N	76	44	W
Morelia	175	19	42	N	101	7	W
Morelos □	177	18	45	N	99	0	W
Morena, Sierra	50	38	20	N	4	0	W
Moresby I.	154	52	30	N	131	40	W
Morgan City	168	29	40	N	91	15	W
Morganton	165	35	46	N	81	48	W
Morgantown	164	39	39	N	79	58	W
Moriguchi	106	34	44	N	135	34	E
Morlaix	36	48	36	N	3	52	W
Mornington	117	38	15	S	145	5	E
Moro G.	112	6	30	N	123	0	E
Morocco ■	126	32	0	N	5	50	W
Moroleón	177	20	8	N	101	12	W
Morón	178	22	8	N	78	39	W
Morotai	113	2	10	N	128	30	E
Morrilton	168	35	10	N	92	45	W
Morrinhos	188	17	45	S	49	10	W
Morris	153	49	25	N	97	22	W
Morristown	165	36	18	N	83	20	W
Mortes, R. das →	188	11	45	S	50	44	W
Mortlake	119	38	5	S	142	50	E
Moruya	117	35	58	S	150	3	E
Morvern	30	56	38	N	5	44	W
Morwell	117	38	10	S	146	22	E
Moscos Is.	94	14	0	N	97	30	E
Moscow = Moskva	68	55	45	N	37	35	E
Moscow	171	46	45	N	116	59	W
Mosel →	42	50	22	N	7	36	E
Moselle = Mosel →	42	50	22	N	7	36	E
Mosgiel	123	45	53	S	170	21	E
Mosjøen	65	65	51	N	13	12	E
Moskva	68	55	45	N	37	35	E
Mosquera	184	2	35	N	78	24	W
Mosquitos, Golfo de los	179	9	15	N	81	10	W
Moss Vale	117	34	32	S	150	25	E
Mosselbaai	136	34	11	S	22	8	E
Mossman	121	16	21	S	145	15	E
Mossoró	189	5	10	S	37	15	W
Mostaganem	127	35	54	N	0	5	E
Mostar	52	43	22	N	17	50	E
Mosul = Al Mawşil	81	36	15	N	43	5	E
Motala	60	58	32	N	15	1	E
Motherwell	31	55	48	N	4	0	W
Motihari	92	26	30	N	84	55	E
Motueka	123	41	7	S	173	1	E
Motul	177	21	6	N	89	17	W
Moúdhros	55	39	50	N	25	18	E
Moule	180	16	20	N	61	22	W
Moulins	37	46	35	N	3	19	E
Moultrie	170	31	11	N	83	47	W
Moundsville	164	39	53	N	80	43	W
Mount Airy	165	36	31	N	80	37	W
Mount Barker, S. Austral., Australia	119	35	5	S	138	52	E
Mount Barker, W. Austral., Australia	120	34	38	S	117	40	E
Mount Carmel	167	38	20	N	87	48	W
Mount Forest	151	43	59	N	80	43	W
Mount Gambier	119	37	50	S	140	46	E
Mount Isa	120	20	42	S	139	26	E
Mount Lofty Ra.	119	34	35	S	139	5	E
Mount Magnet	120	28	2	S	117	47	E
Mount Maunganui	122	37	40	S	176	14	E
Mount Morgan	121	23	40	S	150	25	E
Mount Pearl	149	47	31	N	52	47	W
Mount Pleasant, Mich., U.S.A.	167	43	35	N	84	47	W
Mount Pleasant, Tex., U.S.A.	168	33	5	N	95	0	W
Mount Sterling	165	38	0	N	84	0	W
Mount Vernon, Ill., U.S.A.	166	38	17	N	88	57	W
Mount Vernon, N.Y., U.S.A.	164	40	57	N	73	49	W
Mount Vernon, Wash., U.S.A.	171	48	25	N	122	20	W
Mount Whaleback	114	23	18	S	119	44	E
Mountain City	172	41	54	N	116	0	W
Mountain View	172	37	26	N	122	5	W
Moura, Australia	121	24	35	S	149	58	E
Moura, Brazil	185	1	32	S	61	38	W
Mourne →	34	54	45	N	7	39	W
Mourne Mts.	34	54	10	N	6	0	W
Moyale	133	3	30	N	39	0	E
Mozambique ■	137	19	0	S	35	0	E
Mozambique Chan.	137	20	0	S	39	0	E
Mu Us Shamo	98	39	0	N	109	0	E
Muaná	188	1	25	S	49	15	W
Muang Chiang Rai	94	19	52	N	99	50	E
Muck	32	56	50	N	6	15	W
Mucuri	189	18	0	S	39	36	W
Mudanjiang	98	44	38	N	129	30	E
Mudgee	117	32	32	S	149	31	E
Muğla	80	37	15	N	28	22	E
Mukden = Shenyang	98	41	50	N	123	25	E
Mukhtuya = Lensk	74	60	48	N	114	55	E
Mukinbudin	120	30	55	S	118	5	E
Muktsar	89	30	30	N	74	30	E
Mulchén	190	37	45	S	72	20	W
Mulgrave	149	45	38	N	61	31	W
Mulhacén	50	37	4	N	3	20	W
Mülheim	42	51	26	N	6	53	E
Mulhouse	37	47	40	N	7	20	E
Mull	30	56	27	N	6	0	W
Muller, Pegunungan	111	0	30	N	113	30	E
Mullet Pen.	34	54	10	N	10	2	W
Mullewa	120	28	29	S	115	30	E
Mullingar	34	53	31	N	7	20	W
Mullumbimby	116	28	30	S	153	30	E
Multan	89	30	15	N	71	36	E
Muna	113	5	0	S	122	30	E
München	43	48	8	N	11	33	E
München-Gladbach = Mönchengladbach	42	51	12	N	6	23	E
Muncie	167	40	10	N	85	20	W
Mundo Novo	189	11	50	S	40	29	W
Mungana	121	17	8	S	144	27	E
Munger	92	25	23	N	86	30	E
Munich = München	43	48	8	N	11	33	E
Munising	150	46	25	N	86	39	W
Munku-Sardyk	74	51	45	N	100	20	E
Münster	42	51	58	N	7	37	E
Munster □	35	52	20	N	8	40	W
Muqdisho	133	2	2	N	45	25	E
Murallón, Cuerro	192	49	48	S	73	30	W
Murchison →	120	27	45	S	114	0	E
Murchison Falls = Kabarega Falls	132	2	15	N	31	30	E
Murcia	51	38	20	N	1	10	W
Murcia □	51	37	50	N	1	30	W
Mureş →	56	46	15	N	20	13	E
Mureşul = Mureş →	56	46	15	N	20	13	E
Murfreesboro	169	35	50	N	86	21	W
Murgon	116	26	15	S	151	54	E
Müritz See	43	53	25	N	12	40	E
Murmansk	69	68	57	N	33	10	E
Muroran	103	42	25	N	141	0	E
Muroto	109	33	18	N	134	9	E
Muroto-Misaki	109	33	15	N	134	10	E
Murphysboro	166	37	50	N	89	20	W
Murray	169	36	40	N	88	20	W
Murray →	119	35	20	S	139	22	E
Murray Bridge	119	35	6	S	139	14	E
Murrumbidgee →	117	34	43	S	143	12	E
Murrurundi	116	31	42	S	150	51	E
Murtoa	119	36	35	S	142	28	E
Murupara	122	38	28	S	176	42	E
Murwillumbah	116	28	18	S	153	27	E
Muş	81	38	45	N	41	30	E
Musashino	107	35	42	N	139	34	E
Muscat = Masqat	83	23	37	N	58	36	E
Muscat & Oman = Oman ■	83	23	0	N	58	0	E

Muscatine	**166**	41 25N	91	5W
Musgrave Ras.	**114**	26 0S	132	0 E
Musi ⟶	**111**	2 20S	104	56 E
Muskegon	**167**	43 15N	86	17W
Muskegon ⟶	**167**	43 25N	86	0W
Muskegon Hts.	**167**	43 12N	86	17W
Muskogee	**168**	35 50N	95	25W
Musselburgh	**31**	55 57N	3	3W
Muswellbrook	**116**	32 16S	150	56 E
Mutare	**137**	18 58S	32	38 E
Mutsu	**103**	41 5N	140	55 E
Mutsu-Wan	**103**	41 5N	140	55 E
Muzaffargarh	**89**	30 5N	71	14 E
Muzaffarnagar	**89**	29 26N	77	40 E
Muzaffarpur	**92**	26 7N	85	23 E
Mwanza	**135**	2 30S	32	58 E
Mweru, L.	**135**	9 0S	28	40 E
My Tho	**95**	10 29N	106	23 E
Myanaung	**93**	18 18N	95	22 E
Myeik Kyunzu	**94**	11 30N	97	30 E
Myingyan	**93**	21 30N	95	20 E
Myitkyina	**93**	25 24N	97	26 E
Mýrdalsjökull	**64**	63 40N	19	6W
Myrtle Point	**171**	43 0N	124	4W
Mysore	**90**	12 17N	76	41 E
Mysore □ = Karnataka □	**90**	13 15N	77	0 E
Naaldwijk	**40**	51 59N	4	13 E
Nabari	**106**	34 37N	136	5 E
Nablus = Nābulus	**80**	32 14N	35	15 E
Nābulus	**80**	32 14N	35	15 E
Nacogdoches	**168**	31 33N	94	39W
Nacozari	**174**	30 24N	109	39W
Nadiad	**91**	22 41N	72	56 E
Nadym	**69**	65 35N	72	42 E
Nagahama	**106**	35 23N	136	16 E
Nagaland □	**93**	26 0N	94	30 E
Nagano	**107**	36 40N	138	10 E
Nagaoka	**105**	37 27N	138	51 E
Nagappattinam	**90**	10 46N	79	51 E
Nagasaki	**108**	32 47N	129	50 E
Nagato	**108**	34 19N	131	5 E
Nagercoil	**90**	8 12N	77	26 E
Nagornyy	**75**	55 58N	124	57 E
Nagoya	**106**	35 10N	136	50 E
Nagpur	**91**	21 8N	79	10 E
Nahanni Butte	**144**	61 2N	123	31W
Nahāvand	**84**	34 10N	48	22 E
Naicam	**152**	52 30N	104	30W
Nain	**147**	56 34N	61	40W
Nainpur	**91**	22 30N	80	10 E
Nairn	**33**	57 35N	3	54W
Nairobi	**132**	1 17S	36	48 E
Naivasha	**132**	0 40S	36	30 E
Najafābād	**85**	32 40N	51	15 E
Najibabad	**89**	29 40N	78	20 E
Naka ⟶	**107**	36 20N	140	36 E
Naka-no-Shima	**104**	29 51N	129	46 E
Nakama	**108**	33 56N	130	43 E
Nakamura	**109**	33 0N	133	0 E
Nakano	**107**	36 45N	138	22 E
Nakanojō	**107**	36 35N	138	51 E
Nakatsu	**108**	33 34N	131	15 E
Nakatsugawa	**106**	35 29N	137	30 E
Nakhichevan A.S.S.R. □	**70**	39 14N	45	30 E
Nakhodka	**75**	42 53N	132	54 E
Nakhon Phanom	**95**	17 23N	104	43 E
Nakhon Ratchasima	**95**	14 59N	102	12 E
Nakhon Sawan	**94**	15 35N	100	10 E
Nakhon Si Thammarat	**96**	8 29N	100	0 E
Nakina	**140**	50 10N	86	40W
Nakskov	**61**	54 50N	11	8 E
Nakuru	**132**	0 15S	36	4 E
Nalchik	**70**	43 30N	43	33 E
Nalgonda	**91**	17 6N	79	15 E
Nam Co	**101**	30 30N	90	45 E
Nam Dinh	**95**	20 25N	106	5 E
Nam-Phan	**95**	10 30N	106	0 E
Nam Tha	**95**	20 58N	101	30 E
Nam Tok	**94**	14 21N	99	4 E
Namaland	**136**	24 30S	17	0 E
Namangan	**71**	41 0N	71	40 E
Nambour	**116**	26 32S	152	58 E
Nambucca Heads	**116**	30 37S	153	0 E
Namerikawa	**106**	36 46N	137	20 E
Namib Desert = Namib-Woestyn	**124**	22 30S	15	0 E
Namib-Woestyn	**124**	22 30S	15	0 E
Namibe	**134**	15 7S	12	11 E
Namibia ■	**136**	22 0S	18	9 E
Nampa	**171**	43 34N	116	34W
Namsos	**65**	64 29N	11	30 E
Namur	**42**	50 27N	4	52 E
Nanaimo	**154**	49 10N	124	0W
Nanango	**116**	26 40S	152	0 E
Nanao	**105**	37 0N	137	0 E
Nanchang	**99**	28 42N	115	55 E
Nanching = Nanjing	**99**	32 2N	118	47 E
Nanching	**99**	32 3N	118	47 E
Nancy	**37**	48 42N	6	12 E
Nanda Devi	**101**	30 23N	79	59 E
Nandan	**109**	34 10N	134	42 E
Nanded	**91**	19 10N	77	20 C
Nandurbar	**91**	21 20N	74	15 E
Nanga Parbat	**89**	35 10N	74	35 E
Nangarhár □	**87**	34 20N	70	0 E
Nanjing	**99**	32 2N	118	47 E
Nanking = Nanching	**99**	32 3N	118	47 E
Nanking = Nanjing	**99**	32 2N	118	47 E
Nankoku	**109**	33 39N	133	44 E
Nanning	**99**	22 48N	108	20 E
Nanping	**99**	26 38N	118	10 E
Nantes	**36**	47 12N	1	33W
Nanticoke	**164**	41 12N	76	1W
Nanton	**155**	50 21N	113	46W
Nanuque	**189**	17 50S	40	21W
Napa	**172**	38 18N	122	17W
Napier	**122**	39 30S	176	56 E
Naples = Nápoli ⟶	**49**	40 50N	14	17 E
Napo ⟶	**186**	3 20S	72	40W
Nápoli	**49**	40 50N	14	17 E
Nara, Japan	**106**	34 40N	135	49 E
Nara, Mali	**130**	15 10N	7	20W
Naracoorte	**119**	36 58S	140	45 E
Narasapur	**92**	16 26N	81	40 E
Narayanganj	**92**	23 40N	90	33 E
Narayanpet	**91**	16 45N	77	30 E
Narbonne	**37**	43 11N	3	0 E
Narita	**107**	35 47N	140	19 E
Narmada ⟶	**91**	21 38N	72	36 E
Narooma	**117**	36 14S	150	4 E
Narrabri	**116**	30 19S	149	46 E
Narrandera	**117**	34 42S	146	31 E
Narrogin	**120**	32 58S	117	14 E
Narromine	**116**	32 12S	148	12 E
Naruto	**109**	34 11N	134	37 E
Narvik	**64**	68 28N	17	26 E
Narym	**71**	59 0N	81	30 E
Naser, Buheirat en	**128**	23 0N	32	30 E
Nashua	**164**	42 50N	71	25W
Nashville	**169**	36 12N	86	46W
Nasik	**91**	19 58N	73	50 E
Nasirabad	**91**	26 15N	74	45 E
Nassau	**178**	25 0N	77	20W
Nasser, L. = Naser, Buheirat en	**128**	23 0N	32	30 E
Nässjö	**60**	57 39N	14	42 E
Natal	**189**	5 47S	35	13W
Natal □	**137**	28 30S	30	30 E
Natashquan	**149**	50 14N	61	46W
Natchez	**168**	31 35N	91	25W
Natchitoches	**168**	31 47N	93	4W
Nathalia	**117**	36 1S	145	13 E
National City	**173**	32 39N	117	7W
Natuna Besar, Kepulauan.	**111**	4 0N	108	15 E
Natuna Selatan, Kepulauan	**111**	2 45N	109	0 E
Nauru ■	**122**	1 0S	166	0 E
Nauta	**186**	4 31S	73	35W
Nautanwa	**92**	27 20N	83	25 E
Nautla	**177**	20 20N	96	50W

Navarra □ **51** 42 40N 1 40W
Navojoa **174** 27 0N 109 30W
Navsari .... **91** 20 57N 72 59 E
Nawabshah .... **88** 26 15N 68 25 E
Nawalgarh .... **89** 27 50N 75 15 E
Náxos .... **55** 37 8N 25 25 E
Näy Band .... **87** 27 20N 52 40 E
Nayakhan .... **73** 61 56N 159 0 E
Nayarit □ **175** 22 0N 105 0W
Ndélé .... **129** 8 25N 20 36 E
Ndjamena .... **131** 12 10N 14 59 E
Ndola .... **135** 13 0S 28 34 E
Neagh, Lough **34** 54 35N 6 25W
Near Is. .... **142** 53 0N 172 0 E
Neath **27** 51 39N 3 49W
Nebraska □ **163** 41 30N 100 0W
Nebraska City **166** 40 40N 95 52W
Nebrodi Mts. .... **49** 37 55N 14 45 E
Neches → **168** 29 55N 93 52W
Neckar → .... **42** 49 31N 8 26 E
Necochea **190** 38 30S 58 50W
Needles, The **24** 50 39N 1 35W
Neenah **167** 44 10N 88 30W
Neepawa **153** 50 15N 99 30W
Negapatam =
  Nagappattinam .... **90** 10 46N 79 51 E
Negeri Sembilan □ ...... **96** 2 45N 102 10 E
Negotin .... **53** 44 16N 22 37 E
Negra, Pta. **186** 6 6S 81 10W
Negro →, Argentina **190** 41 2S 62 47W
Negro →, Brazil **185** 3 0S 60 0W
Negros .... **112** 9 30N 122 40 E
Nehbandān .... **85** 31 35N 60 5 E
Nei Monggol Zizhiqu □ ... **98** 42 0N 112 0 E
Neijiang .... **99** 29 35N 104 55 E
Neiva **184** 2 56N 75 18W
Nellore .... **90** 14 27N 79 59 E
Nelson, Canada **155** 49 30N 117 20W
Nelson, N.Z. .... **123** 41 18S 173 16 E
Nelson, U.K. **28** 53 50N 2 14W
Nelson → **153** 54 33N 98 2W
Néma **126** 16 40N 7 15W
Neman → .... **68** 55 25N 21 10 E
Nemours .... **39** 48 16N 2 40 E
Nemunas = Neman → .... **68** 55 25N 21 10 E
Nemuro .... **103** 43 20N 145 35 E
Nemuro-Kaikyō .... **103** 43 30N 145 30 E
Nenagh **35** 52 52N 8 11W
Nenana **142** 64 30N 149 20W
Nene → .... **29** 52 38N 0 13 E
Neosho **168** 36 56N 94 28W
Neosho → **168** 35 59N 95 10W
Nepal ■ .... **92** 28 0N 84 30 E
Nephi **162** 39 43N 111 52W
Ness, Loch **33** 57 15N 4 30W
Netanya .... **80** 32 20N 34 51 E
Netherlands ■ .... **41** 52 0N 5 30 E
Netherlands Antilles ■ .. **181** 12 15N 69 0W
Netherlands Guiana =
  Surinam ■ **185** 4 0N 56 0W
Nettilling L. **146** 66 30N 71 0W
Netzahualcoyotl, Presa .. **177** 17 10N 93 30W
Neuchâtel .... **44** 47 0N 6 55 E
Neuchâtel, Lac de ...... **44** 46 53N 6 50 E
Neuquén .... **190** 38 55S 68 0 E
Neuse → **165** 35 5N 76 30W
Neusiedler See .... **45** 47 50N 16 47 E
Nevada **166** 37 51N 94 22W
Nevada □ **172** 39 20N 117 0W
Nevada, Sierra, Spain **50** 37 3N 3 15W
Nevada, Sierra, U.S.A. .. **172** 39 0N 120 30W
Nevada City **172** 39 20N 121 0W
Nevada de Sta. Marta, Sa. .. **184** 10 55N 73 50W
Nevers .... **37** 47 0N 3 9 E
New Albany **167** 38 20N 85 50W
New Amsterdam **185** 6 15N 57 36W
New Bedford **164** 41 40N 70 52W
New Bern **165** 35 8N 77 3W
New Braunfels **161** 29 43N 98 9W
New Brighton .... **123** 43 29S 172 43 E

New Britain, Papua N. G. .... **115** 5 50S 150 20 E
New Britain, U.S.A. **164** 41 41N 72 47W
New Brunswick **164** 40 30N 74 28W
New Brunswick □ **148** 46 50N 66 30W
New Caledonia = Nouvelle
  Calédonie .... **122** 21 0S 165 0 E
New Castile = Castilla La
  Nueva **50** 39 45N 3 20W
New Castle, Ind., U.S.A. .. **164** 39 55N 85 23W
New Castle, Pa., U.S.A. .. **164** 41 0N 80 20W
New England Ra. ...... **116** 30 20S 151 45 E
New Forest **24** 50 53N 1 40W
New Glasgow **149** 45 35N 62 36W
New Hampshire □ **164** 43 40N 71 40W
New Haven **164** 41 20N 72 54W
New Hebrides = Vanuatu ■ .. **122** 15 0S 168 0 E
New Iberia **168** 30 2N 91 54W
New Ireland .... **115** 3 20S 151 50 E
New Jersey □ **164** 40 30N 74 10W
New Kensington **164** 40 36N 79 43W
New London **164** 41 23N 72 8W
New Mexico □ **161** 34 30N 106 0W
New Norfolk .... **119** 42 46S 147 2 E
New Orleans **169** 30 0N 90 5W
New Philadelphia **164** 40 29N 81 25W
New Plymouth .... **122** 39 4S 174 5 E
New Providence **178** 25 25N 78 35W
New Radnor **26** 52 15N 3 10W
New Siberian Is. =
  Novosibirskiye Ostrova .... **72** 75 0N 142 0 E
New South Wales □ ...... **116** 33 0S 146 0 E
New Ulm **166** 44 15N 94 30W
New Waterford **149** 46 13N 60 4W
New Westminster **154** 49 13N 122 55W
New York □ **164** 42 40N 76 0W
New York City **164** 40 45N 74 0W
New Zealand ■ .... **122** 40 0S 176 0 E
Newark, N.J., U.S.A. **164** 40 41N 74 12W
Newark, N.Y., U.S.A. **164** 43 2N 77 10W
Newark, Ohio, U.S.A. **167** 40 5N 82 24W
Newark-on-Trent **29** 53 6N 0 48W
Newberry, Mich., U.S.A. .. **150** 46 20N 85 32W
Newberry, S.C., U.S.A. .. **165** 34 17N 81 37W
Newburgh **164** 41 30N 74 1W
Newburyport **164** 42 48N 70 50W
Newcastle, Australia .... **117** 33 0S 151 46 E
Newcastle, Canada **148** 47 1N 65 38W
Newcastle, U.K. **34** 54 13N 5 54W
Newcastle Emlyn **26** 52 2N 4 29W
Newcastle-under-Lyme .. **28** 53 2N 2 15W
Newcastle-upon-Tyne **28** 54 59N 1 37W
Newfoundland □ **149** 53 0N 58 0W
Newhaven .... **25** 50 47N 0 4 E
Newmarket .... **25** 52 15N 0 23 E
Newnan **170** 33 22N 84 48W
Newport, Gwent, U.K. **27** 51 35N 3 0W
Newport, I. of W., U.K. .. **25** 50 42N 1 18W
Newport, Ark., U.S.A. **168** 35 38N 91 15W
Newport, Ky., U.S.A. **167** 39 5N 84 23W
Newport, Oreg., U.S.A. **171** 44 41N 124 2W
Newport, R.I., U.S.A. **164** 41 13N 71 19W
Newport, Vt., U.S.A. **148** 44 57N 72 17W
Newport Beach **173** 33 40N 117 58W
Newport News **165** 37 2N 76 30W
Newquay **27** 50 24N 5 6W
Newry **34** 54 10N 6 20W
Newton, Iowa, U.S.A. **166** 41 40N 93 3W
Newton, Mass., U.S.A. .. **164** 42 21N 71 10W
Newton Abbot **27** 50 32N 3 37W
Newton Stewart **31** 54 57N 4 30W
Newtonmore **33** 57 4N 4 7W
Newtown **26** 52 31N 3 19W
Newtownards **34** 54 37N 5 40W
Ngaoundéré .... **131** 7 15N 13 35 E
Ngoring Hu .... **101** 34 55N 97 5 E
Nguru .... **131** 12 56N 10 29 E
Nha Trang .... **95** 12 16N 109 10 E
Nhill .... **119** 36 18S 141 40 E
Niagara Falls, Canada .. **151** 43 7N 79 5W
Niagara Falls, U.S.A. **164** 43 5N 79 0W

Niamey	131	13 27N	2	6 E
Nias	111	1 0N	97	30 E
Nicaragua ■	179	11 40N	85	30W
Nicaragua, Lago de	179	12 0N	85	30W
Nice	37	43 42N	7	14 E
Nichinan	108	31 38N	131	23 E
Nicobar Is.	8	9 0N	93	0 E
Nicosia	80	35 10N	33	25 E
Nicoya, Pen. de	179	9 45N	85	40W
Nidd →	28	54 1N	1	32W
Niederösterreich □	45	48 25N	15	40 E
Niedersachsen □	42	52 45N	9	0 E
Nieuw Nickerie	185	6 0N	56	59W
Niger ■	131	13 30N	10	0 E
Niger →	131	5 33N	6	33 E
Nigeria ■	131	8 30N	8	0 E
Nii-Jima	107	34 20N	139	15 E
Niigata	103	37 58N	139	0 E
Niihama	109	33 55N	133	16 E
Niimi	109	34 59N	133	28 E
Nijkerk	41	52 13N	5	30 E
Nijmegen	41	51 50N	5	52 E
Nikki	131	9 58N	3	12 E
Nikkō	107	36 45N	139	35 E
Nikolayev	68	46 58N	32	0 E
Nikolayevsk-na-Amur	75	53 8N	140	44 E
Nikolskoye	73	55 12N	166	0 E
Nikšić	52	42 50N	18	57 E
Nīl, Nahr en →	128	30 10N	31	6 E
Nīl el Abyad →	129	15 38N	32	31 E
Nīl el Azraq →	129	15 38N	32	31 E
Nile = Nīl, Nahr en →	128	30 10N	31	6 E
Niles	164	41 8N	80	40W
Nîmes	37	43 50N	4	23 E
Nimule	129	3 32N	32	3 E
Ninawá	81	36 25N	43	10 E
Nineveh = Ninawá	81	36 25N	43	10 E
Ningbo	99	29 51N	121	28 E
Ningde	99	26 38N	119	23 E
Ningpo = Ningbo	99	29 51N	121	28 E
Ningsia Hui A.R. = Ningxia				
Huizu Zizhiqu □	98	38 0N	106	0 E
Ningxia Huizu Zizhiqu □	98	38 0N	106	0 E
Niobrara →	163	42 45N	98	0W
Nioro du Sahel	130	15 15N	9	30W
Niort	36	46 19N	0	29W
Nipawin	152	53 20N	104	0W
Nipigon	150	49 0N	88	17W
Nipigon, L.	150	49 50N	88	30W
Niš	53	43 19N	21	58 E
Nişāb	83	14 25N	46	29 E
Nishinomiya	106	34 45N	135	20 E
Nishio	106	34 52N	137	3 E
Nishiwaki	109	34 59N	134	58 E
Niterói	188	22 52S	43	0W
Nith →	31	55 20N	3	5W
Nitra	59	48 19N	18	4 E
Nivernais	37	47 0N	3	40 E
Nizamabad	91	18 45N	78	7 E
Nizhne Kolymsk	73	68 34N	160	55 E
Nizhneudinsk	74	54 54N	99	3 E
Nizhnevartovsk	69	60 56N	76	38 E
Nizhniy Novgorod = Gorkiy	68	56 20N	44	0 E
Nizhniy Tagil	69	57 55N	59	57 E
Nizhnyaya Tunguska →	74	64 20N	93	0 E
Nizké Tatry	59	48 55N	20	0 E
Nkongsamba	131	4 55N	9	55 E
Noatak	142	67 32N	162	59W
Nobeoka	108	32 36N	131	41 E
Noda	107	35 56N	139	52 E
Nogales	174	31 20N	110	56W
Nōgata	108	33 48N	130	44 E
Nogent-le-Rotrou	39	48 20N	0	50 E
Noi →	94	14 50N	100	15 E
Noirmoutier, Î. de	36	46 58N	2	10W
Nojima-Zaki	107	34 54N	139	53 E
Nok Kundi	88	28 50N	62	45 E
Nome	142	64 30N	165	24W
Nong Khae	95	14 29N	100	53 E
Nong Khai	95	17 50N	102	46 E
Nonoava	174	27 28N	106	44W
Noord Brabant □	40	51 40N	5	0 E
Noord Holland □	40	52 30N	4	45 E
Noordbeveland	40	51 35N	3	50 E
Noordoostpolder	41	52 45N	5	45 E
Noordwijk aan Zee	40	52 14N	4	26 E
Nootka I.	154	49 32N	126	42W
Nord-Trøndelag fylke □	65	64 20N	12	0 E
Nordaustlandet	13	79 14N	23	0 E
Nordegg	155	52 29N	116	5W
Nordkapp	67	71 10N	25	44 E
Nordkinn	67	71 8N	27	40 E
Nordland fylke □	65	65 40N	13	0 E
Nordrhein-Westfalen □	42	51 45N	7	30 E
Nordvik	72	74 2N	111	32 E
Nore →	35	52 40N	7	20W
Norfolk	165	36 40N	76	15W
Norfolk □	29	52 39N	1	0 E
Norfolk I.	122	28 58S	168	3 E
Norilsk	72	69 20N	88	6 E
Norman	168	35 12N	97	30W
Norman Wells	144	65 17N	126	51W
Normandie	39	48 45N	0	10 E
Normandin	151	48 49N	72	31W
Normandy = Normandie	39	48 45N	0	10 E
Normanton	115	17 40S	141	10 E
Norquinco	192	41 51S	70	55W
Norristown	164	40 9N	75	21W
Norrköping	60	58 37N	16	11 E
Norrland □	66	66 50N	18	0 E
Norseman	114	32 8S	121	43 E
Norsk	75	52 30N	130	0 E
North Andaman I.	94	13 15N	92	40 E
North Battleford	152	52 50N	108	17W
North Bay	151	46 20N	79	30W
North Bend	171	43 28N	124	14W
North Berwick	31	56 4N	2	44W
North C.	122	34 23S	173	4 E
North Carolina □	165	35 30N	80	0W
North Channel, Br. Is.	30	55 0N	5	30W
North Channel, Canada	150	46 0N	83	0W
North Dakota □	163	47 30N	100	0W
North Downs	25	51 17N	0	30 E
North European Plain	17	55 0N	20	0 E
North I.	122	38 0S	175	0 E
North Korea ■	98	40 0N	127	0 E
North Minch	32	58 5N	5	55W
North Ossetian A.S.S.R. □	70	43 30N	44	30 E
North Platte	163	41 10N	100	50W
North Platte →	163	41 15N	100	45W
North Pole	12	90 0N	0	0 E
North Ronaldsay	33	59 20N	2	30W
North Saskatchewan →	143	53 15N	105	5W
North Sea	16	56 0N	4	0 E
North Sentinel I.	94	11 35N	92	15 E
North Sporades = Vorіаі				
Sporádhes	55	39 15N	23	30 E
North Sydney	149	46 12N	60	15W
North Tonawanda	164	43 5N	78	50W
North Uist	32	57 40N	7	15W
North Vancouver	154	49 25N	123	3W
North Walsham	29	52 49N	1	22 E
North West Frontier □	89	34 0N	71	0 E
North West Highlands	32	57 35N	5	2W
North West River	147	53 30N	60	10W
North West Territories □	145	67 0N	110	0W
North York Moors	29	54 25N	0	50W
North Yorkshire □	28	54 15N	1	25W
Northallerton	28	54 20N	1	26W
Northam	120	31 35S	116	42 E
Northam, Australia	120	28 27S	114	33 E
Northampton, U.K.	25	52 14N	0	54W
Northampton, U.S.A.	164	42 22N	72	31W
Northampton □	25	52 16N	0	55W
Northcliffe	120	34 39S	116	7 E
Northern Circars	92	17 30N	82	30 E
Northern Ireland □	34	54 45N	7	0W
Northern Territory □	114	16 0S	133	0 E
Northfield	166	44 30N	93	10W
Northland □	122	35 30S	173	30 E

Northumberland □ **28** 55 12N   2 0W
Northumberland Is. .... **121** 21 30S 149 50 E
Northumberland Str. **148** 46 20N 64 0W
Northwich **28** 53 16N   2 30W
Norton Sd. **142** 64 0N 164 0W
Norwalk **164** 41 9N 73 25W
Norway ■.................. **18** 63 0N 11 0 E
Norwegian Sea .... **16** 66 0N   1 0 E
Norwich .... **29** 52 38N   1 17 E
Nos Kaliakra .... **53** 43 21N 28 30 E
Noshiro................... **103** 40 12N 140 0 E
Noss Hd. **33** 58 29N   3 4W
Nossob ⟶ .... **136** 26 55S 20 37 E
Noteć ⟶ .... **58** 52 44N 15 26 E
Notre Dame de Koartac =
  Koartac **146** 60 55N 69 40W
Nottaway ⟶ **140** 51 22N 78 55W
Nottingham **29** 52 57N   1 10W
Nottingham □ **29** 53 10N   1 0W
Nouâdhibou **126** 20 54N 17 0W
Nouâdhibou, Ras **126** 20 50N 17 0W
Nouakchott **126** 18 9N 15 58W
Noumea .... **122** 22 17S 166 30 E
Nouveau Comptoir **140** 53 0N 78 49W
Nouvelle Calédonie .... **122** 21 0S 165 0 E
Nova Friburgo **188** 22 16S 42 30W
Nova Granada **188** 20 30S 49 20W
Nova Lisboa = Huambo ..... **134** 12 42S 15 54 E
Nova Scotia □ **149** 45 10N 63 0W
Novara .... **46** 45 27N   8 36 E
Novaya Sibir, Ostrov ..... **72** 75 10N 150 0 E
Novaya Zemlya............. **69** 75 0N 56 0 E
Novgorod.................. **68** 58 30N 31 25 E
Novi Pazar .... **52** 43 12N 20 28 E
Novi Sad .... **52** 45 18N 19 52 E
Novocherkassk............. **68** 47 27N 40 5 E
Novokuznetsk .... **71** 53 45N 87 10 E
Novomoskovsk .... **68** 54 5N 38 15 E
Novorossiysk.............. **68** 44 43N 37 46 E
Novosibirsk .... **71** 55 0N 83 5 E
Novosibirskiye Ostrova ... **72** 75 0N 142 0 E
Nowgong .... **93** 26 20N 92 50 E
Nowra .... **117** 34 53S 150 35 E
Nowy Sącz................. **59** 49 40N 20 41 E
Noyon .... **38** 49 34N   3 0 E
Nûblya, Es Sahrâ En ...... **129** 21 30N 33 30 E
Nueces ⟶ **161** 27 50N 97 30W
Nueltin L. **145** 60 30N 99 30W
Nueva Gerona............. **178** 21 53N 82 49W
Nueva Rosita **174** 27 57N 101 13W
Nuevitas.................. **178** 21 30N 77 20W
Nuevo Laredo **176** 27 30N 99 30W
Nuevo Leon □ **176** 25 40N 100 0W
Nuhaka.................... **122** 39 3S 177 45 E
Nukey Bluff, Mt........... **118** 32 26S 135 29 E
Nukus .... **70** 42 20N 59 7 E
Nulato.................... **142** 64 40N 158 10W
Nullarbor Plain .... **114** 30 45S 129 0 E
Numan .... **131** 9 29N 12 3 E
Numazu .... **107** 35 7N 138 51 E
Numurkah .... **117** 36 5S 145 26 E
Nuneaton **25** 52 32N   1 29W
Nunivak **142** 60 0N 166 0W
Nunspeet .... **41** 52 21N   5 45 E
Nuoro .... **48** 40 20N   9 20 E
Nuremburg = Nürnberg ..... **43** 49 26N 11 5 E
Nuriootpa .... **119** 34 27S 139 0 E
Nürnberg .... **43** 49 26N 11 5 E
Nurran, L. = Terewah, L...... **116** 29 52S 147 35 E
Nutak **147** 57 28N 61 59W
Nuweveldberge .... **136** 32 10S 21 45 E
Nuyts Arch. .... **118** 32 35S 133 20 E
Nyaake.................... **130** 4 52N   7 37W
Nyainqentanglha Shan ..... **101** 30 0N 90 0 E
Nyasa, L. = Malawi, L..... **137** 12 30S 34 30 E
Nyíregyháza .... **59** 47 58N 21 47 E
Nyngan .... **116** 31 30S 147 8 E
Nysa .... **58** 50 30N 17 22 E

Oahe L. **163** 45 30N 100 25W
Oahu...................... **160** 21 30N 158 0W
Oak Hill.................. **165** 38 0N 81 7W
Oak Park **167** 41 55N 87 45W
Oak Ridge **169** 36 1N 84 12W
Oakengates............... **28** 52 42N   2 29W
Oakey .... **116** 27 25S 151 43 E
Oakham **29** 52 40N   0 43W
Oakland **172** 37 50N 122 18W
Oakridge **171** 43 47N 122 31W
Oamaru .... **123** 45 5S 170 59 E
Oaxaca **177** 17 2N 96 40W
Oaxaca □ **177** 17 0N 96 30W
Ob ⟶ .... **69** 66 45N 69 30 E
Oba....................... **150** 49 4N 84 7W
Obama .... **106** 35 30N 135 45 E
Oban **30** 56 25N   5 30W
Obbia .... **133** 5 25N 48 30 E
Oberhausen .... **42** 51 28N   6 50 E
Oberon .... **117** 33 45S 149 52 E
Oberösterreich □ .... **45** 48 10N 14 0 E
Obi, Is. .... **113** 1 30S 127 30 E
Obihiro .... **103** 42 56N 143 12 E
Obskaya Guba .... **69** 69 0N 73 0 E
Ocala **170** 29 11N 82 5W
Ocampo **174** 28 11N 108 23W
Ocaña **184** 8 15N 73 20W
Occidental, Cordillera ... **184** 5 0N 76 0W
Ocean City................ **164** 39 18N 74 34W
Oceanside **173** 33 13N 117 26W
Ochil Hills. **31** 56 14N   3 40W
Oconee ⟶ **170** 31 58N 82 32W
Oconto **167** 44 52N 87 53W
Ocotlán **175** 20 21N 102 46W
Oda....................... **109** 35 11N 132 30 E
Ódáðahraun **64** 65 5N 17 0W
Odate .... **103** 40 16N 140 34 E
Odawara .... **107** 35 20N 139 6 E
Ödemiş .... **80** 38 15N 28 0 E
Odense .... **61** 55 22N 10 23 E
Oder ⟶ .... **58** 53 33N 14 38 E
Odessa, U.S.A. **161** 31 51N 102 23W
Odessa, U.S.S.R. .... **68** 46 30N 30 45 E
Odra ⟶ .... **58** 53 33N 14 38 E
Odžak..................... **52** 45 3N 18 18 E
Offaly □ **35** 53 15N   7 30W
Offenbach .... **42** 50 6N   8 46 E
Oga-Hantō .... **103** 39 58N 139 47 E
Ogaden .... **133** 7 30N 45 30 E
Ogaki .... **106** 35 21N 136 37 E
Ogbomosho .... **131** 8 1N   4 11 E
Ogden **163** 41 13N 112 1W
Ogdensburg **151** 44 40N 75 27W
Ohio □ .... **167** 40 20N 14 10 E
Ohio ⟶ **167** 38 0N 86 0W
Ohrid .... **52** 41 8N 20 52 E
Ohridsko, Jezero .... **52** 41 8N 20 52 E
Oil City **164** 41 26N 79 40W
Oise ⟶ .... **38** 49 0N   2 4 E
Oisterwijk .... **40** 51 35N   5 12 E
Oita .... **108** 33 14N 131 36 E
Ojos del Salado, Cerro ... **190** 27 0S 68 40W
Oka ⟶ .... **68** 56 20N 43 59 E
Okawa .... **108** 33 9N 130 21 E
Okaya .... **107** 36 0N 138 10 E
Okayama .... **109** 34 40N 133 54 E
Okazaki .... **106** 34 57N 137 10 E
Okeechobee, L. **170** 27 0N 80 50W
Okehampton **27** 50 44N   4 1W
Okha .... **75** 53 40N 143 0 E
Okhotsk .... **75** 59 20N 143 10 E
Okhotsk, Sea of........... **77** 55 0N 145 0 E
Okhotsko Kolymskoye ...... **73** 63 0N 157 0 E
Oki-no-Shima .... **109** 32 44N 132 33 E
Oki-Shotō .... **109** 36 5N 133 15 E
Okinawa-Jima .... **99** 26 32N 128 0 E
Oklahoma □ **161** 35 20N 97 30W
Oklahoma City **161** 35 25N 97 30W
Okmulgee **168** 35 38N 96 0W
Oktabrsk .... **70** 49 28N 57 25 E
Oktyabrskoy Revolyutsii, Os. .. **72** 79 30N 97 0 E

Name	Page	Lat	Long
Oktyabrskoye	**69**	62 28N	66 3 E
Ōkuchi	**108**	32 4N	130 37 E
Okuru	**123**	43 55S	168 55 E
Okushiri-Tō	**103**	42 15N	139 30 E
Olanchito	**179**	15 30N	86 30W
Öland	**61**	56 45N	16 38 E
Olary	**118**	32 18S	140 19 E
Olavarría	**190**	36 55S	60 20W
Old Castile = Castilla La Vieja	**50**	41 55N	4 0W
Old Town	**148**	45 0N	68 41W
Oldenburg	**42**	53 10N	8 10 E
Oldenzaal	**41**	52 19N	6 53 E
Oldham	**28**	53 33N	2 8W
Olds	**155**	51 50N	114 10W
Olekma →	**74**	60 22N	120 42 E
Olekminsk	**74**	60 25N	120 30 E
Olenek	**72**	68 28N	112 18 E
Olenek →	**72**	73 0N	120 10 E
Oléron, Île d'	**36**	45 55N	1 15W
Oleśnica	**58**	51 13N	17 22 E
Olifants →	**137**	24 5S	31 20 E
Ólimbos, Óros	**54**	40 6N	22 23 E
Oliveira	**188**	20 39S	44 50W
Oliver	**155**	49 13N	119 37W
Ollagüe	**187**	21 15S	68 10W
Olney	**167**	38 40N	88 0W
Olomouc	**59**	49 38N	17 12 E
Olsztyn	**58**	53 48N	20 29 E
Olt →	**57**	43 50N	24 40 E
Olympia, Greece	**54**	37 39N	21 39 E
Olympia, U.S.A.	**171**	47 0N	122 58W
Olympic Mts.	**171**	47 50N	123 45W
Olympus, Mt. = Ólimbos, Óros	**54**	40 6N	22 23 E
Olympus, Mt.	**171**	47 52N	123 40W
Omachi	**107**	36 30N	137 50 E
Omae-Zaki	**107**	34 36N	138 14 E
Omagh	**34**	54 36N	7 20W
Omaha	**166**	41 15N	96 0W
Omak	**171**	48 24N	119 31W
Oman ■	**83**	23 0N	58 0 E
Oman, G. of	**83**	24 30N	58 30 E
Omdurmân	**129**	15 40N	32 28 E
Ōme	**107**	35 47N	139 15 E
Omeo	**117**	37 6S	147 36 E
Omihachiman	**106**	35 7N	136 3 E
Omiya	**107**	35 54N	139 38 E
Omo →	**132**	6 25N	36 10 E
Omolon →	**73**	68 42N	158 36 E
Omono-Gawa →	**103**	39 46N	140 3 E
Omsk	**71**	55 0N	73 12 E
Ōmura	**108**	32 56N	130 0 E
Ōmuta	**108**	33 0N	130 26 E
Onega	**68**	64 0N	38 10 E
Onega, L. = Onezhskoye Ozero	**68**	62 0N	35 30 E
Onehunga	**122**	36 55S	174 48 E
Oneida	**164**	43 5N	75 40W
Onekotan, Ostrov	**75**	49 25N	154 45 E
Onezhskoye Ozero	**68**	62 0N	35 30 E
Ongerup	**120**	33 58S	118 28 E
Ongole	**90**	15 33N	80 2 E
Onguren	**74**	53 38N	107 36 E
Onitsha	**131**	6 6N	6 42 E
Ono, Fukui, Japan	**106**	35 59N	136 29 E
Ono, Hyōgo, Japan	**109**	34 51N	134 56 E
Onoda	**108**	34 2N	131 25 E
Onomichi	**109**	34 25N	133 12 E
Onslow	**114**	21 40S	115 12 E
Onslow B.	**165**	34 20N	77 20W
Ontake-San	**106**	35 53N	137 29 E
Ontario	**173**	34 2N	117 40W
Ontario □	**140**	52 0N	88 10W
Ontario, L.	**151**	43 40N	78 0W
Oodnadatta	**118**	27 33S	135 30 E
Ooldea	**114**	30 27S	131 50 E
Oostende	**42**	51 15N	2 50 E
Oosterhout	**40**	51 39N	4 47 E
Oosterschelde	**40**	51 33N	4 0 E
Opala	**73**	51 58N	156 30 E
Opava	**58**	49 57N	17 58 E
Opelousas	**168**	30 35N	92 7W
Ophir	**142**	63 10N	156 40W
Opole	**58**	50 42N	17 58 E
Oporto = Porto	**50**	41 8N	8 40W
Opp	**169**	31 19N	86 13W
Oppland fylke □	**60**	61 15N	9 40 E
Opua	**122**	35 19S	174 9 E
Oradea	**56**	47 2N	21 58 E
Öræfajökull	**64**	64 2N	16 39W
Orai	**91**	25 58N	79 30 E
Oran, Algeria	**127**	35 45N	0 39W
Oran, Argentina	**190**	23 10S	64 20W
Orange, Australia	**117**	33 15S	149 7 E
Orange, France	**37**	44 8N	4 47 E
Orange, U.S.A.	**168**	30 10N	93 50W
Orange → = Oranje →	**136**	28 41S	16 28 E
Orange, C.	**185**	4 20N	51 30W
Orangeburg	**170**	33 35N	80 53W
Oranje →	**136**	28 41S	16 28 E
Oraşul Stalin = Braşov	**57**	45 38N	25 35 E
Orbost	**117**	37 40S	148 29 E
Orchies	**38**	50 28N	3 14 E
Ordos = Mu Us Shamo	**98**	39 0N	109 0 E
Ordu	**81**	40 55N	37 53 E
Ordzhonikidze	**70**	43 0N	44 35 E
Ore Mts. = Erzgebirge	**43**	50 25S	13 0 E
Örebro	**60**	59 20N	15 18 E
Oregon □	**171**	44 0N	121 0W
Oregon City	**171**	45 21N	122 35W
Orel	**68**	52 57N	36 3 E
Orenburg	**70**	51 45N	55 6 E
Orense	**50**	42 19N	7 55W
Orepuki	**123**	46 19S	167 46 E
Orford Ness	**24**	52 6N	1 31 E
Oriental, Cordillera	**184**	6 0N	73 0W
Orillia	**151**	44 40N	79 24W
Orinoco →	**185**	9 15N	61 30W
Orissa □	**92**	20 0N	84 0 E
Oristano	**48**	39 54N	8 35 E
Oristano, Golfo di	**48**	39 50N	8 22 E
Orizaba	**177**	18 51N	97 6W
Orkney Is.	**33**	59 0N	3 0W
Orland	**172**	39 46N	122 12W
Orlando	**170**	28 30N	81 25W
Orléanais	**39**	48 0N	2 0 E
Orléans	**39**	47 54N	1 52 E
Ormara	**88**	25 16N	64 33 E
Ormskirk	**28**	53 35N	2 53W
Örnsköldsvik	**66**	63 17N	18 40 E
Orocué	**184**	4 48N	71 20W
Oroville	**172**	39 31N	121 30W
Orsha	**68**	54 30N	30 25 E
Orsk	**70**	51 12N	58 34 E
Ortegal, C.	**50**	43 43N	7 52W
Orūmīyeh	**81**	37 40N	45 0 E
Orūmīyeh, Daryācheh-ye	**81**	37 50N	45 30 E
Oruro	**187**	18 0S	67 9W
Oruzgān □	**87**	33 30N	66 0 E
Oryakhovo	**53**	43 40N	23 57 E
Osage →	**166**	38 35N	91 57W
Ōsaka	**106**	34 40N	135 30 E
Osceola	**169**	35 40N	90 0W
Ösel = Saaremaa	**68**	58 30N	22 30 E
Osh	**71**	40 37N	72 49 E
Oshawa	**151**	43 50N	78 50W
Oshima	**107**	33 55N	132 14 E
Oshkosh	**167**	44 3N	88 35W
Oshogbo	**131**	7 48N	4 37 E
Osijek	**52**	45 34N	18 41 E
Oskaloosa	**166**	41 18N	92 40W
Oslo	**60**	59 55N	10 45 E
Osmaniye	**80**	37 5N	36 10 E
Osnabrück	**42**	52 16N	8 2 E
Osorno	**190**	40 25S	73 0W
Oss	**41**	51 46N	5 32 E
Ossa, Mt.	**119**	41 52S	146 3 E
Ostend = Oostende	**42**	51 15N	2 50 E
Östergötlands län □	**60**	58 35N	15 45 E
Östersund	**66**	63 10N	14 38 E
Østfold fylke □	**60**	59 25N	11 25 E

Ostfriesische Inseln	**42**	53 45N	7	15 E
Ostia	**46**	41 40N	12	20 E
Ostrava	**59**	49 51N	18	18 E
Ostróda	**58**	53 42N	19	58 E
Ostrofeka	**58**	53 4N	21	32 E
Ostrów Mazowiecka	**58**	52 50N	21	51 E
Ostrów Wielkopolski	**58**	51 36N	17	44 E
Ōsumi-Kaikyō	**104**	30 55N	131	0 E
Ōsumi-Shotō	**104**	30 30N	130	0 E
Oswego	**164**	43 29N	76	30W
Oswestry	**28**	52 52N	3	3W
Ōta	**107**	36 18N	139	22 E
Otago □	**123**	44 44S	169	10 E
Ōtake	**109**	34 12N	132	13 E
Otaki	**122**	40 45S	175	10 E
Otaru	**103**	43 10N	141	0 E
Otaru-Wan = Ishikari-Wan	**103**	43 25N	141	1 E
Otira Gorge	**123**	42 53S	171	33 E
Otoineppu	**103**	44 44N	142	16 E
Otranto	**49**	40 9N	18	28 E
Otranto, C. d'	**49**	40 7N	18	30 E
Otranto, Str. of	**52**	40 15N	18	40 E
Ōtsu	**106**	35 0N	135	50 E
Ottawa, Canada	**151**	45 27N	75	42W
Ottawa, U.S.A.	**166**	38 40N	95	6W
Ottawa ⟶ = Outaouais ⟶	**140**	45 27N	74	8W
Ottawa Is.	**146**	59 35N	80	10W
Otter Rapids, Ont., Canada	**151**	50 11N	81	39W
Otter Rapids, Sask., Canada	**152**	55 38N	104	44W
Ottumwa	**166**	41 0N	92	25W
Otwock	**58**	52 5N	21	20 E
Ouachita ⟶	**168**	31 38N	91	49W
Ouachita Mts.	**168**	34 50N	94	30W
Ouagadougou	**130**	12 25N	1	30W
Ouahran = Oran	**127**	35 45N	0	39W
Ouargla	**127**	31 59N	5	16 E
Oubangi ⟶	**131**	1 0N	17	50 E
Oudenbosch	**40**	51 35N	4	32 E
Oudtshoorn	**136**	33 35S	22	14 E
Ouessant, Île d'	**36**	48 28N	5	6W
Oujda	**127**	34 41N	1	55W
Oulu	**67**	65 1N	25	29 E
Oulujärvi	**67**	64 25N	27	15 E
Oulujoki ⟶	**67**	65 1N	25	30 E
Ouse ⟶	**29**	54 3N	0	7 E
Outaouais ⟶	**140**	45 27N	74	8W
Outer Hebrides	**32**	57 30N	7	40W
Outlook	**152**	51 30N	107	0W
Outreau	**38**	50 40N	1	36 E
Ouyen	**119**	35 1S	142	22 E
Ovalle	**190**	30 33S	71	18W
Overflakkee	**40**	51 44N	4	10 E
Overijssel □	**41**	52 25N	6	35 E
Oviedo	**50**	43 25N	5	50W
Owaka	**123**	46 27S	169	40 E
Owase	**106**	34 7N	136	12 E
Owatonna	**166**	44 3N	93	10W
Owen Sound	**151**	44 35N	80	55W
Owen Stanley Range	**115**	8 30S	147	0 E
Owensboro	**167**	37 40N	87	5W
Owosso	**167**	43 0N	84	10W
Owyhee ⟶	**171**	43 46N	117	2W
Oxford, U.K.	**25**	51 45N	1	15W
Oxford, U.S.A.	**165**	36 19N	78	36W
Oxford □	**25**	51 45N	1	15W
Oxford L.	**153**	54 51N	95	37W
Oxnard	**173**	34 10N	119	14W
Oyabe	**106**	36 47N	136	56 E
Oyama	**107**	36 18N	139	48 E
Oyana	**108**	32 32N	130	30 E
Oyo	**131**	7 46N	3	56 E
Oyonnax	**37**	46 16N	5	40 E
Ozamis	**112**	8 15N	123	50 E
Ozark	**169**	31 29N	85	39W
Ozark Plateau	**168**	37 20N	91	40W
Ozarks, L. of	**166**	38 10N	92	40W
Ozu, Ehime, Japan	**109**	33 30N	132	33 E
Ozu, Kumamoto, Japan	**108**	32 52N	130	52 E

Paarl	**136**	33 45S	18	56 E
Pabna	**92**	24 1N	89	18 E
Pacaraima, Sierra	**185**	4 0N	62	30W
Pacasmayo	**186**	7 20S	79	35W
Pachuca	**177**	20 10N	98	40W
Padang	**111**	1 0S	100	20 E
Pádova	**47**	45 24N	11	52 E
Padstow	**27**	50 33N	4	57W
Padua = Pádova	**47**	45 24N	11	52 E
Paducah	**169**	37 0N	88	40W
Pag	**52**	44 30N	14	50 E
Pagalu = Annobón	**131**	1 25S	5	36 E
Pagastikós Kólpos	**54**	39 15N	23	0 E
Page	**160**	36 57N	111	27W
Pahala	**160**	19 12N	155	29W
Pahang □	**96**	3 30N	102	45 E
Pahiatua	**122**	40 27S	175	50 E
Paignton	**27**	50 26N	3	33W
Painesville	**167**	41 42N	81	18W
Paint Hills = Nouveau Comptoir	**140**	53 0N	78	49W
Painted Desert	**160**	36 0N	111	30W
Paisley	**31**	55 51N	4	27W
Paita	**186**	5 11S	81	9W
Pak Sane	**95**	18 22N	103	39 E
Pakistan ■	**78**	30 0N	70	0 E
Pakistan, East = Bangladesh ■	**92**	24 0N	90	0 E
Pakokku	**93**	21 20N	95	0 E
Pakse	**95**	15 5N	105	52 E
Pakfīā □	**87**	33 0N	69	15 E
Palanpur	**91**	24 10N	72	25 E
Palatka	**170**	29 40N	81	40W
Palawan	**112**	9 30N	118	30 E
Palembang	**111**	3 0S	104	50 E
Palencia	**50**	42 1N	4	34W
Palermo	**48**	38 8N	13	20 E
Palestine	**168**	31 42N	95	35W
Palghat	**90**	10 46N	76	42 E
Pali	**91**	25 50N	73	20 E
Palizada	**177**	18 15N	92	5W
Palk Bay	**90**	9 30N	79	15 E
Palk Strait	**90**	10 0N	79	45 E
Palm Is.	**121**	18 40S	146	35 E
Palm Springs	**173**	33 51N	116	35W
Palma, La	**179**	8 15N	78	0W
Palma de Mallorca	**51**	39 35N	2	39 E
Palma Soriano	**178**	20 15N	76	0W
Palmas, C.	**130**	4 27N	7	46W
Palmer Land	**14**	73 0S	60	0W
Palmerston North	**122**	40 21S	175	39 E
Palmi	**49**	38 21N	15	51 E
Palmira	**184**	3 32N	76	16W
Palmyra = Tudmur	**80**	34 36N	38	15 E
Palo Alto	**172**	37 25N	122	8W
Pamirs	**71**	37 40N	73	0 E
Pamlico Sd.	**165**	35 20N	76	0W
Pampa	**161**	35 35N	100	58W
Pampas	**190**	35 0S	63	0W
Pamplona	**51**	42 48N	1	38W
Panaca	**173**	37 51N	114	23W
Panaji	**91**	15 25N	73	50 E
Panamá	**179**	9 0N	79	25W
Panama ■	**179**	8 48N	79	55W
Panamá, Golfo de	**179**	8 4N	79	20W
Panama Canal	**175**	9 10N	79	37W
Panama City	**169**	30 10N	85	41W
Panay	**112**	11 10N	122	30 E
Pančevo	**52**	44 52N	20	41 E
Pandharpur	**91**	17 41N	75	20 E
Pangfou = Bengbu	**99**	32 58N	117	20 E
Pangkalpinang	**111**	2 0S	106	0 E
Pangnirtung	**146**	66 8N	65	54W
Panjim = Panaji	**91**	15 25N	73	50 E
Panjnad Barrage	**89**	29 22N	71	15 E
Pantelleria	**48**	36 52N	12	0 E
Pánuco	**177**	22 3N	98	10W
Paoting = Baoding	**98**	38 50N	115	28 E
Paot'ou = Baotou	**98**	40 32N	110	2 E
Papien Chiang = Da ⟶	**95**	21 15N	105	20 E
Papua, Gulf of	**115**	9 0S	144	50 E

Papua New Guinea ■	115	8	0S	145	0 E
Pará = Belém	188	1	20S	48	30W
Pará □	188	3	20S	52	0W
Paracatu	188	17	10S	46	50W
Paragua, La	185	6	50N	63	20W
Paraguay ■	191	23	0S	57	0W
Paraguay →	191	27	18S	58	38W
Paraíba = João Pessoa	189	7	10S	34	52W
Paraíba □	189	7	0S	36	0W
Parakou	131	9	25N	2	40 E
Paramaribo	185	5	50N	55	10W
Paraná	190	31	45S	60	30W
Paraná □	191	24	30S	51	0W
Paraná →	190	33	43S	59	15W
Paranaguá	191	25	30S	48	30W
Paranaíba →	188	20	6S	51	4W
Parbhani	91	19	8N	76	52 E
Parecis, Serra dos	187	13	0S	60	0W
Parent	151	47	55N	74	35W
Paria, Golfo de	180	10	20N	62	0W
Parika	185	6	50N	58	20W
Parintins	185	2	40S	56	50W
Pariparit Kyun	94	14	55S	93	45 E
Paris, France	30	48	50N	2	20 E
Paris, Tenn., U.S.A.	169	36	20N	88	20W
Paris, Tex., U.S.A.	168	33	40N	95	30W
Park Range	163	40	0N	106	30W
Parker	173	34	8N	114	16W
Parkersburg	164	39	18N	81	31W
Parkes	117	33	9S	148	11 E
Parma	46	44	50N	10	20 E
Parnaguá	188	10	10S	44	38W
Parnaíba	189	2	54S	41	47W
Parnaíba →	188	3	0S	41	50W
Parnassós	54	38	35N	22	30 E
Pärnu	68	58	28N	24	33 E
Páros	55	37	5N	25	12 E
Parral	190	36	10S	71	52W
Parramatta	117	33	48S	151	1 E
Parras	174	25	30N	102	20W
Parrett →	27	51	7N	2	58W
Parry Is.	12	77	0N	110	0W
Parry Sound	151	45	20N	80	0W
Parsons	166	37	20N	95	17W
Paruro	187	13	45S	71	50W
Parvän □	87	35	0N	69	0 E
Pasadena, Calif., U.S.A.	173	34	5N	118	9W
Pasadena, Tex., U.S.A.	168	29	45N	95	14W
Pasaje	184	3	23S	79	50W
Pascagoula	169	30	21N	88	30W
Pasco	171	46	10N	119	0W
Pasco, Cerro de	186	10	45S	76	10W
Paso Robles	173	35	40N	120	45W
Passero, C.	49	36	42N	15	8 E
Passo Fundo	191	28	10S	52	20W
Pasto	184	1	13N	77	17W
Patagonia	192	45	0S	69	0W
Patan	91	23	54N	72	14 E
Patchogue	164	40	46N	73	1W
Paterson	164	40	55N	74	10W
Pathankot	89	32	18N	75	45 E
Patiala	89	30	23N	76	26 E
Patkai Bum	93	27	0N	95	30 E
Pátmos	55	37	21N	26	36 E
Patna	92	25	35N	85	12 E
Patos, Lag. dos	191	31	20S	51	0 E
Patos de Minas	188	18	35S	46	32W
Pátrai	54	38	14N	21	47 E
Patuca →	179	15	50N	84	18W
Pátzcuaro	175	19	32N	101	36W
Pau	36	43	19N	0	25W
Paulistana	189	8	9S	41	9W
Paulo Afonso	189	9	21S	38	15W
Pavia	46	45	10N	9	10 E
Pavlodar	71	52	33N	77	0 E
Pavlovo	74	63	5N	115	25 E
Pawtucket	164	41	51N	71	22W
Payette	171	44	0N	117	0W
Payne Bay = Bellin	146	60	0N	70	0W
Payne L.	146	59	30N	74	30W
Paynes Find	120	29	15S	117	42 E
Paysandú	191	32	19S	58	8W
Paz, La, Argentina	190	30	50S	59	45W
Paz, La, Bolivia	187	16	20S	68	10W
Paz, La, Mexico	174	24	10N	110	18W
Pazardzhik	53	42	12N	24	20 E
Peace →	145	59	0N	111	25W
Peace River	155	56	15N	117	18W
Peak, The	28	53	24N	1	53W
Peak Hill	116	32	47S	148	11 E
Pearl City	160	21	24N	158	0W
Pearl Harbor	160	21	20N	158	0W
Peary Land	13	82	40N	33	0W
Pebas	186	3	10S	71	46W
Pechenga	69	69	30N	31	25 E
Pechora →	69	68	13N	54	15 E
Pechorskaya Guba	69	68	40N	54	0 E
Pecos	161	31	25N	103	35W
Pecos →	161	29	42N	102	30W
Pécs	59	46	5N	18	15 E
Pedro Afonso	188	9	0S	48	10W
Pedro Juan Caballero	191	22	30S	55	40W
Peebles	31	55	40N	3	12W
Peekskill	164	41	18N	73	57W
Pool	28	54	14N	4	40W
Peel →	144	67	0N	135	0W
Pegasus Bay	123	43	20S	173	10 E
Pegu	93	17	20N	96	29 E
Pegu Yoma	93	19	0N	96	0 E
Pehuajó	190	35	45S	62	0W
Peip'ing = Beijing	98	39	55N	116	20 E
Pekalongan	111	6	53S	109	40 E
Pekan	96	3	30N	103	25 E
Pekanbaru	111	0	30N	101	15 E
Pekin	166	40	35N	89	40W
Peking = Beijing	98	39	55N	116	20 E
Peleng	113	1	20S	123	30 E
Pelly →	144	62	47N	137	19W
Pelly Bay	146	68	38N	89	50W
Peloponnes =					
Pelopónnisos □	54	37	10N	22	0 E
Pelopónnisos □	54	37	10N	22	0 E
Peloro, C.	49	38	15N	15	40 E
Pelorus Sound	123	40	59S	173	59 E
Pelotas	191	31	42S	52	23W
Pelvoux, Massif de	37	44	52N	6	20 E
Pematangsiantar	111	2	57N	99	5 E
Pemba	135	5	0S	39	45 E
Pembroke, Canada	151	45	50N	77	7W
Pembroke, U.K.	27	51	41N	4	57W
Pen-y-Ghent	28	54	10N	2	15W
Penas, G. de	192	47	0S	75	0W
Pench'i = Benxi	98	41	20N	123	48 E
Pendembu	130	9	7N	12	14W
Pendleton	171	45	35N	118	50W
Penetanguishene	151	44	50N	79	55W
Penguin	119	41	8S	146	6 E
Penicuik	31	55	50N	3	14W
Peninsular Malaysia □	96	4	0N	102	0 E
Pennines	28	54	50N	2	20W
Pennsylvania □	164	40	50N	78	0W
Penola	119	37	25S	140	21 E
Penonomé	179	8	31N	80	21W
Penrith, Australia	117	33	43S	150	38 E
Penrith, U.K.	28	54	40N	2	45W
Pensacola	169	30	30N	87	10W
Pensacola Mts.	14	84	0S	40	0W
Penshurst	119	37	49S	142	20 E
Penticton	155	49	30N	119	38W
Pentland Firth	33	58	43N	3	10W
Pentland Hills	31	55	48N	3	25W
Penza	68	53	15N	45	5 E
Penzance	27	50	7N	5	32W
Penzhinskaya Guba	73	61	30N	163	0 E
Peoria	166	40	40N	89	40W
Perak □	96	5	0N	101	0 E
Perche	36	48	31N	1	1 E
Pereira	184	4	49N	75	43W
Perenjori	120	29	26S	116	16 E
Pergamino	190	33	52S	60	30W
Périgueux	36	45	10N	0	42 E
Perlis □	96	6	30N	100	15 E

Name	Page	Lat °	'	N/S	Long °	'	E/W
Perm	69	58	0	N	57	10	E
Pernambuco = Recife	189	8	0	S	35	0	W
Pernambuco □	189	8	0	S	37	0	W
Pernatty Lagoon	118	31	30	S	137	12	E
Pernik	53	42	35	N	23	2	E
Peron Pen.	120	26	0	S	113	10	E
Péronne	38	49	55	N	2	57	E
Perouse Str., La	77	45	40	N	142	0	E
Perpignan	37	42	42	N	2	53	E
Perry, Iowa, U.S.A.	166	41	48	N	94	5	W
Perry, Okla., U.S.A.	168	36	20	N	97	20	W
Persepolis	85	29	55	N	52	50	E
Persia = Iran ■	86	33	0	N	53	0	E
Persian Gulf = Gulf, The	85	27	0	N	50	0	E
Perth, Australia	120	31	57	S	115	52	E
Perth, Canada	151	44	55	N	76	15	W
Perth, U.K.	31	56	24	N	3	27	W
Perth Amboy	164	40	31	N	74	16	W
Peru	167	40	42	N	86	0	W
Peru ■	186	8	0	S	75	0	W
Perúgia	46	43	6	N	12	24	E
Pervouralsk	69	56	55	N	60	0	E
Pésaro	47	43	55	N	12	53	E
Pescara	47	42	28	N	14	13	E
Peshawar	89	34	2	N	71	37	E
Pesqueria →	176	25	54	N	99	11	W
Petah Tiqwa	80	32	6	N	34	53	E
Petaling Jaya	96	3	4	N	101	42	E
Petaluma	172	38	13	N	122	39	W
Petatlán	177	17	31	N	101	16	W
Peterborough, Australia	118	32	58	S	138	51	E
Peterborough, Canada	151	44	20	N	78	20	W
Peterborough, U.K.	25	52	35	N	0	14	W
Peterhead	33	57	30	N	1	49	W
Peterlee	29	54	45	N	1	18	W
Petersburg, Alaska, U.S.A.	143	56	50	N	133	0	W
Petersburg, Va., U.S.A.	164	37	17	N	77	26	W
Petit Goâve	180	18	27	N	72	51	W
Petitsikapau, L.	147	54	37	N	66	25	W
Petlad	91	22	30	N	72	45	E
Petone	123	41	13	S	174	53	E
Petoskey	150	45	22	N	84	57	W
Petrich	53	41	24	N	23	13	E
Petrolia	150	42	54	N	82	9	W
Petrolina	189	9	24	S	40	30	W
Petropavlovsk	71	54	53	N	69	13	E
Petropavlovsk-Kamchatskiy	73	53	3	N	158	43	E
Petrópolis	188	22	33	S	43	9	W
Petrovaradin	52	45	16	N	19	55	E
Petrozavodsk	68	61	41	N	34	20	E
Pevek	73	69	41	N	171	19	E
Pforzheim	42	48	53	N	8	43	E
Phan Rang	95	11	34	N	109	0	E
Phangan, Ko	96	9	45	N	100	0	E
Phenix City	169	32	30	N	85	0	W
Philadelphia	164	40	0	N	75	10	W
Philippi	55	41	1	N	24	16	E
Philippines ■	112	12	0	N	123	0	E
Philippopolis = Plovdiv	53	42	8	N	24	44	E
Phitsanulok	94	16	50	N	100	12	E
Phnom Penh	95	11	33	N	104	55	E
Phoenix	160	33	30	N	112	10	W
Phoenix Is.	123	3	30	S	172	0	W
Phra Chedi Sam Ong	94	15	16	N	98	23	E
Phuket	96	7	52	N	98	22	E
Piacenza	46	45	2	N	9	42	E
Piauí □	188	7	0	S	43	0	W
Picardie	38	50	0	N	2	15	E
Picardie, Plaine de	37	50	0	N	2	0	E
Picardy = Picardie	38	50	0	N	2	15	E
Picayune	169	30	31	N	89	40	W
Pickering	29	54	15	N	0	46	W
Picton, Australia	117	34	12	S	150	34	E
Picton, N.Z.	123	41	18	S	174	3	E
Pictou	149	45	41	N	62	42	W
Pidurutalagala	90	7	10	N	80	50	E
Piedad, La	175	20	20	N	102	1	W
Piedmont = Piemonte □	46	45	0	N	7	30	E
Piedmont Plat.	165	34	0	N	81	30	W
Piedras Negras	174	28	42	N	100	31	W
Piemonte □	46	45	0	N	7	30	E
Pierre	163	44	23	N	100	20	W
Pietermaritzburg	137	29	35	S	30	25	E
Pietrosul	57	47	35	N	24	43	E
Pikeville	165	37	30	N	82	30	W
Pilcomayo →	190	25	21	S	57	42	W
Pilsen = Plzen	43	49	45	N	13	22	E
Pimenta Bueno	187	11	35	S	61	10	W
Pinang □	96	5	20	N	100	20	E
Pinar del Río	178	22	26	N	83	40	W
Pinaroo	119	35	17	S	140	53	E
Pinawa	153	50	9	N	95	50	W
Pincher Creek	155	49	30	N	113	57	W
Pinczów	58	50	30	N	20	35	E
Pindos Óros	54	40	0	N	21	0	E
Pindus Mts. = Pindos Óros	54	40	0	N	21	0	E
Pine Bluff	168	34	10	N	92	0	W
Pine Pass	155	55	25	N	122	42	W
Pineville	168	31	22	N	92	30	W
Ping →	94	15	42	N	100	9	E
Pingdong	99	22	39	N	120	30	E
Pingliang	99	35	35	N	106	31	E
Pingxiang	99	22	6	N	106	46	E
Piniós →	54	37	48	N	21	20	E
Pinjarra	120	32	37	S	115	52	E
Piombino	46	42	54	N	10	30	E
Piotrków Trybunalski	58	51	23	N	19	43	E
Piqua	167	40	10	N	84	10	W
Piracicaba	188	22	45	S	47	40	W
Piræus = Piraiévs	55	37	57	N	23	42	E
Piraiévs	55	37	57	N	23	42	E
Pirapora	188	17	20	S	44	56	W
Pírgos	54	37	40	N	21	27	E
Pirin Planina	53	41	40	N	23	30	E
Pirineos	51	42	40	N	1	0	E
Pisa	46	43	43	N	10	23	E
Pisagua	187	19	40	S	70	15	W
Pisco	186	13	50	S	76	12	W
Pistóia	46	43	57	N	10	53	E
Pitcairn I.	10	25	5	S	130	5	W
Piteå	67	65	20	N	21	25	E
Pitești	57	44	52	N	24	54	E
Pithiviers	39	48	10	N	2	13	E
Pitlochry	33	56	43	N	3	43	W
Pitt I.	154	53	30	N	129	50	W
Pittsburg, Kans., U.S.A.	166	37	21	N	94	43	W
Pittsburg, Tex., U.S.A.	168	32	59	N	94	58	W
Pittsburgh	164	40	25	N	79	55	W
Pittsfield	164	42	28	N	73	17	W
Pittsworth	116	27	41	S	151	37	E
Piura	186	5	15	S	80	38	W
Placentia	149	47	20	N	54	0	W
Placerville	172	38	47	N	120	51	W
Placetas	178	22	15	N	79	44	W
Plainfield	164	40	37	N	74	28	W
Plainview	161	34	10	N	101	40	W
Plaster Rock	148	46	53	N	67	22	W
Plata, La	191	35	0	S	57	55	W
Plata, Río de la	191	34	45	S	57	30	W
Platte →	163	39	16	N	94	50	W
Plattsburg	151	44	41	N	73	30	W
Plauen	43	50	29	N	12	9	E
Pleasantville	164	39	25	N	74	30	W
Plenty, Bay of	122	37	45	S	177	0	E
Plessisville	148	46	14	N	71	47	W
Pleven	53	43	26	N	24	37	E
Płock	58	52	32	N	19	40	E
Ploiești	57	44	57	N	26	5	E
Plovdiv	53	42	8	N	24	44	E
Plymouth	27	50	23	N	4	9	W
Plzen	43	49	45	N	13	22	E
Po →	47	44	57	N	12	4	E
Po Hai = Bo Hai	98	39	0	N	120	0	E
Pobeda	73	65	12	N	146	12	E
Pobedy Pik	71	40	45	N	79	58	E
Pocatello	163	42	50	N	112	25	W
Pochutla	177	15	50	N	96	31	W
Poços de Caldas	188	21	50	S	46	33	W
Podgorica = Titograd	52	42	30	N	19	19	E
Podkamennaya Tunguska →	74	61	50	N	90	13	E
Point Edward	150	43	0	N	82	30	W

Pointe-à-Pitre	**180**	16 10N	61 30W
Pointe Noire	**134**	4 48S	11 53 E
Poissy	**39**	48 55N	2 0 E
Poitiers	**36**	46 35N	0 20 E
Poitou, Plaines et Seuil du	**36**	46 30N	0 1W
Pokaran	**91**	27 0N	71 50 E
Pola = Pula	**52**	44 54N	13 57 E
Poland ■	**58**	52 0N	20 0 E
Polden Hills	**27**	51 7N	2 50W
Polesye	**17**	52 0N	28 10 E
Polillo Is.	**112**	14 56N	122 0 E
Pollyiros	**55**	40 23N	23 25 E
Pollachi	**90**	10 35N	77 0 E
Polotsk	**68**	55 30N	28 50 E
Poltava	**68**	49 35N	34 35 E
Polynesia	**123**	10 0S	162 0W
Pomona	**173**	34 2N	117 49W
Pompano Beach	**170**	26 12N	80 6W
Ponca City	**168**	36 40N	97 5W
Ponce	**180**	18 1N	66 37W
Pond Inlet	**146**	72 40N	77 0W
Pondicherry	**90**	11 59N	79 50 E
Ponnyadaung	**93**	22 0N	94 10 F
Ponoka	**155**	52 42N	113 40W
Pont-Audemer	**39**	49 21N	0 30 E
Ponta Grossa	**191**	25 7S	50 10W
Ponta Pora	**188**	22 20S	55 35W
Pontchartrain, L.	**169**	30 12N	90 0W
Pontefract	**29**	53 42N	1 19W
Pontevedra	**50**	42 26N	8 40W
Pontiac	**167**	42 40N	83 20W
Pontianak	**111**	0 3S	109 15 E
Pontine Is. = Ponziane, Isole	**48**	40 55N	13 0 E
Pontoise	**39**	49 3N	2 5 E
Pontypool	**27**	51 42N	3 1W
Pontypridd	**27**	51 36N	3 21W
Ponziane, Isole	**48**	40 55N	13 0 E
Poochera	**118**	32 43S	134 51 E
Poole	**24**	50 42N	1 58W
Pooley I.	**154**	52 45N	128 15W
Poona = Pune	**91**	18 29N	73 57 E
Poopó, Lago de	**187**	18 30S	67 35W
Popayán	**184**	2 27N	76 36W
Poplar Bluff	**169**	36 45N	90 22W
Popocatépetl, Volcán	**177**	19 2N	98 38W
Porcher I.	**154**	53 50N	130 30W
Porcupine ⟶	**142**	66 35N	145 15W
Pori	**67**	61 29N	21 48 E
Porkkala	**67**	59 59N	24 26 E
Port Adelaide	**119**	34 46S	138 30 E
Port Alberni	**154**	49 40N	124 50W
Port Albert	**115**	38 42S	146 42 E
Port Alfred	**148**	48 18N	70 53W
Port Angeles	**171**	48 7N	123 30W
Port Antonio	**180**	18 10N	76 30W
Port Arthur	**168**	30 0N	94 0W
Port-au-Prince	**180**	18 40N	72 20W
Port Augusta	**118**	32 30S	137 50 E
Port Blair	**94**	11 40N	92 30 E
Port-Cartier	**148**	50 2N	66 50W
Port Chalmers	**123**	45 49S	170 30 E
Port Colborne	**151**	42 50N	79 10W
Port Coquitlam	**154**	49 15N	122 45W
Port Darwin	**192**	51 50S	59 0W
Port-de-Paix	**180**	19 50N	72 50W
Port Elgin	**150**	44 25N	81 25W
Port Elizabeth	**136**	33 58S	25 40 E
Port Erin	**28**	54 5N	4 45W
Port Etienne = Nouâdhibou	**126**	20 54N	17 0W
Port Fairy	**119**	38 22S	142 12 E
Port Glasgow	**30**	55 57N	4 40W
Port Harcourt	**131**	4 40N	7 10 E
Port Harrison = Inoucdjouac	**146**	58 25N	78 15W
Port Hawkesbury	**149**	45 36N	61 22W
Port Hope	**151**	43 56N	78 20W
Port Huron	**167**	43 0N	82 28W
Port Kembla	**117**	34 52S	150 49 E
Port Laoise	**35**	53 2N	7 20W
Port Lavaca	**158**	28 38N	96 38W
Port Lincoln	**119**	34 42S	135 52 E
Port Lyautey = Kenitra	**126**	34 15N	6 40W
Port Macquarie	**116**	31 25S	152 25 E
Port Morant	**180**	17 54N	76 19W
Port Moresby	**115**	9 24S	147 8 E
Port Nelson	**143**	57 3N	92 36W
Port Nolloth	**136**	29 17S	16 52 E
Port Nouveau-Québec	**146**	58 30N	65 59W
Port of Spain	**180**	10 40N	61 31W
Port Phillip B.	**117**	38 10S	144 50 E
Port Pirie	**118**	33 10S	138 1 E
Port Saïd = Bûr Saïd	**128**	31 16N	32 18 E
Port Simpson	**154**	54 30N	130 20W
Port Stanley	**150**	42 40N	81 10W
Port Sudan = Bûr Sûdân	**129**	19 32N	37 9 E
Port Talbot	**27**	51 35N	3 48W
Port Townsend	**171**	48 7N	122 50W
Portadown	**34**	54 27N	6 26W
Portage La Prairie	**153**	49 58N	98 18W
Portarlington	**35**	53 10N	7 10W
Porte, La	**167**	41 36N	86 43W
Porterville	**173**	36 5N	119 0W
Porthcawl	**27**	51 28N	3 42W
Porthmadog	**26**	52 55N	4 13W
Portile de Fier	**56**	44 42N	22 30 E
Portland, Australia	**119**	38 20S	141 35 E
Portland, Maine, U.S.A.	**148**	43 40N	70 15W
Portland, Oreg., U.S.A.	**171**	45 35N	122 40W
Portland, Bill of	**24**	50 31N	2 27W
Portland Prom.	**146**	58 40N	78 33W
Porto	**50**	41 8N	8 40W
Pôrto Alegre	**191**	30 5S	51 10W
Porto Empédocle	**48**	37 18N	13 30 E
Porto Mendes	**191**	24 30S	54 15W
Porto Novo	**131**	6 23N	2 42 E
Pôrto Seguro	**189**	16 26S	39 5W
Pôrto Velho	**187**	8 46S	63 54W
Portoferráio	**46**	42 50N	10 20 E
Portoscuso	**48**	39 12N	8 22 E
Portovlejo	**184**	1 7S	80 28W
Portpatrick	**30**	54 50N	5 7W
Portree	**32**	57 25N	6 11W
Portrush	**34**	55 13N	6 40W
Portsmouth, Domin.	**180**	15 34N	61 27W
Portsmouth, U.K.	**25**	50 48N	1 6W
Portsmouth, N.H., U.S.A.	**164**	43 5N	70 45W
Portsmouth, Ohio, U.S.A.	**167**	38 45N	83 0W
Portsmouth, Va., U.S.A.	**165**	36 50N	76 20W
Porttipahta	**67**	68 5N	26 40 E
Portugal ■	**50**	40 0N	7 0W
Portuguese-Guinea = Guinea-Bissau ■	**130**	12 0N	15 0W
Portuguese Timor ■ = Timor	**113**	9 0S	125 0 E
Portumna	**35**	53 5N	8 12W
Porvenir	**192**	53 10S	70 16W
Posadas	**191**	27 30S	55 50W
Poshan = Boshan	**98**	36 28N	117 49 E
Poste-de-la-Baleine	**140**	55 17N	77 45W
Potchefstroom	**137**	26 41S	27 7 E
Potenza	**49**	40 40N	15 50 E
Potomac ⟶	**165**	38 0N	76 23W
Potosí	**187**	19 38S	65 50W
Potsdam, Germany	**43**	52 23N	13 4 E
Potsdam, U.S.A.	**151**	44 40N	74 59W
Pottsville	**164**	40 39N	76 12W
Pouce Coupé	**155**	55 40N	120 10W
Poughkeepsie	**164**	41 40N	73 57W
Poulaphouca Res.	**35**	53 8N	6 30W
Póvoa de Varzim	**50**	41 25N	8 46W
Powell, L.	**163**	37 25N	110 45W
Powell River	**154**	49 50N	124 35W
Powys □	**26**	52 20N	3 20W
Poyang Hu	**99**	29 10N	116 10 E
Poyarkovo	**75**	49 36N	128 41 E
Poznań	**58**	52 25N	16 55 E
Prachuap Khiri Khan	**94**	11 49N	99 48 E
Prague = Praha	**58**	50 5N	14 22 E
Praha	**58**	50 5N	14 22 E
Prainha, Amazonas, Brazil	**187**	7 10S	60 30W
Prainha, Pará, Brazil	**185**	1 45S	53 30W
Prairie du Chien	**166**	43 1N	91 9W
Prato	**46**	43 53N	11 5 E
Pratt	**161**	37 40N	98 45W

Place				
Prepansko Jezero	52	40 55N	21	0 E
Preparis North Channel	94	15 12N	93	40 E
Preparis South Channel	94	14 36N	93	40 E
Prescott	160	34 35N	112	30W
Preservation Inlet	123	46 8S	166	35 E
Presidencia Roque Saenz Peña	190	26 45S	60	30W
Presidente Prudente	188	22 5S	51	25W
Presidio	161	29 30N	104	20W
Prespa, L. = Prepansko Jezero	52	40 55N	21	0 E
Presque Isle	148	46 40N	68	0W
Preston, Borders, U.K.	28	55 48N	2	18W
Preston, Lancs., U.K.	21	53 46N	2	42W
Prestonpans	31	55 58N	3	0W
Prestwick	31	55 30N	4	38W
Pretoria	137	25 44S	28	12 E
Préveza	55	38 57N	20	47 E
Prichard	169	30 47N	88	5W
Prilep	52	41 21N	21	37 E
Prince Albert	152	53 15N	105	50W
Prince Albert Pen.	145	72 30N	116	0W
Prince Albert Sd.	145	70 25N	115	0W
Prince Charles I.	146	67 47N	76	12W
Prince Edward I. □	148	46 20N	63	20W
Prince George	154	53 55N	122	50W
Prince of Wales I., Canada	145	73 0N	99	0W
Prince of Wales I., U.S.A.	143	55 30N	133	0W
Prince Patrick I.	12	77 0N	120	0W
Prince Rupert	154	54 20N	130	20W
Princess Royal I.	154	53 0N	128	40W
Princeton	155	49 27N	120	30W
Principe, I. de	131	1 37N	7	27 E
Principe da Beira	187	12 20S	64	30W
Pripet = Pripyat →	68	51 20N	30	9 E
Pripet Marshes = Polesye	17	52 0N	28	10 E
Pripyat →	68	51 20N	30	9 E
Pripyat Marshes = Polesye	17	52 0N	28	10 E
Priština	52	42 40N	21	13 E
Privolzhskaya Vozvyshennost	17	51 0N	46	0 E
Prizren	52	42 13N	20	45 E
Proddatur	90	14 45N	78	30 E
Progreso	177	21 17N	89	40W
Prokopyevsk	71	54 0N	86	45 E
Proserpine	121	20 21S	148	36 E
Provence	37	43 40N	5	46 E
Providence	164	41 50N	71	28W
Provo	163	40 16N	111	37W
Prudhoe Bay	142	70 20N	148	20W
Pruszków	58	52 9N	20	49 E
Prut →	57	46 3N	28	10 E
Przemyśl	58	49 50N	22	45 E
Przeworsk	58	50 6N	22	32 E
Pskov	68	57 50N	28	25 E
Pucallpa	186	8 25S	74	30W
Puebla	177	19 3N	98	12W
Puebla □	177	18 50N	98	0W
Pueblo	163	38 20N	104	40W
Puelches	190	38 5S	65	51W
Puente Alto	190	33 32S	70	35W
Puerto Armuelles	179	8 20N	82	51W
Puerto Ayacucho	184	5 40N	67	35W
Puerto Barrios	177	15 40N	88	32W
Puerto Cabello	184	10 28N	68	1W
Puerto Cabezas	179	14 0N	83	30W
Puerto Castilla	179	16 0N	86	0W
Puerto Cortes, C. Rica	179	8 55N	84	0W
Puerto Cortes, Hond.	177	15 51N	88	0W
Puerto Heath	187	12 34S	68	39W
Puerto La Cruz	185	10 13N	64	38W
Puerto Libertad	174	29 55N	112	41W
Puerto Lobos	192	42 0S	65	3W
Puerto Maldonado	187	12 30S	69	10W
Puerto Montt	190	41 28S	73	0W
Puerto Padre	178	21 13N	76	35W
Puerto Pinasco	191	22 36S	57	50W
Puerto Plata	180	19 48N	70	45W
Puerto Quepos	179	9 29N	84	6W
Puerto Rico ■	180	18 15N	66	45W
Puerto Vallarta	175	20 37N	105	15W
Puertollano	50	38 43N	4	7W
Puget Sd.	171	47 15N	122	30W
Púglia □	49	41 0N	16	30 E
Pula	52	44 54N	13	57 E
Pulaski, Tenn., U.S.A.	169	35 10N	87	0W
Pulaski, Va., U.S.A.	165	37 4N	80	49W
Pulicat, L.	90	13 40N	80	15 E
Pullman	171	46 49N	117	10W
Punakha	92	27 42N	89	52 E
Punata	187	17 32S	65	50W
Pune	91	18 29N	73	57 E
Punjab □, India	89	31 0N	76	0 E
Punjab □, Pakistan	89	30 0N	72	0 E
Puno	187	15 55S	70	3W
Punta Alta	190	38 53S	62	4W
Punta Arenas	192	53 10S	71	0W
Punta Gorda	177	16 10N	88	45W
Puntabie	118	32 12S	134	13 E
Puntarenas	179	10 0N	84	50W
Punto Fijo	184	11 50N	70	13W
Puquio	186	14 45S	74	10W
Pur →	69	67 31N	77	55 E
Purbeck, Isle of	24	50 40N	2	5W
Purmerend	40	52 30N	4	58 E
Purnia	92	25 45N	87	31 E
Pursat	95	12 34N	103	50 E
Purus →	185	3 42S	61	28W
Pusan	98	35 5N	129	0 E
Putao	93	27 28N	97	30 E
Putorana, Gory	72	69 0N	95	0 E
Putumayo →	184	3 7S	67	58W
Puy, Le	37	45 2N	3	53 E
Puy-de-Dôme	37	45 46N	2	57 E
Puyallup	171	47 10N	122	22W
Pwllheli	26	52 54N	4	26W
Pyasina →	72	73 30N	87	0 E
Pyatigorsk	70	44 2N	43	6 E
Pyinmana	93	19 45N	96	12 E
Pyŏngyang	98	39 0N	125	30 E
Pyramid L.	172	40 0N	119	30W
Pyrénées	124	42 45N	0	18 E
Qā'emshahr	86	36 30N	52	55 E
Qahremänshahr = Bākhtarān	84	34 23N	47	0 E
Qaidam Pendi	100	37 0N	95	0 E
Qal'at al Akhḍar	82	28 0N	37	10 E
Qamar, Ghubbat al	83	16 20N	52	30 E
Qamdo	101	31 15N	97	6 E
Qandahār	87	31 32N	65	30 E
Qaṣr-e Qand	85	26 15N	60	45 E
Qatar ■	85	25 30N	51	15 E
Qāyen	86	33 40N	59	10 E
Qazvin	81	36 15N	50	0 E
Qena	128	26 10N	32	43 E
Qeshm	85	26 55N	56	10 E
Qilian Shan	100	38 30N	96	0 E
Qingdao	98	36 5N	120	20 E
Qinghai □	101	36 0N	98	0 E
Qinghai Hu	100	36 40N	100	10 E
Qinhuangdao	98	39 56N	119	30 E
Qiqihar	98	47 26N	124	0 E
Qom	86	34 40N	51	0 E
Qomsheh	85	32 0N	51	55 E
Qondūz □	87	36 50N	68	50 E
Qu Xian	99	30 48N	106	58 E
Quang Ngai	95	15 13N	108	58 E
Quantock Hills	27	51 8N	3	10W
Quanzhou	99	24 55N	118	34 E
Quatsino	154	50 30N	127	40W
Queanbeyan	117	35 17S	149	14 E
Québec	148	46 52N	71	13W
Québec □	140	50 0N	70	0W
Queen Alexandra Ra.	15	85 0S	170	0 E
Queen Charlotte	154	53 15N	132	2W
Queen Charlotte Is.	154	53 20N	132	10W
Queen Charlotte Str.	154	51 0N	128	0W
Queen Elizabeth Is.	138	76 0N	95	0W
Queen Mary Land	15	70 0S	95	0 E
Queen Maud G.	145	68 15N	102	30W
Queen Maud Mts.	15	86 0S	160	0W

Queenscliff . . . . **117** 38 16S 144 39 E
Queensland □ . . . . **115** 22 0S 142 0 E
Queenstown, Australia . . . . . . **119** 42 4S 145 35 E
Queenstown, N.Z. . . . . **123** 45 1S 168 40 E
Quelimane . . . . **137** 17 53S 36 58 E
Quelpart = Cheju Do . . . . **99** 33 29N 126 34 E
Querétaro **177** 20 36N 100 23W
Querétaro □ **177** 21 0N 99 55W
Quesnel **154** 53 0N 122 30W
Quetta . . . . **88** 30 15N 66 55 E
Quezaltenango **177** 14 50N 91 30W
Quezon City . . . . **112** 14 38N 121 0 E
Qui Nhon . . . . **95** 13 40N 109 13 E
Quibdo **184** 5 42N 76 40W
Quillabamba **186** 12 50S 72 50W
Quilon . . . . **90** 8 50N 76 38 E
Quilpie . . . . **116** 26 35S 144 11 E
Quimper **36** 48 0N 4 9W
Quincy **172** 39 56N 121 0W
Quincy, Calif., U.S.A. **170** 30 34N 84 34W
Quincy, Fla., U.S.A. **166** 39 55N 91 20W
Quincy, Ill., U.S.A. **164** 42 14N 71 0W
Quincy, Mass., U.S.A. **177** 19 40N 88 30W
Quintana Roo □ . . . . **116** 31 28S 150 40 E
Quirindi **170** 30 49N 83 35W
Quitman **184** 0 15S 78 35W
Quito **189** 4 55S 39 0W
Quixadá . . . . **118** 32 25S 138 0 E
Quorn . . . . **128** 26 7N 34 16 E
Quseir . . . .

Raahe . . . . **67** 64 40N 24 28 E
Raasay **32** 57 25N 6 4W
Rabat **126** 34 2N 6 48W
Rabaul . . . . **115** 4 24S 152 18 E
Rābigh . . . . **82** 22 50N 39 5 E
Race, C. **149** 46 40N 53 5W
Rach Gia . . . . **95** 10 5N 105 5 E
Racibórz . . . . **58** 50 7N 18 18 E
Racine **167** 42 41N 87 51W
Radium Hot Springs **155** 50 35N 116 2W
Radnor Forest **26** 52 17N 3 10W
Radom . . . . **58** 51 23N 21 12 E
Radomir . . . . **53** 42 37N 23 4 E
Radstock **27** 51 17N 2 25W
Radville **152** 49 30N 104 15W
Rae **145** 62 50N 116 3W
Rae Bareli . . . . **92** 26 18N 81 20 E
Raetihi . . . . **122** 39 25S 175 17 E
Rafaela **190** 31 10S 61 30W
Rafḥā . . . . **82** 29 35N 43 35 E
Rafsanjān . . . . **85** 30 30N 56 5 E
Ragama . . . . **90** 7 0N 79 50 E
Raglan . . . . **122** 37 55S 174 55 E
Ragusa . . . . **49** 36 56N 14 42 E
Rahaeng = Tak . . . . **94** 16 52N 99 8 E
Raichur . . . . **91** 16 10N 77 20 E
Rainier, Mt. **171** 46 50N 121 50W
Rainy L. **153** 48 42N 93 10W
Rainy River **153** 48 43N 94 29W
Raipur . . . . **92** 21 17N 81 45 E
Rajahmundry . . . . **92** 17 1N 81 48 E
Rajapalaiyam . . . . **90** 9 25N 77 35 E
Rajasthan □ . . . . **91** 26 45N 73 30 E
Rajasthan Canal . . . . **89** 28 0N 72 0 E
Rajkot . . . . **91** 22 15N 70 56 E
Rajshahi □ . . . . **92** 25 0N 89 0 E
Raleigh **165** 35 47N 78 39W
Raleigh B. **165** 34 50N 76 15W
Rambouillet . . . . **39** 48 40N 1 48 E
Rampur . . . . **89** 28 50N 79 5 E
Ramsey **28** 54 20N 4 21W
Rancagua **190** 34 10S 70 50W
Ranchi . . . . **92** 23 19N 85 27 E
Rangiora . . . . **123** 43 19S 172 36 E
Rangoon . . . . **93** 16 45N 96 20 E
Rangpur . . . . **92** 25 42N 89 22 E
Raniwara . . . . **91** 24 50N 72 10 E
Rankin Inlet **145** 62 30N 93 0W
Rankins Springs . . . . **117** 33 49S 146 14 E

Rannoch, L. **33** 56 41N 4 20W
Rannoch Moor **30** 56 38N 4 48W
Rapid City **163** 44 0N 103 0W
Ras Dashen . . . . **132** 13 8N 38 26 E
Rasa, Punta **192** 40 50S 62 15W
Rasht . . . . **81** 37 20N 49 40 E
Rat Is. . . . . **142** 51 50N 178 15 E
Ratangarh . . . . **89** 28 5N 74 35 E
Rath Luirc **35** 52 21N 8 40W
Rathlin I. **34** 55 18N 6 14W
Ratibor = Racibórz . . . . **58** 50 7N 18 18 E
Ratlam . . . . **91** 23 20N 75 0 E
Ratnagiri . . . . **91** 16 57N 73 18 E
Rattray Hd. **33** 57 38N 1 50W
Raub . . . . **96** 3 47N 101 52 E
Raukumara Ra. . . . . **122** 38 5S 177 55 E
Ravenna . . . . **47** 44 28N 12 15 E
Ravenshoe . . . . **121** 17 37S 145 29 E
Ravensthorpe . . . . **120** 33 35S 120 2 E
Rawalpindi . . . . **89** 33 38N 73 8 E
Rawlins **163** 41 50N 107 20W
Ray, C. **149** 47 33N 59 15W
Raymond **155** 49 30N 112 35W
Hazgrad . . . . **53** 43 33N 26 34 E
Ré, Ile de **36** 46 12N 1 30W
Reading, U.K. **25** 51 27N 0 57W
Reading, U.S.A. **164** 40 20N 75 53W
Reay Forest **32** 58 20N 4 55W
Rebun-Tō . . . . **103** 45 23N 141 2 E
Recife **189** 8 0S 35 0W
Reconquista **190** 29 10S 59 45W
Recreo **190** 29 25S 65 10W
Red → **168** 31 0N 91 40W
Red Bluff **172** 40 11N 122 11W
Red Cliffs . . . . **119** 34 19S 142 11 E
Red Deer **155** 52 20N 113 50W
Red Lake **153** 51 3N 93 49W
Red Oak **166** 41 0N 95 10W
Red Sea . . . . **128** 25 0N 36 0 E
Red Tower Pass = Turnu
    Roşu Pasul . . . . **57** 45 33N 24 17 E
Red Wing **166** 44 32N 92 35W
Redcar **29** 54 37N 1 4W
Redcliff **152** 50 10N 110 50W
Redcliffe . . . . **116** 27 12S 153 0 E
Redding **172** 40 30N 122 25W
Redditch **24** 52 18N 1 57W
Redlands **173** 34 0N 117 11W
Redruth **27** 50 14N 5 14W
Redwater **155** 53 55N 113 6W
Redwood City **172** 37 30N 122 15W
Ree, L. **34** 53 35N 8 0W
Reedley **173** 36 36N 119 27W
Regensburg . . . . **43** 49 1N 12 7 E
Réggio di Calábria . . . . **49** 38 7N 15 38 E
Réggio nell' Emília . . . . **46** 44 42N 10 38 E
Regina **152** 50 27N 104 35W
Rehovot . . . . **80** 31 54N 34 48 E
Reichenbach . . . . **43** 50 36N 12 19 E
Reidsville **165** 36 21N 79 40W
Reims . . . . **39** 49 15N 4 0 E
Reina Adelaida, Arch. **192** 52 20S 74 0W
Reindeer L. **143** 57 15N 102 15W
Reliance **145** 63 0N 109 20W
Remanso **189** 9 41S 42 4W
Remarkable, Mt. . . . . **118** 32 48S 138 10 E
Remscheid . . . . **42** 51 11N 7 12 E
Rendsburg . . . . **42** 54 18N 9 41 E
Renfrew, Canada **151** 45 30N 76 40W
Renfrew, U.K. **31** 55 52N 4 24W
Renkum . . . . **41** 51 58N 5 43 E
Renmark . . . . **119** 34 11S 140 43 E
Rennes **36** 48 7N 1 41W
Reno **172** 39 30N 119 50W
Republic **150** 46 25N 87 59W
Republican → **163** 39 3N 96 48W
Repulse Bay **146** 66 30N 86 30W
Requena **186** 5 5S 73 52W
Resht = Rasht . . . . **81** 37 20N 49 40 E
Resistencia **190** 27 30S 59 0W
Resolution I., Canada **146** 61 30N 65 0W

Resolution I., N.Z.	123	45 40S	166 40 E
Retalhuleu	177	14 33N	91 46W
Réthímnon	55	35 18N	24 30 E
Réunion	9	22 0S	56 0 E
Reval = Tallinn	68	59 22N	24 48 E
Revelstoke	155	51 0N	118 10W
Revilla Gigedo, Is.	139	18 40N	112 0W
Rewa	92	24 33N	81 25 E
Rewari	89	28 15N	76 40 E
Rexburg	163	43 55N	111 50W
Rey Malabo	131	3 45N	8 50 E
Reykjavík	64	64 10N	21 57 E
Reynosa	176	26 5N	98 18W
Rhayader	26	52 19N	3 30W
Rhein →	42	51 52N	6 20 E
Rheinland-Pfalz □	42	50 0N	7 0 E
Rhin = Rhein →	42	51 52N	6 20 E
Rhine = Rhein →	42	51 52N	6 20 E
Rhineland-Palatinate □ = Rheinland-Pfalz □	42	50 0N	7 0 E
Rhinelander	150	45 38N	89 29W
Rhode Island □	164	41 38N	71 37W
Rhodes = Ródhos	55	36 15N	28 10 E
Rhodesia = Zimbabwe ■	137	20 0S	30 0 E
Rhodope Mts. = Rhodopi Planina	53	41 40N	24 20 E
Rhodopi Planina	53	41 40N	24 20 E
Rhön	42	50 24N	9 58 E
Rhondda	27	51 39N	3 30W
Rhône →	37	43 28N	4 42 E
Rhum	32	57 0N	6 20W
Rhyl	26	53 19N	3 29W
Rhymney	27	51 45N	3 17W
Riachão	188	7 20S	46 37W
Riau, Kepulauan	111	0 30N	104 20 E
Ribatejo □	50	39 15N	8 30W
Ribble →	28	54 13N	2 20W
Ribeirão Prêto	188	21 10S	47 50W
Riberalta	187	11 0S	66 0W
Riccarton	123	43 32S	172 37 E
Richland	171	46 15N	119 15W
Richmond, Australia	116	20 43S	143 8 E
Richmond, N.Z.	123	41 20S	173 12 E
Richmond, N. Yorks., U.K.	28	54 24N	1 43W
Richmond, Surrey, U.K.	25	51 28N	0 18W
Richmond, Calif., U.S.A.	172	37 58N	122 21W
Richmond, Ind., U.S.A.	167	39 50N	84 50W
Richmond, Ky., U.S.A.	165	37 40N	84 20W
Richmond, Va., U.S.A.	165	37 33N	77 27W
Richwood	165	38 17N	80 32W
Ridgeway	164	42 56S	147 16 E
Riga	68	56 53N	24 8 E
Rigestān □	87	30 15N	65 0 E
Rigolet	147	54 10N	58 23W
Rijeka	52	45 20N	14 21 E
Rijssen	41	52 19N	6 30 E
Rijswijk	40	52 4N	4 22 E
Rímini	47	44 3N	12 33 E
Rímnicu Vîlcea	57	45 9N	24 21 E
Rimouski	148	48 27N	68 30W
Rinía	55	37 23N	25 13 E
Rio Branco	187	9 58S	67 49W
Rio Claro	180	10 20N	61 25W
Rio Cuarto	190	33 10S	64 25W
Rio de Janeiro	188	23 0S	43 12W
Rio de Janeiro □	188	22 50S	43 0W
Rio Gallegos	192	51 35S	69 15W
Rio Grande	191	32 0S	52 20W
Rio Grande →	161	25 57N	97 9W
Rio Grande do Norte □	189	5 40S	36 0W
Rio Grande do Sul □	191	30 0S	53 0W
Rio Mulatos	187	19 40S	66 50W
Rio Negro	191	26 0S	50 0W
Rio Verde	188	17 50S	51 0W
Riobamba	184	1 50S	78 45W
Riohacha	184	11 33N	72 55W
Rioja, La	190	29 20S	67 0W
Rioja, La □	50	42 20N	2 20W
Riosucio	184	7 27N	77 7W
Ripon	28	54 8N	1 31W
Rishiri-Tō	103	45 11N	141 15 E
Ritchies Archipelago	94	12 5N	94 0 E
Rivas	179	11 30N	85 50W
Riverhead	164	40 53N	72 40W
Riverside	173	34 0N	117 22W
Riverton	153	51 1N	97 0W
Riviera di Levante	46	44 23N	9 15 E
Riviera di Ponente	46	43 50N	7 58 E
Rivière-du-Loup	148	47 50N	69 30W
Riyadh = Ar Riyāḍ	83	24 41N	46 42 E
Roanne	37	46 3N	4 4 E
Roanoke, Ala., U.S.A.	169	33 9N	85 23W
Roanoke, Va., U.S.A.	165	37 19N	79 55W
Roanoke →	165	35 56N	76 43W
Roanoke Rapids	165	36 28N	77 42W
Robinvale	119	34 40S	142 45 E
Roblin	152	51 14N	101 21W
Roboré	187	18 10S	59 45W
Robson, Mt.	155	53 10N	119 10W
Roca, C. da	50	38 40N	9 31W
Rocha	191	34 30S	54 25W
Rochdale	28	53 36N	2 10W
Roche-sur-Yon, La	36	46 40N	1 25W
Rochefort	36	45 56N	0 57W
Rochelle, La	36	46 10N	1 9W
Rochester, Minn., U.S.A.	166	44 1N	92 28W
Rochester, N.H., U.S.A.	164	43 19N	70 57W
Rochester, N.Y., U.S.A.	164	43 10N	77 40W
Rock Hill	165	34 55N	81 2W
Rock Island	166	41 30N	90 35W
Rock Sprs.	163	41 40N	109 10W
Rockall	16	57 37N	13 42W
Rockford	166	42 20N	89 0W
Rockglen	152	49 11N	105 57W
Rockhampton	119	23 22S	150 32 E
Rockingham	120	32 15S	115 38 E
Rockland	148	44 6N	69 6W
Rocky Mount	165	35 55N	77 48W
Rocky Mountain House	155	52 22N	114 55W
Rocky Mts.	138	55 0N	121 0W
Ródhos	55	36 15N	28 10 E
Roebourne	114	20 44S	117 9 E
Roermond	41	51 12N	6 0 E
Roes Welcome Sd.	146	65 0N	87 0W
Rogaland fylke □	60	59 12N	6 20 E
Rogers	168	36 20N	94 5W
Rohri	88	27 45N	68 51 E
Rohtak	89	28 55N	76 43 E
Rojo, C.	177	21 33N	97 20W
Rolla	166	37 56N	91 42W
Roma, Australia	116	26 32S	148 49 E
Roma, Italy	46	41 54N	12 30 E
Romaine →	141	50 18N	63 47W
Roman	57	46 57N	26 55 E
Romana, La	180	18 27N	68 57W
Romania ■	57	46 0N	25 0 E
Romans	37	45 3N	5 3 E
Romanzof, C.	142	62 0N	165 50W
Rome = Roma	46	41 54N	12 30 E
Rome, Ga., U.S.A.	169	34 20N	85 0W
Rome, N.Y., U.S.A.	164	43 14N	75 29W
Romilly	39	48 31N	3 44 E
Romney Marsh	25	51 0N	1 0 E
Rona	32	57 33N	6 0W
Rondônia □	187	11 0S	63 0W
Rong, Koh	95	10 45N	103 15 E
Ronge, L. la	152	55 6N	105 17W
Roosendaal	40	51 32N	4 29 E
Roraima □	185	2 0N	61 30W
Roraima, Mt.	185	5 10N	60 40W
Rosario, Argentina	190	33 0S	60 40W
Rosario, Brazil	188	3 0S	44 15W
Rosario, Mexico	175	22 58N	105 53W
Rosario, Paraguay	191	24 30S	57 35W
Rosário do Sul	191	30 15S	54 55W
Roscommon	34	53 38N	8 11W
Roscommon □	34	53 40N	8 15W
Roscrea	35	52 58N	7 50W
Roseau	180	15 20N	61 24W
Roseburg	171	43 10N	123 20W
Rosenberg	168	29 30N	95 48W
Rosendaël	38	51 3N	2 24 E

Rosetown	**152**	51	35N	107	59W
Roseville	**172**	38	46N	121	17W
Rosewood	**116**	27	38S	152	36 E
Roskilde	**61**	55	38N	12	3 E
Ross on Wye	**24**	51	55N	2	34W
Ross Sea	**15**	74	0S	178	0 E
Rossan Pt.	**34**	54	42N	8	47W
Rossland	**155**	49	6N	117	50W
Rosslare	**35**	52	17N	6	23W
Røssvatnet	**65**	65	45N	14	5 E
Rosthern	**152**	52	40N	106	20W
Rostock	**43**	54	4N	12	9 E
Rostov	**68**	47	15N	39	45 E
Roswell	**161**	33	26N	104	32W
Rosyth	**31**	56	2N	3	26W
Rother →	**25**	50	59N	0	40 E
Rotherham	**29**	53	26N	1	21W
Rothesay	**30**	55	50N	5	3W
Roto	**117**	33	0S	145	30 E
Rotorua	**122**	38	9S	176	16 E
Rotorua, L.	**122**	38	5S	176	18 E
Rotterdam	**40**	51	55N	4	30 E
Rotuma	**122**	12	25S	177	5 E
Roubaix	**37**	50	40N	3	10 E
Rouen	**38**	49	27N	1	4 E
Round Mt.	**116**	30	26S	152	16 E
Roussillon	**37**	42	30N	2	35 E
Rouyn	**151**	48	20N	79	0W
Rovaniemi	**67**	66	29N	25	41 E
Rovno	**68**	50	40N	26	10 E
Ruahine Ra.	**122**	39	55S	176	2 E
Ruapehu	**122**	39	17S	175	35 E
Rub' al Khali	**83**	18	0N	48	0 E
Rubh a' Mhail	**30**	55	55N	6	10W
Rubio	**184**	7	43N	72	22W
Rubtsovsk	**71**	51	30N	81	10 E
Rudnyy	**71**	52	57N	63	7 E
Rudolf, Ostrov	**69**	81	45N	58	30 E
Rufiji →	**135**	7	50S	39	15 E
Rufino	**190**	34	20S	62	50W
Rugby	**25**	52	23N	1	16W
Rügen	**43**	54	22N	13	25 E
Ruhr →	**42**	51	25N	6	44 E
Rukwa L.	**135**	8	0S	32	20 E
Rumania = Romania ■	**57**	46	0N	25	0 E
Rumford	**148**	44	30N	70	30W
Rumoi	**103**	43	56N	141	39W
Runcorn	**28**	53	20N	2	44W
Rupat	**111**	1	45N	101	40 E
Rupert →	**140**	51	29N	78	45W
Rupert House = Fort Rupert ..	**140**	51	30N	78	40W
Ruschuk = Ruse	**53**	43	48N	25	59 E
Ruse	**53**	43	48N	25	59 E
Russell	**152**	50	50N	101	20W
Russellville, Ala., U.S.A.	**169**	34	30N	87	44W
Russellville, Ark., U.S.A.	**168**	35	15N	93	8W
Ruston	**168**	32	30N	92	58W
Rutherglen	**31**	55	50N	4	11W
Rutland I.	**94**	11	25N	92	40 E
Ruwenzori	**132**	0	30N	29	55 E
Rwanda ■	**135**	2	0S	30	0 E
Ryan, L.	**30**	55	0N	5	2W
Ryazan	**68**	54	40N	39	40 E
Rybache	**71**	46	40N	81	20 E
Rybinsk = Andropov	**68**	58	5N	38	50 E
Ryde	**25**	50	44N	1	9W
Rye	**25**	50	57N	0	46 E
Rylstone	**117**	32	46S	149	58 E
Ryōhaku-Sanchi	**106**	36	9N	136	49 E
Ryūgasaki	**107**	35	54N	140	11 E
Rzeszów	**58**	50	5N	21	58 E
Sa Dec	**95**	10	20N	105	46 E
Saar →	**42**	49	41N	6	32 E
Saarbrücken	**42**	49	15N	6	58 E
Saaremaa	**68**	58	30N	22	30 E
Saarland □	**42**	49	15N	7	0 E
Sabadell	**51**	41	28N	2	7 E
Sabae	**106**	35	57N	136	11 E
Sabah □	**112**	6	0N	117	0 E
Sábana de la Mar	**180**	19	7N	69	24W
Sabhah	**127**	27	9N	14	29 E
Sabi →	**137**	18	50S	31	40 E
Sabinas	**174**	27	51N	101	7W
Sabinas Hidalgo, R. →	**176**	26	50N	99	35W
Sabine →	**158**	30	0N	93	35W
Sable, C., Canada	**148**	43	29N	65	38W
Sable, C., U.S.A.	**159**	25	13N	81	0W
Sable I.	**149**	44	0N	60	0W
Sabrina Coast	**15**	68	0S	120	0 E
Sabzevār	**86**	36	15N	57	40 E
Saco	**148**	43	30N	70	27W
Sacramento	**172**	38	33N	121	30 E
Sacramento →	**172**	38	3N	121	56W
Sacramento Mts.	**161**	32	30N	105	30W
Sado, Shima	**103**	38	15N	138	30 E
Safed Koh	**87**	34	0N	70	0 E
Saffron Walden	**25**	52	2N	0	15 E
Safi	**126**	32	18N	9	20W
Saga	**108**	33	15N	130	16 E
Sagami-Nada	**107**	34	58N	139	30 E
Sagami-Wan	**107**	35	15N	139	25 E
Sagamihara	**107**	35	33N	139	25 E
Sagar	**91**	14	14N	75	6 E
Sagara	**107**	34	41N	138	12 E
Saginaw	**167**	43	26N	83	55W
Saginaw B.	**167**	43	50N	83	40W
Saglouc	**146**	62	14N	75	38W
Sagres	**50**	37	0N	8	58W
Sagua la Grande	**178**	22	50N	80	10W
Saguenay →	**148**	48	22N	71	0W
Sahara	**126**	23	0N	5	0 E
Saharanpur	**89**	29	58N	77	33 E
Saharien, Atlas	**127**	33	30N	1	0 E
Sahiwal	**89**	30	45N	73	8 E
Sahuaripa	**174**	29	3N	109	14W
Saigō	**109**	36	12N	133	20 E
Saigon = Thanh Pho Ho Chi Minh	**95**	10	58N	106	40 E
Saijō, Ehime, Japan	**109**	33	55N	133	11 E
Saijō, Hiroshima, Japan	**109**	34	25N	132	45 E
Saikhoa Ghat	**93**	27	50N	95	40 E
Saiki	**108**	32	58N	131	51 E
Saimaa	**67**	61	15N	28	15 E
Şa'in Dezh	**81**	36	40N	46	25 E
St. Abb's Head	**31**	55	55N	2	10W
St. Albans, U.K.	**25**	51	44N	0	19W
St. Albans, U.S.A.	**151**	44	49N	73	7W
St. Alban's Head	**24**	50	34N	2	3W
St. Albert	**155**	53	37N	113	32W
St. Andrews	**31**	56	20N	2	48W
St. Arnaud	**119**	36	40S	143	16 E
St. Asaph	**26**	53	15N	3	27W
St-Augustin-Saguenay	**141**	51	13N	58	38W
St. Augustine	**170**	29	52N	81	20W
St. Austell	**27**	50	20N	4	48W
St. Bee's Hd.	**28**	54	30N	3	38 E
St. Boniface	**153**	49	53N	97	5W
St. Bride's B.	**26**	51	48N	5	15W
St-Brieuc	**36**	48	30N	2	46W
St. Catharines	**151**	43	10N	79	15W
St. Charles	**166**	38	46N	90	30W
St. Christopher-Nevis ■	**180**	17	20N	62	40W
St. Cloud	**156**	45	30N	94	11W
St. Croix	**180**	17	45N	64	45W
St. David's	**26**	51	54N	5	16W
St. David's Head	**26**	51	55N	5	16W
St-Denis	**39**	48	56N	2	22 E
St-Dizier	**37**	48	40N	5	0 E
St. Elias, Mt.	**144**	60	14N	140	50W
St. Elias Mts.	**144**	60	33N	139	28W
St-Étienne	**37**	45	27N	4	22 E
St-Félicien	**151**	48	40N	72	25W
St. Gallen	**44**	47	25N	9	20 E
St. George, Australia	**116**	28	1S	148	30 E
St. George, Bermuda	**180**	32	24N	64	42W
St. Georges, Fr. Gui.	**185**	4	0N	52	0W
St. Georges, Grenada	**180**	12	5N	61	43W
St. George's Channel	**20**	52	0N	6	0W

Name	Page	Lat °	′	N/S	Long °	′	E/W
St. Gotthard P. = San Gottardo, Paso del	**44**	46	33N		8	33 E
St. Helena	**125**	15	55S		5	44W
St. Helena B.	**136**	32	40S		18	10 E
St. Helens, Australia	**119**	41	20S		148	15 E
St. Helens, U.K.	**28**	53	28N		2	44W
St. Helens, U.S.A.	**171**	45	55N		122	50W
St. Helier	**36**	49	11N		2	6W
St-Hyacinthe	**151**	45	40N		72	58W
St. Ives, Cambs., U.K.	**25**	52	20N		0	5W
St. Ives, Cornwall, U.K.	**27**	50	13N		5	29W
St-Jean	**151**	45	20N		73	20W
St-Jérôme	**151**	45	47N		74	0W
St. John	**148**	45	20N		66	8W
St. John's	**149**	47	35N		52	40W
St. John's ~→	**170**	30	20N		81	30W
St. Johnsbury	**148**	44	25N		72	1W
St. Joseph, Mich., U.S.A.	**167**	42	5N		86	30W
St. Joseph, Mo., U.S.A.	**166**	39	46N		94	50W
St. Kilda, N.Z.	**123**	45	53S		170	31 E
St. Kilda, U.K.	**22**	57	9N		8	34W
St. Lawrence	**149**	46	54N		55	23W
St. Lawrence ~→	**148**	49	30N		66	0W
St. Lawrence, Gulf of	**149**	48	25N		62	0W
St. Lawrence I.	**142**	63	0N		170	0W
St. Leonard	**148**	47	12N		67	58W
St-Louis	**130**	16	8N		16	27W
St. Louis	**166**	38	40N		90	12W
St. Lucia ■	**180**	14	0N		60	50W
St. Maarten	**180**	18	0N		63	5W
St-Malo	**36**	48	39N		2	1W
St-Marc	**180**	19	10N		72	41W
St-Martin, I.	**180**	18	0N		63	0W
St. Mary Pk.	**118**	31	32S		138	34 E
St. Marys	**164**	41	27N		78	33W
St. Matthews, I. = Zadetkyi Kyun	**94**	10	0N		98	25 E
St. Michael's Mt.	**27**	50	7N		5	30W
St. Moritz	**44**	46	30N		9	51 E
St-Nazaire	**36**	47	17N		2	12W
St. Neots	**25**	52	14N		0	16W
St-Omer	**38**	50	45N		2	15 E
St. Pascal	**148**	47	32N		69	48W
St. Paul	**166**	44	54N		93	5W
St. Paul, I.	**149**	47	12N		60	9W
St. Petersburg	**170**	27	45N		82	40W
St-Pierre et Miquelon □	**149**	46	55N		56	10W
St-Quentin	**38**	49	50N		3	16 E
St-Raphaël	**37**	43	25N		6	46 E
St-Servan-sur-Mer	**36**	48	38N		2	0W
St. Thomas, Canada	**151**	42	45N		81	10W
St. Thomas, W. Indies	**180**	18	21N		64	55W
St-Tropez	**37**	43	17N		6	38 E
St. Vincent and the Grenadines ■	**180**	13	0N		61	10W
Ste-Adresse	**38**	49	31N		0	5 E
Ste Anne de Beaupré	**148**	47	2N		70	58W
Ste Marie	**180**	14	48N		61	1W
Ste-Rose	**180**	16	20N		61	45W
Ste. Rose du lac	**153**	51	4N		99	30W
Saintes	**36**	45	45N		0	37W
Saintonge	**36**	45	40N		0	50W
Saito	**108**	32	3N		131	24 E
Sajama	**187**	18	7S		69	0W
Sakai	**106**	34	30N		135	30 E
Sakaide	**109**	34	15N		133	50 E
Sakaiminato	**109**	35	38N		133	11 E
Sakakawea, L.	**163**	47	30N		102	0W
Sakata	**103**	38	55N		139	50 E
Sakhalin	**79**	51	0N		143	0 E
Sakhalinskiy Zaliv	**75**	54	0N		141	0 E
Saku	**107**	36	17N		138	31 E
Sakura	**107**	35	43N		140	14 E
Sakurai	**106**	34	30N		135	51 E
Salaberry-de-Valleyfield	**151**	45	15N		74	8W
Salado ~→	**190**	31	40S		60	41W
Salado, R. ~→	**176**	26	52N		99	19W
Salamanca, Spain	**50**	40	58N		5	39W
Salamanca, U.S.A.	**164**	42	10N		78	42W
Salamis	**55**	37	56N		23	30 E
Salcombe	**27**	50	14N		3	47W
Sale	**117**	38	6S		147	6 E
Salem, India	**90**	11	40N		78	11 E
Salem, Mass., U.S.A.	**164**	42	29N		70	53W
Salem, Oreg., U.S.A.	**171**	45	0N		123	0W
Salem, Va., U.S.A.	**165**	37	19N		80	8W
Salerno	**49**	40	40N		14	44 E
Salford	**28**	53	30N		2	17W
Salida	**163**	38	35N		106	0W
Salina, Italy	**49**	38	35N		14	50 E
Salina, U.S.A.	**161**	38	50N		97	40W
Salina Cruz	**177**	16	10N		95	12W
Salinas, Ecuador	**184**	2	10S		80	58W
Salinas, U.S.A.	**173**	36	40N		121	41W
Salinas ~→	**173**	36	45N		121	48W
Salinas Grandes	**190**	30	0S		65	0W
Salisbury = Harare	**137**	17	43S		31	2 E
Salisbury, U.K.	**24**	51	4N		1	48W
Salisbury, Md., U.S.A.	**165**	38	20N		75	38W
Salisbury, N.C., U.S.A.	**165**	35	20N		80	29W
Salisbury Plain	**24**	51	13N		1	50W
Salle, La	**166**	41	20N		89	6W
Salmon	**162**	45	12N		113	56W
Salmon ~→	**171**	45	51N		116	46W
Salmon Arm	**155**	50	40N		119	15W
Salmon River Mts.	**162**	45	0N		114	30W
Salon-de-Provence	**37**	43	39N		5	6 E
Salonica = Thessaloníki	**54**	40	38N		22	58 E
Salop = Shropshire □	**24**	52	36N		2	45W
Salt Fork ~→	**161**	36	37N		97	7W
Salt Lake City	**163**	40	45N		111	58W
Salta	**190**	24	57S		65	25W
Saltcoats	**30**	55	38N		4	47W
Saltillo	**174**	25	25N		101	0W
Salto	**191**	31	27S		57	50W
Salton Sea	**173**	33	20N		115	50W
Salûm	**128**	31	31N		25	7 E
Salvador	**189**	13	0S		38	30W
Salween ~→	**93**	16	31N		97	37 E
Salzburg	**45**	47	48N		13	2 E
Salzburg □	**45**	47	15N		13	0 E
Salzgitter	**43**	52	13N		10	22 E
Sam Neua	**95**	20	29N		104	0 E
Sama	**69**	60	12N		60	22 E
Samangán □	**87**	36	15N		68	3 E
Samar	**112**	12	0N		125	0 E
Samarkand	**70**	39	40N		66	55 E
Sāmarrā	**81**	34	12N		43	52 E
Sambalpur	**92**	21	28N		84	4 E
Sambhal	**89**	28	35N		78	37 E
Sámos	**55**	37	45N		26	50 E
Samothráki	**55**	40	28N		25	28 E
Samsun	**80**	41	15N		36	22 E
Samut Prakan	**95**	13	32N		100	40 E
Samut Sakhon	**94**	13	31N		100	13 E
Samut Songkhram ~→	**94**	13	24N		100	1 E
San Andreas	**172**	38	0N		120	39W
San Andres Mts.	**161**	33	0N		106	45W
San Andrés Tuxtla	**177**	18	27N		95	13W
San Angelo	**161**	31	30N		100	30W
San Antonio, Chile	**190**	33	40S		71	40W
San Antonio, U.S.A.	**161**	29	30N		98	30W
San Antonio, C., Argentina	**191**	36	15S		56	40W
San Antonio, C., Cuba	**178**	21	50N		84	57W
San Antonio de los Baños	**178**	22	54N		82	31W
San Antônio Falls	**182**	9	30S		65	0W
San Antonio Oeste	**192**	40	40S		65	0W
San Bernardino	**173**	34	7N		117	18W
San Bernardino Str.	**112**	13	0N		125	0 E
San Bernardo	**190**	33	40S		70	50W
San Blas, C.	**169**	29	40N		85	12W
San Carlos, Chile	**190**	36	10S		72	0W
San Carlos, Mexico	**174**	29	1N		100	51W
San Carlos, Nic.	**179**	11	12N		84	50W
San Carlos de Bariloche	**192**	41	10S		71	25W
San Clemente I.	**173**	32	53N		118	30W
San Cristóbal, Argentina	**190**	30	20S		61	10W
San Cristóbal, Dom. Rep.	**180**	18	25N		70	6W
San Cristóbal, Venezuela	**184**	16	50N		92	40W
San Cristóbal de las Casas	**177**	16	45N		92	38W
San Diego	**173**	32	43N		117	10W
San Felipe, Chile	**190**	32	43S		70	42W

63

Name	Map	Lat			Long		
San Felipe, Colombia	**184**	1	55N		67	6W	
San Fernando, Chile	**190**	34	30S		71	0W	
San Fernando, Mexico	**174**	30	0N		115	10W	
San Fernando, Trin. & Tob.	**180**	10	20N		61	30W	
San Fernando, U.S.A.	**173**	34	15N		118	29W	
San Fernando de Apure	**184**	7	54N		67	15W	
San Francisco	**172**	37	47N		122	30W	
San Francisco de Macorís	**180**	19	19N		70	15W	
San Francisco del Oro	**174**	26	52N		105	51W	
San Gabriel	**191**	0	36N		77	49W	
San Gottardo, Paso del	**44**	46	33N		8	33 E	
San Ignacio	**187**	16	20S		60	55W	
San Joaquin →	**172**	37	4N		121	51W	
San Jorge, Golfo	**192**	46	0S		66	0W	
San Jorge, G. de	**51**	40	50N		0	55W	
San José, Bolivia	**187**	17	53S		60	50W	
San José, C. Rica	**179**	10	0N		84	2W	
San José, U.S.A.	**172**	37	20N		121	53W	
San José de Mayo	**191**	34	27S		56	40W	
San José del Cabo	**175**	23	3N		109	41W	
San José del Guaviare	**184**	2	35N		72	38W	
San Juan, Argentina	**190**	31	30S		68	30W	
San Juan, Dom. Rep.	**180**	18	49N		71	12W	
San Juan, Puerto Rico	**180**	18	28N		66	8W	
San Juan →	**179**	10	56N		83	42W	
San Juan de los Morros	**184**	9	55N		67	21W	
San Juan Mts.	**163**	38	30N		108	30W	
San Julián	**192**	49	15S		67	45W	
San Leandro	**172**	37	40N		122	6W	
San Lorenzo	**184**	1	15N		78	50W	
San Lucas, C. de	**175**	22	50N		110	0W	
San Luis	**190**	33	20S		66	20W	
San Luis de la Paz	**177**	21	18N		100	31W	
San Luis Obispo	**173**	35	21N		120	38W	
San Luis Potosí	**177**	22	9N		100	59W	
San Luis Potosí □	**177**	22	30N		100	30W	
San Marcos	**177**	14	59N		91	52W	
San Marino ■	**47**	43	56N		12	25 E	
San Mateo	**172**	37	32N		122	19W	
San Matías	**187**	16	25S		58	20W	
San Matías, Golfo	**192**	41	30S		64	0W	
San Miguel	**177**	13	30N		88	12W	
San Miguel de Tucumán	**190**	26	50S		65	20W	
San Pedro →	**175**	21	45N		105	30W	
San Pedro de las Colonias	**174**	25	45N		102	59W	
San Pedro de Macorís	**180**	18	30N		69	18W	
San Pedro Sula	**177**	15	30N		88	0W	
San Rafael, Argentina	**190**	34	40S		68	21W	
San Rafael, U.S.A.	**172**	37	59N		122	32W	
San Roque	**190**	28	25S		58	45W	
San Salvador, Bahamas	**178**	24	0N		74	40W	
San Salvador, El Salv.	**177**	13	40N		89	10W	
San Salvador de Jujuy	**190**	24	10S		64	48W	
San Sebastián	**51**	43	17N		1	58W	
San Valentin, Mte.	**192**	46	30S		73	30W	
Sana'	**82**	15	27N		44	12 E	
Sanandaj	**81**	35	18N		47	1 E	
Sancti-Spíritus	**178**	21	52N		79	33W	
Sanda	**106**	34	53N		135	14 E	
Sandgate	**116**	27	18S		153	3 E	
Sandomierz	**58**	50	40N		21	43 E	
Sandpoint	**171**	48	20N		116	34W	
Sandringham	**29**	52	50N		0	30 E	
Sandstone	**120**	27	59S		119	16 E	
Sandusky	**167**	41	25N		82	40W	
Sandwip Chan.	**93**	22	35N		91	35 E	
Sandy C.	**119**	41	25S		144	45 E	
Sandy Lake	**153**	53	0N		93	15W	
Sanford, Fla., U.S.A.	**170**	28	45N		81	20W	
Sanford, Maine, U.S.A.	**148**	43	28N		70	47W	
Sanford, N.C., U.S.A.	**165**	35	30N		79	10W	
Sangay	**184**	2	0S		78	20W	
Sangihe, P.	**113**	3	45N		125	30 E	
Sangli	**91**	16	55N		74	33 E	
Sangre de Cristo Mts.	**161**	37	0N		105	0W	
Sankuru →	**134**	4	17S		20	25 E	
Sano	**107**	36	19N		139	35 E	
Sanok	**59**	49	35N		22	10 E	
Sanquhar	**31**	55	21N		3	56W	
Sanshui	**99**	23	10N		112	56 E	
Santa Ana, Bolivia	**187**	13	50S		65	40W	
Santa Ana, Mexico	**174**	30	33N		111	7W	
Santa Ana, U.S.A.	**173**	33	48N		117	55W	
Santa Bárbara, Mexico	**174**	26	48N		105	49W	
Santa Bárbara, U.S.A.	**173**	34	25N		119	40W	
Santa Barbara I.	**160**	33	29N		119	2W	
Santa Catarina □	**191**	27	25S		48	30W	
Santa Clara, Cuba	**178**	22	20N		80	0W	
Santa Clara, U.S.A.	**162**	37	21N		122	0W	
Santa Clotilde	**186**	2	33S		73	45W	
Santa Cruz, Bolivia	**187**	17	43S		63	10W	
Santa Cruz, U.S.A.	**172**	36	55N		122	1W	
Santa Cruz, Is.	**122**	10	30S		166	0 E	
Sta. Cruz de Tenerife	**126**	28	28N		16	15W	
Santa Cruz del Sur	**178**	20	44N		78	0W	
Santa Cruz do Sul	**191**	29	42S		52	25W	
Santa Fe, Argentina	**190**	31	35S		60	41W	
Santa Fe, U.S.A.	**161**	35	40N		106	0W	
Santa Inés, I.	**192**	54	0S		73	0W	
Santa Isabel = Rey Malabo	**131**	3	45N		8	50 E	
Santa Lucia Range	**173**	36	0N		121	20W	
Santa Maria, Brazil	**191**	29	40S		53	48W	
Santa Maria, U.S.A.	**173**	34	58N		120	29W	
Santa Maria da Vitória	**188**	13	24S		44	12W	
Santa Maria di Leuca, C.	**49**	39	48N		18	20 E	
Santa Marta	**184**	11	15N		74	13W	
Santa Maura = Levkás	**54**	38	40N		20	43 E	
Santa Monica	**173**	34	0N		118	30W	
Santa Rosa, Argentina	**190**	36	40S		64	17W	
Santa Rosa, U.S.A.	**172**	38	26N		122	43W	
Santa Rosa I., Calif., U.S.A.	**173**	34	0N		120	6W	
Santa Rosa I., Fla., U.S.A.	**169**	30	23N		87	0W	
Santa Rosalia	**174**	27	19N		112	17W	
Santana do Livramento	**191**	30	55S		55	30W	
Santander	**50**	43	27N		3	51W	
Santander Jiménez	**176**	24	13N		98	28W	
Santarém, Brazil	**185**	2	25S		54	42W	
Santarém, Portugal	**50**	39	12N		8	42W	
Santiago, Brazil	**191**	29	11S		54	52W	
Santiago, Chile	**190**	33	24S		70	40W	
Santiago, Panama	**179**	8	0N		81	0W	
Santiago de Compostela	**50**	42	52N		8	37W	
Santiago de Cuba	**178**	20	0N		75	49W	
Santiago de los Cabelleros	**180**	19	30N		70	40W	
Santiago del Estero	**190**	27	50S		64	15W	
Santiago Ixcuintla	**175**	21	50N		105	11W	
Santo Amaro	**189**	12	30S		38	43W	
Santo Ângelo	**191**	28	15S		54	15W	
Santo Domingo	**180**	18	30N		64	54W	
Santo Tomé	**191**	28	40S		56	5W	
Santoña	**50**	43	29N		3	27W	
Santos	**191**	24	0S		46	20W	
São Borja	**191**	28	39S		56	0W	
São Carlos	**188**	22	0S		47	50W	
São Francisco →	**189**	10	30S		36	24W	
São Francisco do Sul	**191**	26	15S		48	36W	
São João del Rei	**188**	21	8S		44	15W	
São José do Rio Prêto	**188**	20	50S		49	20W	
São Leopoldo	**191**	29	50S		51	10W	
São Lourenço	**188**	22	7S		45	3W	
São Luís	**188**	2	39S		44	15W	
São Paulo	**191**	23	32S		46	37W	
São Paulo □	**188**	22	0S		49	0W	
São Paulo de Olivença	**184**	3	27S		68	48W	
São Roque, C. de	**189**	5	30S		35	16W	
São Tomé	**131**	0	10N		6	39 E	
São Tomé & Príncipe ■	**131**	0	12N		6	39 E	
São Vicente, Cabo de	**50**	37	0N		9	0W	
Saône →	**37**	45	44N		4	50 E	
Sapporo	**103**	43	0N		141	21 E	
Sapulpa	**168**	36	0N		96	0W	
Saqqez	**81**	36	15N		46	20 E	
Sar Planina	**52**	42	10N		21	0 E	
Saragossa = Zaragoza	**51**	41	39N		0	53W	
Sarajevo	**52**	43	52N		18	26 E	
Saranac Lake	**151**	44	20N		74	10W	
Sarangani B.	**112**	6	0N		125	13 E	
Saransk	**68**	54	10N		45	10 E	
Sarapul	**69**	56	28N		53	48 E	
Sarasota	**165**	27	20N		82	30W	
Saratoga Springs	**164**	43	5N		73	47W	
Saratov	**68**	51	30N		46	2 E	

Sarawak □	111	2	0N	113 0 E
Sardegna	48	39	57N	9 0 E
Sardinia = Sardegna	48	39	57N	9 0 E
Sargodha	89	32	10N	72 40 E
Sarh	131	9	5N	18 23 E
Sārī	86	36	30N	53 4 E
Sarina	121	21	22S	149 13 E
Sarmiento	192	45	35S	69 5W
Sarnia	150	42	58N	82 23W
Saronikós Kólpos	55	37	45N	23 45 E
Sarre = Saar ──▸	42	49	41N	6 32 E
Sarre, La	151	48	45N	79 15W
Sarthe ──▸	36	47	33N	0 31W
Sasaram	92	24	57N	84 5 E
Sasebo	108	33	10N	129 43 E
Saskatchewan □	152	54	40N	106 0W
Saskatchewan ──▸	152	53	37N	100 40W
Saskatoon	152	52	10N	106 38W
Sassandra	130	5	0N	6 8W
Sássari	48	40	44N	8 33 E
Sata-Misaki	108	30	59N	130 40 E
Satara	91	17	44N	73 58 E
Satmala Hills	91	20	15N	74 40 E
Satna	92	24	35N	80 50 E
Satpura Ra.	91	21	25N	76 10 E
Sattahip	95	12	41N	100 54 E
Satu Mare	56	47	46N	22 55 E
Sauðárkrókur	64	65	45N	19 40W
Saudi Arabia ■	82	26	0N	44 0 E
Sault Ste. Marie, Canada	150	46	30N	84 20W
Sault Ste. Marie, U.S.A.	150	46	27N	84 22W
Saumur	36	47	15N	0 5W
Sava ──▸	52	44	50N	20 26 E
Savanna la Mar	180	18	10N	78 10W
Savannah	170	32	4N	81 4W
Savannah ──▸	170	32	2N	80 53W
Savannakhet	95	16	30N	104 49 E
Savoie □	37	45	26N	6 35 E
Savona	46	44	19N	8 29 E
Sawankhalok	94	17	19N	99 50 E
Sawara	107	35	55N	140 30 E
Sawatch Mts.	163	38	30N	106 30W
Sawu, I.	113	10	35S	121 50 E
Sawu Sea	113	9	30S	121 50 E
Saxony, Lower = Niedersachsen □	42	52	45N	9 0 E
Sayan, Zapadnyy	77	52	30N	94 0 E
Saydā	80	33	35N	35 25 E
Sayḥut	83	15	12N	51 10 E
Sayula	175	19	52N	103 36W
Sazan	52	40	30N	19 20 E
Scafell Pikes	28	54	26N	3 14W
Scalloway	30	60	9N	1 16W
Scandinavia	16	64	0N	12 0 E
Scapa Flow	33	58	52N	3 6W
Scarborough	29	54	17N	0 24W
Schaffhausen	44	47	42N	8 39 E
Schefferville	146	54	48N	66 50W
Schelde ──▸	42	51	15N	4 16 E
Schenectady	164	42	50N	73 58W
Scheveningen	40	52	6N	4 16 E
Schiedam	40	51	55N	4 25 E
Schiermonnikoog	41	53	30N	6 15 E
Schleswig-Holstein □	42	54	10N	9 40 E
Schouten I.	119	42	20S	148 20 E
Schouten Is.	113	1	0S	136 0 E
Schouwen	40	51	43N	3 45 E
Schreiber	150	48	45N	87 20W
Schwäbische Alb	42	48	30N	9 30 E
Schwarzwald	42	48	0N	8 0 E
Schwerin	43	53	37N	11 22 E
Schwyz	44	47	2N	8 39 E
Scilly, Isles of	20	49	55N	6 15W
Scone, Australia	116	32	5S	150 52 E
Scone, U.K.	31	56	25N	3 26W
Scoresbysund	13	70	20N	23 0W
Scotia Sea	14	56	5S	56 0W
Scotland □	23	57	0N	4 0W
Scottsbluff	163	41	55N	103 35W
Scottsdale	119	41	9S	147 31 E
Scranton	164	41	22N	75 41W
Scunthorpe	29	53	35N	0 38W
Scutari = Üsküdar	80	41	0N	29 5 E
Seaforth	150	43	35N	81 25W
Searcy	168	35	15N	91 45W
Seascale	28	54	24N	3 29W
Seattle	171	47	41N	122 15W
Sebastián Vizcaíno, B.	174	28	0N	114 30W
Sebastopol = Sevastopol	68	44	35N	33 30 E
Sebring	170	27	30N	81 26W
Sebta = Ceuta	126	35	52N	5 18W
Sebuku, Teluk	111	4	0N	118 10 E
Sechura, Desierto de	186	6	0S	80 30W
Seclin	38	50	33N	3 2 E
Sedalia	166	38	40N	93 18W
Segamat	96	2	30N	102 50 E
Ségou	130	13	30N	6 16W
Segovia = Coco ──▸	179	15	0N	83 8W
Segovia	50	40	57N	4 10W
Séguéla	130	7	55N	6 40W
Segura ──▸	51	38	6N	0 54W
Seine ──▸	38	49	26N	0 26 E
Seistan	85	30	50N	61 0 E
Seki	106	35	29N	136 55 E
Sekondi-Takoradi	130	4	58N	1 45W
Selangor □	96	3	10N	101 30 E
Selby	29	53	47N	1 5W
Sélibabi	130	15	10N	12 15W
Selkirk, Canada	153	50	10N	96 55W
Selkirk, U.K.	31	55	33N	2 50W
Selkirk Mts.	155	51	15N	117 40W
Selma, Ala., U.S.A.	169	32	30N	87 0W
Selma, Calif., U.S.A.	173	36	39N	119 39W
Selsey Bill	24	50	44N	0 47W
Selvas	187	6	30S	67 0W
Semarang	111	7	0S	110 26 E
Seminole	168	35	15N	96 45W
Semipalatinsk	71	50	30N	80 10 E
Semnān	86	35	55N	53 25 E
Semnān □	86	36	0N	54 0 E
Sendai, Kagoshima, Japan	108	31	50N	130 20 E
Sendai, Miyagi, Japan	103	38	15N	140 53 E
Senegal ■	130	14	30N	14 30W
Senegal ──▸	126	15	48N	16 32W
Senge Khambab = Indus ──▸	88	24	20N	67 47 E
Senhor-do-Bonfim	189	10	30S	40 10W
Senja I.	64	69	15N	17 30 E
Senlis	39	49	13N	2 35 E
Sennâr	129	13	30N	33 35 E
Senneterre	151	48	25N	77 15W
Sens	39	48	11N	3 15 E
Senta	52	45	55N	20 3 E
Seoul = Sôul	98	37	31N	126 58 E
Sept-Îles	148	50	13N	66 22W
Seram	113	3	10S	129 0 E
Seram Sea	113	2	30S	128 30 E
Seremban	96	2	43N	101 53 E
Serena, La	190	29	55S	71 10W
Sereth = Siret ──▸	57	47	58N	26 5 E
Sergipe □	189	10	30S	37 30W
Sérifos	55	37	9N	24 30 E
Serny Zavod	70	39	59N	58 50 E
Serov	69	59	29N	60 35 E
Serowe	137	22	25S	26 43 E
Serpukhov	68	54	55N	37 28 E
Serra do Navio	185	0	59N	52 3W
Sérrai	55	41	5N	23 31 E
Sesheke	134	17	29S	24 13 E
Setana	103	42	26N	139 51 E
Sète	37	43	25N	3 42 E
Sétif	127	36	9N	5 26 E
Seto	106	35	14N	137 6 E
Setonaikai	109	34	20N	133 30 E
Settle	28	54	5N	2 18W
Setúbal	50	38	30N	8 58W
Sevastopol	68	44	35N	33 30 E
Seven Sisters	154	54	56N	128 10W
Severn ──▸, Canada	140	56	2N	87 36W
Severn ──▸, U.K.	24	51	35N	2 38W
Severnaya Zemlya	72	79	0N	100 0 E
Severodinsk	69	64	27N	39 58 E

Name	Page	°	′	N/S	°	′	E/W
Sevilla	50	37	23N		6	0W	
Seville = Sevilla	50	37	23N		6	0W	
Seward	142	60	6N		149	26W	
Seward Pen.	142	65	0N		164	0W	
Seychelles ■	78	5	0S		56	0 E	
Seyðisfjörður	64	65	16N		14	0W	
Seymour	117	37	0S		145	10 E	
Seyne-sur-Mer, La	37	43	7N		5	52 E	
Sézanne	39	48	40N		3	40 E	
Sfax	127	34	49N		10	48 E	
Sfîntu Gheorghe	57	45	52N		25	48 E	
Shaanxi □	99	35	0N		109	0 E	
Shaba □	135	8	0S		25	0 E	
Shache	100	38	20N		77	10 E	
Shaftesbury	24	51	0N		2	12W	
Shahdād	85	30	30N		57	40 E	
Shakhty	68	47	40N		40	16 E	
Shamo = Gobi	98	44	0N		111	0 E	
Shamokin	164	40	47N		76	33W	
Shan □	93	21	30N		98	30 E	
Shandong □	99	36	0N		118	0 E	
Shanghai	99	31	15N		121	26 E	
Shangqiu	99	34	26N		115	36 E	
Shangrao	99	28	25N		117	50 E	
Shangshui	99	33	42N		114	35 E	
Shannon ~►	35	52	35N		9	30W	
Shansi = Shanxi □	98	37	0N		112	0 E	
Shantou	99	23	18N		116	40 E	
Shantung = Shandong □	99	36	0N		118	0 E	
Shanxi □	98	37	0N		112	0 E	
Shaoguan	99	24	48N		113	35 E	
Shaoxing	99	30	0N		120	35 E	
Shaoyang	99	27	14N		111	25 E	
Shap	28	54	32N		2	40W	
Sharjah = Ash Shāriqah	85	25	23N		55	26 E	
Shark B.	120	25	55S		113	32 E	
Sharon	164	41	18N		80	30W	
Shashi	99	30	25N		112	14 E	
Shasta, Mt.	172	41	30N		122	12W	
Shasta L.	172	40	50N		122	15W	
Shaunavon	152	49	35N		108	25W	
Shawano	167	44	45N		88	38W	
Shawinigan	151	46	35N		72	50W	
Shawnee	168	35	15N		97	0W	
Shcherbakov = Andropov	68	58	5N		38	50 E	
Shebele, Wabi ~►	133	2	0N		44	0 E	
Sheboygan	167	43	46N		87	45W	
Sheerness	24	51	26N		0	47 E	
Sheffield	28	53	23N		1	28W	
Shekhupura	89	31	42N		73	58 E	
Shelburne	148	43	47N		65	20W	
Shelby, Mont., U.S.A.	163	48	30N		111	52W	
Shelby, N.C., U.S.A.	165	35	18N		81	34W	
Shelbyville, Ind., U.S.A.	167	39	30N		85	42W	
Shelbyville, Tenn., U.S.A.	169	35	30N		86	25W	
Shelikhova, Zaliv.	73	59	30N		157	0 E	
Shellharbour	117	34	31S		150	51 E	
Shelton	171	47	15N		123	6W	
Shenandoah	166	40	50N		95	25W	
Shensi = Shaanxi □	99	35	0N		109	0 E	
Shenyang	98	41	50N		123	25 E	
Shepparton	117	36	23S		145	26 E	
Sheppey, I. of	24	51	23N		0	50 E	
Sherborne	27	50	56N		2	31W	
Sherbrooke	148	45	28N		71	57W	
Sheridan	163	44	50N		107	0W	
Sherman	168	33	40N		96	35W	
Sherridon	152	55	8N		101	5W	
Sherwood Forest	29	53	5N		1	5W	
Shetland Is.	30	60	30N		1	30W	
Shibâm	83	16	0N		48	36 E	
Shibata	103	37	57N		139	20 E	
Shibetsu	103	44	10N		142	23 E	
Shibukawa	107	36	29N		139	0 E	
Shibushi-Wan	108	31	24N		131	8 E	
Shiel, L.	32	56	48N		5	32W	
Shihchiachuangi = Shijiazhuang	98	38	2N		114	28 E	
Shijiazhuang	98	38	2N		114	28 E	
Shikarpur	88	27	57N		68	39 E	
Shikine-Jima	107	34	19N		139	13 E	
Shikoku	109	33	30N		133	30 E	
Shikoku □	109	33	30N		133	30 E	
Shikoku-Sanchi	109	33	30N		133	30 E	
Shillong	93	25	35N		91	53 E	
Shimabara	108	32	48N		130	20 E	
Shimada	107	34	49N		138	10 E	
Shimizu	107	35	0N		138	30 E	
Shimo-Jima	108	32	15N		130	7 E	
Shimo-Koshiki-Jima	108	31	40N		129	43 E	
Shimoda	107	34	40N		138	57 E	
Shimodate	107	36	20N		139	55 E	
Shimoga	90	13	57N		75	32 E	
Shimonoseki	108	33	58N		131	0 E	
Shin, L.	33	58	7N		4	30W	
Shin-Tone ~►	107	35	44N		140	51 E	
Shinano ~►	105	36	50N		138	30 E	
Shingū	106	33	40N		135	55 E	
Shinji Ko	109	35	26N		132	57 E	
Shinjō	103	38	46N		140	18 E	
Shinminato	106	36	47N		137	4 E	
Shinshiro	106	34	54N		137	30 E	
Shio-no-Misaki	106	33	25N		135	45 E	
Shiogama	103	38	19N		141	1 E	
Shiojiri	107	36	6N		137	58 F	
Shipka	53	42	46N		25	33 E	
Shirane-San, Gumma, Japan	107	36	48N		139	22 E	
Shirane-San, Yamanashi, Japan	107	35	42N		138	9 E	
Shīrāz	85	29	42N		52	30 E	
Shire ~►	137	17	42S		35	19 E	
Shiriya-Zaki	103	41	25N		141	30 E	
Shivpuri	91	25	26N		77	42 E	
Shizuoka	107	35	0N		138	24 E	
Shkoder = Shkodra	52	42	6N		19	20 E	
Shkodra	52	42	6N		19	20 E	
Shkumbini ~►	52	41	5N		19	50 E	
Shō-Gawa ~►	106	36	47N		137	4 E	
Shōbara	109	34	51N		133	1 E	
Shoeburyness	24	51	31N		0	49 E	
Sholapur = Solapur	91	17	43N		75	56 E	
Shoshone	172	43	0N		114	27W	
Shreveport	168	32	30N		93	50W	
Shrewsbury	28	52	42N		2	45W	
Shrirampur	92	22	44N		88	21 E	
Shropshire □	24	52	36N		2	45W	
Shuangyashan	98	46	37N		131	22 E	
Siahan Range	88	27	30N		64	40 E	
Sialkot	89	32	32N		74	30 E	
Siam = Thailand ■	95	16	0N		102	0 E	
Sian = Xi'an	99	34	15N		109	0 E	
Siberia	77	60	0N		100	0 E	
Siberut	111	1	30S		99	0 E	
Sibi	88	29	30N		67	54 E	
Sibiu	57	45	45N		24	9 E	
Sichuan □	99	31	0N		104	0 E	
Sicilia	49	37	30N		14	30 E	
Sicily = Sicilia	49	37	30N		14	30 E	
Sicuani	187	14	21S		71	10W	
Sidi-bel-Abbès	127	35	13N		0	39W	
Sidlaw Hills	31	56	32N		3	10W	
Sidley, Mt.	15	77	2S		126	2W	
Sidmouth	27	50	40N		3	13W	
Sidney	154	48	39N		123	24W	
Sidon = Saydā	80	33	35N		35	25 E	
Sidra, G. of = Surt, Khalīj	127	31	40N		18	30 E	
Siedlce	58	52	10N		22	20 E	
Siena	46	43	20N		11	20 E	
Sierra Blanca Pk.	161	33	20N		105	54W	
Sierra Leone ■	130	9	0N		12	0W	
Sífnos	55	37	0N		24	45 E	
Siglufjörður	64	66	12N		18	55W	
Sihanoukville = Kompong Som	95	10	38N		103	30 E	
Siirt	81	37	57N		41	55 E	
Sikar	89	27	33N		75	10 E	
Sikeston	169	36	52N		89	35W	
Sikhote Alin, Khrebet	75	46	0N		136	0 E	
Síkinos	55	36	40N		25	8 E	
Sikkim □	92	27	50N		88	30 E	
Silchar	93	24	49N		92	48 E	
Silesia = Slask	58	51	0N		16	30 E	

Name	Page	Lat	Long
Siling Co	101	31 50N	89 20 E
Silloth	28	54 53N	3 25W
Simcoe	151	42 50N	80 20W
Simenga	74	62 42N	108 25 E
Simeulue	111	2 45N	95 45 E
Simferopol	68	44 55N	34 3 E
Simi Valley	173	34 16N	118 47W
Simla	89	31 2N	77 9 E
Simplon Pass	44	46 15N	8 0 E
Simushir, Ostrov	75	46 50N	152 30 E
Sinai = Es Sînâ'	128	29 0N	34 0 E
Sinaloa	174	25 50N	108 20W
Sinaloa □	174	25 0N	107 30W
Sincelejo	184	9 18N	75 24W
Sinclair Mills	155	54 5N	121 40W
Sind □	88	26 0N	69 0 E
Sind Sagar Doab	89	32 0N	71 30 E
Singa	129	13 10N	33 57 E
Singapore ■	96	1 17N	103 51 E
Singapore, Straits of	96	1 15N	104 0 E
Singkaling Hkamti	92	26 0N	95 39 E
Singleton	117	32 33S	151 0 E
Singora = Songkhla	97	7 13N	100 37 E
Sinkiang Uighur = Xinjiang Uygur Zizhiqu □	100	42 0N	86 0 E
Sioux City	166	42 32N	96 25W
Sioux Falls	166	43 35N	96 40W
Sioux Lookout	153	50 10N	91 50W
Siping	98	43 8N	124 21 E
Sipora	111	2 18S	99 40 E
Siracusa	49	37 4N	15 17 E
Sirajganj	92	24 25N	89 47 E
Siret →	57	47 58N	26 5 E
Síros	55	37 28N	24 57 E
Sitapur	92	27 38N	80 45 E
Sitka	143	57 9N	135 20W
Sittard	41	51 0N	5 52 E
Sivas	80	39 43N	36 58 E
Siverek	81	37 50N	39 19 E
Sivrihisar	80	39 30N	31 35 E
Sîwa	128	29 11N	25 31 E
Siwalik Range	92	28 0N	83 0 E
Sizewell	24	52 13N	1 38 E
Sjumen = Kolarovgrad	53	43 18N	26 55 E
Skadarsko Jezero	52	42 10N	19 20 E
Skagerrak	60	57 30N	9 0 E
Skagway	143	59 23N	135 20W
Skaraborgs län □	60	58 20N	13 30 E
Skeena →	154	54 9N	130 5W
Skegness	29	53 9N	0 20 E
Skellefte →	66	65 30N	18 30 E
Skellefteå	67	64 45N	20 58 E
Skerries, The	26	53 27N	4 40W
Skiddaw	28	54 39N	3 9W
Skien	60	59 12N	9 35 E
Skierniewice	58	51 58N	20 10 E
Skikda	127	36 50N	6 58 E
Skipton	28	53 57N	2 1W
Skíros	55	38 55N	24 34 E
Skopje	52	42 1N	21 32 E
Skowhegan	148	44 49N	69 40W
Skull	35	51 32N	9 40W
Skye	32	57 15N	6 10W
Skyros = Skíros	55	38 55N	24 34 E
Slaney →	35	52 52N	6 45W
Slask	58	51 0N	16 30 E
Slave →	145	61 18N	113 39W
Slave Coast	124	6 0N	2 30 E
Sleaford	29	53 0N	0 22W
Sliedrecht	40	51 50N	4 45 E
Slieve Aughty	35	53 4N	8 30W
Slieve Bloom	35	53 4N	7 40W
Slieve Donard	34	54 10N	5 57W
Slieve Mish	35	52 12N	9 50W
Slievenamon	35	52 25N	7 37W
Sligo	34	54 17N	8 28W
Sligo □	34	54 10N	8 35W
Sliven	53	42 42N	26 19 E
Slovakian Ore Mts. = Slovenské Rudohorie	59	48 45N	20 0 E
Slovenia = Slovenija □	52	45 58N	14 30 E
Slovenija □	52	45 58N	14 30 E
Slovenské Rudohorie	59	48 45N	20 0 E
Slupsk	58	54 30N	17 3 E
Slyne Hd.	34	53 25N	10 10W
Smara	126	32 9N	8 16W
Smithers	154	54 45N	127 10W
Smithfield	165	35 31N	78 16W
Smiths Falls	151	44 55N	76 0W
Smithton	119	40 53S	145 6 E
Smolensk	68	54 45N	32 0 E
Smolikas, Óros	54	40 9N	20 58 E
Smyrna = İzmir	80	38 25N	27 8 E
Snœfell, Iceland	64	64 48N	15 34W
Snœfell, U.K.	28	54 18N	4 26W
Snœfellsjökull	64	64 49N	23 46W
Snake →	171	46 12N	119 2W
Sneek	41	53 2N	5 40 E
Snowdon	26	53 4N	4 8W
Snowdrift	145	62 24N	110 44W
Snowy Mts.	117	36 30S	148 20 E
Sobat →	129	8 32N	32 40 E
Sobral	177	3 50S	40 20W
Soch'e = Shache	100	38 20N	77 10 E
Sochi	70	43 35N	39 40 E
Société, Is. de la	123	17 0S	151 0W
Society Is. = Société, Is. de la	123	17 0S	151 0W
Socorro	161	34 4N	106 54W
Socotra	78	12 30N	54 0 E
Söderhamn	60	61 18N	17 10 E
Södermanlands län □	60	59 10N	16 30 E
Södertälje	60	59 12N	17 39 E
Sodo	132	7 0N	37 41 E
Sofala	137	33 4S	149 43 E
Sofia = Sofiya	53	42 45N	23 20 E
Sofiya	53	42 45N	23 20 E
Sogn og Fjordane fylke □	60	61 40N	6 0 E
Soissons	39	49 25N	3 19 E
Sôja	109	34 40N	133 45 E
Söke	80	37 48N	27 28 E
Sol Iletsk	70	51 10N	55 0 E
Solapur	91	17 43N	75 56 E
Soledad, Colombia	184	10 55N	74 46W
Soledad, Venezuela	185	8 10N	63 34W
Solent, The	24	50 45N	1 25W
Solesmes	38	50 10N	3 30 E
Solikamsk	69	59 38N	56 50 E
Solimões → = Amazonas →	185	0 5S	50 0W
Sóller	51	39 46N	2 43 E
Sololá	177	14 49N	91 10 E
Solomon Is. ■	122	6 0S	155 0 E
Solţānābād	86	36 29N	58 5 E
Solway Firth	31	54 45N	3 38W
Somali Rep. ■	133	7 0N	47 0 E
Sombor	52	45 46N	19 9 E
Sombrerete	175	23 38N	103 39W
Somerset, Bermuda	180	32 16N	64 55W
Somerset, U.S.A.	169	37 5N	84 40W
Somerset □	27	51 9N	3 0W
Somerset I.	145	73 30N	93 0W
Somme □	36	50 0N	2 20 E
Somport, Puerto de	51	42 48N	0 31W
Søndre Strømfjord	147	66 59N	50 40W
Songkhla	97	7 13N	100 37 E
Sonora □	174	29 20N	110 40W
Soochow = Suzhou	99	31 19N	120 38 E
Sop's Arm	149	49 46N	56 56W
Sør-Rondane	14	72 0S	25 0 E
Sør-Trøndelag fylke □	65	63 0N	10 0 E
Sorata	187	15 50S	68 40W
Sorel	151	46 0N	73 10W
Soria	51	41 43N	2 32W
Sorocaba	191	23 31S	47 27W
Sørøya	67	70 40N	22 30 E
Sorsogon	112	13 0N	124 0 E
Sosnowiec	58	50 20N	19 10 E
Sotteville-lès-Rouen	38	49 24N	1 5 E
Sôul	98	37 31N	126 58 E
Souris, Man., Canada	153	49 40N	100 20W
Souris, P.E.I., Canada	149	46 21N	62 15W

SOU

Name	Page	Lat		Long	
South Africa, Rep. of ■	136	32	0S	17	0 E
South Auckland & Bay of Plenty □	122	38	30S	177	0 E
South Australia □	118	32	0S	139	0 E
South Bend	167	41	38N	86	20W
South Carolina □	165	33	45N	81	0W
South Charleston	165	38	20N	81	40W
South China Sea	77	10	0N	113	0 E
South Dakota □	163	45	0N	100	0W
South Downs	25	50	53N	0	10W
South Georgia	183	54	30S	37	0W
South Glamorgan □	27	51	30N	3	20W
South Haven	167	42	22N	86	20W
South Island	123	44	0S	170	0 E
South Korea ■	98	36	0N	128	0 E
South Orkney Is.	14	63	0S	45	0W
South Platte ~→	163	41	7N	100	42W
South Pole	14	90	0S	0	0 E
South Porcupine	151	48	30N	81	12W
South Ronaldsay	33	58	46N	2	58W
South Sandwich Is.	14	57	0S	27	0W
South Sentinel I.	94	11	1N	92	16 E
South Shetland Is.	14	62	0S	59	0W
South Shields	28	54	59N	1	26W
South Taranaki Bight	122	39	40S	174	5 E
South Uist	32	57	20N	7	15W
South West Africa = Namibia ■	136	22	0S	18	9 E
South West Cape	123	47	16S	167	31 E
South Yemen ■.	83	15	0N	48	0 E
South Yorkshire □	29	53	30N	1	20W
Southampton	25	50	54N	1	23W
Southampton I.	146	64	30N	84	0W
Southend-on-Sea	25	51	32N	0	42 E
Southern Alps	123	43	41S	170	11 E
Southern Cross	120	31	12S	119	15 E
Southern Indian L.	143	57	10N	98	30W
Southern Uplands	31	55	30N	3	3W
Southland □	123	45	51S	168	13 E
Southport, Australia	116	27	58S	153	25 E
Southport, U.K.	28	53	38N	3	1W
Southwold	25	52	19N	1	41 E
Sovetskaya Gavan	75	48	50N	140	0 E
Soviet Union ■ = Union of Soviet Socialist Republics ■	79	60	0N	100	0 E
Sōya-Kaikyō = Perouse Str., La	77	45	40N	142	0 E
Spain ■	50	40	0N	5	0W
Spalding	29	52	47N	0	9W
Spandau	43	52	35N	13	7 E
Spanish Fork	163	40	10N	111	37W
Spanish Town	180	18	0N	76	57W
Sparks	172	39	30N	119	45W
Sparta = Spárti	54	37	5N	22	25 E
Sparta	166	43	55N	90	47W
Spartanburg	165	35	0N	82	0W
Spárti	54	37	5N	22	25 E
Spartivento, C., Calabria, Italy	49	37	56N	16	4 E
Spartivento, C., Sard., Italy	48	38	52N	8	50 E
Spassk-Dalniy	75	44	40N	132	48 E
Speightstown	180	13	15N	59	39W
Spence Bay	145	69	32N	93	32W
Spencer	166	43	5N	95	19W
Spencer G.	119	34	0S	137	20 E
Spenser Mts.	123	42	15S	172	45 E
Sperrin Mts.	34	54	50N	7	0W
Spessart	42	50	10N	9	20 E
Spey ~→	33	57	26N	3	25W
Spézia, La	46	44	8N	9	50 E
Spinazzola	49	40	58N	16	5 E
Spithead	25	50	43N	1	5W
Spitzbergen = Svalbard	13	78	0N	17	0 E
Split	52	43	31N	16	26 E
Splügenpass	44	46	30N	9	20 E
Spokane	171	47	45N	117	25W
Sporyy Navolok, Mys	69	75	50N	68	40 E
Spratly, I.	112	8	20N	112	0 E
Spring Mts.	173	36	20N	115	43W
Springfield, Ill., U.S.A.	166	39	48N	89	40W
Springfield, Mass., U.S.A.	164	42	8N	72	37W
Springfield, Mo., U.S.A.	168	37	15N	93	20W
Springfield, Ohio, U.S.A.	167	39	58N	83	48W
Springfield, Oreg., U.S.A.	171	44	2N	123	0W
Springfield, Tenn., U.S.A.	169	36	35N	86	55W
Springfield, Vt., U.S.A.	164	43	20N	72	30W
Springhill	148	45	40N	64	4W
Springs	137	26	13S	28	25 E
Springwood	117	33	41S	150	33 E
Spurn Hd.	29	53	34N	0	8 E
Squamish	154	49	45N	123	10W
Sredinnyy Khrebet	73	57	0N	160	0 E
Srednekolymsk	73	67	27N	153	40 E
Sremska Mitrovica	52	44	59N	19	33 E
Srepok ~→	95	13	33N	106	16 E
Sretensk	74	52	10N	117	40 E
Sri Lanka ■	90	7	30N	80	50 E
Srinagar	89	34	5N	74	50 E
Stadskanaal	41	53	4N	6	55 E
Staffa	30	56	26N	6	21W
Stafford	28	52	49N	2	9W
Stafford □	28	52	53N	2	10W
Staines	25	51	26N	0	30W
Stalingrad = Volgograd	68	48	40N	44	25 E
Stalino = Donotok	68	48	0N	37	45 E
Stalinogorsk = Novomoskovsk	68	54	5N	38	15 E
Stalybridge	28	53	29N	2	4W
Stamford, U.K.	25	52	39N	0	29W
Stamford, U.S.A.	164	41	5N	73	30W
Stanislav = Ivano-Frankovsk	68	48	40N	24	40 E
Stanley, Canada	152	55	24N	104	22W
Stanley, Falk. Is.	192	51	40S	59	51W
Stanovoy Khrebet	75	55	0N	130	0 E
Stanthorpe	116	28	36S	151	59 E
Stara Planina	53	43	15N	23	0 E
Stara Zagora	53	42	26N	25	39 E
Starkville	169	33	26N	88	48W
Start Pt.	27	50	13N	3	38W
State College	164	40	47N	77	49W
Staten, I. = Estados, I. de los .	192	54	40S	64	30W
Statesboro	170	32	26N	81	46W
Statesville	165	35	48N	80	51W
Staunton	165	38	7N	79	4W
Stavanger	60	58	57N	5	40 E
Staveren	40	52	53N	5	22 E
Stavropol	70	45	5N	42	0 E
Stawell	119	37	5S	142	47 E
Steenwijk	41	52	47N	6	7 E
Stefanie L. = Chew Bahir	132	4	40N	36	50 E
Steiermark □	45	47	26N	15	0 E
Steinbach	153	49	32N	96	40W
Steinkjer	65	63	59N	11	31 E
Stellarton	149	45	32N	62	30W
Stephenville	149	48	31N	58	35W
Stereá Ellás □	54	38	50N	22	0 E
Sterling, Colo., U.S.A.	163	40	40N	103	15W
Sterling, Ill., U.S.A.	166	41	45N	89	45W
Sterlitamak	71	53	40N	56	0 E
Stettin = Szczecin	58	53	27N	14	27 E
Stettler	155	52	19N	112	40W
Steubenville	164	40	21N	80	39W
Stevens Port	166	44	32N	89	34W
Stewart	144	63	19N	139	26W
Stewart I.	123	46	58S	167	54 E
Stikine ~→	144	56	40N	132	30W
Stillwater, Minn., U.S.A.	166	45	3N	92	47W
Stillwater, Okla., U.S.A.	168	36	5N	97	3W
Stillwater Ra.	172	39	45N	118	6W
Stip	53	41	42N	22	10 E
Stirling	31	56	7N	3	57W
Stirling Ra.	120	34	23S	118	0 E
Stockholm	60	59	20N	18	3 E
Stockholms län □	60	59	30N	18	20 E
Stockport	28	53	25N	2	11W
Stockton	172	38	0N	121	20W
Stockton-on-Tees	29	54	34N	1	20W
Stoke-on-Trent	28	53	1N	2	11W
Stonehaven	33	56	58N	2	11W
Stonehenge	24	51	9N	1	45W
Stonewall	153	50	10N	97	19W
Stora Lulevatten	66	67	10N	19	30 E

Name		Lat		Long	
Storavan	66	65 45N	18	10 E	
Store Bœlt	61	55 20N	11	0 E	
Storm B.	119	43 10S	147	30 E	
Storm Lake	166	42 35N	95	11W	
Stornoway	32	58 12N	6	23W	
Storsjön	66	63 12N	14	18 E	
Storuman	66	65 5N	17	10 E	
Stour →, Hereford & Worcs., U.K.	24	52 25N	2	13W	
Stour →, Kent, U.K.	25	51 15N	1	20 E	
Stour →, Suffolk, U.K.	25	51 55N	1	5 E	
Stourbridge	24	52 28N	2	8W	
Stowmarket	25	52 11N	1	0 E	
Strabane	34	54 50N	7	28W	
Stralsund	43	54 17N	13	5 E	
Strangford, L.	34	54 30N	5	37W	
Stranraer	30	54 54N	5	0W	
Strasbourg	37	48 35N	7	42 E	
Stratford, Canada	151	43 23N	81	0W	
Stratford, N.Z.	122	39 20S	174	19 E	
Stratford-on-Avon	24	52 12N	1	42W	
Strath Spey	33	57 15N	3	40W	
Strathalbyn	119	35 13S	138	53 E	
Strathclyde □	30	56 0N	4	50W	
Strathmore	33	56 40N	3	4W	
Strathy Pt.	33	58 35N	4	0W	
Streaky B.	118.	32 51S	134	18 E	
Streator	167	41 9N	88	52W	
Strómboli	49	38 48N	15	12 E	
Stromeferry	32	57 20N	5	33W	
Stromness	33	58 58N	3	18W	
Stronsay	33	59 8N	2	38W	
Stroud	24	51 44N	2	12W	
Strumica	53	41 28N	22	41 E	
Stuart L.	154	54 30N	124	30W	
Stung Treng	95	13 31N	105	58 E	
Sturgeon Bay	167	44 52N	87	20W	
Sturgeon Falls	151	46 25N	79	57W	
Stuttgart, Germany	42	48 46N	9	10 E	
Stuttgart, U.S.A.	168	34 30N	91	33W	
Styria = Steiermark □	45	47 26N	15	0 E	
Suakin	129	19 8N	37	20 E	
Subotica	52	46 6N	19	49 E	
Suchitoto	177	13 56N	89	0W	
Suchou = Suzhou	99	31 19N	120	38 E	
Süchow = Xuzhou	99	34 18N	117	10 E	
Sucre	187	19 0S	65	15W	
Sudan ■	129	15 0N	30	0 E	
Sudbury, Canada	151	46 30N	81	0W	
Sudbury, U.K.	25	52 2N	0	44 E	
Sudetan Mts. = Sudety	58	50 20N	16	45 E	
Sudety	58	50 20N	16	45 E	
Suez = El Suweis	128	29 58N	32	31 E	
Suez Canal = Suweis, Qanâl es	128	31 0N	32	20 E	
Suffolk	165	36 47N	76	33W	
Suffolk □	25	52 16N	1	0 E	
Sugluk = Saglouc	146	62 14N	75	38W	
Suhbaatar	98	50 17N	106	10 E	
Suir →	35	52 15N	7	10W	
Suita	106	34 45N	135	32 E	
Sukhona →	68	60 30N	45	0 E	
Sukhumi	70	43 0N	41	0 E	
Sukkertoppen	147	65 26N	52	55W	
Sukkur	88	27 42N	68	54 E	
Sukkur Barrage	88	27 40N	68	50 E	
Sukumo	109	32 56N	132	44 E	
Sulaiman Range	89	30 30N	69	50 E	
Sulawesi □	113	2 0S	120	0 E	
Sulina	57	45 10N	29	40 E	
Sulitjelma	66	67 9N	16	3 E	
Sullana	186	4 52S	80	39W	
Sullivan	167	39 5N	87	26W	
Sullivan I. = Lambi Kyun	96	10 50N	98	20 E	
Sulphur Springs	168	33 5N	95	36W	
Sulu Arch.	112	6 0N	121	0 E	
Sulu Sea	112	8 0N	120	0 E	
Suluq	128	31 44N	20	14 E	
Sumatera □	111	0 40N	100	20 E	
Sumatra = Sumatera □	111	0 40N	100	20 E	
Sumba	113	9 45S	119	35 E	
Sumbawa	113	8 26S	117	30 E	
Sumburgh Hd.	30	59 52N	1	17W	
Summerland	155	49 32N	119	41W	
Summerside	148	46 24N	63	47W	
Sumoto	109	34 21N	134	54 E	
Sumter	165	33 55N	80	22W	
Sumy	68	50 57N	34	50 E	
Sunbury, Australia	117	37 35S	144	44 E	
Sunbury, U.S.A.	164	40 50N	76	46W	
Sunda, Selat	111	6 20S	105	30 E	
Sundarbans, The	92	22 0N	89	0 E	
Sunderland	28	54 54N	1	22W	
Sundsvall	66	62 23N	17	17 E	
Sungei Patani	96	5 38N	100	29 E	
Sungei Siput	96	4 51N	101	6 E	
Sungurlu	80	40 12N	34	21 E	
Sunnyside	171	46 24N	120	2W	
Sunnyvale	172	37 23N	122	2W	
Suntar	72	62 15N	117	30 E	
Suō-Nada	108	33 50N	131	30 E	
Superior	150	46 45N	92	5W	
Superior, L.	150	47 40N	87	0W	
Suphan Dağı	81	38 54N	42	48 E	
Sūr	80	22 34N	59	32 E	
Surabaja = Surabaya	111	7 17S	112	45 E	
Surabaya	111	7 17S	112	45 E	
Surakarta	111	7 35S	110	48 E	
Surat	91	21 12N	72	55 E	
Surat Thani	96	9 6N	99	20 E	
Suratgarh	89	29 18N	73	55 E	
Surgut	69	61 14N	73	20 E	
Surin	95	14 50N	103	34 E	
Surinam ■	185	4 0N	56	0W	
Surrey □	25	51 16N	0	30W	
Surt	127	31 11N	16	39 E	
Surt, Khalīj	127	31 40N	18	30 E	
Suruga-Wan	107	34 45N	138	30 E	
Susaki	109	33 22N	133	17 E	
Susanville	172	40 28N	120	40W	
Susquehanna →	164	39 33N	76	5W	
Sutherland Falls	123	44 48S	167	46 E	
Sutlej →	89	29 23N	71	3 E	
Sutton-in-Ashfield	29	53 7N	1	20W	
Suva	122	18 6S	178	30 E	
Suwa	107	36 2N	138	8 E	
Suwa-Ko	107	36 3N	138	5 E	
Suwannee →	170	29 18N	83	9W	
Suwanose-Jima	104	29 38N	129	43 E	
Suweis, Qanâl es	128	31 0N	32	20 E	
Suzaka	107	36 39N	138	19 E	
Suzhou	99	31 19N	120	38 E	
Suzu-Misaki	105	37 31N	137	21 E	
Svalbard	13	78 0N	17	0 E	
Svartenhuk Halvø	146	71 50N	54	30W	
Svendborg	61	55 4N	10	35 E	
Sverdlovsk	69	56 50N	60	30 E	
Sverdrup Is.	12	79 0N	97	0W	
Svishtov	53	43 36N	25	23 E	
Svobodnyy	75	51 20N	128	0 E	
Swabian Alps = Schwäbische Alb	42	48 30N	9	30 E	
Swakopmund	136	22 37S	14	30 E	
Swale →	28	54 5N	1	20W	
Swan Hill	117	35 20S	143	33 E	
Swan Hills	155	54 42N	115	24W	
Swan Islands	178	17 22N	83	57W	
Swan River	152	52 10N	101	16W	
Swanage	24	50 36N	1	59W	
Swansea	27	51 37N	3	57W	
Swartberge	136	33 20S	22	0 E	
Swatow = Shantou	99	23 18N	116	40 E	
Swaziland ■	137	26 30S	31	30 E	
Sweden ■	66	57 0N	15	0 E	
Sweetwater	161	32 30N	100	28W	
Swift Current	152	50 20N	107	45W	
Swindon	24	51 33N	1	47W	
Switzerland ■	44	46 30N	8	0 E	
Swords	34	53 27N	6	15W	
Sydney, Australia	117	33 53S	151	10 E	
Sydney, Canada	149	46 7N	60	7W	
Sydney Mines	149	46 18N	60	15W	

Sydprøven	**147**	60 30N	45	35W
Sydra G. of = Surt, Khalīj	**127**	31 40N	18	30 E
Syktyvkar	**69**	61 45N	50	40 E
Sylacauga	**169**	33 10N	86	15W
Sylhet	**92**	24 54N	91	52 E
Sylvan Lake	**155**	52 20N	114	3W
Syracuse	**164**	43 4N	76	11W
Syrdarya →	**71**	46 3N	61	0 E
Syria ■	**80**	35 0N	38	0 E
Syrian Desert	**76**	31 0N	40	0 E
Syzran	**68**	53 12N	48	30 E
Szczecin	**58**	53 27N	14	27 E
Szechwan = Sichuan □	**99**	31 0N	104	0 E
Szeged	**59**	46 16N	20	10 E
Székesfehérvár	**59**	47 15N	18	25 E
Szolnok	**59**	47 10N	20	15 E
Szombathely	**59**	47 14N	16	38 E
Tabacal	**190**	23 15S	64	15W
Ṭābah	**82**	26 55N	42	38 E
Tabasco □	**177**	18 0N	92	40W
Taber	**155**	49 47N	112	8W
Tablas	**112**	12 25N	122	2 E
Table Mt.	**136**	34 0S	18	22 E
Table Top, Mt.	**121**	23 24S	147	11 E
Tabora	**135**	5 2S	32	50 E
Tabrīz	**81**	38 7N	46	20 E
Tabūk	**82**	28 23N	36	36 E
Tachibana-Wan	**108**	32 45N	130	7 E
Tachikawa	**107**	35 42N	139	25 E
Tacna	**187**	18 0S	70	20W
Tacoma	**171**	47 15N	122	30W
Tacuarembó	**191**	31 45S	56	0W
Tademaït, Plateau du	**127**	28 30N	2	30 E
Tadoussac	**148**	48 11N	69	42W
Tadzhik S.S.R. □	**71**	35 30N	70	0 E
Taegu	**98**	35 50N	128	37 E
Taejŏn	**98**	36 20N	127	28 E
Taganrog	**68**	47 12N	38	50 E
Tagish	**144**	60 19N	134	16W
Tagua, La	**184**	0 3N	74	40W
Tagus = Tajo →	**50**	38 40N	9	24W
Tahiti	**123**	17 37S	149	27W
Tahoua	**131**	14 57N	5	16 E
Taibei	**99**	25 4N	121	29 E
T'aichung = Taizhong	**99**	24 12N	120	35 E
Taidong	**99**	22 43N	121	9 E
Taihape	**122**	39 41S	175	48 E
Tailem Bend	**119**	35 12S	139	29 E
Taimyr = Taymyr, Poluostrov .	**72**	75 0N	100	0 E
Tain	**33**	57 49N	4	4W
Tainan	**99**	23 17N	120	18 E
Taínaron, Ákra	**54**	36 22N	22	27 E
T'aipei = Taibei	**99**	25 4N	121	29 E
Taiping	**96**	4 51N	100	44 E
Taisha	**109**	35 24N	132	40 E
Taitao, Pen. de	**192**	46 30S	75	0W
Taiwan ■	**99**	23 30N	121	0 E
Taiyuan	**98**	37 52N	112	33 E
Taizhong	**99**	24 12N	120	35 E
Ta'izz	**83**	13 35N	44	2 E
Tajimi	**106**	35 19N	137	8 E
Tajo →	**50**	38 40N	9	24W
Tak	**94**	16 52N	99	8 E
Takachiho	**108**	32 42N	131	18 E
Takada	**105**	37 7N	138	15 E
Takahashi	**109**	34 51N	133	39 E
Takamatsu	**109**	34 20N	134	5 E
Takaoka	**106**	36 47N	137	0 E
Takapuna	**122**	36 47S	174	47 E
Takasago	**109**	34 45N	134	48 E
Takasaki	**107**	36 20N	139	0 E
Takatsuki	**106**	34 51N	135	37 E
Takawa	**108**	33 38N	130	51 E
Takayama	**106**	36 18N	137	11 E
Takayama-Bonchi	**106**	36 0N	137	18 E
Takefu	**106**	35 50N	136	10 E
Takehara	**109**	34 21N	132	55 E
Taketa	**108**	32 58N	131	24 E
Takhār □	**87**	36 40N	70	0 E
Takla Landing	**154**	55 30N	125	50W
Takla Makan	**76**	39 0N	83	0 E
Taku	**108**	33 18N	130	3 E
Talara	**186**	4 38S	81	18 E
Talaud, Kepulauan	**113**	4 30N	127	10 E
Talca	**190**	35 28S	71	40W
Talcahuano	**190**	36 40S	73	10W
Ṭalesh, Kūhhā-ye	**81**	39 0N	48	30 E
Talguppa	**90**	14 10N	74	45 E
Taliabu	**113**	1 45S	125	0 E
Talkeetna	**142**	62 20N	150	9W
Tall 'Afar	**81**	36 22N	42	27 E
Talladega	**169**	33 28N	86	2W
Tallahassee	**170**	30 25N	84	15W
Tallangatta	**117**	36 15S	147	19 E
Tallinn	**68**	59 22N	24	48 E
Tallulah	**168**	32 25N	91	12W
Tamale	**130**	9 22N	0	50W
Tamana	**108**	32 58N	130	32 E
Tamano	**109**	34 29N	133	59 E
Tamanrasset	**127**	22 50N	5	30 E
Tamar →	**27**	50 33N	4	15W
Tamaulipas □	**176**	24 0N	98	45W
Tambellup	**120**	34 4S	117	37 E
Tambov	**68**	52 45N	41	28 E
Tamgak, Mts.	**127**	19 12N	8	35 E
Tamil Nadu □	**90**	11 0N	77	0 E
Tammerfors = Tampere	**67**	61 30N	23	50 E
Tamo Abu, Pegunungan	**111**	3 10N	115	0 E
Tampa	**170**	27 57N	82	38W
Tampa B.	**170**	27 40N	82	40W
Tampere	**67**	61 30N	23	50 E
Tampico	**177**	22 20N	97	50W
Tamrah	**83**	20 24N	45	25 E
Tamsagbulag	**98**	47 14N	117	21 E
Tamworth, Australia	**116**	31 7S	150	58 E
Tamworth, U.K.	**24**	52 38N	1	41W
Tana →, Kenya	**133**	2 32S	40	31 E
Tana →, Norway	**67**	70 30N	28	23 E
Tana, L.	**132**	13 5N	37	30 E
Tanabe	**106**	33 44N	135	22 E
Tanana	**142**	65 10N	152	15W
Tananarive = Antananarivo	**137**	18 55S	47	31 E
Tanba-Sanchi	**106**	35 7N	135	48 E
Tandil	**190**	37 15S	59	6W
Tando Adam	**88**	25 45N	68	40 E
Tane-ga-Shima	**104**	30 30N	131	0 E
Tanen Tong Dan	**93**	16 30N	98	30 E
Tanezrouft	**127**	23 9N	0	11 E
Tanga	**135**	5 5S	39	2 E
Tanganyika, L.	**135**	6 40S	30	0 E
Tanger	**126**	35 50N	5	49W
Tanggula Shan	**101**	32 40N	92	10 E
Tangier = Tanger	**126**	35 50N	5	49W
Tangshan	**98**	39 38N	118	10 E
Tanimbar, Kepulauan	**113**	7 30S	131	30 E
Taniyama	**108**	31 31N	130	31 E
Tanjore = Thanjavur	**90**	10 48N	79	12 E
Tannu Ola	**74**	51 0N	94	0 E
Tanout	**131**	14 50N	8	55 E
Tanta	**128**	30 45N	30	57 E
Tantung = Dandong	**98**	40 10N	124	20 E
Tanunda	**119**	34 30S	139	0 E
Tanzania ■	**135**	6 40S	34	0 E
Tapa Shan = Daba Shan	**99**	32 0N	109	0 E
Tapachula	**177**	14 54N	92	17W
Tapajós →	**185**	2 24S	54	41W
Tapanui	**123**	45 56S	169	18 E
Tapi →	**91**	21 8N	72	41 E
Tara →	**71**	56 42N	74	36 E
Tarabagatay, Khrebet	**71**	48 0N	83	0 E
Tarābulus, Lebanon	**80**	34 31N	35	50 E
Tarābulus, Libya	**127**	32 49N	13	7 E
Taranaki □	**122**	39 5S	174	51 E
Táranto	**49**	40 30N	17	11 E
Táranto, G. di	**49**	40 0N	17	15 E
Tarapoto	**186**	6 30S	76	20W
Tarare	**37**	45 54N	4	26 E
Tararua Range	**123**	40 45S	175	25 E
Tarauacá	**187**	8 6S	70	48W

Tarbela Dam	**89**	34 8N	72	52 E
Tarbert	**32**	57 54N	6	49W
Tarbes	**36**	43 15N	0	3 E
Tarcoola	**118**	30 44S	134	36 E
Taree	**116**	31 50S	152	30 E
Tarfaya	**126**	27 55N	12	55W
Tarifa	**50**	36 1N	5	36W
Tarija	**187**	21 30S	64	40W
Tarim →	**100**	41 5N	86	40 E
Tarim Pendi	**100**	40 0N	84	0 E
Tarko Sale	**69**	64 55N	77	50 E
Tarn →	**36**	44 5N	1	6 E
Tarnobrzeg	**58**	50 35N	21	41 E
Tarnów	**58**	50 3N	21	0 E
Tarragona	**51**	41 5N	1	17 E
Tarrasa	**51**	41 34N	2	1 E
Tarsus	**80**	36 58N	34	55 E
Tartagal	**190**	22 30S	63	50W
Tarţūs	**80**	34 55N	35	55 E
Tarumizu	**108**	31 29N	130	42 E
Tarutao, Ko	**96**	6 33N	99	40 E
Taschereau	**151**	48 40N	78	40W
Tashi Chho Dzong = Thimphu	**92**	27 31N	89	45 E
Tashkent	**71**	41 20N	69	10 E
Tasman B.	**123**	40 59S	173	25 E
Tasman Mts.	**123**	41 3S	172	25 E
Tasman Sea	**122**	36 0S	160	0 E
Tasmania □	**119**	42 0S	146	30 E
Tatabánya	**59**	47 32N	18	25 E
Tatarsk	**71**	55 14N	76	0 E
Tateshina-Yama	**107**	36 8N	138	11 E
Tateyama	**107**	35 0N	139	50 E
Tatra = Tatry	**59**	49 20N	20	0 E
Tatry	**59**	49 20N	20	0 E
Tatsuno	**109**	34 52N	134	33 E
Tat'ung = Datong	**98**	40 6N	113	18 E
Taubaté	**191**	23 0S	45	36W
Tauern	**45**	47 15N	12	40 E
Taumarunui	**122**	38 53S	175	15 E
Taunggyi	**93**	20 50N	97	0 E
Taungup Taunggya	**93**	18 20N	93	40 E
Taunton, U.K.	**27**	51 1N	3	7W
Taunton, U.S.A.	**164**	41 54N	71	6W
Taunus	**42**	50 15N	8	20 E
Taupo	**122**	38 41S	176	7 E
Taupo, L.	**122**	38 46S	175	55 E
Tauranga	**122**	37 42S	176	11 E
Taurus Mts. = Toros Daglari	**80**	37 0N	35	0 E
Taverny	**39**	49 2N	2	13 E
Tavistock	**27**	50 33N	4	9W
Tavoy	**94**	14 2N	98	12 E
Tawas City	**167**	44 16N	83	31W
Tay →	**33**	56 37N	3	38W
Tayabamba	**186**	8 15S	77	16W
Taylor Mt.	**161**	35 16N	107	36W
Taymā	**82**	27 35N	38	45 E
Taymyr, Poluostrov	**72**	75 0N	100	0 E
Tayshet	**74**	55 58N	98	1 E
Tayside □	**31**	56 25N	3	30W
Taz →	**69**	67 32N	78	40 E
Tbilisi	**70**	41 43N	44	50 E
Tchad ■ = Chad ■	**131**	15 0N	17	15 E
Tchad, L.	**131**	13 30N	14	30 E
Tch'eng-tou = Chengdu	**99**	30 38N	104	2 E
Tch'ung-k'ing = Chongqing	**99**	29 35N	106	25 E
Te Anau, L.	**123**	45 15S	167	45 E
Te Kuiti	**122**	38 20S	175	11 E
Tecuala	**175**	22 23N	105	27W
Tefé	**185**	3 25S	64	50W
Tegal	**111**	6 52S	109	8 E
Tegucigalpa	**179**	14 5N	87	14W
Tehachapi Mts.	**173**	35 0N	118	40W
Tehrān	**86**	35 44N	51	30 E
Tehuacán	**177**	18 27N	97	23W
Tehuantepec	**177**	16 21N	95	13W
Tehuantepec, G. de	**177**	16 0N	94	50W
Tehuantepec, Istmo de	**177**	17 0N	94	30W
Teifi →	**26**	52 4N	4	14W
Teignmouth	**27**	50 33N	3	30W
Tejo →	**50**	38 40N	9	24W
Tekax	**177**	20 12N	89	17W
Tekeli	**71**	44 50N	79	0 E
Tekirdağ	**80**	40 58N	27	30 E
Tel Aviv-Yafo	**80**	32 4N	34	48 E
Tela	**179**	15 40N	87	28W
Telanaipura = Jambi	**111**	1 38S	103	30 E
Telegraph Cr. →	**144**	58 0N	131	10W
Telemark fylke □	**60**	59 25N	8	30 E
Teles Pires →	**187**	7 21S	58	3W
Telford	**28**	52 42N	2	31W
Tell City	**167**	38 0N	86	44W
Teme →	**24**	52 23N	2	15W
Temerloh	**96**	3 27N	102	25 E
Temirtau	**71**	50 5N	72	56 E
Temora	**117**	34 30S	147	30 E
Temosachic	**174**	28 57N	107	51W
Temple	**158**	31 5N	97	22W
Temuco	**190**	38 45S	72	40W
Temuka	**123**	44 14S	171	17 E
Tenali	**91**	16 15N	80	35 E
Tenancingo	**177**	19 0N	99	33W
Tenango	**177**	19 7N	99	33W
Tenby	**27**	51 40N	4	42W
Tenerife	**126**	28 15N	16	35W
Teng Xian	**99**	35 5N	117	10 E
Tennessee □	**169**	36 0N	86	30W
Tennessee →	**169**	37 4N	88	34W
Tenri	**106**	34 39N	135	49 E
Tenryū	**107**	34 52N	137	49 E
Tenryū-Gawa →	**107**	35 39N	137	48 E
Tenterfield	**116**	29 0S	152	0 E
Teófilo Otoni	**189**	17 50S	41	30W
Tepic	**175**	21 30N	104	54W
Terang	**119**	38 15S	142	55 E
Terek →	**70**	44 0N	47	30 E
Terengganu □	**96**	4 55N	103	0 E
Teresina	**188**	5 9S	42	45W
Terewah, L.	**116**	29 52S	147	35 E
Termez	**70**	37 15N	67	15 E
Términos, L. de	**177**	18 37N	91	33W
Terneuzen	**40**	51 20N	3	50 E
Terni	**46**	42 34N	12	38 E
Terrace	**154**	54 30N	128	35W
Terre Haute	**167**	39 28N	87	24W
Terrell	**168**	32 44N	96	19W
Terschelling	**40**	53 25N	5	20 E
Teruel	**51**	40 22N	1	8W
Teshio	**103**	44 53N	141	44 E
Teslin	**144**	60 10N	132	43W
Test →	**24**	51 7N	1	30W
Tete	**137**	16 13S	33	33 E
Teteven	**53**	42 58N	24	17 E
Tétouan	**126**	35 35N	5	21W
Tetuán = Tétouan	**126**	35 35N	5	21W
Teuco →	**190**	25 35S	60	11W
Teutoburger Wald	**42**	52 5N	8	20 E
Tevere →	**46**	41 44N	12	14 E
Tewkesbury	**24**	51 59N	2	8W
Texarkana, Ark., U.S.A.	**168**	33 25N	94	0W
Texarkana, Tex., U.S.A.	**168**	33 25N	94	3W
Texas □	**161**	31 40N	98	30W
Texel	**40**	53 5N	4	50 E
Teziutlán	**177**	19 49N	97	21W
Tezpur	**93**	26 40N	92	45 E
Thabana Ntlenyana	**137**	29 30S	29	16 E
Thailand ■	**95**	16 0N	102	0 E
Thailand, G. of.	**95**	11 30N	101	0 E
Thai Desert	**89**	31 10N	71	30 E
Thame →	**24**	51 35N	1	8W
Thames	**122**	37 7S	175	34 E
Thames →	**25**	51 30N	0	35 E
Thane	**91**	19 12N	72	59 E
Thanh Hoa	**95**	19 48N	105	46 E
Thanh Pho Ho Chi Minh	**95**	10 58N	106	40 E
Thanjavur	**90**	10 48N	79	12 E
Thar Desert	**89**	28 0N	72	0 E
Thásos	**55**	40 40N	24	40 E
Thaungdut	**93**	24 30N	94	40 E
Thazi	**93**	21 0N	96	5 E
The Dalles	**171**	45 40N	121	11W
The Grenadines, Is.	**180**	12 40N	61	20W

The Hague = 's-Gravenhage . **40** 52 7N 4 17 E
The Macumba → .... **118** 27 52S 137 12 E
The Neales → .... **118** 28 8S 136 47 E
The Pas **152** 53 45N 101 15W
The Rock .... **117** 35 15S 147 2 E
The Warburton → ..... **118** 28 4S 137 28 E
Thebes = Thívai ...... **55** 38 19N 23 19 E
Thermaïkos Kólpos .... **54** 40 15N 22 45 E
Thermopolis **163** 43 35N 108 10W
Thessalía □ .... **54** 39 30N 22 0 E
Thessalon **150** 46 20N 83 30W
Thessaloníki .... **54** 40 38N 22 58 E
Thessaly = Thessalía □ ..... **54** 39 30N 22 0 E
Thetford Mines **148** 46 8N 71 18W
Thicket Portage............ **153** 55 19N 97 42W
Thies................ **130** 14 50N 16 51W
Thimphu............. **92** 27 31N 89 45 E
Thionville .... **37** 49 20N 6 10 E
Thíra .... **55** 36 23N 25 27 E
Thirsk **29** 54 15N 1 20W
Thisted .... **61** 56 58N 8 40 E
Thívai .... **55** 38 19N 23 19 E
Thomaston............ **170** 32 54N 84 20W
Thomasville, Ga., U.S.A. **170** 30 50N 84 0W
Thomasville, N.C., U.S.A. **165** 35 55N 80 4W
Thon Buri .... **94** 13 43N 100 29 E
Thornaby on Tees **29** 54 36N 1 19W
Thrace = Thráki □ ...... **55** 41 9N 25 30 E
Thráki □ .... **55** 41 9N 25 30 E
Three Hills **155** 51 43N 113 15W
Three Hummock I. .... **119** 40 25S 144 55 E
Thule **13** 77 40N 69 0W
Thundelarra............ **120** 28 53S 117 7 E
Thunder B. **150** 45 0N 83 20W
Thunder Bay **150** 48 20N 89 15W
Thüringer Wald .... **43** 50 35N 11 0 E
Thurles **35** 52 40N 7 53W
Thursday I. .... **115** 10 30S 142 3 E
Thurso **33** 58 34N 3 31W
Tian Shan .... **100** 43 0N 84 0 E
Tianjin............... **98** 39 8N 117 10 E
Tianshui .... **99** 34 32N 105 40 E
Tiber = Tevere → ..... **46** 41 44N 12 14 E
Tibesti.............. **127** 21 0N 17 30 E
Tibet = Xizang □ .... **101** 32 0N 88 0 E
Tibooburra................ **118** 29 26S 142 1 E
Ticul **177** 20 24N 89 32W
Tiel .... **40** 51 53N 5 26 E
Tien Shan .... **76** 42 0N 80 0 E
Tien-tsin = Tianjin ..... **98** 39 8N 117 10 E
T'ienching = Tianjin .... **98** 39 8N 117 10 E
Tientsin = Tianjin .... **98** 39 8N 117 10 E
Tierra de Campos....... **50** 42 10N 4 50W
Tierra del Fuego □ **192** 54 0S 67 45W
Tiffin **167** 41 8N 83 10W
Tiflis = Tbilisi .... **70** 41 43N 44 50 E
Tifton............... **170** 31 28N 83 32W
Tignish **148** 46 58N 64 2W
Tigris = Dijlah, Nahr → ..... **81** 31 0N 47 25 E
Tijuana **174** 32 32N 117 1W
Tiksi .... **72** 71 40N 128 45 E
Tilburg .... **40** 51 31N 5 6 E
Tilbury .... **25** 51 27N 0 24 E
Tillsonburg............ **151** 42 53N 80 44W
Tílos .... **55** 36 27N 27 27 E
Timaru .... **123** 44 23S 171 14 E
Timbuktu = Tombouctou **130** 16 50N 3 0W
Timișoara .... **56** 45 43N 21 15 E
Timmins **151** 48 28N 81 25W
Timor .... **113** 9 0S 125 0 E
Timor Sea............ **113** 10 0S 127 0 E
Tinaca Pt............. **112** 5 30N 125 25 E
Tindouf.............. **126** 27 42N 8 10W
Tinnevelly = Tirunelveli ...... **90** 8 45N 77 45 E
Tinogasta............ **190** 28 5S 67 32W
Tínos .... **55** 37 33N 25 8 E
Tioman, Pulau .... **96** 2 50N 104 10 E
Tipperary **35** 52 28N 8 10W
Tipperary □ **35** 52 37N 7 55W
Tipton **24** 52 32N 2 4W
Tirana .... **52** 41 18N 19 49 E

Tiraspol .... **68** 46 55N 29 35 E
Tire .... **80** 38 5N 27 50 E
Tirebolu .... **81** 40 58N 38 45 E
Tiree **30** 56 31N 6 55W
Tîrgu Mureș .... **57** 46 31N 24 38 E
Tirol □................ **45** 47 3N 10 43 E
Tiruchchirappalli .... **90** 10 45N 78 45 E
Tirunelveli .... **90** 8 45N 77 45 E
Tisa → .... **59** 45 15N 20 17 E
Tisdale **152** 52 50N 104 0W
Titicaca, L. **187** 15 30S 69 30W
Titograd .... **52** 42 30N 19 19 E
Titov Veles .... **53** 41 46N 21 47 E
Titovo Užice............ **52** 43 55N 19 50 E
Tiverton **27** 50 54N 3 30W
Tívoli .... **46** 41 58N 12 45 E
Tizimín **177** 21 9N 88 9W
Tjirebon = Cirebon .... **111** 6 45S 108 32 E
Tlaxcala □ **177** 19 25N 98 10W
Tlaxiaco............... **177** 17 18N 97 40W
Tlemcen **127** 34 52N 1 21W
To-Shima .... **107** 34 31N 139 17 E
Toamasina .... **137** 18 10S 49 25 E
Toba Kakar .... **88** 31 30N 69 0 E
Tobago **180** 11 10N 60 30W
Tobermory............. **30** 56 37N 6 4W
Tobol'sk .... **69** 58 15N 68 10 E
Tobruk = Tubruq .... **128** 32 7N 23 55 E
Tocantins → **188** 1 45S 49 10W
Toccoa **165** 34 32N 83 17W
Tochigi .... **107** 36 25N 139 45 E
Tocopilla **190** 22 5S 70 10W
Todos Santos **175** 23 27N 110 13W
Tōgane .... **107** 35 33N 140 22 E
Togliatti .... **68** 53 32N 49 24 E
Togo ■ .... **130** 6 15N 1 35 E
Tōhoku □ .... **103** 39 50N 141 45 E
Tōjō .... **109** 34 53N 133 16 E
Tokai .... **106** 35 2N 136 55 E
Tokaj .... **58** 48 8N 21 27 E
Tokara Kaikyō .... **104** 30 0N 130 0 E
Tokat................ **80** 40 22N 36 35 E
Tokelau Is. **123** 9 0S 171 45W
Toki .... **106** 35 18N 137 8 E
Tokoname .... **106** 34 53N 136 51 E
Tokorozawa .... **107** 35 47N 139 28 E
Tokushima .... **109** 34 4N 134 34 E
Tokuyama .... **108** 34 3N 131 50 E
Tōkyō .... **107** 35 45N 139 45 E
Tōkyō-Wan .... **107** 35 25N 139 47 E
Tolbukhin .... **53** 43 37N 27 49 E
Toledo, Spain **50** 39 50N 4 2W
Toledo, U.S.A. **167** 41 37N 83 33W
Tolga .... **127** 34 40N 5 22 E
Tolima, Vol. **184** 4 40N 75 19W
Toluca **177** 19 20N 99 40W
Tomakomai .... **103** 42 38N 141 36 E
Tombigbee → **169** 31 4N 87 58W
Tombouctou **130** 16 50N 3 0W
Tomini, Teluk .... **113** 0 10S 122 0 E
Tomsk................ **71** 56 30N 85 5 E
Tonalá **177** 16 4N 93 45W
Tonantins **184** 2 45S 67 45W
Tonbridge .... **25** 51 12N 0 18 E
Tong Xian .... **98** 39 55N 116 35 E
Tonga ■ **123** 19 50S 174 30W
Tongchuan .... **99** 35 6N 109 3 E
Tonghua............... **98** 41 42N 125 58 E
Tongking, G. of .... **95** 20 0N 108 0 E
Tongue **33** 58 29N 4 25W
Tonk .... **91** 26 6N 75 54 E
Tonkin = Bac Phan .... **95** 22 0N 105 0 E
Tonlé Sap............. **95** 13 0N 104 0 E
Tonopah.............. **172** 38 4N 117 12W
Tonoshō .... **109** 34 29N 134 11 E
Tooele **162** 40 30N 112 20W
Toowoomba .... **116** 27 32S 151 56 E
Topeka **166** 39 3N 95 40W
Toppenish **171** 46 27N 120 16W
Torbay **27** 50 26N 3 31W
Torino .... **46** 45 4N 7 40 E

Tormes →		**50**	41 18N	6 29W
Torne älv →		**67**	65 50N	24 12 E
Torneå = Tornio		**67**	65 50N	24 12 E
Torneträsk		**66**	68 24N	19 15 E
Tornio		**67**	65 50N	24 12 E
Toro, Cerro del		**190**	29 10S	69 50W
Toronto, Australia		**117**	33 0S	151 30 E
Toronto, Canada		**151**	43 39N	79 20W
Toros Daglari		**80**	37 0N	35 0 E
Torquay		**27**	50 27N	3 31W
Torre Annunziata		**49**	40 45N	14 26 E
Tôrre de Moncorvo		**50**	41 12N	7 8W
Torremolinos		**50**	36 38N	4 30W
Torrens, L.		**119**	31 0S	137 50 E
Torreón		**174**	25 33N	103 26W
Torres Vedras		**50**	39 5N	9 15W
Torridge →		**27**	50 51N	4 10W
Torrington		**164**	41 50N	73 9W
Tortosa		**51**	40 49N	0 31 E
Tortosa, C.		**51**	40 41N	0 52 E
Toruń		**58**	53 0N	18 39 E
Tory I.		**34**	55 17N	8 12W
Tosa-Shimizu		**109**	32 52N	132 58 E
Tosa-Wan		**109**	33 15N	133 30 E
Toscana		**46**	43 30N	11 5 E
Tostado		**190**	29 15S	61 50W
Tosu		**109**	33 22N	130 31 E
Totnes		**27**	50 26N	3 41W
Totonicapán		**177**	14 58N	91 12W
Tottori		**109**	35 30N	134 15 E
Toubkal, Djebel		**126**	31 0N	8 0W
Touggourt		**127**	33 6N	6 4 E
Toulon		**37**	43 10N	5 55 E
Toulouse		**36**	43 37N	1 27 E
Toungoo		**93**	19 0N	96 30 E
Touraine		**36**	47 20N	0 30 E
Tourane = Da Nang		**95**	16 4N	108 13 E
Tourcoing		**38**	50 42N	3 10 E
Tournai		**42**	50 35N	3 25 E
Tours		**36**	47 22N	0 40 E
Townsville		**121**	19 15S	146 45 E
Towson		**164**	39 26N	76 34W
Toyama		**106**	36 40N	137 15 E
Toyama-Wan		**105**	37 0N	137 30 E
Toyohashi		**106**	34 45N	137 25 E
Toyokawa		**106**	34 48N	137 27 E
Toyonaka		**106**	34 50N	135 28 E
Toyooka		**109**	35 35N	134 48 E
Toyota		**106**	35 3N	137 7 E
Tozeur		**127**	33 56N	8 8 E
Trabzon		**81**	41 0N	39 45 E
Tracy		**172**	37 46N	121 27W
Trafalgar, C.		**50**	36 10N	6 2W
Trail		**155**	49 5N	117 40W
Tralee		**35**	52 16N	9 42W
Tralee B.		**35**	52 17N	9 55W
Tran Ninh, Cao Nguyen		**95**	19 30N	103 10 E
Trangan		**113**	6 40S	134 20 E
Trangie		**116**	32 4S	148 0 E
Transantarctic Mts.		**15**	85 0S	170 ' 0W
Transcona		**153**	49 55N	97 0W
Transilvania		**57**	46 19N	25 0 E
Transkei		**137**	32 15S	28 15 E
Transvaal □		**137**	25 0S	29 0 E
Transylvania = Transilvania		**57**	46 19N	25 0 E
Transylvanian Alps		**17**	45 30N	25 0 E
Trápani		**48**	38 1N	12 30 E
Traralgon		**117**	38 12S	146 34 E
Trasimeno, L.		**46**	43 10N	12 5 E
Travers, Mt.		**123**	42 1S	172 45 E
Traverse City		**167**	44 45N	85 39W
Travnik		**52**	44 17N	17 39 E
Tredegar		**27**	51 47N	3 16W
Tregaron		**26**	52 14N	3 56W
Treinta y Tres		**191**	33 16S	54 17W
Trelew		**192**	43 10S	65 20W
Trenque Lauquen		**190**	36 5S	62 45W
Trent →		**29**	53 33N	0 44W
Trentino-Alto Adige □		**47**	46 30N	11 0 E
Trento		**47**	46 5N	11 8 E
Trenton, Canada		**151**	44 10N	77 34W
Trenton, Mo., U.S.A.		**166**	40 5N	93 37W
Trenton, N.J., U.S.A.		**164**	40 15N	74 41W
Tréport, Le		**38**	50 3N	1 20 E
Tres Arroyos		**190**	38 26S	60 20W
Três Lagoas		**188**	20 50S	51 43W
Tres Montes, C.		**192**	46 50S	75 30W
Tres Puntas, C.		**192**	47 0S	66 0W
Treviso		**47**	45 40N	12 15 E
Trichinopoly = Tiruchchirappalli		**90**	10 45N	78 45 E
Trichur		**90**	10 30N	76 18 E
Trier		**42**	49 45N	6 37 E
Trieste		**47**	45 39N	13 45 E
Trikkala		**54**	39 34N	21 47 E
Trincomalee		**90**	8 38N	81 15 E
Trinidad, Bolivia		**187**	14 46S	64 50W
Trinidad, Colombia		**184**	5 25N	71 40W
Trinidad, Cuba		**178**	21 48N	80 0W
Trinidad, Uruguay		**191**	33 30S	56 50W
Trinidad, U.S.A.		**163**	37 15N	104 30W
Trinidad & Tobago ■		**180**	10 30N	61 20W
Trinity →		**168**	30 30N	95 0W
Trinity Mts.		**172**	40 20N	118 50W
Tripoli = Tarābulus, Lebanon		**80**	34 31N	35 50 E
Tripoli = Tarābulus, Libya		**127**	32 49N	13 7 E
Trípolis		**54**	37 31N	22 25 E
Tripura □		**93**	24 0N	92 0 E
Trivandrum		**90**	8 41N	77 0 E
Trois-Riviéres		**151**	46 25N	72 34W
Troitsk		**71**	54 10N	61 35 E
Trollhättan		**60**	58 17N	12 20 E
Tromsø		**66**	69 40N	18 56 E
Trondheim		**65**	63 36N	10 25 E
Trossachs, The		**31**	56 14N	4 24W
Trotternish		**32**	57 32N	6 15W
Trouville		**38**	49 21N	0 5 E
Trowbridge		**24**	51 18N	2 12W
Troy, Ala., U.S.A.		**169**	31 50N	85 58W
Troy, N.Y., U.S.A.		**164**	42 45N	73 39W
Troyes		**39**	48 19N	4 3 E
Trucial States = United Arab Emirates ■		**85**	23 50N	54 0 E
Trujillo, Hond.		**179**	16 0N	86 0W
Trujillo, Peru		**186**	8 6S	79 0W
Trujillo, Venezuela		**184**	9 22N	70 38W
Trundle		**117**	32 53S	147 35 E
Trung-Phan		**95**	16 0N	108 0 E
Truro, Canada		**149**	45 21N	63 14W
Truro, U.K.		**27**	50 17N	5 2W
Tselinograd		**71**	51 10N	71 30 E
Tsinan = Jinan		**98**	36 38N	117 1 E
Tsinghai = Qinghai □		**101**	36 0N	98 0 E
Tsingtao = Qingdao		**98**	36 5N	120 20 E
Tsu		**106**	34 45N	136 25 E
Tsuchiura		**107**	36 5N	140 15 E
Tsugaru-Kaikyō		**103**	41 35N	141 0 E
Tsukumi		**108**	33 4N	131 52 E
Tsukushi-Sanchi		**108**	33 25N	130 30 E
Tsuruga		**106**	35 45N	136 2 E
Tsurugi-San		**109**	33 51N	134 6 E
Tsuruoka		**103**	38 44N	139 50 E
Tsushima, Gifu, Japan		**106**	35 10N	136 43 E
Tsushima, Nagasaki, Japan		**104**	34 20N	129 20 E
Tuamotu Arch.		**123**	17 0S	144 0W
Tubarão		**191**	28 30S	49 0W
Tubruq		**128**	32 7N	23 55 E
Tubuai Is.		**123**	25 0S	150 0W
Tucacas		**184**	10 48N	68 19W
Tucson		**160**	32 14N	110 59W
Tucumcari		**161**	35 12N	103 45W
Tucupita		**185**	9 2N	62 3W
Tucuruí		**188**	3 42S	49 44W
Tudmur		**80**	34 36N	38 15 E
Tuktoyaktuk		**144**	69 27N	133 2W
Tula, Mexico		**177**	23 0N	99 43W
Tula, U.S.S.R.		**68**	54 13N	37 38 E
Tulare		**173**	36 15N	119 26W
Tulcán		**184**	0 48N	77 43W
Tullahoma		**169**	35 23N	86 12W
Tullamore		**35**	53 17N	7 30W
Tully		**121**	17 56S	145 55 E

TUL

Name	Ref	Lat	Long
Tulsa	168	36 10N	96 0W
Tulua	184	4 6N	76 11W
Tuma →	179	13 6N	84 35W
Tumaco	184	1 50N	78 45W
Tumatumari	185	5 20N	58 55W
Tumbarumba	117	35 44S	148 0 E
Túmbes	186	3 37S	80 27W
Tumkur	90	13 18N	77 6 E
Tummel, L.	33	56 43N	3 55W
Tummo	127	22 45N	14 8 E
Tump	88	26 7N	62 16 E
Tumucumaque, Serra	188	2 0N	55 0W
Tumut	117	35 16S	148 13 E
Tunbridge Wells	25	51 7N	0 16 E
Tundzha →	53	41 40N	26 35 E
Tunis	127	36 50N	10 11 E
Tunisia ■	127	33 30N	9 10 E
Tunja	184	5 33N	73 25W
Tunxi	99	29 42N	118 25 E
Tupelo	169	34 15N	88 42W
Tupiza	187	21 30S	65 40W
Tupper L.	151	44 18N	74 30W
Tuque, La	151	47 30N	72 50W
Túquerres	184	1 5N	77 37W
Tura	92	25 30N	90 16 E
Turayf	82	31 41N	38 39 E
Turfan = Turpan	100	43 58N	89 10 E
Turfan Depression = Turpan Hami	100	42 40N	89 25 E
Tŭrgovishte	53	43 17N	26 38 E
Turgutlu	80	38 30N	27 48 E
Turin = Torino	46	45 4N	7 40 E
Turkana, L.	132	3 30N	36 5 E
Turkestan	71	43 17N	68 16 E
Turkey ■	80	39 0N	36 0 E
Turkmen S.S.R. □	70	39 0N	59 0 E
Turks Is.	180	21 20N	71 20W
Turku	67	60 30N	22 19 E
Turlock	172	37 30N	120 55W
Turnagain, C.	122	40 28S	176 38 E
Turnhout	42	51 19N	4 57 E
Tŭrnovo	53	43 5N	25 41 E
Turnu Rosu Pasul	57	45 33N	24 17 E
Turnu-Severin	56	44 39N	22 41 E
Turpan	100	43 58N	89 10 E
Turpan Hami	100	42 40N	89 25 E
Turukhansk	74	65 21N	88 5 E
Tuscaloosa	169	33 13N	87 31W
Tuscany = Toscana	46	43 30N	11 5 E
Tuskegee	169	32 24N	85 39W
Tutrakan	53	44 2N	26 40 E
Tuvalu ■	122	8 0S	178 0 E
Tuxpan	177	20 57N	97 24W
Tuxtla Gutiérrez	177	16 45N	93 7W
Tuy Hoa	95	13 5N	109 10 E
Tuyen Hoa	95	17 50N	106 10 E
Tuz Gölü	80	38 45N	33 30 E
Tūz Khurmātū	81	34 56N	44 38 E
Tuzla	52	44 34N	18 41 E
Tweed →	31	55 42N	2 10W
Tweed Heads	116	28 10S	153 31 E
Twin Falls	172	42 30N	114 30W
Two Harbors	156	47 1N	91 40W
Tyler	168	32 18N	95 18W
Tyne →	28	54 58N	1 28W
Tyne & Wear □	28	54 55N	1 35W
Tynemouth	28	55 1N	1 27W
Tyrol = Tirol □	45	47 3N	10 43 E
Tyrrhenian Sea	48	40 0N	12 30 E
Tyumen	69	57 11N	65 29 E
Tzukong = Zigong	99	29 15N	104 48 E
Uaupés	184	0 8S	67 5W
Ubangi = Oubangi →	131	1 0N	17 50 E
Ube	108	33 56N	131 15 E
Uberaba	188	19 50S	47 55W
Uberlândia	188	19 0S	48 20W
Ubon Ratchathani	95	15 15N	104 50 E
Ucayali →	186	4 30S	73 30W
Uchi Lake	153	51 5N	92 35W
Uchiura-Wan	103	42 25N	140 40 E
Uchur →	75	58 48N	130 35 E
Udaipur	91	24 36N	73 44 E
Uddevalla	60	58 21N	11 55 E
Údine	47	46 5N	13 10 E
Udmurt A.S.S.R. □	69	57 30N	52 30 E
Udon Thani	95	17 29N	102 46 E
Ueda	107	36 24N	138 16 E
Uelen	73	66 10N	170 0W
Uelzen	43	53 0N	10 33 E
Ueno	106	34 45N	136 8 E
Ufa	69	54 45N	55 55 E
Uganda ■	132	2 0N	32 0 E
Uinta Mts.	163	40 45N	110 30W
Uithuizen	41	53 24N	6 41 E
Uji	106	34 53N	135 48 E
Ujjain	91	23 9N	75 43 E
Újpest	59	47 32N	19 6 E
Ujung Pandang	113	5 10S	119 20 E
Ukiah	172	39 10N	123 9W
Ukrainian S.S.R. □	68	49 0N	32 0 E
Ulaanbaatar	98	47 55N	106 53 E
Ulan Bator = Ulaanbaatar	98	47 55N	106 53 E
Ulan Ude	74	51 45N	107 40 E
Ulcinj	52	41 58N	19 10 E
Ulhasnagar	91	19 15N	73 10 E
Ulladulla	117	35 21S	150 29 E
Ullapool	32	57 54N	5 10W
Ullswater	28	54 35N	2 52W
Ulm	42	48 23N	10 0 E
Ulster □	34	54 35N	6 30W
Ulverston	28	54 13N	3 7W
Ulverstone	119	41 11S	146 11 E
Ulyanovsk	68	54 20N	48 25 E
Ulyasutay	100	47 56N	97 28 E
Umbrella Mts	123	45 35S	169 5 E
Umbria □	46	42 53N	12 30 E
Ume älv →	66	63 45N	20 20 E
Umeå	66	63 45N	20 20 E
Umm al Qaywayn	85	25 30N	55 35 E
Umm Lajj	82	25 0N	37 23 E
Umnak	142	53 20N	168 20W
Umpang	94	16 3N	98 54 E
Umtata	137	31 36S	28 49 E
Unalaska	142	53 40N	166 40W
Ungava B.	146	59 30N	67 30W
Ungava Pen.	146	60 0N	74 0W
União da Vitória	191	26 13S	51 5W
Unimak	142	55 0N	164 0W
Union City	169	36 25N	89 0W
Union of Soviet Socialist Republics ■	79	60 0N	100 0 E
Uniontown	164	39 54N	79 45W
United Arab Emirates ■	85	23 50N	54 0 E
United Kingdom ■	18	55 0N	3 0W
United States of America ■	139	37 0N	96 0W
Unity	152	52 30N	109 5W
Unnao	92	26 35N	80 30 E
Unst	30	60 50N	0 55W
Uozu	106	36 48N	137 24 E
Upata	185	8 1N	62 24W
Upper Austria = Oberösterreich □	45	48 10N	14 0 E
Upper Hutt	123	41 8S	175 5 E
Upper Taimyr →	72	74 15N	99 48 E
Upper Volta ■ = Burkina Faso ■	130	12 0N	1 0W
Uppsala	60	59 53N	17 38 E
Uppsala län □	60	60 0N	17 30 E
Ur	84	30 55N	46 25 E
Uracara	185	2 20S	57 50W
Urakawa	103	42 9N	142 47 E
Ural →	70	47 0N	51 48 E
Ural Mts. = Uralskie Gory	69	60 0N	59 0 E
Uralsk	70	51 20N	51 20 E
Uralskie Gory	69	60 0N	59 0 E
Uranium City	145	59 34N	108 37W
Urawa	107	35 50N	139 40 E
Urbana, Ill., U.S.A.	167	40 7N	88 12W
Urbana, Ohio, U.S.A.	167	40 9N	83 44W

Name	Pg	Lat	Long
Urbana, La	184	7 8N	66 56W
Urcos	187	13 40S	71 38W
Ures	174	29 26N	110 24W
Urfa	81	37 12N	38 50 E
Urgench	70	41 40N	60 41 E
Uribia	184	11 43N	72 16W
Urk	41	52 39N	5 36 E
Urmia = Orūmīyeh	81	37 40N	45 0 E
Urmia, L. = Orūmīyeh, Daryācheh-ye	81	37 50N	45 30 E
Uruapan	175	19 30N	102 0W
Uruçuí	188	7 20S	44 28W
Uruguaiana	191	29 50S	57 0W
Uruguay ■	191	32 30S	56 30W
Uruguay ~►	191	34 12S	58 18W
Urumchi = Ürümqi	100	43 45N	87 45 E
Ürümqi	100	43 45N	87 45 E
Urup, Os.	75	46 0N	151 0 E
Usa	108	33 31N	131 21 E
Uşak	80	38 43N	29 28 E
Usfan	82	21 58N	39 27 E
Ushant = Ouessant, Île d'	36	48 28N	5 6W
Ushibuka	108	32 11N	130 1 E
Ushuaia	192	54 50S	68 23W
Usk ~►	26	51 37N	2 56W
Üsküdar	80	41 0N	29 5 E
Usolye Sibirskoye	74	52 48N	103 40 E
Uspenskiy	71	48 41N	72 43 E
Ussuriysk	75	43 48N	131 59 E
Ust-Aldan = Batamay	74	63 30N	129 15 E
Ust-Ilimsk	74	58 3N	102 39 E
Ust-Kamchatsk	73	56 10N	162 28 E
Ust-Kamenogorsk	71	50 0N	82 36 E
Ust Maya	75	60 30N	134 28 E
Ust Olenek	72	73 0N	119 48 E
Ust Port	69	69 40N	84 26 E
Ust Urt = Ustyurt, Plato	70	44 0N	55 0 E
Ust Vorkuta	69	67 24N	64 0 E
Ústí nad Labem	58	50 41N	14 3 E
Ustica	48	38 42N	13 10 E
Ustinov	69	56 51N	53 14 E
Ustyurt, Plato	70	44 0N	55 0 E
Usu	100	44 27N	84 40 E
Usuki	108	33 8N	131 49 E
Usumbura = Bujumbura	135	3 16S	29 18 E
Utah □	163	39 30N	111 30W
Utah, L.	163	40 10N	111 58W
Uthai Thani	94	15 22N	100 3 E
Utica	164	43 5N	75 18W
Uto	108	32 41N	130 40 E
Utrecht	40	52 5N	5 8 E
Utrecht □	40	52 6N	5 7 E
Utrera	50	37 12N	5 48W
Utsunomiya	107	36 30N	139 50 E
Uttar Pradesh □	92	27 0N	80 0 E
Uttoxeter	28	52 53N	1 50W
Uusikaupunki	66	60 47N	21 25 E
Uvalde	161	29 15N	99 48W
Uvs Nuur	74	50 20N	92 30 E
Uwajima	109	33 10N	132 35 E
Uzbek S.S.R. □	70	41 30N	65 0 E
Vaal ~►	137	29 4S	23 38 E
Vaals	41	50 46N	6 1 E
Vaasa	67	63 6N	21 38 E
Vác	58	47 49N	19 10 E
Vach ~►	69	60 45N	76 45 E
Vadodara	91	22 20N	73 10 E
Vadsø	67	70 3N	29 50 E
Váh ~►	59	47 55N	18 0 E
Vaigach	69	70 10N	59 0 E
Val d'Or	151	48 7N	77 47W
Valahia	57	44 35N	25 0 E
Valcheta	192	40 40S	66 8W
Valdés, Pen.	192	42 30S	63 45W
Valdez	142	61 14N	146 17W
Valdivia	190	39 50S	73 14W
Valdosta	170	30 50N	83 20W
Valence	37	44 57N	4 54 E
Valencia, Spain	51	39 27N	0 23W
Valencia, Venezuela	184	10 11N	68 0W
Valencia □	51	39 20N	0 40W
Valencia, Albufera de	51	39 20N	0 27W
Valencia, G. de	51	39 30N	0 20 E
Valencia de Alcántara	50	39 25N	7 14W
Valenciennes	38	50 20N	3 34 E
Valentia I.	35	51 54N	10 22W
Valera	184	9 19N	70 37W
Valkenswaard	41	51 21N	5 29 E
Valladolid, Mexico	177	20 41N	88 12W
Valladolid, Spain	50	41 38N	4 43W
Valle d'Aosta □	46	45 45N	7 22 E
Valle de la Pascua	184	9 13N	66 0W
Valle de Santiago	177	20 23N	101 12W
Vallecas	50	40 23N	3 41W
Vallejo	172	38 12N	122 15W
Valletta	49	35 54N	14 30 E
Valley City	163	46 57N	98 0W
Valley View	155	40 39N	76 33W
Valona = Vlóra	52	40 32N	19 28 E
Valparaíso, Chile	190	33 2S	71 40W
Valparaíso, Mexico	175	22 46N	103 34W
Valsad	91	20 40N	72 58 E
Van	81	38 30N	43 20 E
Van, L. = Van Gölü	81	38 30N	43 0 E
Van Buren, Canada	148	47 10N	67 55W
Van Buren, U.S.A.	168	35 28N	94 18W
Van Gölü	81	38 30N	43 0 E
Van Wert	167	40 52N	84 31W
Vancouver, Canada	154	49 15N	123 10W
Vancouver, U.S.A.	171	45 44N	122 41W
Vancouver I.	154	49 50N	126 0W
Vandalia	166	38 57N	89 4W
Vanderhoof	154	54 0N	124 0W
Vänern	60	58 47N	13 30 E
Vanier	151	45 27N	75 40W
Vankarem	73	67 51N	175 50 E
Vännäs	66	63 58N	19 48 E
Vannes	36	47 40N	2 47W
Vanua Levu	122	16 33S	179 15 E
Vanuatu ■	122	15 0S	168 0 E
Varanasi	92	25 22N	83 0 E
Varangerfjorden	67	70 3N	29 25 E
Varaždin	52	46 20N	16 20 E
Vardak □	87	34 0N	68 0 E
Vardø	67	70 23N	31 5 E
Värmland	60	60 0N	13 30 E
Varna	53	43 13N	27 56 E
Vascongadas	50	42 50N	2 45W
Västerås	60	59 37N	16 38 E
Västmanlands län □	60	59 45N	16 20 E
Vatnajökull	64	64 30N	16 48W
Vatra-Dornei	57	47 22N	25 22 E
Vättern	60	58 25N	14 30 E
Vaygach, Ostrov	69	70 0N	60 0 E
Veendam	41	53 5N	6 52 E
Vega, La	180	19 20N	70 30W
Veghel	41	51 37N	5 32 E
Vegreville	155	53 30N	112 5W
Vela, La	184	11 27N	69 34W
Vellore	90	12 57N	79 10 E
Venado Tuerto	190	33 50S	62 0W
Vendôme	39	47 47N	1 3 E
Véneto □	47	45 40N	12 0 E
Venézia	47	45 27N	12 20 E
Venézia, Golfo di	47	45 20N	13 0 E
Venezuela ■	184	8 0N	65 0W
Venezuela, Golfo de	184	11 30N	71 0W
Vengurla	91	15 53N	73 45 E
Venice = Venézia	47	45 27N	12 20 E
Venlo	41	51 22N	6 11 E
Venraij	41	51 31N	6 0 E
Ventnor	24	50 35N	1 12W
Ventoux	37	44 10N	5 17 E
Ventura	173	34 16N	119 18W
Veracruz	177	19 10N	96 10W
Veracruz □	177	19 20N	96 40W
Verde, R. ~►	175	15 59N	97 50W
Verdun	37	49 12N	5 24 E
Vereeniging	137	26 38S	27 57 E

Name	Map	Lat°	Lat′	N/S	Long°	Long′	E/W
Verkhoyansk	**72**	67	35N		133	25	E
Verkhoyanskiy Khrebet	**72**	66	0N		129	0	E
Vermilion	**152**	53	20N		110	50W	
Vermont □	**164**	43	40N		72	50W	
Verneuil-sur-Avre	**39**	48	45N		0	55	E
Vernon, Canada	**155**	50	20N		119	15W	
Vernon, France	**39**	49	5N		1	30	E
Vernon, U.S.A.	**161**	34	10N		99	20W	
Verona	**46**	45	27N		11	0	E
Versailles	**39**	48	48N		2	8	E
Vert, C.	**130**	14	45N		17	30W	
Verviers	**42**	50	37N		5	52	E
Vest-Agder fylke □	**60**	58	30N		7	15	E
Vesterålen	**64**	68	45N		15	0	E
Vestfjorden	**64**	67	55N		14	0	E
Vestfold fylke □	**60**	59	15N		10	0	E
Vestspitsbergen	**13**	78	40N		17	0	E
Vesuvio	**49**	40	50N		14	22	E
Vesuvius, Mt. = Vesuvio	**49**	40	50N		14	22	E
Viacha	**187**	16	39S		68	18W	
Viborg	**61**	56	27N		9	23	E
Vicenza	**47**	45	32N		11	31	E
Vichy	**37**	46	9N		3	26	E
Vicksburg	**169**	32	22N		90	56W	
Victor Harbor	**119**	35	30S		138	37	E
Victoria, Canada	**154**	48	30N		123	25W	
Victoria, Chile	**190**	38	13S		72	20W	
Victoria, U.S.A.	**158**	28	50N		97	0W	
Victoria □	**117**	37	0S		144	0	E
Victoria, L.	**132**	1	0S		33	0	E
Victoria de las Tunas	**178**	20	58N		76	59W	
Victoria Falls	**137**	17	58S		25	52	E
Victoria I.	**145**	71	0N		111	0W	
Victoria Ld.	**15**	75	0S		160	0	E
Victoriaville	**148**	46	4N		71	56W	
Vidalia	**170**	32	13N		82	25W	
Vidin	**53**	43	59N		22	50	E
Viedma	**192**	40	50S		63	0W	
Vienna = Wien	**45**	48	12N		16	22	E
Vienne	**37**	45	31N		4	53	E
Vienne →	**36**	47	13N		0	5	E
Vientiane	**95**	17	58N		102	36	E
Vientos, Paso de los	**180**	20	0N		74	0W	
Vietnam ■	**95**	19	0N		106	0	E
Vigo	**50**	42	12N		8	41W	
Vijayawada	**92**	16	31N		80	39	E
Vila Real de Santo António	**50**	37	10N		7	28W	
Vilhelmina	**66**	64	35N		16	39	E
Vilhena	**187**	12	40S		60	5W	
Villa Bella	**187**	10	25S		65	22W	
Villa Bens = Tarfaya	**126**	27	55N		12	55W	
Villa Cisneros = Dakhla	**126**	23	50N		15	53W	
Villa Dolores	**190**	31	58S		65	15W	
Villa María	**190**	32	20S		63	10W	
Villa Montes	**187**	21	10S		63	30W	
Villaguay	**190**	32	0S		59	0W	
Villahermosa	**177**	17	59N		92	55W	
Villanueva de la Serena	**50**	38	59N		5	50W	
Villarreal	**51**	39	55N		0	3W	
Villarrica	**191**	39	15S		72	15W	
Villazón	**187**	22	0S		65	35W	
Ville Platte	**168**	30	45N		92	17W	
Villefranche-sur-Saône	**37**	45	59N		4	43	E
Villers-Cotterêts	**39**	49	15N		3	4	E
Vilnius	**68**	54	38N		25	19	E
Vilskutskogo, Proliv	**72**	78	0N		103	0	E
Vilyuy →	**74**	64	24N		126	26	E
Vilyuysk	**74**	63	40N		121	35	E
Viña del Mar	**190**	33	0S		71	30W	
Vincennes	**167**	38	42N		87	29W	
Vindhya Ra.	**91**	22	50N		77	0	E
Vinh	**95**	18	45N		105	38	E
Vinita	**168**	36	40N		95	12W	
Vinkovci	**52**	45	19N		18	48	E
Vinnitsa	**68**	49	15N		28	30	E
Viramgam	**91**	23	5N		72	0	E
Virden	**153**	49	50N		100	56W	
Vire	**36**	48	50N		0	53W	
Vírgenes, C.	**192**	52	19S		68	21W	
Virgin →	**173**	36	50N		114	10W	
Virgin Is.	**180**	18	40N		64	30W	
Virginia	**156**	47	30N		92	32W	
Virginia □	**165**	37	45N		78	0W	
Virginia Beach	**165**	36	54N		75	58W	
Visalia	**173**	36	25N		119	18W	
Visby	**60**	57	37N		18	18	E
Viscount Melville Sd.	**145**	74	10N		108	0W	
Višegrad	**52**	43	47N		19	17	E
Vishakhapatnam	**92**	17	45N		83	20	E
Vistula = Wisła →	**58**	54	22N		18	55	E
Vitebsk	**68**	55	10N		30	15	E
Viti Levu	**122**	17	30S		177	30	E
Vitim →	**74**	59	26N		112	34	E
Vitória, Brazil	**189**	20	20S		40	22W	
Vitória, Spain	**50**	42	50N		2	41W	
Vitória da Conquista	**189**	14	51S		40	51W	
Vizianagaram	**92**	18	6N		83	30	E
Vlaardingen	**40**	51	55N		4	21	E
Vladimir	**68**	56	15N		40	30	E
Vladivostok	**75**	43	10N		131	53	E
Vlieland	**40**	53	16N		4	55	E
Vlissingen	**40**	51	26N		3	34	E
Vlóra	**52**	40	32N		19	28	E
Vltava →	**59**	50	21N		14	30	E
Vogelkop	**113**	1	25S		133	0	E
Vogels Berg, mt.	**42**	50	37N		9	30	E
Vohimena, Tanjon' i	**137**	25	36S		45	8	E
Voi	**133**	3	25S		38	32	E
Volendam	**40**	52	30N		5	4	E
Volga →	**68**	48	30N		46	0	E
Volga Hts. = Privolzhskaya Vozvyshennost	**17**	51	0N		46	0	E
Volgograd	**68**	48	40N		44	25	E
Vollenhove	**41**	52	40N		5	58	E
Vologda	**68**	59	10N		40	0	E
Vólos	**54**	39	24N		22	59	E
Volsk	**68**	52	5N		47	22	E
Volta →	**130**	5	46N		0	41	E
Volta, L.	**130**	7	30N		0	15	E
Volta Redonda	**188**	22	31S		44	5W	
Voorburg	**40**	52	5N		4	24	E
Vopnafjörður	**64**	65	45N		14	40W	
Vorîai Sporádhes	**55**	39	15N		23	30	E
Voronezh	**68**	51	40N		39	10	E
Voroshilovgrad	**68**	48	38N		39	15	E
Vosges	**37**	48	20N		7	10	E
Vostochnyy Sayan	**74**	54	0N		96	0	E
Vrangelya, Ostrov	**73**	71	0N		180	0	E
Vranje	**53**	42	34N		21	54	E
Vratsa	**53**	43	13N		23	30	E
Vršac	**52**	45	8N		21	18	E
Vught	**40**	51	38N		5	20	E
Vulcan	**155**	50	25N		113	15W	
Vyborg	**68**	60	43N		28	47	E
Vychegda →	**69**	61	18N		46	36	E
Vychodné Beskydy	**59**	49	30N		22	0	E
Wa	**130**	10	7N		2	25W	
Waal →	**41**	51	59N		4	30	E
Waalwijk	**40**	51	42N		5	4	E
Wabash	**167**	40	48N		85	46W	
Wabash →	**167**	37	46N		88	2W	
Wąbrzeźno	**58**	53	16N		18	57	E
Waco	**168**	31	33N		97	5W	
Wâd Medanî	**129**	14	28N		33	30	E
Waddenzee	**40**	53	6N		5	10	E
Waddington, Mt.	**154**	51	23N		125	15W	
Waddinxveen	**40**	52	2N		4	40	E
Wadena	**152**	51	57N		103	47W	
Wadi Halfa	**129**	21	53N		31	19	E
Wageningen	**41**	51	58N		5	40	E
Wager Bay	**146**	65	56N		90	49W	
Wagga Wagga	**117**	35	7S		147	24	E
Wagin	**120**	33	17S		117	25	E
Waigeo	**113**	0	20S		130	40	E
Waihi	**122**	37	23S		175	52	E
Waikerie	**119**	34	9S		140	0	E
Waikokopu	**122**	39	3S		177	52	E
Waimate	**123**	44	45S		171	3	E
Wainwright, Canada	**152**	52	50N		110	50W	

Name					
Wainwright, U.S.A.	**142**	70	39N	160	1W
Waipara	**123**	43	3S	172	46 E
Waipu	**122**	35	59S	174	29 E
Waipukurau	**122**	40	1S	176	33 E
Wairoa	**122**	39	3S	177	25 E
Waitara	**122**	38	59S	174	15 E
Wajima	**105**	37	30N	137	0 E
Wajir	**133**	1	42N	40	5 E
Wakasa-Wan	**106**	35	40N	135	30 E
Wakatipu, L.	**123**	45	5 S	168	33 E
Wakayama	**106**	34	15N	135	15 E
Wakefield, N.Z.	**123**	41	24S	173	5 E
Wakefield, U.K.	**28**	53	41N	1	31W
Wakkanai	**103**	45	28N	141	35 E
Wałbrzych	**58**	50	45N	16	18 E
Walcha	**116**	30	55S	151	31 E
Walcheren	**40**	51	30N	3	35 E
Wales □	**26**	52	30N	3	30W
Walgett	**116**	30	0S	148	5 E
Walkerton	**151**	44	10N	81	10W
Walla Walla	**171**	46	3N	118	25W
Wallaceburg	**150**	42	34N	82	23W
Wallachia = Valahia	**57**	44	35N	25	0 E
Wallangarra	**116**	28	56S	151	58 E
Wallaroo	**119**	33	56S	137	39 E
Wallasey	**28**	53	26N	3	2W
Wallerawang	**117**	33	25S	150	4 E
Wallis & Futuna	**122**	13	18S	176	10W
Wallowa, Mts.	**171**	45	20N	117	30W
Wallsend, Australia	**117**	32	55S	151	40 E
Wallsend, U.K.	**28**	54	59N	1	30W
Walney, Isle of	**28**	54	5N	3	15W
Walpole	**120**	34	58S	116	44 E
Walsall	**24**	52	36N	1	59W
Walvis Bay	**136**	23	0S	14	28 E
Wana	**88**	32	20N	69	32 E
Wanaka L.	**123**	44	33S	169	7 E
Wang Saphung	**95**	17	18N	101	46 E
Wanganui	**122**	39	56S	175	3 E
Wangaratta	**117**	36	21S	146	19 E
Wanxian	**99**	30	42N	108	20 E
Warabi	**107**	35	49N	139	41 E
Warangal	**91**	17	58N	79	35 E
Warburton	**117**	37	47S	145	42 E
Wardha	**91**	20	45N	78	39 E
Wardha →	**91**	19	57N	79	11 E
Warialda	**116**	29	29S	150	33 E
Warley	**24**	52	30N	2	0W
Warner Mts.	**172**	41	30N	120	20W
Waroona	**120**	32	50S	115	58 E
Warracknabeal	**119**	36	9S	142	26 E
Warragul	**117**	38	10S	145	58 E
Warrego →	**116**	30	24S	145	21 E
Warrego Ra.	**121**	24	58S	146	0 E
Warren, Australia	**116**	31	42S	147	51 E
Warren, Ark., U.S.A.	**168**	33	35N	92	3W
Warren, Mich., U.S.A.	**167**	42	31N	83	2W
Warren, Ohio, U.S.A.	**164**	41	18N	80	52W
Warren, Pa., U.S.A.	**164**	41	52N	79	10W
Warrenpoint	**34**	54	7N	6	15W
Warrensburg	**166**	38	45N	93	45W
Warrington, U.K.	**28**	53	25N	2	38W
Warrington, U.S.A.	**169**	30	22N	87	16W
Warrnambool	**119**	38	25S	142	30 E
Warsaw = Warszawa	**58**	52	13N	21	0 E
Warszawa	**58**	52	13N	21	0 E
Warta →	**58**	52	35N	14	39 E
Warthe = Warta →	**58**	52	35N	14	39 E
Warwick, Australia	**116**	28	10S	152	1 E
Warwick, U.K.	**24**	52	17N	1	36W
Warwick, U.S.A.	**164**	41	43N	71	25W
Warwick □	**24**	52	20N	1	30W
Wasatch Ra.	**163**	40	30N	111	15W
Wasco	**173**	35	37N	119	16W
Wash, The	**29**	52	58N	0	20 E
Washim	**91**	20	3N	77	0 E
Washington, D.C., U.S.A.	**165**	38	52N	77	0W
Washington, Ind., U.S.A.	**167**	38	40N	87	8W
Washington, Mo., U.S.A.	**166**	38	35N	91	1W
Washington, Pa., U.S.A.	**164**	40	10N	80	20W
Washington □	**171**	47	45N	120	30W
Wassenaar	**40**	52	8N	4	24 E
Waterbury	**164**	41	32N	73	0W
Waterford	**35**	52	16N	7	8W
Waterford □	**35**	52	10N	7	40W
Waterloo, Canada	**151**	43	30N	80	32W
Waterloo, U.S.A.	**166**	42	27N	92	20W
Watertown, N.Y., U.S.A.	**151**	43	58N	75	57W
Watertown, Wis., U.S.A.	**167**	43	15N	88	45W
Waterville	**148**	44	35N	69	40W
Watling I. = San Salvador	**178**	24	0N	74	40W
Watrous	**152**	51	40N	105	25W
Watson Lake	**144**	60	6N	128	49W
Watsonville	**173**	36	55N	121	49W
Watubela, Kepulauan	**113**	4	28S	131	35 E
Wauchope	**116**	31	28S	152	45 E
Waukegan	**167**	42	22N	87	54W
Waukesha	**167**	43	0N	88	15W
Wausau	**166**	44	57N	89	40W
Wauwatosa	**167**	43	6N	87	59W
Waveney →	**25**	52	24N	1	20 E
Wâw	**129**	7	45N	28	1 E
Waxahachie	**168**	32	22N	96	53W
Waycross	**170**	31	12N	82	25W
Waynesboro, Pa., U.S.A.	**164**	39	46N	77	32W
Waynesboro, Va., U.S.A.	**165**	38	4N	78	57W
Waynesville	**165**	35	31N	83	0W
Wazirabad	**89**	32	30N	74	8 E
Weald, The	**25**	51	7N	0	9 E
Webo = Nyaake	**130**	4	52N	7	37W
Weddell Sea	**14**	72	30S	40	0W
Wedderburn	**117**	36	26S	143	33 E
Wee Waa	**116**	30	11S	149	26 E
Weert	**41**	51	15N	5	43 E
Weesp	**40**	52	18N	5	2 E
Weifang	**98**	36	47N	119	10 E
Weiser	**171**	44	10N	117	0W
Welbourn Hill	**118**	27	21S	134	6 E
Welch	**165**	37	29N	81	36W
Welland	**151**	43	0N	79	15W
Welland →	**29**	52	43N	0	10W
Wellingborough	**25**	52	18N	0	41W
Wellington, Australia	**116**	32	35S	148	59 E
Wellington, N.Z.	**123**	41	19S	174	46 E
Wellington, Salop, U.K.	**28**	52	42N	2	31W
Wellington, Somerset, U.K.	**27**	50	58N	3	13W
Wellington □	**123**	40	8S	175	36 E
Wellington, I.	**192**	49	30S	75	0W
Wells, Norfolk, U.K.	**29**	52	57N	0	51 E
Wells, Somerset, U.K.	**27**	51	12N	2	39W
Wells, U.S.A.	**172**	41	8N	115	0W
Wellsville, N.Y., U.S.A.	**164**	42	9N	77	53W
Wellsville, Ohio, U.S.A.	**164**	40	36N	80	40W
Welshpool	**26**	52	40N	3	9W
Wem	**28**	52	52N	2	45W
Wenatchee	**171**	47	30N	120	17W
Wenchow = Wenzhou	**99**	28	0N	120	38 E
Wensleydale	**28**	54	18N	2	0W
Wentworth	**119**	34	2S	141	54 E
Wenzhou	**99**	28	0N	120	38 E
Werribee	**117**	37	54S	144	40 E
Werris Creek	**116**	31	18S	150	38 E
Weser →	**42**	53	33N	8	30 E
West Bengal □	**92**	23	0N	88	0 E
West Bromwich	**24**	52	32N	2	1W
West Falkland	**192**	51	40S	60	0W
West Frankfort	**166**	37	56N	89	0W
West Germany ■	**42**	52	0N	9	0 E
West Glamorgan □	**27**	51	40N	3	55W
West Memphis	**169**	35	5N	90	11W
West Midlands □	**24**	52	30N	1	55W
West Palm Beach	**170**	26	44N	80	3W
West Schelde → = Westerschelde →	**40**	51	25N	3	25 E
West Siberian Plain	**76**	62	0N	75	0 E
West Sussex □	**25**	50	55N	0	30W
West Virginia □	**165**	39	0N	81	0W
West Yorkshire □	**28**	53	45N	1	40W
Western Australia □	**114**	25	0S	118	0 E
Western Ghats	**90**	14	0N	75	0 E
Western Isles □	**32**	57	30N	7	10W
Western Sahara ■	**126**	25	0N	13	0W

Western Samoa ■ **123** 14 0S 172 0W
Westerschelde → . . . . **40** 51 25N 3 25 E
Westerwald . . . . **42** 50 39N 8 0 E
Westfriesche Eilanden. . . . . . . **40** 53 20N 5 10 E
Westland □ . . . . **123** 43 33S 169 59 E
Westland Bight . . . . **123** 42 55S 170 5 E
Westlock **155** 54 9N 113 55W
Westmeath □ **34** 53 30N 7 30W
Westminster **164** 39 34N 77 1W
Weston **165** 39 3N 80 29W
Weston-super-Mare **27** 51 20N 2 59W
Westport . . . . **123** 41 46S 171 37 E
Westray **33** 59 18N 3 0W
Wetar . . . . **113** 7 30S 126 30 E
Wetaskiwin **155** 52 55N 113 24W
Wewaka **168** 35 10N 96 35W
Wexford **35** 52 20N 6 28W
Wexford □ **35** 52 20N 6 25W
Weyburn **152** 49 40N 103 50W
Weymouth **27** 50 36N 2 28W
Whakatane . . . . **122** 37 57S 177 1 E
Whale Cove **145** 62 11N 92 36W
Whalsay **30** 60 22N 1 0W
Whangamomona . . . . **122** 39 8S 174 44 E
Whangarei . . . . **122** 35 43S 174 21 E
Wharfe → **29** 53 55N 1 30W
Wheeler Pk. **172** 38 57N 114 15W
Wheeling **164** 40 2N 80 41W
Whernside **28** 54 14N 2 24W
Whitby **29** 54 29N 0 37W
Whitchurch **28** 52 58N 2 42W
White →, Ark., U.S.A. **168** 33 53N 91 3W
White →, Ind., U.S.A. **167** 38 25N 87 45W
White →, S. Dak., U.S.A. . . . **163** 43 45N 99 30W
White Cliffs . . . . **118** 30 50S 143 10 E
White Mts. **157** 44 15N 71 15W
White Park = Nll el
  Abyad → . . . . **129** 15 38N 32 31 E
White Russia = Byelorussian
  S.S.R. □ . . . . **68** 53 30N 27 0 E
White Sea = Beloye More . . . . **69** 66 30N 38 0 E
Whitecliffs . . . . **123** 43 26S 171 55 E
Whitehaven **28** 54 33N 3 35W
Whitehorse **144** 60 43N 135 3W
Whitney, Mt. **173** 36 35N 118 14W
Whitstable . . . . **25** 51 21N 1 2 E
Whitsunday I. . . . . **121** 20 15S 149 4 E
Whittier **142** 60 46N 148 48W
Whyalla . . . . **118** 33 2S 137 30 E
Wichita **158** 37 40N 97 20W
Wichita Falls **161** 33 57N 98 30W
Wick **33** 58 26N 3 5W
Wickepin . . . . **120** 32 50S 117 30 E
Wicklow **35** 53 0N 6 2W
Wicklow □ **35** 52 59N 6 25W
Wicklow Mts. **35** 53 0N 6 30W
Widnes **28** 53 22N 2 44W
Wieluń . . . . **58** 51 15N 18 34 E
Wien . . . . **45** 48 12N 16 22 E
Wiesbaden . . . . **42** 50 7N 8 17 E
Wigan **28** 53 33N 2 38W
Wight, I. of **25** 50 40N 1 20W
Wigtown **31** 54 52N 4 27W
Wigtown B. **31** 54 46N 4 15W
Wilcannia . . . . **118** 31 30S 143 26 E
Wildwood **164** 38 59N 74 46W
Wilhelmshaven . . . . **42** 53 30N 8 9 E
Wilkes Barre **164** 41 15N 75 52W
Wilkes Sub-Glacial Basin . . . . **15** 75 0S 130 0 E
Wilkie **152** 52 27N 108 42W
Willamina **171** 45 9N 123 32W
Willemstad **181** 12 5N 69 0W
Williams L. **154** 51 48N 90 45W
Williamsburg **165** 37 17N 76 44W
Williamson **165** 37 46N 82 17W
Williamsport. **164** 41 18N 77 1W
Williamstown . . . . **117** 37 51S 144 52 E
Williston **163** 48 10N 103 35W
Willits **172** 39 28N 123 17W
Willmar **156** 45 5N 95 0W
Wilmette **167** 42 6N 87 44W

Wilmington, Del., U.S.A. **164** 39 45N 75 32W
Wilmington, N.C., U.S.A. **165** 34 14N 77 54W
Wilson. **165** 35 44N 77 54W
Wilsons Promontory . . . . **117** 38 55S 146 25 E
Wilton **24** 51 5N 1 52W
Wiltshire □ **24** 51 20N 2 0W
Wiluna . . . . **120** 26 36S 120 14 E
Wimereux. . . . . **38** 50 45N 1 37 E
Winchester, U.K. **25** 51 4N 1 19W
Winchester, Ind., U.S.A. **167** 40 10N 84 56W
Winchester, Ky., U.S.A. **165** 38 0N 84 8W
Winchester, Va., U.S.A. **164** 39 14N 78 8W
Wind River Range **163** 43 0N 109 30W
Windermere. **28** 54 24N 2 56W
Windermere, L. **28** 54 20N 2 57W
Windhoek. . . . . **136** 22 35S 17 4 E
Windsor, Australia . . . . **117** 33 37S 150 50 E
Windsor, Nfld., Canada **149** 48 57N 55 40W
Windsor, Ont., Canada **150** 42 18N 83 0W
Windsor, U.K. **25** 51 28N 0 36W
Windward Is. **181** 13 0N 63 0W
Windward Passage =
  Vientos, Paso de los. **180** 20 0N 74 0W
Winisk → **140** 55 17N 85 5W
Winkler **153** 49 10N 97 56W
Winnemucca **172** 41 0N 117 45W
Winnfield **168** 31 57N 92 38W
Winnipeg **153** 49 54N 97 9W
Winnipeg, L. **153** 52 0N 97 0W
Winnipegosis L. **153** 52 30N 100 0W
Winona **166** 44 2N 91 39W
Winooski **151** 44 31N 73 11W
Winschoten . . . . **41** 53 9N 7 3 E
Winslow **161** 35 2N 110 41W
Winston-Salem **165** 36 7N 80 15W
Winter Haven **170** 28 0N 81 42W
Winter Park **170** 28 34N 81 19W
Winterswijk . . . . **41** 51 58N 6 43 E
Winterthur . . . . **44** 47 30N 8 44 E
Wirral **28** 53 25N 3 0W
Wisbech . . . . **29** 52 39N 0 10 E
Wisconsin □ **166** 44 30N 90 0W
Wisconsin → **166** 43 0N 91 15W
Wisconsin Rapids **166** 44 25N 89 50W
Wishaw **31** 55 46N 3 55W
Wisła → . . . . **58** 54 22N 18 55 E
Witham → **29** 53 3N 0 8W
Withernsea . . . . **29** 53 43N 0 2 E
Witney **24** 51 47N 1 29W
Włocławek . . . . **58** 52 40N 19 3 E
Wodonga . . . . **117** 36 5S 146 50 E
Wokam . . . . **113** 5 45S 134 28 E
Woking **25** 51 18N 0 33W
Wolin. . . . . **58** 53 50N 14 37 E
Wollaston L. **145** 58 7N 103 10W
Wollaston Pen. **145** 69 30N 115 0W
Wollongong . . . . **117** 34 25S 150 54 E
Wolverhampton **24** 52 35N 2 6W
Wondai . . . . **116** 26 20S 151 49 E
Wŏnsan . . . . **98** 39 11N 127 27 E
Wonthaggi . . . . **117** 38 37S 145 37 E
Woodburn . . . . **116** 29 6S 153 23 E
Woodenbong . . . . **116** 28 24S 152 39 E
Woodend . . . . **117** 37 20S 144 33 E
Woodland **172** 38 40N 121 50W
Woods, L. of the **153** 49 15N 94 45W
Woodstock, N.B., Canada . . . **148** 46 11N 67 37W
Woodstock, Ont., Canada . . . **151** 43 10N 80 45W
Woolgoolga . . . . **116** 30 6S 153 11 E
Woomera . . . . **118** 31 30S 137 10 E
Woonsocket **164** 42 0N 71 30W
Wooroloo . . . . **120** 31 48S 116 18 E
Worcester, U.K. **24** 52 12N 2 12W
Worcester, U.S.A. **164** 42 14N 71 49W
Workington **28** 54 39N 3 34W
Worksop. **29** 53 19N 1 9W
Wormerveer . . . . **40** 52 30N 4 46 E
Worms . . . . **42** 49 37N 8 21 E
Worthing **25** 50 49N 0 21W
Worthington **166** 43 35N 95 36W
Wou-han = Wuhan. . . . . **99** 30 31N 114 18 E

Woy Woy	**117**	33 30S	151	19 E
Wrangel I.	**138**	71 0N	180	0 E
Wrangell	**143**	56 30N	132	25W
Wrangell Mts.	**142**	61 40N	143	30W
Wrath, C.	**32**	58 38N	5	0W
Wrekin, The	**28**	52 41N	2	35W
Wrexham	**26**	53 5N	3	0W
Wrigley	**144**	63 16N	123	37W
Wrocław	**58**	51 5N	17	5 E
Września	**58**	52 21N	17	36 E
Wu Jiang ⟶	**99**	29 40N	107	20 E
Wubin	**120**	30 6S	116	37 E
Wuhan	**99**	30 31N	114	18 E
Wuhsi = Wuxi	**99**	31 33N	120	18 E
Wuhu	**99**	31 22N	118	21 E
Wulumuchi = Ürümqi	**100**	43 45N	87	45 E
Wuppertal	**42**	51 15N	7	8 E
Würzburg	**42**	49 46N	9	55 E
Wutongqiao	**99**	29 22N	103	50 E
Wuxi	**99**	31 33N	120	18 E
Wuzhong	**98**	38 2N	106	12 E
Wuzhou	**99**	23 30N	111	18 E
Wyalkatchem	**120**	31 8S	117	22 E
Wyandotte	**167**	42 14N	83	13W
Wycheproof	**119**	36 0S	143	17 E
Wye ⟶	**27**	51 36N	2	40W
Wyndham	**114**	15 33S	128	3 E
Wynnum	**116**	27 27S	153	9 E
Wynyard	**152**	51 45N	104	10W
Wyoming □	**163**	42 48N	109	0W
Wytheville	**165**	37 0N	81	3W
Xánthi	**55**	41 10N	24	58 E
Xapuri	**187**	10 35S	68	35W
Xenia	**167**	39 42N	83	57W
Xiamen	**99**	24 25N	118	4 E
Xi'an	**99**	34 15N	109	0 E
Xiangfan	**99**	32 2N	112	8 E
Xiangtan	**99**	27 51N	112	54 E
Xiao Hinggan Ling	**98**	49 0N	127	0 E
Xigazê	**101**	29 5N	88	45 E
Xingtai	**98**	37 3N	114	32 E
Xingu ⟶	**188**	1 30S	51	53W
Xining	**98**	36 34N	101	40 E
Xinjiang Uygur Zizhiqu □	**100**	42 0N	86	0 E
Xinxiang	**99**	35 18N	113	50 E
Xinyang	**99**	32 6N	114	3 E
Xinzhu	**99**	24 49N	120	57 E
Xique-Xique	**188**	10 50S	42	40W
Xizang □	**101**	32 0N	88	0 E
Xuanhua	**98**	40 40N	115	2 E
Xuchang	**99**	34 2N	113	48 E
Xuzhou	**99**	34 18N	117	10 E
Ya'an	**99**	29 58N	103	5 E
Yablonovy Khrebet	**74**	53 0N	114	0 E
Yablonovy Ra. = Yablonovy				
Khrebet	**74**	53 0N	114	0 E
Yacuiba	**187**	22 0S	63	43W
Yaizu	**107**	34 52N	138	20 E
Yakima	**171**	46 42N	120	30W
Yaku-Jima	**104**	30 20N	130	30 E
Yakut A.S.S.R. □	**72**	62 0N	130	0 E
Yakutat	**143**	59 29N	139	44W
Yakutsk	**75**	62 5N	129	50 E
Yalgoo	**120**	28 16S	116	39 E
Yalinga	**129**	6 33N	23	10 E
Yamaga	**108**	33 1N	130	41 E
Yamagata	**103**	38 15N	140	15 E
Yamaguchi	**108**	34 10N	131	32 E
Yamal, Poluostrov	**69**	71 0N	70	0 E
Yamato	**107**	35 27N	139	25 E
Yamatotakada	**106**	34 31N	135	45 E
Yamazaki	**109**	35 0N	134	32 E
Yamba	**116**	29 26S	153	23 E
Yambol	**53**	42 30N	26	36 E
Yamdena	**113**	7 45S	131	20 E

Yame	**108**	33 13N	130	35 E
Yamma-Yamma, L.	**118**	26 16S	141	20 E
Yampa ⟶	**163**	40 37N	108	59W
Yamuna ⟶	**92**	25 30N	81	53 E
Yamzho Yumco	**101**	28 48N	90	35 E
Yana ⟶	**72**	71 30N	136	0 E
Yanagawa	**108**	33 10N	130	24 E
Yanai	**109**	33 58N	132	7 E
Yanco	**117**	34 38S	146	27 E
Yangch'ü = Taiyuan	**98**	37 52N	112	33 E
Yangquan	**98**	37 58N	113	31 E
Yangtze Kiang = Chang				
Jiang ⟶	**99**	31 48N	121	10 E
Yanji	**98**	42 59N	129	30 E
Yantai	**98**	37 34N	121	22 E
Yao	**106**	34 32N	135	36 E
Yaoundé	**131**	3 50N	11	35 E
Yaqui ⟶	**174**	27 37N	110	39W
Yare ⟶	**25**	52 36N	1	28 E
Yarensk	**69**	61 10N	49	8 E
Yarkand = Shache	**100**	38 20N	77	10 E
Yarmouth	**148**	43 50N	66	7W
Yaroslavl	**68**	57 35N	39	55 E
Yarram	**117**	38 29S	146	9 E
Yashiro-Jima	**109**	33 55N	132	15 E
Yass	**117**	34 49S	148	54 E
Yasugi	**109**	35 26N	133	15 E
Yatsushiro	**108**	32 30N	130	40 E
Yavari ⟶	**186**	4 21S	70	2W
Yavatmal	**91**	20 20N	78	15 E
Yawatahama	**109**	33 27N	132	24 E
Yazd	**85**	31 55N	54	27 E
Yazoo ⟶	**169**	32 35N	90	50W
Yazoo City	**169**	32 48N	90	28W
Ye Xian	**98**	37 8N	119	57 E
Yegros	**191**	26 20S	56	25W
Yell	**30**	60 35N	1	5W
Yellow Sea	**99**	35 0N	123	0 E
Yellowhead P.	**155**	52 53N	118	25W
Yellowknife	**145**	62 27N	114	29W
Yellowstone ⟶	**163**	47 58N	103	59W
Yellowstone National Park	**163**	44 35N	110	0W
Yemen ■	**82**	15 0N	44	0 E
Yenisey ⟶	**69**	71 50N	82	40 E
Yeniseyskiy Zaliv	**69**	72 20N	81	0 E
Yeo ⟶	**27**	51 10N	3	0W
Yeola	**91**	20 0N	74	30 E
Yeovil	**27**	50 57N	2	38W
Yeppoon	**121**	23 5S	150	47 E
Yerevan	**70**	40 10N	44	31 E
Yes Tor	**27**	50 41N	3	59W
Yetman	**116**	28 56S	150	48 E
Yezd = Yazd	**85**	31 55N	54	27 E
Yiannitsa	**54**	40 46N	22	24 E
Yibin	**99**	28 45N	104	32 E
Yichang	**99**	30 40N	111	20 E
Yichun	**98**	47 44N	128	52 E
Yilan	**99**	24 51N	121	44 E
Yinchuan	**98**	38 30N	106	15 E
Yingkou	**98**	40 37N	122	18 E
Yingtan	**99**	28 12N	117	0 E
Yining	**100**	43 58N	81	10 E
Ylthion	**54**	36 46N	22	34 E
Yiyang	**99**	28 45N	112	16 E
Yogyakarta	**111**	7 49S	110	22 E
Yōkaichiba	**107**	35 42N	140	33 E
Yokkaichi	**106**	35 0N	136	38 E
Yokohama	**107**	35 27N	139	28 E
Yokosuka	**107**	35 20N	139	40 E
Yokote	**103**	39 20N	140	30 E
Yonago	**109**	35 25N	133	19 E
Yoneshiro ⟶	**103**	40 15N	140	15 E
Yonezawa	**103**	37 57N	140	4 E
Yongji	**99**	34 52N	110	28 E
Yonkers	**164**	40 57N	73	51W
York, Australia	**120**	31 52S	116	47 E
York, U.K.	**29**	53 58N	1	7W
York, U.S.A.	**164**	39 57N	76	43W
Yorke Pen.	**119**	34 50S	137	40 E
Yorkshire Wolds	**29**	54 0N	0	30W
Yorkton	**152**	51 11N	102	28W

Yosemite National Park 172 38 0N 119 30W
Youghal 35 51 58N 7 51W
Young .... 117 34 19S 148 18 E
Younghusband Pen. .... 119 36 0S 139 25 E
Youngstown 164 41 7N 80 41W
Yuba City 172 39 12N 121 37W
Yūbari.................... 103 43 4N 141 59 E
Yūbetsu .... 103 43 13N 144 5 E
Yucatán □ 177 20 50N 89 0W
Yucatán, Canal de 178 22 0N 86 30W
Yucatan Str. = Yucatán,
Canal de 178 22 0N 86 30W
Yuci..................... 98 37 42N 112 46 E
Yugoslavia ■............. 52 44 0N 20 0 E
Yukon → 142 65 30N 150 0W
Yukon Territory □ 144 63 0N 135 0W
Yuma 173 32 45N 114 37W
Yunnan □................. 101 25 0N 102 30 E
Yuribei .... 69 71 8N 76 58 E
Yurimaguas 186 5 55S 76 7W
Yushu .... 101 33 5N 96 55 E
Yuzhno-Sakhalinsk......... 75 46 58N 142 45 E
Yvetot .... 38 49 37N 0 44 E

Zaandam .... 40 52 26N 4 49 E
Zabaykalskiy .... 74 49 40N 117 25 E
Zabid .... 82 14 0N 43 10 E
Zābol .... 85 31 0N 61 32 E
Zābol □ .... 87 32 0N 67 0 E
Zabrze .... 58 50 18N 18 50 E
Zacapa................... 177 14 59N 89 31W
Zacatecas 175 22 47N 102 35W
Zacatecas □.............. 175 23 0N 103 0W
Zacatecoluca 177 13 29N 88 51W
Zadar .... 52 44 8N 15 14 E
Zadetkyi Kyun .... 94 10 0N 98 25 E
Zagreb .... 52 45 50N 16 0 E
Zāhedān .... 86 29 30N 60 50 E
Zahlah .... 80 33 52N 35 50 E
Zaïre ■ .... 134 3 0S 23 0 E
Zaïre → .... 134 6 4S 12 24 E
Zákinthos .... 54 37 47N 20 57 E
Zambeze → .... 135 18 55S 36 4 E
Zambezi = Zambeze → ..... 135 18 55S 36 4 E
Zambia ■................. 135 15 0S 28 0 E
Zamboanga................ 112 6 59N 122 3 E
Zamora, Mexico 175 20 0N 102 21W
Zamora, Spain 50 41 30N 5 45W
Zandvoort .... 40 52 22N 4 32 E
Zanesville 167 39 56N 82 2W
Zanjan .... 81 36 40N 48 35 E
Zante = Zákinthos .... 54 37 47N 20 57 E
Zanzibar................. 135 6 12S 39 12 E
Zaouiet El-Kala = Bordj Omar
Driss .... 127 28 10N 6 40 E
Zaouiet Reggane .... 127 26 32N 0 3 E
Zapadnaya Dvina → .... 68 57 4N 24 3 E
Západné Beskydy .... 59 49 30N 19 0 E
Zapala 190 39 0S 70 5W
Zaporozhye............... 68 47 50N 35 10 E
Zaragoza, Mexico 174 28 29N 100 55W

Zaragoza, Spain.......... 51 41 39N 0 53W
Zaranj................... 87 30 55N 61 55 E
Zaria .... 131 11 0N 7 40 E
Zaruma................... 184 3 40S 79 38W
Zaskar Mountains......... 89 33 15N 77 30 E
Zavitinsk................ 75 50 10N 129 20 E
Zaysan, Oz............... 71 48 0N 83 0 E
Zayü .... 101 28 48N 97 27 E
Zduńska Wola .... 58 51 37N 18 59 E
Zeebrugge .... 42 51 19N 3 12 E
Zeeland □ .... 40 51 30N 3 50 E
Zeila .... 133 11 21N 43 30 E
Zeist .... 40 52 5N 5 15 E
Zemlya Frantsa Iosifa.... 13 81 0N 55 0 E
Zentsūji .... 109 34 14N 133 47 E
Zeya .... 75 53 48N 127 14 E
Zêzere → 50 39 28N 8 20W
Zhanghua .... 99 24 6N 120 29 E
Zhangjiakou .... 98 40 48N 114 55 E
Zhangzhou .... 99 24 30N 117 35 E
Zhanjiang................ 99 21 15N 110 20 E
Zhdanov.................. 68 47 5N 37 31 E
Zhejiang □............... 99 29 0N 120 0 E
Zhengzhou .... 99 34 45N 113 34 E
Zhenjiang................ 99 32 11N 119 26 E
Zhenyuan................. 99 27 4N 108 21 E
Zhijiang .... 99 27 27N 109 42 E
Zhitomir .... 68 50 20N 28 40 E
Zhumadian .... 99 32 59N 114 2 E
Zhupanovo .... 73 53 40N 159 52 E
Zhuzhou.................. 99 27 49N 113 12 E
Zibo .... 98 36 47N 118 3 E
Zielona Góra .... 58 51 57N 15 31 E
Zierikzee .... 40 51 40N 3 55 E
Zigong .... 99 29 15N 104 48 E
Žile .... 80 40 15N 35 52 E
Žilina .... 59 49 12N 18 42 E
Zimbabwe .... 137 20 16S 30 54 E
Zimbabwe ■............... 137 20 0S 30 0 E
Zinder .... 131 13 48N 9 0 E
Zipaquirá 184 5 0N 74 0W
Zitácuaro 175 19 24N 100 22W
Zlatograd .... 53 41 22N 25 7 E
Zlatoust .... 69 55 10N 59 40 E
Zlin = Gottwaldov........ 59 49 14N 17 40 E
Zomba .... 137 15 22S 35 19 E
Zonguldak................ 80 41 28N 31 50 E
Zorritos 186 3 43S 80 40W
Zoutkamp .... 41 53 20N 6 18 E
Zrenjanin .... 52 45 22N 20 23 E
Zufar .... 83 17 40N 54 0 E
Zug .... 44 47 10N 8 31 E
Zuid-Holland □........... 40 52 0N 4 35 E
Zuidhorn .... 41 53 15N 6 23 E
Zungeru .... 131 9 48N 6 8 E
Zunyi.................... 99 27 42N 106 53 E
Zürich .... 44 47 22N 8 32 E
Zutphen .... 41 52 9N 6 12 E
Zuwārah .... 127 32 58N 12 1 E
Zvolen .... 59 48 33N 19 10 E
Zwickau .... 43 50 43N 12 30 E
Zwolle .... 41 52 31N 6 6 E
Zyryanovsk .... 71 49 43N 84 20 E